# Family Maps
of
# Hamilton County, Illinois
Deluxe Edition

*With Homesteads, Roads, Waterways, Towns, Cemeteries, Railroads, and More*

# Family Maps
of
## Hamilton County, Illinois
### Deluxe Edition

*With Homesteads, Roads, Waterways, Towns, Cemeteries, Railroads, and More*

by Gregory A. Boyd, J.D.

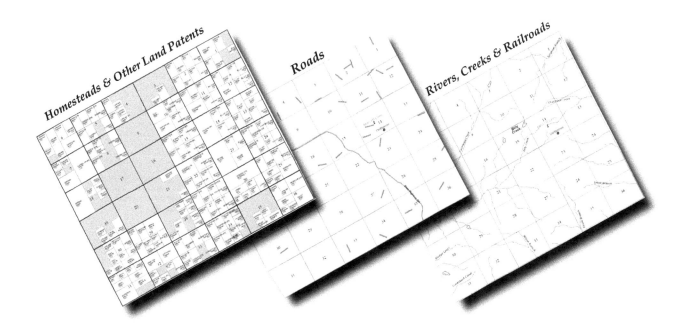

*Featuring* **3** *Maps Per Township...*

*Arphax Publishing Co.*
*www.arphax.com*

**Family Maps of Hamilton County, Illinois, Deluxe Edition: With Homesteads, Roads, Waterways, Towns, Cemeteries, Railroads, and More.**
by Gregory A. Boyd, J.D.


ISBN 1-4203-1440-8

Published by Arphax Publishing Co., 2210 Research Park Blvd., Norman, Oklahoma, USA  73069
www.arphax.com


First Edition

ATTENTION HISTORICAL & GENEALOGICAL SOCIETIES, UNIVERSITIES, COLLEGES, CORPORATIONS, FAMILY REUNION COORDINATORS, AND PROFESSIONAL ORGANIZATIONS: Quantity discounts are available on bulk purchases of this book. For information, please contact Arphax Publishing Co., at the address listed above, or at (405) 366-6181, or visit our web-site at www.arphax.com and contact us through the "Bulk Sales" link.

—LEGAL—

The contents of this book rely on data published by the United States Government and its various agencies and departments, including but not limited to the General Land Office–Bureau of Land Management, the Department of the Interior, and the U.S. Census Bureau. The author has relied on said government agencies or re-sellers of its data, but makes no guarantee of the data's accuracy or of its representation herein, neither in its text nor maps. Said maps have been proportioned and scaled in a manner reflecting the author's primary goal—to make patentee names readable. This book will assist in the discovery of possible relationships between people, places, locales, rivers, streams, cemeteries, etc., but "proving" those relationships or exact geographic locations of any of the elements contained in the maps will require the use of other source material, which could include, but not be limited to:  land patents, surveys, the patentees' applications, professionally drawn road-maps, etc.

Neither the author nor publisher makes any claim that the contents herein represent a complete or accurate record of the data it presents and disclaims any liability for reader's use of the book's contents.  Many circumstances exist where human, computer, or data delivery errors could cause records to have been missed or to be inaccurately represented herein. Neither the author nor publisher shall assume any liability whatsoever for errors, inaccuracies, omissions or other inconsistencies herein.

This book is dedicated to my wonderful family:

*Vicki, Jordan, & Amy Boyd*

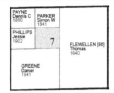

# Contents

## - Part I -

## The Big Picture

## - Part II -

## Township Map Groups

*(each Map Group contains a Patent Index, Patent Map, Road Map, & Historical Map)*

# Appendices

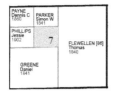

# Preface

The quest for the discovery of my ancestors' origins, migrations, beliefs, and life-ways has brought me rewards that I could never have imagined. The *Family Maps* series of books is my first effort to share with historical and genealogical researchers, some of the tools that I have developed to achieve my research goals. I firmly believe that this effort will allow many people to reap the same sorts of treasures that I have.

The Illinois State Archives (much like the Federal Government's Bureau of Land Management) has given genealogists and historians an incredible gift by virtue of its enormous database housed on its web-site at www.cyberdriveillinois.com. There, you can search for and find over half-a-million descriptions of original land-purchases in Illinois.

This Illinois Archives site is in a small class of truly unique web-sites that present such a vast collection of records for FREE. But, the site is not for the faint of heart, nor is it for those unwilling or unable to to sift through and analyze the thousands of records that exist for most counties.

My immediate goal with this series is to spare you the hundreds of hours of work that it would take you to map the Land Patents for this county. Every Hamilton County homestead or land patent that I have gleaned from the Illinos State Archives database is mapped here (at least ones that can be). Consequently, I can usually show you in an instant, where your ancestor's land is located, as well as the names of nearby land-owners.

Originally, that was my primary goal. But after speaking to other genealogists, it became clear that there was much more that they wanted. Taking their advice set me back almost a full year, but I think you will agree it was worth the wait. Because now, you can learn so much more.

Now, this book answers these sorts of questions:

- Are there any variant spellings for surnames that I have missed in searching Illinois land-records?
- Where is my family's traditional home-place?
- What cemeteries are near Grandma's house?
- My Granddad used to swim in such-and-such-Creek—where is that?
- How close is this little community to that one?
- Are there any other people with the same surname who bought land in the county?
- How about cousins and in-laws—did they buy land in the area?

**And these are just for starters!**

The rules for using the *Family Maps* books are simple, but the strategies for success are many. Some techniques are apparent on first use, but many are gained with time and experience. Please take the time to notice the roads, cemeteries, creek-names, family names, and unique first-names throughout the whole county. You cannot imagine what YOU might be the first to discover.

I hope to learn that many of you have answered age-old research questions within these pages or that you have discovered relationships previously not even considered. When these sorts of things happen to you, will you please let me hear about it? I would like nothing better. My contact information can always be found at www.arphax.com.

One more thing: please read the "How To Use This Book" chapter; it starts on the next page. This will give you the very best chance to find the treasures that lie within these pages.

My family and I wish you the very best of luck, both in life, and in your research.      Greg Boyd

How to Use This Book - A Graphical Summary

## Part I
# "The Big Picture"

**Map A** ▸ *Counties in the State*
**Map B** ▸ *Surrounding Counties*
**Map C** ▸ *Congressional Townships (Map Groups) in the County*
**Map D** ▸ *Cities & Towns in the County*
**Map E** ▸ *Cemeteries in the County*
**Surnames in the County** ▸ *Number of Land-Parcels for Each Surname*
**Surname/Township Index** ▸ *Directs you to Township Map Groups in Part II*

*The Surname/Township Index can direct you to any number of* **Township Map Groups**

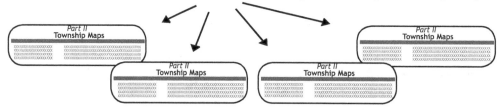

## Part II
# Township Map Groups
*(1 for each Township in the County)*

Each Township Map Group contains all four of of the following tools . . .

**Land Patent Index** ▸ *Every-name Index of Patents Mapped in this Township*
**Land Patent Map** ▸ *Map of Patents as listed in above Index*
**Road Map** ▸ *Map of Roads, City-centers, and Cemeteries in the Township*
**Historical Map** ▸ *Map of Railroads, Lakes, Rivers, Creeks, City-Centers, and Cemeteries*

# Appendices

**Appendix A** ▸ *Illinois State Archives Abbreviations*
**Appendix B** ▸ *Section-Parts / Aliquot Parts (a comprehensive list)*
**Appendix C** ▸ *Multi-patentee Groups (Individuals within Buying Groups)*

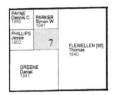

# How to Use This Book

The two "Parts" of this *Family Maps* volume seek to answer two different types of questions. Part I deals with broad questions like: what counties surround Hamilton County, are there any ASHCRAFTs in Hamilton County, and if so, in which Townships or Maps can I find them? Ultimately, though, Part I should point you to a particular Township Map Group in Part II.

Part II concerns itself with details like: where exactly is this family's land, who else bought land in the area, and what roads and streams run through the land, or are located nearby. The Chart on the opposite page, and the remainder of this chapter attempt to convey to you the particulars of these two "parts", as well as how best to use them to achieve your research goals.

## Part I
### "The Big Picture"

Within Part I, you will find five "Big Picture" maps and two county-wide surname tools.

These include:

• Map A - Where Hamilton County lies within the state
• Map B - Counties that surround Hamilton County
• Map C - Congressional Townships of Hamilton County (+ Map Group Numbers)
• Map D - Cities & Towns of Hamilton County (with Index)
• Map E - Cemeteries of Hamilton County (with Index)
• Surnames in Hamilton County Patents (with Parcel-counts for each surname)
• Surname/Township Index (with Parcel-counts for each surname by Township)

The five "Big-Picture" Maps are fairly self-explanatory, yet should not be overlooked. This is particularly true of Maps "C", "D", and "E", all of which show Hamilton County and its Congressional Townships (and their assigned Map Group Numbers).

Let me briefly explain this concept of Map Group Numbers. These are a device completely of our own invention. They were created to help you quickly locate maps without having to remember the full legal name of the various Congressional Townships. It is simply easier to remember "Map Group 1" than a legal name like: "Township 9-North Range 6-West, 5th Principal Meridian." But the fact is that the TRUE legal name for these Townships IS terribly important. These are the designations that others will be familiar with and you will need to accurately record them in your notes. This is why both Map Group numbers AND legal descriptions of Townships are almost always displayed together.

Map "C" will be your first intoduction to "Map Group Numbers", and that is all it contains: legal Township descriptions and their assigned Map Group Numbers. Once you get further into your research, and more immersed in the details, you will likely want to refer back to Map "C" from time to time, in order to regain your bearings on just where in the county you are researching.

Remember, township boundaries are a completely artificial device, created to standardize land descriptions. But do not let them become a boundary in your mind when choosing which townships to research. Your relative's in-laws, children, cousins, siblings, and mamas and papas, might just as easily have lived in the township next to the one your grandfather lived in—rather than in the one where he actually lived. So Map "C" can be your guide to which other Townships/ Map Groups you likewise ought to analyze.

Of course, the same holds true for County lines; this is the purpose behind Map "B". It shows you surrounding counties that you may want to consider for further reserarch.

Map "D", the Cities and Towns map, is the first map with an index. Map "E" is the second (Cemeteries). Both, Maps "D" and "E" give you broad views of City (or Cemetery) locations in the County. But they go much further by pointing you toward pertinent Township Map Groups so you can locate the patents, roads, and waterways located near a particular city or cemetery.

Once you are familiar with these *Family Maps* volumes and the county you are researching, the "Surnames In Hamilton County" chapter (or its sister chapter in other volumes) is where you'll likely start your future research sessions. Here, you can quickly scan its few pages and see if anyone in the county possesses the surnames you are researching. The "Surnames in Hamilton County" list shows only two things: surnames and the number of parcels of land we have located for that surname in Hamilton County. But whether or not you immediately locate the surnames you are researching, please do not go any further without taking a few moments to scan ALL the surnames in these very few pages.

You cannot imagine how many lost ancestors are waiting to be found by someone willing to take just a little longer to scan the "Surnames In Hamilton County" list. Misspellings and typographical errors abound in most any index of this sort. Don't miss out on finding your Kinard that was written Rynard or Cox that was written Lox. If it looks funny or wrong, it very often is. And one of those little errors may well be your relative.

Now, armed with a surname and the knowledge that it has one or more entries in this book, you are ready for the "Surname/Township Index." Unlike the "Surnames In Hamilton County", which has only one line per Surname, the "Surname/Township Index" contains one line-item for each Township Map Group in which each surname is found. In other words, each line represents a different Township Map Group that you will need to review.

Specifically, each line of the Surname/Township

Index contains the following four columns of information:

1. Surname
2. Township Map Group Number (these Map Groups are found in Part II)
3. Parcels of Land (number of them with the given Surname within the Township)
4. Meridian/Township/Range (the legal description for this Township Map Group)

The key column here is that of the Township Map Group Number. While you should definitely record the Meridian, Township, and Range, you can do that later. Right now, you need to dig a little deeper. That Map Group Number tells you where in Part II that you need to start digging.

But before you leave the "Surname/Township Index", do the same thing that you did with the "Surnames in Hamilton County" list: take a moment to scan the pages of the Index and see if there are similarly spelled or misspelled surnames that deserve your attention. Here again, is an easy opportunity to discover grossly misspelled family names with very little effort. Now you are ready to turn to . . .

## Part II
## "Township Map Groups"

You will normally arrive here in Part II after being directed to do so by one or more "Map Group Numbers" in the Surname/Township Index of Part I.

Each Map Group represents a set of four tools dedicated to a single Congressional Township that is either wholly or partially within the county. If you are trying to learn all that you can about a particular family or their land, then these tools should usually be viewed in the order they are presented.

These four tools include:

1. a Land Patent Index
2. a Land Patent Map
3. a Road Map, and
4. an Historical Map

As I mentioned earlier, each grouping of this sort is assigned a Map Group Number. So, let's now move on to a discussion of the four tools that make up one of these Township Map Groups.

## Land Patent Index

Each Township Map Group's Index begins with a title, something along these lines:

**MAP GROUP 1: Index to Land Patents**
**Township 16-North Range 5-West (2nd PM)**

The Index contains eight (8) columns. They are:
1. ID (a unique ID number for this Individual and a corresponding Parcel of land in this Township)
2. Individual in Patent (name)
3. Sec. (Section), and
4. Sec. Part (Section Part, or Aliquot Part)
5. Purchase Date (Patent)
6. Sale Type (IL Archives Abbreviation).
7. IL Aliquot Part (more on this, below).
8. For More Info: varying information which often requires you to turn to Appendices A or C for clarification..

While most of these eight columns are self-explanatory, I will take a few moments to explain the "Sec. Part." "Purchase Date," "Sale Type, "IL Aliquot Part," and "For More Info" columns.

The "Sec. Part" column refers to what surveryors and other land professionals refer to as an Aliquot Part. The origins and use of such a term mean little to a non-surveyor, and I have chosen to simply call these sub-sections of land what they are: a "Section Part". No matter what we call them, what we are referring to are things like a quarter-section or half-section or quarter-quarter-section. See Appendix "B" for most of the "Section Parts" you will come across (and many you will not) and what size land-parcel they represent.

In the volumes in this series which rely on Illinois Archives data rather than on that of the Bureau of Land Management, this value is our translation of that Aliquot Part as recorded by the Illinois

Archives. Because the Archives chose to add much additional information to that value (more on this, below), sometimes the underlying Section Part is not ascertainable with complete certainty.

In short, the Sec. Part column will tell you where we mapped the parcel, whether or not that is where it actually lies. In the vast majority of cases, we feel like we will hit the spot.

The "Purchase Date" column displays just that: the date on which the patentee signed the necessary documents in the relevant Land Office, in order to seek his or her land-claim. This value differs from that stored in the BLM databases (and in our books based on them) where the "Issue date" is given---the "issue-date" is a later date on which the Federal Government effectively finalized the transaction.

The "Sale Type" column offers an abbreviation which you can locate in Appendix A. The vast majority of the patents here will be noted as an "FD" (Federal) sale-type.

The "IL Aliquot Part" column is one which we include as a response to the problem we identified above: sometimes we cannot ascertain the true location of the land based on the the Illinois Archive's stated "Aliquot Part." We do not state this as any sort of criticism: I challenge anyone to read a few hundred of these patents (particularly in urban areas or along rivers or canals) and try to come up with a standard way to describe the legal descriptions they contain---frankly, such a chore is beyond that which most of us would choose to entertain.

The Archives had a hard-time deciphering these legal descriptions, as did we. And because of this confession, we repeat, verbatim, the "IL Aliquot Part" in each Patent-Index so you may see what source information we used in our decision-making. We acknowledge that you may come to a different conclusion as to where some of these parcels actually lie.

A couple of final points need be made with regard to this "IL Aliquot Part" column.

First, if the meaning of its contents are not readily

apparent, then it is likely you have come across one of the numerous examples wherein the Archives tacked on information not technically belonging to a standard legal description (and yet existed in the underlying patent). For instance, you may find a value like "NWNANDWRR." I hate to tell you, but this could mean several things: the northwest-quarter section, north and west of Rock River, being one reasonable intepretation, but there could be others. See Appendix "A" for the numerous abbreviations used in these descriptions.

Next, if the "IL Aliquot Part" entry contains the words "Lot" or "Block" or begins with either "L" or "B" and is then followed by a number (and sometimes an alphabetic character), then this is a lot. Its whereabouts within a section cannot be ascertained with the legal description alone, and so we cannot map them with the resources we possess. This does not thwart the uses for which we contemplate this series will be used, but we want you to be aware that you will need to locate plat-maps from the individual counties if you need to more precisely locate land within lots. We do list the lots out for you in the map, so you can know which section they fall within.

The "For More Info" column of the Index is variable in its content from one patent to another, as is the case with the underlying data provided by the Illinois Archives. There are three primary possible items you may find here, as evinced by looking at a sample of the Legend which accompanies each Patent-Map Index:

### LEGEND

"For More Info . . . " column
| |
|---|
| **G** = Group (Multi-Patentee Patent, see Appendix "C") |
| **R** = Residence |
| **S** = Social Status |

Below, I will explain what each of these items means to you as a researcher.

### G = Group

**(Multi-Patentee Patent, see Appendix "C")**
A "G" designation means that the Patent was issued to a GROUP of people (Multi-patentees). The

"G" will always be followed by a number. Some such groups were quite large and it was impractical if not impossible to display each individual in our maps without unduly affecting readability. EACH person in the group is named in the Index, but they won't all be found on the Map. You will find the name of only person listed in such a Group on the map with the Group number next to it, enclosed in [square brackets]. That square bracket [ ] is your key to locating patents on the patent map.

To find all the members of the Group you can either scan the Index for all people with the same Group Number or you can simply refer to Appendix "C" where all members of the Group are listed next to their number.

### R = Residence

Though only a fraction of the patents here contain this wonderful bit of data, those which do, offer up a nice windfall to many researchers. This value comes from the language in patents which often includes words like "John Smith of Franklin County" or some similiar verbiage. There are people identified as having been "from" numerous states. If the location is within Illinois, usually we are given simply the county name.

### S = Social Status

Again, most patents are not accompanied by this information, but those which do, will contain a value that can be looked-up in the Abbreviations found in Appendix "C."

## Land Patent Map

On the first two-page spread following each Township's Index to Land Patents, you'll find the corresponding Land Patent Map. And here lies the real heart of our work. For the first time anywhere, researchers will be able to observe and analyze, on a grand scale, most of the original land-owners for an area AND see them mapped in proximity to each one another.

We encourage you to make vigorous use of the accompanying Index described above, but then later, to abandon it, and just stare at these maps for a while. This is a great way to catch misspellings or to find collateral kin you'd not known were in the area.

Each Land Patent Map represents one Congressional Township containing approximately 36-square miles. Each of these square miles is labeled by an accompanying Section Number (1 through 36, in most cases). Keep in mind, that this book concerns itself solely with Hamilton County's patents. Townships which creep into one or more other counties will not be shown in their entirety in any one book. You will need to consult other books, as they become available, in order to view other countys' patents, cities, cemeteries, etc.

But getting back to Hamilton County: each Land Patent Map contains a Statistical Chart that looks like the following:

### Township Statistics

| | | |
|---|---|---|
| Parcels Mapped | : | 173 |
| Number of Patents | : | 163 |
| Number of Individuals | : | 152 |
| Patentees Identified | : | 151 |
| Number of Surnames | : | 137 |
| Multi-Patentee Parcels | : | 4 |
| Oldest Patent Date | : | 11/27/1820 |
| Most Recent Patent | : | 9/28/1917 |
| Block/Lot Parcels | : | 0 |
| Cities and Towns | : | 6 |
| Cemeteries | : | 6 |

This information may be of more use to a social statistician or historian than a genealogist, but I think all three will find it interesting.

Most of the statistics are self-explanatory, and what is not, was described in the above discussion of the Index's Legend, but I do want to mention a few of them that may affect your understanding of the Land Patent Maps.

First of all, Patents often contain more than one Parcel of land, so it is common for there to be more Parcels than Patents. Also, the Number of Individuals will more often than not, not match the number of Patentees. A Patentee is literally the person or PERSONS named in a patent. So, a Patent may have a multi-person Patentee or a single-person patentee. Nonetheless, we account for all these individuals in our indexes.

On the lower-righthand side of the Patent Map is a Legend which describes various features in the map, including Section Boundaries, Patent (land) Boundaries, Lots (numbered), and Multi-Patentee Group Numbers. You'll also find a "Helpful Hints" Box that will assist you.

*One important note: though the vast majority of Patents mapped in this series will prove to be reasonably accurate representations of their actual locations, we cannot claim this for patents lying along state and county lines, or waterways, or that have been platted (lots). Shifting boundaries and sparse legal descriptions in the Illinois Archives data make this a reality that we have nonetheless tried to overcome by estimating these patents' locations the best that we can.*

### Road Map

On the two-page spread following each Patent Map you will find a Road Map covering the exact same area (the same Congressional Township).

For me, fully exploring the past means that every once in a while I must leave the library and travel to the actual locations where my ancestors once walked and worked the land. Our Township Road Maps are a great place to begin such a quest.

Keep in mind that the scaling and proportion of these maps was chosen in order to squeeze hundreds of people-names, road-names, and place-names into tinier spaces than you would traditionally see. These are not professional road-maps, and like any secondary genealogical source, should be looked upon as an entry-way to original sources—in this case, original patents and applications, professionally produced maps and surveys, etc.

Both our Road Maps and Historical Maps contain cemeteries and city-centers, along with a listing of these on the left-hand side of the map. I should note that I am showing you city center-points, rather than city-limit boundaries, because in many instances, this will represent a place where settlement began. This may be a good time to mention that many cemeteries are located on private property, Always check with a local historical or genealogical society to see if a particular cemetery is publicly accessible (if it is not obviously so). As a final point, look for your surnames among the road-names. You will often be surprised by what you find.

## Historical Map

The third and final map in each Map Group is our attempt to display what each Township might have looked like before the advent of modern roads. In frontier times, people were usually more determined to settle near rivers and creeks than they were near roads, which were often few and far between. As was the case with the Road Map, we've included the same cemeteries and city-centers. We've also included railroads, many of which came along before most roads.

While some may claim "Historical Map" to be a bit of a misnomer for this tool, we settled for this label simply because it was almost as accurate as saying "Railroads, Lakes, Rivers, Cities, and Cemeteries," and it is much easier to remember.

*In Closing . . .*

By way of example, here is *A Really Good Way to Use a Township Map Group.* First, find the person you are researching in the Township's Index to Land Patents, which will direct you to the proper Section and parcel on the Patent Map. But before leaving the Index, scan all the patents within it, looking for other names of interest. Now, turn to the Patent Map and locate your parcels of land. Pay special attention to the names of patent-holders who own land surrounding your person of interest. Next, turn the page and look at the same Section(s) on the Road Map. Note which roads are closest to your parcels and also the names of nearby towns

and cemeteries. Using other resources, you may be able to learn of kin who have been buried here, plus, you may choose to visit these cemeteries the next time you are in the area.

Finally, turn to the Historical Map. Look once more at the same Sections where you found your research subject's land. Note the nearby streams, creeks, and other geographical features. You may be surprised to find family names were used to name them, or you may see a name you haven't heard mentioned in years and years—and a new research possibility is born.

Many more techniques for using these *Family Maps* volumes will no doubt be discovered. If from time to time, you will navigate to Hamilton County's web-page at www.arphax.com (use the "Research" link), you can learn new tricks as they become known (or you can share ones you have employed). But for now, you are ready to get started. So, go, and good luck.

---

Postscript: these "Illinois Archives" editions, though substantially similar to their "GLO" (General Land Office) counterparts, do have a few important differences. First, Illinois has indexed far more patents (for Illinois, of course) than has the GLO and second, the Illinois data contains the residences for numerous patentees. In order to make room for this latter benefit, we have, by necessity, had to remove some features that are present in the GLO indexes: for example the noting of cancellations, overlaps, re-issues, and the like. We think the trade-off is a minor one and that on balance, the increased research value is enormous.

# – Part I –

# The Big Picture

## Map A - Where Hamilton County, Illinois Lies Within the State

Legend

———— State Boundary

———— County Boundaries

▭ Hamilton County, Illinois

Helpful Hints

1 We start with Map "A" which simply shows us where within the State this county lies.

2 Map "B" zooms in further to help us more easily identify surrounding Counties.

3 Map "C" zooms in even further to reveal the Congressional Townships that either lie within or intersect Hamilton County

## Map B - Hamilton County, Illinois and Surrounding Counties

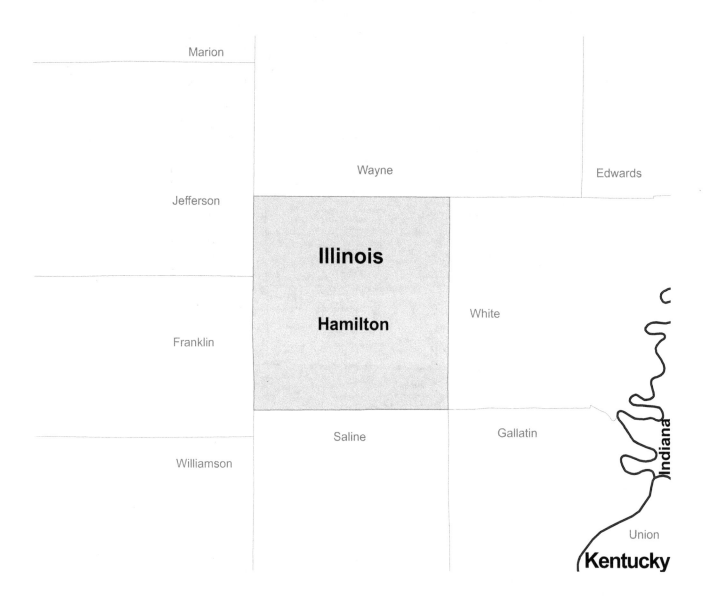

——— Legend ———

**——** State Boundaries (when applicable)

——— County Boundary

——— Helpful Hints ———

1  Many Patent-holders and their families settled across county lines. It is always a good idea to check nearby counties for your families.

2  Refer to Map "A" to see a broader view of where this County lies within the State, and Map "C" to see which Congressional Townships lie within Hamilton County.

# Map C - Congressional Townships of Hamilton County, Illinois

| | | |
|---|---|---|
| **Map Group 1**<br>Township 3-S Range 5-E | **Map Group 2**<br>Township 3-S Range 6-E | **Map Group 3**<br>Township 3-S Range 7-E |
| **Map Group 4**<br>Township 4-S Range 5-E | **Map Group 5**<br>Township 4-S Range 6-E | **Map Group 6**<br>Township 4-S Range 7-E |
| **Map Group 7**<br>Township 5-S Range 5-E | **Map Group 8**<br>Township 5-S Range 6-E | **Map Group 9**<br>Township 5-S Range 7-E |
| **Map Group 10**<br>Township 6-S Range 5-E | **Map Group 11**<br>Township 6-S Range 6-E | **Map Group 12**<br>Township 6-S Range 7-E |
| **Map Group 13**<br>Township 7-S Range 5-E | **Map Group 14**<br>Township 7-S Range 6-E | **Map Group 15**<br>Township 7-S Range 7-E |

─────── Legend ───────

Hamilton County, Illinois

Congressional Townships

─────── Helpful Hints ───────

1  Many Patent-holders and their families settled across county lines. It is always a good idea to check nearby counties for your families (See Map "B").

2  Refer to Map "A" to see a broader view of where this county lies within the State, and Map "B" for a view of the counties surrounding Hamilton County.

## Map D Index:  Cities & Towns of Hamilton County, Illinois

The following represents the Cities and Towns of Hamilton County, along with the corresponding Map Group in which each is found. Cities and Towns are displayed in both the Road and Historical maps in the Group.

| City/Town | Map Group No. |
|---|---|
| Aden | 3 |
| Belle Prairie City | 2 |
| Blairsville | 6 |
| Braden | 10 |
| Broughton | 15 |
| Bungay | 6 |
| Cornerville | 13 |
| Dahlgren | 4 |
| Dale | 11 |
| Delafield | 4 |
| Diamond City | 8 |
| Flint | 7 |
| Garrison | 2 |
| Hoodville | 8 |
| Jamestown (historical) | 9 |
| Jefferson City (historical) | 6 |
| Logansport (historical) | 9 |
| Lovilla | 4 |
| McLeansboro | 8 |
| New London (historical) | 6 |
| Nipper Corner | 9 |
| Olga | 11 |
| Piopolis | 5 |
| Rectorville (historical) | 15 |
| Rural Hill | 10 |
| Thackeray | 9 |
| Thurber | 9 |
| Tuckers Corners | 10 |
| University | 13 |
| Walpole | 14 |
| West Rural Hill | 10 |

# Map D - Cities & Towns of Hamilton County, Illinois

| | | |
|---|---|---|
| **Map Group 1**<br>Township 3-S Range 5-E | ● Garrison<br>**Map Group 2**<br>Township 3-S Range 6-E<br>Belle Prairie City ● | ● Aden<br>**Map Group 3**<br>Township 3-S Range 7-E |
| ● Dahlgren<br>**Map Group 4**<br>Township 4-S Range 5-E<br>● Lovilla<br>Delafield● | ● Piopolis<br>**Map Group 5**<br>Township 4-S Range 6-E | **Map Group 6**<br>Township 4-S Range 7-E<br>Bungay ●<br>● Blairsville　● New London<br>(historical)<br>● Jefferson City<br>(historical) |
| **Map Group 7**<br>Township 5-S Range 5-E<br>Flint ● | Diamond City ●　● McLeansboro<br>**Map Group 8**<br>Township 5-S Range 6-E<br>● Hoodville | ● Thackeray<br>Logansport ●<br>(historical)<br>●Thurber<br>**Map Group 9**<br>Township 5-S Range 7-E<br>Nipper Corner ●　　Jamestown<br>(historical) ● |
| **Map Group 10**<br>Township 6-S Range 5-E　Braden ●<br>Tuckers Corners ●<br>●West Rural Hill<br>● Rural Hill | **Map Group 11**<br>Township 6-S Range 6-E<br>● Olga　　　　Dale●<br> | **Map Group 12**<br>Township 6-S Range 7-E |
| University ●<br>**Map Group 13**<br>Township 7-S Range 5-E<br>● Comerville | Walpole ●<br>**Map Group 14**<br>Township 7-S Range 6-E | Broughton ●　**Map Group 15**<br>Township 7-S Range 7-E<br>● Rectorville<br>(historical) |

── Legend ──

Hamilton County, Illinois

Congressional Townships

Copyright © 2007 Boyd IT, Inc. All Rights Reserved

── Helpful Hints ──

**1** Cities and towns are marked only at their center-points as published by the USGS and/or NationalAtlas.gov. This often enables us to more closely approximate where these might have existed when first settled.

**2** To see more specifically where these Cities & Towns are located within the county, refer to both the Road and Historical maps in the Map-Group referred to above. See also, the Map "D" Index on the opposite page.

# Map E Index:  Cemeteries of Hamilton County, Illinois

The following represents many of the Cemeteries of Hamilton County, along with the corresponding Township Map Group in which each is found. Cemeteries are displayed in both the Road and Historical maps in the Map Groups referred to below.

| Cemetery | Map Group No. |
|---|---|
| Arterberry Cem. | 9 |
| Atchison Cem. | 1 |
| Atchisson Cem. | 7 |
| Barker Cem. | 14 |
| Bethel Cem. | 4 |
| Big Hill Cem. | 12 |
| Bright Cem. | 7 |
| Cartwright Cem. | 10 |
| Cherry Grove Cem. | 5 |
| Clark Cem. | 12 |
| Cook Cem. | 15 |
| Crisel Cem. | 4 |
| Crisel Cem. | 8 |
| Crouch Cem. | 2 |
| Digby Cem. | 11 |
| Fitzsimons Cem. | 4 |
| Garrison Cem. | 2 |
| Gholson Cem. | 15 |
| Glenview Memorial Gardens | 8 |
| Good Hope Cem. | 13 |
| Gunter Cem. | 7 |
| Hopkins Cem. | 9 |
| Hutson Cem. | 8 |
| Independent Order of Oddfellows Cem | 4 |
| Independent Order of Oddfellows Cem | 8 |
| Keasler Cem. | 15 |
| Knights Prairie Cem. | 10 |
| Lampley Cem. | 10 |
| Lantham Cem. | 15 |
| Marys Chapel Cem. | 11 |
| Morris Cem. | 15 |
| Mount Nebo Cem. | 7 |
| Munsell Cem. | 9 |
| New Hope Cem. | 9 |
| Old Brush Harbor Cem. | 9 |
| Pleasant Hill Cem. | 1 |
| Presley Cem. | 8 |
| Preston Cem. | 4 |
| Prince Cem. | 9 |
| Rawls Cem. | 2 |
| Roberts Cem. | 14 |
| Saint Johns Cem. | 4 |
| Springer Cem. | 6 |
| Union Hill Cem. | 8 |
| Webb Cem. | 9 |
| Winn Cem. | 13 |
| Wolfe Cem. | 15 |

# Map E - Cemeteries of Hamilton County, Illinois

| | | |
|---|---|---|
| ⚲ Atchison<br><br>**Map Group 1**<br>Township 3-S Range 5-E<br>Pleasant Hill ⚲ | Garrison ⚲<br><br>**Map Group 2**<br>Township 3-S Range 6-E<br>⚲ Rawls<br>⚲ Crouch | **Map Group 3**<br>Township 3-S Range 7-E |
| Independent<br>Order of<br>Oddfellows ⚲<br>⚲<br>Saint<br>Johns     ⚲ Bethel<br>⚲ Crisel<br>⚲Fitzsimons<br>⚲ Preston<br><br>**Map Group 4**<br>Township 4-S Range 5-E | **Map Group 5**<br>Township 4-S Range 6-E<br>Cherry Grove ⚲ | **Map Group 6**<br>Township 4-S Range 7-E<br>Springer ⚲ |
| ⚲Mount Nebo<br>⚲ Atchisson<br>Gunter ⚲<br>Bright ⚲<br>**Map Group 7**<br>Township 5-S Range 5-E | ⚲Glenview Memorial    ⚲ Crisel<br>Gardens<br>⚲ Union Hill    Independent<br>Order of<br>⚲ Oddfellows<br>**Map Group 8**    Hutson ⚲<br>Township 5-S Range 6-E<br>⚲Presley | ⚲ New Hope    Hopkins ⚲<br>Arterberry ⚲<br>Prince ⚲<br>Old Brush Harbor ⚲    ⚲Munsell<br>**Map Group 9**<br>Township 5-S Range 7-E<br>Webb ⚲ |
| Knights Prairie ⚲<br>Cartwright ⚲<br>**Map Group 10**<br>Township 6-S Range 5-E<br>⚲ Lampley | ⚲ Marys Chapel<br><br>Digby ⚲<br>**Map Group 11**<br>Township 6-S Range 6-E | ⚲ Clark<br><br>**Map Group 12**<br>Township 6-S Range 7-E<br>Big Hill ⚲ |
| **Map Group 13**<br>Township 7-S Range 5-E<br>⚲Good Hope<br>Winn ⚲ | Barker ⚲<br><br>**Map Group 14**<br>Township 7-S Range 6-E<br>Roberts ⚲ | **Map Group 15**    Cook ⚲<br>Township 7-S Range 7-E    Morris ⚲<br>Wolfe⚲<br>⚲ Lantham<br>Gholson ⚲    Keasler ⚲ |

───── Legend ─────

☐ Hamilton County, Illinois

☐ Congressional Townships

───── Helpful Hints ─────

1  Cemeteries are marked at locations as published by the USGS and/or NationalAtlas.gov.

2  To see more specifically where these Cemeteries are located, refer to the Road & Historical maps in the Map-Group referred to above. See also, the Map "E" Index on the opposite page to make sure you don't miss any of the Cemeteries located within this Congressional township.

# Surnames in Hamilton County, Illinois Patents

The following list represents the surnames that we have located in Hamilton County, Illinois Patents and the number of parcels that we have mapped for each one. Here is a quick way to determine the existence (or not) of Patents to be found in the subsequent indexes and maps of this volume.

| Surname | # of Land Parcels | Surname | # of Land Parcels | Surname | # of Land Parcels | Surname | # of Land Parcels |
|---|---|---|---|---|---|---|---|
| AARON | 5 | BENTLEY | 1 | CAMP | 1 | CRISAL | 3 |
| ACORD | 4 | BENTLY | 1 | CAMPBELL | 31 | CRISEL | 8 |
| ADAIR | 2 | BENTON | 3 | CANNADY | 1 | CRISELL | 1 |
| ADAMS | 7 | BESTEM | 3 | CANNEDEY | 1 | CROOK | 3 |
| ADARE | 4 | BETTS | 2 | CANNON | 2 | CROSS | 11 |
| ADCOCK | 2 | BICKERSTAFF | 1 | CANTRELL | 4 | CROUCH | 24 |
| ADDCOCK | 1 | BICKERSTUFF | 1 | CAPE | 3 | CROUSE | 2 |
| AKERS | 1 | BIGERSTAFF | 3 | CARGIL | 4 | CRUME | 1 |
| ALBIN | 2 | BIGGERSTAFF | 13 | CARGILL | 3 | CULLY | 2 |
| ALDEN | 1 | BILDERBACK | 1 | CARLISLE | 7 | CUMMUNGS | 1 |
| ALEXANDER | 2 | BISHOP | 5 | CARLTON | 2 | CUMPTON | 2 |
| ALLAN | 2 | BLACK | 4 | CARNER | 1 | CUSIC | 1 |
| ALLEN | 61 | BLADES | 3 | CARPENTER | 15 | DAEN | 1 |
| ALLENDUKER | 1 | BLAKE | 7 | CARR | 3 | DAILEY | 13 |
| ANDERSON | 15 | BOLARJACK | 2 | CARROLL | 2 | DAILY | 12 |
| ANGELMENT | 1 | BOND | 4 | CARTER | 6 | DALE | 13 |
| ANSELMANT | 1 | BOSLEY | 1 | CASKEY | 1 | DAMON | 4 |
| ANSELMENT | 5 | BOSTER | 8 | CATE | 1 | DANIEL | 1 |
| ARON | 1 | BOURLAND | 2 | CATES | 8 | DARNALL | 16 |
| ARTEBERRY | 1 | BOWEN | 7 | CATTSEL | 1 | DARNEL | 2 |
| ARTESBERRY | 1 | BOWERS | 2 | CAVANAUGH | 1 | DARNELL | 4 |
| ASHBY | 1 | BOYD | 6 | CHARLES | 2 | DAVIS | 65 |
| ASKEY | 4 | BOYER | 6 | CHEEK | 6 | DAWES | 1 |
| ATCHINSON | 1 | BOYLES | 1 | CHENNAULT | 2 | DAWSEN | 1 |
| ATCHISON | 10 | BRADEN | 52 | CHOISSER | 3 | DAWSON | 1 |
| ATCHISSON | 4 | BRADFOR | 1 | CHOSSER | 1 | DAY | 1 |
| ATERBERRY | 1 | BRADFORD | 1 | CLARK | 17 | DEAN | 4 |
| ATTEBERRY | 1 | BRADLEY | 9 | CLEAVELAND | 1 | DEBOARD | 1 |
| ATTERBURY | 1 | BRADSHAN | 1 | CLEAVELIN | 1 | DEEN | 9 |
| AVANT | 2 | BRANDON | 4 | CLICK | 1 | DEER | 1 |
| AVERETT | 1 | BRATLETT | 1 | CLIFFE | 1 | DEETS | 1 |
| AYD | 19 | BREMER | 1 | CLOSE | 1 | DELAP | 1 |
| BACHTOLD | 1 | BRENCK | 1 | CLOUD | 2 | DENNY | 8 |
| BACK | 1 | BRIAN | 2 | CLUCK | 5 | DENTON | 2 |
| BACKLE | 1 | BRIANT | 1 | COALS | 1 | DEUVALL | 3 |
| BADGER | 1 | BRILL | 3 | COATS | 1 | DEWITT | 3 |
| BAGLY | 1 | BRINK | 3 | COBB | 2 | DIAL | 1 |
| BAILEY | 9 | BRISTOL | 8 | COFFEE | 1 | DIGBY | 6 |
| BAILY | 1 | BRISTON | 1 | COFFER | 3 | DILL | 1 |
| BAKER | 2 | BROCKWAY | 3 | COFFEY | 3 | DILLARDRICK | 1 |
| BALLARD | 2 | BROOKENS | 1 | COFFMAN | 1 | DITSON | 3 |
| BANES | 3 | BROOKINS | 14 | COKER | 31 | DIXON | 7 |
| BARKER | 30 | BROOKS | 2 | COLLINS | 14 | DOBBS | 5 |
| BARNES | 5 | BROWN | 6 | COLLUP | 1 | DOCHOR | 1 |
| BARNET | 3 | BROYLES | 1 | COLVERT | 1 | DOCKER | 3 |
| BARNETT | 4 | BRUMLEY | 2 | COMPTON | 1 | DODDS | 3 |
| BARRETT | 1 | BRUMLY | 1 | CONNELLEY | 1 | DONIPHAN | 2 |
| BARRON | 1 | BRUMMER | 3 | CONNELLY | 1 | DOUGHTY | 2 |
| BARROW | 1 | BRYANT | 9 | CONNETT | 1 | DOUGLAS | 2 |
| BARTLETT | 2 | BUCHE | 1 | COOK | 14 | DOUGLASS | 8 |
| BAUMGARDNER | 1 | BUCK | 12 | COONS | 5 | DRAKE | 2 |
| BAYLES | 1 | BULLIN | 1 | COOPER | 3 | DREW | 11 |
| BEARD | 5 | BUMGARDENER | 1 | CORDER | 1 | DUCKWORTH | 8 |
| BEARDEN | 5 | BUNNETT | 3 | CORGILL | 2 | DUKES | 3 |
| BEATY | 2 | BURGESS | 1 | CORKY | 1 | DUN | 1 |
| BECKERSTAFF | 1 | BURLISON | 2 | CORN | 3 | DURAM | 1 |
| BECKWITH | 1 | BURNETT | 9 | COTES | 4 | DURHAM | 3 |
| BEECHER | 1 | BURTON | 15 | COTTINGHAM | 3 | ECHOLDS | 1 |
| BELL | 3 | BYHOVER | 1 | CRABTREE | 2 | ECHOLS | 4 |
| BELT | 8 | CAIN | 2 | CRAIG | 3 | EDDY | 1 |
| BENBROOK | 7 | CALDWELL | 1 | CRAWFORD | 1 | EDWARDS | 4 |
| BENNETT | 2 | CALVIN | 3 | CREEKMAN | 2 | ELLIS | 14 |

| Surname | # of Land Parcels | Surname | # of Land Parcels | Surname | # of Land Parcels | Surname | # of Land Parcels |
|---|---|---|---|---|---|---|---|
| EMMERSON | 5 | GOFF | 2 | HAYS | 2 | JONES | 13 |
| EPPERSON | 1 | GOINS | 1 | HAYTER | 3 | JUDD | 3 |
| ERWIN | 1 | GOODNER | 1 | HEARD | 51 | KANADA | 2 |
| ESSARY | 2 | GOODRIDGE | 7 | HEARIN | 1 | KANE | 1 |
| ESTERS | 1 | GORDON | 2 | HEIL | 3 | KANFURANN | 1 |
| ESTES | 6 | GORE | 1 | HENSLEY | 2 | KARCHER | 8 |
| ESWEICE | 1 | GOSSETT | 1 | HENSON | 1 | KAUFMAN | 7 |
| EUBANKS | 5 | GOTT | 5 | HERD | 1 | KAUGHMAN | 1 |
| EUILINSTINE | 3 | GOUDY | 1 | HERRINGTON | 1 | KEARBY | 2 |
| EWING | 1 | GOWDY | 6 | HIATT | 2 | KEASLER | 3 |
| EZELL | 1 | GRACE | 1 | HICKS | 2 | KEENEY | 2 |
| FAIRWEATHER | 2 | GRANT | 3 | HIDE | 1 | KELLEY | 5 |
| FAIRWEATHERS | 2 | GRAVENER | 1 | HIGGINS | 1 | KELLY | 5 |
| FAN | 2 | GRAVES | 6 | HILL | 3 | KENDALL | 1 |
| FANN | 5 | GRAY | 4 | HILLMAN | 2 | KENEDY | 2 |
| FANNING | 1 | GREATHOUSE | 1 | HILLYER | 2 | KENIDAY | 1 |
| FARMER | 8 | GREEN | 13 | HILMAN | 2 | KENNEDDY | 3 |
| FARRIS | 8 | GREENLER | 2 | HINDMAN | 2 | KESLER | 9 |
| FARRISS | 1 | GREGG | 3 | HINES | 1 | KING | 2 |
| FAULKNER | 10 | GRIFFIN | 2 | HINSON | 2 | KINGTON | 3 |
| FELLOWES | 1 | GRIFFITH | 4 | HITE | 2 | KINNEAR | 2 |
| FENTCH | 1 | GRIMES | 10 | HOBBS | 1 | KIRCHER | 1 |
| FIELDS | 2 | GRINESTAFF | 1 | HODGES | 1 | KIRK | 1 |
| FILDS | 1 | GRISWOLD | 15 | HOELZTS | 1 | KIRKPATRICK | 1 |
| FISHER | 10 | GROCE | 2 | HOGAN | 1 | KIRKSEA | 1 |
| FITZGERRALD | 3 | GROSS | 1 | HOGG | 6 | KISKEY | 1 |
| FLANIKIN | 1 | GROVES | 1 | HOLADAY | 2 | KITEHEY | 1 |
| FLANINKIN | 3 | GUIRE | 1 | HOLDERLY | 2 | KNIGHT | 9 |
| FLANNIKEN | 1 | GULLIO | 4 | HOLLADAY | 3 | KNOWLES | 3 |
| FLANNIKIN | 6 | GUNTER | 1 | HOLLAND | 11 | KNYKENDALL | 1 |
| FLAT | 1 | HADLEY | 1 | HOLLEMAN | 1 | KOGER | 1 |
| FLATT | 1 | HAGUE | 1 | HOLLEY | 2 | KRISSELL | 1 |
| FLINT | 24 | HALEY | 1 | HOLLOWAY | 1 | KUYKENDALL | 4 |
| FLOYD | 3 | HALL | 42 | HOOD | 8 | LACK | 1 |
| FORD | 4 | HALLER | 2 | HOOVER | 1 | LAM | 1 |
| FORESTER | 3 | HALLEY | 5 | HOPSON | 4 | LAMBERT | 4 |
| FOSTER | 12 | HAMILTON | 13 | HOWARD | 4 | LAMBUD | 1 |
| FOUTCH | 1 | HAMONTREE | 2 | HUBBELL | 1 | LAMKIN | 1 |
| FRAZIER | 5 | HAMPTON | 1 | HUFF | 2 | LANE | 62 |
| FREIZE | 1 | HANAGAN | 1 | HUFFSTATLAR | 1 | LANES | 1 |
| FRY | 2 | HANCOCK | 2 | HUFFSTATLER | 2 | LANGLEY | 2 |
| FUEL | 1 | HANCOK | 1 | HUGHES | 1 | LANHAM | 4 |
| FULLER | 3 | HANDEESTER | 1 | HUGHS | 2 | LANSDEN | 1 |
| FUNKHOUSER | 1 | HANELSON | 1 | HUHLEIN | 1 | LASATER | 19 |
| GAGE | 1 | HANNAGAN | 1 | HUNGATE | 16 | LASLEY | 1 |
| GAINES | 4 | HANNIKIN | 1 | HUNSINGER | 1 | LASSATER | 1 |
| GALBRAITH | 3 | HANSDMAN | 1 | HUNT | 11 | LASSWELL | 4 |
| GALBREATH | 2 | HARDESTER | 2 | HUNTER | 6 | LASWELL | 1 |
| GALLAHARE | 1 | HARDESTY | 6 | HUTCHINSON | 1 | LAWLER | 1 |
| GALLIHER | 1 | HARDGE | 4 | HUTSON | 10 | LAWS | 5 |
| GARISON | 1 | HARDISBY | 1 | HYDE | 1 | LEAKY | 1 |
| GARNET | 1 | HARDISTY | 13 | HYSSIS | 1 | LEARNED | 3 |
| GARRISON | 31 | HARDY | 3 | HYTEN | 4 | LEE | 7 |
| GARVIN | 5 | HARISTY | 1 | HYTER | 1 | LEECH | 2 |
| GATES | 5 | HARMISON | 5 | INGRAM | 7 | LEONARD | 1 |
| GATHIN | 1 | HARPER | 11 | INMAN | 6 | LESLEY | 1 |
| GATLIN | 1 | HARRAILSON | 2 | IRBY | 7 | LEWALLEN | 1 |
| GATTIN | 1 | HARRELSON | 7 | IRLY | 3 | LEWIS | 23 |
| GEORGE | 1 | HARRIS | 7 | IRVIN | 22 | LINGLEY | 1 |
| GERSBACSSER | 1 | HARRISON | 4 | IRVINE | 1 | LITTLE | 2 |
| GETTINGS | 1 | HARROWOOD | 2 | IRWIN | 5 | LLOYD | 1 |
| GHOLSEN | 2 | HARTESTER | 2 | JACK | 3 | LOCKHART | 5 |
| GHOLSON | 14 | HARVESTER | 3 | JAMES | 3 | LOCKWOOD | 12 |
| GHOLSTEN | 1 | HARWOOD | 1 | JANEY | 2 | LOGSDEN | 4 |
| GHORMLEY | 4 | HATCHET | 1 | JANSON | 1 | LONE | 1 |
| GIBBS | 8 | HATCHETT | 4 | JESTEES | 1 | LONG | 4 |
| GIBSON | 7 | HAWKES | 1 | JOHNS | 10 | LORIE | 1 |
| GILL | 10 | HAWLEY | 1 | JOHNSEN | 8 | LOURY | 1 |
| GILLAHAN | 1 | HAWTHORN | 1 | JOHNSON | 92 | LOWERY | 1 |
| GLAZE | 2 | HAYNES | 2 | JOHNSTON | 3 | LOWREY | 7 |

| Surname | # of Land Parcels | Surname | # of Land Parcels | Surname | # of Land Parcels | Surname | # of Land Parcels |
|---|---|---|---|---|---|---|---|
| LOWRY | 11 | MCMURTRY | 6 | PEER | 2 | ROBINSON | 3 |
| LOYD | 7 | MCNABB | 1 | PEIRCE | 1 | ROGER | 1 |
| LUSTER | 1 | MCNAMER | 1 | PEMBERTON | 11 | ROGERS | 13 |
| LYNCH | 2 | MCNEMAR | 2 | PENNINGTON | 3 | ROHRER | 5 |
| MABERRY | 1 | MCTHOMAS | 1 | PERRY | 2 | ROMINE | 7 |
| MALON | 1 | MECKE | 1 | PERRYMAN | 4 | ROO | 1 |
| MALOND | 1 | MELLON | 1 | PETER | 1 | RORER | 1 |
| MALONE | 11 | MELTON | 3 | PETERS | 3 | ROSBOROUGH | 6 |
| MAN | 2 | METCALF | 12 | PETMAN | 1 | ROSE | 4 |
| MANGIS | 3 | METHERY | 2 | PGLESHY | 1 | ROSS | 8 |
| MANIER | 1 | MEYER | 1 | PHELPS | 2 | RUBANACKER | 1 |
| MANN | 1 | MEZO | 4 | PHILIPS | 3 | RUBENAKER | 1 |
| MANNERS | 1 | MILLER | 12 | PHILLIPS | 1 | RUDE | 1 |
| MANNING | 3 | MILLS | 1 | PHIPPS | 3 | RUEBENACKER | 1 |
| MANSELL | 2 | MILLSBAUGH | 1 | PIERCE | 1 | RUMSEY | 1 |
| MARGRAVE | 1 | MILLSPAUGH | 9 | PINER | 1 | RUPARD | 1 |
| MARICLE | 2 | MINTON | 1 | PINKSTON | 1 | RUSH | 1 |
| MARKEL | 1 | MITCHEL | 1 | PITMAN | 1 | RUSSARD | 1 |
| MARQUIS | 2 | MITCHELL | 13 | PITTMAN | 1 | RUSSELL | 8 |
| MARSH | 3 | MIZE | 1 | PLUNCKETT | 2 | RUTTER | 1 |
| MARSHALL | 11 | MOBLEY | 2 | POOL | 1 | SACKBERGER | 2 |
| MARTELL | 1 | MONDAY | 3 | PORCTOR | 1 | SALLEE | 1 |
| MARTIN | 19 | MOORE | 34 | PORTER | 17 | SALLENGER | 2 |
| MATHENY | 3 | MOORES | 1 | POWELL | 18 | SANDERS | 2 |
| MATLOCK | 5 | MOORMAN | 1 | PRATT | 2 | SARRELLS | 2 |
| MAUG | 1 | MOOTHY | 2 | PRESLEY | 8 | SAUER | 1 |
| MAULDEN | 2 | MORGAN | 4 | PRICE | 1 | SCARLET | 1 |
| MAULDING | 31 | MORRIS | 14 | PRIMM | 2 | SCHLODER | 1 |
| MAY | 1 | MOSS | 1 | PRINCE | 15 | SCHOOLCRAFT | 6 |
| MAYBERRY | 48 | MOTT | 2 | PROCOT | 1 | SCHUSTER | 1 |
| MAYHALL | 1 | MOULDING | 3 | PROCTER | 1 | SCORVOIER | 1 |
| MAYNARD | 1 | MOUTRAY | 1 | PROCTOR | 15 | SCOTT | 8 |
| MCBRIDE | 1 | MUNDAY | 2 | PROMMEL | 1 | SCRUGGS | 2 |
| MCBROOM | 2 | MUNSELL | 9 | PRYOR | 2 | SCUDAMORE | 2 |
| MCBROWN | 5 | MURPHY | 4 | PUCKETT | 1 | SEAL | 2 |
| MCCAWLLEY | 1 | MUSGRAVE | 16 | PULLIAM | 2 | SEPHENS | 3 |
| MCCAY | 1 | MUSGROVE | 5 | PULLIAN | 1 | SEXTON | 1 |
| MCCLEUR | 1 | MUSKGRAVE | 1 | PYNOR | 1 | SHAFFER | 2 |
| MCCLUER | 1 | MYERS | 6 | QUARLES | 1 | SHANNON | 1 |
| MCCLURE | 2 | MYRES | 1 | RAFFERTY | 3 | SHARP | 1 |
| MCCLUSKY | 4 | NANCE | 1 | RAMBEAU | 1 | SHASTEEN | 2 |
| MCCOBGAN | 1 | NASH | 1 | RAMBO | 1 | SHEESTER | 1 |
| MCCOLGAN | 6 | NATION | 3 | RANKIN | 8 | SHELBY | 1 |
| MCCOMB | 1 | NATIONS | 3 | RAPARD | 1 | SHELTON | 25 |
| MCCOMBS | 2 | NEILSON | 1 | RATHBONE | 5 | SHERLEY | 1 |
| MCCONNER | 1 | NELSON | 1 | RAWLS | 10 | SHIPLEY | 1 |
| MCCOY | 12 | NEWMAN | 3 | RAY | 7 | SHIRBEY | 2 |
| MCCREERY | 1 | NICHOLAS | 1 | REBANACKER | 2 | SHIRLEY | 7 |
| MCDANIEL | 7 | NORMAN | 1 | REBINAKER | 1 | SHOEMAKER | 2 |
| MCDONALD | 5 | ODEL | 1 | RECTOR | 1 | SHUMAKER | 1 |
| MCDOWELL | 2 | ODELL | 3 | REED | 17 | SHUSTER | 4 |
| MCFARLAND | 7 | ODLE | 12 | REES | 1 | SIGLER | 13 |
| MCGEHEE | 1 | OGDEN | 2 | REID | 2 | SIMMONS | 1 |
| MCGENNIS | 1 | OGDON | 1 | REINER | 1 | SIMS | 10 |
| MCGILL | 3 | OGLESBAY | 1 | REYNOLDS | 1 | SINK | 2 |
| MCGINNIS | 1 | OGLESBY | 3 | RHORER | 1 | SINKS | 1 |
| MCGUIER | 1 | OHUMACHT | 1 | RICE | 8 | SLOAN | 1 |
| MCGUIRE | 5 | OLIVER | 3 | RICH | 7 | SLOO | 10 |
| MCILVANE | 1 | ONEAL | 5 | RICHARDS | 6 | SMALLWOOD | 1 |
| MCINTOSH | 1 | ORGAN | 2 | RICHARDSON | 13 | SMITH | 53 |
| MCKENZIE | 7 | ORMSBY | 2 | RICHE | 1 | SMITHPELTER | 2 |
| MCKINGY | 1 | ORR | 1 | RICHESON | 1 | SMITHPETER | 8 |
| MCKINLEY | 1 | PAGE | 9 | RIDDLE | 1 | SNEAD | 7 |
| MCKINSIE | 1 | PARKER | 2 | RIDGWAY | 1 | SNEED | 5 |
| MCKINZIE | 4 | PARMER | 1 | RILEY | 8 | SNIDER | 3 |
| MCKNIGHT | 12 | PATE | 4 | RITCHEY | 8 | SNOVER | 1 |
| MCLEAN | 6 | PATRIDGE | 1 | RITCHY | 3 | SNOW | 2 |
| MCLIN | 1 | PATTELLO | 1 | RIVES | 2 | SPAIN | 4 |
| MCMAHAN | 9 | PATTON | 3 | ROBB | 1 | SPENCER | 3 |
| MCMAHON | 2 | PECK | 3 | ROBERTS | 10 | SPILLER | 4 |

| Surname | # of Land Parcels | Surname | # of Land Parcels |
|---|---|---|---|
| SPRINGER | 1 | TWIGG | 8 |
| SPURIEN | 3 | TWIGGS | 1 |
| STADDEN | 1 | TYLER | 2 |
| STALL | 3 | ULMER | 1 |
| STANDERFER | 2 | UPTON | 16 |
| STANFIELD | 8 | VALENTINE | 4 |
| STANTON | 1 | VALETINE | 1 |
| STARNATER | 4 | VARNELL | 4 |
| STEELE | 4 | VAUGH | 1 |
| STEELLE | 3 | VAUGHAN | 1 |
| STEERMAN | 4 | VAUGHN | 1 |
| STELLE | 7 | VENABLES | 1 |
| STEPENSON | 2 | VICK | 2 |
| STEPHENS | 19 | VICKERS | 9 |
| STEPHENSON | 7 | VIOLETT | 1 |
| STEVENS | 3 | VISE | 7 |
| STEWART | 2 | WALLER | 13 |
| STILLE | 2 | WALLIS | 2 |
| STOCKER | 2 | WARD | 4 |
| STOKES | 1 | WARFIELD | 2 |
| STONE | 1 | WATSON | 2 |
| STOREY | 1 | WAUGH | 5 |
| STORY | 3 | WAYBERRY | 1 |
| STOVALL | 7 | WEBB | 15 |
| STRAWMAT | 1 | WEEKS | 3 |
| STROTHER | 1 | WELDIN | 2 |
| STULL | 8 | WELLS | 1 |
| STURMAN | 20 | WESNER | 1 |
| SULIVAN | 2 | WESTON | 3 |
| SULLINGER | 1 | WHEELER | 39 |
| SULLIVAN | 7 | WHITAKER | 2 |
| SUMMERS | 1 | WHITE | 47 |
| SUTTON | 1 | WHITEAKER | 2 |
| SWAIN | 1 | WHITESIDE | 1 |
| SWEARINGEN | 1 | WHITTINGTON | 1 |
| SWEARINGER | 2 | WHORLOW | 3 |
| SWEET | 1 | WIGGINS | 1 |
| SWEETEN | 1 | WILBANKS | 2 |
| TALLEE | 3 | WILKEY | 6 |
| TALLER | 3 | WILKINS | 1 |
| TALLEY | 1 | WILLIAMS | 26 |
| TANNER | 1 | WILLIAMSEN | 3 |
| TATE | 11 | WILLIAMSON | 1 |
| TAYLOR | 15 | WILLIS | 8 |
| TEDFORD | 4 | WILSON | 19 |
| TEMPLES | 1 | WILTON | 1 |
| TESHLEY | 1 | WINCHESTER | 1 |
| THIERRY | 6 | WINKLER | 1 |
| THOMAS | 26 | WINN | 2 |
| THOMASON | 2 | WITT | 1 |
| THOMPSON | 8 | WOLF | 2 |
| THORP | 2 | WOOD | 1 |
| THRASHER | 1 | WOODRIDGE | 1 |
| TICKNER | 1 | WOODROW | 1 |
| TINER | 3 | WOODRUFF | 5 |
| TIPSCORD | 1 | WOOLRIDGE | 1 |
| TODD | 3 | WOOLSEY | 2 |
| TOLLEY | 1 | WOOSLEY | 1 |
| TOWNSEND | 2 | WORTH | 2 |
| TRAMEL | 5 | WORTON | 1 |
| TRAMMEL | 6 | WRAY | 1 |
| TRAMMELL | 1 | WRIGHT | 18 |
| TRAMMELS | 3 | YARWOOD | 1 |
| TROTTER | 6 | YORK | 21 |
| TROUSDALE | 1 | YOUNG | 10 |
| TROUT | 4 | ZACHMAMN | 1 |
| TUBMAN | 1 | ZACHMAN | 3 |
| TUNSEND | 1 | ZACHMANN | 1 |
| TURNER | 9 | ZACHRMAN | 1 |
| TURRENLIN | 1 | ZACKMAN | 1 |

# Surname/Township Index

This Index allows you to determine which *Township Map Group(s)* contain individuals with the following surnames. Each *Map Group* has a corresponding full-name index of all individuals who obtained patents for land within its Congressional township's borders. After each index you will find the Patent Map to which it refers, and just thereafter, you can view the township's Road Map and Historical Map, with the latter map displaying streams, railroads, and more.

So, once you find your Surname here, proceed to the Index at the beginning of the **Map Group** indicated below.

| Surname | Map Group | Parcels of Land | Meridian/Township/Range | | |
|---------|-----------|-----------------|------|------|------|
| AARON | **13** | 4 | 3rd PM | 7-S | 5-E |
| " " | **14** | 1 | 3rd PM | 7-S | 6-E |
| ACORD | **7** | 3 | 3rd PM | 5-S | 5-E |
| " " | **8** | 1 | 3rd PM | 5-S | 6-E |
| ADAIR | **4** | 1 | 3rd PM | 4-S | 5-E |
| " " | **7** | 1 | 3rd PM | 5-S | 5-E |
| ADAMS | **14** | 4 | 3rd PM | 7-S | 6-E |
| " " | **6** | 3 | 3rd PM | 4-S | 7-E |
| ADARE | **7** | 4 | 3rd PM | 5-S | 5-E |
| ADCOCK | **4** | 2 | 3rd PM | 4-S | 5-E |
| ADDCOCK | **4** | 1 | 3rd PM | 4-S | 5-E |
| AKERS | **6** | 1 | 3rd PM | 4-S | 7-E |
| ALBIN | **9** | 2 | 3rd PM | 5-S | 7-E |
| ALDEN | **15** | 1 | 3rd PM | 7-S | 7-E |
| ALEXANDER | **6** | 1 | 3rd PM | 4-S | 7-E |
| " " | **12** | 1 | 3rd PM | 6-S | 7-E |
| ALLAN | **8** | 2 | 3rd PM | 5-S | 6-E |
| ALLEN | **9** | 19 | 3rd PM | 5-S | 7-E |
| " " | **8** | 12 | 3rd PM | 5-S | 6-E |
| " " | **7** | 8 | 3rd PM | 5-S | 5-E |
| " " | **14** | 8 | 3rd PM | 7-S | 6-E |
| " " | **11** | 4 | 3rd PM | 6-S | 6-E |
| " " | **15** | 4 | 3rd PM | 7-S | 7-E |
| " " | **12** | 3 | 3rd PM | 6-S | 7-E |
| " " | **10** | 2 | 3rd PM | 6-S | 5-E |
| " " | **13** | 1 | 3rd PM | 7-S | 5-E |
| ALLENDUKER | **6** | 1 | 3rd PM | 4-S | 7-E |
| ANDERSON | **8** | 8 | 3rd PM | 5-S | 6-E |
| " " | **9** | 4 | 3rd PM | 5-S | 7-E |
| " " | **13** | 2 | 3rd PM | 7-S | 5-E |
| " " | **12** | 1 | 3rd PM | 6-S | 7-E |
| ANGELMENT | **2** | 1 | 3rd PM | 3-S | 6-E |
| ANSELMANT | **2** | 1 | 3rd PM | 3-S | 6-E |
| ANSELMENT | **4** | 4 | 3rd PM | 4-S | 5-E |
| " " | **5** | 1 | 3rd PM | 4-S | 6-E |
| ARON | **13** | 1 | 3rd PM | 7-S | 5-E |
| ARTEBERRY | **9** | 1 | 3rd PM | 5-S | 7-E |
| ARTESBERRY | **9** | 1 | 3rd PM | 5-S | 7-E |
| ASHBY | **1** | 1 | 3rd PM | 3-S | 5-E |
| ASKEY | **8** | 3 | 3rd PM | 5-S | 6-E |
| " " | **5** | 1 | 3rd PM | 4-S | 6-E |
| ATCHINSON | **1** | 1 | 3rd PM | 3-S | 5-E |
| ATCHISON | **1** | 5 | 3rd PM | 3-S | 5-E |
| " " | **7** | 5 | 3rd PM | 5-S | 5-E |

| Surname | Map Group | Parcels of Land | Meridian/Township/Range | | |
|---|---|---|---|---|---|
| ATCHISSON | **1** | 2 | 3rd PM | 3-S | 5-E |
| " " | **4** | 1 | 3rd PM | 4-S | 5-E |
| " " | **7** | 1 | 3rd PM | 5-S | 5-E |
| ATERBERRY | **9** | 1 | 3rd PM | 5-S | 7-E |
| ATTEBERRY | **9** | 1 | 3rd PM | 5-S | 7-E |
| ATTERBURY | **9** | 1 | 3rd PM | 5-S | 7-E |
| AVANT | **6** | 1 | 3rd PM | 4-S | 7-E |
| " " | **9** | 1 | 3rd PM | 5-S | 7-E |
| AVERETT | **12** | 1 | 3rd PM | 6-S | 7-E |
| AYD | **5** | 15 | 3rd PM | 4-S | 6-E |
| " " | **2** | 2 | 3rd PM | 3-S | 6-E |
| " " | **4** | 2 | 3rd PM | 4-S | 5-E |
| BACHTOLD | **1** | 1 | 3rd PM | 3-S | 5-E |
| BACK | **9** | 1 | 3rd PM | 5-S | 7-E |
| BACKLE | **4** | 1 | 3rd PM | 4-S | 5-E |
| BADGER | **9** | 1 | 3rd PM | 5-S | 7-E |
| BAGLY | **12** | 1 | 3rd PM | 6-S | 7-E |
| BAILEY | **6** | 9 | 3rd PM | 4-S | 7-E |
| BAILY | **6** | 1 | 3rd PM | 4-S | 7-E |
| BAKER | **10** | 2 | 3rd PM | 6-S | 5-E |
| BALLARD | **12** | 2 | 3rd PM | 6-S | 7-E |
| BANES | **10** | 3 | 3rd PM | 6-S | 5-E |
| BARKER | **14** | 15 | 3rd PM | 7-S | 6-E |
| " " | **10** | 8 | 3rd PM | 6-S | 5-E |
| " " | **15** | 4 | 3rd PM | 7-S | 7-E |
| " " | **4** | 1 | 3rd PM | 4-S | 5-E |
| " " | **9** | 1 | 3rd PM | 5-S | 7-E |
| " " | **11** | 1 | 3rd PM | 6-S | 6-E |
| BARNES | **8** | 2 | 3rd PM | 5-S | 6-E |
| " " | **9** | 2 | 3rd PM | 5-S | 7-E |
| " " | **11** | 1 | 3rd PM | 6-S | 6-E |
| BARNET | **8** | 3 | 3rd PM | 5-S | 6-E |
| BARNETT | **7** | 2 | 3rd PM | 5-S | 5-E |
| " " | **9** | 1 | 3rd PM | 5-S | 7-E |
| " " | **11** | 1 | 3rd PM | 6-S | 6-E |
| BARRETT | **7** | 1 | 3rd PM | 5-S | 5-E |
| BARRON | **8** | 1 | 3rd PM | 5-S | 6-E |
| BARROW | **8** | 1 | 3rd PM | 5-S | 6-E |
| BARTLETT | **4** | 2 | 3rd PM | 4-S | 5-E |
| BAUMGARDNER | **8** | 1 | 3rd PM | 5-S | 6-E |
| BAYLES | **4** | 1 | 3rd PM | 4-S | 5-E |
| BEARD | **6** | 3 | 3rd PM | 4-S | 7-E |
| " " | **9** | 2 | 3rd PM | 5-S | 7-E |
| BEARDEN | **4** | 5 | 3rd PM | 4-S | 5-E |
| BEATY | **6** | 1 | 3rd PM | 4-S | 7-E |
| " " | **12** | 1 | 3rd PM | 6-S | 7-E |
| BECKERSTAFF | **9** | 1 | 3rd PM | 5-S | 7-E |
| BECKWITH | **5** | 1 | 3rd PM | 4-S | 6-E |
| BEECHER | **2** | 1 | 3rd PM | 3-S | 6-E |
| BELL | **4** | 1 | 3rd PM | 4-S | 5-E |
| " " | **7** | 1 | 3rd PM | 5-S | 5-E |
| " " | **15** | 1 | 3rd PM | 7-S | 7-E |
| BELT | **4** | 8 | 3rd PM | 4-S | 5-E |
| BENBROOK | **9** | 6 | 3rd PM | 5-S | 7-E |
| " " | **7** | 1 | 3rd PM | 5-S | 5-E |
| BENNETT | **13** | 2 | 3rd PM | 7-S | 5-E |
| BENTLEY | **10** | 1 | 3rd PM | 6-S | 5-E |
| BENTLY | **10** | 1 | 3rd PM | 6-S | 5-E |
| BENTON | **8** | 3 | 3rd PM | 5-S | 6-E |
| BESTEM | **4** | 3 | 3rd PM | 4-S | 5-E |

| Surname | Map Group | Parcels of Land | Meridian/Township/Range | | |
|---|---|---|---|---|---|
| BETTS | **11** | 2 | 3rd PM | 6-S | 6-E |
| BICKERSTAFF | **6** | 1 | 3rd PM | 4-S | 7-E |
| BICKERSTUFF | **9** | 1 | 3rd PM | 5-S | 7-E |
| BIGERSTAFF | **9** | 3 | 3rd PM | 5-S | 7-E |
| BIGGERSTAFF | **9** | 12 | 3rd PM | 5-S | 7-E |
| " " | **5** | 1 | 3rd PM | 4-S | 6-E |
| BILDERBACK | **10** | 1 | 3rd PM | 6-S | 5-E |
| BISHOP | **1** | 4 | 3rd PM | 3-S | 5-E |
| " " | **10** | 1 | 3rd PM | 6-S | 5-E |
| BLACK | **5** | 2 | 3rd PM | 4-S | 6-E |
| " " | **9** | 2 | 3rd PM | 5-S | 7-E |
| BLADES | **11** | 2 | 3rd PM | 6-S | 6-E |
| " " | **14** | 1 | 3rd PM | 7-S | 6-E |
| BLAKE | **12** | 7 | 3rd PM | 6-S | 7-E |
| BOLARJACK | **12** | 2 | 3rd PM | 6-S | 7-E |
| BOND | **5** | 4 | 3rd PM | 4-S | 6-E |
| BOSLEY | **4** | 1 | 3rd PM | 4-S | 5-E |
| BOSTER | **7** | 7 | 3rd PM | 5-S | 5-E |
| " " | **4** | 1 | 3rd PM | 4-S | 5-E |
| BOURLAND | **8** | 1 | 3rd PM | 5-S | 6-E |
| " " | **9** | 1 | 3rd PM | 5-S | 7-E |
| BOWEN | **7** | 4 | 3rd PM | 5-S | 5-E |
| " " | **4** | 3 | 3rd PM | 4-S | 5-E |
| BOWERS | **5** | 1 | 3rd PM | 4-S | 6-E |
| " " | **9** | 1 | 3rd PM | 5-S | 7-E |
| BOYD | **7** | 2 | 3rd PM | 5-S | 5-E |
| " " | **8** | 2 | 3rd PM | 5-S | 6-E |
| " " | **10** | 2 | 3rd PM | 6-S | 5-E |
| BOYER | **9** | 6 | 3rd PM | 5-S | 7-E |
| BOYLES | **4** | 1 | 3rd PM | 4-S | 5-E |
| BRADEN | **10** | 47 | 3rd PM | 6-S | 5-E |
| " " | **14** | 3 | 3rd PM | 7-S | 6-E |
| " " | **7** | 1 | 3rd PM | 5-S | 5-E |
| " " | **15** | 1 | 3rd PM | 7-S | 7-E |
| BRADFOR | **8** | 1 | 3rd PM | 5-S | 6-E |
| BRADFORD | **4** | 1 | 3rd PM | 4-S | 5-E |
| BRADLEY | **6** | 9 | 3rd PM | 4-S | 7-E |
| BRADSHAN | **13** | 1 | 3rd PM | 7-S | 5-E |
| BRANDON | **10** | 2 | 3rd PM | 6-S | 5-E |
| " " | **11** | 2 | 3rd PM | 6-S | 6-E |
| BRATLETT | **4** | 1 | 3rd PM | 4-S | 5-E |
| BREMER | **5** | 1 | 3rd PM | 4-S | 6-E |
| BRENCK | **4** | 1 | 3rd PM | 4-S | 5-E |
| BRIAN | **14** | 2 | 3rd PM | 7-S | 6-E |
| BRIANT | **9** | 1 | 3rd PM | 5-S | 7-E |
| BRILL | **12** | 3 | 3rd PM | 6-S | 7-E |
| BRINK | **4** | 3 | 3rd PM | 4-S | 5-E |
| BRISTOL | **4** | 8 | 3rd PM | 4-S | 5-E |
| BRISTON | **4** | 1 | 3rd PM | 4-S | 5-E |
| BROCKWAY | **2** | 2 | 3rd PM | 3-S | 6-E |
| " " | **3** | 1 | 3rd PM | 3-S | 7-E |
| BROOKENS | **4** | 1 | 3rd PM | 4-S | 5-E |
| BROOKINS | **4** | 9 | 3rd PM | 4-S | 5-E |
| " " | **7** | 5 | 3rd PM | 5-S | 5-E |
| BROOKS | **7** | 2 | 3rd PM | 5-S | 5-E |
| BROWN | **13** | 4 | 3rd PM | 7-S | 5-E |
| " " | **4** | 1 | 3rd PM | 4-S | 5-E |
| " " | **8** | 1 | 3rd PM | 5-S | 6-E |
| BROYLES | **10** | 1 | 3rd PM | 6-S | 5-E |
| BRUMLEY | **11** | 2 | 3rd PM | 6-S | 6-E |

| Surname | Map Group | Parcels of Land | Meridian/Township/Range | | |
|---|---|---|---|---|---|
| BRUMLY | **8** | 1 | 3rd PM | 5-S | 6-E |
| BRUMMER | **5** | 3 | 3rd PM | 4-S | 6-E |
| BRYANT | **7** | 6 | 3rd PM | 5-S | 5-E |
| " " | **9** | 2 | 3rd PM | 5-S | 7-E |
| " " | **8** | 1 | 3rd PM | 5-S | 6-E |
| BUCHE | **6** | 1 | 3rd PM | 4-S | 7-E |
| BUCK | **6** | 10 | 3rd PM | 4-S | 7-E |
| " " | **2** | 2 | 3rd PM | 3-S | 6-E |
| BULLIN | **10** | 1 | 3rd PM | 6-S | 5-E |
| BUMGARDENER | **8** | 1 | 3rd PM | 5-S | 6-E |
| BUNNETT | **11** | 3 | 3rd PM | 6-S | 6-E |
| BURGESS | **7** | 1 | 3rd PM | 5-S | 5-E |
| BURLISON | **10** | 2 | 3rd PM | 6-S | 5-E |
| BURNETT | **11** | 7 | 3rd PM | 6-S | 6-E |
| " " | **13** | 1 | 3rd PM | 7-S | 5-E |
| " " | **14** | 1 | 3rd PM | 7-S | 6-E |
| BURTON | **4** | 6 | 3rd PM | 4-S | 5-E |
| " " | **7** | 4 | 3rd PM | 5-S | 5-E |
| " " | **8** | 3 | 3rd PM | 5-S | 6-E |
| " " | **10** | 2 | 3rd PM | 6-S | 5-E |
| BYHOVER | **5** | 1 | 3rd PM | 4-S | 6-E |
| CAIN | **9** | 1 | 3rd PM | 5-S | 7-E |
| " " | **10** | 1 | 3rd PM | 6-S | 5-E |
| CALDWELL | **8** | 1 | 3rd PM | 5-S | 6-E |
| CALVIN | **10** | 2 | 3rd PM | 6-S | 5-E |
| " " | **7** | 1 | 3rd PM | 5-S | 5-E |
| CAMP | **5** | 1 | 3rd PM | 4-S | 6-E |
| CAMPBELL | **7** | 16 | 3rd PM | 5-S | 5-E |
| " " | **9** | 9 | 3rd PM | 5-S | 7-E |
| " " | **8** | 3 | 3rd PM | 5-S | 6-E |
| " " | **6** | 2 | 3rd PM | 4-S | 7-E |
| " " | **10** | 1 | 3rd PM | 6-S | 5-E |
| CANNADY | **1** | 1 | 3rd PM | 3-S | 5-E |
| CANNEDEY | **1** | 1 | 3rd PM | 3-S | 5-E |
| CANNON | **4** | 2 | 3rd PM | 4-S | 5-E |
| CANTRELL | **13** | 2 | 3rd PM | 7-S | 5-E |
| " " | **14** | 2 | 3rd PM | 7-S | 6-E |
| CAPE | **4** | 3 | 3rd PM | 4-S | 5-E |
| CARGIL | **8** | 4 | 3rd PM | 5-S | 6-E |
| CARGILL | **11** | 2 | 3rd PM | 6-S | 6-E |
| " " | **8** | 1 | 3rd PM | 5-S | 6-E |
| CARLISLE | **10** | 7 | 3rd PM | 6-S | 5-E |
| CARLTON | **7** | 2 | 3rd PM | 5-S | 5-E |
| CARNER | **13** | 1 | 3rd PM | 7-S | 5-E |
| CARPENTER | **10** | 4 | 3rd PM | 6-S | 5-E |
| " " | **8** | 2 | 3rd PM | 5-S | 6-E |
| " " | **11** | 2 | 3rd PM | 6-S | 6-E |
| " " | **12** | 2 | 3rd PM | 6-S | 7-E |
| " " | **3** | 1 | 3rd PM | 3-S | 7-E |
| " " | **7** | 1 | 3rd PM | 5-S | 5-E |
| " " | **9** | 1 | 3rd PM | 5-S | 7-E |
| " " | **13** | 1 | 3rd PM | 7-S | 5-E |
| " " | **15** | 1 | 3rd PM | 7-S | 7-E |
| CARR | **7** | 3 | 3rd PM | 5-S | 5-E |
| CARROLL | **8** | 2 | 3rd PM | 5-S | 6-E |
| CARTER | **6** | 4 | 3rd PM | 4-S | 7-E |
| " " | **10** | 2 | 3rd PM | 6-S | 5-E |
| CASKEY | **4** | 1 | 3rd PM | 4-S | 5-E |
| CATE | **4** | 1 | 3rd PM | 4-S | 5-E |
| CATES | **1** | 4 | 3rd PM | 3-S | 5-E |

| Surname | Map Group | Parcels of Land | Meridian/Township/Range | | |
|---|---|---|---|---|---|
| CATES (Cont'd) | **4** | 4 | 3rd PM | 4-S | 5-E |
| CATTSEL | **13** | 1 | 3rd PM | 7-S | 5-E |
| CAVANAUGH | **13** | 1 | 3rd PM | 7-S | 5-E |
| CHARLES | **11** | 2 | 3rd PM | 6-S | 6-E |
| CHEEK | **9** | 6 | 3rd PM | 5-S | 7-E |
| CHENNAULT | **11** | 2 | 3rd PM | 6-S | 6-E |
| CHOISSER | **7** | 3 | 3rd PM | 5-S | 5-E |
| CHOSSER | **4** | 1 | 3rd PM | 4-S | 5-E |
| CLARK | **7** | 4 | 3rd PM | 5-S | 5-E |
| " " | **11** | 4 | 3rd PM | 6-S | 6-E |
| " " | **8** | 3 | 3rd PM | 5-S | 6-E |
| " " | **12** | 3 | 3rd PM | 6-S | 7-E |
| " " | **13** | 2 | 3rd PM | 7-S | 5-E |
| " " | **10** | 1 | 3rd PM | 6-S | 5-E |
| CLEAVELAND | **15** | 1 | 3rd PM | 7-S | 7-E |
| CLEAVELIN | **9** | 1 | 3rd PM | 5-S | 7-E |
| CLICK | **10** | 1 | 3rd PM | 6-S | 5-E |
| CLIFFE | **2** | 1 | 3rd PM | 3-S | 6-E |
| CLOSE | **3** | 1 | 3rd PM | 3-S | 7-E |
| CLOUD | **9** | 2 | 3rd PM | 5-S | 7-E |
| CLUCK | **8** | 2 | 3rd PM | 5-S | 6-E |
| " " | **10** | 2 | 3rd PM | 6-S | 5-E |
| " " | **11** | 1 | 3rd PM | 6-S | 6-E |
| COALS | **5** | 1 | 3rd PM | 4-S | 6-E |
| COATS | **5** | 1 | 3rd PM | 4-S | 6-E |
| COBB | **8** | 1 | 3rd PM | 5-S | 6-E |
| " " | **11** | 1 | 3rd PM | 6-S | 6-E |
| COFFEE | **14** | 1 | 3rd PM | 7-S | 6-E |
| COFFER | **13** | 2 | 3rd PM | 7-S | 5-E |
| " " | **14** | 1 | 3rd PM | 7-S | 6-E |
| COFFEY | **13** | 2 | 3rd PM | 7-S | 5-E |
| " " | **10** | 1 | 3rd PM | 6-S | 5-E |
| COFFMAN | **5** | 1 | 3rd PM | 4-S | 6-E |
| COKER | **7** | 12 | 3rd PM | 5-S | 5-E |
| " " | **9** | 10 | 3rd PM | 5-S | 7-E |
| " " | **8** | 9 | 3rd PM | 5-S | 6-E |
| COLLINS | **1** | 8 | 3rd PM | 3-S | 5-E |
| " " | **4** | 5 | 3rd PM | 4-S | 5-E |
| " " | **13** | 1 | 3rd PM | 7-S | 5-E |
| COLLUP | **5** | 1 | 3rd PM | 4-S | 6-E |
| COLVERT | **7** | 1 | 3rd PM | 5-S | 5-E |
| COMPTON | **13** | 1 | 3rd PM | 7-S | 5-E |
| CONNELLEY | **9** | 1 | 3rd PM | 5-S | 7-E |
| CONNELLY | **9** | 1 | 3rd PM | 5-S | 7-E |
| CONNETT | **7** | 1 | 3rd PM | 5-S | 5-E |
| COOK | **4** | 6 | 3rd PM | 4-S | 5-E |
| " " | **15** | 5 | 3rd PM | 7-S | 7-E |
| " " | **10** | 2 | 3rd PM | 6-S | 5-E |
| " " | **9** | 1 | 3rd PM | 5-S | 7-E |
| COONS | **11** | 5 | 3rd PM | 6-S | 6-E |
| COOPER | **9** | 2 | 3rd PM | 5-S | 7-E |
| " " | **2** | 1 | 3rd PM | 3-S | 6-E |
| CORDER | **13** | 1 | 3rd PM | 7-S | 5-E |
| CORGILL | **11** | 2 | 3rd PM | 6-S | 6-E |
| CORKY | **4** | 1 | 3rd PM | 4-S | 5-E |
| CORN | **10** | 3 | 3rd PM | 6-S | 5-E |
| COTES | **4** | 3 | 3rd PM | 4-S | 5-E |
| " " | **5** | 1 | 3rd PM | 4-S | 6-E |
| COTTINGHAM | **8** | 3 | 3rd PM | 5-S | 6-E |
| CRABTREE | **10** | 2 | 3rd PM | 6-S | 5-E |

| Surname | Map Group | Parcels of Land | Meridian/Township/Range |
|---|---|---|---|
| CRAIG | **9** | 3 | 3rd PM 5-S 7-E |
| CRAWFORD | **9** | 1 | 3rd PM 5-S 7-E |
| CREEKMAN | **10** | 2 | 3rd PM 6-S 5-E |
| CRISAL | **4** | 3 | 3rd PM 4-S 5-E |
| CRISEL | **4** | 6 | 3rd PM 4-S 5-E |
| " " | **8** | 1 | 3rd PM 5-S 6-E |
| " " | **9** | 1 | 3rd PM 5-S 7-E |
| CRISELL | **5** | 1 | 3rd PM 4-S 6-E |
| CROOK | **9** | 3 | 3rd PM 5-S 7-E |
| CROSS | **4** | 10 | 3rd PM 4-S 5-E |
| " " | **1** | 1 | 3rd PM 3-S 5-E |
| CROUCH | **2** | 15 | 3rd PM 3-S 6-E |
| " " | **5** | 5 | 3rd PM 4-S 6-E |
| " " | **1** | 2 | 3rd PM 3-S 5-E |
| " " | **4** | 2 | 3rd PM 4-S 5-E |
| CROUSE | **12** | 2 | 3rd PM 6-S 7-E |
| CRUME | **7** | 1 | 3rd PM 5-S 5-E |
| CULLY | **10** | 2 | 3rd PM 6-S 5-E |
| CUMMUNGS | **11** | 1 | 3rd PM 6-S 6-E |
| CUMPTON | **7** | 2 | 3rd PM 5-S 5-E |
| CUSIC | **9** | 1 | 3rd PM 5-S 7-E |
| DAEN | **14** | 1 | 3rd PM 7-S 6-E |
| DAILEY | **5** | 10 | 3rd PM 4-S 6-E |
| " " | **7** | 1 | 3rd PM 5-S 5-E |
| " " | **8** | 1 | 3rd PM 5-S 6-E |
| " " | **10** | 1 | 3rd PM 6-S 5-E |
| DAILY | **5** | 8 | 3rd PM 4-S 6-E |
| " " | **8** | 3 | 3rd PM 5-S 6-E |
| " " | **6** | 1 | 3rd PM 4-S 7-E |
| DALE | **8** | 11 | 3rd PM 5-S 6-E |
| " " | **4** | 1 | 3rd PM 4-S 5-E |
| " " | **7** | 1 | 3rd PM 5-S 5-E |
| DAMON | **4** | 4 | 3rd PM 4-S 5-E |
| DANIEL | **11** | 1 | 3rd PM 6-S 6-E |
| DARNALL | **10** | 16 | 3rd PM 6-S 5-E |
| DARNEL | **10** | 2 | 3rd PM 6-S 5-E |
| DARNELL | **10** | 4 | 3rd PM 6-S 5-E |
| DAVIS | **14** | 23 | 3rd PM 7-S 6-E |
| " " | **9** | 11 | 3rd PM 5-S 7-E |
| " " | **6** | 7 | 3rd PM 4-S 7-E |
| " " | **7** | 7 | 3rd PM 5-S 5-E |
| " " | **4** | 6 | 3rd PM 4-S 5-E |
| " " | **15** | 5 | 3rd PM 7-S 7-E |
| " " | **5** | 2 | 3rd PM 4-S 6-E |
| " " | **8** | 2 | 3rd PM 5-S 6-E |
| " " | **2** | 1 | 3rd PM 3-S 6-E |
| " " | **13** | 1 | 3rd PM 7-S 5-E |
| DAWES | **13** | 1 | 3rd PM 7-S 5-E |
| DAWSEN | **7** | 1 | 3rd PM 5-S 5-E |
| DAWSON | **4** | 1 | 3rd PM 4-S 5-E |
| DAY | **1** | 1 | 3rd PM 3-S 5-E |
| DEAN | **10** | 2 | 3rd PM 6-S 5-E |
| " " | **11** | 1 | 3rd PM 6-S 6-E |
| " " | **14** | 1 | 3rd PM 7-S 6-E |
| DEBOARD | **12** | 1 | 3rd PM 6-S 7-E |
| DEEN | **14** | 7 | 3rd PM 7-S 6-E |
| " " | **10** | 1 | 3rd PM 6-S 5-E |
| " " | **11** | 1 | 3rd PM 6-S 6-E |
| DEER | **14** | 1 | 3rd PM 7-S 6-E |
| DEETS | **8** | 1 | 3rd PM 5-S 6-E |

| Surname | Map Group | Parcels of Land | Meridian/Township/Range | | |
|---|---|---|---|---|---|
| DELAP | **12** | 1 | 3rd PM | 6-S | 7-E |
| DENNY | **9** | 6 | 3rd PM | 5-S | 7-E |
| " " | **12** | 2 | 3rd PM | 6-S | 7-E |
| DENTON | **5** | 2 | 3rd PM | 4-S | 6-E |
| DEUVALL | **11** | 3 | 3rd PM | 6-S | 6-E |
| DEWITT | **7** | 2 | 3rd PM | 5-S | 5-E |
| " " | **4** | 1 | 3rd PM | 4-S | 5-E |
| DIAL | **8** | 1 | 3rd PM | 5-S | 6-E |
| DIGBY | **11** | 6 | 3rd PM | 6-S | 6-E |
| DILL | **7** | 1 | 3rd PM | 5-S | 5-E |
| DILLARDRICK | **4** | 1 | 3rd PM | 4-S | 5-E |
| DITSON | **7** | 3 | 3rd PM | 5-S | 5-E |
| DIXON | **4** | 6 | 3rd PM | 4-S | 5-E |
| " " | **7** | 1 | 3rd PM | 5-S | 5-E |
| DOBBS | **9** | 3 | 3rd PM | 5-S | 7-E |
| " " | **2** | 1 | 3rd PM | 3-S | 6-E |
| " " | **5** | 1 | 3rd PM | 4-S | 6-E |
| DOCHOR | **12** | 1 | 3rd PM | 6-S | 7-E |
| DOCKER | **9** | 2 | 3rd PM | 5-S | 7-E |
| " " | **12** | 1 | 3rd PM | 6-S | 7-E |
| DODDS | **6** | 3 | 3rd PM | 4-S | 7-E |
| DONIPHAN | **5** | 1 | 3rd PM | 4-S | 6-E |
| " " | **8** | 1 | 3rd PM | 5-S | 6-E |
| DOUGHTY | **4** | 2 | 3rd PM | 4-S | 5-E |
| DOUGLAS | **14** | 1 | 3rd PM | 7-S | 6-E |
| " " | **15** | 1 | 3rd PM | 7-S | 7-E |
| DOUGLASS | **15** | 8 | 3rd PM | 7-S | 7-E |
| DRAKE | **7** | 1 | 3rd PM | 5-S | 5-E |
| " " | **10** | 1 | 3rd PM | 6-S | 5-E |
| DREW | **9** | 6 | 3rd PM | 5-S | 7-E |
| " " | **6** | 3 | 3rd PM | 4-S | 7-E |
| " " | **8** | 2 | 3rd PM | 5-S | 6-E |
| DUCKWORTH | **10** | 7 | 3rd PM | 6-S | 5-E |
| " " | **11** | 1 | 3rd PM | 6-S | 6-E |
| DUKES | **6** | 3 | 3rd PM | 4-S | 7-E |
| DUN | **14** | 1 | 3rd PM | 7-S | 6-E |
| DURAM | **11** | 1 | 3rd PM | 6-S | 6-E |
| DURHAM | **14** | 2 | 3rd PM | 7-S | 6-E |
| " " | **11** | 1 | 3rd PM | 6-S | 6-E |
| ECHOLDS | **8** | 1 | 3rd PM | 5-S | 6-E |
| ECHOLS | **8** | 4 | 3rd PM | 5-S | 6-E |
| EDDY | **6** | 1 | 3rd PM | 4-S | 7-E |
| EDWARDS | **11** | 3 | 3rd PM | 6-S | 6-E |
| " " | **15** | 1 | 3rd PM | 7-S | 7-E |
| ELLIS | **6** | 5 | 3rd PM | 4-S | 7-E |
| " " | **2** | 3 | 3rd PM | 3-S | 6-E |
| " " | **4** | 3 | 3rd PM | 4-S | 5-E |
| " " | **5** | 2 | 3rd PM | 4-S | 6-E |
| " " | **9** | 1 | 3rd PM | 5-S | 7-E |
| EMMERSON | **7** | 3 | 3rd PM | 5-S | 5-E |
| " " | **4** | 1 | 3rd PM | 4-S | 5-E |
| " " | **11** | 1 | 3rd PM | 6-S | 6-E |
| EPPERSON | **7** | 1 | 3rd PM | 5-S | 5-E |
| ERWIN | **9** | 1 | 3rd PM | 5-S | 7-E |
| ESSARY | **11** | 2 | 3rd PM | 6-S | 6-E |
| ESTERS | **4** | 1 | 3rd PM | 4-S | 5-E |
| ESTES | **2** | 5 | 3rd PM | 3-S | 6-E |
| " " | **4** | 1 | 3rd PM | 4-S | 5-E |
| ESWEICE | **2** | 1 | 3rd PM | 3-S | 6-E |
| EUBANKS | **2** | 4 | 3rd PM | 3-S | 6-E |

| Surname | Map Group | Parcels of Land | Meridian/Township/Range | | |
|---|---|---|---|---|---|
| EUBANKS (Cont'd) | **5** | 1 | 3rd PM | 4-S | 6-E |
| EUILINSTINE | **11** | 3 | 3rd PM | 6-S | 6-E |
| EWING | **11** | 1 | 3rd PM | 6-S | 6-E |
| EZELL | **3** | 1 | 3rd PM | 3-S | 7-E |
| FAIRWEATHER | **11** | 1 | 3rd PM | 6-S | 6-E |
| " " | **12** | 1 | 3rd PM | 6-S | 7-E |
| FAIRWEATHERS | **12** | 2 | 3rd PM | 6-S | 7-E |
| FAN | **7** | 2 | 3rd PM | 5-S | 5-E |
| FANN | **7** | 4 | 3rd PM | 5-S | 5-E |
| " " | **10** | 1 | 3rd PM | 6-S | 5-E |
| FANNING | **13** | 1 | 3rd PM | 7-S | 5-E |
| FARMER | **4** | 5 | 3rd PM | 4-S | 5-E |
| " " | **6** | 2 | 3rd PM | 4-S | 7-E |
| " " | **7** | 1 | 3rd PM | 5-S | 5-E |
| FARRIS | **9** | 5 | 3rd PM | 5-S | 7-E |
| " " | **6** | 3 | 3rd PM | 4-S | 7-E |
| FARRISS | **9** | 1 | 3rd PM | 5-S | 7-E |
| FAULKNER | **4** | 6 | 3rd PM | 4-S | 5-E |
| " " | **10** | 3 | 3rd PM | 6-S | 5-E |
| " " | **11** | 1 | 3rd PM | 6-S | 6-E |
| FELLOWES | **7** | 1 | 3rd PM | 5-S | 5-E |
| FENTCH | **14** | 1 | 3rd PM | 7-S | 6-E |
| FIELDS | **9** | 2 | 3rd PM | 5-S | 7-E |
| FILDS | **6** | 1 | 3rd PM | 4-S | 7-E |
| FISHER | **10** | 10 | 3rd PM | 6-S | 5-E |
| FITZGERRALD | **9** | 3 | 3rd PM | 5-S | 7-E |
| FLANIKIN | **13** | 1 | 3rd PM | 7-S | 5-E |
| FLANINKIN | **13** | 2 | 3rd PM | 7-S | 5-E |
| " " | **10** | 1 | 3rd PM | 6-S | 5-E |
| FLANNIKEN | **13** | 1 | 3rd PM | 7-S | 5-E |
| FLANNIKIN | **13** | 4 | 3rd PM | 7-S | 5-E |
| " " | **10** | 2 | 3rd PM | 6-S | 5-E |
| FLAT | **2** | 1 | 3rd PM | 3-S | 6-E |
| FLATT | **2** | 1 | 3rd PM | 3-S | 6-E |
| FLINT | **10** | 14 | 3rd PM | 6-S | 5-E |
| " " | **11** | 6 | 3rd PM | 6-S | 6-E |
| " " | **7** | 2 | 3rd PM | 5-S | 5-E |
| " " | **8** | 2 | 3rd PM | 5-S | 6-E |
| FLOYD | **9** | 2 | 3rd PM | 5-S | 7-E |
| " " | **13** | 1 | 3rd PM | 7-S | 5-E |
| FORD | **12** | 2 | 3rd PM | 6-S | 7-E |
| " " | **8** | 1 | 3rd PM | 5-S | 6-E |
| " " | **15** | 1 | 3rd PM | 7-S | 7-E |
| FORESTER | **7** | 2 | 3rd PM | 5-S | 5-E |
| " " | **13** | 1 | 3rd PM | 7-S | 5-E |
| FOSTER | **10** | 6 | 3rd PM | 6-S | 5-E |
| " " | **7** | 4 | 3rd PM | 5-S | 5-E |
| " " | **4** | 2 | 3rd PM | 4-S | 5-E |
| FOUTCH | **14** | 1 | 3rd PM | 7-S | 6-E |
| FRAZIER | **7** | 5 | 3rd PM | 5-S | 5-E |
| FREIZE | **8** | 1 | 3rd PM | 5-S | 6-E |
| FRY | **2** | 1 | 3rd PM | 3-S | 6-E |
| " " | **5** | 1 | 3rd PM | 4-S | 6-E |
| FUEL | **7** | 1 | 3rd PM | 5-S | 5-E |
| FULLER | **9** | 2 | 3rd PM | 5-S | 7-E |
| " " | **5** | 1 | 3rd PM | 4-S | 6-E |
| FUNKHOUSER | **6** | 1 | 3rd PM | 4-S | 7-E |
| GAGE | **4** | 1 | 3rd PM | 4-S | 5-E |
| GAINES | **4** | 2 | 3rd PM | 4-S | 5-E |
| " " | **7** | 1 | 3rd PM | 5-S | 5-E |

| Surname | Map Group | Parcels of Land | Meridian/Township/Range |
|---|---|---|---|
| GAINES (Cont'd) | **14** | 1 | 3rd PM 7-S 6-E |
| GALBRAITH | **13** | 3 | 3rd PM 7-S 5-E |
| GALBREATH | **13** | 2 | 3rd PM 7-S 5-E |
| GALLAHARE | **5** | 1 | 3rd PM 4-S 6-E |
| GALLIHER | **11** | 1 | 3rd PM 6-S 6-E |
| GARISON | **2** | 1 | 3rd PM 3-S 6-E |
| GARNET | **10** | 1 | 3rd PM 6-S 5-E |
| GARRISON | **1** | 8 | 3rd PM 3-S 5-E |
| " " | **2** | 8 | 3rd PM 3-S 6-E |
| " " | **6** | 7 | 3rd PM 4-S 7-E |
| " " | **9** | 6 | 3rd PM 5-S 7-E |
| " " | **8** | 2 | 3rd PM 5-S 6-E |
| GARVIN | **10** | 3 | 3rd PM 6-S 5-E |
| " " | **7** | 2 | 3rd PM 5-S 5-E |
| GATES | **11** | 3 | 3rd PM 6-S 6-E |
| " " | **9** | 2 | 3rd PM 5-S 7-E |
| GATHIN | **5** | 1 | 3rd PM 4-S 6-E |
| GATLIN | **5** | 1 | 3rd PM 4-S 6-E |
| GATTIN | **5** | 1 | 3rd PM 4-S 6-E |
| GEORGE | **15** | 1 | 3rd PM 7-S 7-E |
| GERSBACSSER | **6** | 1 | 3rd PM 4-S 7-E |
| GETTINGS | **9** | 1 | 3rd PM 5-S 7-E |
| GHOLSEN | **15** | 2 | 3rd PM 7-S 7-E |
| GHOLSON | **15** | 11 | 3rd PM 7-S 7-E |
| " " | **14** | 2 | 3rd PM 7-S 6-E |
| " " | **12** | 1 | 3rd PM 6-S 7-E |
| GHOLSTEN | **13** | 1 | 3rd PM 7-S 5-E |
| GHORMLEY | **5** | 3 | 3rd PM 4-S 6-E |
| " " | **4** | 1 | 3rd PM 4-S 5-E |
| GIBBS | **7** | 8 | 3rd PM 5-S 5-E |
| GIBSON | **15** | 7 | 3rd PM 7-S 7-E |
| GILL | **4** | 10 | 3rd PM 4-S 5-E |
| GILLAHAN | **7** | 1 | 3rd PM 5-S 5-E |
| GLAZE | **5** | 2 | 3rd PM 4-S 6-E |
| GOFF | **8** | 2 | 3rd PM 5-S 6-E |
| GOINS | **4** | 1 | 3rd PM 4-S 5-E |
| GOODNER | **1** | 1 | 3rd PM 3-S 5-E |
| GOODRIDGE | **4** | 7 | 3rd PM 4-S 5-E |
| GORDON | **9** | 2 | 3rd PM 5-S 7-E |
| GORE | **7** | 1 | 3rd PM 5-S 5-E |
| GOSSETT | **12** | 1 | 3rd PM 6-S 7-E |
| GOTT | **12** | 5 | 3rd PM 6-S 7-E |
| GOUDY | **9** | 1 | 3rd PM 5-S 7-E |
| GOWDY | **10** | 4 | 3rd PM 6-S 5-E |
| " " | **8** | 1 | 3rd PM 5-S 6-E |
| " " | **9** | 1 | 3rd PM 5-S 7-E |
| GRACE | **5** | 1 | 3rd PM 4-S 6-E |
| GRANT | **8** | 3 | 3rd PM 5-S 6-E |
| GRAVENER | **1** | 1 | 3rd PM 3-S 5-E |
| GRAVES | **14** | 3 | 3rd PM 7-S 6-E |
| " " | **13** | 2 | 3rd PM 7-S 5-E |
| " " | **7** | 1 | 3rd PM 5-S 5-E |
| GRAY | **13** | 2 | 3rd PM 7-S 5-E |
| " " | **9** | 1 | 3rd PM 5-S 7-E |
| " " | **14** | 1 | 3rd PM 7-S 6-E |
| GREATHOUSE | **12** | 1 | 3rd PM 6-S 7-E |
| GREEN | **6** | 3 | 3rd PM 4-S 7-E |
| " " | **7** | 3 | 3rd PM 5-S 5-E |
| " " | **5** | 2 | 3rd PM 4-S 6-E |
| " " | **9** | 2 | 3rd PM 5-S 7-E |

| Surname | Map Group | Parcels of Land | Meridian/Township/Range | | |
|---|---|---|---|---|---|
| GREEN (Cont'd) | 10 | 2 | 3rd PM | 6-S | 5-E |
| " " | 2 | 1 | 3rd PM | 3-S | 6-E |
| GREENLER | 9 | 2 | 3rd PM | 5-S | 7-E |
| GREGG | 15 | 3 | 3rd PM | 7-S | 7-E |
| GRIFFIN | 7 | 2 | 3rd PM | 5-S | 5-E |
| GRIFFITH | 12 | 4 | 3rd PM | 6-S | 7-E |
| GRIMES | 14 | 5 | 3rd PM | 7-S | 6-E |
| " " | 12 | 4 | 3rd PM | 6-S | 7-E |
| " " | 15 | 1 | 3rd PM | 7-S | 7-E |
| GRINESTAFF | 10 | 1 | 3rd PM | 6-S | 5-E |
| GRISWOLD | 14 | 15 | 3rd PM | 7-S | 6-E |
| GROCE | 5 | 1 | 3rd PM | 4-S | 6-E |
| " " | 8 | 1 | 3rd PM | 5-S | 6-E |
| GROSS | 12 | 1 | 3rd PM | 6-S | 7-E |
| GROVES | 12 | 1 | 3rd PM | 6-S | 7-E |
| GUIRE | 4 | 1 | 3rd PM | 4-S | 5-E |
| GULLIO | 6 | 4 | 3rd PM | 4-S | 7-E |
| GUNTER | 7 | 1 | 3rd PM | 5-S | 5-E |
| HADLEY | 15 | 1 | 3rd PM | 7-S | 7-E |
| HAGUE | 1 | 1 | 3rd PM | 3-S | 5-E |
| HALEY | 15 | 1 | 3rd PM | 7-S | 7-E |
| HALL | 2 | 8 | 3rd PM | 3-S | 6-E |
| " " | 14 | 8 | 3rd PM | 7-S | 6-E |
| " " | 7 | 7 | 3rd PM | 5-S | 5-E |
| " " | 10 | 7 | 3rd PM | 6-S | 5-E |
| " " | 13 | 4 | 3rd PM | 7-S | 5-E |
| " " | 4 | 3 | 3rd PM | 4-S | 5-E |
| " " | 1 | 2 | 3rd PM | 3-S | 5-E |
| " " | 5 | 2 | 3rd PM | 4-S | 6-E |
| " " | 9 | 1 | 3rd PM | 5-S | 7-E |
| HALLER | 2 | 2 | 3rd PM | 3-S | 6-E |
| HALLEY | 4 | 5 | 3rd PM | 4-S | 5-E |
| HAMILTON | 10 | 7 | 3rd PM | 6-S | 5-E |
| " " | 12 | 3 | 3rd PM | 6-S | 7-E |
| " " | 7 | 2 | 3rd PM | 5-S | 5-E |
| " " | 4 | 1 | 3rd PM | 4-S | 5-E |
| HAMONTREE | 7 | 2 | 3rd PM | 5-S | 5-E |
| HAMPTON | 9 | 1 | 3rd PM | 5-S | 7-E |
| HANAGAN | 9 | 1 | 3rd PM | 5-S | 7-E |
| HANCOCK | 11 | 1 | 3rd PM | 6-S | 6-E |
| " " | 13 | 1 | 3rd PM | 7-S | 5-E |
| HANCOK | 13 | 1 | 3rd PM | 7-S | 5-E |
| HANDEESTER | 12 | 1 | 3rd PM | 6-S | 7-E |
| HANELSON | 10 | 1 | 3rd PM | 6-S | 5-E |
| HANNAGAN | 9 | 1 | 3rd PM | 5-S | 7-E |
| HANNIKIN | 10 | 1 | 3rd PM | 6-S | 5-E |
| HANSDMAN | 4 | 1 | 3rd PM | 4-S | 5-E |
| HARDESTER | 12 | 1 | 3rd PM | 6-S | 7-E |
| " " | 14 | 1 | 3rd PM | 7-S | 6-E |
| HARDESTY | 12 | 3 | 3rd PM | 6-S | 7-E |
| " " | 15 | 2 | 3rd PM | 7-S | 7-E |
| " " | 7 | 1 | 3rd PM | 5-S | 5-E |
| HARDGE | 8 | 4 | 3rd PM | 5-S | 6-E |
| HARDISBY | 14 | 1 | 3rd PM | 7-S | 6-E |
| HARDISTY | 12 | 5 | 3rd PM | 6-S | 7-E |
| " " | 15 | 5 | 3rd PM | 7-S | 7-E |
| " " | 14 | 3 | 3rd PM | 7-S | 6-E |
| HARDY | 5 | 1 | 3rd PM | 4-S | 6-E |
| " " | 7 | 1 | 3rd PM | 5-S | 5-E |
| " " | 8 | 1 | 3rd PM | 5-S | 6-E |

| Surname | Map Group | Parcels of Land | Meridian/Township/Range | | |
|---|---|---|---|---|---|
| HARISTY | **14** | 1 | 3rd PM | 7-S | 6-E |
| HARMISON | **7** | 5 | 3rd PM | 5-S | 5-E |
| HARPER | **7** | 9 | 3rd PM | 5-S | 5-E |
| " " | **8** | 2 | 3rd PM | 5-S | 6-E |
| HARRAILSON | **7** | 2 | 3rd PM | 5-S | 5-E |
| HARRELSON | **10** | 5 | 3rd PM | 6-S | 5-E |
| " " | **7** | 2 | 3rd PM | 5-S | 5-E |
| HARRIS | **11** | 5 | 3rd PM | 6-S | 6-E |
| " " | **10** | 1 | 3rd PM | 6-S | 5-E |
| " " | **13** | 1 | 3rd PM | 7-S | 5-E |
| HARRISON | **7** | 2 | 3rd PM | 5-S | 5-E |
| " " | **12** | 1 | 3rd PM | 6-S | 7-E |
| " " | **13** | 1 | 3rd PM | 7-S | 5-E |
| HARROWOOD | **12** | 2 | 3rd PM | 6-S | 7-E |
| HARTESTER | **14** | 2 | 3rd PM | 7-S | 6-E |
| HARVESTER | **14** | 3 | 3rd PM | 7-S | 6-E |
| HARWOOD | **7** | 1 | 3rd PM | 5-S | 5-E |
| HATCHET | **10** | 1 | 3rd PM | 6-S | 5-E |
| HATCHETT | **10** | 4 | 3rd PM | 6-S | 5-E |
| HAWKES | **7** | 1 | 3rd PM | 5-S | 5-E |
| HAWLEY | **8** | 1 | 3rd PM | 5-S | 6-E |
| HAWTHORN | **9** | 1 | 3rd PM | 5-S | 7-E |
| HAYNES | **6** | 1 | 3rd PM | 4-S | 7-E |
| " " | **8** | 1 | 3rd PM | 5-S | 6-E |
| HAYS | **8** | 2 | 3rd PM | 5-S | 6-E |
| HAYTER | **9** | 3 | 3rd PM | 5-S | 7-E |
| HEARD | **8** | 22 | 3rd PM | 5-S | 6-E |
| " " | **11** | 17 | 3rd PM | 6-S | 6-E |
| " " | **6** | 4 | 3rd PM | 4-S | 7-E |
| " " | **5** | 3 | 3rd PM | 4-S | 6-E |
| " " | **10** | 2 | 3rd PM | 6-S | 5-E |
| " " | **13** | 2 | 3rd PM | 7-S | 5-E |
| " " | **12** | 1 | 3rd PM | 6-S | 7-E |
| HEARIN | **9** | 1 | 3rd PM | 5-S | 7-E |
| HEIL | **5** | 3 | 3rd PM | 4-S | 6-E |
| HENSLEY | **10** | 2 | 3rd PM | 6-S | 5-E |
| HENSON | **14** | 1 | 3rd PM | 7-S | 6-E |
| HERD | **8** | 1 | 3rd PM | 5-S | 6-E |
| HERRINGTON | **11** | 1 | 3rd PM | 6-S | 6-E |
| HIATT | **9** | 2 | 3rd PM | 5-S | 7-E |
| HICKS | **10** | 1 | 3rd PM | 6-S | 5-E |
| " " | **14** | 1 | 3rd PM | 7-S | 6-E |
| HIDE | **10** | 1 | 3rd PM | 6-S | 5-E |
| HIGGINS | **13** | 1 | 3rd PM | 7-S | 5-E |
| HILL | **7** | 1 | 3rd PM | 5-S | 5-E |
| " " | **8** | 1 | 3rd PM | 5-S | 6-E |
| " " | **9** | 1 | 3rd PM | 5-S | 7-E |
| HILLMAN | **4** | 2 | 3rd PM | 4-S | 5-E |
| HILLYER | **6** | 2 | 3rd PM | 4-S | 7-E |
| HILMAN | **4** | 2 | 3rd PM | 4-S | 5-E |
| HINDMAN | **7** | 2 | 3rd PM | 5-S | 5-E |
| HINES | **4** | 1 | 3rd PM | 4-S | 5-E |
| HINSON | **11** | 1 | 3rd PM | 6-S | 6-E |
| " " | **14** | 1 | 3rd PM | 7-S | 6-E |
| HITE | **8** | 2 | 3rd PM | 5-S | 6-E |
| HOBBS | **4** | 1 | 3rd PM | 4-S | 5-E |
| HODGES | **7** | 1 | 3rd PM | 5-S | 5-E |
| HOELZTS | **2** | 1 | 3rd PM | 3-S | 6-E |
| HOGAN | **2** | 1 | 3rd PM | 3-S | 6-E |
| HOGG | **11** | 3 | 3rd PM | 6-S | 6-E |

| Surname | Map Group | Parcels of Land | Meridian/Township/Range | | |
|---|---|---|---|---|---|
| HOGG (Cont'd) | **14** | 2 | 3rd PM | 7-S | 6-E |
| " " | **8** | 1 | 3rd PM | 5-S | 6-E |
| HOLADAY | **2** | 2 | 3rd PM | 3-S | 6-E |
| HOLDERLY | **13** | 2 | 3rd PM | 7-S | 5-E |
| HOLLADAY | **13** | 2 | 3rd PM | 7-S | 5-E |
| " " | **2** | 1 | 3rd PM | 3-S | 6-E |
| HOLLAND | **7** | 3 | 3rd PM | 5-S | 5-E |
| " " | **5** | 2 | 3rd PM | 4-S | 6-E |
| " " | **6** | 2 | 3rd PM | 4-S | 7-E |
| " " | **1** | 1 | 3rd PM | 3-S | 5-E |
| " " | **8** | 1 | 3rd PM | 5-S | 6-E |
| " " | **13** | 1 | 3rd PM | 7-S | 5-E |
| " " | **14** | 1 | 3rd PM | 7-S | 6-E |
| HOLLEMAN | **10** | 1 | 3rd PM | 6-S | 5-E |
| HOLLEY | **6** | 2 | 3rd PM | 4-S | 7-E |
| HOLLOWAY | **15** | 1 | 3rd PM | 7-S | 7-E |
| HOOD | **8** | 5 | 3rd PM | 5-S | 6-E |
| " " | **15** | 3 | 3rd PM | 7-S | 7-E |
| HOOVER | **8** | 1 | 3rd PM | 5-S | 6-E |
| HOPSON | **9** | 4 | 3rd PM | 5-S | 7-E |
| HOWARD | **12** | 3 | 3rd PM | 6-S | 7-E |
| " " | **15** | 1 | 3rd PM | 7-S | 7-E |
| HUBBELL | **9** | 1 | 3rd PM | 5-S | 7-E |
| HUFF | **4** | 1 | 3rd PM | 4-S | 5-E |
| " " | **13** | 1 | 3rd PM | 7-S | 5-E |
| HUFFSTATLAR | **7** | 1 | 3rd PM | 5-S | 5-E |
| HUFFSTATLER | **13** | 2 | 3rd PM | 7-S | 5-E |
| HUGHES | **12** | 1 | 3rd PM | 6-S | 7-E |
| HUGHS | **12** | 2 | 3rd PM | 6-S | 7-E |
| HUHLEIN | **2** | 1 | 3rd PM | 3-S | 6-E |
| HUNGATE | **10** | 10 | 3rd PM | 6-S | 5-E |
| " " | **7** | 6 | 3rd PM | 5-S | 5-E |
| HUNSINGER | **4** | 1 | 3rd PM | 4-S | 5-E |
| HUNT | **6** | 3 | 3rd PM | 4-S | 7-E |
| " " | **7** | 3 | 3rd PM | 5-S | 5-E |
| " " | **10** | 2 | 3rd PM | 6-S | 5-E |
| " " | **11** | 2 | 3rd PM | 6-S | 6-E |
| " " | **9** | 1 | 3rd PM | 5-S | 7-E |
| HUNTER | **8** | 4 | 3rd PM | 5-S | 6-E |
| " " | **10** | 1 | 3rd PM | 6-S | 5-E |
| " " | **11** | 1 | 3rd PM | 6-S | 6-E |
| HUTCHINSON | **11** | 1 | 3rd PM | 6-S | 6-E |
| HUTSON | **8** | 8 | 3rd PM | 5-S | 6-E |
| " " | **11** | 2 | 3rd PM | 6-S | 6-E |
| HYDE | **10** | 1 | 3rd PM | 6-S | 5-E |
| HYSSIS | **8** | 1 | 3rd PM | 5-S | 6-E |
| HYTEN | **6** | 4 | 3rd PM | 4-S | 7-E |
| HYTER | **6** | 1 | 3rd PM | 4-S | 7-E |
| INGRAM | **5** | 4 | 3rd PM | 4-S | 6-E |
| " " | **8** | 3 | 3rd PM | 5-S | 6-E |
| INMAN | **4** | 6 | 3rd PM | 4-S | 5-E |
| IRBY | **13** | 7 | 3rd PM | 7-S | 5-E |
| IRLY | **13** | 3 | 3rd PM | 7-S | 5-E |
| IRVIN | **7** | 17 | 3rd PM | 5-S | 5-E |
| " " | **8** | 2 | 3rd PM | 5-S | 6-E |
| " " | **2** | 1 | 3rd PM | 3-S | 6-E |
| " " | **4** | 1 | 3rd PM | 4-S | 5-E |
| " " | **6** | 1 | 3rd PM | 4-S | 7-E |
| IRVINE | **7** | 1 | 3rd PM | 5-S | 5-E |
| IRWIN | **2** | 4 | 3rd PM | 3-S | 6-E |

| Surname | Map Group | Parcels of Land | Meridian/Township/Range | | |
|---|---|---|---|---|---|
| IRWIN (Cont'd) | **7** | 1 | 3rd PM | 5-S | 5-E |
| JACK | **7** | 3 | 3rd PM | 5-S | 5-E |
| JAMES | **1** | 3 | 3rd PM | 3-S | 5-E |
| JANEY | **7** | 2 | 3rd PM | 5-S | 5-E |
| JANSON | **7** | 1 | 3rd PM | 5-S | 5-E |
| JESTEES | **12** | 1 | 3rd PM | 6-S | 7-E |
| JOHNS | **13** | 10 | 3rd PM | 7-S | 5-E |
| JOHNSEN | **11** | 5 | 3rd PM | 6-S | 6-E |
| " " | **7** | 2 | 3rd PM | 5-S | 5-E |
| " " | **10** | 1 | 3rd PM | 6-S | 5-E |
| JOHNSON | **10** | 49 | 3rd PM | 6-S | 5-E |
| " " | **11** | 15 | 3rd PM | 6-S | 6-E |
| " " | **7** | 14 | 3rd PM | 5-S | 5-E |
| " " | **15** | 5 | 3rd PM | 7-S | 7-E |
| " " | **4** | 4 | 3rd PM | 4-S | 5-E |
| " " | **13** | 2 | 3rd PM | 7-S | 5-E |
| " " | **6** | 1 | 3rd PM | 4-S | 7-E |
| " " | **9** | 1 | 3rd PM | 5-S | 7-E |
| " " | **12** | 1 | 3rd PM | 6-S | 7-E |
| JOHNSTON | **10** | 3 | 3rd PM | 6-S | 5-E |
| JONES | **10** | 3 | 3rd PM | 6-S | 5-E |
| " " | **14** | 3 | 3rd PM | 7-S | 6-E |
| " " | **11** | 2 | 3rd PM | 6-S | 6-E |
| " " | **13** | 2 | 3rd PM | 7-S | 5-E |
| " " | **6** | 1 | 3rd PM | 4-S | 7-E |
| " " | **8** | 1 | 3rd PM | 5-S | 6-E |
| " " | **9** | 1 | 3rd PM | 5-S | 7-E |
| JUDD | **4** | 3 | 3rd PM | 4-S | 5-E |
| KANADA | **1** | 2 | 3rd PM | 3-S | 5-E |
| KANE | **14** | 1 | 3rd PM | 7-S | 6-E |
| KANFURANN | **2** | 1 | 3rd PM | 3-S | 6-E |
| KARCHER | **4** | 5 | 3rd PM | 4-S | 5-E |
| " " | **1** | 2 | 3rd PM | 3-S | 5-E |
| " " | **2** | 1 | 3rd PM | 3-S | 6-E |
| KAUFMAN | **5** | 5 | 3rd PM | 4-S | 6-E |
| " " | **2** | 2 | 3rd PM | 3-S | 6-E |
| KAUGHMAN | **5** | 1 | 3rd PM | 4-S | 6-E |
| KEARBY | **6** | 2 | 3rd PM | 4-S | 7-E |
| KEASLER | **15** | 3 | 3rd PM | 7-S | 7-E |
| KEENEY | **15** | 2 | 3rd PM | 7-S | 7-E |
| KELLEY | **13** | 3 | 3rd PM | 7-S | 5-E |
| " " | **7** | 2 | 3rd PM | 5-S | 5-E |
| KELLY | **7** | 4 | 3rd PM | 5-S | 5-E |
| " " | **2** | 1 | 3rd PM | 3-S | 6-E |
| KENDALL | **4** | 1 | 3rd PM | 4-S | 5-E |
| KENEDY | **1** | 2 | 3rd PM | 3-S | 5-E |
| KENIDAY | **1** | 1 | 3rd PM | 3-S | 5-E |
| KENNEDDY | **1** | 3 | 3rd PM | 3-S | 5-E |
| KESLER | **15** | 9 | 3rd PM | 7-S | 7-E |
| KING | **4** | 2 | 3rd PM | 4-S | 5-E |
| KINGTON | **10** | 3 | 3rd PM | 6-S | 5-E |
| KINNEAR | **11** | 2 | 3rd PM | 6-S | 6-E |
| KIRCHER | **4** | 1 | 3rd PM | 4-S | 5-E |
| KIRK | **9** | 1 | 3rd PM | 5-S | 7-E |
| KIRKPATRICK | **8** | 1 | 3rd PM | 5-S | 6-E |
| KIRKSEA | **1** | 1 | 3rd PM | 3-S | 5-E |
| KISKEY | **4** | 1 | 3rd PM | 4-S | 5-E |
| KITEHEY | **12** | 1 | 3rd PM | 6-S | 7-E |
| KNIGHT | **13** | 9 | 3rd PM | 7-S | 5-E |
| KNOWLES | **5** | 3 | 3rd PM | 4-S | 6-E |

| Surname | Map Group | Parcels of Land | Meridian/Township/Range | | |
|---|---|---|---|---|---|
| KNYKENDALL | **4** | 1 | 3rd PM | 4-S | 5-E |
| KOGER | **5** | 1 | 3rd PM | 4-S | 6-E |
| KRISSELL | **5** | 1 | 3rd PM | 4-S | 6-E |
| KUYKENDALL | **4** | 4 | 3rd PM | 4-S | 5-E |
| LACK | **7** | 1 | 3rd PM | 5-S | 5-E |
| LAM | **9** | 1 | 3rd PM | 5-S | 7-E |
| LAMBERT | **9** | 3 | 3rd PM | 5-S | 7-E |
| " " | **7** | 1 | 3rd PM | 5-S | 5-E |
| LAMBUD | **7** | 1 | 3rd PM | 5-S | 5-E |
| LAMKIN | **13** | 1 | 3rd PM | 7-S | 5-E |
| LANE | **9** | 21 | 3rd PM | 5-S | 7-E |
| " " | **14** | 20 | 3rd PM | 7-S | 6-E |
| " " | **5** | 7 | 3rd PM | 4-S | 6-E |
| " " | **8** | 6 | 3rd PM | 5-S | 6-E |
| " " | **13** | 5 | 3rd PM | 7-S | 5-E |
| " " | **6** | 3 | 3rd PM | 4-S | 7-E |
| LANES | **13** | 1 | 3rd PM | 7-S | 5-E |
| LANGLEY | **7** | 2 | 3rd PM | 5-S | 5-E |
| LANHAM | **15** | 4 | 3rd PM | 7-S | 7-E |
| LANSDEN | **9** | 1 | 3rd PM | 5-S | 7-E |
| LASATER | **12** | 8 | 3rd PM | 6-S | 7-E |
| " " | **6** | 4 | 3rd PM | 4-S | 7-E |
| " " | **9** | 2 | 3rd PM | 5-S | 7-E |
| " " | **13** | 2 | 3rd PM | 7-S | 5-E |
| " " | **15** | 2 | 3rd PM | 7-S | 7-E |
| " " | **11** | 1 | 3rd PM | 6-S | 6-E |
| LASLEY | **7** | 1 | 3rd PM | 5-S | 5-E |
| LASSATER | **13** | 1 | 3rd PM | 7-S | 5-E |
| LASSWELL | **11** | 3 | 3rd PM | 6-S | 6-E |
| " " | **14** | 1 | 3rd PM | 7-S | 6-E |
| LASWELL | **14** | 1 | 3rd PM | 7-S | 6-E |
| LAWLER | **2** | 1 | 3rd PM | 3-S | 6-E |
| LAWS | **13** | 4 | 3rd PM | 7-S | 5-E |
| " " | **14** | 1 | 3rd PM | 7-S | 6-E |
| LEAKY | **8** | 1 | 3rd PM | 5-S | 6-E |
| LEARNED | **4** | 3 | 3rd PM | 4-S | 5-E |
| LEE | **7** | 4 | 3rd PM | 5-S | 5-E |
| " " | **10** | 2 | 3rd PM | 6-S | 5-E |
| " " | **6** | 1 | 3rd PM | 4-S | 7-E |
| LEECH | **8** | 1 | 3rd PM | 5-S | 6-E |
| " " | **9** | 1 | 3rd PM | 5-S | 7-E |
| LEONARD | **11** | 1 | 3rd PM | 6-S | 6-E |
| LESLEY | **7** | 1 | 3rd PM | 5-S | 5-E |
| LEWALLEN | **11** | 1 | 3rd PM | 6-S | 6-E |
| LEWIS | **5** | 7 | 3rd PM | 4-S | 6-E |
| " " | **13** | 5 | 3rd PM | 7-S | 5-E |
| " " | **14** | 5 | 3rd PM | 7-S | 6-E |
| " " | **10** | 3 | 3rd PM | 6-S | 5-E |
| " " | **11** | 2 | 3rd PM | 6-S | 6-E |
| " " | **4** | 1 | 3rd PM | 4-S | 5-E |
| LINGLEY | **6** | 1 | 3rd PM | 4-S | 7-E |
| LITTLE | **14** | 2 | 3rd PM | 7-S | 6-E |
| LLOYD | **9** | 1 | 3rd PM | 5-S | 7-E |
| LOCKHART | **14** | 3 | 3rd PM | 7-S | 6-E |
| " " | **8** | 1 | 3rd PM | 5-S | 6-E |
| " " | **11** | 1 | 3rd PM | 6-S | 6-E |
| LOCKWOOD | **7** | 9 | 3rd PM | 5-S | 5-E |
| " " | **8** | 3 | 3rd PM | 5-S | 6-E |
| LOGSDEN | **7** | 4 | 3rd PM | 5-S | 5-E |
| LONE | **14** | 1 | 3rd PM | 7-S | 6-E |

| Surname | Map Group | Parcels of Land | Meridian/Township/Range |
|---------|-----------|-----------------|-------------------------|
| LONG | **8** | 4 | 3rd PM  5-S  6-E |
| LORIE | **8** | 1 | 3rd PM  5-S  6-E |
| LOURY | **4** | 1 | 3rd PM  4-S  5-E |
| LOWERY | **4** | 1 | 3rd PM  4-S  5-E |
| LOWREY | **4** | 6 | 3rd PM  4-S  5-E |
| " " | **7** | 1 | 3rd PM  5-S  5-E |
| LOWRY | **4** | 10 | 3rd PM  4-S  5-E |
| " " | **7** | 1 | 3rd PM  5-S  5-E |
| LOYD | **9** | 5 | 3rd PM  5-S  7-E |
| " " | **6** | 2 | 3rd PM  4-S  7-E |
| LUSTER | **6** | 1 | 3rd PM  4-S  7-E |
| LYNCH | **13** | 2 | 3rd PM  7-S  5-E |
| MABERRY | **9** | 1 | 3rd PM  5-S  7-E |
| MALON | **9** | 1 | 3rd PM  5-S  7-E |
| MALOND | **6** | 1 | 3rd PM  4-S  7-E |
| MALONE | **9** | 11 | 3rd PM  5-S  7-E |
| MAN | **11** | 2 | 3rd PM  6-S  6-E |
| MANGIS | **7** | 1 | 3rd PM  5-S  5-E |
| " " | **8** | 1 | 3rd PM  5-S  6-E |
| " " | **9** | 1 | 3rd PM  5-S  7-E |
| MANIER | **11** | 1 | 3rd PM  6-S  6-E |
| MANN | **11** | 1 | 3rd PM  6-S  6-E |
| MANNERS | **10** | 1 | 3rd PM  6-S  5-E |
| MANNING | **8** | 3 | 3rd PM  5-S  6-E |
| MANSELL | **9** | 2 | 3rd PM  5-S  7-E |
| MARGRAVE | **12** | 1 | 3rd PM  6-S  7-E |
| MARICLE | **13** | 2 | 3rd PM  7-S  5-E |
| MARKEL | **9** | 1 | 3rd PM  5-S  7-E |
| MARQUIS | **7** | 2 | 3rd PM  5-S  5-E |
| MARSH | **8** | 3 | 3rd PM  5-S  6-E |
| MARSHALL | **8** | 10 | 3rd PM  5-S  6-E |
| " " | **7** | 1 | 3rd PM  5-S  5-E |
| MARTELL | **1** | 1 | 3rd PM  3-S  5-E |
| MARTIN | **6** | 7 | 3rd PM  4-S  7-E |
| " " | **4** | 6 | 3rd PM  4-S  5-E |
| " " | **7** | 2 | 3rd PM  5-S  5-E |
| " " | **13** | 2 | 3rd PM  7-S  5-E |
| " " | **9** | 1 | 3rd PM  5-S  7-E |
| " " | **14** | 1 | 3rd PM  7-S  6-E |
| MATHENY | **10** | 2 | 3rd PM  6-S  5-E |
| " " | **8** | 1 | 3rd PM  5-S  6-E |
| MATLOCK | **12** | 3 | 3rd PM  6-S  7-E |
| " " | **9** | 2 | 3rd PM  5-S  7-E |
| MAUG | **14** | 1 | 3rd PM  7-S  6-E |
| MAULDEN | **7** | 2 | 3rd PM  5-S  5-E |
| MAULDING | **5** | 13 | 3rd PM  4-S  6-E |
| " " | **7** | 9 | 3rd PM  5-S  5-E |
| " " | **4** | 6 | 3rd PM  4-S  5-E |
| " " | **10** | 2 | 3rd PM  6-S  5-E |
| " " | **8** | 1 | 3rd PM  5-S  6-E |
| MAY | **7** | 1 | 3rd PM  5-S  5-E |
| MAYBERRY | **12** | 36 | 3rd PM  6-S  7-E |
| " " | **11** | 7 | 3rd PM  6-S  6-E |
| " " | **9** | 5 | 3rd PM  5-S  7-E |
| MAYHALL | **4** | 1 | 3rd PM  4-S  5-E |
| MAYNARD | **5** | 1 | 3rd PM  4-S  6-E |
| MCBRIDE | **7** | 1 | 3rd PM  5-S  5-E |
| MCBROOM | **9** | 1 | 3rd PM  5-S  7-E |
| " " | **12** | 1 | 3rd PM  6-S  7-E |
| MCBROWN | **9** | 5 | 3rd PM  5-S  7-E |

| Surname | Map Group | Parcels of Land | Meridian/Township/Range | | |
|---|---|---|---|---|---|
| MCCAWLLEY | **12** | 1 | 3rd PM | 6-S | 7-E |
| MCCAY | **4** | 1 | 3rd PM | 4-S | 5-E |
| MCCLEUR | **4** | 1 | 3rd PM | 4-S | 5-E |
| MCCLUER | **4** | 1 | 3rd PM | 4-S | 5-E |
| MCCLURE | **4** | 2 | 3rd PM | 4-S | 5-E |
| MCCLUSKY | **10** | 4 | 3rd PM | 6-S | 5-E |
| MCCOBGAN | **9** | 1 | 3rd PM | 5-S | 7-E |
| MCCOLGAN | **6** | 6 | 3rd PM | 4-S | 7-E |
| MCCOMB | **14** | 1 | 3rd PM | 7-S | 6-E |
| MCCOMBS | **11** | 2 | 3rd PM | 6-S | 6-E |
| MCCONNER | **4** | 1 | 3rd PM | 4-S | 5-E |
| MCCOY | **7** | 8 | 3rd PM | 5-S | 5-E |
| " " | **4** | 4 | 3rd PM | 4-S | 5-E |
| MCCREERY | **13** | 1 | 3rd PM | 7-S | 5-E |
| MCDANIEL | **5** | 2 | 3rd PM | 4-S | 6-E |
| " " | **10** | 2 | 3rd PM | 6-S | 5-E |
| " " | **11** | 2 | 3rd PM | 6-S | 6-E |
| " " | **7** | 1 | 3rd PM | 5-S | 5-E |
| MCDONALD | **7** | 2 | 3rd PM | 5-S | 5-E |
| " " | **8** | 1 | 3rd PM | 5-S | 6-E |
| " " | **11** | 1 | 3rd PM | 6-S | 6-E |
| " " | **13** | 1 | 3rd PM | 7-S | 5-E |
| MCDOWELL | **12** | 2 | 3rd PM | 6-S | 7-E |
| MCFARLAND | **13** | 4 | 3rd PM | 7-S | 5-E |
| " " | **8** | 2 | 3rd PM | 5-S | 6-E |
| " " | **7** | 1 | 3rd PM | 5-S | 5-E |
| MCGEHEE | **6** | 1 | 3rd PM | 4-S | 7-E |
| MCGENNIS | **7** | 1 | 3rd PM | 5-S | 5-E |
| MCGILL | **14** | 2 | 3rd PM | 7-S | 6-E |
| " " | **11** | 1 | 3rd PM | 6-S | 6-E |
| MCGINNIS | **7** | 1 | 3rd PM | 5-S | 5-E |
| MCGUIER | **11** | 1 | 3rd PM | 6-S | 6-E |
| MCGUIRE | **11** | 5 | 3rd PM | 6-S | 6-E |
| MCILVANE | **12** | 1 | 3rd PM | 6-S | 7-E |
| MCINTOSH | **6** | 1 | 3rd PM | 4-S | 7-E |
| MCKENZIE | **12** | 6 | 3rd PM | 6-S | 7-E |
| " " | **15** | 1 | 3rd PM | 7-S | 7-E |
| MCKINGY | **12** | 1 | 3rd PM | 6-S | 7-E |
| MCKINLEY | **5** | 1 | 3rd PM | 4-S | 6-E |
| MCKINSIE | **12** | 1 | 3rd PM | 6-S | 7-E |
| MCKINZIE | **12** | 2 | 3rd PM | 6-S | 7-E |
| " " | **10** | 1 | 3rd PM | 6-S | 5-E |
| " " | **15** | 1 | 3rd PM | 7-S | 7-E |
| MCKNIGHT | **4** | 6 | 3rd PM | 4-S | 5-E |
| " " | **9** | 6 | 3rd PM | 5-S | 7-E |
| MCLEAN | **8** | 6 | 3rd PM | 5-S | 6-E |
| MCLIN | **9** | 1 | 3rd PM | 5-S | 7-E |
| MCMAHAN | **12** | 8 | 3rd PM | 6-S | 7-E |
| " " | **8** | 1 | 3rd PM | 5-S | 6-E |
| MCMAHON | **4** | 1 | 3rd PM | 4-S | 5-E |
| " " | **12** | 1 | 3rd PM | 6-S | 7-E |
| MCMURTRY | **12** | 3 | 3rd PM | 6-S | 7-E |
| " " | **15** | 3 | 3rd PM | 7-S | 7-E |
| MCNABB | **7** | 1 | 3rd PM | 5-S | 5-E |
| MCNAMER | **8** | 1 | 3rd PM | 5-S | 6-E |
| MCNEMAR | **8** | 2 | 3rd PM | 5-S | 6-E |
| MCTHOMAS | **2** | 1 | 3rd PM | 3-S | 6-E |
| MECKE | **4** | 1 | 3rd PM | 4-S | 5-E |
| MELLON | **7** | 1 | 3rd PM | 5-S | 5-E |
| MELTON | **13** | 3 | 3rd PM | 7-S | 5-E |

| Surname | Map Group | Parcels of Land | Meridian/Township/Range | | |
|---|---|---|---|---|---|
| METCALF | **9** | 11 | 3rd PM | 5-S | 7-E |
| " " | **7** | 1 | 3rd PM | 5-S | 5-E |
| METHERY | **10** | 2 | 3rd PM | 6-S | 5-E |
| MEYER | **15** | 1 | 3rd PM | 7-S | 7-E |
| MEZO | **11** | 3 | 3rd PM | 6-S | 6-E |
| " " | **10** | 1 | 3rd PM | 6-S | 5-E |
| MILLER | **12** | 5 | 3rd PM | 6-S | 7-E |
| " " | **7** | 3 | 3rd PM | 5-S | 5-E |
| " " | **10** | 2 | 3rd PM | 6-S | 5-E |
| " " | **2** | 1 | 3rd PM | 3-S | 6-E |
| " " | **4** | 1 | 3rd PM | 4-S | 5-E |
| MILLS | **10** | 1 | 3rd PM | 6-S | 5-E |
| MILLSBAUGH | **12** | 1 | 3rd PM | 6-S | 7-E |
| MILLSPAUGH | **12** | 9 | 3rd PM | 6-S | 7-E |
| MINTON | **5** | 1 | 3rd PM | 4-S | 6-E |
| MITCHEL | **8** | 1 | 3rd PM | 5-S | 6-E |
| MITCHELL | **8** | 7 | 3rd PM | 5-S | 6-E |
| " " | **5** | 3 | 3rd PM | 4-S | 6-E |
| " " | **9** | 3 | 3rd PM | 5-S | 7-E |
| MIZE | **11** | 1 | 3rd PM | 6-S | 6-E |
| MOBLEY | **10** | 1 | 3rd PM | 6-S | 5-E |
| " " | **11** | 1 | 3rd PM | 6-S | 6-E |
| MONDAY | **1** | 3 | 3rd PM | 3-S | 5-E |
| MOORE | **7** | 9 | 3rd PM | 5-S | 5-E |
| " " | **8** | 6 | 3rd PM | 5-S | 6-E |
| " " | **10** | 6 | 3rd PM | 6-S | 5-E |
| " " | **4** | 4 | 3rd PM | 4-S | 5-E |
| " " | **9** | 4 | 3rd PM | 5-S | 7-E |
| " " | **5** | 3 | 3rd PM | 4-S | 6-E |
| " " | **6** | 2 | 3rd PM | 4-S | 7-E |
| MOORES | **12** | 1 | 3rd PM | 6-S | 7-E |
| MOORMAN | **10** | 1 | 3rd PM | 6-S | 5-E |
| MOOTHY | **2** | 2 | 3rd PM | 3-S | 6-E |
| MORGAN | **4** | 4 | 3rd PM | 4-S | 5-E |
| MORRIS | **8** | 6 | 3rd PM | 5-S | 6-E |
| " " | **12** | 4 | 3rd PM | 6-S | 7-E |
| " " | **4** | 2 | 3rd PM | 4-S | 5-E |
| " " | **11** | 1 | 3rd PM | 6-S | 6-E |
| " " | **15** | 1 | 3rd PM | 7-S | 7-E |
| MOSS | **5** | 1 | 3rd PM | 4-S | 6-E |
| MOTT | **14** | 2 | 3rd PM | 7-S | 6-E |
| MOULDING | **8** | 2 | 3rd PM | 5-S | 6-E |
| " " | **5** | 1 | 3rd PM | 4-S | 6-E |
| MOUTRAY | **5** | 1 | 3rd PM | 4-S | 6-E |
| MUNDAY | **1** | 2 | 3rd PM | 3-S | 5-E |
| MUNSELL | **9** | 7 | 3rd PM | 5-S | 7-E |
| " " | **8** | 2 | 3rd PM | 5-S | 6-E |
| MURPHY | **8** | 4 | 3rd PM | 5-S | 6-E |
| MUSGRAVE | **6** | 7 | 3rd PM | 4-S | 7-E |
| " " | **5** | 5 | 3rd PM | 4-S | 6-E |
| " " | **8** | 3 | 3rd PM | 5-S | 6-E |
| " " | **9** | 1 | 3rd PM | 5-S | 7-E |
| MUSGROVE | **6** | 3 | 3rd PM | 4-S | 7-E |
| " " | **5** | 1 | 3rd PM | 4-S | 6-E |
| " " | **9** | 1 | 3rd PM | 5-S | 7-E |
| MUSKGRAVE | **8** | 1 | 3rd PM | 5-S | 6-E |
| MYERS | **5** | 2 | 3rd PM | 4-S | 6-E |
| " " | **9** | 2 | 3rd PM | 5-S | 7-E |
| " " | **2** | 1 | 3rd PM | 3-S | 6-E |
| " " | **6** | 1 | 3rd PM | 4-S | 7-E |

| Surname | Map Group | Parcels of Land | Meridian/Township/Range | | |
|---------|-----------|-----------------|------|------|------|
| MYRES | **5** | 1 | 3rd PM | 4-S | 6-E |
| NANCE | **7** | 1 | 3rd PM | 5-S | 5-E |
| NASH | **10** | 1 | 3rd PM | 6-S | 5-E |
| NATION | **6** | 1 | 3rd PM | 4-S | 7-E |
| " " | **7** | 1 | 3rd PM | 5-S | 5-E |
| " " | **9** | 1 | 3rd PM | 5-S | 7-E |
| NATIONS | **4** | 1 | 3rd PM | 4-S | 5-E |
| " " | **9** | 1 | 3rd PM | 5-S | 7-E |
| " " | **12** | 1 | 3rd PM | 6-S | 7-E |
| NEILSON | **10** | 1 | 3rd PM | 6-S | 5-E |
| NELSON | **9** | 1 | 3rd PM | 5-S | 7-E |
| NEWMAN | **7** | 2 | 3rd PM | 5-S | 5-E |
| " " | **8** | 1 | 3rd PM | 5-S | 6-E |
| NICHOLAS | **7** | 1 | 3rd PM | 5-S | 5-E |
| NORMAN | **2** | 1 | 3rd PM | 3-S | 6-E |
| ODEL | **13** | 1 | 3rd PM | 7-S | 5-E |
| ODELL | **13** | 2 | 3rd PM | 7-S | 5-E |
| " " | **10** | 1 | 3rd PM | 6-S | 5-E |
| ODLE | **13** | 12 | 3rd PM | 7-S | 5-E |
| OGDEN | **14** | 2 | 3rd PM | 7-S | 6-E |
| OGDON | **14** | 1 | 3rd PM | 7-S | 6-E |
| OGLESBAY | **10** | 1 | 3rd PM | 6-S | 5-E |
| OGLESBY | **8** | 1 | 3rd PM | 5-S | 6-E |
| " " | **10** | 1 | 3rd PM | 6-S | 5-E |
| " " | **15** | 1 | 3rd PM | 7-S | 7-E |
| OHUMACHT | **14** | 1 | 3rd PM | 7-S | 6-E |
| OLIVER | **7** | 3 | 3rd PM | 5-S | 5-E |
| ONEAL | **1** | 3 | 3rd PM | 3-S | 5-E |
| " " | **7** | 1 | 3rd PM | 5-S | 5-E |
| " " | **8** | 1 | 3rd PM | 5-S | 6-E |
| ORGAN | **13** | 2 | 3rd PM | 7-S | 5-E |
| ORMSBY | **8** | 2 | 3rd PM | 5-S | 6-E |
| ORR | **9** | 1 | 3rd PM | 5-S | 7-E |
| PAGE | **10** | 5 | 3rd PM | 6-S | 5-E |
| " " | **7** | 4 | 3rd PM | 5-S | 5-E |
| PARKER | **4** | 1 | 3rd PM | 4-S | 5-E |
| " " | **11** | 1 | 3rd PM | 6-S | 6-E |
| PARMER | **1** | 1 | 3rd PM | 3-S | 5-E |
| PATE | **7** | 4 | 3rd PM | 5-S | 5-E |
| PATRIDGE | **14** | 1 | 3rd PM | 7-S | 6-E |
| PATTELLO | **9** | 1 | 3rd PM | 5-S | 7-E |
| PATTON | **4** | 2 | 3rd PM | 4-S | 5-E |
| " " | **14** | 1 | 3rd PM | 7-S | 6-E |
| PECK | **7** | 2 | 3rd PM | 5-S | 5-E |
| " " | **9** | 1 | 3rd PM | 5-S | 7-E |
| PEER | **2** | 2 | 3rd PM | 3-S | 6-E |
| PEIRCE | **9** | 1 | 3rd PM | 5-S | 7-E |
| PEMBERTON | **13** | 11 | 3rd PM | 7-S | 5-E |
| PENNINGTON | **14** | 3 | 3rd PM | 7-S | 6-E |
| PERRY | **5** | 2 | 3rd PM | 4-S | 6-E |
| PERRYMAN | **9** | 4 | 3rd PM | 5-S | 7-E |
| PETER | **6** | 1 | 3rd PM | 4-S | 7-E |
| PETERS | **6** | 3 | 3rd PM | 4-S | 7-E |
| PETMAN | **8** | 1 | 3rd PM | 5-S | 6-E |
| PGLESHY | **10** | 1 | 3rd PM | 6-S | 5-E |
| PHELPS | **8** | 2 | 3rd PM | 5-S | 6-E |
| PHILIPS | **10** | 3 | 3rd PM | 6-S | 5-E |
| PHILLIPS | **10** | 1 | 3rd PM | 6-S | 5-E |
| PHIPPS | **9** | 3 | 3rd PM | 5-S | 7-E |
| PIERCE | **11** | 1 | 3rd PM | 6-S | 6-E |

| Surname | Map Group | Parcels of Land | Meridian/Township/Range |
|---|---|---|---|
| PINER | **10** | 1 | 3rd PM 6-S 5-E |
| PINKSTON | **4** | 1 | 3rd PM 4-S 5-E |
| PITMAN | **11** | 1 | 3rd PM 6-S 6-E |
| PITTMAN | **8** | 1 | 3rd PM 5-S 6-E |
| PLUNCKETT | **7** | 1 | 3rd PM 5-S 5-E |
| " " | **8** | 1 | 3rd PM 5-S 6-E |
| POOL | **7** | 1 | 3rd PM 5-S 5-E |
| PORCTOR | **9** | 1 | 3rd PM 5-S 7-E |
| PORTER | **15** | 14 | 3rd PM 7-S 7-E |
| " " | **4** | 1 | 3rd PM 4-S 5-E |
| " " | **9** | 1 | 3rd PM 5-S 7-E |
| " " | **14** | 1 | 3rd PM 7-S 6-E |
| POWELL | **15** | 6 | 3rd PM 7-S 7-E |
| " " | **12** | 5 | 3rd PM 6-S 7-E |
| " " | **2** | 2 | 3rd PM 3-S 6-E |
| " " | **5** | 2 | 3rd PM 4-S 6-E |
| " " | **9** | 2 | 3rd PM 5-S 7-E |
| " " | **1** | 1 | 3rd PM 3-S 5-E |
| PRATT | **8** | 2 | 3rd PM 5-S 6-E |
| PRESLEY | **11** | 5 | 3rd PM 6-S 6-E |
| " " | **8** | 3 | 3rd PM 5-S 6-E |
| PRICE | **7** | 1 | 3rd PM 5-S 5-E |
| PRIMM | **9** | 2 | 3rd PM 5-S 7-E |
| PRINCE | **9** | 11 | 3rd PM 5-S 7-E |
| " " | **12** | 4 | 3rd PM 6-S 7-E |
| PROCOT | **6** | 1 | 3rd PM 4-S 7-E |
| PROCTER | **8** | 1 | 3rd PM 5-S 6-E |
| PROCTOR | **8** | 7 | 3rd PM 5-S 6-E |
| " " | **9** | 5 | 3rd PM 5-S 7-E |
| " " | **6** | 3 | 3rd PM 4-S 7-E |
| PROMMEL | **5** | 1 | 3rd PM 4-S 6-E |
| PRYOR | **14** | 2 | 3rd PM 7-S 6-E |
| PUCKETT | **3** | 1 | 3rd PM 3-S 7-E |
| PULLIAM | **14** | 2 | 3rd PM 7-S 6-E |
| PULLIAN | **14** | 1 | 3rd PM 7-S 6-E |
| PYNOR | **10** | 1 | 3rd PM 6-S 5-E |
| QUARLES | **9** | 1 | 3rd PM 5-S 7-E |
| RAFFERTY | **8** | 3 | 3rd PM 5-S 6-E |
| RAMBEAU | **8** | 1 | 3rd PM 5-S 6-E |
| RAMBO | **8** | 1 | 3rd PM 5-S 6-E |
| RANKIN | **6** | 4 | 3rd PM 4-S 7-E |
| " " | **9** | 4 | 3rd PM 5-S 7-E |
| RAPARD | **12** | 1 | 3rd PM 6-S 7-E |
| RATHBONE | **8** | 5 | 3rd PM 5-S 6-E |
| RAWLS | **2** | 5 | 3rd PM 3-S 6-E |
| " " | **4** | 3 | 3rd PM 4-S 5-E |
| " " | **5** | 2 | 3rd PM 4-S 6-E |
| RAY | **9** | 7 | 3rd PM 5-S 7-E |
| REBANACKER | **2** | 1 | 3rd PM 3-S 6-E |
| " " | **5** | 1 | 3rd PM 4-S 6-E |
| REBINAKER | **2** | 1 | 3rd PM 3-S 6-E |
| RECTOR | **13** | 1 | 3rd PM 7-S 5-E |
| REED | **7** | 14 | 3rd PM 5-S 5-E |
| " " | **4** | 3 | 3rd PM 4-S 5-E |
| REES | **5** | 1 | 3rd PM 4-S 6-E |
| REID | **7** | 2 | 3rd PM 5-S 5-E |
| REINER | **12** | 1 | 3rd PM 6-S 7-E |
| REYNOLDS | **4** | 1 | 3rd PM 4-S 5-E |
| RHORER | **6** | 1 | 3rd PM 4-S 7-E |
| RICE | **10** | 7 | 3rd PM 6-S 5-E |

| Surname | Map Group | Parcels of Land | Meridian/Township/Range |
|---|---|---|---|
| RICE (Cont'd) | **11** | 1 | 3rd PM 6-S 6-E |
| RICH | **5** | 7 | 3rd PM 4-S 6-E |
| RICHARDS | **5** | 6 | 3rd PM 4-S 6-E |
| RICHARDSON | **7** | 6 | 3rd PM 5-S 5-E |
| " " | **4** | 3 | 3rd PM 4-S 5-E |
| " " | **2** | 2 | 3rd PM 3-S 6-E |
| " " | **8** | 2 | 3rd PM 5-S 6-E |
| RICHE | **1** | 1 | 3rd PM 3-S 5-E |
| RICHESON | **14** | 1 | 3rd PM 7-S 6-E |
| RIDDLE | **4** | 1 | 3rd PM 4-S 5-E |
| RIDGWAY | **15** | 1 | 3rd PM 7-S 7-E |
| RILEY | **9** | 5 | 3rd PM 5-S 7-E |
| " " | **15** | 3 | 3rd PM 7-S 7-E |
| RITCHEY | **7** | 3 | 3rd PM 5-S 5-E |
| " " | **8** | 3 | 3rd PM 5-S 6-E |
| " " | **5** | 1 | 3rd PM 4-S 6-E |
| " " | **14** | 1 | 3rd PM 7-S 6-E |
| RITCHY | **14** | 2 | 3rd PM 7-S 6-E |
| " " | **9** | 1 | 3rd PM 5-S 7-E |
| RIVES | **14** | 2 | 3rd PM 7-S 6-E |
| ROBB | **7** | 1 | 3rd PM 5-S 5-E |
| ROBERTS | **14** | 7 | 3rd PM 7-S 6-E |
| " " | **9** | 3 | 3rd PM 5-S 7-E |
| ROBINSON | **2** | 2 | 3rd PM 3-S 6-E |
| " " | **9** | 1 | 3rd PM 5-S 7-E |
| ROGER | **6** | 1 | 3rd PM 4-S 7-E |
| ROGERS | **4** | 7 | 3rd PM 4-S 5-E |
| " " | **5** | 3 | 3rd PM 4-S 6-E |
| " " | **11** | 2 | 3rd PM 6-S 6-E |
| " " | **8** | 1 | 3rd PM 5-S 6-E |
| ROHRER | **10** | 3 | 3rd PM 6-S 5-E |
| " " | **4** | 1 | 3rd PM 4-S 5-E |
| " " | **6** | 1 | 3rd PM 4-S 7-E |
| ROMINE | **5** | 4 | 3rd PM 4-S 6-E |
| " " | **8** | 3 | 3rd PM 5-S 6-E |
| ROO | **4** | 1 | 3rd PM 4-S 5-E |
| RORER | **6** | 1 | 3rd PM 4-S 7-E |
| ROSBOROUGH | **10** | 6 | 3rd PM 6-S 5-E |
| ROSE | **10** | 3 | 3rd PM 6-S 5-E |
| " " | **6** | 1 | 3rd PM 4-S 7-E |
| ROSS | **4** | 5 | 3rd PM 4-S 5-E |
| " " | **1** | 3 | 3rd PM 3-S 5-E |
| RUBANACKER | **2** | 1 | 3rd PM 3-S 6-E |
| RUBENAKER | **5** | 1 | 3rd PM 4-S 6-E |
| RUDE | **10** | 1 | 3rd PM 6-S 5-E |
| RUEBENACKER | **4** | 1 | 3rd PM 4-S 5-E |
| RUMSEY | **13** | 1 | 3rd PM 7-S 5-E |
| RUPARD | **15** | 1 | 3rd PM 7-S 7-E |
| RUSH | **3** | 1 | 3rd PM 3-S 7-E |
| RUSSARD | **15** | 1 | 3rd PM 7-S 7-E |
| RUSSELL | **11** | 5 | 3rd PM 6-S 6-E |
| " " | **1** | 3 | 3rd PM 3-S 5-E |
| RUTTER | **10** | 1 | 3rd PM 6-S 5-E |
| SACKBERGER | **13** | 2 | 3rd PM 7-S 5-E |
| SALLEE | **7** | 1 | 3rd PM 5-S 5-E |
| SALLENGER | **8** | 2 | 3rd PM 5-S 6-E |
| SANDERS | **14** | 2 | 3rd PM 7-S 6-E |
| SARRELLS | **13** | 2 | 3rd PM 7-S 5-E |
| SAUER | **8** | 1 | 3rd PM 5-S 6-E |
| SCARLET | **11** | 1 | 3rd PM 6-S 6-E |

| Surname | Map Group | Parcels of Land | Meridian/Township/Range |
|---|---|---|---|
| SCHLODER | **4** | 1 | 3rd PM 4-S 5-E |
| SCHOOLCRAFT | **11** | 3 | 3rd PM 6-S 6-E |
| " " | **14** | 2 | 3rd PM 7-S 6-E |
| " " | **15** | 1 | 3rd PM 7-S 7-E |
| SCHUSTER | **2** | 1 | 3rd PM 3-S 6-E |
| SCORVOIER | **7** | 1 | 3rd PM 5-S 5-E |
| SCOTT | **8** | 3 | 3rd PM 5-S 6-E |
| " " | **4** | 2 | 3rd PM 4-S 5-E |
| " " | **10** | 1 | 3rd PM 6-S 5-E |
| " " | **11** | 1 | 3rd PM 6-S 6-E |
| " " | **14** | 1 | 3rd PM 7-S 6-E |
| SCRUGGS | **7** | 2 | 3rd PM 5-S 5-E |
| SCUDAMORE | **2** | 2 | 3rd PM 3-S 6-E |
| SEAL | **7** | 2 | 3rd PM 5-S 5-E |
| SEPHENS | **8** | 3 | 3rd PM 5-S 6-E |
| SEXTON | **6** | 1 | 3rd PM 4-S 7-E |
| SHAFFER | **7** | 2 | 3rd PM 5-S 5-E |
| SHANNON | **11** | 1 | 3rd PM 6-S 6-E |
| SHARP | **8** | 1 | 3rd PM 5-S 6-E |
| SHASTEEN | **14** | 2 | 3rd PM 7-S 6-E |
| SHEESTER | **4** | 1 | 3rd PM 4-S 5-E |
| SHELBY | **6** | 1 | 3rd PM 4-S 7-E |
| SHELTON | **1** | 16 | 3rd PM 3-S 5-E |
| " " | **4** | 4 | 3rd PM 4-S 5-E |
| " " | **9** | 4 | 3rd PM 5-S 7-E |
| " " | **7** | 1 | 3rd PM 5-S 5-E |
| SHERLEY | **10** | 1 | 3rd PM 6-S 5-E |
| SHIPLEY | **1** | 1 | 3rd PM 3-S 5-E |
| SHIRBEY | **7** | 1 | 3rd PM 5-S 5-E |
| " " | **8** | 1 | 3rd PM 5-S 6-E |
| SHIRLEY | **8** | 3 | 3rd PM 5-S 6-E |
| " " | **5** | 2 | 3rd PM 4-S 6-E |
| " " | **7** | 2 | 3rd PM 5-S 5-E |
| SHOEMAKER | **7** | 2 | 3rd PM 5-S 5-E |
| SHUMAKER | **7** | 1 | 3rd PM 5-S 5-E |
| SHUSTER | **4** | 4 | 3rd PM 4-S 5-E |
| SIGLER | **12** | 13 | 3rd PM 6-S 7-E |
| SIMMONS | **4** | 1 | 3rd PM 4-S 5-E |
| SIMS | **7** | 6 | 3rd PM 5-S 5-E |
| " " | **10** | 4 | 3rd PM 6-S 5-E |
| SINK | **4** | 2 | 3rd PM 4-S 5-E |
| SINKS | **4** | 1 | 3rd PM 4-S 5-E |
| SLOAN | **12** | 1 | 3rd PM 6-S 7-E |
| SLOO | **8** | 5 | 3rd PM 5-S 6-E |
| " " | **5** | 2 | 3rd PM 4-S 6-E |
| " " | **7** | 2 | 3rd PM 5-S 5-E |
| " " | **4** | 1 | 3rd PM 4-S 5-E |
| SMALLWOOD | **9** | 1 | 3rd PM 5-S 7-E |
| SMITH | **11** | 20 | 3rd PM 6-S 6-E |
| " " | **14** | 9 | 3rd PM 7-S 6-E |
| " " | **10** | 7 | 3rd PM 6-S 5-E |
| " " | **13** | 4 | 3rd PM 7-S 5-E |
| " " | **5** | 3 | 3rd PM 4-S 6-E |
| " " | **7** | 3 | 3rd PM 5-S 5-E |
| " " | **8** | 3 | 3rd PM 5-S 6-E |
| " " | **1** | 2 | 3rd PM 3-S 5-E |
| " " | **15** | 2 | 3rd PM 7-S 7-E |
| SMITHPELTER | **5** | 2 | 3rd PM 4-S 6-E |
| SMITHPETER | **5** | 4 | 3rd PM 4-S 6-E |
| " " | **6** | 4 | 3rd PM 4-S 7-E |

| Surname | Map Group | Parcels of Land | Meridian/Township/Range | | |
|---------|-----------|-----------------|------|------|------|
| SNEAD | **6** | 5 | 3rd PM | 4-S | 7-E |
| " " | **9** | 2 | 3rd PM | 5-S | 7-E |
| SNEED | **7** | 3 | 3rd PM | 5-S | 5-E |
| " " | **6** | 2 | 3rd PM | 4-S | 7-E |
| SNIDER | **9** | 2 | 3rd PM | 5-S | 7-E |
| " " | **8** | 1 | 3rd PM | 5-S | 6-E |
| SNOVER | **7** | 1 | 3rd PM | 5-S | 5-E |
| SNOW | **7** | 2 | 3rd PM | 5-S | 5-E |
| SPAIN | **13** | 4 | 3rd PM | 7-S | 5-E |
| SPENCER | **7** | 3 | 3rd PM | 5-S | 5-E |
| SPILLER | **10** | 4 | 3rd PM | 6-S | 5-E |
| SPRINGER | **6** | 1 | 3rd PM | 4-S | 7-E |
| SPURIEN | **7** | 3 | 3rd PM | 5-S | 5-E |
| STADDEN | **8** | 1 | 3rd PM | 5-S | 6-E |
| STALL | **1** | 2 | 3rd PM | 3-S | 5-E |
| " " | **4** | 1 | 3rd PM | 4-S | 5-E |
| STANDERFER | **5** | 2 | 3rd PM | 4-S | 6-E |
| STANFIELD | **11** | 5 | 3rd PM | 6-S | 6-E |
| " " | **8** | 3 | 3rd PM | 5-S | 6-E |
| STANTON | **8** | 1 | 3rd PM | 5-S | 6-E |
| STARNATER | **1** | 4 | 3rd PM | 3-S | 5-E |
| STEELE | **4** | 4 | 3rd PM | 4-S | 5-E |
| STEELLE | **7** | 2 | 3rd PM | 5-S | 5-E |
| " " | **8** | 1 | 3rd PM | 5-S | 6-E |
| STEERMAN | **4** | 4 | 3rd PM | 4-S | 5-E |
| STELLE | **7** | 6 | 3rd PM | 5-S | 5-E |
| " " | **10** | 1 | 3rd PM | 6-S | 5-E |
| STEPENSON | **7** | 2 | 3rd PM | 5-S | 5-E |
| STEPHENS | **8** | 12 | 3rd PM | 5-S | 6-E |
| " " | **11** | 4 | 3rd PM | 6-S | 6-E |
| " " | **9** | 2 | 3rd PM | 5-S | 7-E |
| " " | **5** | 1 | 3rd PM | 4-S | 6-E |
| STEPHENSON | **8** | 4 | 3rd PM | 5-S | 6-E |
| " " | **10** | 3 | 3rd PM | 6-S | 5-E |
| STEVENS | **8** | 1 | 3rd PM | 5-S | 6-E |
| " " | **9** | 1 | 3rd PM | 5-S | 7-E |
| " " | **15** | 1 | 3rd PM | 7-S | 7-E |
| STEWART | **9** | 1 | 3rd PM | 5-S | 7-E |
| " " | **10** | 1 | 3rd PM | 6-S | 5-E |
| STILLE | **7** | 2 | 3rd PM | 5-S | 5-E |
| STOCKER | **9** | 2 | 3rd PM | 5-S | 7-E |
| STOKES | **7** | 1 | 3rd PM | 5-S | 5-E |
| STONE | **12** | 1 | 3rd PM | 6-S | 7-E |
| STOREY | **15** | 1 | 3rd PM | 7-S | 7-E |
| STORY | **12** | 3 | 3rd PM | 6-S | 7-E |
| STOVALL | **15** | 4 | 3rd PM | 7-S | 7-E |
| " " | **12** | 3 | 3rd PM | 6-S | 7-E |
| STRAWMAT | **9** | 1 | 3rd PM | 5-S | 7-E |
| STROTHER | **7** | 1 | 3rd PM | 5-S | 5-E |
| STULL | **1** | 6 | 3rd PM | 3-S | 5-E |
| " " | **2** | 1 | 3rd PM | 3-S | 6-E |
| " " | **7** | 1 | 3rd PM | 5-S | 5-E |
| STURMAN | **4** | 19 | 3rd PM | 4-S | 5-E |
| " " | **6** | 1 | 3rd PM | 4-S | 7-E |
| SULIVAN | **7** | 2 | 3rd PM | 5-S | 5-E |
| SULLINGER | **8** | 1 | 3rd PM | 5-S | 6-E |
| SULLIVAN | **7** | 4 | 3rd PM | 5-S | 5-E |
| " " | **8** | 2 | 3rd PM | 5-S | 6-E |
| " " | **14** | 1 | 3rd PM | 7-S | 6-E |
| SUMMERS | **7** | 1 | 3rd PM | 5-S | 5-E |

| Surname | Map Group | Parcels of Land | Meridian/Township/Range |
|---|---|---|---|
| SUTTON | **2** | 1 | 3rd PM 3-S 6-E |
| SWAIN | **13** | 1 | 3rd PM 7-S 5-E |
| SWEARINGEN | **9** | 1 | 3rd PM 5-S 7-E |
| SWEARINGER | **7** | 2 | 3rd PM 5-S 5-E |
| SWEET | **14** | 1 | 3rd PM 7-S 6-E |
| SWEETEN | **14** | 1 | 3rd PM 7-S 6-E |
| TALLEE | **11** | 3 | 3rd PM 6-S 6-E |
| TALLER | **7** | 3 | 3rd PM 5-S 5-E |
| TALLEY | **4** | 1 | 3rd PM 4-S 5-E |
| TANNER | **6** | 1 | 3rd PM 4-S 7-E |
| TATE | **13** | 11 | 3rd PM 7-S 5-E |
| TAYLOR | **10** | 6 | 3rd PM 6-S 5-E |
| " " | **6** | 4 | 3rd PM 4-S 7-E |
| " " | **2** | 3 | 3rd PM 3-S 6-E |
| " " | **11** | 2 | 3rd PM 6-S 6-E |
| TEDFORD | **5** | 4 | 3rd PM 4-S 6-E |
| TEMPLES | **7** | 1 | 3rd PM 5-S 5-E |
| TESHLEY | **5** | 1 | 3rd PM 4-S 6-E |
| THIERRY | **4** | 5 | 3rd PM 4-S 5-E |
| " " | **1** | 1 | 3rd PM 3-S 5-E |
| THOMAS | **6** | 14 | 3rd PM 4-S 7-E |
| " " | **9** | 8 | 3rd PM 5-S 7-E |
| " " | **7** | 3 | 3rd PM 5-S 5-E |
| " " | **4** | 1 | 3rd PM 4-S 5-E |
| THOMASON | **2** | 1 | 3rd PM 3-S 6-E |
| " " | **11** | 1 | 3rd PM 6-S 6-E |
| THOMPSON | **6** | 8 | 3rd PM 4-S 7-E |
| THORP | **4** | 1 | 3rd PM 4-S 5-E |
| " " | **7** | 1 | 3rd PM 5-S 5-E |
| THRASHER | **7** | 1 | 3rd PM 5-S 5-E |
| TICKNER | **14** | 1 | 3rd PM 7-S 6-E |
| TINER | **7** | 2 | 3rd PM 5-S 5-E |
| " " | **11** | 1 | 3rd PM 6-S 6-E |
| TIPSCORD | **2** | 1 | 3rd PM 3-S 6-E |
| TODD | **7** | 1 | 3rd PM 5-S 5-E |
| " " | **8** | 1 | 3rd PM 5-S 6-E |
| " " | **9** | 1 | 3rd PM 5-S 7-E |
| TOLLEY | **4** | 1 | 3rd PM 4-S 5-E |
| TOWNSEND | **8** | 1 | 3rd PM 5-S 6-E |
| " " | **11** | 1 | 3rd PM 6-S 6-E |
| TRAMEL | **5** | 5 | 3rd PM 4-S 6-E |
| TRAMMEL | **5** | 6 | 3rd PM 4-S 6-E |
| TRAMMELL | **5** | 1 | 3rd PM 4-S 6-E |
| TRAMMELS | **5** | 3 | 3rd PM 4-S 6-E |
| TROTTER | **2** | 4 | 3rd PM 3-S 6-E |
| " " | **1** | 2 | 3rd PM 3-S 5-E |
| TROUSDALE | **12** | 1 | 3rd PM 6-S 7-E |
| TROUT | **9** | 2 | 3rd PM 5-S 7-E |
| " " | **11** | 1 | 3rd PM 6-S 6-E |
| " " | **12** | 1 | 3rd PM 6-S 7-E |
| TUBMAN | **8** | 1 | 3rd PM 5-S 6-E |
| TUNSEND | **8** | 1 | 3rd PM 5-S 6-E |
| TURNER | **4** | 4 | 3rd PM 4-S 5-E |
| " " | **11** | 3 | 3rd PM 6-S 6-E |
| " " | **1** | 2 | 3rd PM 3-S 5-E |
| TURRENLIN | **10** | 1 | 3rd PM 6-S 5-E |
| TWIGG | **14** | 8 | 3rd PM 7-S 6-E |
| TWIGGS | **14** | 1 | 3rd PM 7-S 6-E |
| TYLER | **6** | 2 | 3rd PM 4-S 7-E |
| ULMER | **9** | 1 | 3rd PM 5-S 7-E |

| Surname | Map Group | Parcels of Land | Meridian/Township/Range | | |
|---|---|---|---|---|---|
| UPTON | **6** | 14 | 3rd PM | 4-S | 7-E |
| " " | **5** | 1 | 3rd PM | 4-S | 6-E |
| " " | **9** | 1 | 3rd PM | 5-S | 7-E |
| VALENTINE | **10** | 4 | 3rd PM | 6-S | 5-E |
| VALETINE | **10** | 1 | 3rd PM | 6-S | 5-E |
| VARNELL | **12** | 2 | 3rd PM | 6-S | 7-E |
| " " | **9** | 1 | 3rd PM | 5-S | 7-E |
| " " | **15** | 1 | 3rd PM | 7-S | 7-E |
| VAUGH | **8** | 1 | 3rd PM | 5-S | 6-E |
| VAUGHAN | **8** | 1 | 3rd PM | 5-S | 6-E |
| VAUGHN | **5** | 1 | 3rd PM | 4-S | 6-E |
| VENABLES | **6** | 1 | 3rd PM | 4-S | 7-E |
| VICK | **4** | 2 | 3rd PM | 4-S | 5-E |
| VICKERS | **12** | 9 | 3rd PM | 6-S | 7-E |
| VIOLETT | **9** | 1 | 3rd PM | 5-S | 7-E |
| VISE | **7** | 7 | 3rd PM | 5-S | 5-E |
| WALLER | **13** | 5 | 3rd PM | 7-S | 5-E |
| " " | **10** | 4 | 3rd PM | 6-S | 5-E |
| " " | **5** | 3 | 3rd PM | 4-S | 6-E |
| " " | **2** | 1 | 3rd PM | 3-S | 6-E |
| WALLIS | **8** | 2 | 3rd PM | 5-S | 6-E |
| WARD | **8** | 3 | 3rd PM | 5-S | 6-E |
| " " | **7** | 1 | 3rd PM | 5-S | 5-E |
| WARFIELD | **2** | 1 | 3rd PM | 3-S | 6-E |
| " " | **3** | 1 | 3rd PM | 3-S | 7-E |
| WATSON | **15** | 2 | 3rd PM | 7-S | 7-E |
| WAUGH | **1** | 4 | 3rd PM | 3-S | 5-E |
| " " | **4** | 1 | 3rd PM | 4-S | 5-E |
| WAYBERRY | **12** | 1 | 3rd PM | 6-S | 7-E |
| WEBB | **9** | 9 | 3rd PM | 5-S | 7-E |
| " " | **12** | 5 | 3rd PM | 6-S | 7-E |
| " " | **8** | 1 | 3rd PM | 5-S | 6-E |
| WEEKS | **10** | 3 | 3rd PM | 6-S | 5-E |
| WELDIN | **8** | 2 | 3rd PM | 5-S | 6-E |
| WELLS | **8** | 1 | 3rd PM | 5-S | 6-E |
| WESNER | **9** | 1 | 3rd PM | 5-S | 7-E |
| WESTON | **8** | 3 | 3rd PM | 5-S | 6-E |
| WHEELER | **9** | 22 | 3rd PM | 5-S | 7-E |
| " " | **11** | 9 | 3rd PM | 6-S | 6-E |
| " " | **12** | 6 | 3rd PM | 6-S | 7-E |
| " " | **8** | 2 | 3rd PM | 5-S | 6-E |
| WHITAKER | **5** | 2 | 3rd PM | 4-S | 6-E |
| WHITE | **8** | 21 | 3rd PM | 5-S | 6-E |
| " " | **6** | 15 | 3rd PM | 4-S | 7-E |
| " " | **11** | 8 | 3rd PM | 6-S | 6-E |
| " " | **7** | 3 | 3rd PM | 5-S | 5-E |
| WHITEAKER | **5** | 2 | 3rd PM | 4-S | 6-E |
| WHITESIDE | **7** | 1 | 3rd PM | 5-S | 5-E |
| WHITTINGTON | **7** | 1 | 3rd PM | 5-S | 5-E |
| WHORLOW | **13** | 3 | 3rd PM | 7-S | 5-E |
| WIGGINS | **13** | 1 | 3rd PM | 7-S | 5-E |
| WILBANKS | **4** | 1 | 3rd PM | 4-S | 5-E |
| " " | **7** | 1 | 3rd PM | 5-S | 5-E |
| WILKEY | **4** | 5 | 3rd PM | 4-S | 5-E |
| " " | **1** | 1 | 3rd PM | 3-S | 5-E |
| WILKINS | **12** | 1 | 3rd PM | 6-S | 7-E |
| WILLIAMS | **8** | 8 | 3rd PM | 5-S | 6-E |
| " " | **4** | 4 | 3rd PM | 4-S | 5-E |
| " " | **7** | 3 | 3rd PM | 5-S | 5-E |
| " " | **9** | 3 | 3rd PM | 5-S | 7-E |

| Surname | Map Group | Parcels of Land | Meridian/Township/Range |
|---|---|---|---|
| WILLIAMS (Cont'd) | **11** | 3 | 3rd PM 6-S 6-E |
| " " | **13** | 2 | 3rd PM 7-S 5-E |
| " " | **6** | 1 | 3rd PM 4-S 7-E |
| " " | **14** | 1 | 3rd PM 7-S 6-E |
| " " | **15** | 1 | 3rd PM 7-S 7-E |
| WILLIAMSEN | **1** | 3 | 3rd PM 3-S 5-E |
| WILLIAMSON | **10** | 1 | 3rd PM 6-S 5-E |
| WILLIS | **5** | 5 | 3rd PM 4-S 6-E |
| " " | **8** | 2 | 3rd PM 5-S 6-E |
| " " | **9** | 1 | 3rd PM 5-S 7-E |
| WILSON | **9** | 12 | 3rd PM 5-S 7-E |
| " " | **15** | 3 | 3rd PM 7-S 7-E |
| " " | **6** | 1 | 3rd PM 4-S 7-E |
| " " | **7** | 1 | 3rd PM 5-S 5-E |
| " " | **8** | 1 | 3rd PM 5-S 6-E |
| " " | **14** | 1 | 3rd PM 7-S 6-E |
| WILTON | **7** | 1 | 3rd PM 5-S 5-E |
| WINCHESTER | **9** | 1 | 3rd PM 5-S 7-E |
| WINKLER | **12** | 1 | 3rd PM 6-S 7-E |
| WINN | **13** | 2 | 3rd PM 7-S 5-E |
| WITT | **8** | 1 | 3rd PM 5-S 6-E |
| WOLF | **5** | 1 | 3rd PM 4-S 6-E |
| " " | **13** | 1 | 3rd PM 7-S 5-E |
| WOOD | **15** | 1 | 3rd PM 7-S 7-E |
| WOODRIDGE | **8** | 1 | 3rd PM 5-S 6-E |
| WOODROW | **6** | 1 | 3rd PM 4-S 7-E |
| WOODRUFF | **5** | 3 | 3rd PM 4-S 6-E |
| " " | **8** | 2 | 3rd PM 5-S 6-E |
| WOOLRIDGE | **8** | 1 | 3rd PM 5-S 6-E |
| WOOLSEY | **13** | 1 | 3rd PM 7-S 5-E |
| " " | **14** | 1 | 3rd PM 7-S 6-E |
| WOOSLEY | **12** | 1 | 3rd PM 6-S 7-E |
| WORTH | **4** | 1 | 3rd PM 4-S 5-E |
| " " | **7** | 1 | 3rd PM 5-S 5-E |
| WORTON | **6** | 1 | 3rd PM 4-S 7-E |
| WRAY | **9** | 1 | 3rd PM 5-S 7-E |
| WRIGHT | **9** | 6 | 3rd PM 5-S 7-E |
| " " | **12** | 6 | 3rd PM 6-S 7-E |
| " " | **10** | 5 | 3rd PM 6-S 5-E |
| " " | **11** | 1 | 3rd PM 6-S 6-E |
| YARWOOD | **4** | 1 | 3rd PM 4-S 5-E |
| YORK | **6** | 16 | 3rd PM 4-S 7-E |
| " " | **9** | 5 | 3rd PM 5-S 7-E |
| YOUNG | **15** | 7 | 3rd PM 7-S 7-E |
| " " | **8** | 2 | 3rd PM 5-S 6-E |
| " " | **1** | 1 | 3rd PM 3-S 5-E |
| ZACHMAMN | **5** | 1 | 3rd PM 4-S 6-E |
| ZACHMAN | **5** | 3 | 3rd PM 4-S 6-E |
| ZACHMANN | **5** | 1 | 3rd PM 4-S 6-E |
| ZACHRMAN | **2** | 1 | 3rd PM 3-S 6-E |
| ZACKMAN | **5** | 1 | 3rd PM 4-S 6-E |

# – Part II –

# Township Map Groups

## Map Group 1: Index to Land Patents

## Township 3-South Range 5-East (3rd PM)

After you locate an individual in this Index, take note of the Section and Section Part then proceed to the Land Patent map on the pages immediately following. You should have no difficulty locating the corresponding parcel of land.

The "For More Info" Column will lead you to more information about the underlying Patents. See the *Legend* at right, and the "How to Use this Book" chapter, for more information.

```
                   LEGEND
        "For More Info . . . " column
G = Group (Multi-Patentee Patent, see Appendix "C")
R = Residence
S = Social Status
```

*See Appendix A for list of abbreviations used by the Illinois State Archives in describing the place and nature of these land patents.*

*Note: if the Abbreviations contain "L", "BL", "LOT", or "BLOCK", the exact whereabouts of the parcel within the section is not known.*

| ID | Individual in Patent | Sec. | Sec. Part | Purchase Date | Sale Type | IL Aliquot Part | For More Info . . . |
|----|----------------------|------|-----------|---------------|-----------|-----------------|---------------------|
| 105 | ASHBY, William A | 22 | NWSW | 1841-01-29 | FD | NWSW | R:HAMILTON |
| 82 | " " | 22 | NWSW | 1841-01-29 | FD | NWSW | R:HAMILTON |
| 26 | ATCHINSON, James A | 21 | W½SE | 1852-06-15 | FD | W2SE | |
| 27 | ATCHISON, James A | 21 | NESW | 1844-07-30 | FD | NESW | R:HAMILTON |
| 28 | " " | 21 | SESW | 1847-06-09 | FD | SESW | R:HAMILTON |
| 71 | ATCHISON, Joseph T | 33 | S½NW | 1851-04-02 | FD | S2NW | |
| 70 | " " | 32 | SENE | 1851-04-02 | FD | SENE | |
| 72 | " " | 33 | SWNE | 1851-04-04 | FD | SWNE | |
| 29 | ATCHISSON, James A | 28 | NWNE | 1849-05-19 | FD | NWNE | R:HAMILTON |
| 30 | " " | 29 | NWNE | 1854-03-27 | FD | NWNE | R:HAMILTON |
| 60 | " " | 29 | NWNE | 1854-03-27 | FD | NWNE | R:HAMILTON |
| 25 | BACHTOLD, Jacob | 36 | SWNE | 1852-03-01 | FD | SWNE | R:HAMILTON |
| 37 | BISHOP, James J | 30 | S½SE | 1855-06-22 | FD | S2SE | R:HAMILTON |
| 36 | " " | 30 | NWNE | 1855-06-22 | FD | NWNE | R:HAMILTON |
| 35 | " " | 30 | NENW | 1855-06-22 | FD | NENW | R:HAMILTON |
| 34 | " " | 19 | E½SW | 1855-06-22 | FD | E2SW | R:HAMILTON |
| 122 | CANNADY, William W | 28 | NWSE | 1854-03-28 | FD | NWSE | R:HAMILTON |
| 54 | CANNEDEY, Joel L | 28 | S½SE | 1853-12-21 | FD | S2SE | R:HAMILTON |
| 51 | CATES, Jasper N | 32 | SWSW | 1854-08-02 | FD | SWSW | R:HAMILTON |
| 50 | " " | 32 | N½SW | 1854-10-11 | FD | N2SW | R:HAMILTON |
| 52 | CATES, Jasper Newton | 32 | SESW | 1852-06-26 | FD | SESW | |
| 53 | " " | 32 | SWSE | 1852-06-26 | FD | SWSE | |
| 95 | COLLINS, Samuel M | 28 | NESE | 1854-02-22 | FD | NESE | R:HAMILTON |
| 92 | " " | 27 | NWSW | 1854-02-22 | FD | NWSW | R:HAMILTON |
| 93 | " " | 27 | SWSW | 1854-03-30 | FD | SWSW | R:HAMILTON |
| 94 | " " | 28 | N½NE | 1854-09-18 | FD | N2NE | R:HAMILTON |
| 99 | " " | 34 | NWNW | 1854-09-18 | FD | NWNW | R:HAMILTON |
| 98 | " " | 33 | N½NW | 1854-09-18 | FD | N2NW | R:HAMILTON |
| 97 | " " | 28 | S½SW | 1854-09-18 | FD | S2SW | R:HAMILTON |
| 96 | " " | 28 | NESW | 1854-09-18 | FD | NESW | R:HAMILTON |
| 4 | CROSS, Benjamin | 20 | NENW | 1854-06-24 | FD | NENW | R:WAYNE |
| 104 | CROUCH, Wamen B | 36 | SENE | 1854-01-06 | FD | SENE | R:HAMILTON |
| 103 | " " | 36 | N½SE | 1854-01-06 | FD | N2SE | R:HAMILTON |
| 79 | DAY, Marcus | 20 | NENE | 1853-12-07 | FD | NENE | |
| 24 | GARRISON, Henry G | 22 | NE | 1854-02-08 | FD | NE | G:16 |
| 33 | GARRISON, James | 33 | SESW | 1854-10-12 | FD | SESW | R:HAMILTON |
| 24 | GARRISON, John A | 22 | NE | 1854-02-08 | FD | NE | G:16 |
| 83 | GARRISON, Nathan | 22 | SWSW | 1840-06-19 | FD | SWSW | R:HAMILTON |
| 81 | " " | 21 | SESE | 1844-07-30 | FD | SESE | R:HAMILTON |
| 85 | " " | 28 | NENE | 1851-02-25 | FD | NENE | R:HAMILTON |
| 80 | " " | 21 | NESE | 1852-06-11 | FD | NESE | |
| 82 | " " | 22 | NWSW | 1852-06-11 | FD | NWSW | |
| 105 | " " | 22 | NWSW | 1852-06-11 | FD | NWSW | |
| 84 | " " | 27 | NWNW | 1854-01-16 | FD | NWNW | R:HAMILTON |
| 55 | GOODNER, John A C | 30 | NESW | 1854-05-24 | FD | NESW | R:JEFFERSON |
| 101 | GRAVENER, Thomas H | 34 | SENW | 1853-12-14 | FD | SENW | R:HAMILTON |

| ID | Individual in Patent | Sec. | Sec. Part | Purchase Date | Sale Type | IL Aliquot Part | For More Info . . . |
|---|---|---|---|---|---|---|---|
| 108 | HAGUE, William H | 30 | NENE | 1852-09-01 | FD | NENE | |
| 110 | HALL, William | 36 | SESE | 1852-02-23 | FD | SESE | R:HAMILTON |
| 111 | " " | 36 | SWSE | 1854-06-05 | FD | SWSE | R:HAMILTON |
| 100 | HOLLAND, Thomas G | 30 | SESW | 1852-09-01 | FD | SESW | |
| 112 | JAMES, William P | 22 | E½NW | 1854-09-21 | FD | E2NW | R:GALLATIN |
| 114 | " " | 22 | SW | 1854-09-21 | FD | SW | R:GALLATIN |
| 113 | " " | 22 | NESW | 1854-09-21 | FD | NESW | R:GALLATIN |
| 1 | KANADA, Archibald | 28 | E½NW | 1855-03-26 | FD | E2NW | R:HAMILTON |
| 2 | " " | 28 | SWNE | 1855-03-26 | FD | SWNE | R:HAMILTON |
| 19 | KARCHER, Ernest | 35 | SWSE | 1852-02-25 | FD | SWSE | R:HAMILTON |
| 18 | " " | 35 | SESW | 1854-01-02 | FD | SESW | R:HAMILTON |
| 9 | KENEDY, Edmond T | 28 | NWNW | 1854-02-15 | FD | NWNW | R:HAMILTON |
| 10 | KENEDY, Edmund L | 21 | SWSW | 1854-11-10 | FD | SWSW | R:HAMILTON |
| 59 | KENIDAY, John Shaw | 27 | SWNW | 1853-04-11 | FD | SWNW | |
| 12 | KENNEDDY, Edmund T | 29 | NENE | 1854-03-27 | FD | NENE | R:HAMILTON |
| 11 | " " | 28 | SWNW | 1854-04-10 | FD | SWNW | R:HAMILTON |
| 58 | KENNEDDY, John S | 28 | SENE | 1854-03-27 | FD | SENE | R:HAMILTON |
| 57 | KIRKSEA, John | 27 | E½NW | 1854-03-24 | FD | E2NW | R:HAMILTON |
| 56 | MARTELL, John B | 20 | NWNE | 1853-09-24 | FD | NWNE | |
| 15 | MONDAY, Elias | 22 | W½SE | 1849-05-19 | FD | W2SE | |
| 14 | " " | 22 | SESW | 1849-05-19 | FD | SESW | |
| 13 | " " | 22 | NESE | 1849-05-19 | FD | NESE | |
| 17 | MUNDAY, Elias | 23 | NWSW | 1855-04-06 | FD | NWSW | R:HAMILTON |
| 16 | " " | 22 | SESE | 1855-04-06 | FD | SESE | R:HAMILTON |
| 23 | ONEAL, George | 21 | NWNW | 1854-09-18 | FD | NWNW | R:JEFFERSON |
| 22 | " " | 21 | NE | 1854-09-18 | FD | NE | R:JEFFERSON |
| 21 | " " | 21 | E½NW | 1854-09-18 | FD | E2NW | R:JEFFERSON |
| 32 | PARMER, James A | 31 | E½SE | 1859-04-13 | FD | E2SE | |
| 42 | " " | 31 | E½SE | 1859-04-13 | FD | E2SE | |
| 86 | POWELL, Nelson | 36 | NESW | 1854-01-16 | FD | NESW | R:HAMILTON |
| 38 | RICHE, James M | 31 | SWSW | 1837-02-10 | FD | SWSW | R:JEFFERSON |
| 116 | ROSS, William P S | 31 | NWSW | 1854-10-11 | FD | NWSW | R:HAMILTON |
| 115 | " " | 31 | E½NW | 1854-10-11 | FD | E2NW | R:HAMILTON |
| 117 | " " | 31 | SWNW | 1854-10-11 | FD | SWNW | R:HAMILTON |
| 39 | RUSSELL, James | 29 | W½SW | 1854-10-01 | FD | W2SW | R:HAMILTON |
| 40 | " " | 30 | N½SE | 1854-10-01 | FD | N2SE | R:HAMILTON |
| 41 | " " | 30 | SWSE | 1854-10-01 | FD | SWSE | R:HAMILTON |
| 30 | SHELTON, John W | 29 | NWNE | 1854-12-11 | FD | NWNE | R:HAMILTON |
| 60 | " " | 29 | NWNE | 1854-12-11 | FD | NWNE | R:HAMILTON |
| 69 | SHELTON, Joseph | 33 | W½SW | 1833-12-30 | FD | W2SW | R:HAMILTON |
| 61 | " " | 30 | NWNW | 1836-08-11 | FD | NWNW | R:HAMILTON |
| 64 | " " | 32 | NENW | 1852-06-15 | FD | NENW | R:HAMILTON |
| 63 | " " | 32 | E½SE | 1852-06-15 | FD | E2SE | |
| 66 | " " | 32 | NWSE | 1852-06-15 | FD | NWSE | |
| 68 | " " | 33 | NESW | 1852-06-15 | FD | NESW | R:HAMILTON |
| 67 | " " | 32 | SWNE | 1852-06-15 | FD | SWNE | |
| 62 | " " | 30 | SWNE | 1853-09-19 | FD | SWNE | R:HAMILTON |
| 65 | " " | 32 | NWNE | 1854-02-13 | FD | NWNE | R:HAMILTON |
| 74 | SHELTON, Leonard C | 29 | E½SE | 1854-10-12 | FD | E2SE | R:HAMILTON |
| 73 | " " | 28 | NWSW | 1854-10-12 | FD | NWSW | R:HAMILTON |
| 75 | " " | 29 | SENE | 1854-10-12 | FD | SENE | R:HAMILTON |
| 77 | " " | 29 | W½NW | 1854-10-12 | FD | W2NW | R:HAMILTON |
| 78 | " " | 32 | NENE | 1854-10-12 | FD | NENE | R:HAMILTON |
| 120 | " " | 29 | SENW | 1854-10-12 | FD | SENW | R:HAMILTON |
| 76 | " " | 29 | SENW | 1854-10-12 | FD | SENW | R:HAMILTON |
| 102 | SHIPLEY, Thomas | 31 | NWNW | 1854-01-16 | FD | NWNW | R:HAMILTON |
| 89 | SMITH, Peter | 29 | SESW | 1851-11-25 | FD | SESW | R:HAMILTON |
| 90 | " " | 29 | SWSE | 1851-11-25 | FD | SWSE | R:HAMILTON |
| 43 | STALL, James | 31 | SENE | 1849-09-14 | FD | SENE | G:36 |
| 42 | " " | 31 | E½SE | 1849-09-14 | FD | E2SE | G:36 |
| 32 | " " | 31 | E½SE | 1849-09-14 | FD | E2SE | G:36 |
| 43 | STALL, Lawrence | 31 | SENE | 1849-09-14 | FD | SENE | G:36 |
| 42 | " " | 31 | E½SE | 1849-09-14 | FD | E2SE | G:36 |
| 32 | " " | 31 | E½SE | 1849-09-14 | FD | E2SE | G:36 |
| 121 | STARNATER, William | 29 | SWNE | 1848-02-05 | FD | SWNE | |
| 119 | " " | 29 | NWSE | 1848-02-05 | FD | NWSE | |
| 76 | " " | 29 | SENW | 1848-02-05 | FD | SENW | |
| 120 | " " | 29 | SENW | 1848-02-05 | FD | SENW | |
| 118 | " " | 29 | NESW | 1848-02-05 | FD | NESW | |
| 3 | STULL, Archibald | 31 | E½SW | 1853-04-20 | FD | E2SW | |
| 45 | STULL, James | 31 | NENE | 1852-08-19 | FD | NENE | |
| 44 | " " | 30 | SESE | 1852-08-19 | FD | SESE | |
| 46 | " " | 31 | W½NE | 1852-08-19 | FD | W2NE | |

| ID | Individual in Patent | Sec. | Sec. Part | Purchase Date | Sale Type | IL Aliquot Part | For More Info . . . |
|----|---------------------|------|-----------|---------------|-----------|-----------------|---------------------|
| 87 | STULL, Nicholas | 31 | NWSE | 1837-02-08 | FD | NWSE | R:HAMILTON |
| 88 | " " | 31 | SWSE | 1839-01-03 | FD | SWSE | R:HAMILTON |
| 20 | THIERRY, Francis R | 33 | E½SE | 1851-02-25 | FD | E2SE | |
| 91 | TROTTER, Robert | 33 | SWSE | 1852-03-08 | FD | SWSE | R:HAMILTON |
| 109 | TROTTER, William H | 34 | NESW | 1853-10-31 | FD | NESW | R:HAMILTON |
| 107 | TURNER, William D | 23 | SWNW | 1853-12-23 | FD | SWNW | |
| 106 | " " | 23 | NWNW | 1853-12-23 | FD | NWNW | R:HAMILTON |
| 8 | WAUGH, Charles | 34 | W½SW | 1851-08-20 | FD | W2SW | |
| 7 | " " | 34 | SWNW | 1851-08-20 | FD | SWNW | |
| 5 | " " | 33 | SENE | 1851-08-20 | FD | SENE | |
| 6 | " " | 34 | SESW | 1854-02-02 | FD | SESW | R:HAMILTON |
| 31 | WILKEY, James A J | 33 | NWSE | 1853-03-15 | FD | NWSE | |
| 49 | WILLIAMSEN, Jarvis | 20 | W½NW | 1854-10-09 | FD | W2NW | R:JEFFERSON |
| 47 | " " | 19 | E½NE | 1854-10-09 | FD | E2NE | R:JEFFERSON |
| 48 | " " | 20 | SENW | 1854-10-09 | FD | SENW | R:JEFFERSON |
| 123 | YOUNG, William | 34 | NWSW | 1855-10-18 | FD | NWSW | R:OHIO |

## Patent Map

T3-S  R5-E
3rd PM Meridian

Map  Group  1

### Township Statistics

| | | |
|---|---|---|
| Parcels Mapped | : | 123 |
| Number of Patents | : | 1 |
| Number of Individuals | : | 61 |
| Patentees Identified | : | 59 |
| Number of Surnames | : | 48 |
| Multi-Patentee Parcels | : | 3 |
| Oldest Patent Date | : | 12/30/1833 |
| Most Recent Patent | : | 4/13/1859 |
| Block/Lot Parcels | : | 0 |
| Cities and Towns | : | 0 |
| Cemeteries | : | 2 |

Note: the area contained in this map amounts to far less than a full Township. Therefore, its contents are completely on this single page (instead of a "normal" 2-page spread).

N

### Legend

———————  Patent Boundary

━━━━━━━  Section Boundary

No Patents Found
(or Outside County)

1., 2., 3., ...   Lot Numbers
(when beside a name)

[ ]   Group Number
(see Appendix "C")

**Scale**:  Section = 1 mile  X  1 mile
(generally, with some exceptions)

## Road Map

### T3-S  R5-E
### 3rd PM Meridian

Map  Group  1

Note: the area contained in this map amounts to far less than a full Township. Therefore, its contents are completely on this single page (instead of a "normal" 2-page spread).

### Cities & Towns
None

### Cemeteries
Atchison Cemetery
Pleasant Hill Cemetery

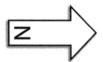

### Legend

| | |
|---|---|
| ——————— | Section Lines |
| ═══════ | Interstates |
| ▬▬▬▬▬ | Highways |
| ——————— | Other Roads |
| ● | Cities/Towns |
| ⚐ | Cemeteries |

**Scale**: Section = 1 mile X 1 mile
(generally, with some exceptions)

31

30

19

County Road 2350

County Road 2200

County Road 2400N

County Road 100

32

29

20

County Road 200

33

28

21

Pleasant Hill Cem.

Atchison Cem.

County Road 2100

County Road 2225

County Road 2300

County Road 275

34

27

22

County Road 325

County Road 2125

County Road 2200

County Road 2315

County Road 2325

County Road 400

35

26

23

County Road 500

36

25

24

County Road 8

County Road 2250

County Road 2350

County Road 600

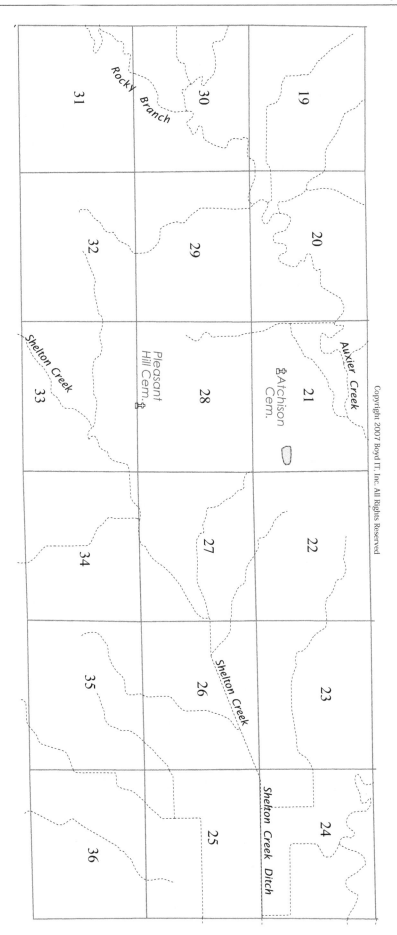

31

Rocky Branch

30

19

32

29

20

Shelton Creek

Pleasant Hill Cem.

33

28

Auxier Creek

Atchison Cem.

21

34

27

22

35

Shelton Creek

26

23

36

25

Shelton Creek Ditch

24

Note: the area contained in this map amounts to far less than a full Township. Therefore, its contents are completely on this single page (instead of a "normal" 2-page spread).

### Cities & Towns
None

### Cemeteries
Atchison Cemetery
Pleasant Hill Cemetery

N

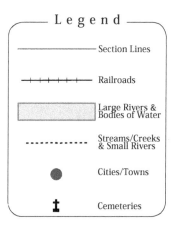

Legend

———— Section Lines

+++++ Railroads

▭ Large Rivers & Bodies of Water

- - - - - Streams/Creeks & Small Rivers

● Cities/Towns

✝ Cemeteries

**Scale**: Section = 1 mile  X  1 mile
(there are some exceptions)

## Map Group 2: Index to Land Patents

## Township 3-South Range 6-East (3rd PM)

After you locate an individual in this Index, take note of the Section and Section Part then proceed to the Land Patent map on the pages immediately following. You should have no difficulty locating the corresponding parcel of land.

The "For More Info" Column will lead you to more information about the underlying Patents. See the *Legend* at right, and the "How to Use this Book" chapter, for more information.

```
                    LEGEND
           "For More Info . . . " column
G = Group  (Multi-Patentee Patent, see Appendix "C")
R = Residence
S = Social Status

See Appendix A for list of abbreviations used by the
Illinois State Archives in describing the place and
nature of these land patents.

Note: if the Abbreviations contain "L", "BL", "LOT",
or "BLOCK", the exact whereabouts of the parcel within
the section is not known.
```

| ID | Individual in Patent | Sec. | Sec. Part | Purchase Date | Sale Type | IL Aliquot Part | For More Info . . . |
|----|---------------------|------|-----------|---------------|-----------|-----------------|---------------------|
| 223 | ANGELMENT, Urban | 32 | SWNW | 1848-08-21 | FD | SWNW | R:HAMILTON |
| 224 | ANSELMANT, Urban | 32 | NWSW | 1841-08-16 | FD | NWSW | R:HAMILTON |
| 191 | AYD, John J | 28 | SWSW | 1843-12-21 | FD | SWSW | R:HAMILTON |
| 192 | AYD, John Leonard | 28 | NWSW | 1848-10-25 | FD | NWSW | R:HAMILTON |
| 159 | BEECHER, Edwin | 22 | E½SW | 1853-12-24 | FD | E2SW | |
| 170 | BROCKWAY, Henry W | 24 | SW | 1818-11-13 | FD | SW | R:NEW YORK |
| 169 | " " | 24 | E½ | 1818-11-13 | FD | E2 | R:NEW YORK |
| 128 | BUCK, Warner | 28 | SE | 1817-11-24 | FD | SE | G:5 |
| 231 | BUCK, Warner Jr | 24 | NW | 1818-12-15 | FD | NW | R:WHITE |
| 174 | CLIFFE, James | 30 | E½SE | 1818-07-27 | FD | E2SE | R:GALLATIN |
| 221 | COOPER, Thomas | 24 | SENW | 1853-05-06 | FD | SENW | |
| 128 | CROUCH, Adam | 28 | SE | 1817-11-24 | FD | SE | G:5 |
| 149 | CROUCH, Cloyd | 33 | W½SW | 1840-02-12 | FD | W2SW | R:HAMILTON |
| 146 | " " | 32 | NESE | 1840-02-12 | FD | NESE | R:HAMILTON |
| 147 | " " | 33 | E½SW | 1842-06-04 | FD | E2SW | R:HAMILTON |
| 148 | " " | 33 | W½NW | 1842-06-04 | FD | W2NW | R:HAMILTON |
| 144 | " " | 22 | SWNE | 1854-01-07 | FD | SWNE | R:HAMILTON |
| 145 | " " | 22 | W½NW | 1854-01-09 | FD | W2NW | R:HAMILTON |
| 143 | " " | 21 | SEN½ | 1855-03-27 | FD | S2NE | R:HAMILTON |
| 150 | CROUCH, Cloyed | 32 | SESE | 1845-08-01 | FD | SESE | R:HAMILTON |
| 225 | CROUCH, Walter Buck | 33 | E½NE | 1842-06-04 | FD | E2NE | R:HAMILTON |
| 226 | " " | 33 | W½SE | 1842-06-04 | FD | W2SE | R:HAMILTON |
| 227 | CROUCH, Warner Buck | 33 | E½NW | 1840-02-12 | FD | E2NW | R:HAMILTON |
| 230 | " " | 33 | SWNE | 1848-09-13 | FD | SWNE | R:HAMILTON |
| 228 | " " | 33 | NESE | 1853-03-07 | FD | NESE | |
| 229 | " " | 33 | NWNE | 1853-03-07 | FD | NWNE | |
| 232 | DAVIS, William C H | 31 | NWNE | 1852-03-01 | FD | NWNE | R:HAMILTON |
| 201 | DOBBS, Josiah | 30 | SESE | 1833-05-18 | FD | SESE | R:HAMILTON |
| 137 | ELLIS, Benjamin | 33 | W½NE | 1818-10-07 | FD | W2NE | R:GALLATIN |
| 234 | ELLIS, William | 28 | SW | 1818-08-20 | FD | SW | R:WHITE |
| 233 | " " | 24 | NENW | 1849-03-07 | FD | NENW | R:WAYNE |
| 239 | ESTES, William | 35 | SWNW | 1848-02-22 | FD | SWNW | |
| 240 | " " | 35 | SWNW | 1848-02-22 | FD | SWNW | |
| 236 | " " | 35 | N½SW | 1848-02-22 | FD | N2SW | |
| 238 | " " | 35 | SESW | 1848-02-22 | FD | SESW | |
| 240 | " " | 35 | SWNW | 1849-12-19 | FD | SWNW | |
| 239 | " " | 35 | SWNW | 1849-12-19 | FD | SWNW | |
| 237 | " " | 35 | NWSW | 1849-12-19 | FD | NWSW | |
| 235 | " " | 35 | E½SW | 1849-12-19 | FD | E2SW | |
| 129 | ESWEICE, Albert | 32 | SWSW | 1853-04-05 | FD | SWSW | R:HAMILTON |
| 188 | EUBANKS, John | 34 | NWNW | 1848-09-13 | FD | NWNW | R:WHITE |
| 187 | " " | 34 | N½SW | 1852-02-24 | FD | N2SW | |
| 190 | " " | 34 | SWNW | 1852-02-24 | FD | SWNW | |
| 189 | " " | 34 | SESW | 1852-02-24 | FD | SESW | |
| 124 | FLAT, Aaron | 25 | NENE | 1853-04-04 | FD | NENE | R:WAYNE |
| 125 | FLATT, Aaron | 23 | NENE | 1854-02-09 | FD | NENE | R:HAMILTON |

| ID | Individual in Patent | Sec. | Sec. Part | Purchase Date | Sale Type | IL Aliquot Part | For More Info . . . |
|---|---|---|---|---|---|---|---|
| 203 | FRY, Leonard | 29 | NESW | 1852-03-01 | FD | NESW | R:HAMILTON |
| 216 | GARISON, Seman | 23 | SWNW | 1848-04-12 | FD | SWNW | R:HAMILTON |
| 152 | GARRISON, David | 23 | NWNW | 1844-07-15 | FD | NWNWLS | R:HAMILTON |
| 153 | "            " | 23 | SWSW | 1852-04-14 | FD | SWSW | |
| 151 | "            " | 22 | SESE | 1852-04-14 | FD | SESE | |
| 154 | "            " | 26 | N½NW | 1852-04-14 | FD | N2NW | |
| 214 | GARRISON, Samuel | 29 | NESE | 1833-02-09 | FD | NESE | R:HAMILTON |
| 218 | GARRISON, Seman | 23 | SWNE | 1854-11-25 | FD | SWNE | R:HAMILTON |
| 217 | "            " | 23 | SESW | 1854-11-25 | FD | SESW | R:HAMILTON |
| 219 | GARRISON, Simeon | 23 | NWSW | 1844-07-15 | FD | NWSWLS | R:HAMILTON |
| 241 | GREEN, William | 22 | NE | 1818-11-30 | FD | NE | R:WHITE |
| 156 | HALL, David H | 23 | NESW | 1853-05-28 | FD | NESW | |
| 157 | "            " | 23 | NWNE | 1853-05-28 | FD | NWNEVOID | |
| 158 | "            " | 23 | SENW | 1853-05-28 | FD | SENW | |
| 155 | "            " | 23 | NENW | 1853-12-30 | FD | NENW | |
| 197 | "            " | 23 | NENW | 1853-12-30 | FD | NENW | |
| 167 | HALL, Henry C | 30 | NWSE | 1854-01-17 | FD | NWSE | R:HAMILTON |
| 168 | HALL, Henry Carroll | 30 | NESE | 1852-01-14 | FD | NESE | R:HAMILTON |
| 176 | HALL, James | 34 | SWSW | 1852-04-29 | FD | SWSW | |
| 175 | "            " | 34 | SESE | 1852-04-29 | FD | SESE | |
| 198 | HALLER, Joseph L | 32 | SWNE | 1841-08-16 | FD | SWNE | R:HAMILTON |
| 199 | "            " | 32 | W½SE | 1841-08-16 | FD | W2SE | R:HAMILTON |
| 130 | HOELZTS, Anselmus | 32 | NENE | 1843-08-02 | FD | NENE | R:HAMILTON |
| 213 | HOGAN, Robert J | 22 | NWSW | 1853-10-22 | FD | NWSW | R:HAMILTON |
| 138 | HOLADAY, Caleb | 32 | NWNW | 1842-01-08 | FD | NWNW | R:HAMILTON |
| 209 | HOLADAY, Nancy | 29 | SESW | 1842-06-04 | FD | SESW | R:HAMILTON S:F |
| 139 | HOLLADAY, Caleb | 31 | NENE | 1836-12-06 | FD | NENE | R:HAMILTON |
| 162 | HUHLEIN, Gerhard | 21 | NESW | 1839-06-06 | FD | NESW | R:POPE |
| 135 | IRVIN, Barthen | 34 | SENW | 1840-10-03 | FD | SENW | R:HARDIN |
| 134 | IRWIN, Barthea | 34 | SENE | 1853-02-09 | FD | SENE | |
| 136 | IRWIN, Barthew | 34 | SWNE | 1854-10-27 | FD | SWNE | R:HAMILTON |
| 215 | IRWIN, Samuel H | 24 | E½SW | 1854-10-27 | FD | E2SW | R:HAMILTON |
| 242 | IRWIN, William | 32 | NESW | 1836-12-15 | FD | NESW | R:HAMILTON |
| 131 | KANFURANN, Anson | 32 | E½NW | 1841-08-16 | FD | E2NW | R:HAMILTON |
| 220 | KARCHER, Solomon | 34 | NENW | 1843-08-23 | FD | NENW | R:HAMILTON |
| 161 | KAUFMAN, Felix | 32 | NWNE | 1854-01-24 | FD | NWNE | R:HAMILTON |
| 212 | KAUFMAN, Philip | 32 | SESW | 1853-11-14 | FD | SESW | R:HAMILTON |
| 177 | KELLY, James | 31 | NE | 1818-09-23 | FD | NE | R:SHAWNEETOWN |
| 207 | LAWLER, Michael Kelly | 29 | SESE | 1837-02-28 | FD | SESE | R:GALLATIN |
| 243 | MCTHOMAS, William | 23 | SENE | 1855-05-18 | FD | SENE | R:WAYNE |
| 179 | MILLER, James | 20 | NENW | 1855-05-05 | FD | NENW | R:HAMILTON |
| 171 | MOOTHY, Hiram | 34 | S½SE | 1844-08-13 | FD | S2SELS | R:HAMILTON |
| 172 | "            " | 35 | SWSW | 1844-08-13 | FD | SWSWLS | R:HAMILTON |
| 204 | MYERS, Martin | 23 | W½NW | 1820-01-29 | FD | W2NW | R:WHITE |
| 205 | NORMAN, Mary | 27 | NENE | 1855-09-10 | FD | NENE | R:HAMILTON S:F |
| 126 | PEER, Abram | 22 | NWSE | 1854-02-15 | FD | NWSE | R:HAMILTON |
| 127 | "            " | 22 | SWSE | 1854-02-27 | FD | SWSE | R:WAYNE |
| 211 | POWELL, Nelson | 31 | SWSE | 1853-10-04 | FD | SWSE | R:HAMILTON |
| 210 | "            " | 31 | NESE | 1853-10-04 | FD | NESE | R:HAMILTON |
| 140 | RAWLS, Canna | 31 | NESW | 1852-03-01 | FD | NESW | R:HAMILTON S:F |
| 141 | "            " | 31 | SENW | 1852-03-01 | FD | SENW | R:HAMILTON S:F |
| 142 | RAWLS, Carma | 31 | SESW | 1854-01-13 | FD | SESW | R:HAMILTON S:F |
| 180 | RAWLS, James | 30 | SWSE | 1846-01-15 | FD | SWSE | R:HAMILTON |
| 181 | "            " | 31 | SWSW | 1855-05-07 | FD | SWSW | R:HAMILTON |
| 163 | REBANACKER, Godfrey | 31 | SWNE | 1849-02-20 | FD | SWNE | R:HAMILTON |
| 164 | REBINAKER, Godfrey | 31 | SENE | 1853-09-24 | FD | SENE | R:HAMILTON |
| 182 | RICHARDSON, James | 20 | NENE | 1853-02-10 | FD | NENE | |
| 183 | "            " | 21 | NWNW | 1853-02-10 | FD | NWNW | |
| 208 | ROBINSON, Michael M | 25 | SW | 1854-09-22 | FD | SW | R:GALLATIN |
| 222 | ROBINSON, Thomas M | 25 | NW | 1854-09-22 | FD | NW | R:GALLATIN |
| 165 | RUBANACKER, Godfrey | 31 | NWSE | 1851-04-05 | FD | NWSE | R:HAMILTON |
| 193 | SCHUSTER, John | 30 | SENE | 1851-04-05 | FD | SENE | R:HAMILTON |
| 195 | SCUDAMORE, Joseph B | 22 | E½NW | 1853-12-07 | FD | E2NW | R:HAMILTON |
| 196 | "            " | 22 | SWSW | 1855-04-09 | FD | SWSW | R:HAMILTON |
| 202 | STULL, Lawrence | 22 | NW | 1819-09-18 | FD | NW | R:WHITE |
| 178 | SUTTON, James M | 20 | NWNE | 1854-06-02 | FD | NWNE | R:HAMILTON |
| 185 | TAYLOR, James | 22 | NESE | 1848-03-17 | FD | NESE | |
| 186 | "            " | 22 | NWNE | 1848-03-17 | FD | NWNE | |
| 184 | "            " | 22 | E½NE | 1848-03-17 | FD | E2NE | |
| 155 | THOMASON, Joseph C | 23 | NENW | 1852-08-25 | FD | NENW | |
| 197 | "            " | 23 | NENW | 1852-08-25 | FD | NENW | |
| 166 | TIPSCORD, Griffin | 29 | SE | 1819-02-17 | FD | SE | R:WHITE |
| 133 | TROTTER, Archibald | 21 | NWNE | 1853-08-24 | FD | NWNE | |

| ID | Individual in Patent | Sec. | Sec. Part | Purchase Date | Sale Type | IL Aliquot Part | For More Info . . . |
|----|----------------------|------|-----------|---------------|-----------|-----------------|---------------------|
| 132 | TROTTER, Archibald (Cont'd) | 21 | NENW | 1856-08-21 | FD | NENW | |
| 173 | TROTTER, Isam | 34 | NWNE | 1852-01-14 | FD | NWNE | R:HAMILTON |
| 200 | TROTTER, Joseph | 21 | NENE | 1855-10-03 | FD | NENE | R:HAMILTON |
| 160 | WALLER, Eli | 29 | SW | 1818-08-21 | FD | SW | R:WHITE |
| 194 | WARFIELD, John | 34 | N½SE | 1836-12-14 | FD | N2SE | R:HAMILTON |
| 206 | ZACHRMAN, Marzell | 32 | SENE | 1842-08-30 | FD | SENE | R:HAMILTON |

Copyright 2007 Boyd IT, Inc. All Rights Reserved

**Section 19**

**Section 20**
MILLER James 1855
SUTTON James M 1854
RICHARDSON James 1853
RICHARDSON James 1853

**Section 21**
HUHLEIN Gerhard 1839
TROTTER Archibald 1856
TROTTER Archibald 1853
TROTTER Joseph 1855
CROUCH Cloyd 1855

**Section 30**
SCHUSTER John 1851
HALL Henry Carroll 1854
HALL Henry C 1854
CLIFFE 1818
DOBBS James 1818
DOBBS Josiah 1833

**Section 31**
RAWLS James 1855
RAWLS Carna 1854
RAWLS Carna 1852
RAWLS Carna 1852
RAWLS Carna 1854
DAVIS, HOLLADAY William C H Caleb 1836
KELLY James 1818
REBINAKER Godfrey 1849
REBINAKER Godfrey 1853
RUBANACKER Godfrey 1851
RAWLS James 1846
POWELL Nelson 1853
POWELL Nelson 1853

**Section 32**
ESWEICE Albert 1853
ANSELMANT Urhan 1841
ANGELMENT Urhan 1848
KAUFMAN Philip 1853
IRWIN William 1836
KANTURANN Anson 1841
HOLLADAY Felix 1854
HOLLADAY Caleb 1842
WALLER Eli 1818
FRY Leonard 1852
HOLADAY Nancy 1842
HALLER Joseph L 1841
HALLER Joseph L 1841
KAUFMAN Samuel 1854
TIPSCORD Griffin 1819
ZACHRMAN Marzell 1842
LAWLER Michael Kelly 1837

**Section 29**

**Section 33**
CROUCH Cloyd 1840
CROUCH Cloyd 1840
CROUCH Cloyd 1842
CROUCH Cloyd 1842
CROUCH Warner Buck 1842
CROUCH Walter Buck 1842
CROUCH Warner Buck 1853
HOELZTS Anselmus 1843
AYD John J 1843
AYD John Leonard 1848
GARRISON Joseph D 1845

**Section 28**
ELLIS William 1818
CROUCH [5] Adam 1817
CROUCH Warner Buck 1818
ELLIS Benjamin 1853
CROUCH 1848

**Section 22**
SCUDAMORE Joseph B 1855
SCUDAMORE Joseph B 1853
HOGAN Robert J 1853
BEECHER Edwin 1853
PEER Abram 1854
PEER Abram 1854
CROUCH Cloyd 1854
STULL Lawrence 1819
TAYLOR James 1848
TAYLOR James 1848
TAYLOR David 1852
TAYLOR Seman 1848
GREEN William 1818
MYERS Martin 1820
GARRISON Seman 1848

**Section 34**
HALL James 1852
HALL James 1852
EUBANKS John 1852
EUBANKS John 1852
EUBANKS John 1848
EUBANKS John 1852
KARCHER Solomon 1843
IRVIN Barthea 1840
WARFIELD John 1836
MOOTHY Hiram 1844
HALL James 1852
TROTTER Isam 1852
IRWIN Barthea 1854
IRWIN Barthea 1853

**Section 27**
NORMAN Mary 1855
GARRISON David 1852
GARRISON Simeon 1844
GARRISON David 1852
GARRISON David 1854
GARRISON David 1852
HALL David H 1853
HALL David H 1853
GARRISON Seman 1854

**Section 35**
MOOTHY Hiram 1844
ESTES William 1848
ESTES William 1849
ESTES William 1849
ESTES William 1848

**Section 23**
GARRISON David L HALL 1844 David H 1844
HALL David H 1852
HALL David H
THOMASON Joseph D
FLATT Aaron 1854
MCTHOMAS William 1855
GARRISON Seman 1854

**Section 26**

**Section 24**
BROCKWAY Henry W 1818

**Section 25**
ROBINSON Michael M 1854
ROBINSON Thomas M 1854
BROCKWAY Henry W 1818
IRWIN Samuel H 1854
BUCK Warner Jr 1818
ELLIS William 1849
COOPER Thomas 1853

**Section 36**
FLAT Aaron 1853

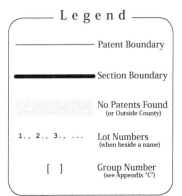

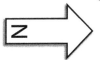

## Township Statistics

| | | |
|---|---|---|
| Parcels Mapped | : | 120 |
| Number of Patents | : | 1 |
| Number of Individuals | : | 82 |
| Patentees Identified | : | 81 |
| Number of Surnames | : | 59 |
| Multi-Patentee Parcels | : | 1 |
| Oldest Patent Date | : | 11/24/1817 |
| Most Recent Patent | : | 8/21/1856 |
| Block/Lot Parcels | : | 0 |
| Cities and Towns | : | 2 |
| Cemeteries | : | 3 |

Note: the area contained in this map amounts to far less than a full Township. Therefore, its contents are completely on this single page (instead of a "normal" 2-page spread).

### Legend

— Patent Boundary

— Section Boundary

No Patents Found
(or Outside County)

1., 2., 3., ... Lot Numbers
(when beside a name)

[ ] Group Number
(see Appendix "C")

**Scale**: Section = 1 mile X 1 mile
(generally, with some exceptions)

## Road Map

### T3-S R6-E
### 3rd PM Meridian

Map Group 2

Note: the area contained in this map amounts to far less than a full Township. Therefore, its contents are completely on this single page (instead of a "normal" 2-page spread).

### Cities & Towns
Belle Prairie City
Garrison

### Cemeteries
Crouch Cemetery
Garrison Cemetery
Rawls Cemetery

### Legend
— Section Lines
═ Interstates
━ Highways
— Other Roads
● Cities/Towns
☖ Cemeteries

**Scale**: Section = 1 mile X 1 mile
(generally, with some exceptions)

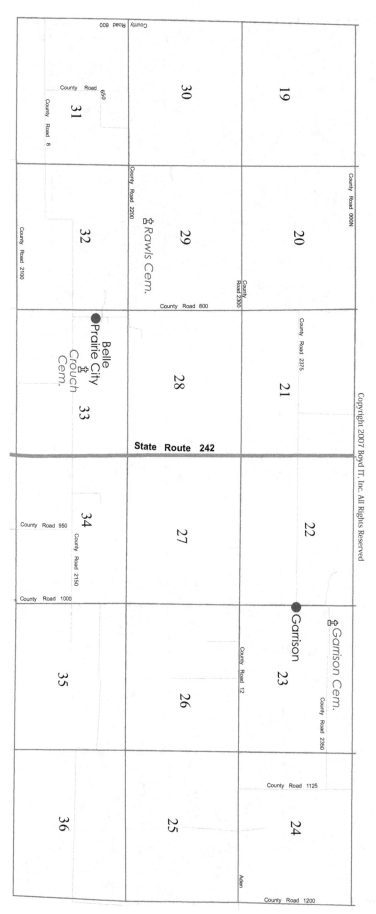

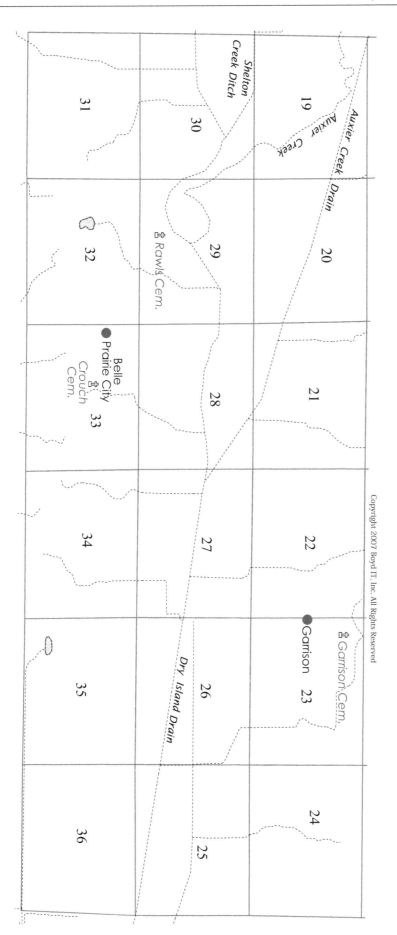

## Historical Map

T3-S R6-E
3rd PM Meridian

Map Group 2

Note: the area contained in this map amounts to far less than a full Township. Therefore, its contents are completely on this single page (instead of a "normal" 2-page spread).

### Cities & Towns
Belle Prairie City
Garrison

### Cemeteries
Crouch Cemetery
Garrison Cemetery
Rawls Cemetery

### Legend
———— Section Lines

+++++ Railroads

Large Rivers & Bodies of Water

- - - - - - Streams/Creeks & Small Rivers

● Cities/Towns

† Cemeteries

**Scale**: Section = 1 mile X 1 mile
(there are some exceptions)

## Map Group 3: Index to Land Patents

## Township 3-South Range 7-East (3rd PM)

After you locate an individual in this Index, take note of the Section and Section Part then proceed to the Land Patent map on the pages immediately following. You should have no difficulty locating the corresponding parcel of land.

The "For More Info" Column will lead you to more information about the underlying Patents. See the *Legend* at right, and the "How to Use this Book" chapter, for more information.

```
LEGEND
          "For More Info . . . " column
G = Group   (Multi-Patentee Patent, see Appendix "C")
R = Residence
S = Social Status

See Appendix A for list of abbreviations used by the
Illinois State Archives in describing the place and
nature of these land patents.

Note: if the Abbreviations contain "L", "BL", "LOT",
or "BLOCK", the exact whereabouts of the parcel within
the section is not known.
```

| ID | Individual in Patent | Sec. | Sec. Part | Purchase Date | Sale Type | IL Aliquot Part | For More Info . . . |
|-----|---------------------|------|-----------|---------------|-----------|-----------------|---------------------|
| 246 | BROCKWAY, Henry W | 19 | NW | 1818-11-13 | FD | NW | R:NEW YORK |
| 245 | CARPENTER, Chester | 30 | NENW | 1858-01-08 | FD | NENW | |
| 244 | CLOSE, Arthur | 28 | SENE | 1852-05-07 | FD | SENE | |
| 250 | EZELL, Thomas | 19 | SW | 1818-11-05 | FD | SW | R:WHITE |
| 248 | PUCKETT, Pleasant J | 28 | NESE | 1844-04-30 | FD | NESE | R:WAYNE S:A |
| 249 | RUSH, Samuel | 36 | SE | 1818-11-07 | FD | SE | R:OHIO |
| 247 | WARFIELD, John W | 28 | NWNE | 1854-02-21 | FD | NWNE | R:HAMILTON |

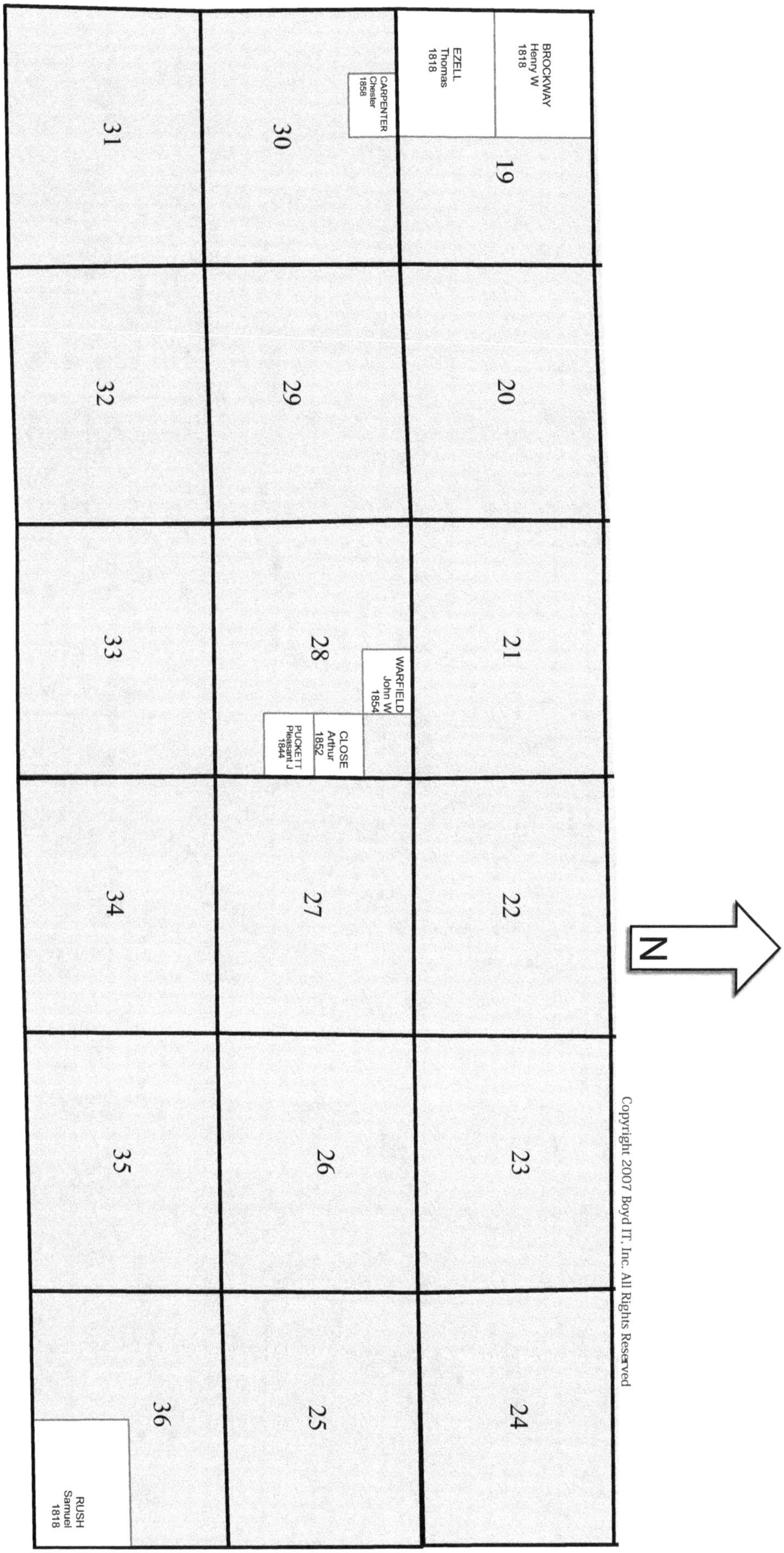

31

30

CARPENTER
Chester
1858

EZELL
Thomas
1818

BROCKWAY
Henry W
1818

19

32

29

20

33

28

WARFIELD
John W
1854

CLOSE
Arthur
1852

PUCKETT
Pleasant J
1844

21

34

27

22

35

26

23

36

RUSH
Samuel
1818

25

24

## Patent Map

### T3-S R7-E
### 3rd PM Meridian

Map Group 3

## Township Statistics

| | | |
|---|---|---|
| Parcels Mapped | : | 7 |
| Number of Patents | : | 1 |
| Number of Individuals | : | 7 |
| Patentees Identified | : | 7 |
| Number of Surnames | : | 7 |
| Multi-Patentee Parcels | : | 0 |
| Oldest Patent Date | : | 11/5/1818 |
| Most Recent Patent | : | 1/8/1858 |
| Block/Lot Parcels | : | 0 |
| Cities and Towns | : | 1 |
| Cemeteries | : | 0 |

Note: the area contained in this map amounts to far less than a full Township. Therefore, its contents are completely on this single page (instead of a "normal" 2-page spread).

## Legend

——————— Patent Boundary

━━━━━━━ Section Boundary

No Patents Found
(or Outside County)

1., 2., 3., ... Lot Numbers
(when beside a name)

[ ] Group Number
(see Appendix "C")

**Scale**: Section = 1 mile X 1 mile
(generally, with some exceptions)

## Road Map

T3-S  R7-E
3rd PM Meridian

Map  Group  3

Note: the area contained in this map amounts to far less than a full Township. Therefore, its contents are completely on this single page (instead of a "normal" 2-page spread).

### Cities & Towns
Aden

### Cemeteries
None

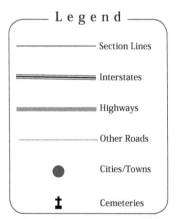

**Legend**

——————— Section Lines

═══════ Interstates

━━━━━━━ Highways

——————— Other Roads

● Cities/Towns

✝ Cemeteries

**Scale**: Section = 1 mile X 1 mile
(generally, with some exceptions)

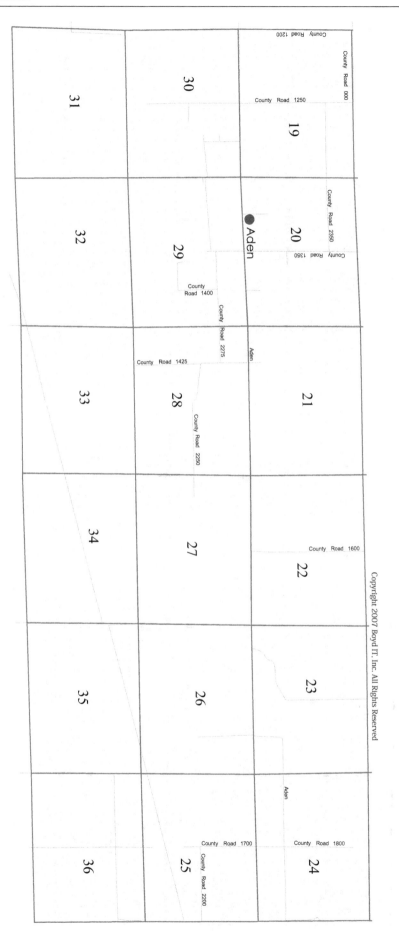

County Road 1200

County Road 000

County Road 1250

County Road 2350

County Road 1350

County Road 1400

County Road 2275

County Road 1425

County Road 2250

County Road 1600

County Road 1700

County Road 1800

County Road 2200

Aden

30  31  19

32  29  20  Aden

33  28  21

34  27  22

35  26  23

36  25  24

Copyright 2007 Boyd IT, Inc. All Rights Reserved

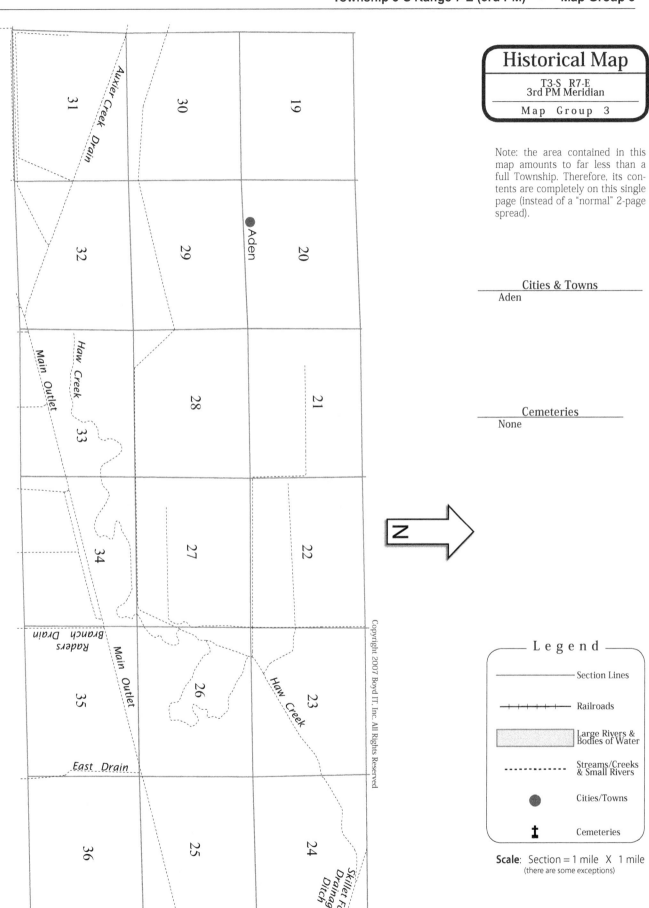

**Historical Map**

T3-S  R7-E
3rd PM Meridian

Map  Group  3

Note: the area contained in this map amounts to far less than a full Township. Therefore, its contents are completely on this single page (instead of a "normal" 2-page spread).

Cities & Towns
Aden

Cemeteries
None

Legend

———— Section Lines

++++++ Railroads

Large Rivers &
Bodies of Water

---------- Streams/Creeks
& Small Rivers

● Cities/Towns

✝ Cemeteries

**Scale**: Section = 1 mile  X  1 mile
(there are some exceptions)

## Map Group 4: Index to Land Patents

## Township 4-South Range 5-East (3rd PM)

After you locate an individual in this Index, take note of the Section and Section Part then proceed to the Land Patent map on the pages immediately following. You should have no difficulty locating the corresponding parcel of land.

The "For More Info" Column will lead you to more information about the underlying Patents. See the *Legend* at right, and the "How to Use this Book" chapter, for more information.

```
┌─────────────────────────────────────────────────────┐
│                      LEGEND                          │
│            "For More Info . . . " column             │
│  ──────────────────────────────────────────────      │
│  G = Group  (Multi-Patentee Patent, see Appendix "C")│
│  R = Residence                                       │
│  S = Social Status                                   │
│                                                      │
│  See Appendix A for list of abbreviations used by the│
│  Illinois State Archives in describing the place and │
│  nature of these land patents.                       │
│                                                      │
│  Note: if the Abbreviations contain "L", "BL", "LOT",│
│  or "BLOCK", the exact whereabouts of the parcel     │
│  within the section is not known.                    │
└─────────────────────────────────────────────────────┘
```

| ID | Individual in Patent | Sec. | Sec. Part | Purchase Date | Sale Type | IL Aliquot Part | For More Info . . . |
|----|----------------------|------|-----------|---------------|-----------|-----------------|---------------------|
| 495 | ADAIR, Philip | 36 | W½SW | 1839-12-03 | FD | W2SW | R:HAMILTON |
| 346 | ADCOCK, Isaac | 33 | NWNE | 1853-06-06 | FD | NWNE | |
| 347 | " " | 33 | SENE | 1853-11-04 | FD | SENE | R:HAMILTON |
| 348 | ADDCOCK, Isaac | 33 | SWNE | 1851-01-09 | FD | SWNE | R:HAMILTON |
| 423 | ANSELMENT, Joseph | 12 | SENE | 1853-08-20 | FD | SENE | R:HAMILTON |
| 422 | " " | 12 | NENE | 1854-04-20 | FD | NENE | R:HAMILTON |
| 586 | ANSELMENT, Urban | 11 | SWNE | 1853-03-01 | FD | SWNE | R:HAMILTON |
| 585 | " " | 11 | NWNE | 1853-08-20 | FD | NWNE | R:HAMILTON |
| 351 | ATCHISSON, James A | 4 | SWNW | 1854-02-13 | FD | SWNW | R:HAMILTON |
| 265 | AYD, Alexander | 10 | E½NE | 1853-08-31 | FD | E2NE | |
| 266 | " " | 3 | SESE | 1854-02-01 | FD | SESE | R:HAMILTON |
| 424 | BACKLE, Joseph | 12 | SWNW | 1854-06-10 | FD | SWNW | R:HAMILTON |
| 551 | BARKER, Thomas | 35 | SENW | 1845-11-08 | FD | SENW | R:HAMILTON |
| 536 | BARTLETT, Sarah Jane | 31 | SENE | 1842-01-06 | FD | SENE | R:HAMILTON S:F |
| 550 | BARTLETT, Stephen H | 32 | NWNW | 1839-04-20 | FD | NWNW | R:HAMILTON |
| 384 | BAYLES, Jesse | 31 | NW | 1818-08-04 | FD | NW | R:WHITE |
| 496 | BEARDEN, Philip Wimn | 19 | E½SW | 1840-06-19 | FD | E2SW | R:HAMILTON |
| 498 | BEARDEN, Philip Winn | 19 | W½NE | 1837-02-25 | FD | W2NE | R:KENTUCKY |
| 499 | " " | 19 | W½SE | 1838-12-17 | FD | W2SE | R:HAMILTON |
| 497 | " " | 19 | SENW | 1838-12-17 | FD | SENW | R:HAMILTON |
| 500 | " " | 29 | NWNE | 1850-07-31 | FD | NWNE | R:HAMILTON |
| 410 | BELL, Johnson | 16 | L13 | 1840-08-15 | SC | LOT13 | |
| 411 | " " | 16 | L14 | 1840-08-15 | SC | LOT14 | |
| 275 | BELT, Andrew J | 5 | NWNW | 1854-11-11 | FD | NWNW | R:HAMILTON |
| 555 | BELT, Thomas | 9 | SWSW | 1851-05-14 | FD | SWSW | |
| 554 | " " | 8 | SESE | 1851-05-14 | FD | SESE | |
| 553 | " " | 8 | SENE | 1854-05-01 | FD | SENE | R:HAMILTON |
| 552 | " " | 8 | NESE | 1854-05-04 | FD | NESE | R:HAMILTON |
| 574 | BELT, Thomas Jr | 9 | NWNW | 1849-03-13 | FD | NWNW | R:HAMILTON |
| 575 | " " | 9 | SWNW | 1852-03-29 | FD | SWNW | R:HAMILTON |
| 579 | BELT, Thomas Sen | 9 | SWSE | 1851-06-24 | FD | SWSE | R:HAMILTON |
| 535 | BESTEM, Sarah | 34 | SESE | 1854-09-21 | FD | SESE | R:HAMILTON S:F |
| 534 | " " | 2 | W½SE | 1854-09-21 | FD | W2SE | R:HAMILTON S:F |
| 533 | " " | 2 | NWNW | 1854-09-21 | FD | NWNW | R:HAMILTON S:F |
| 448 | BOSLEY, Luke | 4 | NWSW | 1849-08-20 | FD | NWSW | R:HAMILTON |
| 330 | BOSTER, George | 35 | SW | 1849-10-25 | FD | SW | |
| 277 | BOWEN, Anthony W | 20 | NWSW | 1854-05-23 | FD | NWSW | R:OHIO |
| 296 | BOWEN, Columbus | 27 | N½NW | 1853-11-28 | FD | N2NW | R:OHIO |
| 295 | " " | 20 | NENW | 1854-05-23 | FD | NENW | R:OHIO |
| 510 | BOYLES, Reuben Davis | 30 | SW | 1839-07-01 | FD | SW | R:FRANKLIN |
| 355 | BRADFORD, James | 32 | NWSW | 1852-07-07 | FD | NWSW | |
| 487 | BRATLETT, Nelson | 31 | E½SW | 1839-09-10 | FD | E2SW | R:HAMILTON |
| 262 | BRENCK, Albert | 2 | SESW | 1852-03-22 | FD | SESW | R:HAMILTON |
| 264 | BRINK, Albert | 2 | SWNE | 1853-12-07 | FD | SWNE | R:HAMILTON |
| 263 | " " | 11 | NENE | 1854-06-07 | FD | NENE | R:HAMILTON |
| 286 | BRINK, Benjamin | 11 | SENE | 1853-04-12 | FD | SENE | R:HAMILTON |

| ID | Individual in Patent | Sec. | Sec. Part | Purchase Date | Sale Type | IL Aliquot Part | For More Info . . . |
|----|---------------------|------|-----------|---------------|-----------|-----------------|---------------------|
| 308 | BRISTOL, Elias H | 10 | W½SE | 1853-04-18 | FD | W2SE | |
| 309 | " " | 3 | SESW | 1853-08-11 | FD | SESW | |
| 462 | BRISTOL, Mary Ann | 10 | NESW | 1853-04-18 | FD | NESW | S:F |
| 556 | BRISTOL, Thomas | 11 | S½SE | 1853-03-31 | FD | S2SE | |
| 558 | " " | 14 | N½NE | 1853-03-31 | FD | N2NE | |
| 557 | " " | 13 | NWNW | 1853-09-16 | FD | NWNW | |
| 559 | " " | 14 | NWNW | 1854-02-24 | FD | NWNW | R:HAMILTON |
| 621 | BRISTOL, Thomas Sen | 11 | SESW | 1853-04-12 | FD | SESW | |
| 580 | " " | 11 | SESW | 1853-04-12 | FD | SESW | |
| 581 | BRISTON, Thomas Sen | 14 | NENW | 1853-04-12 | FD | NENWVOID | |
| 463 | BROOKENS, Milton | 23 | W½NW | 1853-12-31 | FD | W2NW | R:HAMILTON |
| 453 | BROOKINS, Marion | 22 | SENW | 1854-09-18 | FD | SENW | R:JEFFERSON |
| 454 | " " | 22 | W½SW | 1854-09-18 | FD | W2SW | R:JEFFERSON |
| 452 | " " | 22 | SEN½ | 1854-09-18 | FD | S2NE | R:JEFFERSON |
| 450 | " " | 22 | E½SE | 1854-09-18 | FD | E2SE | R:JEFFERSON |
| 451 | " " | 22 | NESW | 1854-09-18 | FD | NESW | R:JEFFERSON |
| 466 | BROOKINS, Milton | 15 | SW | 1854-09-18 | FD | SW | R:HAMILTON |
| 465 | " " | 15 | N½SE | 1854-09-18 | FD | N2SE | R:HAMILTON |
| 467 | " " | 23 | NENW | 1854-09-18 | FD | NENW | R:HAMILTON |
| 464 | " " | 14 | SENW | 1854-09-18 | FD | SENW | R:HAMILTON |
| 630 | " " | 15 | SW | 1854-09-18 | FD | SW | R:HAMILTON |
| 276 | BROWN, Anthony M | 19 | SENE | 1844-05-21 | FD | SENE | R:WAYNE |
| 562 | BURTON, Thomas | 28 | E½NW | 1839-04-20 | FD | E2NW | R:HAMILTON |
| 564 | " " | 28 | NWNW | 1839-04-20 | FD | NWNW | R:HAMILTON |
| 561 | " " | 18 | SWSE | 1850-01-21 | FD | SWSE | R:HAMILTON |
| 563 | " " | 28 | NWNE | 1851-02-11 | FD | NWNE | R:HAMILTON |
| 565 | " " | 28 | SWNE | 1852-09-01 | FD | SWNE | |
| 560 | " " | 18 | SESE | 1853-12-30 | FD | SESE | R:HAMILTON |
| 594 | CANNON, William | 20 | SWNW | 1841-12-20 | FD | SWNW | R:HAMILTON |
| 595 | " " | 33 | NENE | 1848-05-30 | FD | NENE | R:HAMILTON |
| 345 | CAPE, Hiram | 34 | NWSW | 1846-11-20 | FD | NWSW | R:HAMILTON |
| 343 | " " | 34 | NE | 1847-12-01 | FD | NE | |
| 344 | " " | 34 | NESE | 1853-02-12 | FD | NESE | R:HAMILTON |
| 525 | CASKEY, Samuel | 18 | SENE | 1850-02-09 | FD | SENE | R:HAMILTON |
| 566 | CATE, Thomas | 5 | E½NW | 1840-06-19 | FD | E2NW | R:HAMILTON |
| 312 | CATES, Ephraim E | 5 | NESW | 1841-01-29 | FD | NESW | R:HAMILTON |
| 314 | CATES, Ephraim Sen | 6 | E½SE | 1848-10-27 | FD | E2SE | R:HAMILTON |
| 356 | CATES, James | 5 | NWSW | 1837-02-08 | FD | NWSW | R:JEFFERSON |
| 567 | CATES, Thomas | 5 | SWNW | 1837-02-08 | FD | SWNW | R:JEFFERSON |
| 596 | CHOSSER, William | 33 | NESW | 1851-06-06 | FD | NESW | |
| 597 | COLLINS, William | 21 | NESE | 1851-01-18 | FD | NESE | R:HAMILTON |
| 598 | " " | 22 | N½NE | 1854-12-02 | FD | N2NE | R:HAMILTON |
| 620 | COLLINS, William Iii | 15 | SWSE | 1852-07-10 | FD | SWSE | |
| 625 | COLLINS, William Jr | 28 | NWSE | 1852-10-07 | FD | NWSE | |
| 624 | " " | 15 | SESE | 1854-03-18 | FD | SESE | R:HAMILTON |
| 360 | COOK, James | 21 | SENW | 1850-06-03 | FD | SENW | |
| 358 | " " | 21 | NWNE | 1850-06-03 | FD | NWNE | |
| 361 | " " | 21 | SWNE | 1850-06-03 | FD | SWNE | |
| 359 | " " | 21 | NWSE | 1850-06-03 | FD | NWSE | |
| 357 | " " | 21 | NESW | 1854-10-25 | FD | NESW | R:HAMILTON |
| 599 | COOK, William | 15 | NWNE | 1854-10-25 | FD | NWNE | R:HAMILTON |
| 526 | CORKY, Samuel | 16 | L7 | 1841-07-19 | SC | L7 | |
| 313 | COTES, Ephraim E | 5 | NWSE | 1851-12-23 | FD | NWSE | R:HAMILTON |
| 474 | COTES, Nancy | 7 | N½SE | 1851-12-23 | FD | N2SE | R:HAMILTON S:F |
| 568 | COTES, Thomas | 5 | NWNE | 1854-02-25 | FD | NWNE | R:HAMILTON |
| 325 | CRISAL, George A | 10 | NWSW | 1854-06-19 | FD | NWSW | R:HAMILTON |
| 326 | " " | 9 | SENE | 1854-06-19 | FD | SENE | R:HAMILTON |
| 580 | CRISAL, William J | 11 | SESW | 1852-12-08 | FD | SESW | |
| 621 | " " | 11 | SESW | 1852-12-08 | FD | SESW | |
| 328 | CRISEL, George A | 10 | SWNW | 1851-12-06 | FD | SWNW | R:HAMILTON |
| 329 | " " | 9 | NENE | 1854-10-11 | FD | NENE | R:HAMILTON |
| 327 | " " | 10 | NWNW | 1855-05-05 | FD | NWNW | R:HAMILTON |
| 336 | CRISEL, Henry | 3 | NWSW | 1855-05-05 | FD | NWSW | R:HAMILTON |
| 622 | CRISEL, William J | 11 | NWSW | 1853-04-18 | FD | NWSW | |
| 623 | " " | 11 | SWSW | 1853-12-30 | FD | SWSW | R:HAMILTON |
| 281 | CROSS, Asel | 20 | SENE | 1839-04-25 | FD | SENE | R:HAMILTON |
| 283 | " " | 27 | SWNW | 1852-03-16 | FD | SWNW | |
| 282 | " " | 27 | SENW | 1853-12-02 | FD | SENW | R:HAMILTON |
| 396 | CROSS, John | 26 | NWNW | 1853-08-03 | FD | NWNW | R:HAMILTON G:11 |
| 393 | CROSS, John C | 27 | E½SW | 1848-02-19 | FD | E2SW | |
| 395 | " " | 27 | W½SE | 1848-02-19 | FD | W2SE | |
| 396 | " " | 26 | NWNW | 1853-08-03 | FD | NWNW | R:HAMILTON G:11 |
| 392 | " " | 26 | NENW | 1854-02-10 | FD | NENW | R:HAMILTON |

| ID | Individual in Patent | Sec. | Sec. Part | Purchase Date | Sale Type | IL Aliquot Part | For More Info . . . |
|----|---------------------|------|-----------|---------------|-----------|-----------------|---------------------|
| 391 | CROSS, John C (Cont'd) | 23 | SESW | 1854-04-06 | FD | SESW | R:HAMILTON |
| 394 | " " | 27 | SWNE | 1855-04-12 | FD | SWNE | R:HAMILTON |
| 397 | CROSS, John Calvin | 27 | NWSW | 1851-01-04 | FD | NWSW | R:HAMILTON |
| 293 | CROUCH, Cloyd | 1 | N½NW | 1854-04-19 | FD | N2NW | R:HAMILTON |
| 294 | " " | 3 | NESW | 1854-04-19 | FD | NESW | R:HAMILTON G:12 |
| 506 | DALE, Quintilla | 14 | SWNW | 1854-06-16 | FD | SWNW | R:HAMILTON S:F |
| 337 | DAMON, Henry | 21 | SWSE | 1851-02-18 | FD | SWSE | R:HAMILTON |
| 492 | DAMON, Owen Lewis | 32 | SWNE | 1842-09-21 | FD | SWNE | R:WAYNE |
| 491 | " " | 32 | NESE | 1842-09-21 | FD | NESE | R:WAYNE |
| 493 | " " | 33 | N½SE | 1854-02-28 | FD | N2SE | R:HAMILTON |
| 606 | DAVIS, William | 20 | SESE | 1847-05-19 | FD | SESE | R:HAMILTON |
| 605 | " " | 20 | NWSE | 1850-05-31 | FD | NWSE | R:HAMILTON |
| 607 | " " | 20 | SWNE | 1853-09-12 | FD | SWNE | R:HAMILTON |
| 458 | DAVIS, William C | 1 | W½SE | 1854-10-09 | FD | W2SE | R:HAMILTON |
| 590 | " " | 1 | NESW | 1854-10-09 | FD | NESW | R:HAMILTON |
| 592 | " " | 1 | W½SE | 1854-10-09 | FD | W2SE | R:HAMILTON |
| 591 | " " | 1 | SESE | 1854-10-09 | FD | SESE | R:HAMILTON |
| 461 | DAWSON, Martin S | 16 | L16 | 1840-09-01 | SC | LOT16 | |
| 573 | DEWITT, Thomas J | 31 | W½SW | 1839-04-16 | FD | W2SW | R:HAMILTON |
| 280 | DILLARDRICK, Arthur | 7 | SW | 1851-08-25 | FD | SW | |
| 285 | DIXON, Azariah | 32 | NESW | 1851-01-22 | FD | NESW | R:HAMILTON |
| 569 | DIXON, Thomas | 17 | NWNW | 1848-10-27 | FD | NWNW | R:HAMILTON |
| 570 | " " | 17 | SWNW | 1853-04-01 | FD | SWNW | |
| 583 | DIXON, Tilmon | 32 | S½SW | 1842-07-18 | FD | S2SW | R:HAMILTON |
| 588 | DIXON, Wilkerson | 7 | NWNW | 1854-01-10 | FD | NWNW | R:JEFFERSON |
| 589 | DIXON, Wilkinson | 7 | SWNW | 1847-01-04 | FD | SWNW | R:JEFFERSON |
| 520 | DOUGHTY, Robert | 17 | NESE | 1852-07-23 | FD | NESELS | R:HAMILTON |
| 521 | " " | 17 | NWSE | 1852-10-30 | FD | NWSEVOID | |
| 362 | ELLIS, James | 35 | NWSE | 1849-10-05 | FD | NWSE | |
| 363 | " " | 35 | S½SE | 1849-10-05 | FD | S2SE | |
| 364 | " " | 35 | SWNE | 1849-10-05 | FD | SWNE | |
| 608 | EMMERSON, William | 34 | S½SW | 1854-09-22 | FD | S2SW | R:HAMILTON |
| 399 | ESTERS, John | 31 | NWNE | 1852-03-27 | FD | NWNE | R:HAMILTON |
| 400 | ESTES, John | 31 | NENE | 1853-04-08 | FD | NENE | R:HAMILTON |
| 614 | FARMER, William | 34 | N½NW | 1851-01-10 | FD | N2NW | |
| 613 | " " | 28 | SESE | 1851-01-10 | FD | SESE | |
| 612 | " " | 27 | SWSW | 1851-01-10 | FD | SWSW | |
| 615 | " " | 34 | NWSE | 1853-10-20 | FD | NWSE | R:HAMILTON |
| 616 | " " | 34 | SWNW | 1855-11-08 | FD | SWNW | R:HAMILTON |
| 477 | FAULKNER, Nancy Jane | 26 | SENW | 1853-06-16 | FD | SENW | S:F |
| 476 | " " | 26 | NWSE | 1853-06-16 | FD | NWSE | S:F |
| 475 | " " | 26 | N½SW | 1853-06-16 | FD | N2SW | S:F |
| 508 | FAULKNER, Rebecca | 27 | E½SE | 1853-06-16 | FD | E2SE | S:F |
| 507 | " " | 26 | SWNW | 1853-06-16 | FD | SWNW | S:F |
| 509 | " " | 27 | SENE | 1853-06-16 | FD | SENE | S:F |
| 349 | FOSTER, Isaac | 31 | SESE | 1837-02-08 | FD | SESE | R:HAMILTON |
| 571 | FOSTER, Thomas | 17 | S½SW | 1854-06-06 | FD | S2SW | R:HAMILTON |
| 307 | GAGE, Ebenezer | 36 | NWNE | 1854-06-08 | FD | NWNE | R:HAMILTON |
| 488 | GAINES, Newcomb | 32 | SESE | 1839-04-29 | FD | SESE | R:HAMILTON |
| 489 | " " | 32 | W½SE | 1839-04-29 | FD | W2SE | R:HAMILTON |
| 385 | GHORMLEY, Jesse C | 25 | SESE | 1855-05-01 | FD | SESE | R:HAMILTON |
| 647 | GILL, Henry | 9 | NWSE | 1854-09-23 | FD | NWSE | R:GALLATIN |
| 341 | " " | 9 | SWNE | 1854-09-23 | FD | SWNE | R:GALLATIN |
| 339 | " " | 9 | E½SE | 1854-09-23 | FD | E2SE | R:GALLATIN |
| 338 | " " | 10 | S½SW | 1854-09-23 | FD | S2SW | R:GALLATIN |
| 340 | " " | 9 | NWSE | 1854-09-23 | FD | NWSE | R:GALLATIN |
| 433 | GILL, Richard | 12 | SWSW | 1854-09-23 | FD | SWSW | R:GALLATIN |
| 516 | " " | 2 | SESE | 1854-09-23 | FD | SESE | R:GALLATIN |
| 514 | " " | 12 | SWNE | 1854-09-23 | FD | SWNE | R:GALLATIN |
| 513 | " " | 12 | NWNW | 1854-09-23 | FD | NWNW | R:GALLATIN |
| 512 | " " | 12 | N½SE | 1854-09-23 | FD | N2SE | R:GALLATIN |
| 511 | " " | 12 | E½NE | 1854-09-23 | FD | E2NE | R:GALLATIN |
| 515 | " " | 12 | SWSW | 1854-09-23 | FD | SWSW | R:GALLATIN |
| 350 | GOINS, Isaac | 34 | SENW | 1855-11-08 | FD | SENW | R:HAMILTON |
| 447 | GOODRIDGE, Lorenzo | 33 | W½SW | 1839-04-26 | FD | W2SW | R:HAMILTON |
| 441 | " " | 20 | SWSE | 1851-03-21 | FD | SWSE | R:HAMILTON |
| 442 | " " | 23 | NESW | 1853-07-28 | FD | NESW | |
| 445 | " " | 23 | W½SE | 1853-07-28 | FD | W2SE | |
| 443 | " " | 23 | SENW | 1853-07-28 | FD | SENW | |
| 444 | " " | 23 | SESE | 1854-05-13 | FD | SESE | R:HAMILTON |
| 446 | " " | 26 | N½NE | 1854-05-13 | FD | N2NE | R:HAMILTON |
| 527 | GUIRE, Samuel | 15 | E½NE | 1853-12-10 | FD | E2NE | R:HAMILTON |
| 617 | HALL, William | 1 | NENE | 1852-02-23 | FD | NENE | R:HAMILTON |

| ID | Individual in Patent | Sec. | Sec. Part | Purchase Date | Sale Type | IL Aliquot Part | For More Info . . . |
|----|---------------------|------|-----------|---------------|-----------|-----------------|---------------------|
| 619 | HALL, William (Cont'd) | 2 | SENW | 1853-09-06 | FD | SENW | R:HAMILTON |
| 618 | " | 1 | NWNE | 1854-01-16 | FD | NWNE | R:HAMILTON |
| 297 | HALLEY, Cornelius | 26 | S½SW | 1851-05-06 | FD | S2SW | |
| 298 | " " | 26 | SWSE | 1851-05-06 | FD | SWSE | |
| 299 | " " | 35 | NENW | 1851-05-06 | FD | NENW | |
| 354 | HALLEY, James B | 35 | W½NW | 1842-12-01 | FD | W2NW | R:HAMILTON |
| 528 | HALLEY, Samuel | 26 | NESE | 1853-10-28 | FD | NESE | R:HAMILTON |
| 609 | HAMILTON, William F | 35 | NWNE | 1853-05-19 | FD | NWNE | R:JEFFERSON |
| 587 | HANSDMAN, Urban | 11 | E½NW | 1853-01-22 | FD | E2NW | |
| 546 | HILLMAN, Squire | 16 | L8 | 1850-07-22 | SC | LOT8SENE | |
| 547 | " " | 18 | NWNE | 1855-05-16 | FD | NWNE | R:HAMILTON |
| 548 | HILMAN, Squire | 16 | L4 | 1840-08-22 | SC | L4 | |
| 549 | " " | 18 | SWNE | 1852-03-06 | FD | SWNE | |
| 490 | HINES, Oliver P | 36 | NENE | 1862-06-07 | FD | NENE | |
| 311 | HOBBS, Elisha | 16 | L15 | 1840-12-23 | SC | LOT15 | |
| 310 | " " | 16 | L10 | 1840-12-23 | SC | LOT10 | |
| 334 | HUFF, Gransberry | 19 | NENW | 1841-11-22 | FD | NENW | R:HAMILTON |
| 600 | HUNSINGER, William D | 19 | SWNW | 1851-12-02 | FD | SWNW | R:HAMILTON |
| 460 | INMAN, Martin | 12 | NENW | 1854-09-07 | FD | NENW | R:GALLATIN |
| 456 | " " | 1 | SESW | 1854-09-18 | FD | SESW | R:GALLATIN |
| 455 | " " | 1 | NENW | 1854-09-18 | FD | NENW | R:GALLATIN |
| 458 | " " | 1 | W½SE | 1854-09-18 | FD | W2SE | R:GALLATIN |
| 457 | " " | 1 | W½NE | 1854-09-18 | FD | W2NE | R:GALLATIN |
| 459 | " " | 12 | E½SW | 1854-09-18 | FD | E2SW | R:GALLATIN |
| 592 | " " | 1 | W½SE | 1854-09-18 | FD | W2SE | R:GALLATIN |
| 428 | IRVIN, Julia | 31 | NESE | 1839-06-25 | FD | NESE | R:HAMILTON S:F |
| 387 | JOHNSON, Jesse | 11 | NWSE | 1843-09-04 | FD | NWSE | R:HAMILTON |
| 388 | " " | 11 | SWNE | 1843-09-04 | FD | SWNE | R:HAMILTON |
| 389 | " " | 16 | L9 | 1850-07-22 | SC | LOT9NESE | |
| 406 | JOHNSON, John P | 26 | NENE | 1855-04-26 | FD | NENE | R:POPE |
| 291 | JUDD, Chester | 28 | NESE | 1854-05-20 | FD | NESE | R:HAMILTON |
| 292 | " " | 28 | SWSE | 1854-05-20 | FD | SWSE | R:HAMILTON |
| 331 | JUDD, Giles | 28 | E½NE | 1852-04-01 | FD | E2NE | R:HAMILTON |
| 317 | KARCHER, Ernest | 2 | NWNE | 1852-02-25 | FD | NWNE | R:HAMILTON |
| 316 | " " | 2 | NENW | 1852-02-25 | FD | NENW | R:HAMILTON |
| 542 | KARCHER, Solomon | 1 | NWSW | 1852-02-25 | FD | NWSW | R:HAMILTON |
| 544 | " " | 2 | SWNW | 1854-01-02 | FD | SWNW | R:HAMILTON |
| 543 | " " | 2 | NWSW | 1854-02-07 | FD | NWSW | R:HAMILTON |
| 408 | " " | 2 | NWSW | 1854-02-07 | FD | NWSW | R:HAMILTON |
| 429 | " " | 2 | NWSW | 1854-02-07 | FD | NWSW | R:HAMILTON |
| 258 | KENDALL, Abel Ray | 5 | SESW | 1849-01-26 | FD | SESW | R:HAMILTON |
| 421 | KING, Jordin | 20 | NWNE | 1854-10-24 | FD | NWNE | R:HAMILTON |
| 420 | " " | 17 | SWSE | 1854-10-24 | FD | SWSE | R:HAMILTON |
| 545 | KIRCHER, Solomon | 1 | S½NW | 1853-01-22 | FD | S2NW | |
| 530 | KISKEY, Samuel | 16 | L6 | 1840-09-01 | SC | L6 | |
| 529 | " " | 16 | L12 | 1840-09-01 | SC | LOT12 | |
| 254 | KNYKENDALL, Abel | 8 | NWNW | 1839-11-01 | FD | NWNW | R:HAMILTON |
| 255 | KUYKENDALL, Abel | 5 | E½NE | 1854-05-01 | FD | E2NE | R:HAMILTON |
| 256 | " " | 5 | SWNE | 1854-05-01 | FD | SWNE | R:HAMILTON |
| 257 | " " | 5 | SWSE | 1854-10-11 | FD | SWSE | R:HAMILTON |
| 259 | KUYKENDALL, Able | 7 | SENE | 1851-11-26 | FD | SENE | R:HAMILTON |
| 284 | LEARNED, Austin | 3 | S½NW | 1855-05-05 | FD | S2NW | R:HAMILTON |
| 418 | LEARNED, Jones G | 10 | SWNE | 1855-05-05 | FD | SWNE | R:HAMILTON |
| 417 | " " | 10 | E½NW | 1855-05-05 | FD | E2NW | R:HAMILTON |
| 294 | LEWIS, Wilson | 3 | NESW | 1854-04-19 | FD | NESW | R:HAMILTON G:12 |
| 402 | LOURY, John | 18 | W½NW | 1840-06-19 | FD | W2NW | R:JEFFERSON |
| 434 | LOWERY, Light W | 17 | NENE | 1852-01-05 | FD | NENE | R:HAMILTON |
| 305 | LOWREY, David | 21 | NENE | 1850-12-23 | FD | NENE | R:HAMILTON |
| 306 | " " | 21 | SENE | 1851-01-18 | FD | SENE | R:HAMILTON |
| 304 | " " | 17 | SENW | 1853-02-15 | FD | SENW | |
| 436 | LOWREY, Light W | 17 | NWNE | 1849-01-26 | FD | NWNE | R:HAMILTON |
| 435 | " " | 17 | NENW | 1849-01-26 | FD | NENW | R:HAMILTON |
| 437 | " " | 17 | SENE | 1853-02-15 | FD | SENE | |
| 303 | LOWRY, David Jr | 17 | SWNE | 1854-05-01 | FD | SWNE | R:HAMILTON |
| 403 | LOWRY, John | 18 | SENW | 1853-01-13 | FD | SENW | R:HAMILTON |
| 404 | " " | 9 | NWSW | 1854-10-11 | FD | NWSW | R:HAMILTON |
| 440 | LOWRY, Light W | 8 | SWSE | 1850-01-28 | FD | SWSE | R:HAMILTON |
| 438 | " " | 8 | NWSE | 1854-10-11 | FD | NWSE | R:HAMILTON |
| 439 | " " | 8 | SWNE | 1854-10-11 | FD | SWNE | R:HAMILTON |
| 473 | LOWRY, Moses F | 15 | SWNE | 1853-01-11 | FD | SWNE | |
| 472 | " " | 15 | NWSE | 1855-05-14 | FD | NWSE | R:HAMILTON |
| 644 | LOWRY, Young Squire | 22 | SWNW | 1850-05-21 | FD | SWNW | R:HAMILTON |
| 643 | " " | 22 | N½NW | 1850-12-23 | FD | N2NW | R:HAMILTON |

| ID | Individual in Patent | Sec. | Sec. Part | Purchase Date | Sale Type | IL Aliquot Part | For More Info . . . |
|---|---|---|---|---|---|---|---|
| 267 | MARTIN, Alexander H | 7 | SWNE | 1841-07-09 | FD | SWNE | R:HAMILTON |
| 405 | MARTIN, John | 4 | SWNE | 1854-06-06 | FD | SWNE | R:HAMILTON |
| 524 | MARTIN, Samuel A | 5 | E½SE | 1854-02-23 | FD | E2SE | |
| 577 | MARTIN, Thomas | 7 | E½NW | 1845-03-28 | FD | E2NW | R:JEFFERSON |
| 578 | "          " | 7 | SESE | 1847-11-05 | FD | SESE | R:HAMILTON |
| 582 | MARTIN, Thomas T | 6 | SENE | 1851-12-23 | FD | SENE | R:HAMILTON |
| 301 | MAULDING, Daniel M | 36 | NWSE | 1851-02-22 | FD | NWSE | R:HAMILTON |
| 300 | "          " | 36 | NESE | 1854-10-25 | FD | NESE | R:HAMILTON |
| 503 | MAULDING, Presley | 36 | NESW | 1850-12-02 | FD | NESW | |
| 504 | "          " | 36 | SEN½ | 1850-12-02 | FD | S2NE | |
| 505 | "          " | 36 | SENW | 1850-12-02 | FD | SENW | |
| 502 | "          " | 36 | NENW | 1854-10-10 | FD | NENW | R:HAMILTON |
| 342 | MAYHALL, Henry | 3 | SWSW | 1855-05-05 | FD | SWSW | R:HAMILTON |
| 541 | MCCAY, Simon | 21 | SESW | 1849-05-30 | FD | SESW | R:HAMILTON |
| 601 | MCCLEUR, William D | 30 | NW | 1850-07-24 | FD | NW | |
| 602 | MCCLUER, William D | 18 | NENE | 1850-07-24 | FD | NENE | R:HAMILTON |
| 603 | MCCLURE, William D | 19 | SWSW | 1851-12-08 | FD | SWSW | R:HAMILTON |
| 604 | "          " | 20 | SESW | 1852-10-28 | FD | SESW | R:HAMILTON |
| 630 | MCCONNER, William | 15 | SW | 1850-05-14 | FD | SW | |
| 466 | "          " | 15 | SW | 1850-05-14 | FD | SW | |
| 369 | MCCOY, James | 31 | NENW | 1852-09-29 | FD | NENW | |
| 426 | MCCOY, Joseph | 31 | S½NW | 1843-06-17 | FD | S2NW | R:HARDIN |
| 425 | "          " | 31 | NWNW | 1852-03-20 | FD | NWNW | |
| 540 | MCCOY, Simon D | 21 | SWSW | 1846-08-29 | FD | SWSW | R:HAMILTON |
| 370 | MCKNIGHT, James | 18 | NESE | 1851-12-20 | FD | NESE | R:HAMILTON |
| 371 | "          " | 18 | NWSE | 1852-07-31 | FD | NWSE | R:HAMILTON |
| 383 | MCKNIGHT, Jefferson | 17 | NWSW | 1854-06-22 | FD | NWSW | R:HAMILTON |
| 382 | MCKNIGHT, Jefferson M | 17 | NESW | 1854-03-29 | FD | NESW | R:HAMILTON |
| 611 | MCKNIGHT, William F | 32 | SWNW | 1853-04-21 | FD | SWNW | R:HAMILTON |
| 610 | "          " | 31 | SWNE | 1853-04-21 | FD | SWNE | R:HAMILTON |
| 287 | MCMAHON, Benjamin | 8 | SESW | 1850-03-06 | FD | SESW | R:HAMILTON |
| 289 | MECKE, Charles W | 27 | NENE | 1870-11-21 | FD | NENE | |
| 274 | MILLER, Anderson | 21 | NENW | 1853-11-23 | FD | NENW | R:HAMILTON |
| 335 | MOORE, Haywood P | 22 | SENE | 1851-08-07 | FD | SENE | |
| 642 | MOORE, Willis | 30 | NE | 1841-09-17 | FD | NE | R:HAMILTON |
| 641 | "          " | 29 | NWNW | 1841-09-17 | FD | NWNW | R:HAMILTON |
| 640 | "          " | 20 | SWSW | 1842-01-12 | FD | SWSW | R:HAMILTON |
| 323 | MORGAN, Frisby | 18 | W½SW | 1836-08-10 | FD | W2SW | R:HAMILTON |
| 324 | "          " | 19 | NWNW | 1837-02-25 | FD | NWNW | R:HAMILTON |
| 322 | "          " | 16 | L5 | 1840-06-29 | SC | L5 | |
| 321 | "          " | 16 | L11 | 1840-06-29 | SC | LOT11 | |
| 584 | MORGAN, Trisby | 18 | E½SW | 1840-06-19 | FD | E2SW | R:HAMILTON |
| 368 | MORRIS, James M | 10 | SESE | 1853-01-13 | FD | SESE | |
| 367 | "          " | 10 | NESE | 1853-03-01 | FD | NESE | |
| 401 | NATIONS, John H | 10 | NWNE | 1854-02-02 | FD | NWNE | R:HAMILTON |
| 407 | PARKER, John | 32 | E½NW | 1839-04-20 | FD | E2NW | R:HAMILTON |
| 531 | PATTON, Samuel | 16 | L3 | 1850-07-22 | SC | LOT3NENW | |
| 532 | "          " | 9 | SESW | 1854-04-25 | FD | SESW | R:HAMILTON |
| 537 | PINKSTON, William | 6 | SWSE | 1849-09-29 | FD | SWSE | R:HAMILTON G:31 |
| 572 | PORTER, Thomas G | 33 | SESW | 1853-01-13 | FD | SESW | |
| 373 | RAWLS, James | 1 | SENE | 1848-09-28 | FD | SENE | R:HAMILTON |
| 372 | "          " | 1 | NESE | 1853-09-19 | FD | NESE | R:HAMILTON |
| 374 | "          " | 1 | SWNE | 1854-02-13 | FD | SWNE | R:HAMILTON |
| 340 | REED, Zepariah B | 9 | NWSE | 1850-07-19 | FD | NWSE | |
| 647 | "          " | 9 | NWSE | 1850-07-19 | FD | NWSE | |
| 646 | "          " | 9 | NESW | 1850-07-19 | FD | NESW | |
| 645 | "          " | 9 | E½NW | 1850-07-19 | FD | E2NW | |
| 375 | REYNOLDS, James | 31 | NWSE | 1839-10-17 | FD | NWSE | R:HAMILTON |
| 252 | RICHARDSON, A H | 19 | NWSW | 1840-10-08 | FD | NWSW | R:OHIO S:I |
| 251 | "          " | 19 | NENE | 1840-10-08 | FD | NENE | R:OHIO S:I |
| 253 | RICHARDSON, Aaron H | 19 | E½SE | 1842-01-12 | FD | E2SE | R:HAMILTON |
| 288 | RIDDLE, Charles H | 31 | SWSE | 1839-01-28 | FD | SWSE | R:HAMILTON |
| 376 | ROGERS, James | 29 | NENW | 1848-07-19 | FD | NENW | R:HAMILTON |
| 413 | ROGERS, Jonathan | 20 | NENE | 1839-02-08 | FD | NENE | R:HAMILTON |
| 416 | "          " | 29 | SWSE | 1840-05-25 | FD | SWSE | R:HAMILTON |
| 479 | "          " | 29 | SWSE | 1840-05-25 | FD | SWSE | R:HAMILTON |
| 415 | "          " | 20 | SENW | 1849-01-12 | FD | SENW | R:HAMILTON |
| 412 | "          " | 17 | SESE | 1849-01-26 | FD | SESE | R:HAMILTON |
| 414 | "          " | 20 | NESW | 1849-02-23 | FD | NESW | R:HAMILTON |
| 419 | ROGERS, Jones | 29 | SWNE | 1837-03-29 | FD | SWNE | R:HAMILTON |
| 593 | ROHRER, William C | 25 | W½ | 1854-10-10 | FD | W2 | R:HENDERSON |
| 537 | ROO, Shelton | 6 | SWSE | 1849-09-29 | FD | SWSE | R:HAMILTON G:31 |
| 427 | ROSS, Joseph Wilson | 6 | NWSE | 1840-12-05 | FD | NWSE | R:HAMILTON |

| ID | Individual in Patent | Sec. | Sec. Part | Purchase Date | Sale Type | IL Aliquot Part | For More Info . . . |
|---|---|---|---|---|---|---|---|
| 523 | ROSS, Sally Moseley | 6 | SWSW | 1836-10-26 | FD | SWSW | R:HAMILTON S:F |
| 522 | " " | 6 | NESW | 1836-10-26 | FD | NESW | R:HAMILTON S:F |
| 632 | ROSS, William P S | 6 | SESW | 1837-10-31 | FD | SESW | R:HAMILTON |
| 631 | " " | 6 | NWNW | 1854-02-27 | FD | NWNW | R:HAMILTON |
| 333 | RUEBENACKER, Gottfrie | 2 | NESW | 1852-03-26 | FD | NESW | R:HAMILTON |
| 408 | SCHLODER, John | 2 | NWSW | 1861-02-25 | FD | NWSWLS | |
| 543 | " " | 2 | NWSW | 1861-02-25 | FD | NWSWLS | |
| 429 | " " | 2 | NWSW | 1861-02-25 | FD | NWSWLS | |
| 319 | SCOTT, Francis | 35 | NESE | 1844-09-03 | FD | NESE | |
| 320 | " " | 35 | SENE | 1844-09-03 | FD | SENE | |
| 408 | SHEESTER, Leon | 2 | NWSW | 1853-03-04 | FD | NWSW | R:HAMILTON |
| 543 | " " | 2 | NWSW | 1853-03-04 | FD | NWSW | R:HAMILTON |
| 429 | " " | 2 | NWSW | 1853-03-04 | FD | NWSW | R:HAMILTON |
| 261 | SHELTON, Abraham | 6 | SWNW | 1852-02-12 | FD | SWNW | |
| 260 | " " | 6 | NWSW | 1852-02-12 | FD | NWSW | |
| 538 | SHELTON, Silvester A | 6 | E½NW | 1849-01-01 | FD | E2NW | |
| 539 | " " | 6 | W½NE | 1849-01-01 | FD | W2NE | |
| 431 | SHUSTER, Leon | 11 | NWNW | 1853-03-09 | FD | NWNW | |
| 430 | " " | 11 | NESE | 1853-09-03 | FD | NESE | |
| 432 | " " | 12 | NWSW | 1853-09-03 | FD | NWSW | |
| 433 | " " | 12 | SWSW | 1853-09-14 | FD | SWSW | R:HAMILTON |
| 515 | " " | 12 | SWSW | 1853-09-14 | FD | SWSW | R:HAMILTON |
| 365 | SIMMONS, James H | 26 | SESE | 1871-05-10 | FD | SESE | |
| 390 | SINK, Jesse | 33 | SESE | 1854-04-20 | FD | SESE | R:HAMILTON |
| 494 | SINK, Peter | 34 | NESW | 1854-04-20 | FD | NESW | R:HAMILTON |
| 386 | SINKS, Jesse J | 33 | SWSE | 1855-04-04 | FD | SWSE | R:HAMILTON |
| 576 | SLOO, Thomas Jr | 29 | | 1817-09-15 | FD | SERSA | R:CINCINATTI |
| 377 | STALL, James | 6 | NENE | 1849-09-14 | FD | NENE | G:36 |
| 377 | STALL, Lawrence | 6 | NENE | 1849-09-14 | FD | NENE | G:36 |
| 381 | STEELE, James | 21 | SWNW | 1848-06-19 | FD | SWNW | R:HAMILTON |
| 379 | " " | 21 | NWNW | 1848-12-23 | FD | NWNW | R:HAMILTON |
| 380 | " " | 21 | NWSW | 1848-12-23 | FD | NWSW | R:HAMILTON |
| 378 | " " | 20 | NESE | 1849-02-20 | FD | NESE | R:HAMILTON |
| 268 | STEERMAN, Alexander M | 8 | SWNW | 1848-11-16 | FD | SWNW | R:HAMILTON |
| 366 | STEERMAN, James K | 20 | NWNW | 1849-01-22 | FD | NWNW | R:HAMILTON |
| 478 | STEERMAN, Nathan D | 29 | E½SE | 1836-06-17 | FD | E2SE | R:HAMILTON |
| 479 | " " | 29 | SWSE | 1837-03-30 | FD | SWSE | R:HAMILTON |
| 416 | " " | 29 | SWSE | 1837-03-30 | FD | SWSE | R:HAMILTON |
| 273 | STURMAN, Alexander | 8 | NENW | 1849-08-20 | FD | NENW | R:HAMILTON |
| 269 | STURMAN, Alexander M | 7 | N½NE | 1839-07-23 | FD | N2NE | R:GALLATIN |
| 270 | " " | 8 | NESW | 1851-04-19 | FD | NESW | R:HAMILTON |
| 272 | " " | 8 | SENW | 1851-12-23 | FD | SENW | R:HAMILTON |
| 271 | " " | 8 | NWSW | 1854-02-10 | FD | NWSW | R:HAMILTON |
| 482 | STURMAN, Nathan D | 28 | SWNW | 1840-03-07 | FD | SWNW | R:HAMILTON |
| 483 | " " | 28 | W½SW | 1840-06-19 | FD | W2SW | R:HAMILTON |
| 485 | " " | 32 | NWNE | 1840-06-19 | FD | NWNE | R:HAMILTON |
| 481 | " " | 28 | SESW | 1849-03-20 | FD | SESW | R:HAMILTON |
| 480 | " " | 28 | NESW | 1851-01-18 | FD | NESW | R:HAMILTON |
| 484 | " " | 32 | NENE | 1853-03-23 | FD | NENE | |
| 638 | STURMAN, William | 33 | W½NW | 1836-10-17 | FD | W2NW | R:HAMILTON |
| 635 | " " | 32 | SENE | 1837-03-29 | FD | SENE | R:HAMILTON |
| 637 | " " | 33 | SENW | 1838-05-26 | FD | SENW | R:HAMILTON |
| 634 | " " | 29 | SENW | 1852-01-19 | FD | SENW | |
| 636 | " " | 33 | NENW | 1852-04-03 | FD | NENW | |
| 628 | STURMAN, William M | 29 | S½SW | 1836-10-18 | FD | S2SW | R:HAMILTON |
| 627 | " " | 29 | E½NE | 1839-04-20 | FD | E2NE | R:HAMILTON |
| 629 | " " | 29 | SWNW | 1852-01-19 | FD | SWNW | R:HAMILTON |
| 501 | TALLEY, Pleasant | 15 | NW | 1852-10-20 | FD | NW | S:F |
| 318 | THIERRY, Francis R | 4 | N½NE | 1851-02-25 | FD | N2NE | |
| 468 | THIERRY, Mirabin | 3 | N½NE | 1852-02-27 | FD | N2NE | |
| 471 | " " | 3 | SWNE | 1852-02-27 | FD | SWNE | |
| 469 | " " | 3 | NENW | 1852-02-27 | FD | NENW | |
| 470 | " " | 3 | SENE | 1854-10-25 | FD | SENE | R:HAMILTON |
| 409 | THOMAS, John | 16 | L2 | 1840-09-07 | SC | L2 | |
| 398 | THORP, John D | 12 | E½SE | 1854-10-01 | FD | E2SE | R:JEFFERSON |
| 302 | TOLLEY, Daniel | 36 | SESW | 1850-12-18 | FD | SESW | R:HAMILTON |
| 651 | TURNER, Zephaniah | 8 | SWSW | 1854-01-25 | FD | SWSW | R:HAMILTON |
| 650 | " " | 4 | SWSW | 1854-10-11 | FD | SWSW | R:HAMILTON |
| 648 | " " | 4 | SENE | 1854-10-11 | FD | SENE | R:HAMILTON |
| 649 | " " | 4 | SENW | 1854-10-11 | FD | SENW | R:HAMILTON |
| 278 | VICK, Arthur D | 18 | NENW | 1854-01-07 | FD | NENW | R:KENTUCKY |
| 279 | " " | 7 | SWSE | 1854-01-07 | FD | SWSE | R:KENTUCKY |
| 290 | WAUGH, Charles | 3 | NWNW | 1854-10-25 | FD | NWNW | R:HAMILTON |

| ID | Individual in Patent | Sec. | Sec. Part | Purchase Date | Sale Type | IL Aliquot Part | For More Info . . . |
|-----|----------------------|------|-----------|---------------|-----------|-----------------|---------------------|
| 449 | WILBANKS, Luke S | 30 | SE | 1850-04-02 | FD | SE | |
| 353 | WILKEY, James A J | 3 | SWSE | 1854-10-11 | FD | SWSE | R:HAMILTON |
| 352 | " " | 3 | N½SE | 1854-10-11 | FD | N2SE | R:HAMILTON |
| 518 | WILKEY, Richard | 4 | E½SW | 1851-11-18 | FD | E2SW | |
| 519 | " " | 4 | W½SE | 1851-11-18 | FD | W2SE | |
| 517 | " " | 4 | E½SE | 1854-06-06 | FD | E2SE | R:HAMILTON |
| 486 | WILLIAMS, Nathan | 36 | SWNE | 1851-06-03 | FD | SWNE | |
| 639 | WILLIAMS, William | 4 | NWNW | 1853-10-19 | FD | NWNW | R:HAMILTON |
| 626 | WILLIAMS, William K | 4 | NENW | 1854-03-02 | FD | NENW | R:HAMILTON |
| 633 | WILLIAMS, William R | 36 | SESE | 1854-02-24 | FD | SESE | R:HAMILTON |
| 332 | WORTH, Gorham A | 29 | SE | 1817-09-15 | FD | SE | |
| 315 | YARWOOD, Ephraim | 35 | NENE | 1853-10-31 | FD | NENE | R:HAMILTON |

## Patent Map

T4-S R5-E
3rd PM Meridian

Map Group 4

## Township Statistics

| | | |
|---|---|---|
| Parcels Mapped | : | 401 |
| Number of Patents | : | 1 |
| Number of Individuals | : | 226 |
| Patentees Identified | : | 224 |
| Number of Surnames | : | 148 |
| Multi-Patentee Parcels | : | 4 |
| Oldest Patent Date | : | 9/15/1817 |
| Most Recent Patent | : | 5/10/1871 |
| Block/Lot Parcels | : | 15 |
| Cities and Towns | : | 3 |
| Cemeteries | : | 6 |

**Section 6**
- ROSS, William P S 1854
- SHELTON, Silvester A 1849
- SHELTON, Silvester A 1849
- STALL [36], James 1849
- BELT, Andrew J 1854
- CATE, Thomas 1840
- SHELTON, Abraham 1852
- MARTIN, Thomas T 1851
- CATES, Thomas 1837
- SHELTON, Abraham 1852
- ROSS, Sally Moseley 1836
- ROSS, Joseph Wilson 1840
- CATES, Ephraim Sen 1848
- CATES, James 1837
- ROSS, Sally Moseley 1836
- ROSS, William P S 1837
- ROO [31], Shelton 1849

**Section 5**
- COTES, Thomas 1854
- KUYKENDALL, Abel 1854
- KUYKENDALL, Abel 1854
- CATES, Ephraim E 1841
- CATES, Ephraim E 1851
- COTES, Ephraim E 1851
- KENDALL, Abel Ray 1849
- KUYKENDALL, Abel 1854
- MARTIN, Samuel A 1854

**Section 4**
- WILLIAMS, William 1853
- WILLIAMS, William K 1854
- THIERRY, Francis R 1851
- ATCHISSON, James A 1854
- TURNER, Zephaniah 1854
- MARTIN, John 1854
- TURNER, Zephaniah 1854
- BOSLEY, Luke 1849
- WILKEY, Richard 1851
- WILKEY, Richard 1851
- WILKEY, Richard 1854
- TURNER, Zephaniah 1854

**Section 7**
- DIXON, Wilkerson 1854
- DIXON, Wilkinson 1847
- MARTIN, Thomas 1845
- STURMAN, Alexander M 1839
- MARTIN, Alexander H 1841
- KUYKENDALL, Able 1851
- COTES, Nancy 1851
- DILLARDRICK, Arthur 1851
- VICK, Arthur D 1854
- MARTIN, Thomas 1847

**Section 8**
- KNYKENDALL, Abel 1839
- STURMAN, Alexander 1849
- STEERMAN, Alexander M 1848
- STURMAN, Alexander M 1851
- LOWRY, Light W 1854
- STURMAN, Alexander M 1854
- STURMAN, Alexander M 1851
- LOWRY, Light W 1854
- BELT, Thomas 1854
- BELT, Thomas 1854
- TURNER, Zephaniah 1854
- MCMAHON, Benjamin 1850
- LOWRY, Light W 1850
- BELT, Thomas 1851

**Section 9**
- BELT, Thomas Jr 1849
- REED, Zepariah B 1850
- CRISEL, George A 1854
- BELT, Thomas Jr 1852
- GILL, Henry 1854
- CRISAL, George A 1854
- LOWRY, John 1854
- REED, Zepariah B 1850
- GILL, Henry 1854
- REED, Zepariah B 1850
- GILL, Henry 1854
- BELT, Thomas 1851
- PATTON, Samuel 1854
- BELT, Thomas Sen 1851

**Section 18**
- LOURY, John 1840
- VICK, Arthur D 1854
- HILLMAN, Squire 1855
- MCCLUER, William D 1850
- LOWRY, John 1853
- HILMAN, Squire 1852
- CASKEY, Samuel 1850
- MORGAN, Frisby 1836
- MORGAN, Trisby 1840
- MCKNIGHT, James 1852
- MCKNIGHT, James 1851
- BURTON, Thomas 1850
- BURTON, Thomas 1853

**Section 17**
- DIXON, Thomas 1848
- LOWREY, Light W 1849
- LOWREY, Light W 1849
- LOWERY, Light W 1852
- DIXON, Thomas 1853
- LOWREY, David 1853
- LOWRY, David Jr 1854
- LOWREY, Light W 1853
- MCKNIGHT, Jefferson 1854
- MCKNIGHT, Jefferson M 1854
- DOUGHTY, Robert 1852
- DOUGHTY, Robert 1852
- FOSTER, Thomas 1854
- KING, Jordin 1854
- ROGERS, Jonathan 1849

**Lots-Sec. 16**
|  |  |  |
|---|---|---|
| L2 | THOMAS, John | 1840 |
| L3 | PATTON, Samuel | 1850 |
| L4 | HILMAN, Squire | 1840 |
| L5 | MORGAN, Frisby | 1840 |
| L6 | KISKEY, Samuel | 1840 |
| L7 | CORKY, Samuel | 1841 |
| L8 | HILLMAN, Squire | 1850 |
| L9 | JOHNSON, Jesse | 1850 |
| L10 | HOBBS, Elisha | 1840 |
| L11 | MORGAN, Frisby | 1840 |
| L12 | KISKEY, Samuel | 1840 |
| L13 | BELL, Johnson | 1840 |
| L14 | BELL, Johnson | 1840 |
| L15 | HOBBS, Elisha | 1840 |
| L16 | DAWSON, Martin S | 1840 |

**Section 19**
- MORGAN, Frisby 1837
- HUFF, Gransberry 1841
- BEARDEN, Philip Winn 1837
- RICHARDSON, A H 1840
- HUNSINGER, William D 1851
- BEARDEN, Philip Winn 1838
- BROWN, Anthony M 1844
- RICHARDSON, A H 1840
- BEARDEN, Philip Wimn 1840
- BEARDEN, Philip Winn 1838
- RICHARDSON, Aaron H 1842
- MCCLURE, William D 1851

**Section 20**
- STEERMAN, James K 1849
- BOWEN, Columbus 1854
- KING, Jordin 1854
- ROGERS, Jonathan 1839
- CANNON, William 1841
- ROGERS, Jonathan 1849
- DAVIS, William 1853
- CROSS, Asel 1854
- BOWEN, Anthony W 1854
- ROGERS, Jonathan 1849
- DAVIS, William 1850
- STEELE, James 1849
- MOORE, Willis 1842
- MCCLURE, William D 1852
- GOODRIDGE, Lorenzo 1851
- DAVIS, William 1847

**Section 21**
- STEELE, James 1848
- MILLER, Anderson 1853
- COOK, James 1850
- LOWREY, David 1850
- STEELE, James 1848
- COOK, James 1850
- COOK, James 1850
- LOWREY, David 1851
- STEELE, James 1848
- COOK, James 1854
- COOK, James 1850
- COLLINS, William 1851
- MCCOY, Simon D 1846
- MCCAY, Simon 1849
- DAMON, Henry 1851

**Section 30**
- MCCLEUR, William D 1850
- MOORE, Willis 1841
- BOYLES, Reuben Davis 1839
- WILBANKS, Luke S 1850

**Section 29**
- MOORE, Willis 1841
- ROGERS, James 1848
- BEARDEN, Philip Winn 1850
- STURMAN, William M 1839
- STURMAN, William M 1852
- STURMAN, William 1852
- ROGERS, Jones 1837
- STEERMAN, Nathan D 1836
- WORTH, Gotham A
- STEERMAN, Nathan D 1837
- ROGERS, Jonathan 1840
- STURMAN, William M 1836

**Section 28**
- BURTON, Thomas 1839
- BURTON, Thomas 1839
- BURTON, Thomas 1851
- JUDD, Giles 1852
- STURMAN, Nathan D 1840
- BURTON, Thomas 1852
- STURMAN, Nathan D 1851
- COLLINS, William Jr 1852
- JUDD, Chester 1854
- STURMAN, Nathan D 1840
- STURMAN, Nathan D 1849
- JUDD, Chester 1854
- FARMER, William 1851

**Section 31**
- MCCOY, Joseph 1852
- MCCOY, James 1852
- BAYLES, Jesse 1852
- MCCOY, Joseph 1818
- MCCOY, Joseph 1843
- ESTERS, John 1852
- ESTES, John 1853
- MCKNIGHT, William F 1853
- BARTLETT, Sarah Jane 1842
- REYNOLDS, James 1839
- IRVIN, Julia 1839
- DEWITT, Thomas J 1839
- BRATLETT, Nelson 1839
- RIDDLE, Charles H 1839
- FOSTER, Isaac 1837

**Section 32**
- BARTLETT, Stephen H 1839
- STURMAN, Nathan D 1840
- STURMAN, Nathan D 1853
- MCKNIGHT, William F 1853
- PARKER, John 1839
- DAMON, Owen Lewis 1842
- STURMAN, William 1837
- DAMON, Owen Lewis 1842
- BRADFORD, James 1852
- DIXON, Azariah 1851
- GAINES, Newcomb 1839
- GAINES, Newcomb 1839
- DIXON, Tilmon 1842

**Section 33**
- STURMAN, William 1836
- STURMAN, William 1852
- ADCOCK, Isaac 1853
- CANNON, William 1848
- STURMAN, William 1838
- ADDCOCK, Isaac 1851
- ADCOCK, Isaac 1853
- CHOSSER, William 1851
- DAMON, Owen Lewis 1854
- GOODRIDGE, Lorenzo 1839
- PORTER, Thomas G 1853
- SINKS, Jesse J 1855
- SINK, Jesse 1854

| | | | | | | | | | |
|---|---|---|---|---|---|---|---|---|---|
| WAUGH Charles 1854 | THIERRY Mirabin 1852 | THIERRY Mirabin 1852 | | BESTEM Sarah 1854 | KARCHER Ernest 1852 | KARCHER Ernest 1852 | | CROUCH Cloyd 1854 | INMAN Martin 1854 | INMAN HALL Martin William 1854 1854 | HALL William 1852 |

**Section 3 / 2 / 1 area:**

- WAUGH Charles 1854
- THIERRY Mirabin 1852
- THIERRY Mirabin 1852
- BESTEM Sarah 1854
- KARCHER Ernest 1852
- KARCHER Ernest 1852
- CROUCH Cloyd 1854
- INMAN Martin 1854
- INMAN HALL Martin / William 1854 / 1854
- HALL William 1852
- LEARNED Austin 1855
- THIERRY Mirabin 1852
- THIERRY Mirabin 1854
- KARCHER Solomon 1854
- HALL William 1853
- **2**
- BRINK Albert 1853
- KIRCHER Solomon 1853
- RAWLS James 1854
- RAWLS James 1848
- CRISEL Henry 1855
- CROUCH [12] Cloyd 1854
- **3**
- WILKEY James A J 1854
- SCHLODER John 1861 / KARCHER Solomon 1854
- RUEBENACKER Gottfrie 1852 / SHEESTER Leon 1853
- BESTEM Sarah 1854
- KARCHER Solomon 1852
- DAVIS William C 1854
- DAVIS William C 1854
- RAWLS James 1853
- MAYHALL Henry 1855
- BRISTOL Elias H 1853
- WILKEY James A J 1854
- AYD Alexander 1854
- BRENCK Albert 1852
- GILL Richard 1854
- INMAN Martin 1854
- INMAN Martin 1854
- DAVIS William C 1854

**Section 10 / 11 / 12 area:**

- CRISEL George A 1855
- NATIONS John H 1854
- LEARNED Jones G 1855
- SHUSTER Leon 1853
- HANSDMAN Urban 1853
- ANSELMENT Urban 1853
- BRINK Albert 1854
- GILL Richard 1854
- INMAN Martin 1854
- ANSELMENT Joseph 1854 / GILL Richard 1854
- CRISEL George A 1851
- LEARNED Jones G 1855
- AYD Alexander 1853
- ANSELMENT Urban 1853
- JOHNSON Jesse 1843
- BRINK Benjamin 1853
- BACKLE Joseph 1854
- **12**
- GILL Richard 1854
- ANSELMENT Joseph 1853
- CRISAL George A 1854
- BRISTOL Mary Ann 1853
- **10**
- MORRIS James M 1853
- CRISEL William J 1853
- **11**
- JOHNSON Jesse 1843
- SHUSTER Leon 1853
- SHUSTER Leon 1853
- INMAN Martin 1854
- GILL Richard 1854
- THORP John D 1854
- GILL Henry 1854
- BRISTOL Elias H 1853
- MORRIS James M 1853
- CRISEL William J 1853
- BRISTOL Thomas Sen 1853 / CRISAL William J 1852
- BRISTOL Thomas 1853
- SHUSTER Leon / GILL 1853 / Richard 1854

**Section 15 / 14 / 13 area:**

- TALLEY Pleasant 1852
- COOK William 1854
- GUIRE Samuel 1853
- BRISTOL Thomas 1854
- BRISTON Thomas Sen 1853
- BRISTOL Thomas 1853
- BRISTOL Thomas 1853
- **15**
- LOWRY Moses F 1853
- DALE Quintilla 1854
- BROOKINS Milton 1854
- **14**
- **13**
- MCCONNER William 1850
- LOWRY Moses F 1855
- BROOKINS Milton 1854
- BROOKINS Milton 1854
- COLLINS William Iii 1852
- COLLINS William Jr 1854

**Section 22 / 23 / 24 area:**

- LOWRY Young Squire 1850
- COLLINS William 1854
- BROOKINS Milton 1854
- LOWRY Young Squire 1850
- BROOKINS Marion 1854
- BROOKINS Marion 1854
- MOORE Haywood P 1851
- BROOKENS Milton 1853
- GOODRIDGE Lorenzo 1853
- **23**
- **24**
- BROOKINS Marion 1854
- BROOKINS Marion 1854
- **22**
- BROOKINS Marion 1854
- GOODRIDGE Lorenzo 1853
- GOODRIDGE Lorenzo 1853
- CROSS John C 1854
- GOODRIDGE Lorenzo 1854

**Section 27 / 26 / 25 area:**

- BOWEN Columbus 1853
- MECKE Charles W 1870
- CROSS [11] John C 1853
- CROSS John C 1854
- GOODRIDGE Lorenzo 1854
- JOHNSON John P 1855
- CROSS Asel 1852
- CROSS Asel 1853
- CROSS John C 1855
- FAULKNER Rebecca 1853
- FAULKNER Rebecca 1853
- FAULKNER Nancy Jane 1853
- ROHRER William C 1854
- **25**
- CROSS John Calvin 1851
- CROSS John C 1848
- **27**
- FAULKNER Rebecca 1853
- FAULKNER Nancy Jane 1853
- **26**
- FAULKNER Nancy Jane 1853
- HALLEY Samuel 1853
- FARMER William 1851
- CROSS John C 1848
- HALLEY Cornelius 1851
- HALLEY Cornelius 1851
- SIMMONS James H 1871
- GHORMLEY Jesse C 1855

**Section 34 / 35 / 36 area:**

- FARMER William 1851
- HALLEY James B 1842
- HALLEY Cornelius 1851
- HAMILTON William F 1853
- YARWOOD Ephraim 1853
- MAULDING Presley 1854
- GAGE Ebenezer 1854
- HINES Oliver P 1862
- FARMER William 1855
- CAPE Hiram 1847
- GOINS Isaac 1855
- **34**
- BARKER Thomas 1845
- ELLIS James 1849
- SCOTT Francis 1844
- MAULDING Presley 1850
- **36**
- WILLIAMS Nathan 1851
- MAULDING Presley 1850
- CAPE Hiram 1846
- SINK Peter 1854
- FARMER William 1853
- CAPE Hiram 1853
- **35**
- ELLIS James 1849
- SCOTT Francis 1844
- MAULDING Presley 1850
- MAULDING Daniel M 1851
- MAULDING Daniel M 1854
- EMMERSON William 1854
- BESTEM Sarah 1854
- BOSTER George 1849
- ELLIS James 1849
- ADAIR Philip 1839
- TOLLEY Daniel 1850
- WILLIAMS William R 1854

---

## Helpful Hints

1. This Map's INDEX can be found on the preceding pages.

2. Refer to Map "C" to see where this Township lies within Hamilton County, Illinois.

3. Numbers within square brackets [ ] denote a multi-patentee land parcel (multi-owner). Refer to Appendix "C" for a full list of members in this group.

4. Areas that look to be crowded with Patentees usually indicate multiple sales of the same parcel (re-issues), cancellations or voided transactions (that we map, anyway) or overlapping parcels. We opt to show even these ambiguous parcels, which oftentimes lead to research avenues not yet taken.

---

## Legend

- —— Patent Boundary
- ▬▬ Section Boundary
- No Patents Found (or Outside County)
- 1., 2., 3., ... Lot Numbers (when beside a name)
- [ ] Group Number (see Appendix "C")

**Scale**: Section = 1 mile X 1 mile (generally, with some exceptions)

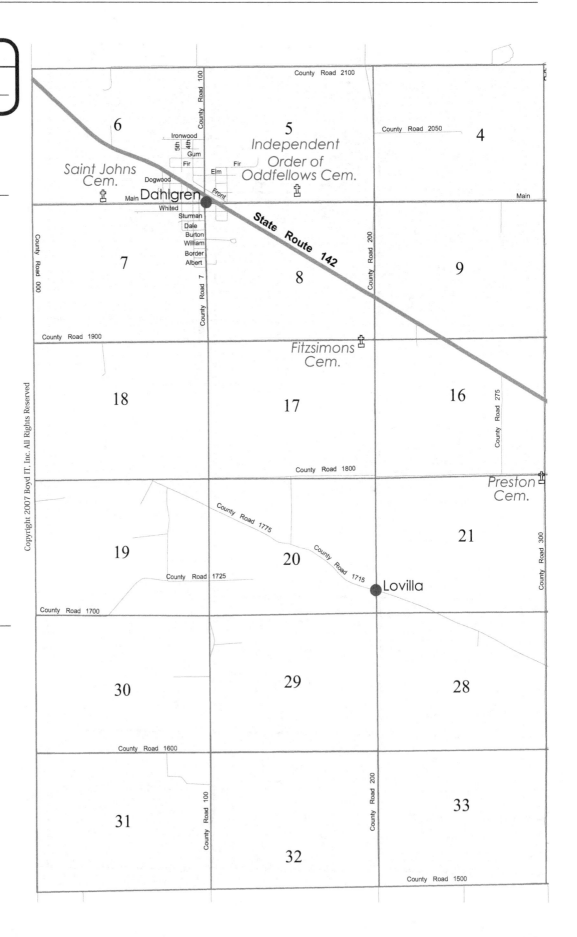

## Road Map

### T4-S R5-E
### 3rd PM Meridian

### Map Group 4

**Cities & Towns**

Dahlgren
Delafield
Lovilla

**Cemeteries**

Bethel Cemetery
Crisel Cemetery
Fitzsimons Cemetery
Preston Cemetery
Saint Johns Cemetery
Independent Order of
Oddfellows Cemetery

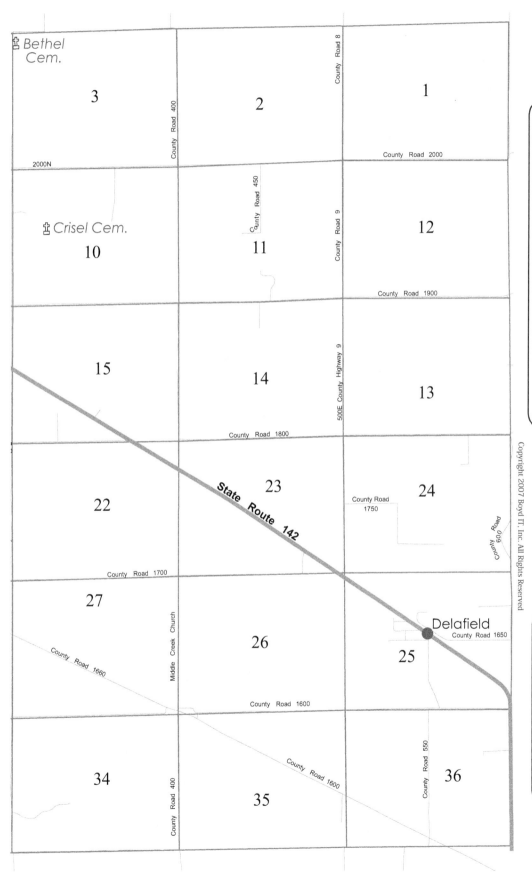

☦ *Bethel Cem.*

3

2

County Road 8

1

County Road 2000

2000N

☦ *Crisel Cem.*

10

County Road 450

11

County Road 9

12

County Road 1900

15

14

500E County Highway 9

13

County Road 1800

23

State Route 142

24

County Road 1750

22

County Road 600 Road

County Road 1700

27

Middle Creek Church

26

Delafield

County Road 1650

25

County Road 1660

County Road 1600

34

County Road 400

35

County Road 1600

County Road 550

36

## Helpful Hints

1. This road map has a number of uses, but primarily it is to help you: a) find the present location of land owned by your ancestors (at least the general area), b) find cemeteries and city-centers, and c) estimate the route/roads used by Census-takers & tax-assessors.

2. If you plan to travel to Hamilton County to locate cemeteries or land parcels, please pick up a modern travel map for the area before you do. Mapping old land parcels on modern maps is not as exact a science as you might think. Just the slightest variations in public land survey coordinates, estimates of parcel boundaries, or road-map deviations can greatly alter a map's representation of how a road either does or doesn't cross a particular parcel of land.

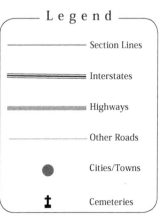

### L e g e n d

———— Section Lines

═══ Interstates

━━━ Highways

———— Other Roads

● Cities/Towns

☦ Cemeteries

**Scale**: Section = 1 mile  X  1 mile
(generally, with some exceptions)

## Historical Map

T4-S  R5-E
3rd PM Meridian

Map Group 4

### Cities & Towns
Dahlgren
Delafield
Lovilla

### Cemeteries
Bethel Cemetery
Crisel Cemetery
Fitzsimons Cemetery
Preston Cemetery
Saint Johns Cemetery
Independent Order of
   Oddfellows Cemetery

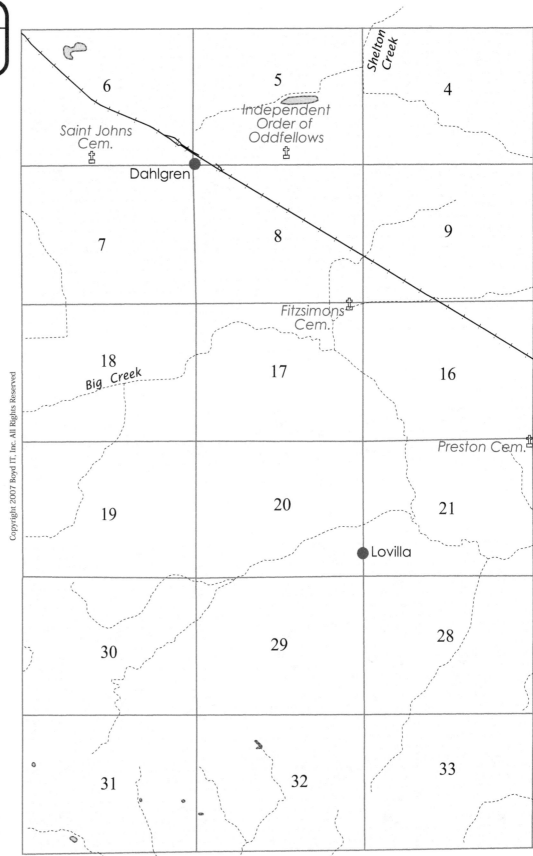

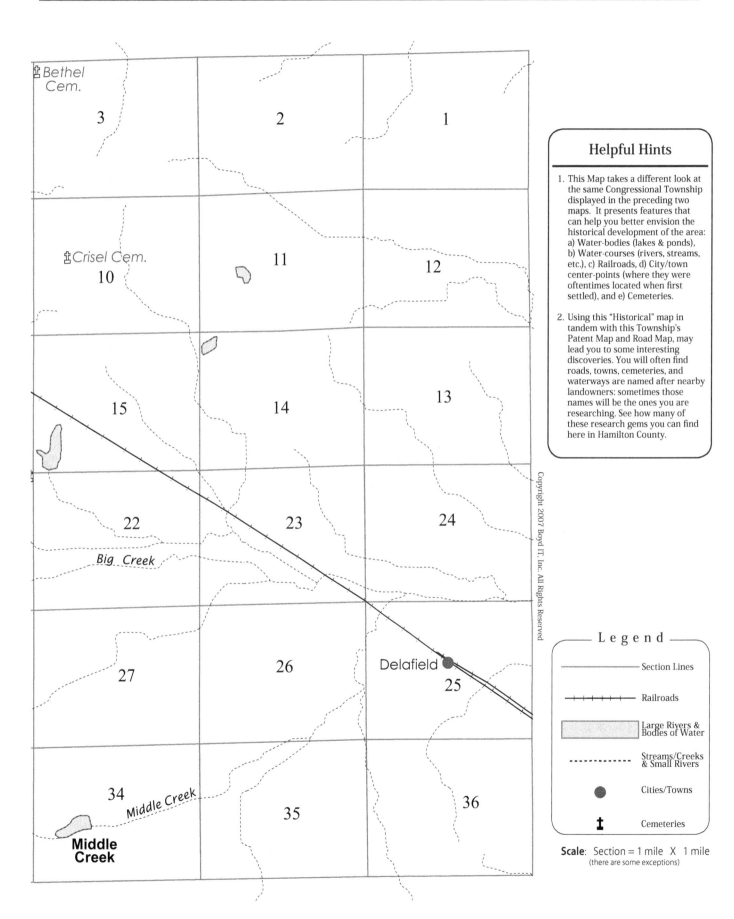

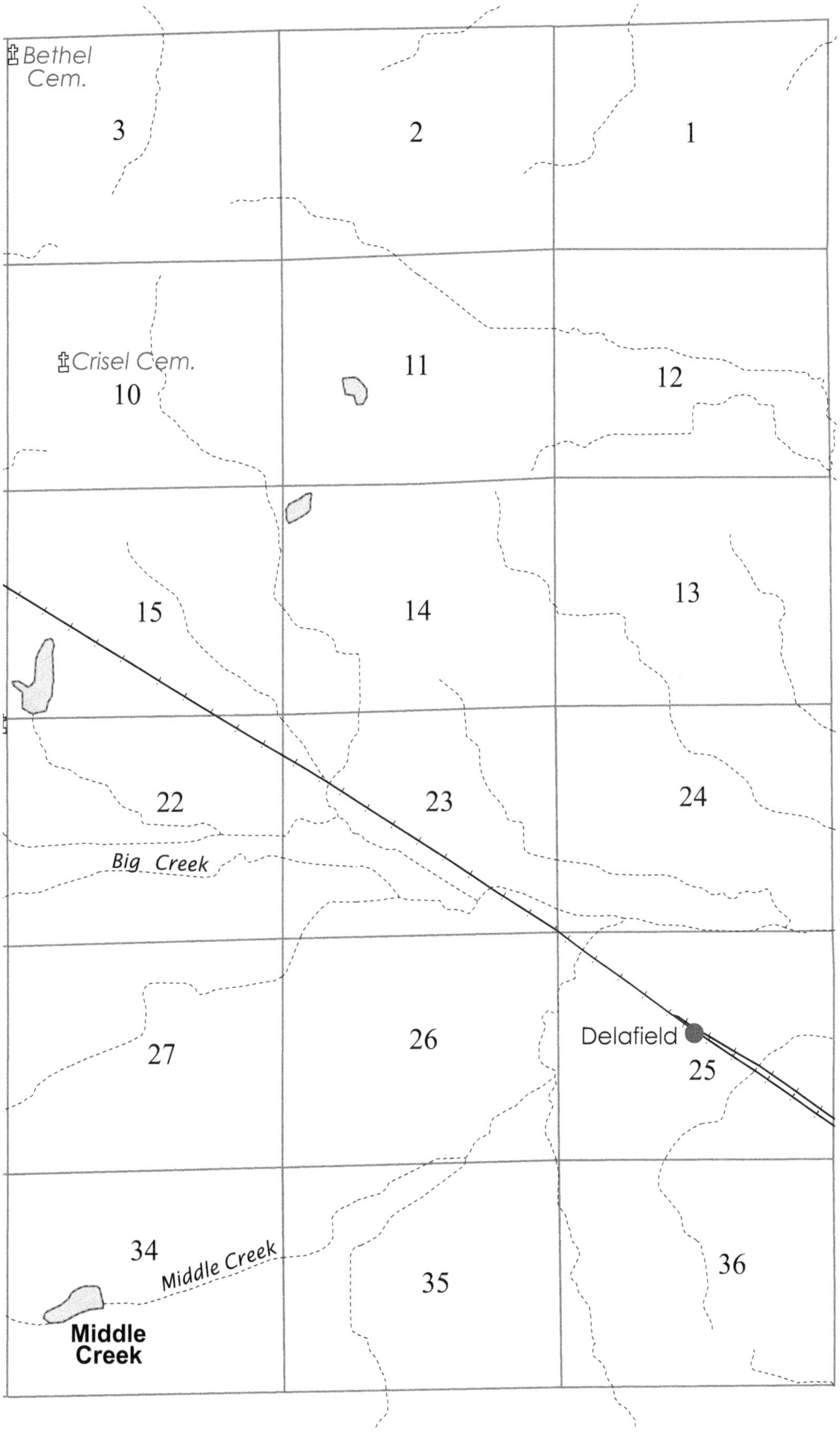
Bethel Cem.
3
2
1
Crisel Cem.
10
11
12
15
14
13
22
23
24
Big Creek
27
26
Delafield
25
34
Middle Creek
35
36
Middle Creek



## Helpful Hints

1. This Map takes a different look at the same Congressional Township displayed in the preceding two maps. It presents features that can help you better envision the historical development of the area: a) Water-bodies (lakes & ponds), b) Water-courses (rivers, streams, etc.), c) Railroads, d) City/town center-points (where they were oftentimes located when first settled), and e) Cemeteries.

2. Using this "Historical" map in tandem with this Township's Patent Map and Road Map, may lead you to some interesting discoveries. You will often find roads, towns, cemeteries, and waterways are named after nearby landowners: sometimes those names will be the ones you are researching. See how many of these research gems you can find here in Hamilton County.

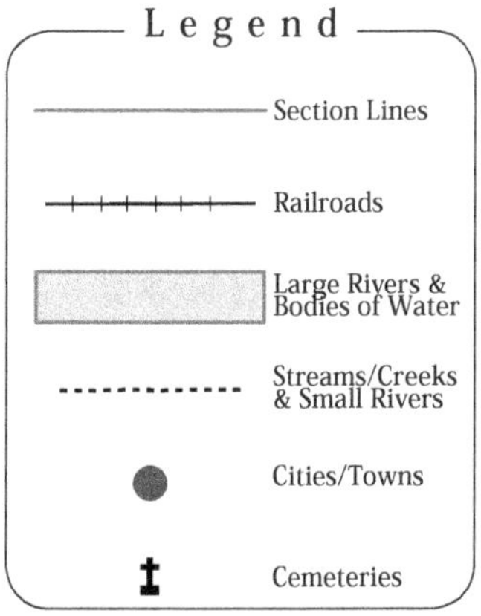
Legend
Section Lines
Railroads
Large Rivers & Bodies of Water
Streams/Creeks & Small Rivers
Cities/Towns
Cemeteries

**Scale**: Section = 1 mile X 1 mile
(there are some exceptions)

## Map Group 5: Index to Land Patents

## Township 4-South Range 6-East (3rd PM)

After you locate an individual in this Index, take note of the Section and Section Part then proceed to the Land Patent map on the pages immediately following. You should have no difficulty locating the corresponding parcel of land.

The "For More Info" Column will lead you to more information about the underlying Patents. See the *Legend* at right, and the "How to Use this Book" chapter, for more information.

```
          LEGEND
     "For More Info . . . " column
G = Group  (Multi-Patentee Patent, see Appendix "C")
R = Residence
S = Social Status

See Appendix A for list of abbreviations used by the
Illinois State Archives in describing the place and
nature of these land patents.

Note: if the Abbreviations contain "L", "BL", "LOT",
or "BLOCK", the exact whereabouts of the parcel within
the section is not known.
```

| ID | Individual in Patent | Sec. | Sec. Part | Purchase Date | Sale Type | IL Aliquot Part | For More Info . . . |
|----|----------------------|------|-----------|---------------|-----------|-----------------|---------------------|
| 767 | ANSELMENT, John | 8 | N½SW | 1854-01-27 | FD | N2SW | R:HAMILTON |
| 665 | ASKEY, Andrew J | 22 | NENE | 1853-10-01 | FD | NENE | R:HAMILTON |
| 672 | AYD, Charles | 20 | SENW | 1849-02-23 | FD | SENW | R:HAMILTON |
| 680 | AYD, Charles W | 4 | SENW | 1854-01-17 | FD | SENW | R:HAMILTON |
| 683 | AYD, Charles William | 4 | SWNW | 1841-08-16 | FD | SWNW | R:HAMILTON |
| 684 | " " | 4 | SWSW | 1848-12-30 | FD | SWSW | R:HAMILTON |
| 685 | AYD, Christine | 17 | NESE | 1841-11-22 | FD | NESE | R:HAMILTON S:F |
| 693 | AYD, Edward | 17 | NWSW | 1849-03-08 | FD | NWSW | R:HAMILTON |
| 709 | AYD, Emilia | 17 | SENE | 1849-08-20 | FD | SENE | R:HAMILTON S:F |
| 794 | AYD, John Jacob | 5 | NWNE | 1845-08-05 | FD | NWNE | R:HAMILTON |
| 800 | AYD, John Kaieton | 17 | W½SE | 1841-08-16 | FD | W2SE | R:HAMILTON |
| 797 | " " | 17 | E½SW | 1841-08-16 | FD | E2SW | R:HAMILTON |
| 798 | " " | 17 | SENW | 1841-08-16 | FD | SENW | R:HAMILTON |
| 799 | " " | 17 | SWNE | 1841-08-16 | FD | SWNE | R:HAMILTON |
| 801 | AYD, John Keyton | 3 | E½NE | 1844-08-13 | FD | E2NE | R:HAMILTON |
| 806 | AYD, John Leonard | 4 | NWSW | 1841-11-22 | FD | NWSW | R:HAMILTON |
| 805 | " " | 17 | NENW | 1853-12-30 | FD | NENW | R:HAMILTON |
| 690 | BECKWITH, Dennis | 34 | E½NE | 1823-12-29 | FD | E2NE | R:HAMILTON |
| 832 | BIGGERSTAFF, Lewis L | 35 | NWSW | 1853-01-21 | FD | NWSW | G:3 |
| 832 | BIGGERSTAFF, Lucy | 35 | NWSW | 1853-01-21 | FD | NWSW | G:3 |
| 832 | BIGGERSTAFF, Mary E | 35 | NWSW | 1853-01-21 | FD | NWSW | G:3 |
| 832 | BIGGERSTAFF, Milo M | 35 | NWSW | 1853-01-21 | FD | NWSW | G:3 |
| 770 | BLACK, John | 8 | E½NW | 1853-11-17 | FD | E2NW | R:HAMILTON |
| 771 | " " | 8 | W½NE | 1853-11-17 | FD | W2NE | R:HAMILTON |
| 773 | BOND, John | 33 | N½NE | 1850-12-29 | FD | N2NE | R:HAMILTON |
| 774 | " " | 33 | SENE | 1851-10-18 | FD | SENE | R:HAMILTON |
| 772 | " " | 30 | SWSW | 1854-01-30 | FD | SWSW | R:FRANKLIN |
| 840 | BOND, Marstin | 33 | SW | 1818-05-20 | FD | SW | R:KENTUCKY |
| 826 | BOWERS, Lemuel Gomer | 34 | NWNE | 1851-05-01 | FD | NWNE | R:HAMILTON |
| 874 | BREMER, Tobias | 8 | SWNE | 1853-08-25 | FD | SWNE | R:HAMILTON |
| 673 | BRUMMER, Charles | 18 | NWSE | 1843-08-14 | FD | NWSE | R:HAMILTON |
| 775 | BRUMMER, John C | 17 | SWNW | 1854-07-24 | FD | SWNW | R:HAMILTON |
| 875 | BRUMMER, Tobias | 18 | NESE | 1851-04-05 | FD | NESE | R:HAMILTON |
| 659 | BYHOVER, Amelium | 17 | SWSW | 1854-11-14 | FD | SWSW | R:HAMILTON |
| 886 | CAMP, William | 24 | NENW | 1853-08-26 | FD | NENW | R:HAMILTON |
| 866 | COALS, Solomon | 23 | SWSW | 1851-12-16 | FD | SWSW | R:HAMILTON |
| 867 | COATS, Solomon | 14 | SWSE | 1853-11-19 | FD | SWSE | R:HAMILTON |
| 668 | COFFMAN, Charles A | 8 | NWNE | 1853-08-25 | FD | NWNE | R:HAMILTON |
| 776 | COLLUP, John | 3 | W½NW | 1842-01-07 | FD | W2NW | R:HAMILTON |
| 868 | COTES, Solomon | 23 | NENE | 1853-09-19 | FD | NENE | R:HAMILTON |
| 674 | CRISELL, Charles | 35 | SWNW | 1853-03-08 | FD | SWNW | R:HAMILTON |
| 687 | CROUCH, Cloyd | 2 | E½NW | 1854-01-07 | FD | E2NW | R:HAMILTON |
| 688 | " " | 5 | SWNE | 1854-01-10 | FD | SWNE | R:HAMILTON |
| 877 | CROUCH, Wamen B | 8 | NWSE | 1854-01-06 | FD | NWSE | R:HAMILTON |
| 878 | " " | 8 | SESE | 1854-01-06 | FD | SESE | R:HAMILTON |
| 876 | " " | 17 | NENE | 1854-01-06 | FD | NENE | R:HAMILTON |

| ID | Individual in Patent | Sec. | Sec. Part | Purchase Date | Sale Type | IL Aliquot Part | For More Info . . . |
|----|----------------------|------|-----------|---------------|-----------|-----------------|---------------------|
| 652 | DAILEY, Abner | 23 | SESW | 1853-11-02 | FD | SESW | R:HAMILTON |
| 661 | DAILEY, Anderson | 33 | SWNW | 1839-04-17 | FD | SWNW | R:HAMILTON |
| 660 | " " | 32 | NESE | 1851-03-19 | FD | NESE | R:HAMILTON |
| 815 | DAILEY, John W | 33 | SWNE | 1853-11-09 | FD | SWNE | R:HAMILTON |
| 828 | DAILEY, Levi | 27 | SWSW | 1850-12-29 | FD | SWSW | R:HAMILTON |
| 827 | " " | 27 | SESW | 1854-03-13 | FD | SESW | R:HAMILTON |
| 888 | DAILEY, William | 27 | SESE | 1847-05-24 | FD | SESE | R:HAMILTON |
| 889 | " " | 35 | NWNW | 1847-05-24 | FD | NWNW | R:HAMILTON |
| 890 | " " | 35 | SENW | 1851-11-06 | FD | SENW | R:HAMILTON |
| 887 | " " | 27 | NESE | 1855-03-27 | FD | NESE | R:HAMILTON |
| 662 | DAILY, Anderson | 33 | E½NW | 1836-12-15 | FD | E2NW | R:HAMILTON |
| 663 | " " | 33 | NWNW | 1849-10-31 | FD | NWNW | R:HAMILTON |
| 664 | " " | 34 | NESW | 1852-04-01 | FD | NESW | R:MASSAC |
| 811 | DAILY, John Sen | 28 | SWSW | 1836-12-15 | FD | SWSW | R:HAMILTON |
| 830 | DAILY, Levi | 28 | SESE | 1849-10-31 | FD | SESE | R:HAMILTON |
| 829 | " " | 28 | NESE | 1851-10-18 | FD | NESE | R:HAMILTON |
| 891 | DAILY, William | 26 | SWSW | 1836-12-15 | FD | SWSW | R:HAMILTON |
| 892 | " " | 35 | NENW | 1852-10-15 | FD | NENW | |
| 881 | DAVIS, William C | 6 | E½NW | 1852-06-30 | FD | E2NW | |
| 882 | " " | 6 | NWSW | 1854-01-16 | FD | NWSW | R:HAMILTON |
| 653 | DENTON, Abram | 24 | SWNW | 1853-11-22 | FD | SWNW | R:HAMILTON |
| 658 | DENTON, Alvey | 14 | SWSW | 1854-06-06 | FD | SWSW | R:HAMILTON |
| 777 | DOBBS, John | 26 | NESE | 1852-10-27 | FD | NESEVOID | |
| 715 | DONIPHAN, George | 5 | W½ | 1853-03-07 | FD | W2 | |
| 841 | ELLIS, Martin Elmore | 22 | NESW | 1851-06-13 | FD | NESW | R:HAMILTON |
| 842 | " " | 22 | SWNE | 1851-06-13 | FD | SWNE | R:HAMILTON |
| 738 | EUBANKS, James | 3 | SE | 1852-02-24 | FD | SE | |
| 686 | FRY, Christopher | 19 | N½SE | 1854-10-13 | FD | N2SE | R:HAMILTON |
| 725 | FULLER, George W | 31 | NWNW | 1854-03-29 | FD | NWNW | R:GALLATIN |
| 739 | GALLAHARE, James F | 26 | SWSE | 1852-01-07 | FD | SWSE | R:HAMILTON |
| 698 | GATHIN, Edwin Jr | 25 | NENW | 1853-11-22 | FD | NENW | R:HAMILTON |
| 694 | GATLIN, Edward | 25 | NWNW | 1851-11-06 | FD | NWNW | |
| 695 | GATTIN, Edward | 25 | SENW | 1852-05-11 | FD | SENW | |
| 857 | GHORMLEY, Nancy | 31 | W½NE | 1848-09-10 | FD | W2NE | S:F |
| 855 | " " | 30 | SWSE | 1848-09-10 | FD | SWSE | S:F |
| 856 | " " | 31 | NENE | 1848-09-10 | FD | NENE | S:F |
| 779 | GLAZE, John | 30 | E½NW | 1859-06-27 | FD | E2NW | |
| 780 | " " | 30 | NE | 1859-06-27 | FD | NE | |
| 726 | GRACE, George W | 23 | W½NE | 1851-01-31 | FD | W2NE | R:HAMILTON |
| 831 | GREEN, Lewis | 24 | E½SW | 1821-12-06 | FD | E2SW | R:HAMILTON |
| 893 | GREEN, William | 23 | SESE | 1837-08-18 | FD | SESE | R:WHITE |
| 727 | GROCE, George W | 23 | NENW | 1851-04-19 | FD | NENW | R:HAMILTON |
| 895 | HALL, William | 8 | SWSW | 1854-10-09 | FD | SWSW | R:HAMILTON |
| 894 | " " | 17 | NWNW | 1854-10-09 | FD | NWNW | R:HAMILTON |
| 757 | HARDY, Jeduthun P | 26 | NWSW | 1836-05-19 | FD | NWSW | R:HAMILTON |
| 675 | HEARD, Charles H | 25 | SWSW | 1853-03-07 | FD | SWSW | R:HAMILTON |
| 785 | HEARD, John H | 16 | L3 | 1850-05-13 | SC | LOT3NENW | |
| 789 | " " | 16 | L8 | 1850-05-13 | SC | LOT8NWSW | |
| 788 | " " | 16 | L7 | 1850-05-13 | SC | LOT7NESW | |
| 786 | " " | 16 | L4 | 1850-05-13 | SC | LOT4NWNW | |
| 784 | " " | 16 | L2 | 1850-05-13 | SC | LOT2W2NE | |
| 783 | " " | 16 | L12 | 1850-05-13 | SC | LOT12E2SE | |
| 782 | " " | 16 | L11 | 1850-05-13 | SC | LOT11W2SE | |
| 781 | " " | 16 | L1 | 1850-05-13 | SC | LOT1E2NE | |
| 787 | " " | 16 | L5 | 1850-05-13 | SC | LOT5SWNW | |
| 790 | " " | 16 | L6 | 1850-05-15 | SC | LOT6SENW | |
| 791 | " " | 25 | NENE | 1855-06-11 | FD | NENE | R:HAMILTON |
| 677 | HEIL, Charles | 20 | SENE | 1854-05-25 | FD | SENE | R:HAMILTON |
| 678 | " " | 20 | SWNE | 1854-11-14 | FD | SWNE | R:HAMILTON |
| 676 | " " | 20 | NENE | 1854-11-14 | FD | NENE | R:HAMILTON |
| 667 | HOLLAND, Berryman | 32 | SWSW | 1854-04-12 | FD | SWSW | R:HAMILTON |
| 666 | " " | 32 | NWNE | 1854-04-12 | FD | NWNE | R:HAMILTON |
| 778 | INGRAM, John F | 36 | SENE | 1853-11-07 | FD | SENE | R:HAMILTON |
| 814 | INGRAM, John T | 36 | W½NW | 1852-10-21 | FD | W2NWVOID | |
| 812 | " " | 25 | SESW | 1852-10-21 | FD | SESWVOID | |
| 813 | " " | 36 | NENW | 1852-10-21 | FD | NENWVOID | |
| 670 | KAUFMAN, Charles A | 7 | SESW | 1851-02-14 | FD | SESW | R:HAMILTON |
| 669 | " " | 7 | NWNW | 1851-08-07 | FD | NWNW | R:HAMILTON |
| 847 | KAUFMAN, Mathias | 4 | NESW | 1842-11-23 | FD | NESW | R:HAMILTON |
| 766 | KAUFMAN, Philip | 32 | SWNE | 1854-10-13 | FD | SWNE | R:HAMILTON |
| 858 | " " | 32 | E½NE | 1854-10-13 | FD | E2NE | R:HAMILTON |
| 859 | " " | 32 | SWNE | 1854-10-13 | FD | SWNE | R:HAMILTON |
| 764 | " " | 32 | E½NE | 1854-10-13 | FD | E2NE | R:HAMILTON |

| ID | Individual in Patent | Sec. | Sec. Part | Purchase Date | Sale Type | IL Aliquot Part | For More Info . . . |
|---|---|---|---|---|---|---|---|
| 671 | KAUGHMAN, Charles A | 7 | SWSW | 1843-09-04 | FD | SWSW | R:HAMILTON |
| 803 | KNOWLES, John | 26 | NENE | 1852-10-29 | FD | NENE | |
| 804 | "            " | 26 | SEN½ | 1852-10-29 | FD | S2NE | |
| 802 | "            " | 25 | SWNW | 1852-10-29 | FD | SWNW | |
| 821 | KOGER, Joseph | 25 | NESE | 1853-03-09 | FD | NESE | R:HAMILTON |
| 679 | KRISSELL, Charles | 34 | NESE | 1851-12-09 | FD | NESE | |
| 742 | LANE, James | 24 | SENW | 1848-12-27 | FD | SENW | G:29 |
| 746 | "        " | 24 | SENW | 1848-12-27 | FD | SENW | G:29 |
| 743 | "        " | 24 | E½SE | 1848-12-27 | FD | E2SE | G:29 |
| 744 | "        " | 24 | NWSE | 1848-12-27 | FD | NWSE | G:29 |
| 745 | "        " | 24 | SEN½ | 1849-03-17 | FD | S2NE | G:29 |
| 747 | "        " | 24 | W½SE | 1849-03-17 | FD | W2SE | G:29 |
| 746 | "        " | 24 | SENW | 1849-04-05 | FD | SENW | R:HAMILTON |
| 742 | "        " | 24 | SENW | 1849-04-05 | FD | SENW | R:HAMILTON |
| 755 | "        " | 13 | SWSE | 1854-09-25 | FD | SWSE | R:HAMILTON |
| 741 | "        " | 13 | SWSE | 1854-09-25 | FD | SWSE | R:HAMILTON |
| 740 | "        " | 13 | E½SE | 1854-09-25 | FD | E2SE | R:HAMILTON |
| 905 | LEWIS, Wilson | 6 | NENE | 1854-01-09 | FD | NENE | |
| 904 | "         " | 6 | E½SE | 1854-01-09 | FD | E2SE | |
| 906 | "         " | 6 | NWSE | 1854-01-09 | FD | NWSE | |
| 907 | "         " | 6 | SENE | 1854-01-09 | FD | SENE | |
| 903 | "         " | 31 | SESE | 1854-01-09 | FD | SESE | |
| 901 | "         " | 31 | SESE | 1854-01-09 | FD | SESE | |
| 909 | "         " | 6 | W½NE | 1854-01-10 | FD | W2NE | R:HAMILTON |
| 908 | "         " | 6 | SWSE | 1854-04-19 | FD | SWSE | R:HAMILTON |
| 717 | MAULDING, George | 3 | NWSW | 1842-06-04 | FD | NWSW | R:HAMILTON |
| 720 | "            " | 4 | E½SE | 1848-10-23 | FD | E2SE | |
| 719 | "            " | 4 | E½NE | 1848-10-23 | FD | E2NE | |
| 722 | "            " | 4 | SWSE | 1853-03-22 | FD | SWSE | R:HAMILTON |
| 721 | "            " | 4 | SESW | 1853-03-22 | FD | SESW | R:HAMILTON |
| 718 | "            " | 3 | SWSW | 1853-03-22 | FD | SWSW | R:HAMILTON |
| 716 | "            " | 10 | NWNW | 1853-03-22 | FD | NWNW | R:HAMILTON |
| 756 | MAULDING, Jarret | 3 | SESE | 1854-02-09 | FD | SESE | R:HAMILTON |
| 825 | MAULDING, Keeling | 9 | NESE | 1854-10-03 | FD | NESE | R:HAMILTON |
| 900 | MAULDING, William | 31 | SWNE | 1853-08-29 | FD | SWNE | R:HAMILTON |
| 883 | MAULDING, William C | 31 | NESW | 1853-12-14 | FD | NESW | R:HAMILTON |
| 884 | "              " | 31 | NWSE | 1854-10-07 | FD | NWSE | R:HAMILTON |
| 885 | "              " | 31 | S½SW | 1854-10-07 | FD | S2SW | R:HAMILTON |
| 807 | MAYNARD, John | 32 | S½SE | 1852-01-02 | FD | S2SE | |
| 820 | MCDANIEL, Joseph H | 24 | NWNW | 1853-11-22 | FD | NWNW | R:HAMILTON |
| 759 | "             " | 24 | NENE | 1855-05-10 | FD | NENE | R:HAMILTON |
| 819 | "             " | 24 | NENE | 1855-05-10 | FD | NENE | R:HAMILTON |
| 691 | MCKINLEY, Ebenezer | 3 | W½NE | 1842-06-04 | FD | W2NE | R:HAMILTON |
| 839 | MINTON, Marinda | 25 | NESW | 1851-02-24 | FD | NESW | R:HAMILTON S:F |
| 734 | MITCHELL, Ichabod | 36 | E½SW | 1852-01-30 | FD | E2SW | |
| 735 | "            " | 36 | SENW | 1852-01-30 | FD | SENW | |
| 736 | "            " | 36 | SWSE | 1852-01-30 | FD | SWSE | |
| 750 | MOORE, James | 28 | SWSE | 1852-09-22 | FD | SWSE | |
| 760 | MOORE, Jesse | 35 | SESW | 1851-11-11 | FD | SESW | |
| 761 | "        " | 36 | NENE | 1852-12-06 | FD | NENE | |
| 692 | MOSS, Ebenzer | 24 | NWSW | 1851-02-11 | FD | NWSW | R:HAMILTON |
| 903 | MOULDING, William | 31 | SESE | 1850-05-31 | FD | SESE | |
| 901 | "             " | 31 | SESE | 1850-05-31 | FD | SESE | |
| 733 | MOUTRAY, Hiram | 2 | W½NW | 1851-06-02 | FD | W2NW | R:HAMILTON |
| 743 | MUSGRAVE, Robert J | 24 | E½SE | 1848-12-27 | FD | E2SE | G:29 |
| 744 | "              " | 24 | NWSE | 1848-12-27 | FD | NWSE | G:29 |
| 742 | "              " | 24 | SENW | 1848-12-27 | FD | SENW | G:29 |
| 746 | "              " | 24 | SENW | 1848-12-27 | FD | SENW | G:29 |
| 747 | "              " | 24 | W½SE | 1849-03-17 | FD | W2SE | G:29 |
| 745 | "              " | 24 | SEN½ | 1849-03-17 | FD | S2NE | G:29 |
| 730 | MUSGROVE, Hannah | 26 | NWNE | 1851-02-14 | FD | NWNE | R:HAMILTON S:F |
| 729 | MYERS, George W | 36 | W½NE | 1850-07-31 | FD | W2NE | |
| 728 | "          " | 25 | W½SE | 1850-07-31 | FD | W2SE | |
| 737 | MYRES, Jacob P | 25 | SESE | 1854-11-18 | FD | SESE | R:HAMILTON |
| 654 | PERRY, Abram | 23 | SENW | 1836-03-28 | FD | SENW | R:HAMILTON |
| 655 | "        " | 35 | SWNE | 1853-05-16 | FD | SWNE | R:HAMILTON |
| 809 | POWELL, John Nagly | 4 | W½NE | 1852-08-30 | FD | W2NE | |
| 808 | "             " | 4 | NWSE | 1852-08-30 | FD | NWSE | |
| 819 | PROMMEL, Jerret | 24 | NENE | 1849-09-14 | FD | NENE | R:HAMILTON |
| 759 | "            " | 24 | NENE | 1849-09-14 | FD | NENE | R:HAMILTON |
| 752 | RAWLS, James | 6 | SWNW | 1848-09-28 | FD | SWNW | R:HAMILTON |
| 751 | "        " | 6 | NWNW | 1854-06-17 | FD | NWNW | R:HAMILTON |
| 762 | REBANACKER, Jhnatz | 20 | N½NW | 1843-08-14 | FD | N2NW | R:HAMILTON |

| ID | Individual in Patent | Sec. | Sec. Part | Purchase Date | Sale Type | IL Aliquot Part | For More Info . . . |
|----|---------------------|------|-----------|---------------|-----------|-----------------|---------------------|
| 854 | REES, Murphy | 34 | SWNE | 1851-06-02 | FD | SWNE | |
| 702 | RICH, Elias | 34 | NWSE | 1853-03-18 | FD | NWSE | R:HAMILTON |
| 753 | RICH, James | 22 | NWSE | 1849-02-19 | FD | NWSE | |
| 758 | RICH, Jeremiah | 35 | NENE | 1852-12-01 | FD | NENE | |
| 810 | RICH, John | 26 | NENW | 1847-09-02 | FD | NENW | R:HAMILTON |
| 880 | RICH, Washington | 36 | SESE | 1853-02-21 | FD | SESE | |
| 879 | " " | 36 | NESE | 1853-11-17 | FD | NESE | R:HAMILTON |
| 902 | RICH, William | 26 | NWNW | 1849-05-26 | FD | NWNW | R:HAMILTON |
| 833 | RICHARDS, Lewis | 35 | SESE | 1845-01-28 | FD | SESE | R:HAMILTON |
| 834 | " " | 35 | SWSE | 1851-11-24 | FD | SWSE | R:HAMILTON |
| 835 | " " | 36 | NWSE | 1853-11-16 | FD | NWSE | R:HAMILTON |
| 896 | RICHARDS, William I | 13 | NESW | 1853-08-29 | FD | NESW | R:HAMILTON |
| 897 | RICHARDS, William J | 35 | N½SE | 1848-10-24 | FD | N2SE | |
| 898 | " " | 36 | W½SW | 1848-10-24 | FD | W2SW | |
| 793 | RITCHEY, John J | 16 | L9 | 1850-05-13 | SC | LOT9SWSW | |
| 792 | " " | 16 | L10 | 1850-05-13 | SC | LOT10SESW | |
| 824 | ROGERS, Joseph | 25 | W½NE | 1848-02-28 | FD | W2NE | |
| 823 | " " | 25 | SENE | 1848-02-28 | FD | SENE | |
| 822 | " " | 24 | SWSE | 1848-02-28 | FD | SWSE | |
| 681 | ROMINE, Charles W | 5 | SESE | 1853-12-22 | FD | SESE | R:HAMILTON |
| 682 | " " | 5 | W½SE | 1853-12-22 | FD | W2SE | R:HAMILTON |
| 749 | ROMINE, James M | 8 | W½NW | 1853-11-17 | FD | W2NW | |
| 748 | " " | 7 | E½NE | 1854-01-09 | FD | E2NE | R:HAMILTON |
| 713 | RUBENAKER, Francis | 20 | NWNE | 1854-06-05 | FD | NWNE | R:HAMILTON |
| 864 | SHIRLEY, Russel | 34 | SWSE | 1852-09-16 | FD | SWSE | |
| 863 | " " | 34 | SESW | 1852-09-16 | FD | SESW | |
| 871 | SLOO, Thomas Jr | 34 | SW | 1818-05-30 | FD | SW | R:CINCINATTI |
| 870 | " " | 33 | SE | 1818-05-30 | FD | SE | R:CINCINATTI |
| 768 | SMITH, John B | 34 | NW | 1848-02-21 | FD | NW | |
| 765 | SMITH, Joseph B | 32 | NWSE | 1857-06-17 | FD | NWSE | |
| 818 | " " | 32 | NWSE | 1857-06-17 | FD | NWSE | |
| 862 | SMITH, Richard W | 26 | NW | 1819-03-05 | FD | NW | R:WHITE |
| 848 | SMITHPELTER, Michael | 22 | S½SE | 1849-05-19 | FD | S2SEVOID | |
| 849 | " " | 27 | E½NE | 1849-05-19 | FD | E2NEVOID | |
| 852 | " " | 27 | E½NE | 1849-05-19 | FD | E2NEVOID | |
| 850 | " " | 22 | S½SE | 1849-05-19 | FD | S2SEVOID | |
| 849 | SMITHPETER, Michael | 27 | E½NE | 1850-05-24 | FD | E2NE | |
| 848 | " " | 22 | S½SE | 1850-05-24 | FD | S2SE | |
| 852 | " " | 27 | E½NE | 1850-05-24 | FD | E2NE | |
| 850 | " " | 22 | S½SE | 1850-05-24 | FD | S2SE | |
| 853 | " " | 27 | NWNE | 1851-01-27 | FD | NWNE | R:HAMILTON |
| 851 | " " | 26 | SWNW | 1851-10-01 | FD | SWNW | R:HAMILTON |
| 763 | STANDERFER, Job | 31 | E½NW | 1853-03-14 | FD | E2NW | |
| 769 | STANDERFER, John B | 30 | SESW | 1854-05-17 | FD | SESW | R:HAMILTON |
| 899 | STEPHENS, William L | 24 | SWSW | 1849-05-18 | FD | SWSW | R:HAMILTON |
| 657 | TEDFORD, Alexander S | 31 | SWSW | 1852-06-05 | FD | SWSW | |
| 656 | " " | 31 | NWSW | 1853-11-09 | FD | NWSW | R:HAMILTON |
| 724 | TEDFORD, George P | 31 | SENE | 1852-05-18 | FD | SENE | |
| 723 | " " | 31 | NESE | 1853-11-09 | FD | NESE | R:HAMILTON |
| 714 | TESHLEY, Francis | 22 | NESE | 1839-10-16 | FD | NESE | R:HAMILTON |
| 696 | TRAMEL, Edward | 23 | SENE | 1852-12-01 | FD | SENE | |
| 705 | TRAMEL, Elijah | 23 | W½NW | 1849-10-08 | FD | W2NW | |
| 701 | " " | 22 | SENE | 1849-10-08 | FD | SENE | |
| 703 | " " | 22 | SENE | 1849-10-08 | FD | SENE | |
| 704 | " " | 23 | NWSW | 1849-10-08 | FD | NWSW | |
| 860 | TRAMEL, Philip | 35 | NWNE | 1853-09-12 | FD | NWNE | R:HAMILTON |
| 697 | TRAMMEL, Edward | 3 | E½NW | 1855-03-26 | FD | E2NW | R:HAMILTON |
| 708 | TRAMMEL, Elijah | 23 | W½SE | 1848-02-16 | FD | W2SE | |
| 707 | " " | 23 | NESW | 1848-02-16 | FD | NESW | |
| 706 | " " | 23 | NESE | 1848-02-16 | FD | NESE | |
| 754 | TRAMMEL, James | 24 | NWNE | 1855-05-31 | FD | NWNE | R:HAMILTON |
| 861 | TRAMMEL, Philip | 25 | NWSW | 1851-08-30 | FD | NWSW | R:HAMILTON |
| 755 | TRAMMELL, Janett | 13 | SWSE | 1853-09-19 | FD | SWSE | R:HAMILTON S:F |
| 741 | " " | 13 | SWSE | 1853-09-19 | FD | SWSE | R:HAMILTON S:F |
| 712 | TRAMMELS, Fields | 26 | SENW | 1851-02-22 | FD | SENW | |
| 711 | " " | 26 | NWSE | 1851-02-22 | FD | NWSE | |
| 710 | " " | 26 | E½SW | 1851-02-22 | FD | E2SW | |
| 689 | UPTON, David | 24 | SESE | 1852-01-02 | FD | SESE | R:HAMILTON |
| 865 | VAUGHN, Samuel | 35 | NESW | 1851-10-27 | FD | NESW | R:HAMILTON |
| 836 | WALLER, Lewis | 6 | E½SW | 1854-10-05 | FD | E2SW | R:HAMILTON |
| 838 | " " | 7 | NENW | 1854-10-05 | FD | NENW | R:HAMILTON |
| 837 | " " | 6 | NWNE | 1854-10-05 | FD | NWNE | R:HAMILTON |
| 796 | WHITAKER, John K | 35 | SENE | 1851-04-11 | FD | SENE | R:HAMILTON |

| ID | Individual in Patent | Sec. | Sec. Part | Purchase Date | Sale Type | IL Aliquot Part | For More Info . . . |
|-----|----------------------|------|-----------|---------------|-----------|-----------------|---------------------|
| 795 | WHITAKER, John K (Cont'd) | 27 | N½SW | 1854-10-10 | FD | N2SW | R:HAMILTON |
| 873 | WHITEAKER, Thomas | 8 | SWSE | 1839-06-11 | FD | SWSE | R:GALLATIN |
| 872 | "            " | 17 | NWNE | 1839-06-11 | FD | NWNE | R:GALLATIN |
| 703 | WILLIS, Eli | 22 | SENE | 1852-04-16 | FD | SENEVOID | |
| 701 | "        " | 22 | SENE | 1852-04-16 | FD | SENEVOID | |
| 700 | WILLIS, Eli S | 26 | SESE | 1851-02-06 | FD | SESE | R:HAMILTON |
| 699 | "      " | 14 | SESW | 1852-08-16 | FD | SESW | |
| 732 | WILLIS, Hardy C | 27 | W½SE | 1840-03-26 | FD | W2SE | R:HAMILTON |
| 731 | "           " | 27 | SWNE | 1840-03-26 | FD | SWNE | R:HAMILTON |
| 869 | WOLF, Stephen | 5 | NESE | 1853-03-23 | FD | NESE | R:HAMILTON |
| 858 | WOODRUFF, Job | 32 | E½NE | 1851-02-28 | FD | E2NE | |
| 764 | "        " | 32 | E½NE | 1851-02-28 | FD | E2NE | |
| 765 | "        " | 32 | NWSE | 1851-02-28 | FD | NWSE | |
| 766 | "        " | 32 | SWNE | 1851-02-28 | FD | SWNE | |
| 818 | "        " | 32 | NWSE | 1851-02-28 | FD | NWSE | |
| 859 | "        " | 32 | SWNE | 1851-02-28 | FD | SWNE | |
| 843 | ZACHMAMN, Marzell | 5 | SENE | 1850-06-01 | FD | SENE | R:HAMILTON |
| 817 | ZACHMAN, John | 8 | SESW | 1853-02-21 | FD | SESW | R:HAMILTON |
| 816 | "         " | 17 | SESE | 1854-01-07 | FD | SESE | R:HAMILTON |
| 844 | ZACHMAN, Marzell | 5 | NENE | 1853-06-01 | FD | NENE | R:HAMILTON |
| 845 | ZACHMANN, Marzell | 4 | NENW | 1853-03-23 | FD | NENW | R:HAMILTON |
| 846 | ZACKMAN, Marzell | 4 | NWNW | 1841-08-16 | FD | NWNW | R:HAMILTON |

## Patent Map

**T4-S R6-E**
**3rd PM Meridian**

Map Group 5

## Township Statistics

| | | |
|---|---|---|
| Parcels Mapped | : | 258 |
| Number of Patents | : | 1 |
| Number of Individuals | : | 156 |
| Patentees Identified | : | 153 |
| Number of Surnames | : | 102 |
| Multi-Patentee Parcels | : | 6 |
| Oldest Patent Date | : | 5/20/1818 |
| Most Recent Patent | : | 6/27/1859 |
| Block/Lot Parcels | : | 12 |
| Cities and Towns | : | 1 |
| Cemeteries | : | 1 |

### Section 6
RAWLS James 1854
RAWLS James 1848
DAVIS William C 1854
DAVIS William C 1852
WALLER Lewis 1854
WALLER Lewis 1854
LEWIS Wilson 1854
LEWIS Wilson 1854
LEWIS Wilson 1854
LEWIS Wilson 1854
LEWIS Wilson 1854
LEWIS Wilson 1854

### Section 5
DONIPHAN George 1853
AYD John Jacob 1845
CROUCH Cloyd 1854
ROMINE Charles W 1853
ZACHMAN Marzell 1853
ZACHMAMN Marzell 1850
WOLF Stephen 1853
ROMINE Charles W 1853

### Section 4
ZACKMAN Marzell 1841
AYD Charles William 1841
ZACHMANN Marzell 1853
AYD Charles W 1854
POWELL John Nagly 1852
POWELL John Nagly 1852
AYD John Leonard 1841
KAUFMAN Mathias 1842
AYD Charles William 1848
MAULDING George 1853
MAULDING George 1853
MAULDING George 1848
MAULDING George 1848

### Section 7
KAUFMAN Charles A 1851
WALLER Lewis 1854
ROMINE James M 1854
KAUGHMAN Charles A 1843
KAUFMAN Charles A 1851

### Section 8
ROMINE James M 1853
BLACK John 1853
COFFMAN Charles A 1853
BREMER Tobias 1853
BLACK John 1853
ANSELMENT John 1854
CROUCH Wamen B 1854
HALL William 1854
ZACHMAN John 1853
WHITEAKER Thomas 1839
CROUCH Wamen B 1854

### Section 9
MAULDING Keeling 1854

### Section 18
BRUMMER Charles 1843
BRUMMER Tobias 1851

### Section 17
HALL William 1854
AYD John Leonard 1853
WHITEAKER Thomas 1839
CROUCH Wamen B 1854
BRUMMER John C 1854
AYD John Kaieton 1841
AYD John Kaieton 1841
AYD Emilia 1849
AYD Edward 1849
AYD John Kaieton 1841
AYD John Kaieton 1841
AYD Christine 1841
BYHOVER Amelium 1854
ZACHMAN John 1854

### Lots-Sec. 16 / Section 16
```
Lots-Sec. 16
-------------------
L1    HEARD, John H    1850
L2    HEARD, John H    1850
L3    HEARD, John H    1850
L4    HEARD, John H    1850
L5    HEARD, John H    1850
L6    HEARD, John H    1850
L7    HEARD, John H    1850
L8    HEARD, John H    1850
L9    RITCHEY, John J  1850
L10   RITCHEY, John J  1850
L11   HEARD, John H    1850
L12   HEARD, John H    1850
```

### Section 19

### Section 20
REBANACKER Jhnatz 1843
RUBENAKER Francis 1854
HEIL Charles 1854
AYD Charles 1849
HEIL Charles 1854
HEIL Charles 1854
FRY Christopher 1854

### Section 21

### Section 30
GLAZE John 1859
GLAZE John 1859
GLAZE John 1859

### Section 29

### Section 28
DAILY Levi 1851
DAILY John Sen 1836
MOORE James 1852
DAILY Levi 1849

### Section 31
BOND John 1854
STANDERFER John B 1854
GHORMLEY Nancy 1848
FULLER George W 1854
STANDERFER Job 1853
GHORMLEY Nancy 1848
GHORMLEY Nancy 1848
MAULDING William 1853
TEDFORD George P 1852
TEDFORD Alexander S 1853
MAULDING William C 1853
MAULDING William C 1854
TEDFORD George P 1853
TEDFORD Alexander S 1852
MAULDING William C 1854
MOULDING LEWIS William Wilson 1850 1854

### Section 32
HOLLAND Berryman 1854
KAUFMAN Philip 1854
WOODRUFF Job 1851
WOODRUFF Job 1851
KAUFMAN Philip 1854
WOODRUFF Job 1851
SMITH Joseph B 1857
DAILEY Anderson 1851
HOLLAND Berryman 1854
MAYNARD John 1852

### Section 33
DAILY Anderson 1849
DAILY Anderson 1836
BOND John 1850
DAILEY Anderson 1839
DAILEY John W 1853
BOND John 1851
BOND Marstin 1818
SLOO Thomas Jr 1818

## Helpful Hints

1. This Map's INDEX can be found on the preceding pages.

2. Refer to Map "C" to see where this Township lies within Hamilton County, Illinois.

3. Numbers within square brackets [ ] denote a multi-patentee land parcel (multi-owner). Refer to Appendix "C" for a full list of members in this group.

4. Areas that look to be crowded with Patentees usually indicate multiple sales of the same parcel (re-issues), cancellations or voided transactions (that we map, anyway) or overlapping parcels. We opt to show even these ambiguous parcels, which oftentimes lead to research avenues not yet taken.

### Section 3
- COLLUP John 1842
- TRAMMEL Edward 1855
- MCKINLEY Ebenezer 1842
- AYD John Keyton 1844
- MAULDING George 1842
- 3
- EUBANKS James 1852
- MAULDING George 1853
- MAULDING Jarret 1854

### Section 2
- MOUTRAY Hiram 1851
- CROUCH Cloyd 1854
- 2

### Section 1
- 1

### Section 10
- MAULDING George 1853
- 10

### Section 11
- 11

### Section 12
- 12

### Section 15
- 15

### Section 14
- 14
- DENTON Alvey 1854
- WILLIS Eli S 1852
- COATS Solomon 1853

### Section 13
- 13
- RICHARDS William I 1853
- TRAMMELL LANE Janett 1853
- LANE James 1854
- LANE James 1854

### Section 22
- 22
- ASKEY Andrew J 1853
- ELLIS Martin Elmore 1851
- TRAMEL Elijah
- WILLIS1849 Eli 1852
- ELLIS Martin Elmore 1851
- RICH James 1849
- TESHLEY Francis 1839
- SMITHPETER Michael 1849
- SMITHPELTER Michael 1850

### Section 23
- TRAMEL Elijah 1849
- GROCE George W 1851
- GRACE George W 1851
- COTES Solomon 1853
- PERRY Abram 1836
- 23
- TRAMEL Edward 1852
- TRAMEL Elijah 1849
- TRAMMEL Elijah 1848
- TRAMMEL Elijah 1848
- TRAMMEL Elijah 1848
- COALS Solomon 1851
- DAILEY Abner 1853
- GREEN William 1837

### Section 24
- MCDANIEL Joseph H 1853
- CAMP William 1853
- TRAMMEL James 1855
- PROMMEL Jerret 1849
- MCDANIEL Joseph II 1855
- DENTON Abram 1853
- LANE [29] James 1848
- LANE James 1849
- LANE [29] James 1849
- MOSS Ebenzer 1851
- 24
- GREEN Lewis 1821
- STEPHENS William L 1849
- LANE [29] James 1848
- LANE [29] James 1848
- LANE [29] James ROGERS Joseph 1849 / 1848
- UPTON David 1852

### Section 25
- GATLIN Edward 1851
- GATHIN Edwin Jr 1853
- ROGERS Joseph 1848
- HEARD John H 1855
- KNOWLES John 1852
- GATTIN Edward 1852
- ROGERS Joseph 1848
- TRAMMEL Philip 1851
- MINTON Marinda 1851
- 25
- MYERS George W 1850
- KOGER Joseph 1853
- HEARD Charles H 1853
- INGRAM John T 1852
- MYRES Jacob P 1854

### Section 26
- RICH William 1849
- SMITH Richard W 1819
- RICH John 1847
- MUSGROVE Hannah 1851
- KNOWLES John 1852
- SMITHPETER Michael 1851
- TRAMMELS Fields 1851
- KNOWLES John 1852
- HARDY Jeduthun P 1836
- 26
- TRAMMELS Fields 1851
- TRAMMELS Fields 1851
- DOBBS John 1852
- DAILY William 1836
- GALLAHARE James F 1852
- WILLIS Eli S 1851

### Section 27
- SMITHPETER Michael 1851
- SMITHPELTER Michael 1850
- WILLIS Hardy C 1840
- SMITHPETER Michael 1850
- WHITAKER John K 1854
- 27
- DAILEY William 1855
- DAILEY Levi 1850
- DAILEY Levi 1854
- WILLIS Hardy C 1840
- DAILEY William 1847

### Section 34
- SMITH John B 1848
- BOWERS Lemuel Gomer 1851
- BECKWITH Dennis 1823
- REES Murphy 1851
- 34
- SLOO Thomas Jr 1818
- DAILY Anderson 1852
- RICH Elias 1853
- KRISSELL Charles 1851
- SHIRLEY Russel 1852
- SHIRLEY Russel 1852

### Section 35
- DAILEY William 1847
- DAILY William 1852
- TRAMEL Philip 1853
- RICH Jeremiah 1852
- CRISELL Charles 1853
- DAILEY William 1851
- PERRY Abram 1853
- WHITAKER John K 1851
- BIGGERSTAFF [3] Lewis L 1853
- VAUGHN Samuel 1851
- 35
- RICHARDS William J 1848
- MOORE Jesse 1851
- RICHARDS Lewis 1851
- RICHARDS Lewis 1845

### Section 36
- INGRAM John T 1852
- MOORE Jesse 1852
- INGRAM John T 1852
- MITCHELL Ichabod 1852
- MYERS George W 1850
- INGRAM John F 1853
- RICHARDS William J 1848
- 36
- RICHARDS Lewis 1853
- RICH Washington 1853
- MITCHELL Ichabod 1852
- MITCHELL Ichabod 1852
- RICH Washington 1853

### Legend
- ———— Patent Boundary
- ▬▬▬▬ Section Boundary
- No Patents Found (or Outside County)
- 1., 2., 3., ... Lot Numbers (when beside a name)
- [ ] Group Number (see Appendix "C")

**Scale**: Section = 1 mile X 1 mile (generally, with some exceptions)

## Road Map

T4-S R6-E
3rd PM Meridian

Map Group 5

### Cities & Towns
Piopolis

### Cemeteries
Cherry Grove Cemetery

County Road 600

County Road 2000

County Road 850

County Road 2050

County Road 875

6

5

4

County Road 1950

County Road 650

County Road 700

County Road 800

7

8

9

County Road 1900

Piopolis

County Road 715

County Road 1850

County Road 725

County Road 775

17

16

State Route 242

18

County Road 1800

County Road 675

County Road 1750

19

20

21

30

29

28

County Road 1600

31

32

County Road 1550

33

County Road 19

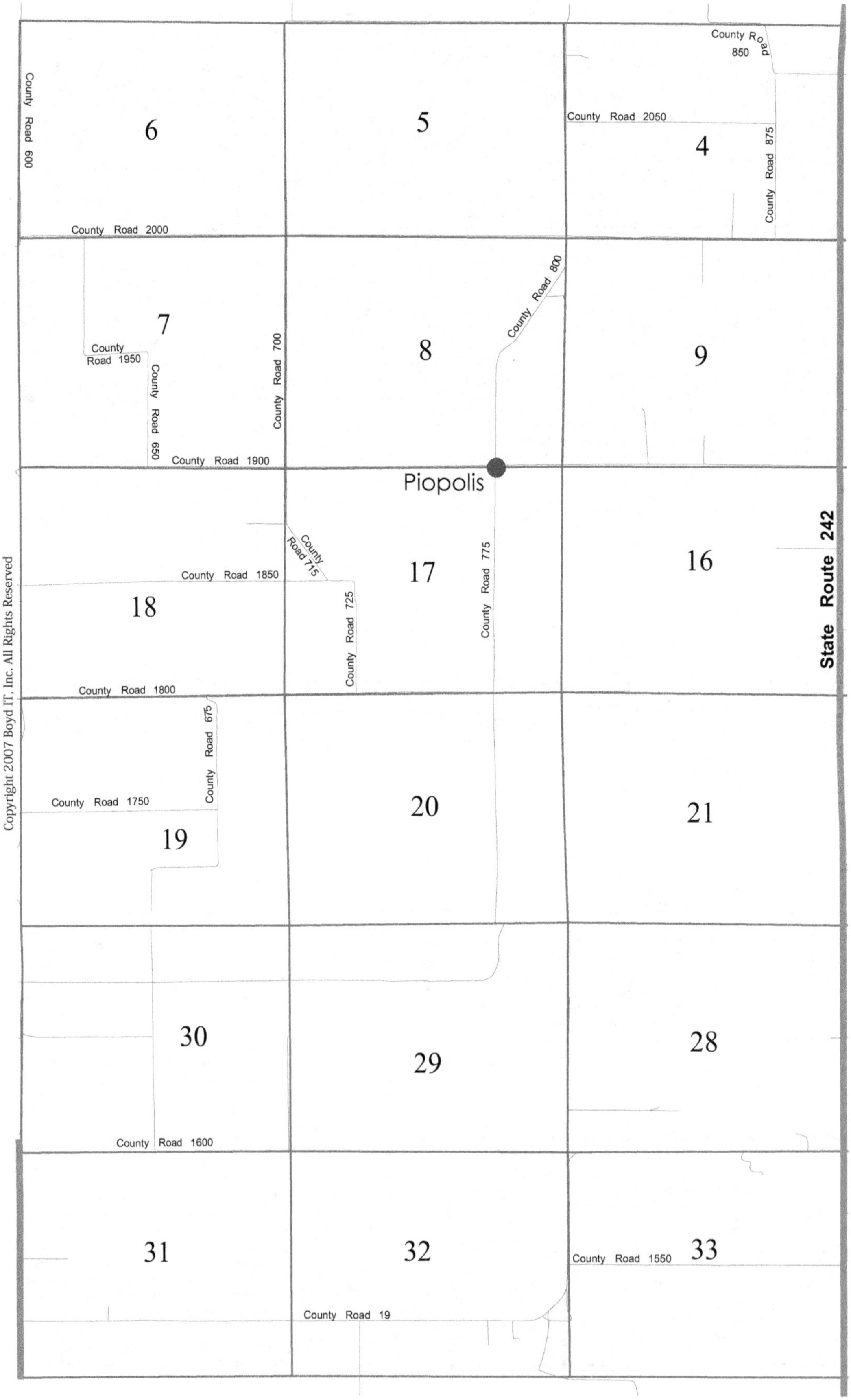

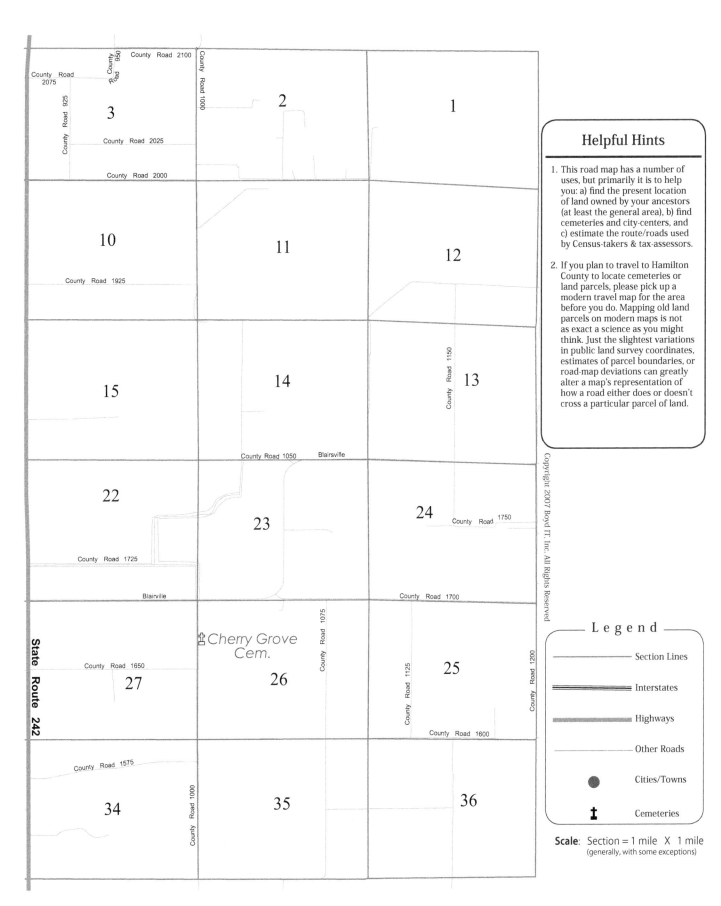

## Helpful Hints

1. This road map has a number of uses, but primarily it is to help you: a) find the present location of land owned by your ancestors (at least the general area), b) find cemeteries and city-centers, and c) estimate the route/roads used by Census-takers & tax-assessors.

2. If you plan to travel to Hamilton County to locate cemeteries or land parcels, please pick up a modern travel map for the area before you do. Mapping old land parcels on modern maps is not as exact a science as you might think. Just the slightest variations in public land survey coordinates, estimates of parcel boundaries, or road-map deviations can greatly alter a map's representation of how a road either does or doesn't cross a particular parcel of land.

### Legend

| | |
|---|---|
| ——————— | Section Lines |
| ━━━━━━━ | Interstates |
| ━━━━━━━ | Highways |
| ——————— | Other Roads |
| ● | Cities/Towns |
| ✝ | Cemeteries |

**Scale**: Section = 1 mile X 1 mile
(generally, with some exceptions)

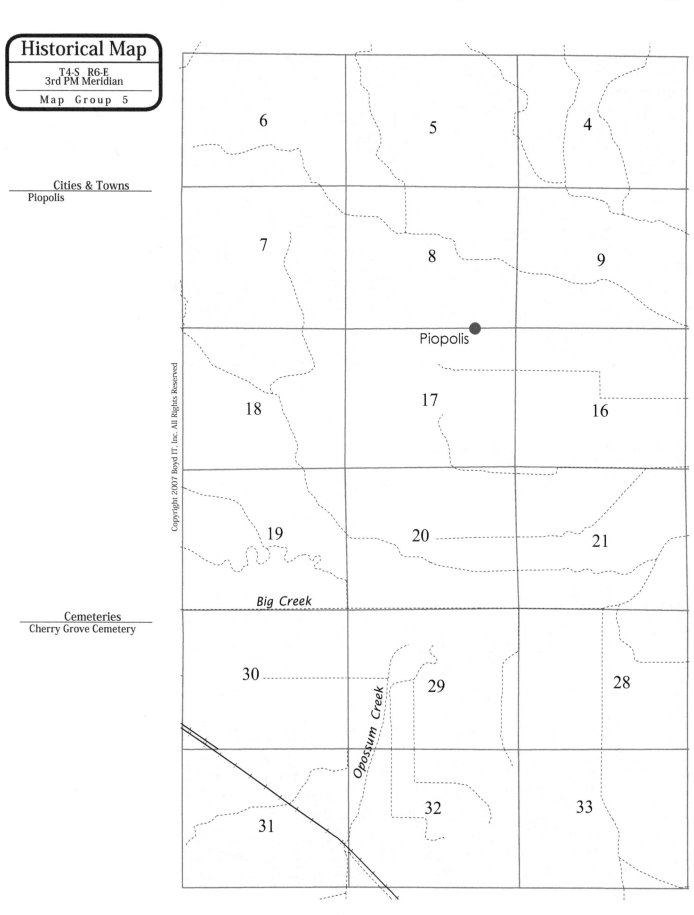

### Historical Map

T4-S  R6-E
3rd PM Meridian

Map Group 5

Cities & Towns
Piopolis

Cemeteries
Cherry Grove Cemetery

6

5

4

7

8

9

Piopolis

18

17

16

19

20

21

Big Creek

30

29

28

Opossum Creek

31

32

33

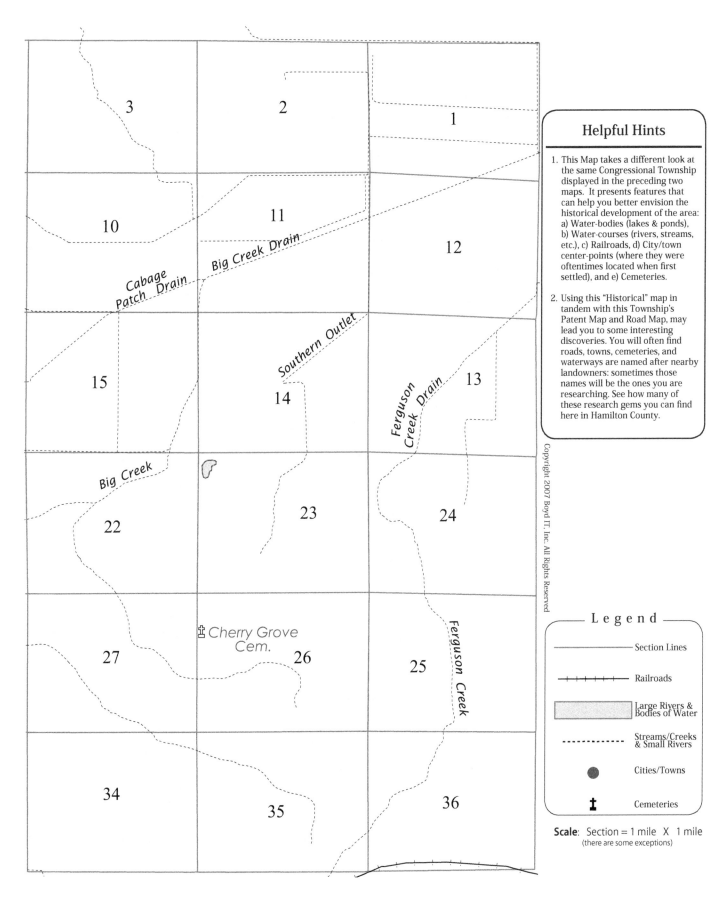

3

2

1

10

11

Big Creek Drain

12

Cabage Patch Drain

15

Southern Outlet

14

Ferguson Creek Drain

13

Big Creek

22

23

24

✝ Cherry Grove Cem.

27

26

25

Ferguson Creek

34

35

36

Legend

———— Section Lines

+++++++ Railroads

▭ Large Rivers & Bodies of Water

- - - - - - Streams/Creeks & Small Rivers

● Cities/Towns

✝ Cemeteries

**Scale**: Section = 1 mile  X  1 mile
(there are some exceptions)

## Map Group 6: Index to Land Patents

## Township 4-South Range 7-East (3rd PM)

After you locate an individual in this Index, take note of the Section and Section Part then proceed to the Land Patent map on the pages immediately following. You should have no difficulty locating the corresponding parcel of land.

The "For More Info" Column will lead you to more information about the underlying Patents. See the *Legend* at right, and the "How to Use this Book" chapter, for more information.

```
                        LEGEND
              "For More Info . . ." column
G = Group  (Multi-Patentee Patent, see Appendix "C")
R = Residence
S = Social Status

See Appendix A for list of abbreviations used by the
Illinois State Archives in describing the place and
nature of these land patents.

Note: if the Abbreviations contain "L", "BL", "LOT",
or "BLOCK", the exact whereabouts of the parcel within
the section is not known.
```

| ID | Individual in Patent | Sec. | Sec. Part | Purchase Date | Sale Type | IL Aliquot Part | For More Info . . . |
|----|---------------------|------|-----------|---------------|-----------|-----------------|---------------------|
| 933 | ADAMS, Daniel | 33 | SWSW | 1853-03-31 | FD | SWSW | |
| 934 | " " | 34 | SWNE | 1854-01-04 | FD | SWNE | R:HAMILTON |
| 1156 | ADAMS, William C | 28 | NESW | 1854-01-09 | FD | NESW | R:HAMILTON |
| 1106 | " " | 28 | NESW | 1854-01-09 | FD | NESW | R:HAMILTON |
| 1136 | AKERS, Thomas | 12 | SWNE | 1853-03-18 | FD | SWNE | R:HAMILTON |
| 1087 | ALEXANDER, Mastin E | 30 | NESE | 1839-05-20 | FD | NESE | R:GALLATIN |
| 1154 | " " | 30 | NESE | 1839-05-20 | FD | NESE | R:GALLATIN |
| 1115 | ALLENDUKER, Robert | 16 | L8 | 1843-03-30 | SC | L8 | |
| 1016 | AVANT, John | 31 | SESE | 1851-07-21 | FD | SESE | |
| 949 | BAILEY, Faphart | 23 | SENE | 1838-11-28 | FD | SENE | R:WHITE |
| 953 | BAILEY, Gaephart | 24 | NENW | 1854-10-13 | FD | NENW | R:HAMILTON |
| 954 | " " | 24 | NWNE | 1854-10-13 | FD | NWNE | R:HAMILTON |
| 955 | BAILEY, Geaphart | 14 | SESE | 1848-11-21 | FD | SESE | R:HAMILTON |
| 957 | " " | 24 | SWNW | 1848-11-21 | FD | SWNW | R:HAMILTON |
| 958 | " " | 29 | NWNE | 1851-02-08 | FD | NWNE | R:HAMILTON |
| 956 | " " | 23 | SWNE | 1853-12-26 | FD | SWNE | R:HAMILTON |
| 960 | BAILEY, Geophart | 24 | NWSW | 1853-03-14 | FD | NWSW | R:HAMILTON |
| 959 | " " | 24 | NWNW | 1853-03-14 | FD | NWNW | R:HAMILTON |
| 946 | BAILY, Elizabeth | 23 | NENE | 1837-07-19 | FD | NENE | R:WHITE S:F |
| 1117 | BEARD, Robert M | 32 | NWNW | 1849-11-17 | FD | NWNW | R:HAMILTON |
| 1116 | " " | 31 | NENE | 1849-11-17 | FD | NENE | R:HAMILTON |
| 1154 | BEARD, William | 30 | NESE | 1854-02-04 | FD | NESE | R:HAMILTON |
| 1087 | " " | 30 | NESE | 1854-02-04 | FD | NESE | R:HAMILTON |
| 1149 | BEATY, William A | 18 | NWSW | 1853-11-29 | FD | NWSW | R:HAMILTON |
| 1124 | BICKERSTAFF, Samuel | 36 | SW | 1819-05-05 | FD | SW | R:WHITE |
| 962 | BRADLEY, George | 29 | SWSE | 1844-10-15 | FD | SWSE | R:HAMILTON |
| 964 | " " | 32 | NWNE | 1844-12-21 | FD | NWNE | R:HAMILTON |
| 961 | " " | 29 | SESE | 1850-01-01 | FD | SESE | R:HAMILTON |
| 965 | " " | 32 | SENE | 1850-01-09 | FD | SENE | R:HAMILTON |
| 1099 | " " | 32 | SENE | 1850-01-09 | FD | SENE | R:HAMILTON |
| 966 | " " | 32 | SWNE | 1852-01-21 | FD | SWNE | R:HAMILTON |
| 967 | " " | 33 | N½NW | 1854-10-12 | FD | N2NW | R:HAMILTON |
| 963 | " " | 32 | NENE | 1854-10-12 | FD | NENE | R:HAMILTON |
| 969 | " " | 33 | W½NE | 1854-10-12 | FD | W2NE | R:HAMILTON |
| 968 | " " | 33 | SWNW | 1854-10-12 | FD | SWNW | R:HAMILTON |
| 1017 | BUCHE, John | 22 | SESW | 1841-02-27 | FD | SESW | R:HAMILTON |
| 1020 | BUCK, John | 22 | SWSW | 1848-03-20 | FD | SWSW | R:HAMILTON |
| 1021 | " " | 27 | N½NW | 1853-02-01 | FD | N2NW | |
| 1018 | " " | 21 | SE | 1854-09-23 | FD | SE | R:HAMILTON |
| 1022 | " " | 28 | NENE | 1854-09-23 | FD | NENE | R:HAMILTON |
| 1023 | " " | 28 | SEN½ | 1854-09-23 | FD | S2NE | R:HAMILTON |
| 1019 | " " | 22 | NWNW | 1855-03-27 | FD | NWNW | R:HAMILTON |
| 1037 | BUCK, John J | 28 | NWNE | 1853-03-09 | FD | NWNE | |
| 1040 | BUCK, John Joseph | 28 | SWNE | 1850-02-02 | BLD | SWNE | R:HAMILTON |
| 1038 | " " | 28 | NWSE | 1851-02-11 | FD | NWSE | R:HAMILTON |
| 1039 | " " | 28 | SENW | 1851-02-11 | FD | SENW | R:HAMILTON |

| ID | Individual in Patent | Sec. | Sec. Part | Purchase Date | Sale Type | IL Aliquot Part | For More Info . . . |
|---|---|---|---|---|---|---|---|
| 950 | CAMPBELL, Felix | 30 | SESW | 1854-10-03 | FD | SESW | R:HAMILTON |
| 951 | " " | 30 | W½SW | 1854-10-03 | FD | W2SW | R:HAMILTON |
| 1061 | CARTER, Joseph | 14 | NESE | 1848-11-20 | FD | NESE | R:HAMILTON |
| 1059 | " " | 13 | SWSE | 1851-05-14 | FD | SWSE | |
| 1060 | " " | 13 | W½SW | 1851-05-14 | FD | W2SW | |
| 1058 | " " | 13 | SESW | 1851-05-14 | FD | SESW | |
| 970 | DAILY, George | 15 | NENE | 1853-03-08 | FD | NENE | |
| 971 | DAVIS, George W | 34 | NESW | 1851-09-18 | FD | NESW | R:HAMILTON |
| 972 | " " | 34 | NWSW | 1854-01-14 | FD | NWSW | R:HAMILTON |
| 973 | " " | 34 | SESW | 1854-01-14 | FD | SESW | R:HAMILTON |
| 1025 | DAVIS, John | 12 | SENW | 1849-03-05 | FD | SENW | R:HAMILTON |
| 1024 | " " | 12 | NWSW | 1849-03-05 | FD | NWSW | R:HAMILTON |
| 1085 | DAVIS, Lucy | 12 | NESW | 1843-10-01 | FD | NESW | R:HAMILTON S:F |
| 1148 | DAVIS, Washington | 34 | SWSW | 1853-03-04 | FD | SWSW | |
| 1139 | DODDS, Thomas | 28 | NWSW | 1854-10-11 | FD | NWSW | R:HAMILTON |
| 1138 | " " | 28 | NWNW | 1854-11-15 | FD | NWNW | R:HAMILTON |
| 1137 | " " | 28 | N½NW | 1854-11-15 | FD | N2NW | R:HAMILTON |
| 913 | DREW, Alford | 20 | SESW | 1851-01-27 | FD | SESW | R:HAMILTON |
| 1140 | DREW, Thomas | 19 | NESE | 1853-05-17 | FD | NESE | R:HAMILTON |
| 1141 | " " | 19 | SENE | 1853-11-18 | FD | SENE | R:HAMILTON |
| 1114 | DUKES, Robert Allen | 19 | SESE | 1841-02-26 | FD | SESE | R:HAMILTON |
| 1157 | DUKES, William | 29 | NWNW | 1837-07-10 | FD | NWNW | R:HAMILTON |
| 1158 | " " | 29 | SWNW | 1839-05-20 | FD | SWNW | R:HAMILTON |
| 978 | EDDY, Henry | 30 | E½NE | 1839-05-20 | FD | E2NE | R:GALLATIN |
| 923 | ELLIS, Caleb | 11 | N½SW | 1854-10-14 | FD | N2SW | R:HAMILTON |
| 924 | " " | 11 | SWSW | 1854-10-14 | FD | SWSW | R:HAMILTON |
| 995 | ELLIS, James | 12 | SWNW | 1855-04-09 | FD | SWNW | R:HAMILTON |
| 1089 | ELLIS, Mastin Elmore | 29 | NWSW | 1851-01-08 | FD | NWSW | R:HAMILTON |
| 1088 | " " | 29 | NENW | 1851-02-22 | FD | NENW | R:HAMILTON |
| 1028 | FARMER, John | 21 | SWNW | 1836-08-23 | FD | SWNW | R:HAMILTON |
| 1027 | " " | 20 | SENE | 1837-09-09 | FD | SENE | R:HAMILTON |
| 1161 | FARRIS, William | 13 | W½SE | 1854-10-05 | FD | W2SE | R:HAMILTON |
| 1159 | " " | 12 | S½SW | 1854-10-05 | FD | S2SW | R:HAMILTON |
| 1160 | " " | 13 | E½NW | 1854-10-05 | FD | E2NW | R:HAMILTON |
| 1162 | FILDS, William | 25 | SENW | 1851-02-08 | FD | SENW | R:HAMILTON |
| 1177 | FUNKHOUSER, William M | 6 | NWSW | 1853-12-07 | FD | NWSW | R:WHITE |
| 914 | GARRISON, Andrew J | 36 | SENE | 1854-01-02 | FD | SENE | R:HAMILTON |
| 1007 | GARRISON, Jefferson | 30 | S½SE | 1849-03-29 | FD | S2SE | R:HAMILTON |
| 1005 | " " | 19 | NWSW | 1851-02-05 | FD | NWSW | R:HAMILTON |
| 1008 | " " | 30 | SWNE | 1851-02-22 | FD | SWNE | R:HAMILTON |
| 1006 | " " | 20 | SWSW | 1851-09-19 | FD | SWSW | R:HAMILTON |
| 1004 | " " | 19 | NESW | 1852-12-17 | FD | NESW | |
| 1009 | " " | 19 | SENW | 1853-11-21 | FD | SENW | R:HAMILTON G:17 |
| 1009 | GARRISON, William | 19 | SENW | 1853-11-21 | FD | SENW | R:HAMILTON G:17 |
| 1062 | GERSBACSSER, Joseph | 24 | SENE | 1855-04-12 | FD | SENE | R:HAMILTON |
| 979 | GREEN, Henry | 29 | NWSE | 1837-07-10 | FD | NWSE | R:HAMILTON |
| 1183 | GREEN, William R | 19 | NWNE | 1853-11-21 | FD | NWNE | R:HAMILTON |
| 1184 | GREEN, William Riley | 19 | SWNW | 1851-02-08 | FD | SWNW | R:HAMILTON |
| 994 | " " | 19 | SWNW | 1851-02-08 | FD | SWNW | R:HAMILTON |
| 1180 | GULLIO, William P | 31 | SENW | 1848-12-14 | FD | SENW | |
| 1178 | " " | 31 | NWSE | 1848-12-14 | FD | NWSE | |
| 1181 | " " | 31 | SWNE | 1848-12-14 | FD | SWNE | |
| 1179 | " " | 31 | SENE | 1848-12-14 | FD | SENE | |
| 947 | HAYNES, Elizabeth | 13 | SWNW | 1853-05-06 | FD | SWNW | S:F |
| 925 | HEARD, Charles H | 30 | NESW | 1853-10-28 | FD | NESW | R:HAMILTON |
| 927 | " " | 30 | SWNW | 1853-10-28 | FD | SWNW | R:HAMILTON |
| 926 | " " | 30 | NWNW | 1853-11-15 | FD | NWNW | R:HAMILTON |
| 1036 | HEARD, John H | 16 | L7 | 1850-07-01 | SC | LOT7SWNE | |
| 1035 | " " | 16 | L6 | 1850-07-01 | SC | LOT6SENW | |
| 1034 | " " | 16 | L5 | 1850-07-01 | SC | LOT5SWNW | |
| 1033 | " " | 16 | L4 | 1850-07-01 | SC | LOT4NWNW | R:HAMILTON |
| 1032 | " " | 16 | L3 | 1850-07-01 | SC | LOT3NENW | |
| 1030 | " " | 16 | L12 | 1850-07-01 | SC | LOT12NWSW | |
| 1031 | " " | 16 | L2 | 1850-07-01 | SC | LOT2NWNE | |
| 1029 | " " | 16 | L1 | 1850-07-01 | SC | LOT1NENE | |
| 917 | HILLYER, Charles T | 13 | NESW | 1858-03-09 | FD | NESW | |
| 929 | " " | 13 | NESW | 1858-03-09 | FD | NESW | |
| 928 | " " | 13 | N½SE | 1858-03-09 | FD | N2SE | |
| 916 | " " | 13 | N½SE | 1858-03-09 | FD | N2SE | |
| 930 | HOLLAND, Christopher | 10 | SESW | 1851-12-06 | FD | SESW | |
| 931 | " " | 15 | NENW | 1851-12-06 | FD | NENW | |
| 915 | HOLLEY, Anna | 25 | SESE | 1839-05-31 | FD | SESE | R:HAMILTON S:F |
| 932 | HOLLEY, Christopher | 36 | N½NE | 1837-06-22 | FD | N2NE | R:HAMILTON |

| ID | Individual in Patent | Sec. | Sec. Part | Purchase Date | Sale Type | IL Aliquot Part | For More Info . . . |
|---|---|---|---|---|---|---|---|
| 1011 | HUNT, Jesse | 32 | SESE | 1853-09-16 | FD | SESE | R:HAMILTON |
| 1012 | " " | 32 | SWSE | 1854-07-25 | FD | SWSE | R:HAMILTON |
| 1010 | " " | 31 | W½NW | 1854-10-12 | FD | W2NW | R:HAMILTON |
| 1166 | HYTEN, William | 27 | NWSE | 1845-01-07 | FD | NWSE | R:HAMILTON |
| 1167 | " " | 27 | SWNW | 1847-06-11 | FD | SWNW | R:HAMILTON |
| 1169 | " " | 28 | SWSE | 1851-02-20 | FD | SWSE | R:HAMILTON |
| 1168 | " " | 28 | SENE | 1853-03-05 | FD | SENE | R:HAMILTON |
| 1170 | HYTER, William | 27 | SENW | 1851-12-15 | FD | SENW | R:HAMILTON |
| 1171 | IRVIN, William | 25 | NWSW | 1846-08-25 | FD | NWSW | R:HAMILTON |
| 1086 | JOHNSON, Martin | 22 | SWNE | 1852-02-03 | FD | SWNE | |
| 996 | JONES, James | 20 | NESW | 1854-10-26 | FD | NESW | R:HAMILTON |
| 1164 | KEARBY, William H | 25 | N½NW | 1851-06-02 | FD | N2NW | |
| 1165 | " " | 26 | NWNE | 1853-03-09 | FD | NWNE | |
| 998 | LANE, James | 19 | NWNW | 1854-09-25 | FD | NWNW | R:HAMILTON |
| 936 | " " | 18 | SWSW | 1854-09-25 | FD | SWSW | R:HAMILTON |
| 997 | " " | 18 | SWSW | 1854-09-25 | FD | SWSW | R:HAMILTON |
| 1042 | LANE, John | 22 | NESW | 1834-02-17 | FD | NESW | R:HAMILTON |
| 1000 | LASATER, James M | 30 | NWSE | 1857-06-09 | FD | NWSE | |
| 999 | " " | 18 | NESE | 1857-06-09 | FD | NESE | |
| 1147 | LASATER, W L | 15 | SWNW | 1853-02-08 | FD | SWNW | S:I |
| 1175 | LASATER, William P | 23 | NWNW | 1857-06-09 | FD | NWNW | |
| 1182 | " " | 23 | NWNW | 1857-06-09 | FD | NWNW | |
| 994 | LEE, James E | 19 | SWNW | 1854-11-27 | FD | SWNW | R:HAMILTON |
| 1184 | " " | 19 | SWNW | 1854-11-27 | FD | SWNW | R:HAMILTON |
| 975 | LINGLEY, Hacket | 28 | SWSW | 1860-08-15 | FD | SWSW | |
| 993 | LOYD, James D | 27 | NWNE | 1853-10-25 | FD | NWNE | R:HAMILTON |
| 992 | " " | 27 | NESE | 1853-12-30 | FD | NESE | R:HAMILTON |
| 974 | LUSTER, Griffith | 24 | SWNE | 1853-06-09 | FD | SWNE | R:HARDIN |
| 1176 | MALOND, William Logan | 34 | SWSE | 1853-03-26 | FD | SWSE | R:HAMILTON |
| 1105 | MARTIN, Nathaniel | 10 | SWSE | 1841-02-20 | FD | SWSE | R:HAMILTON |
| 1128 | MARTIN, Samuel | 15 | SESE | 1839-11-09 | FD | SESE | R:HAMILTON |
| 1119 | MARTIN, Samuel A | 10 | NWSE | 1839-08-27 | FD | NWSE | R:HAMILTON |
| 1120 | " " | 16 | L16 | 1839-09-07 | SC | LOT16 | |
| 1121 | " " | 26 | NESW | 1850-07-01 | FD | NESW | |
| 1122 | " " | 26 | SEN½ | 1850-07-01 | FD | S2NE | |
| 1123 | " " | 26 | SENW | 1850-07-01 | FD | SENW | |
| 1044 | MCCOLGAN, John | 15 | N½SE | 1849-03-12 | FD | N2SE | |
| 1043 | " " | 14 | NWSW | 1849-03-12 | FD | NWSW | |
| 1046 | " " | 15 | NWNE | 1849-03-12 | FD | NWNE | R:HAMILTON |
| 1048 | " " | 15 | SWNE | 1849-03-12 | FD | SWNE | |
| 1047 | " " | 15 | SENW | 1853-01-14 | FD | SENW | |
| 1045 | " " | 15 | NESW | 1854-09-06 | FD | NESW | R:HAMILTON |
| 921 | MCGEHEE, Benjamin W | 13 | SESE | 1855-05-02 | FD | SESE | R:WHITE |
| 918 | MCINTOSH, Benjamin B | 34 | NWSE | 1853-05-18 | FD | NWSE | |
| 1002 | MOORE, James M | 31 | NWNE | 1853-11-23 | FD | NWNE | R:HAMILTON |
| 1001 | " " | 31 | NENW | 1853-11-23 | FD | NENW | R:HAMILTON |
| 1049 | MUSGRAVE, John | 26 | NENE | 1837-12-09 | FD | NENE | R:HAMILTON |
| 1100 | MUSGRAVE, Moses | 32 | SESW | 1853-11-29 | FD | SESW | R:HAMILTON |
| 1097 | " " | 32 | N½SE | 1854-10-03 | FD | N2SE | R:HAMILTON |
| 1098 | " " | 32 | NESW | 1854-10-03 | FD | NESW | R:HAMILTON |
| 1101 | " " | 32 | SWNW | 1854-10-03 | FD | SWNW | R:HAMILTON |
| 1102 | " " | 32 | W½SW | 1854-10-03 | FD | W2SW | R:HAMILTON |
| 965 | " " | 32 | SENE | 1854-10-03 | FD | SENE | R:HAMILTON |
| 1099 | " " | 32 | SENE | 1854-10-03 | FD | SENE | R:HAMILTON |
| 1026 | MUSGROVE, John E | 27 | SWSW | 1844-11-04 | FD | SWSW | R:HAMILTON |
| 1103 | MUSGROVE, Moses | 31 | E½SW | 1850-06-10 | FD | E2SW | |
| 1104 | " " | 31 | SWSE | 1850-06-10 | FD | SWSE | |
| 991 | MYERS, Jacob Perry | 30 | SENW | 1851-01-31 | FD | SENW | R:HAMILTON |
| 1142 | NATION, Thomas | 31 | NWSW | 1851-06-09 | FD | NWSW | |
| 1091 | PETER, Michael Smith | 20 | SESE | 1837-07-10 | FD | SESE | R:HAMILTON |
| 1093 | PETERS, Michael Smith | 29 | SWSW | 1848-01-24 | FD | SWSW | |
| 1094 | " " | 32 | NENW | 1848-01-24 | FD | NENW | |
| 1092 | " " | 29 | E½SW | 1848-01-24 | FD | E2SW | |
| 1127 | PROCOT, Samuel M | 15 | W½SW | 1851-08-26 | FD | W2SW | G:32 |
| 1127 | PROCTOR, Samuel L M | 15 | W½SW | 1851-08-26 | FD | W2SW | G:32 |
| 1125 | " " | 15 | SESW | 1851-08-26 | FD | SESW | |
| 1126 | " " | 15 | SWSE | 1851-08-26 | FD | SWSE | |
| 1013 | RANKIN, Jesse | 25 | SWNW | 1836-08-09 | FD | SWNW | R:HAMILTON |
| 1187 | RANKIN, Wilson | 33 | NESW | 1851-03-22 | FD | NESW | R:HAMILTON |
| 1189 | " " | 33 | SENW | 1853-03-04 | FD | SENW | |
| 1188 | " " | 33 | NWSW | 1853-03-31 | FD | NWSW | |
| 1135 | RHORER, Susan | 20 | NESE | 1847-02-18 | FD | NESE | R:HAMILTON S:F |
| 1113 | ROGER, Richard | 18 | SWNW | 1855-03-29 | FD | SWNW | R:HAMILTON |

| ID | Individual in Patent | Sec. | Sec. Part | Purchase Date | Sale Type | IL Aliquot Part | For More Info . . . |
|---|---|---|---|---|---|---|---|
| 1050 | ROHRER, John | 21 | NWNW | 1847-05-08 | FD | NWNW | R:HAMILTON |
| 952 | RORER, Francis M | 20 | NENE | 1853-01-17 | FD | NENE | |
| 980 | ROSE, Henry | 12 | SENE | 1855-05-02 | FD | SENE | R:WHITE |
| 981 | SEXTON, Henry | 21 | E½SW | 1839-09-25 | FD | E2SW | R:WHITE |
| 1185 | SHELBY, William | 26 | NWSE | 1841-02-20 | FD | NWSE | R:HAMILTON |
| 1095 | SMITHPETER, Michael | 21 | NWSW | 1847-01-26 | FD | NWSW | R:HAMILTON |
| 1096 | " | 29 | SENW | 1850-08-24 | FD | SENW | R:HAMILTON |
| 1130 | SMITHPETER, Sarah | 21 | SWSW | 1839-02-05 | FD | SWSW | R:HAMILTON S:F |
| 1129 | " | 20 | SWSE | 1841-03-17 | FD | SWSE | R:HAMILTON S:F |
| 945 | SNEAD, Elijah | 16 | L9 | 1839-09-16 | SC | L9 | |
| 948 | SNEAD, Ezekiel | 27 | SEN½ | 1841-03-11 | FD | S2NE | R:HAMILTON |
| 1053 | SNEAD, John | 27 | NENE | 1848-02-21 | FD | NENE | R:HAMILTON |
| 1052 | " | 26 | SWNW | 1852-01-20 | FD | SWNW | R:WAYNE |
| 1051 | " | 26 | NWNW | 1853-01-14 | FD | NWNW | |
| 1132 | SNEED, Seborn | 22 | NWNE | 1846-02-06 | FD | NWNE | R:HAMILTON |
| 1133 | SNEED, Seburn | 34 | SENW | 1848-09-15 | FD | SENW | R:HAMILTON |
| 1090 | SPRINGER, Matthew W | 21 | NENE | 1855-04-14 | FD | NENE | R:HAMILTON |
| 912 | STURMAN, Alexander M | 8 | N½NE | 1854-04-13 | FD | N2NE | R:HAMILTON |
| 1131 | TANNER, Sarah | 21 | NWNE | 1847-09-11 | FD | NWNE | R:HAMILTON S:F |
| 919 | TAYLOR, Benjamin H | 13 | SEN½ | 1853-03-09 | FD | S2NE | R:HAMILTON |
| 1054 | TAYLOR, John | 13 | NWNE | 1853-03-09 | FD | NWNE | R:HAMILTON |
| 1112 | TAYLOR, Rane Carter | 11 | SWSE | 1853-03-09 | FD | SWSE | R:HAMILTON |
| 1111 | " | 11 | SESW | 1853-03-09 | FD | SESW | R:HAMILTON |
| 1074 | THOMAS, Lewis | 14 | SWSE | 1848-03-08 | FD | SWSE | R:HAMILTON |
| 1073 | " | 14 | SWNW | 1853-03-01 | FD | SWNW | |
| 1070 | THOMAS, Lewis F | 33 | E½SE | 1852-03-30 | FD | E2SE | R:HAMILTON |
| 1072 | " | 33 | W½SE | 1852-04-28 | FD | W2SE | |
| 1071 | " | 33 | SESW | 1853-05-30 | FD | SESW | R:HAMILTON |
| 1110 | THOMAS, Peter F | 34 | SWNW | 1846-08-25 | FD | SWNW | R:HAMILTON |
| 1156 | " | 28 | NESW | 1849-09-28 | FD | NESW | R:HAMILTON |
| 1106 | " | 28 | NESW | 1849-09-28 | FD | NESW | R:HAMILTON |
| 1107 | " | 28 | SESE | 1851-02-06 | FD | SESE | R:HAMILTON |
| 1109 | " | 34 | NWNW | 1852-08-11 | FD | NWNW | R:HAMILTON |
| 1108 | " | 33 | E½NE | 1854-01-04 | FD | E2NE | R:HAMILTON |
| 1172 | THOMAS, William L | 22 | NENE | 1854-03-28 | FD | NENE | R:HAMILTON |
| 1174 | THOMAS, William Leroy | 23 | NWNE | 1839-11-26 | FD | NWNE | R:HAMILTON |
| 1173 | " | 23 | NENW | 1848-03-08 | FD | NENW | R:HAMILTON |
| 1182 | " | 23 | NWNW | 1848-11-24 | FD | NWNW | R:HAMILTON |
| 1175 | " | 23 | NWNW | 1848-11-24 | FD | NWNW | R:HAMILTON |
| 911 | THOMPSON, Adam | 13 | NWNW | 1852-01-09 | FD | NWNW | R:HAMILTON |
| 1080 | THOMPSON, Lewis | 16 | L15 | 1839-07-20 | SC | LOT15 | |
| 1079 | " | 16 | L14 | 1839-07-20 | SC | LOT14 | |
| 1081 | " | 16 | L10 | 1839-08-30 | SC | LOT10 | |
| 1084 | " | 21 | E½NW | 1847-06-12 | FD | E2NW | R:HAMILTON |
| 1082 | " | 16 | L11 | 1850-07-01 | SC | LOT11NESW | |
| 1083 | " | 16 | L13 | 1850-07-01 | SC | LOT13SWSW | |
| 1076 | " | 14 | NENE | 1853-03-07 | FD | NENE | |
| 1075 | " | 11 | SESE | 1853-03-07 | FD | SESE | |
| 1078 | " | 14 | NWNE | 1854-10-13 | FD | NWNE | R:HAMILTON |
| 1077 | " | 14 | NENW | 1854-10-13 | FD | NENW | R:HAMILTON |
| 1186 | THOMPSON, William | 14 | SENE | 1849-12-26 | FD | SENE | R:HAMILTON |
| 929 | TYLER, Austin | 13 | NESW | 1854-10-23 | FD | NESW | R:WHITE |
| 917 | " | 13 | NESW | 1854-10-23 | FD | NESW | R:WHITE |
| 928 | " | 13 | N½SE | 1854-10-23 | FD | N2SE | R:WHITE |
| 916 | " | 13 | N½SE | 1854-10-23 | FD | N2SE | R:WHITE |
| 939 | UPTON, David | 22 | NWSW | 1834-02-19 | FD | NWSW | R:HAMILTON |
| 940 | " | 22 | SWNW | 1839-12-14 | FD | SWNW | R:HAMILTON |
| 938 | " | 19 | W½SE | 1841-03-08 | FD | W2SE | R:HAMILTON |
| 937 | " | 19 | S½SW | 1851-01-18 | FD | S2SW | R:HAMILTON |
| 936 | " | 18 | SWSW | 1854-01-18 | FD | SWSW | R:HAMILTON |
| 997 | " | 18 | SWSW | 1854-01-18 | FD | SWSW | R:HAMILTON |
| 935 | " | 18 | SESW | 1854-01-18 | FD | SESW | R:HAMILTON |
| 976 | UPTON, Hannah | 30 | NENW | 1842-01-22 | FD | NENW | R:HAMILTON S:F |
| 977 | UPTON, Haunah | 30 | NWNE | 1841-03-08 | FD | NWNE | R:HAMILTON S:F |
| 1055 | UPTON, John | 29 | E½NE | 1838-11-08 | FD | E2NE | R:HAMILTON |
| 1056 | " | 29 | SWNE | 1839-02-05 | FD | SWNE | R:HAMILTON |
| 1041 | UPTON, John Jr | 29 | NESE | 1839-09-06 | FD | NESE | R:HAMILTON |
| 1063 | UPTON, Joseph | 22 | SENW | 1847-06-12 | FD | SENW | R:HAMILTON |
| 1064 | " | 22 | W½SE | 1852-12-04 | FD | W2SE | |
| 1065 | " | 23 | SWNW | 1854-02-15 | FD | SWNW | R:HAMILTON |
| 920 | VENABLES, Benjamin | 12 | E½SE | 1852-02-09 | FD | E2SE | |
| 983 | WHITE, Hugh | 15 | SENE | 1853-01-14 | FD | SENE | |
| 982 | " | 14 | SWSW | 1853-01-14 | FD | SWSW | |

| ID | Individual in Patent | Sec. | Sec. Part | Purchase Date | Sale Type | IL Aliquot Part | For More Info . . . |
|---|---|---|---|---|---|---|---|
| 1068 | WHITE, Lewis B | 27 | SESW | 1853-02-01 | FD | SESW | |
| 1066 | " " | 26 | S½SE | 1853-02-12 | FD | S2SE | |
| 1069 | " " | 35 | NENW | 1853-02-12 | FD | NENW | |
| 1067 | " " | 26 | SESW | 1853-02-12 | FD | SESW | |
| 1144 | WHITE, Thomas | 14 | NWSE | 1845-10-18 | FD | NWSE | R:HAMILTON |
| 1146 | " " | 14 | SWNE | 1849-03-05 | FD | SWNE | |
| 1145 | " " | 14 | SENW | 1849-03-05 | FD | SENW | |
| 1143 | " " | 14 | E½SW | 1849-03-05 | FD | E2SW | |
| 1152 | WHITE, William B | 27 | SWSE | 1853-01-22 | FD | SWSE | |
| 1153 | " " | 34 | NWNE | 1853-01-22 | FD | NWNE | |
| 1151 | " " | 22 | SENE | 1855-04-02 | FD | SENE | R:HAMILTON |
| 1150 | " " | 22 | NESE | 1855-04-02 | FD | NESE | R:HAMILTON |
| 1155 | WHITE, William Bryan | 27 | N½SW | 1851-01-06 | FD | N2SW | R:HAMILTON |
| 1163 | WILLIAMS, William G | 31 | SWSW | 1849-04-26 | FD | SWSW | R:HAMILTON |
| 1003 | WILSON, James M | 22 | NENW | 1851-04-25 | FD | NENW | |
| 1134 | WOODROW, Stephen | 13 | NENE | 1851-06-02 | FD | NENE | R:WHITE |
| 910 | WORTON, Abner | 25 | NESW | 1853-01-21 | FD | NESW | |
| 922 | YORK, Branson | 36 | SWNE | 1837-02-07 | FD | SWNE | R:HAMILTON |
| 941 | YORK, Edmond C | 23 | SENW | 1853-03-09 | FD | SENW | R:HAMILTON |
| 942 | YORK, Edmun | 36 | SENW | 1852-02-02 | FD | SENW | R:HAMILTON |
| 943 | YORK, Eli | 36 | NESW | 1833-06-05 | FD | NESW | R:HAMILTON |
| 944 | " " | 36 | NWSW | 1836-09-26 | FD | NWSW | R:HAMILTON |
| 988 | YORK, Iram | 36 | NWSE | 1836-09-26 | FD | NWSE | R:HAMILTON |
| 986 | " " | 35 | SWSE | 1837-03-15 | FD | SWSE | R:HAMILTON |
| 989 | " " | 36 | SESE | 1840-05-29 | FD | SESE | R:HAMILTON |
| 990 | " " | 36 | SWSE | 1851-04-21 | FD | SWSE | R:HARDIN |
| 987 | " " | 36 | NESE | 1853-02-28 | FD | NESE | R:HAMILTON |
| 984 | YORK, Iram B | 25 | SWSW | 1853-03-08 | FD | SWSW | |
| 985 | " " | 26 | NESE | 1853-03-31 | FD | NESE | |
| 1014 | YORK, Jesse | 35 | SESE | 1848-09-11 | FD | SESE | |
| 1015 | " " | 36 | S½SW | 1848-09-11 | FD | S2SW | |
| 1057 | YORK, John | 35 | NWNE | 1853-03-01 | FD | NWNE | |
| 1118 | YORK, Romeley J | 35 | NESE | 1853-02-01 | FD | NESE | R:HAMILTON |

## Patent Map

T4-S R7-E
3rd PM Meridian

Map Group 6

### Township Statistics

| | | |
|---|---|---|
| Parcels Mapped | : | 280 |
| Number of Patents | : | 1 |
| Number of Individuals | : | 145 |
| Patentees Identified | : | 145 |
| Number of Surnames | : | 88 |
| Multi-Patentee Parcels | : | 2 |
| Oldest Patent Date | : | 5/5/1819 |
| Most Recent Patent | : | 8/15/1860 |
| Block/Lot Parcels | : | 16 |
| Cities and Towns | : | 4 |
| Cemeteries | : | 1 |

**Section 6**
FUNKHOUSER William M 1853

**Section 5**

**Section 4**

**Section 7**

**Section 8**
STURMAN Alexander M 1854

**Section 9**

**Section 18**
ROGER Richard 1855
BEATY William A 1853
UPTON David 1854
LANE James 1854
UPTON David 1854

**Section 17**
LASATER James M 1857

**Section 16**
Lots-Sec. 16
--------
| L1 | HEARD, John H | 1850 |
| L2 | HEARD, John H | 1850 |
| L3 | HEARD, John H | 1850 |
| L4 | HEARD, John H | 1850 |
| L5 | HEARD, John H | 1850 |
| L6 | HEARD, John H | 1850 |
| L7 | HEARD, John H | 1850 |
| L8 | ALLENDUKER, Robert | 1843 |
| L9 | SNEAD, Elijah | 1839 |
| L10 | THOMPSON, Lewis | 1839 |
| L11 | THOMPSON, Lewis | 1850 |
| L12 | HEARD, John H | 1850 |
| L13 | THOMPSON, Lewis | 1850 |
| L14 | THOMPSON, Lewis | 1839 |
| L15 | THOMPSON, Lewis | 1839 |
| L16 | MARTIN, Samuel A | 1839 |

**Section 19**
LANE James 1854
GREEN William R 1853
DREW Thomas 1853
GREEN William Riley 1853
LEE James E 1854
GARRISON [17] Jefferson 1853
GARRISON Jefferson 1851
GARRISON Jefferson 1852
UPTON David 1841
DREW Thomas 1853
UPTON David 1851
DUKES Robert Allen 1841

**Section 20**
RORER Francis M 1853
FARMER John 1837
JONES James 1854
RHORER Susan 1847
GARRISON Jefferson 1851
DREW Alford 1851
SMITHPETER Sarah 1841
PETER Michael Smith 1837

**Section 21**
ROHRER John 1847
THOMPSON Lewis 1847
TANNER Sarah 1847
SPRINGER Matthew W 1855
FARMER John 1836
SMITHPETER Michael 1847
SEXTON Henry 1839
BUCK John 1854
SMITHPETER Sarah 1839

**Section 30**
HEARD Charles H 1853
UPTON Hannah 1842
UPTON Haunah 1841
HEARD Charles H 1853
MYERS Jacob Perry 1851
GARRISON Jefferson 1851
EDDY Henry 1839
HEARD Charles H 1853
LASATER James M 1857
ALEXANDER Mastin E
BEARD William 1854
CAMPBELL Felix 1854
CAMPBELL Felix 1854
GARRISON Jefferson 1849

**Section 29**
DUKES William 1837
ELLIS Mastin Elmore 1851
BAILEY Geaphart 1851
UPTON John 1838
DUKES William 1839
SMITHPETER Michael 1850
UPTON John 1839
BEARD 1839
ELLIS Mastin Elmore 1851
GREEN Henry 1837
UPTON John Jr 1839
PETERS Michael Smith 1848
PETERS Michael Smith 1848
BRADLEY George 1844
BRADLEY George 1850

**Section 28**
DODDS Thomas 1854
DODDS Thomas 1854
BUCK John J 1853
BUCK John 1854
BUCK John Joseph 1851
BUCK John Joseph 1850
HYTEN William 1853
BUCK John 1854
DODDS Thomas 1854
THOMAS Peter F
ADAMS 1849
William C 1854
BUCK John Joseph 1851
LINGLEY Hacket 1860
HYTEN William 1851
THOMAS Peter F 1851

**Section 31**
HUNT Jesse 1854
MOORE James M 1853
MOORE James M 1853
BEARD Robert M 1849
GULLIO William P 1848
GULLIO William P 1848
GULLIO William P 1848
NATION Thomas 1851
GULLIO William P 1848
WILLIAMS William G 1849
MUSGROVE Moses 1850
MUSGROVE Moses 1850
AVANT John 1851

**Section 32**
BEARD Robert M 1849
PETERS Michael Smith 1848
BRADLEY George 1844
BRADLEY George 1854
MUSGRAVE Moses 1854
BRADLEY George 1852
MUSGRAVE Moses 1854
BRADLEY George 1850
MUSGRAVE Moses 1854
MUSGRAVE Moses 1854
MUSGRAVE Moses 1854
MUSGRAVE Moses 1853
HUNT Jesse 1854
HUNT Jesse 1853

**Section 33**
BRADLEY George 1854
BRADLEY George 1854
RANKIN Wilson 1853
BRADLEY George 1854
THOMAS Peter F 1854
BRADLEY George 1854
RANKIN Wilson 1853
RANKIN Wilson 1851
ADAMS Daniel 1853
THOMAS Lewis F 1853
THOMAS Lewis F 1852
THOMAS Lewis F 1852

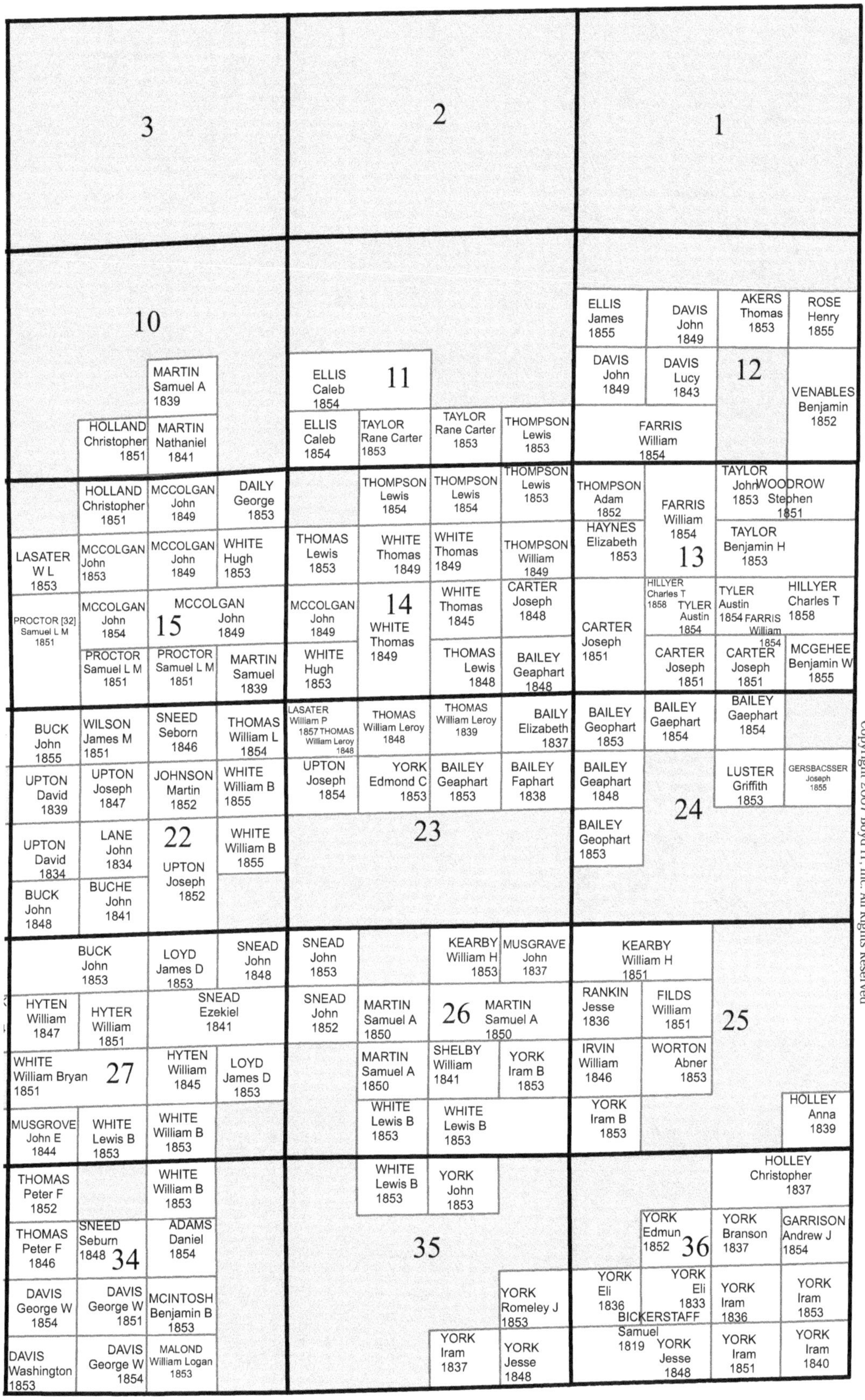

## Map Sections (top row)

**3**

**2**

**1**

## Section 10 / 11 / 12 area

**10**

MARTIN Samuel A 1839

HOLLAND Christopher 1851

MARTIN Nathaniel 1841

**11**

ELLIS Caleb 1854

ELLIS Caleb 1854

TAYLOR Rane Carter 1853

TAYLOR Rane Carter 1853

THOMPSON Lewis 1853

ELLIS James 1855

DAVIS Thomas 1849

AKERS Thomas 1853

ROSE Henry 1855

DAVIS John 1849

DAVIS Lucy 1843

**12**

VENABLES Benjamin 1852

FARRIS William 1854

## Section 13 / 14 / 15 area

HOLLAND Christopher 1851

MCCOLGAN John 1849

DAILY George 1853

LASATER W L 1853

MCCOLGAN John 1853

MCCOLGAN John 1849

WHITE Hugh 1853

PROCTOR [32] Samuel L M 1851

MCCOLGAN John 1854

**15** MCCOLGAN John 1849

PROCTOR Samuel L M 1851

PROCTOR Samuel L M 1851

MARTIN Samuel 1839

THOMAS Lewis 1853

WHITE Thomas 1849

WHITE Thomas 1849

MCCOLGAN John 1849

**14** WHITE Thomas 1849

WHITE Hugh 1853

THOMPSON Lewis 1854

THOMPSON Lewis 1854

THOMPSON Lewis 1853

WHITE Thomas 1845

CARTER Joseph 1848

THOMAS Lewis 1848

THOMPSON Adam 1852

HAYNES Elizabeth 1853

CARTER Joseph 1851

BAILEY Geaphart 1848

TAYLOR John 1853

FARRIS William 1854

WOODROW Stephen 1851

TAYLOR Benjamin H 1853

HILLYER Charles T 1858

TYLER Austin 1854

TYLER Austin 1854

FARRIS William 1854

HILLYER Charles T 1858

**13**

CARTER Joseph 1851

CARTER Joseph 1851

MCGEHEE Benjamin W 1855

## Section 22 / 23 / 24 area

BUCK John 1855

WILSON James M 1851

SNEED Seborn 1846

THOMAS William L 1854

UPTON David 1839

UPTON Joseph 1847

JOHNSON Martin 1852

WHITE William B 1855

UPTON David 1834

LANE John 1834

**22** UPTON Joseph 1852

WHITE William B 1855

BUCK John 1848

BUCHE John 1841

LASATER William P 1857 THOMAS William Leroy 1848

THOMAS William Leroy 1848

THOMAS William Leroy 1839

BAILY Elizabeth 1837

UPTON Joseph 1854

YORK Edmond C 1853

BAILEY Geaphart 1853

BAILEY Faphart 1838

**23**

BAILEY Geophart 1853

BAILEY Geophart 1854

BAILEY Geaphart 1848

BAILEY Geophart 1853

BAILEY Gaephart 1854

BAILEY Gaephart 1854

LUSTER Griffith 1853

GERSBACSSER Joseph 1855

**24**

## Section 26 / 27 / 25 area

BUCK John 1853

LOYD James D 1853

SNEAD John 1848

SNEAD John 1853

KEARBY William H 1853

MUSGRAVE John 1837

KEARBY William H 1851

HYTEN William 1847

HYTER William 1851

SNEAD Ezekiel 1841

SNEAD John 1852

MARTIN Samuel A 1850

**26** MARTIN Samuel A 1850

RANKIN Jesse 1836

FILDS William 1851

**25**

WHITE William Bryan 1851

**27**

HYTEN William 1845

LOYD James D 1853

MARTIN Samuel A 1850

SHELBY William 1841

YORK Iram B 1853

IRVIN William 1846

WORTON Abner 1853

MUSGROVE John E 1844

WHITE Lewis B 1853

WHITE William B 1853

WHITE Lewis B 1853

WHITE Lewis B 1853

YORK Iram B 1853

HOLLEY Anna 1839

## Section 34 / 35 / 36 area

THOMAS Peter F 1852

WHITE William B 1853

WHITE Lewis B 1853

YORK John 1853

HOLLEY Christopher 1837

THOMAS Peter F 1846

SNEED Seburn 1848 **34**

ADAMS Daniel 1854

**35**

YORK Edmun 1852

YORK Branson 1837

GARRISON Andrew J 1854

DAVIS George W 1854

DAVIS George W 1851

MCINTOSH Benjamin B 1853

YORK Romeley J 1853

YORK Eli 1836

YORK Eli 1833

YORK Iram 1836

YORK Iram 1853

DAVIS Washington 1853

DAVIS George W 1854

MALOND William Logan 1853

YORK Iram 1837

YORK Jesse 1848

BICKERSTAFF Samuel 1819

YORK Jesse 1848

YORK Iram 1851

YORK Iram 1840

**36**

## Helpful Hints

1. This Map's INDEX can be found on the preceding pages.

2. Refer to Map "C" to see where this Township lies within Hamilton County, Illinois.

3. Numbers within square brackets [ ] denote a multi-patentee land parcel (multi-owner). Refer to Appendix "C" for a full list of members in this group.

4. Areas that look to be crowded with Patentees usually indicate multiple sales of the same parcel (re-issues), cancellations or voided transactions (that we map, anyway) or overlapping parcels. We opt to show even these ambiguous parcels, which oftentimes lead to research avenues not yet taken.

## Legend

— Patent Boundary

— Section Boundary

No Patents Found (or Outside County)

1., 2., 3., ... Lot Numbers (when beside a name)

[ ] Group Number (see Appendix "C")

**Scale**: Section = 1 mile X 1 mile (generally, with some exceptions)

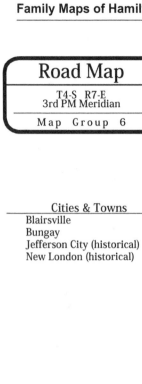

## Road Map

T4-S R7-E
3rd PM Meridian

Map Group 6

### Cities & Towns

Blairsville
Bungay
Jefferson City (historical)
New London (historical)

### Cemeteries

Springer Cemetery

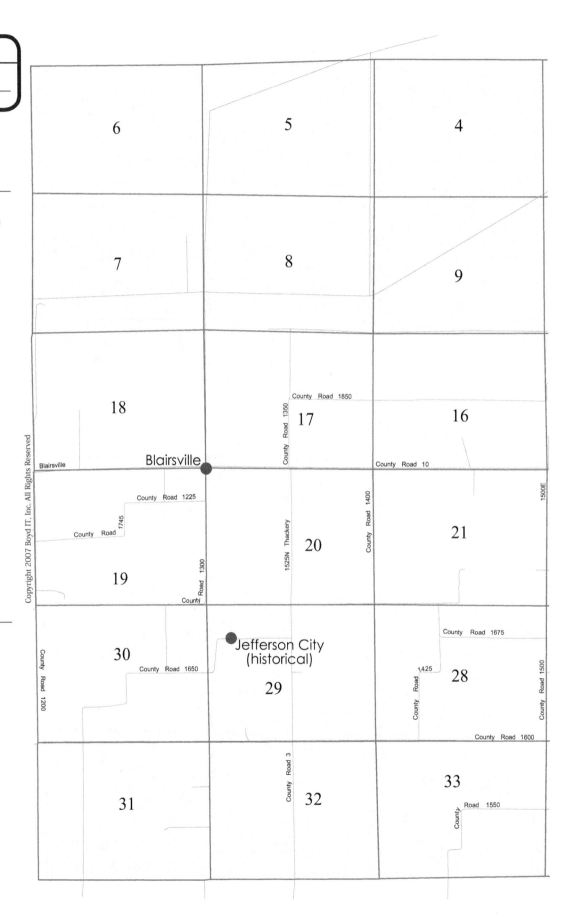

3

2

1

Raders Branch

County Road 1915

11

County Road 1950

12

County Road 1750

County Road 1930

10

County Road 1900

County Road 1870

County Road 1860

Bungay

County Road 1875

15

14

13

County Road 151

County Road 1800

Blairsville

New London
(historical)

County Road 1700

County Road 1775

✝ Springer
Cem.

22

23

24

County
Road 1725

26

County Road 1650

27

25

County Road 1625

County Road
1610

County Road
1575

County Road

36

County Road 1

34

35

## Helpful Hints

1. This road map has a number of uses, but primarily it is to help you: a) find the present location of land owned by your ancestors (at least the general area), b) find cemeteries and city-centers, and c) estimate the route/roads used by Census-takers & tax-assessors.

2. If you plan to travel to Hamilton County to locate cemeteries or land parcels, please pick up a modern travel map for the area before you do. Mapping old land parcels on modern maps is not as exact a science as you might think. Just the slightest variations in public land survey coordinates, estimates of parcel boundaries, or road-map deviations can greatly alter a map's representation of how a road either does or doesn't cross a particular parcel of land.

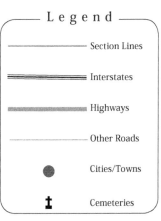

### L e g e n d

——————— Section Lines

═══════ Interstates

━━━━━━━ Highways

——————— Other Roads

● Cities/Towns

✝ Cemeteries

**Scale**: Section = 1 mile X 1 mile
(generally, with some exceptions)

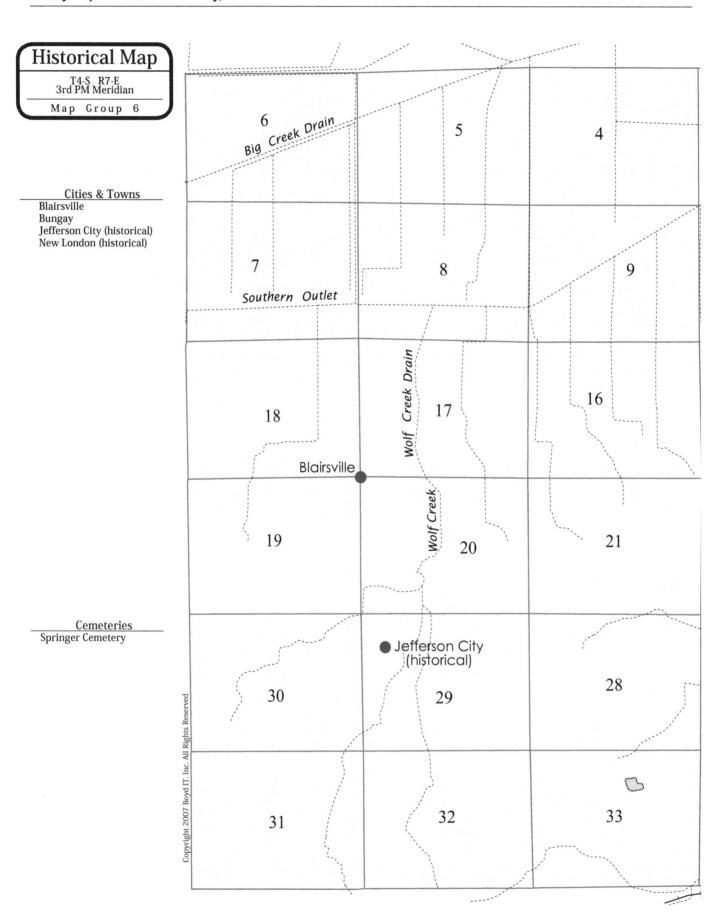

## Historical Map

T4-S R7-E
3rd PM Meridian

Map Group 6

### Cities & Towns
Blairsville
Bungay
Jefferson City (historical)
New London (historical)

### Cemeteries
Springer Cemetery

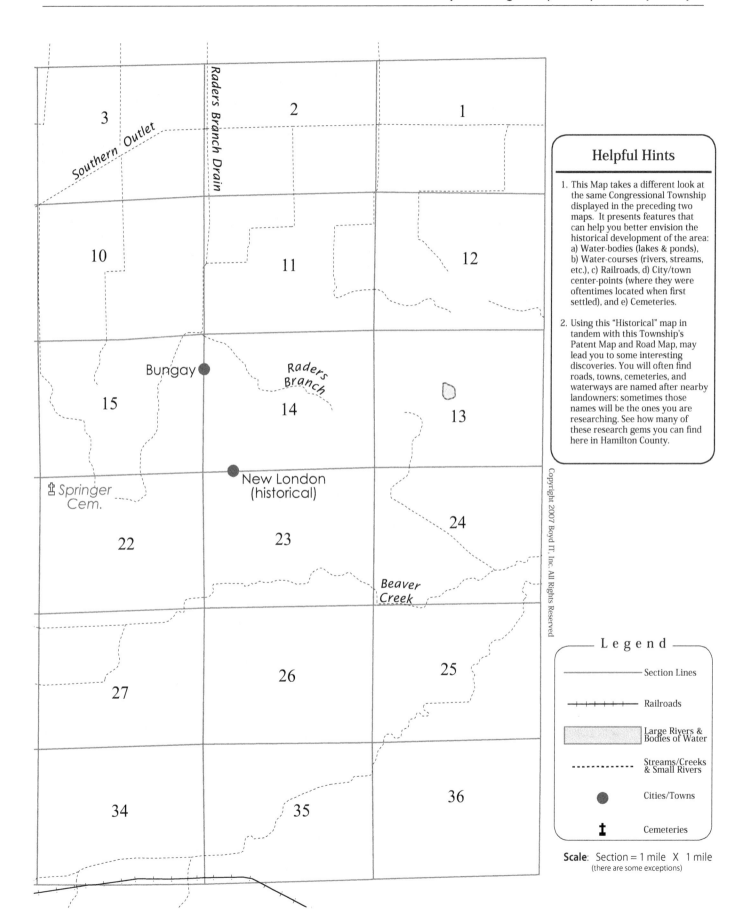

3

*Southern Outlet*

*Raders Branch Drain*

2

1

10

11

12

Bungay ●

*Raders Branch*

15

14

13

⚑ *Springer Cem.*

New London
(historical) ●

22

23

24

27

26

Beaver
Creek

25

34

35

36

## Helpful Hints

1. This Map takes a different look at the same Congressional Township displayed in the preceding two maps. It presents features that can help you better envision the historical development of the area: a) Water-bodies (lakes & ponds), b) Water-courses (rivers, streams, etc.), c) Railroads, d) City/town center-points (where they were oftentimes located when first settled), and e) Cemeteries.

2. Using this "Historical" map in tandem with this Township's Patent Map and Road Map, may lead you to some interesting discoveries. You will often find roads, towns, cemeteries, and waterways are named after nearby landowners: sometimes those names will be the ones you are researching. See how many of these research gems you can find here in Hamilton County.

### L e g e n d

| | |
|---|---|
| ——————— | Section Lines |
| ＋＋＋＋＋ | Railroads |
| ▭ | Large Rivers & Bodies of Water |
| - - - - - - - | Streams/Creeks & Small Rivers |
| ● | Cities/Towns |
| ⚑ | Cemeteries |

**Scale**: Section = 1 mile X 1 mile
(there are some exceptions)

## Map Group 7: Index to Land Patents

## Township 5-South Range 5-East (3rd PM)

After you locate an individual in this Index, take note of the Section and Section Part then proceed to the Land Patent map on the pages immediately following. You should have no difficulty locating the corresponding parcel of land.

The "For More Info" Column will lead you to more information about the underlying Patents. See the *Legend* at right, and the "How to Use this Book" chapter, for more information.

```
┌─────────────────────────────────────────────┐
│              LEGEND                          │
│       "For More Info . . . " column          │
│ ───────────────────────────────────────────  │
│ G = Group  (Multi-Patentee Patent, see       │
│            Appendix "C")                     │
│ R = Residence                                │
│ S = Social Status                            │
│                                              │
│ See Appendix A for list of abbreviations     │
│ used by the Illinois State Archives in       │
│ describing the place and nature of these     │
│ land patents.                                │
│                                              │
│ Note: if the Abbreviations contain "L", "BL",│
│ "LOT", or "BLOCK", the exact whereabouts of  │
│ the parcel within the section is not known.  │
└─────────────────────────────────────────────┘
```

| ID | Individual in Patent | Sec. | Sec. Part | Purchase Date | Sale Type | IL Aliquot Part | For More Info . . . |
|---|---|---|---|---|---|---|---|
| 1466 | ACORD, Martin | 28 | NWSE | 1853-03-07 | FD | NWSE | |
| 1465 | " " | 28 | NENW | 1853-11-11 | FD | NENW | R:HAMILTON |
| 1467 | " " | 28 | SWNE | 1855-08-16 | FD | SWNE | R:HAMILTON |
| 1268 | ADAIR, Demis | 5 | SESE | 1849-11-07 | FD | SESE | R:HAMILTON |
| 1521 | ADARE, Philip | 9 | SESW | 1837-10-24 | FD | SESW | R:HAMILTON |
| 1518 | " " | 16 | NWNW | 1838-08-04 | SC | NWNW | |
| 1519 | " " | 16 | SWNW | 1839-01-30 | SC | SWNW | |
| 1520 | " " | 17 | SESE | 1840-04-27 | FD | SESE | R:HAMILTON |
| 1232 | ALLEN, Calvin Young | 13 | NWNW | 1853-09-03 | FD | NWNW | |
| 1231 | " " | 12 | SWSW | 1853-09-03 | FD | SWSW | |
| 1436 | ALLEN, Joseph | 24 | NWNE | 1852-07-27 | FD | NWNE | |
| 1447 | ALLEN, Josiah | 13 | SWNE | 1837-04-13 | FD | SWNE | R:HAMILTON |
| 1378 | ALLEN, William B | 24 | NENW | 1848-09-29 | FD | NENW | G:2 |
| 1376 | " " | 13 | SESW | 1848-09-29 | FD | SESW | G:2 |
| 1377 | " " | 13 | W½SW | 1848-09-29 | FD | W2SW | G:2 |
| 1602 | ALLEN, William Bright | 13 | NESW | 1851-01-02 | FD | NESW | R:HAMILTON |
| 1221 | ATCHISON, Barton | 9 | W½NW | 1830-10-28 | FD | W2NW | R:JEFFERSON |
| 1240 | ATCHISON, Charles | 9 | NWSW | 1848-12-19 | FD | NWSW | |
| 1237 | " " | 9 | E½NW | 1848-12-19 | FD | E2NW | |
| 1241 | " " | 9 | SWNE | 1848-12-19 | FD | SWNE | |
| 1445 | " " | 9 | NWSW | 1848-12-19 | FD | NWSW | |
| 1238 | " " | 9 | E½NW | 1848-12-19 | FD | E2NW | |
| 1242 | " " | 9 | SWNE | 1848-12-19 | FD | SWNE | |
| 1237 | " " | 9 | E½NW | 1849-03-13 | FD | E2NW | |
| 1238 | " " | 9 | E½NW | 1849-03-13 | FD | E2NW | |
| 1239 | " " | 9 | NWSE | 1849-03-13 | FD | NWSE | |
| 1241 | " " | 9 | SWNE | 1849-03-13 | FD | SWNE | |
| 1242 | " " | 9 | SWNE | 1849-03-13 | FD | SWNE | |
| 1445 | ATCHISON, Joseph T | 9 | NWSW | 1849-03-13 | FD | NWSW | R:HAMILTON |
| 1240 | " " | 9 | NWSW | 1849-03-13 | FD | NWSW | R:HAMILTON |
| 1243 | ATCHISSON, Charles | 16 | L3 | 1851-02-12 | SC | L3NENW | |
| 1244 | BARNETT, Charles C | 10 | E½SE | 1853-11-23 | FD | E2SE | |
| 1245 | " " | 11 | W½SW | 1853-11-23 | FD | W2SW | |
| 1442 | BARRETT, John | 12 | SENW | 1853-12-07 | FD | SENW | R:MASSAC |
| 1393 | " " | 12 | SENW | 1853-12-07 | FD | SENW | R:MASSAC |
| 1566 | BELL, Thomas | 5 | SESW | 1836-11-03 | FD | SESW | R:HAMILTON |
| 1288 | BENBROOK, Ezekiel G | 33 | NESE | 1853-08-27 | FD | NESE | R:HAMILTON |
| 1213 | BOSTER, Andrew J | 18 | NWSW | 1853-11-21 | FD | NWSW | R:HAMILTON |
| 1214 | " " | 18 | SENW | 1853-12-15 | FD | SENW | R:HAMILTON |
| 1212 | " " | 17 | S½SW | 1854-10-04 | FD | S2SW | R:HAMILTON |
| 1261 | BOSTER, Daniel | 7 | E½SW | 1839-12-06 | FD | E2SW | R:HAMILTON |
| 1449 | BOSTER, George | 5 | SWSE | 1840-04-08 | FD | SWSE | R:HAMILTON |
| 1289 | " " | 5 | SWSE | 1840-04-08 | FD | SWSE | R:HAMILTON |
| 1290 | " " | 7 | E½NE | 1850-12-06 | FD | E2NE | |
| 1291 | " " | 8 | W½NW | 1850-12-06 | FD | W2NW | |
| 1256 | BOWEN, Columbus | 15 | N½NE | 1853-11-28 | FD | N2NE | R:OHIO |

| ID | Individual in Patent | Sec. | Sec. Part | Purchase Date | Sale Type | IL Aliquot Part | For More Info . . . |
|----|---------------------|------|-----------|---------------|-----------|-----------------|---------------------|
| 1255 | BOWEN, Columbus (Cont'd) | 10 | W½SE | 1853-11-28 | FD | W2SE | R:OHIO |
| 1257 | " " | 15 | NWSW | 1854-05-22 | FD | NWSW | R:OHIO |
| 1258 | " " | 15 | SWNE | 1854-05-23 | FD | SWNE | R:OHIO |
| 1601 | BOYD, William | 24 | NWSE | 1841-10-01 | FD | NWSE | R:HAMILTON |
| 1600 | " " | 24 | NESE | 1850-04-24 | FD | NESE | R:HAMILTON |
| 1203 | BRADEN, Alfred | 36 | SWSE | 1852-12-03 | FD | SWSE | |
| 1459 | BROOKINS, Madison | 10 | S½NW | 1854-09-18 | FD | S2NW | R:JEFFERSON |
| 1632 | " " | 10 | SENW | 1854-09-18 | FD | SENW | R:JEFFERSON |
| 1437 | " " | 10 | SWNE | 1854-09-18 | FD | SWNE | R:JEFFERSON |
| 1458 | " " | 10 | N½NW | 1854-09-18 | FD | N2NW | R:JEFFERSON |
| 1460 | " " | 10 | SENW | 1854-09-18 | FD | SENW | R:JEFFERSON |
| 1461 | " " | 10 | SWNE | 1854-09-18 | FD | SWNE | R:JEFFERSON |
| 1462 | " " | 3 | W½SW | 1854-09-18 | FD | W2SW | R:JEFFERSON |
| 1344 | BROOKS, Isaac | 14 | E½SW | 1853-12-03 | FD | E2SW | R:HAMILTON |
| 1394 | BROOKS, John | 14 | W½SW | 1853-01-25 | FD | W2SW | R:HAMILTON |
| 1360 | BRYANT, James H | 28 | SWSE | 1851-09-01 | FD | SWSE | R:HAMILTON |
| 1477 | BRYANT, Mary C | 27 | SWSW | 1853-04-13 | FD | SWSW | S:F |
| 1606 | BRYANT, William | 27 | W½NW | 1852-07-27 | FD | W2NW | |
| 1605 | " " | 27 | NWSW | 1852-07-27 | FD | NWSW | |
| 1603 | " " | 22 | SWSW | 1852-07-27 | FD | SWSW | |
| 1604 | " " | 27 | NENW | 1853-07-18 | FD | NENW | |
| 1388 | " " | 27 | NENW | 1853-07-18 | FD | NENW | |
| 1448 | BURGESS, Josiah | 25 | NENW | 1851-11-14 | FD | NENW | |
| 1317 | BURTON, Henry | 32 | NENW | 1851-11-14 | FD | NENW | |
| 1358 | BURTON, James | 16 | L10 | 1854-01-24 | SC | LOT10NWSE | |
| 1395 | BURTON, John | 36 | SWSW | 1836-06-16 | FD | SWSW | R:HAMILTON |
| 1609 | BURTON, William | 23 | NENE | 1853-01-24 | FD | NENE | R:HAMILTON |
| 1608 | " " | 16 | L9 | 1854-01-24 | SC | LOT9NESE | |
| 1607 | " " | 16 | L16 | 1854-01-24 | SC | LOT16SESE | |
| 1359 | CALVIN, James | 33 | SWSW | 1851-09-08 | FD | SWSW | R:HAMILTON |
| 1514 | CAMPBELL, Patrick | 11 | NWSE | 1854-06-30 | FD | NWSE | R:HAMILTON |
| 1592 | CAMPBELL, Wallace A | 18 | NESE | 1583-12-28 | FD | NESE | R:HAMILTON |
| 1587 | " " | 17 | NWNE | 1583-12-28 | FD | NWNE | R:HAMILTON |
| 1597 | " " | 8 | SWSE | 1583-12-28 | FD | SWSE | R:HAMILTON |
| 1586 | " " | 17 | N½SE | 1851-09-09 | FD | N2SE | |
| 1590 | " " | 17 | SWSE | 1851-09-09 | FD | SWSE | R:HAMILTON |
| 1585 | " " | 17 | E½NE | 1851-09-09 | FD | E2NE | |
| 1589 | " " | 17 | SWNW | 1854-01-14 | FD | SWNW | R:HAMILTON |
| 1588 | " " | 17 | SWNE | 1854-02-15 | FD | SWNE | R:HAMILTON |
| 1595 | " " | 18 | SWSW | 1854-10-02 | FD | SWSW | R:HAMILTON |
| 1593 | " " | 18 | NWSE | 1854-10-02 | FD | NWSE | R:HAMILTON |
| 1591 | " " | 18 | E½SW | 1854-10-02 | FD | E2SW | R:HAMILTON |
| 1594 | " " | 18 | SENE | 1854-10-04 | FD | SENE | R:HAMILTON |
| 1596 | " " | 20 | NWNE | 1855-03-29 | FD | NWNE | R:HAMILTON |
| 1611 | CAMPBELL, William | 34 | E½SW | 1851-04-18 | FD | E2SW | |
| 1612 | " " | 34 | SESW | 1851-04-18 | FD | SESW | |
| 1259 | CARLTON, Cornelius | 17 | E½NW | 1853-12-05 | FD | E2NW | R:HAMILTON |
| 1260 | " " | 17 | NWNW | 1854-10-02 | FD | NWNW | R:HAMILTON |
| 1248 | CARPENTER, Chester | 3 | NWSW | 1858-01-08 | FD | NWSW | |
| 1265 | CARR, Daniel W | 24 | NWSW | 1853-03-12 | FD | NWSW | |
| 1621 | CARR, William H | 14 | N½NE | 1852-10-26 | FD | N2NE | |
| 1620 | " " | 13 | NWSE | 1853-03-21 | FD | NWSE | R:HAMILTON |
| 1629 | CHOISSER, William Jr | 29 | NWSE | 1854-10-09 | FD | NWSE | R:HAMILTON |
| 1628 | " " | 29 | NESW | 1854-10-09 | FD | NESW | R:HAMILTON |
| 1200 | " " | 29 | E½NW | 1854-10-09 | FD | E2NW | R:HAMILTON |
| 1202 | " " | 29 | NWSE | 1854-10-09 | FD | NWSE | R:HAMILTON |
| 1201 | " " | 29 | NESW | 1854-10-09 | FD | NESW | R:HAMILTON |
| 1627 | " " | 29 | E½NW | 1854-10-09 | FD | E2NW | R:HAMILTON |
| 1353 | CLARK, Jacksen | 4 | SWNW | 1855-03-29 | FD | SWNW | R:WILLIAMSON |
| 1354 | CLARK, Jacob Scott | 18 | W½NW | 1844-09-03 | FD | W2NW | |
| 1384 | CLARK, John A | 25 | NWNW | 1852-12-02 | FD | NWNW | |
| 1385 | " " | 35 | NENW | 1853-09-05 | FD | NENW | |
| 1193 | COKER, Abram B | 11 | SESW | 1853-12-03 | FD | SESW | R:HAMILTON |
| 1194 | " " | 11 | SWSE | 1853-12-03 | FD | SWSE | R:HAMILTON |
| 1233 | COKER, Catharine | 1 | NWSW | 1852-08-31 | FD | NWSW | S:F |
| 1234 | " " | 1 | SWNW | 1852-08-31 | FD | SWNW | S:F |
| 1235 | " " | 2 | NESE | 1852-08-31 | FD | NESE | S:F |
| 1236 | " " | 2 | SENE | 1852-08-31 | FD | SENE | S:F |
| 1442 | COKER, Joseph | 12 | SENW | 1851-03-14 | FD | SENW | |
| 1441 | " " | 12 | N½SW | 1851-03-14 | FD | N2SW | |
| 1393 | " " | 12 | SENW | 1851-03-14 | FD | SENW | |
| 1443 | " " | 12 | SWNE | 1851-03-14 | FD | SWNE | |
| 1440 | " " | 1 | SEN½ | 1851-04-23 | FD | S2NE | |

| ID | Individual in Patent | Sec. | Sec. Part | Purchase Date | Sale Type | IL Aliquot Part | For More Info . . . |
|---|---|---|---|---|---|---|---|
| 1613 | COKER, William | 2 | N½NE | 1852-12-02 | FD | N2NE | |
| 1614 | "           " | 2 | NWSE | 1853-12-29 | FD | NWSE | R:HAMILTON |
| 1626 | COLVERT, William J | 32 | NWNW | 1852-02-09 | FD | NWNW | |
| 1292 | CONNETT, George | 4 | NWNW | 1854-04-13 | FD | NWNW | R:HAMILTON |
| 1318 | CRUME, Henry | 8 | NENE | 1836-06-06 | FD | NENE | R:HAMILTON |
| 1273 | CUMPTON, Eisha | 29 | SESE | 1853-08-27 | FD | SESE | R:HAMILTON |
| 1276 | CUMPTON, Elisha | 29 | SWSE | 1855-08-15 | FD | SWSE | R:HAMILTON |
| 1584 | DAILEY, Vincent | 12 | SENE | 1851-03-19 | FD | SENE | R:HAMILTON |
| 1262 | DALE, Daniel | 24 | SENE | 1850-04-30 | FD | SENE | R:HAMILTON |
| 1280 | DAVIS, Elizabeth | 3 | SWSW | 1849-11-10 | FD | SWSW | S:F G:14 |
| 1278 | "           " | 3 | E½SW | 1849-11-10 | FD | E2SW | S:F G:14 |
| 1279 | "           " | 3 | SWSE | 1849-11-10 | FD | SWSE | S:F G:14 |
| 1279 | DAVIS, Joseph | 3 | SWSE | 1849-11-10 | FD | SWSE | S:F G:14 |
| 1280 | "           " | 3 | SWSW | 1849-11-10 | FD | SWSW | S:F G:14 |
| 1278 | "           " | 3 | E½SW | 1849-11-10 | FD | E2SW | S:F G:14 |
| 1494 | DAVIS, Nehemiah | 6 | E½SW | 1838-07-03 | FD | E2SWNT | R:OHIO |
| 1495 | "           " | 7 | | 1838-07-03 | FD | W2SWNT | R:OHIO |
| 1495 | "           " | 7 | | 1838-07-03 | FD | W2NWNT | R:OHIO |
| 1493 | "           " | 6 | | 1838-07-03 | FD | W2SENT | R:OHIO |
| 1544 | DAVIS, Rueben | 7 | SENW | 1853-08-13 | FD | SENW | R:HAMILTON |
| 1468 | DAWSEN, Martin S | 9 | SWSW | 1854-10-09 | FD | SWSW | R:HAMILTON |
| 1598 | "           " | 9 | SWSW | 1854-10-09 | FD | SWSW | R:HAMILTON |
| 1532 | DEWITT, Richard | 9 | NESW | 1843-12-01 | FD | NESW | |
| 1567 | DEWITT, Thomas J | 8 | SEN½ | 1840-11-30 | FD | S2NE | R:HAMILTON |
| 1269 | DILL, Dorcas | 34 | W½SE | 1851-11-14 | FD | W2SE | S:F |
| 1382 | DITSON, Jesse | 23 | E½NW | 1818-06-24 | FD | E2NW | R:WHITE |
| 1381 | "           " | 23 | E½NE | 1818-07-08 | FD | E2NE | R:WHITE |
| 1491 | "           " | 23 | W½NW | 1818-07-17 | FD | W2NW | R:WHITE |
| 1383 | "           " | 23 | W½NW | 1818-07-17 | FD | W2NW | R:WHITE |
| 1583 | DIXON, Tilmon | 16 | L2 | 1854-03-20 | SC | LOT2NWNE | |
| 1399 | DRAKE, John | 32 | SESE | 1854-10-27 | FD | SESE | R:HAMILTON |
| 1616 | EMMERSON, William | 3 | N½NE | 1854-09-22 | FD | N2NE | R:HAMILTON |
| 1618 | "           " | 3 | S½SE | 1854-09-22 | FD | S2SE | R:HAMILTON |
| 1617 | "           " | 3 | NENW | 1854-09-22 | FD | NENW | R:HAMILTON |
| 1246 | EPPERSON, Charles | 2 | NENW | 1852-12-22 | FD | NENW | |
| 1346 | FAN, Isaac | 23 | SWNE | 1851-01-04 | FD | SWNE | R:HAMILTON |
| 1345 | "           " | 16 | L14 | 1854-03-27 | SC | LOT14SESW | |
| 1522 | FAN, Philip | 16 | L15 | 1854-03-27 | SC | LOT15SWSE | |
| 1332 | FANN, Hiram | 24 | SENW | 1853-08-02 | FD | SENW | |
| 1523 | FANN, Philip | 23 | NENW | 1852-08-21 | FD | NENW | |
| 1524 | "           " | 23 | NWNE | 1852-08-21 | FD | NWNE | |
| 1525 | "           " | 25 | SWNE | 1853-02-05 | FD | SWNE | |
| 1456 | FARMER, Litteberry | 2 | W½SW | 1851-08-20 | FD | W2SW | |
| 1619 | FELLOWES, William | 26 | SEN½ | 1838-06-01 | FD | S2NE | R:KENTUCKY |
| 1401 | FLINT, John | 35 | NESE | 1836-08-10 | FD | NESE | R:HAMILTON |
| 1402 | "           " | 36 | N½SW | 1852-12-27 | FD | N2SW | |
| 1222 | FORESTER, Benjamin | 20 | S½SE | 1853-08-20 | FD | S2SE | |
| 1223 | "           " | 29 | N½NE | 1853-08-20 | FD | N2NE | |
| 1263 | FOSTER, Daniel | 25 | NWSE | 1853-04-18 | FD | NWSE | |
| 1274 | FOSTER, Elijah | 16 | L6 | 1854-03-27 | SC | LOT6SENW | |
| 1348 | FOSTER, Isaac | 5 | SWSW | 1839-08-21 | FD | SWSW | R:FRANKLIN G:15 |
| 1347 | "           " | 6 | SESE | 1839-10-14 | FD | SESE | R:HAMILTON |
| 1301 | FRAZIER, George W A | 28 | SENE | 1853-04-11 | FD | SENE | |
| 1298 | "           " | 21 | SESW | 1853-11-11 | FD | SESW | R:HAMILTON |
| 1300 | "           " | 28 | NWNE | 1854-03-25 | FD | NWNE | R:HAMILTON |
| 1299 | "           " | 28 | NENE | 1854-09-26 | FD | NENE | R:HAMILTON |
| 1307 | FRAZIER, George W S | 28 | NESE | 1853-04-11 | FD | NESE | |
| 1217 | FUEL, Anna | 8 | NESE | 1854-10-23 | FD | NESE | R:HAMILTON S:F |
| 1496 | GAINES, Newcomb | 5 | NWNE | 1839-04-29 | FD | NWNE | R:HAMILTON |
| 1386 | GARVIN, John B | 22 | E½NE | 1830-10-19 | FD | E2NE | R:HAMILTON |
| 1396 | GARVIN, John Bush | 26 | W½NW | 1831-11-30 | FD | W2NW | R:HAMILTON |
| 1351 | GIBBS, Isaac P | 7 | SWSE | 1853-09-12 | FD | SWSE | R:HAMILTON |
| 1350 | "           " | 18 | NENW | 1853-11-21 | FD | NENW | R:HAMILTON |
| 1406 | GIBBS, John | 8 | NWSW | 1839-12-26 | FD | NWSW | R:HAMILTON |
| 1405 | "           " | 8 | NESW | 1841-06-24 | FD | NESW | R:HAMILTON |
| 1404 | "           " | 7 | E½SE | 1848-10-16 | FD | E2SE | |
| 1403 | "           " | 18 | N½NE | 1848-10-16 | FD | N2NE | |
| 1407 | "           " | 8 | SENW | 1853-05-30 | FD | SENW | |
| 1498 | GIBBS, Nicholas | 8 | NWSE | 1841-06-24 | FD | NWSE | R:HAMILTON |
| 1254 | GILLAHAN, Clemons | 24 | SESW | 1851-11-14 | FD | SESW | |
| 1397 | GORE, John C | 14 | SW | 1817-12-29 | FD | SW | R:WHITE |
| 1497 | GRAVES, Newcomb | 5 | NENE | 1849-10-24 | FD | NENE | R:HAMILTON |
| 1535 | GREEN, Richmond | 13 | E½NW | 1851-03-25 | FD | E2NW | |

| ID | Individual in Patent | Sec. | Sec. Part | Purchase Date | Sale Type | IL Aliquot Part | For More Info . . . |
|---|---|---|---|---|---|---|---|
| 1536 | GREEN, Richmond (Cont'd) | 13 | NWNE | 1851-03-25 | FD | NWNE | |
| 1534 | " " | 12 | SESW | 1851-03-25 | FD | SESW | |
| 1270 | GRIFFIN, Edam | 34 | NWSW | 1583-08-27 | FD | NWSW | R:HAMILTON |
| 1271 | " " | 34 | SWNW | 1583-08-27 | FD | SWNW | R:HAMILTON |
| 1195 | GUNTER, Alexander J | 14 | SEN½ | 1852-09-24 | FD | S2NE | |
| 1408 | HALL, John | 26 | SWSE | 1836-05-12 | FD | SWSE | R:HAMILTON |
| 1411 | " " | 35 | NENE | 1836-05-12 | FD | NENE | R:HAMILTON |
| 1409 | " " | 32 | E½SW | 1851-08-21 | FD | E2SW | |
| 1410 | " " | 32 | SENW | 1851-08-21 | FD | SENW | |
| 1400 | HALL, John F | 33 | SESE | 1853-10-29 | FD | SESE | R:HAMILTON |
| 1483 | HALL, Nancy | 36 | NWNW | 1853-02-03 | FD | NWNW | S:F |
| 1529 | HALL, Price | 36 | SWNW | 1853-06-11 | FD | SWNW | R:WILLIAMSON |
| 1357 | HAMILTON, James B | 32 | W½SE | 1854-09-20 | FD | W2SE | R:HAMILTON |
| 1488 | HAMILTON, Nathaniel | 33 | SWSE | 1853-05-05 | FD | SWSE | R:HAMILTON |
| 1623 | HAMONTREE, William | 12 | NWNE | 1852-08-12 | FD | NWNE | |
| 1622 | " " | 12 | NENW | 1852-08-12 | FD | NENW | |
| 1412 | HARDESTY, John | 35 | NE | 1818-03-23 | FD | NE | R:WHITE |
| 1565 | HARDY, Thomas Allen | 35 | SENE | 1836-10-24 | FD | SENE | R:HAMILTON |
| 1434 | HARMISON, Jonathan | 22 | NESE | 1836-05-30 | FD | NESE | R:HAMILTON |
| 1489 | HARMISON, Nathaniel | 22 | W½NE | 1830-10-20 | FD | W2NE | R:FRANKLIN |
| 1383 | " " | 23 | W½NW | 1831-11-14 | FD | W2NW | R:HAMILTON |
| 1491 | " " | 23 | W½NW | 1831-11-14 | FD | W2NW | R:HAMILTON |
| 1492 | " " | 26 | NESW | 1836-08-10 | FD | NESW | R:HAMILTON |
| 1490 | " " | 23 | NWSW | 1836-08-10 | FD | NWSW | R:HAMILTON |
| 1281 | HARPER, Ellis B | 1 | NW | 1854-10-26 | FD | NW | R:POPE S:F |
| 1282 | " " | 2 | E½NE | 1854-10-26 | FD | E2NE | R:POPE S:F |
| 1295 | HARPER, George | 24 | NESW | 1851-03-25 | FD | NESW | R:HAMILTON |
| 1294 | " " | 23 | NWSE | 1851-04-26 | FD | NWSE | R:HAMILTON |
| 1296 | " " | 24 | SESE | 1853-03-02 | FD | SESE | R:HAMILTON |
| 1303 | HARPER, George W | 25 | NWNE | 1851-03-25 | FD | NWNE | R:HAMILTON |
| 1302 | " " | 24 | SWSE | 1851-03-25 | FD | SWSE | R:HAMILTON |
| 1361 | HARPER, James M | 13 | SWNW | 1853-12-16 | FD | SWNW | R:HAMILTON |
| 1463 | HARPER, Mark | 25 | NESE | 1852-08-18 | FD | NESE | |
| 1224 | HARRAILSON, Benjamin | 33 | E½SW | 1849-08-20 | FD | E2SW | |
| 1225 | " " | 33 | NWSE | 1849-08-20 | FD | NWSE | |
| 1308 | HARRELSON, Gideo N | 33 | NENE | 1856-07-31 | FD | NENE | R:HAMILTON |
| 1309 | " " | 33 | NENE | 1856-07-31 | FD | NENE | R:HAMILTON |
| 1309 | HARRELSON, Gideon | 33 | NENE | 1853-02-22 | FD | NENE | |
| 1308 | " " | 33 | NENE | 1853-02-22 | FD | NENE | |
| 1310 | " " | 34 | NWNW | 1853-11-01 | FD | NWNW | R:HAMILTON |
| 1226 | HARRISON, Benjamin | 33 | NWSW | 1849-08-20 | FD | NWSW | |
| 1311 | HARRISON, Gideon | 28 | SESE | 1853-04-07 | FD | SESE | R:HAMILTON |
| 1453 | HARWOOD, Leroy B | 4 | NENW | 1854-06-06 | FD | NENW | R:HAMILTON |
| 1598 | HAWKES, Walter S | 9 | SWSW | 1856-10-25 | FD | SWSW | |
| 1468 | " " | 9 | SWSW | 1856-10-25 | FD | SWSW | |
| 1349 | HILL, Isaac | 20 | E½NE | 1819-08-17 | FD | E2NE | R:WHITE |
| 1533 | " " | 20 | E½NE | 1819-08-17 | FD | E2NE | R:WHITE |
| 1349 | HILL, Richard | 20 | E½NE | 1837-03-07 | FD | E2NE | R:HAMILTON |
| 1533 | " " | 20 | E½NE | 1837-03-07 | FD | E2NE | R:HAMILTON |
| 1413 | HINDMAN, John | 20 | NESE | 1853-10-22 | FD | NESE | R:HAMILTON |
| 1414 | " " | 21 | NWSW | 1854-05-22 | FD | NWSW | R:HAMILTON |
| 1335 | HODGES, Hiram | 5 | W½NW | 1820-02-14 | FD | W2NW | R:WHITE |
| 1229 | HOLLAND, Berryman | 2 | SENW | 1853-09-19 | FD | SENW | |
| 1230 | " " | 2 | W½NW | 1853-09-19 | FD | W2NW | |
| 1228 | " " | 2 | NESW | 1853-09-19 | FD | NESW | |
| 1415 | HUFFSTATLAR, John | 14 | SWNW | 1852-09-09 | FD | SWNW | |
| 1247 | HUNGATE, Charles | 26 | SENW | 1836-06-11 | FD | SENW | R:HAMILTON |
| 1297 | HUNGATE, Christopher | 22 | SWNW | 1853-10-17 | FD | SWNW | R:HAMILTON |
| 1250 | " " | 22 | SWNW | 1853-10-17 | FD | SWNW | R:HAMILTON |
| 1249 | " " | 22 | NWNW | 1853-10-25 | FD | NWNW | R:HAMILTON |
| 1444 | HUNGATE, Joseph | 26 | SE | 1818-10-01 | FD | SE | R:KENTUCKY |
| 1624 | HUNGATE, William | 15 | SE | 1816-11-16 | FD | SE | R:WHITE |
| 1625 | " " | 23 | E½SW | 1818-07-23 | FD | E2SW | R:WHITE |
| 1305 | HUNT, George W | 36 | W½NE | 1853-01-27 | FD | W2NE | |
| 1219 | " " | 36 | SENW | 1854-10-13 | FD | SENW | R:HAMILTON |
| 1304 | " " | 36 | SENW | 1854-10-13 | FD | SENW | R:HAMILTON |
| 1478 | HUNT, Mary | 36 | NENW | 1853-05-05 | FD | NENW | R:HAMILTON S:F |
| 1191 | IRVIN, Abraham | 5 | NWSW | 1836-09-26 | FD | NWSW | R:HAMILTON |
| 1190 | " " | 5 | NENW | 1836-11-03 | FD | NENW | R:HAMILTON |
| 1192 | " " | 6 | E½SE | 1838-02-08 | FD | E2SE | R:HAMILTON |
| 1321 | IRVIN, Henry H | 15 | W½NW | 1830-05-12 | FD | W2NW | R:HAMILTON |
| 1320 | " " | 15 | SWSW | 1853-04-26 | FD | SWSW | R:HAMILTON |
| 1322 | " " | 16 | L8 | 1853-10-27 | SC | LOT8SENE | |

| ID | Individual in Patent | Sec. | Sec. Part | Purchase Date | Sale Type | IL Aliquot Part | For More Info . . . |
|---|---|---|---|---|---|---|---|
| 1319 | IRVIN, Henry H (Cont'd) | 15 | NENW | 1853-11-14 | FD | NENW | R:HAMILTON |
| 1323 | " " | 16 | L7 | 1854-02-04 | SC | LOT7SENE | |
| 1325 | " " | 9 | SW | 1854-10-03 | FD | SW | R:HAMILTON |
| 1324 | " " | 9 | NESE | 1854-10-03 | FD | NESE | R:HAMILTON |
| 1326 | IRVIN, Henry Howel | 15 | SENW | 1836-11-03 | FD | SENW | R:HAMILTON |
| 1327 | " " | 5 | SENW | 1838-01-02 | FD | SENW | R:HAMILTON |
| 1331 | IRVIN, Henry Wells | 4 | S½SW | 1842-08-03 | FD | S2SW | R:HAMILTON |
| 1449 | IRVIN, Julia | 5 | SWSE | 1840-02-01 | FD | SWSE | R:HAMILTON S:F |
| 1289 | " " | 5 | SWSE | 1840-02-01 | FD | SWSE | R:HAMILTON S:F |
| 1545 | IRVIN, Runyon | 6 | NWNE | 1836-11-03 | FD | NWNE | R:HAMILTON |
| 1546 | " " | 6 | NWNW | 1838-02-08 | FD | NWNW | R:HAMILTON |
| 1547 | " " | 6 | SWNE | 1838-06-25 | FD | SWNE | R:HAMILTON |
| 1548 | " " | 6 | SWNW | 1840-02-01 | FD | SWNW | R:HAMILTON |
| 1549 | IRVINE, Runyon | 6 | E½NW | 1829-08-21 | FD | E2NW | R:HAMILTON |
| 1328 | IRWIN, Henry | 16 | NENE | 1838-08-04 | SC | NENE | |
| 1428 | JACK, John O | 29 | S½NE | 1854-01-14 | FD | S2NEVOID | |
| 1427 | " " | 28 | W½NW | 1854-01-14 | FD | W2NWVOID | |
| 1426 | " " | 28 | W½NW | 1854-01-14 | FD | W2NWVOID | |
| 1426 | " " | 28 | W½NW | 1855-06-01 | FD | W2NW | |
| 1427 | " " | 28 | W½NW | 1855-06-01 | FD | W2NW | |
| 1429 | " " | 29 | SEN½ | 1855-06-01 | FD | S2NE | |
| 1485 | JANEY, Nathan | 23 | W½SW | 1818-08-10 | FD | W2SW | R:WHITE |
| 1484 | " " | 22 | SE | 1818-08-10 | FD | SE | R:WHITE |
| 1538 | JANSON, Robert Henry | 31 | NENW | 1847-06-28 | FD | NENW | R:HAMILTON |
| 1286 | JOHNSEN, Enoch S | 19 | S½SW | 1854-10-04 | FD | S2SW | R:HAMILTON |
| 1287 | " " | 30 | N½NW | 1854-10-04 | FD | N2NW | R:HAMILTON |
| 1252 | JOHNSON, Christopher | 30 | SENW | 1853-12-15 | FD | SENW | R:HAMILTON |
| 1251 | " " | 30 | NESW | 1854-10-10 | FD | NESW | R:HAMILTON |
| 1334 | JOHNSON, Hiram G | 31 | SWSW | 1853-11-14 | FD | SWSW | R:HAMILTON |
| 1333 | " " | 31 | NWSW | 1854-03-01 | FD | NWSW | R:HAMILTON |
| 1416 | JOHNSON, John K | 32 | SWSW | 1854-09-26 | FD | SWSW | R:HAMILTON |
| 1417 | JOHNSON, John Kent | 31 | SESW | 1851-05-02 | FD | SESW | R:HAMILTON |
| 1435 | JOHNSON, Jonathan | 13 | SENE | 1854-09-18 | FD | SENE | R:SALINE |
| 1537 | JOHNSON, Robert H | 30 | SWSW | 1583-12-27 | FD | SWSW | R:HAMILTON |
| 1542 | JOHNSON, Robert Henry | 31 | W½NW | 1851-02-25 | FD | W2NW | |
| 1541 | " " | 31 | SENW | 1851-02-25 | FD | SENW | |
| 1540 | " " | 31 | NESW | 1851-02-25 | FD | NESW | |
| 1539 | " " | 30 | SESW | 1853-04-21 | FD | SESW | R:HAMILTON |
| 1509 | JOHNSON, Zopher | 30 | NWSW | 1853-12-15 | FD | NWSW | R:HAMILTON |
| 1681 | " " | 30 | NWSW | 1853-12-15 | FD | NWSW | R:HAMILTON |
| 1682 | " " | 30 | SWNW | 1853-12-15 | FD | SWNW | R:HAMILTON |
| 1507 | KELLEY, Oliver P | 31 | NWNE | 1853-12-12 | FD | NWNE | R:HAMILTON |
| 1508 | " " | 31 | SEN½ | 1854-03-11 | FD | S2NE | R:HAMILTON |
| 1510 | KELLY, Oliver P | 30 | W½SE | 1854-09-18 | FD | W2SE | R:HAMILTON |
| 1511 | " " | 31 | NWSE | 1854-09-18 | FD | NWSE | R:HAMILTON |
| 1681 | " " | 30 | NWSW | 1854-09-18 | FD | NWSW | R:HAMILTON |
| 1509 | " " | 30 | NWSW | 1854-09-18 | FD | NWSW | R:HAMILTON |
| 1512 | " " | 32 | SWNW | 1854-09-18 | FD | SWNW | R:HAMILTON |
| 1631 | LACK, William | 25 | S½NW | 1851-11-14 | FD | S2NW | |
| 1336 | LAMBERT, Hiram | 28 | SENW | 1854-06-16 | FD | SENW | R:HAMILTON |
| 1316 | LAMBUD, Henderson | 4 | NESW | 1853-12-20 | FD | NESW | R:HAMILTON |
| 1421 | LANGLEY, John | 3 | SESE | 1844-09-24 | FD | SESE | R:HAMILTON |
| 1550 | LANGLEY, Sally | 10 | NENE | 1851-04-23 | FD | NENE | R:HAMILTON S:F |
| 1571 | LASLEY, Thomas P | 11 | W½NW | 1853-12-03 | FD | W2NW | R:HAMILTON |
| 1364 | LEE, James M | 35 | SWNW | 1854-09-23 | FD | SWNW | R:HAMILTON |
| 1672 | " " | 34 | NENE | 1854-09-23 | FD | NENE | R:HAMILTON |
| 1363 | " " | 34 | NESE | 1854-09-23 | FD | NESE | R:HAMILTON |
| 1362 | " " | 34 | NENE | 1854-09-23 | FD | NENE | R:HAMILTON |
| 1531 | LEE, Rebecca | 34 | NWNE | 1854-11-02 | FD | NWNE | R:HAMILTON S:F |
| 1572 | LESLEY, Thomas P | 1 | SESW | 1853-01-15 | FD | SESW | |
| 1387 | LOCKWOOD, John B | 23 | SWSE | 1850-02-27 | FD | SWSE | R:HAMILTON |
| 1392 | " " | 27 | SENW | 1854-09-18 | FD | SENW | R:HAMILTON |
| 1388 | " " | 27 | NENW | 1854-09-18 | FD | NENW | R:HAMILTON |
| 1389 | " " | 27 | NWNE | 1854-09-18 | FD | NWNE | R:HAMILTON |
| 1391 | " " | 27 | SEN½ | 1854-09-18 | FD | S2NE | R:HAMILTON |
| 1604 | " " | 27 | NENW | 1854-09-18 | FD | NENW | R:HAMILTON |
| 1390 | " " | 27 | NWSE | 1854-09-18 | FD | NWSE | R:HAMILTON |
| 1552 | LOCKWOOD, Samuel D | 26 | NESE | 1836-08-10 | FD | NESE | R:HAMILTON |
| 1551 | " " | 26 | NENW | 1837-05-08 | FD | NENW | R:HAMILTON |
| 1562 | LOCKWOOD, Susan M | 15 | SENE | 1837-07-18 | FD | SENE | R:HAMILTON S:F |
| 1576 | LOGSDEN, Thomas R | 19 | SWNE | 1854-09-29 | FD | SWNE | R:GALLATIN |
| 1573 | " " | 19 | E½NE | 1854-09-29 | FD | E2NE | R:GALLATIN |
| 1575 | " " | 19 | S½NW | 1854-09-29 | FD | S2NW | R:GALLATIN |

| ID | Individual in Patent | Sec. | Sec. Part | Purchase Date | Sale Type | IL Aliquot Part | For More Info . . . |
|---|---|---|---|---|---|---|---|
| 1574 | LOGSDEN, Thomas R (Cont'd) | 19 | N½SW | 1854-09-29 | FD | N2SW | R:GALLATIN |
| 1196 | LOWREY, Alexander | 4 | NWNE | 1854-03-07 | FD | NWNE | R:HAMILTON |
| 1197 | LOWRY, Alexander | 4 | SWNE | 1854-03-01 | FD | SWNE | R:HAMILTON |
| 1306 | MANGIS, George W | 14 | N½NW | 1854-03-31 | FD | N2NW | R:HAMILTON |
| 1516 | MARQUIS, Perry G | 20 | NW | 1854-08-17 | FD | NW | R:HAMILTON |
| 1517 | " " | 21 | SWSW | 1855-03-28 | FD | SWSW | R:HAMILTON |
| 1264 | MARSHALL, Daniel | 26 | NWNW | 1837-05-08 | FD | NWNW | R:HAMILTON |
| 1266 | MARTIN, David | 2 | NWNW | 1852-12-16 | FD | NWNW | R:FRANKLIN |
| 1285 | MARTIN, Enoch | 8 | NWNE | 1839-12-30 | FD | NWNE | R:HAMILTON |
| 1563 | MAULDEN, Temperance | 21 | NESW | 1854-09-18 | FD | NESW | R:HAMILTON |
| 1564 | " " | 21 | NW | 1854-09-18 | FD | NW | R:HAMILTON |
| 1210 | MAULDING, Ambrose | 13 | NE | 1817-08-11 | FD | NE | R:WHITE |
| 1211 | " " | 13 | SE | 1819-05-04 | FD | SE | R:WHITE |
| 1284 | MAULDING, Enness | 12 | NW | 1819-05-25 | FD | NW | R:WHITE |
| 1369 | MAULDING, James | 23 | SWSW | 1836-06-13 | FD | SWSW | R:HAMILTON |
| 1368 | " " | 22 | SESE | 1851-12-10 | FD | SESE | R:HAMILTON |
| 1370 | " " | 27 | NENE | 1851-12-10 | FD | NENE | R:HAMILTON |
| 1433 | MAULDING, John W | 13 | SW | 1818-08-28 | FD | SW | R:FRANKLIN |
| 1457 | MAULDING, Lorenzo D | 22 | N½SW | 1854-05-01 | FD | N2SW | R:HAMILTON |
| 1630 | MAULDING, William L | 25 | SENE | 1853-12-15 | FD | SENE | R:HAMILTON |
| 1530 | MAY, Rachel | 24 | SWNE | 1846-12-05 | FD | SWNE | R:HAMILTON S:F |
| 1216 | MCBRIDE, Andrew Ross | 6 | W½SW | 1836-10-27 | FD | W2SW | R:TENNESSEE |
| 1638 | MCCOY, William | 7 | W½NE | 1853-06-06 | FD | W2NE | |
| 1637 | " " | 7 | NENW | 1853-11-23 | FD | NENW | R:HAMILTON |
| 1633 | " " | 10 | W½NW | 1853-12-01 | FD | W2NW | R:HAMILTON |
| 1639 | " " | 9 | E½NE | 1853-12-01 | FD | E2NE | R:HAMILTON |
| 1460 | " " | 10 | SENW | 1853-12-20 | FD | SENW | R:HAMILTON |
| 1636 | " " | 5 | NESE | 1853-12-20 | FD | NESE | R:HAMILTON |
| 1634 | " " | 4 | NWSW | 1853-12-20 | FD | NWSW | R:HAMILTON |
| 1635 | " " | 4 | S½NW | 1853-12-20 | FD | S2NW | R:HAMILTON |
| 1632 | " " | 10 | SENW | 1853-12-20 | FD | SENW | R:HAMILTON |
| 1293 | MCDANIEL, George H | 22 | SWSE | 1854-10-13 | FD | SWSE | R:HAMILTON |
| 1663 | MCDONALD, Mary A | 1 | NENE | 1848-12-27 | FD | NENE | S:F |
| 1476 | " " | 36 | SESE | 1848-12-27 | FD | SESE | S:F |
| 1475 | " " | 1 | NENE | 1848-12-27 | FD | NENE | S:F |
| 1312 | MCFARLAND, Gilbert | 12 | S½SE | 1839-03-28 | FD | S2SE | R:HAMILTON |
| 1640 | MCGENNIS, William | 8 | SWSW | 1854-02-28 | FD | SWSW | R:HAMILTON |
| 1641 | MCGINNIS, William | 8 | SESW | 1851-12-09 | FD | SESW | R:HAMILTON |
| 1218 | MCNABB, Archibald W | 10 | SENE | 1853-12-06 | FD | SENE | R:HAMILTON |
| 1570 | MELLON, Thomas | 22 | SESW | 1853-03-28 | FD | SESW | |
| 1452 | METCALF, Lee | 27 | SENE | 1853-11-18 | FD | SENE | R:HAMILTON |
| 1424 | MILLER, John | 24 | NENE | 1851-12-20 | FD | NENE | |
| 1423 | " " | 13 | SWSE | 1851-12-20 | FD | SWSE | |
| 1422 | " " | 13 | E½SE | 1851-12-20 | FD | E2SE | |
| 1205 | MOORE, Alfred | 35 | NESW | 1836-06-28 | FD | NESW | R:HAMILTON |
| 1208 | " " | 35 | SESW | 1847-05-27 | FD | SESW | R:HAMILTON |
| 1209 | " " | 35 | W½SE | 1850-04-05 | FD | W2SE | |
| 1207 | " " | 35 | SESE | 1850-04-05 | FD | SESE | |
| 1206 | " " | 35 | SENW | 1851-06-10 | FD | SENW | |
| 1204 | " " | 34 | SWNE | 1853-04-07 | FD | SWNE | R:HAMILTON |
| 1379 | MOORE, Jeremiah | 24 | NE | 1819-11-01 | FD | NE | R:WHITE |
| 1425 | MOORE, John | 35 | SW | 1819-06-01 | FD | SW | R:WHITE |
| 1610 | MOORE, William C | 34 | SESE | 1853-10-28 | FD | SESE | R:HAMILTON |
| 1215 | NANCE, Andrew | 23 | SE | 1816-11-16 | FD | SE | R:WHITE |
| 1418 | NATION, John L | 16 | L1 | 1853-12-05 | SC | LOT1NENE | |
| 1420 | NEWMAN, John L | 1 | NESW | 1852-01-07 | FD | NESW | |
| 1419 | " " | 1 | N½SE | 1852-01-07 | FD | N2SE | |
| 1479 | NICHOLAS, Mathew | 23 | SENW | 1852-03-04 | FD | SENW | |
| 1451 | OLIVER, Lanson | 3 | SENE | 1849-11-01 | FD | SENE | R:HAMILTON |
| 1450 | " " | 3 | NESE | 1854-11-27 | FD | NESE | R:HAMILTON |
| 1642 | OLIVER, William | 3 | NWSE | 1849-10-23 | FD | NWSE | R:HAMILTON |
| 1250 | ONEAL, George | 22 | SWNW | 1854-09-18 | FD | SWNW | R:JEFFERSON |
| 1297 | " " | 22 | SWNW | 1854-09-18 | FD | SWNW | R:JEFFERSON |
| 1543 | PAGE, Robert | 28 | SWSW | 1836-06-22 | FD | SWSW | R:HAMILTON |
| 1559 | PAGE, Silas M | 32 | SWNE | 1854-10-27 | FD | SWNE | R:HAMILTON |
| 1561 | PAGE, Silas Mercer | 32 | SENE | 1851-09-04 | FD | SENE | R:HAMILTON |
| 1560 | " " | 32 | NESE | 1853-10-31 | FD | NESE | R:HAMILTON |
| 1314 | PATE, Hamilton | 19 | SE | 1854-09-21 | FD | SE | R:FRANKLIN |
| 1315 | " " | 20 | SW | 1854-09-21 | FD | SW | R:FRANKLIN |
| 1371 | PATE, James | 21 | SE | 1854-09-18 | FD | SE | R:HAMILTON |
| 1372 | " " | 21 | W½SE | 1854-09-18 | FD | W2SE | R:HAMILTON |
| 1658 | PECK, William T | 11 | SENW | 1853-12-06 | FD | SENW | R:HAMILTON |
| 1558 | " " | 11 | NESW | 1853-12-20 | FD | NESW | R:HAMILTON |

| ID | Individual in Patent | Sec. | Sec. Part | Purchase Date | Sale Type | IL Aliquot Part | For More Info . . . |
|---|---|---|---|---|---|---|---|
| 1657 | PECK, William T (Cont'd) | 11 | NESW | 1853-12-20 | FD | NESW | R:HAMILTON |
| 1464 | PLUNCKETT, Martha | 25 | NENE | 1852-03-04 | FD | NENE | S:F |
| 1513 | POOL, Orval | 14 | SWSE | 1853-02-28 | FD | SWSE | R:GALLATIN |
| 1480 | PRICE, Michael | 26 | NWNE | 1851-09-08 | FD | NWNE | |
| 1678 | REED, Zephaniah | 27 | NESE | 1853-03-17 | FD | NESE | |
| 1676 | REED, Zephaniah B | 36 | E½NE | 1850-04-11 | FD | E2NE | |
| 1677 | " " | 36 | N½SE | 1850-04-11 | FD | N2SE | |
| 1669 | " " | 25 | SWSW | 1851-01-21 | FD | SWSW | R:HAMILTON |
| 1668 | " " | 25 | NESW | 1853-06-07 | FD | NESW | R:HAMILTON |
| 1673 | " " | 34 | NENW | 1853-07-07 | FD | NENW | R:HAMILTON |
| 1666 | " " | 20 | NWSE | 1853-10-11 | FD | NWSE | R:HAMILTON |
| 1664 | " " | 16 | L12 | 1853-10-30 | SC | LOT12NWSW | |
| 1665 | " " | 16 | L11 | 1853-11-11 | SC | LOT11NESW | |
| 1670 | " " | 27 | SESE | 1854-01-07 | FD | SESE | R:HAMILTON |
| 1667 | " " | 20 | SWNE | 1854-02-04 | FD | SWNE | R:HAMILTON |
| 1672 | " " | 34 | NENE | 1854-09-20 | FD | NENE | R:HAMILTON |
| 1674 | " " | 35 | NWNW | 1854-09-20 | FD | NWNW | R:HAMILTON |
| 1675 | " " | 35 | SWSE | 1854-09-20 | FD | SWSE | R:HAMILTON |
| 1362 | " " | 34 | NENE | 1854-09-20 | FD | NENE | R:HAMILTON |
| 1671 | " " | 27 | SESW | 1854-09-20 | FD | SESW | R:HAMILTON |
| 1679 | REID, Zephaniak B | 26 | NWSW | 1842-06-04 | FD | NWSW | R:HAMILTON |
| 1680 | " | 26 | SESW | 1842-06-04 | FD | SESW | R:HAMILTON |
| 1199 | RICHARDSON, Alexander | 9 | SESE | 1833-11-05 | FD | SESE | R:FRANKLIN |
| 1198 | " " | 11 | SESE | 1851-10-06 | FD | SESE | |
| 1352 | RICHARDSON, Isaac | 7 | NWSE | 1854-10-04 | FD | NWSE | R:HAMILTON |
| 1649 | RICHARDSON, William | 1 | SWSW | 1851-12-06 | FD | SWSW | R:HAMILTON |
| 1647 | " " | 1 | N½NW | 1852-09-22 | FD | N2NW | |
| 1648 | " " | 1 | SENW | 1854-09-28 | FD | SENW | R:HAMILTON |
| 1366 | RITCHEY, James M | 3 | SWNE | 1854-10-05 | FD | SWNE | R:HAMILTON |
| 1367 | " " | 3 | W½NW | 1854-10-05 | FD | W2NW | R:HAMILTON |
| 1365 | " " | 3 | SENW | 1854-10-05 | FD | SENW | R:HAMILTON |
| 1430 | ROBB, John T | 8 | SESE | 1854-03-31 | FD | SESE | R:INDIANA |
| 1283 | SALLEE, Ellis | 34 | SWSW | 1854-07-26 | FD | SWSW | R:HAMILTON S:F |
| 1373 | SCORVOIER, James R | 18 | SWNE | 1840-04-27 | FD | SWNE | R:HAMILTON |
| 1556 | SCRUGGS, Sarah | 23 | NESE | 1852-03-04 | FD | NESE | S:F |
| 1557 | " " | 23 | SENE | 1852-03-04 | FD | SENE | S:F |
| 1330 | SEAL, Henry | 10 | NWNE | 1853-11-28 | FD | NWNE | R:HAMILTON |
| 1329 | " " | 10 | NENW | 1853-11-28 | FD | NENW | R:HAMILTON |
| 1481 | SHAFFER, Michael | 4 | E½NE | 1854-04-04 | FD | E2NE | R:OHIO |
| 1482 | " " | 4 | N½SE | 1854-04-04 | FD | N2SE | R:OHIO |
| 1599 | SHELTON, William B | 17 | SENW | 1854-02-11 | FD | SENW | R:HAMILTON |
| 1499 | SHIRBEY, Nimrod | 14 | N½SE | 1839-06-10 | FD | N2SE | R:HAMILTON |
| 1500 | SHIRLEY, Nimrod | 14 | SE | 1818-08-08 | FD | SE | R:WHITE |
| 1501 | " " | 14 | SESE | 1852-01-15 | FD | SESE | |
| 1650 | SHOEMAKER, William | 26 | NWSE | 1836-05-14 | FD | NWSE | R:HAMILTON |
| 1651 | " " | 26 | SESE | 1836-05-14 | FD | SESE | R:HAMILTON |
| 1380 | SHUMAKER, Jeremiah | 25 | NWSW | 1852-03-10 | FD | NWSW | |
| 1474 | SIMS, Martin | 31 | NENE | 1851-07-23 | FD | NENE | |
| 1473 | " " | 30 | SESE | 1853-11-11 | FD | SESE | R:HAMILTON |
| 1472 | " " | 30 | NESE | 1854-09-19 | FD | NESE | R:HAMILTON |
| 1471 | " " | 30 | NE | 1854-09-19 | FD | NE | R:HAMILTON |
| 1469 | " " | 29 | NWSW | 1854-09-19 | FD | NWSW | R:HAMILTON |
| 1470 | " " | 29 | W½NW | 1854-09-19 | FD | W2NW | R:HAMILTON |
| 1568 | SLOO, Thomas Jr | 2 | NW | 1818-05-30 | FD | NW | R:CINCINATTI |
| 1569 | " | 3 | | 1818-06-03 | FD | NERSA | R:CINCINATTI |
| 1304 | SMITH, Artemissa | 36 | SENW | 1851-05-07 | FD | SENW | R:HAMILTON |
| 1219 | " " | 36 | SENW | 1851-05-07 | FD | SENW | R:HAMILTON |
| 1461 | SMITH, Joseph B | 10 | SWNE | 1857-06-17 | FD | SWNE | |
| 1437 | " " | 10 | SWNE | 1857-06-17 | FD | SWNE | |
| 1438 | " " | 9 | NWNE | 1857-06-17 | FD | NWNE | |
| 1645 | SNEED, William P | 33 | SWNE | 1853-03-24 | FD | SWNE | |
| 1643 | " " | 33 | NWNE | 1853-05-05 | FD | NWNE | R:HAMILTON |
| 1341 | " " | 33 | NWNE | 1853-05-05 | FD | NWNE | R:HAMILTON |
| 1644 | " " | 33 | SENE | 1853-06-23 | FD | SENE | R:HAMILTON |
| 1652 | SNOVER, William | 5 | SENE | 1853-08-18 | FD | SENE | R:HAMILTON |
| 1653 | SNOW, William | 16 | L13 | 1840-05-02 | SC | LOT13 | |
| 1654 | " " | 5 | SWNE | 1853-08-09 | FD | SWNE | R:HAMILTON |
| 1253 | SPENCER, Christopher | 17 | N½SW | 1853-12-09 | FD | N2SW | R:HAMILTON |
| 1515 | SPENCER, Peledge H | 21 | E½NE | 1853-11-14 | FD | E2NE | |
| 1615 | SPENCER, William D | 6 | NESE | 1854-10-24 | FD | NESE | R:HAMILTON |
| 1627 | SPURIEN, Alexander | 29 | E½NW | 1853-11-11 | FD | E2NWVOID | |
| 1628 | " " | 29 | NESW | 1853-11-11 | FD | NESWVOID | |
| 1629 | " " | 29 | NWSE | 1853-11-11 | FD | NWSEVOID | |

| ID | Individual in Patent | Sec. | Sec. Part | Purchase Date | Sale Type | IL Aliquot Part | For More Info . . . |
|---|---|---|---|---|---|---|---|
| 1201 | SPURIEN, Alexander (Cont'd) | 29 | NESW | 1853-11-11 | FD | NESWVOID | |
| 1202 | " | 29 | NWSE | 1853-11-11 | FD | NWSEVOID | |
| 1200 | " | 29 | E½NW | 1853-11-11 | FD | E2NWVOID | |
| 1553 | STEELLE, Samuel | 1 | S½SE | 1850-07-29 | FD | S2SE | |
| 1554 | " | 12 | NENE | 1850-07-29 | FD | NENE | |
| 1356 | STELLE, Jacob | 2 | SESW | 1852-09-28 | FD | SESW | |
| 1355 | " | 11 | NENW | 1852-09-28 | FD | NENW | |
| 1578 | STELLE, Thompson | 11 | SENE | 1852-01-29 | FD | SENE | R:HAMILTON |
| 1577 | " | 11 | NWNE | 1853-10-25 | FD | NWNE | R:HAMILTON |
| 1580 | " | 2 | SWSE | 1853-10-25 | FD | SWSE | R:HAMILTON |
| 1579 | " | 11 | SWNE | 1853-12-06 | FD | SWNE | R:HAMILTON |
| 1375 | STEPENSON, James | 29 | NESE | 1853-11-11 | FD | NESE | |
| 1374 | " | 28 | NWSW | 1853-11-11 | FD | NWSW | |
| 1581 | STILLE, Thompson | 11 | NENE | 1839-01-05 | FD | NENE | R:HAMILTON |
| 1582 | " | 2 | SESE | 1852-02-20 | FD | SESE | R:HAMILTON |
| 1431 | STOKES, John T | 24 | W½NW | 1852-03-04 | FD | W2NW | |
| 1398 | STROTHER, John D | 9 | NW | 1819-01-04 | FD | NW | |
| 1646 | STULL, William R | 3 | NESW | 1854-03-25 | FD | NESW | R:WAYNE |
| 1502 | SULIVAN, Noah | 18 | SWSE | 1851-04-08 | FD | SWSE | R:HAMILTON |
| 1503 | " | 19 | NWNW | 1853-07-28 | FD | NWNW | R:HAMILTON |
| 1267 | SULLIVAN, David | 18 | SESE | 1853-12-01 | FD | SESE | R:HAMILTON |
| 1505 | SULLIVAN, Noah | 8 | NENW | 1839-12-25 | FD | NENW | R:HAMILTON |
| 1504 | " | 19 | NWNE | 1853-07-12 | FD | NWNE | |
| 1506 | SULLIVAN, Noan | 19 | NENW | 1854-01-09 | FD | NENW | R:HAMILTON |
| 1277 | SUMMERS, Elisha | 4 | W½NW | 1854-10-02 | FD | W2NW | R:FRANKLIN |
| 1655 | SWEARINGER, William | 23 | SESE | 1851-11-14 | FD | SESE | |
| 1656 | " | 24 | SWSW | 1851-11-14 | FD | SWSW | |
| 1376 | TALLER, James | 13 | SESW | 1848-09-29 | FD | SESW | G:2 |
| 1377 | " | 13 | W½SW | 1848-09-29 | FD | W2SW | G:2 |
| 1378 | " | 24 | NENW | 1848-09-29 | FD | NENW | G:2 |
| 1432 | TEMPLES, John | 14 | SENW | 1853-03-26 | FD | SENW | R:HAMILTON |
| 1661 | THOMAS, William | 22 | NWSE | 1852-05-24 | FD | NWSE | |
| 1659 | " | 15 | E½SW | 1852-05-24 | FD | E2SW | |
| 1660 | " | 22 | E½NW | 1852-05-24 | FD | E2NW | |
| 1446 | THORP, Joseph | 5 | NESW | 1839-07-26 | FD | NESW | R:HAMILTON |
| 1662 | THRASHER, William | 31 | NESE | 1851-12-15 | FD | NESE | |
| 1455 | TINER, Lewis | 32 | NWNE | 1853-10-26 | FD | NWNE | R:HAMILTON |
| 1454 | " | 29 | S½SW | 1853-10-26 | FD | S2SW | R:HAMILTON |
| 1227 | TODD, Benjamin | 19 | NENE | 1853-11-18 | FD | NENE | R:HAMILTON |
| 1275 | VISE, Eliphas H | 28 | SESW | 1853-10-12 | FD | SESW | R:HAMILTON |
| 1343 | VISE, Hosea | 33 | SWNW | 1836-08-30 | FD | SWNW | R:HAMILTON |
| 1643 | " | 33 | NWNE | 1851-12-04 | FD | NWNEVOID | |
| 1337 | " | 32 | NENE | 1851-12-04 | FD | NENEVOID | |
| 1338 | " | 32 | NENE | 1851-12-04 | FD | NENEVOID | |
| 1339 | " | 33 | E½NE | 1851-12-04 | FD | E2NEVOID | |
| 1341 | " | 33 | NWNE | 1851-12-04 | FD | NWNEVOID | |
| 1337 | " | 32 | NENE | 1852-11-12 | FD | NENE | |
| 1338 | " | 32 | NENE | 1852-11-12 | FD | NENE | |
| 1340 | " | 33 | N½NW | 1852-11-12 | FD | N2NW | |
| 1342 | " | 33 | SENW | 1852-11-12 | FD | SENW | |
| 1555 | WARD, Samuel | 26 | SWSW | 1851-05-28 | FD | SWSW | |
| 1526 | WHITE, Preston | 25 | SESE | 1850-02-25 | FD | SESE | R:HAMILTON |
| 1527 | " | 25 | SESW | 1852-03-04 | FD | SESW | R:HAMILTON |
| 1528 | " | 25 | SWSE | 1853-03-02 | FD | SWSE | R:HAMILTON |
| 1558 | WHITESIDE, Sarah | 11 | NESW | 1837-03-22 | FD | NESW | R:GALLATIN S:F |
| 1657 | " | 11 | NESW | 1837-03-22 | FD | NESW | R:GALLATIN S:F |
| 1220 | WHITTINGTON, Azariah | 4 | S½SE | 1851-12-19 | FD | S2SE | |
| 1348 | WILBANKS, Robert A D | 5 | SWSW | 1839-08-21 | FD | SWSW | R:FRANKLIN G:15 |
| 1487 | WILLIAMS, Nathan | 12 | NWSE | 1840-04-15 | FD | NWSE | R:HAMILTON |
| 1486 | " | 1 | NWNE | 1851-06-03 | FD | NWNE | |
| 1475 | WILLIAMS, Wylie | 1 | NENE | 1851-04-14 | FD | NENE | |
| 1663 | " | 1 | NENE | 1851-04-14 | FD | NENE | |
| 1439 | WILSON, Joseph C | 11 | NESE | 1854-02-09 | FD | NESE | R:HAMILTON |
| 1272 | WILTON, Edward | 9 | SWSE | 1853-08-02 | FD | SWSE | |
| 1313 | WORTH, Gorham A | 3 | NE | 1818-06-03 | FD | NE | |

## Patent Map

**T5-S  R5-E**
**3rd PM Meridian**

**Map  Group  7**

## Township Statistics

| | | |
|---|---|---|
| Parcels Mapped | : | 493 |
| Number of Patents | : | 1 |
| Number of Individuals | : | 273 |
| Patentees Identified | : | 271 |
| Number of Surnames | : | 182 |
| Multi-Patentee Parcels | : | 7 |
| Oldest Patent Date | : | 8/27/1583 |
| Most Recent Patent | : | 1/8/1858 |
| Block/Lot Parcels | : | 14 |
| Cities and Towns | : | 1 |
| Cemeteries | : | 4 |

**Section 6**
IRVIN Runyon 1838 — IRVINE Runyon 1829 — IRVIN Runyon 1836
IRVIN Runyon 1840 — IRVIN Runyon 1838
MCBRIDE Andrew Ross 1836 — DAVIS Nehemiah 1838 — SPENCER William D 1854
DAVIS Nehemiah 1838 — FOSTER Isaac 1839

**Section 5**
HODGES Hiram 1820 — IRVIN Abraham 1836 — GAINES Newcomb 1839 — GRAVES Newcomb 1849
IRVIN Henry Howel 1838 — SNOW William 1853 — SNOVER William 1853
IRVIN Abraham 1836 — THORP Joseph 1839 — MCCOY William 1853
FOSTER [15] Isaac 1839 — IRVIN Abraham 1838 — BELL Thomas 1836 — BOSTER George 1840 — IRVIN Julia 1840 — ADAIR Demis 1849

**Section 4**
CONNETT George 1854 — HARWOOD Leroy B 1854 — LOWREY Alexander 1854
SUMMERS Elisha 1854 — MCCOY William 1853 — LOWRY Alexander 1854 — SHAFFER Michael 1854
CLARK Jacksen 1855
MCCOY William 1853 — LAMBUD Henderson 1853 — SHAFFER Michael 1854
IRVIN Henry Wells 1842 — WHITTINGTON Azariah 1851

**Section 7**
DAVIS Nehemiah 1838 — MCCOY William 1853 — BOSTER George 1850 — BOSTER George 1850
DAVIS Rueben 1853 — MCCOY William 1853
DAVIS Nehemiah 1838 — RICHARDSON Isaac 1854
BOSTER Daniel 1839 — GIBBS Isaac P 1853 — GIBBS John 1848 — GIBBS John 1839 — MCGENNIS William 1854

**Section 8**
SULLIVAN Noah 1839 — MARTIN Enoch 1839 — CRUME Henry 1836
GIBBS John 1853 — DEWITT Thomas J 1840
GIBBS John 1841 — GIBBS Nicholas 1841 — FUEL Anna 1854
MCGINNIS William 1851 — CAMPBELL Wallace A 1583 — ROBB John T 1854

**Section 9**
ATCHISON Barton 1830 — ATCHISON Charles 1849 — SMITH Joseph B 1857 — MCCOY William 1853
STROTHER John D 1819 — ATCHISON Charles 1849 — ATCHISON Charles 1848
ATCHISON Joseph T 1849 — DEWITT Richard 1843 — ATCHISON Charles 1849 — IRVIN Henry H 1854
ATCHISON Charles 1848 — IRVIN Henry H — DAWSEN Martin S 1854 — ADARE Philip 1837 — WILTON Edward 1853 — RICHARDSON Alexander 1833
HAWKES 1854 Walter S 1856

**Section 18**
CLARK Jacob Scott 1844 — GIBBS Isaac P 1853 — GIBBS John 1848
BOSTER Andrew J 1853 — SCORVOIER James R 1840 — CAMPBELL Wallace A 1854
BOSTER Andrew J 1853 — CAMPBELL Wallace A 1854 — CAMPBELL Wallace A 1583
CAMPBELL Wallace A 1854 — SULIVAN Noah 1851

**Section 17**
CARLTON Cornelius 1854 — CARLTON Cornelius 1853 — CAMPBELL Wallace A 1853
CAMPBELL Wallace A 1854 — SHELTON William B 1854 — CAMPBELL Wallace A 1854 — CAMPBELL Wallace A 1851
SPENCER Christopher 1853 — CAMPBELL Wallace A 1851
SULLIVAN David 1853 — BOSTER Andrew J 1854 — CAMPBELL Wallace A 1851 — ADARE Philip 1840

**Section 16**
ADARE Philip 1838 — IRWIN Henry 1838
ADAREL Philip 1839
Lots-Sec. 16
L1 NATION, John L 1853
L2 DIXON, Tilmon 1854
L3 ATCHISSON, Charles 1851
L6 FOSTER, Elijah 1854
L7 IRVIN, Henry H 1854
L8 IRVIN, Henry H 1853
L9 BURTON, William 1854
L10 BURTON, James 1854
L11 REED, Zephaniah B 1853
L12 REED, Zephaniah B 1853
L13 SNOW, William 1840
L14 FAN, Isaac 1854
L15 FAN, Philip 1854
L16 BURTON, William 1854

**Section 19**
SULLIVAN Noah 1853 — SULLIVAN Noah 1854 — SULLIVAN Noah 1853 — TODD Benjamin 1853
LOGSDEN Thomas R 1854 — LOGSDEN Thomas R 1854 — LOGSDEN Thomas R 1854
LOGSDEN Thomas R 1854 — PATE Hamilton 1854
JOHNSEN Enoch S 1854 — PATE Hamilton 1854

**Section 20**
MARQUIS Perry G 1854 — CAMPBELL Wallace A 1855
HILL Isaac 1819 — HILL Richard 1837
REED Zephaniah B 1854
PATE Hamilton 1854 — REED Zephaniah B 1853 — HINDMAN John 1853
FORESTER Benjamin 1853

**Section 21**
MAULDEN Temperance 1854 — SPENCER Peledge H 1853
HINDMAN John 1854 — MAULDEN Temperance 1854
MARQUIS Perry G 1855 — FRAZIER George W A 1853 — PATE James 1854 — PATE James 1854

**Section 30**
JOHNSEN Enoch S 1854 — SIMS Martin 1854
JOHNSON Zopher 1853 — JOHNSON Christopher 1853
JOHNSON Zopher 1853 — JOHNSON Christopher 1854 — SIMS Martin 1854
KELLY Oliver P 1854
JOHNSON Robert H 1583 — JOHNSON Robert Henry 1853 — KELLY Oliver P 1854 — SIMS Martin 1853

**Section 29**
SIMS Martin 1854 — CHOISSER William Jr 1854 — FORESTER Benjamin 1853
SIMS Martin 1854 — SPURIEN Alexander 1853 — JACK John O 1855 — JACK John O 1854
CHOISSER William Jr 1854 — SPURIEN Alexander 1853 — SPURIEN Alexander 1853 — CHOISSER William Jr 1854 — STEPENSON James 1853
SIMS Martin 1854 — TINER Lewis 1853 — CUMPTON Elisha 1855 — CUMPTON Eisha 1853

**Section 28**
JACK John O 1854 — ACORD Martin 1853 — FRAZIER George W A 1854 — FRAZIER George W A 1854
JACK John O 1855 — LAMBERT Hiram 1854 — ACORD Martin 1855 — FRAZIER George W A 1853
STEPENSON James 1853 — ACORD Martin 1853 — FRAZIER George W S 1853
PAGE Robert 1836 — VISE Eliphas H 1853 — BRYANT James H 1851 — HARRISON Gideon 1853

**Section 31**
JANSON Robert Henry 1847 — KELLEY Oliver P 1853 — SIMS Martin 1851
JOHNSON Robert Henry 1851 — JOHNSON Robert Henry 1851 — KELLEY Oliver P 1854
JOHNSON Hiram G 1854 — JOHNSON Robert Henry 1851 — KELLY Oliver P 1854 — THRASHER William 1851
JOHNSON Hiram G 1853 — JOHNSON John Kent 1851

**Section 32**
COLVERT William J 1852 — BURTON Henry 1851 — TINER Lewis 1853 — VISE Hosea 1851
KELLY Oliver P 1854 — HALL John 1851 — PAGE Silas M 1854 — PAGE Silas Mercer 1851
HAMILTON James B 1854
HALL John 1851 — JOHNSON John K 1854

**Section 33**
VISE Hosea 1852 — VISE Hosea 1836 — SNEED William P 1853 — HARRELSON Gideon 1853 — VISE Hosea 1851
VISE Hosea 1836 — VISE Hosea 1852 — SNEED William P 1853 — SNEED William P 1853
PAGE Silas Mercer 1853 — HARRISON Benjamin 1849 — HARRAILSON Benjamin 1849 — BENBROOK Ezekiel G 1853
CALVIN James 1851 — HARRAILSON Benjamin 1849 — HAMILTON Nathaniel 1853 — HALL John F 1853
DRAKE John 1854

Copyright 2007 Boyd IT, Inc. All Rights Reserved

## Map

**Section 3**
EMMERSON William 1854
EMMERSON William 1854
WORTH Gorham A 1818
MARTIN David 1852
SLOO Thomas Jr 1818
EPPERSON Charles 1852
COKER William 1852
HARPER Ellis B 1854

RITCHEY James M 1854
RITCHEY James M 1854 **3**
SLOO
RITCHEY James M 1854
OLIVER Lanson 1849
HOLLAND Berryman 1853
HOLLAND Berryman 1853
**2**
COKER Catharine 1852

BROOKINS Madison 1854
STULL 1818 Thomas Jr
William R 1854
OLIVER Lanson 1854
HOLLAND Berryman 1853
COKER William 1853
COKER Catharine 1852

CARPENTER Chester 1858
DAVIS [14] Elizabeth 1849
DAVIS [14] Elizabeth 1849
EMMERSON William 1854
DAVIS [14] Elizabeth 1849
LANGLEY John 1844
FARMER Litteberry 1851
STELLE Jacob 1852
STELLE Thompson 1853
STILLE Thompson 1852

**Section 1**
HARPER Ellis B
RICHARDSON William 1854
WILLIAMS Nathan 1851
WILLIAMS Wylie 1851
MCDONALD Mary A 1848
COKER Catharine 1852
RICHARDSON William 1854
**1**
COKER Joseph 1851
COKER Catharine 1852
NEWMAN John L 1852
NEWMAN John L 1852
RICHARDSON William 1851
LESLEY Thomas P 1853
STEELLE Samuel 1850

**Section 10**
MCCOY William 1853
BROOKINS Madison 1854
SEAL Henry 1853
SEAL Henry 1853
LANGLEY Sally 1851
LASLEY Thomas P 1853
STELLE Jacob 1852
STELLE Thompson 1853
STILLE Thompson 1839

BROOKINS Madison 1854
BROOKINS Madison 1854
SMITH 1854
MCNABB Archibald W 1853
PECK William T 1853 **11**
STELLE Thompson 1853
STELLE Thompson 1852

BROOKINS Madison 1854
MCCOY William 1853
SMITH Joseph B 1857
**10**
WHITESIDE Sarah 1837
PECK William T 1853
CAMPBELL Patrick 1854
WILSON Joseph C 1854

BOWEN Columbus 1853
BARNETT Charles C 1853
BARNETT Charles C 1853
COKER Abram B 1853
COKER Abram B 1853
RICHARDSON Alexander 1851

**Section 12**
MAULDING Enness 1819
HAMONTREE William 1852
HAMONTREE William 1852
STEELLE Samuel 1850
BARRETT COKER Joseph 1853
COKER Joseph 1851
DAILEY Vincent 1851
COKER Joseph 1851 **12**
WILLIAMS Nathan 1840
ALLEN Calvin Young 1853
GREEN Richmond 1851
MCFARLAND Gilbert 1839

**Section 15**
IRVIN Henry H 1830
IRVIN Henry H 1853
BOWEN Columbus 1853
MANGIS George W 1854
CARR William H 1852

IRVIN Henry Howel 1836
BOWEN Columbus 1854
LOCKWOOD Susan M 1837
HUFFSTATLAR John 1852
TEMPLES John 1853 **14**
GUNTER Alexander J 1852

BOWEN Columbus 1854
THOMAS William 1852
**15**
HUNGATE William 1816
BROOKS John 1853
BROOKS Isaac 1853
GORE John C 1817
SHIRBEY SHIRLEY Nimrod Nimrod 1818 1839

IRVIN Henry H 1853
POOL Orval 1853
SHIRLEY Nimrod 1852

**Section 13**
ALLEN Calvin Young 1853
GREEN Richmond 1851
GREEN Richmond 1851
MAULDING Ambrose 1817
HARPER James M 1853 **13**
ALLEN Josiah 1837
JOHNSON Jonathan 1854
ALLEN William Bright 1851
CARR William H 1853
MILLER John 1851
MAULDING John W 1818
TALLER [2] James 1848
TALLER [2] James 1848
MILLER John 1851
MAULDING Ambrose 1819

**Section 22**
HUNGATE Christopher 1853
THOMAS William 1852
HARMISON Nathaniel 1830
GARVIN John B 1830
ONEAL George 1854
HUNGATE Christopher 1853
**22**
MAULDING Lorenzo D 1854
THOMAS William 1852
HARMISON Jonathan 1836
JANEY Nathan 1818

BRYANT William 1852
MELLON Thomas 1853
MCDANIEL George H 1854
MAULDING James 1851

**Section 23**
HARMISON Nathaniel 1831
FANN Philip 1852
FANN Philip 1852
BURTON William 1853
DITSON
DITSON Jesse 1818
DITSON Jesse 1818
NICHOLAS Mathew 1852
FAN Isaac 1851
Jesse 1818
SCRUGGS Sarah 1852
HARMISON Nathaniel 1836
JANEY Nathan 1818 1836
**23**
SCRUGGS Sarah 1852
HARPER George 1851
NANCE Andrew 1816
MAULDING James 1836
MAULDING James 1836
HUNGATE William 1818
LOCKWOOD John B 1850
SWEARINGER William 1851

**Section 24**
STOKES John T 1852
TALLER [2] James 1848
ALLEN Joseph 1852
MILLER John 1851
MOORE Jeremiah 1819
FANN Hiram 1853 **24**
MAY Rachel 1846
DALE Daniel 1850
CARR Daniel W 1853
HARPER George 1851
BOYD William 1841
BOYD William 1850
SWEARINGER William 1851
GILLAHAN Clemons 1851
HARPER George W 1851
HARPER George 1853

**Section 27**
BRYANT William 1852
BRYANT William 1851
LOCKWOOD John B 1854
LOCKWOOD John B 1854
MAULDING James 1851
LOCKWOOD John B 1854
LOCKWOOD John B 1854
METCALF Lee 1853
**27**
LOCKWOOD John B 1854
REED Zephaniah 1853
BRYANT William 1852
REED Zephaniah B 1854
REED Zephaniah B 1854
BRYANT Mary C 1853

**Section 26**
MARSHALL Daniel 1837
LOCKWOOD Samuel D 1837
PRICE Michael 1851
GARVIN John Bush 1831
HUNGATE Charles 1836
FELLOWES William 1838 **26**
REID Zephaniak 1842
HARMISON Nathaniel 1836
SHOEMAKER William 1836
HUNGATE Joseph 1818
LOCKWOOD Samuel D 1836
WARD Samuel 1851
REID Zephaniak B 1842
HALL John 1836
SHOEMAKER William 1836

**Section 25**
CLARK John A 1852
BURGESS Josiah 1851
HARPER George W 1851
PLUNCKETT Martha 1852
LACK William 1851
FANN Philip 1853 **25**
MAULDING William L 1853
SHUMAKER Jeremiah 1852
REED Zephaniah B 1853
FOSTER Daniel 1853
HARPER Mark 1852
REED Zephaniah B 1851
WHITE Preston 1852
WHITE Preston 1853
WHITE Preston 1850

**Section 34**
HARRELSON Gideon 1853
REED Zephaniah B 1853
LEE Rebecca 1854
LEE James M 1854
REED Zephaniah B 1854
CLARK John A 1853
REED Zephaniah B 1854
GRIFFIN Edam 1583
**34**
MOORE Alfred 1853
LEE James M 1854
GRIFFIN Edam 1583
CAMPBELL William 1851
DILL Dorcas 1851
LEE James M 1854
SALLEE Ellis 1854
CAMPBELL William 1851
MOORE William C 1853

**Section 35**
HARDESTY John 1818
HALL John 1836
MOORE Alfred 1854
**35**
HARDY Thomas Allen 1836
MOORE Alfred 1836
MOORE Alfred 1850
FLINT John 1836
MOORE John 1819
MOORE Alfred 1847
REED Zephaniah B 1854
MOORE Alfred 1850

**Section 36**
HALL Nancy 1853
HUNT Mary 1853
HUNT George W 1853
REED Zephaniah B 1850
HALL Price 1853
HUNT George W 1854
SMITH Artemissa 1851
FLINT John 1852
**36**
REED Zephaniah B 1850
BURTON John 1836
BRADEN Alfred 1852
MCDONALD Mary A 1848

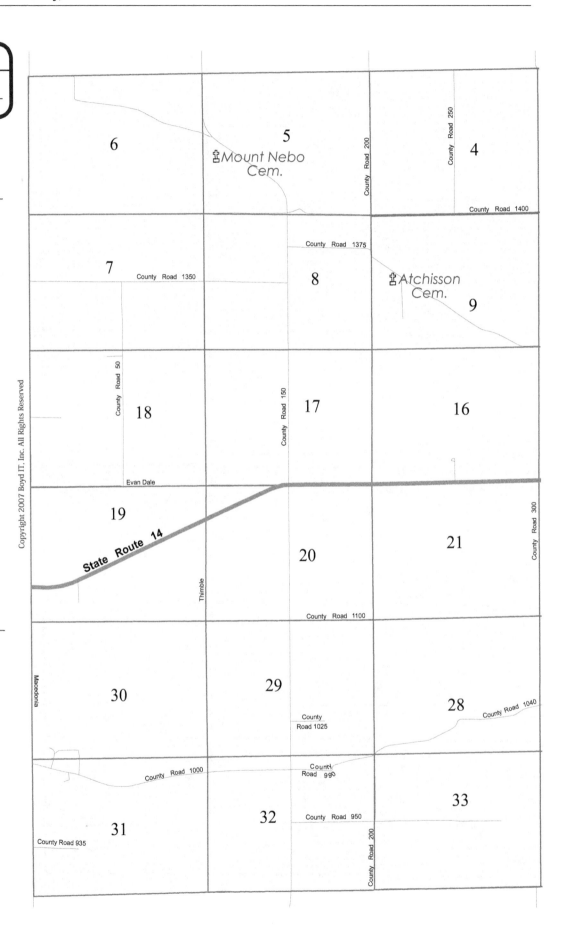

**Road Map**

T5-S R5-E
3rd PM Meridian

Map Group 7

**Cities & Towns**

Flint

**Cemeteries**

Atchisson Cemetery
Bright Cemetery
Gunter Cemetery
Mount Nebo Cemetery

Copyright 2007 Boyd IT, Inc. All Rights Reserved

6

5

⚓Mount Nebo Cem.

County Road 250

4

County Road 200

County Road 1400

7

County Road 1350

County Road 1375

8

⚓Atchisson Cem.

9

County Road 50

18

County Road 150

17

16

Evan Dale

19

State Route 14

20

Thimble

21

County Road 300

County Road 1100

Macedonia

30

29

County Road 1025

28

County Road 1040

County Road 1000

County Road 990

33

31

County Road 935

32

County Road 950

County Road 200

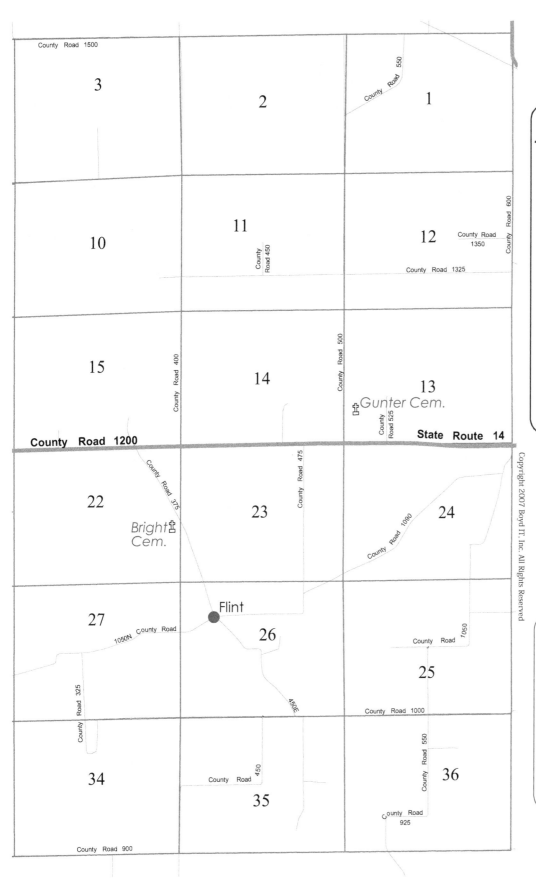

County Road 1500

3

2

County Road 550

1

10

11

County Road 450

County Road 600

12

County Road 1350

County Road 1325

15

County Road 400

14

County Road 500

13

Gunter Cem.

County Road 525

County Road 1200

State Route 14

22

County Road 375

23

County Road 475

24

County Road 1090

Bright Cem.

Flint

27

County Road

1050N

26

County Road 1050

County Road 325

450 E

25

County Road 1000

34

County Road 450

35

County Road 925

County Road 550

36

County Road 900

### Helpful Hints

1. This road map has a number of uses, but primarily it is to help you: a) find the present location of land owned by your ancestors (at least the general area), b) find cemeteries and city-centers, and c) estimate the route/roads used by Census-takers & tax-assessors.

2. If you plan to travel to Hamilton County to locate cemeteries or land parcels, please pick up a modern travel map for the area before you do. Mapping old land parcels on modern maps is not as exact a science as you might think. Just the slightest variations in public land survey coordinates, estimates of parcel boundaries, or road-map deviations can greatly alter a map's representation of how a road either does or doesn't cross a particular parcel of land.

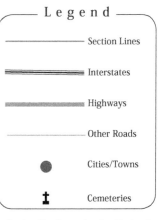

### Legend

————— Section Lines

══════ Interstates

━━━━━ Highways

————— Other Roads

● Cities/Towns

✝ Cemeteries

**Scale**: Section = 1 mile X 1 mile
(generally, with some exceptions)

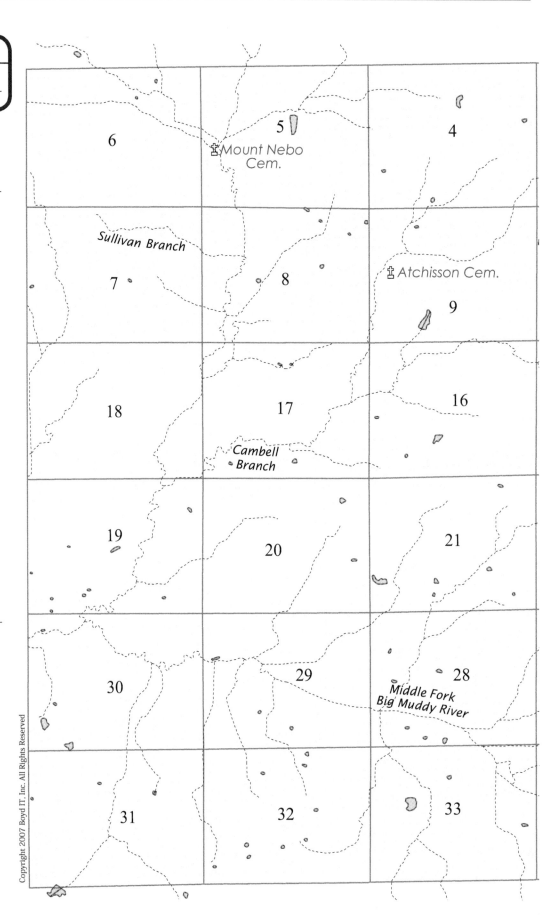

## Historical Map

T5-S R5-E
3rd PM Meridian

Map Group 7

### Cities & Towns
Flint

### Cemeteries
Atchisson Cemetery
Bright Cemetery
Gunter Cemetery
Mount Nebo Cemetery

6

5

4

☖ *Mount Nebo Cem.*

*Sullivan Branch*

7

8

☖ *Atchisson Cem.*

9

18

17

16

*Cambell Branch*

19

20

21

30

29

28

*Middle Fork Big Muddy River*

31

32

33

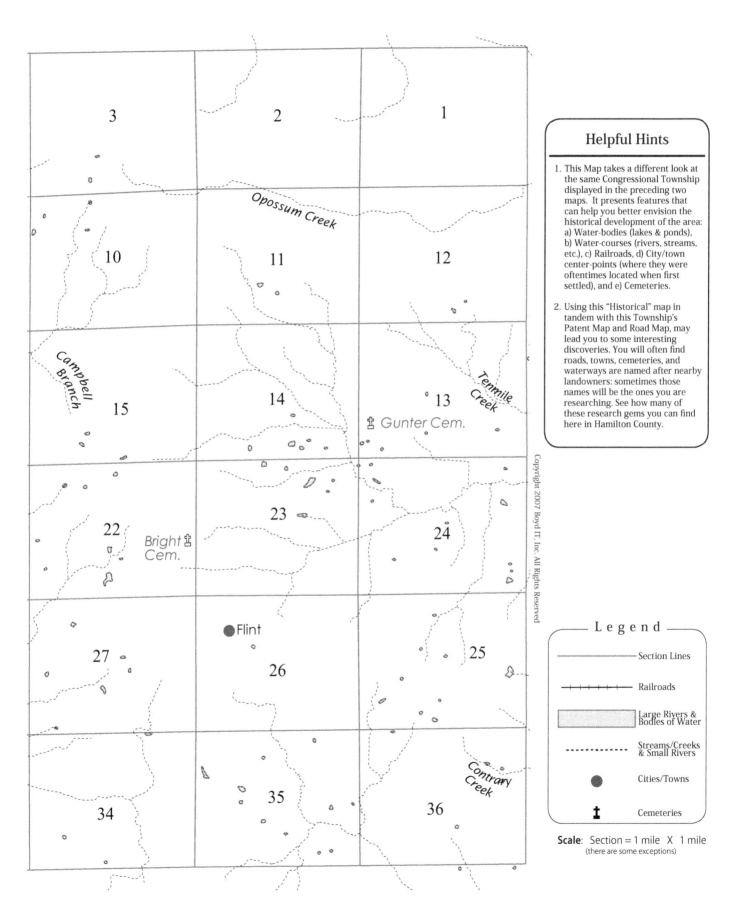

3

2

1

Opossum Creek

10

11

12

Campbell Branch

15

14

13

Tenmile Creek

✝ Gunter Cem.

22

Bright ✝ Cem.

23

24

●Flint

27

26

25

34

35

36

Contrary Creek

## Helpful Hints

1. This Map takes a different look at the same Congressional Township displayed in the preceding two maps. It presents features that can help you better envision the historical development of the area: a) Water-bodies (lakes & ponds), b) Water-courses (rivers, streams, etc.), c) Railroads, d) City/town center-points (where they were oftentimes located when first settled), and e) Cemeteries.

2. Using this "Historical" map in tandem with this Township's Patent Map and Road Map, may lead you to some interesting discoveries. You will often find roads, towns, cemeteries, and waterways are named after nearby landowners: sometimes those names will be the ones you are researching. See how many of these research gems you can find here in Hamilton County.

### Legend

|                          |                              |
| ------------------------ | ---------------------------- |
| ————————                 | Section Lines                |
| +++++++++                | Railroads                    |
| ▭                        | Large Rivers & Bodies of Water |
| - - - - - - -            | Streams/Creeks & Small Rivers |
| ●                        | Cities/Towns                 |
| ✝                        | Cemeteries                   |

**Scale**: Section = 1 mile X 1 mile
(there are some exceptions)

# Map Group 8: Index to Land Patents

# Township 5-South Range 6-East (3rd PM)

After you locate an individual in this Index, take note of the Section and Section Part then proceed to the Land Patent map on the pages immediately following. You should have no difficulty locating the corresponding parcel of land.

The "For More Info" Column will lead you to more information about the underlying Patents. See the *Legend* at right, and the "How to Use this Book" chapter, for more information.

```
                    LEGEND
          "For More Info . . . " column
G = Group  (Multi-Patentee Patent, see Appendix "C")
R = Residence
S = Social Status

See Appendix A for list of abbreviations used by the
Illinois State Archives in describing the place and
nature of these land patents.

Note: if the Abbreviations contain "L", "BL", "LOT",
or "BLOCK", the exact whereabouts of the parcel within
the section is not known.
```

| ID | Individual in Patent | Sec. | Sec. Part | Purchase Date | Sale Type | IL Aliquot Part | For More Info . . . |
|----|---------------------|------|-----------|---------------|-----------|-----------------|---------------------|
| 1946 | ACORD, Martin | 36 | SENE | 1853-10-20 | FD | SENE | R:HAMILTON |
| 1909 | ALLAN, Joseph | 29 | NENW | 1852-04-14 | FD | NENW | |
| 1700 | " " | 20 | SESW | 1852-04-14 | FD | SESW | |
| 1908 | " " | 20 | SESW | 1852-04-14 | FD | SESW | |
| 1808 | ALLEN, James | 9 | NENW | 1837-04-22 | FD | NENW | R:HAMILTON |
| 1809 | " " | 9 | NWNE | 1837-04-22 | FD | NWNE | R:HAMILTON |
| 1880 | ALLEN, Joseph | 8 | NESE | 1850-12-20 | FD | NESE | R:HAMILTON |
| 1916 | " " | 8 | NESE | 1850-12-20 | FD | NESE | R:HAMILTON |
| 1912 | " " | 29 | N½SE | 1852-06-29 | FD | N2SE | |
| 1914 | " " | 32 | SESE | 1853-01-11 | FD | SESE | |
| 1915 | " " | 32 | W½SE | 1853-01-11 | FD | W2SE | |
| 1917 | " " | 8 | SWNE | 1853-02-24 | FD | SWNE | R:HAMILTON |
| 1910 | " " | 20 | NESW | 1854-01-07 | FD | NESW | R:HAMILTON |
| 1913 | " " | 29 | SENW | 1854-01-07 | FD | SENW | R:HAMILTON |
| 1911 | " " | 20 | SENW | 1855-05-19 | FD | SENW | R:HAMILTON |
| 1924 | ALLEN, Larken B | 25 | NWSE | 1851-01-11 | FD | NWSE | R:HAMILTON |
| 1941 | ALLEN, Mark | 25 | SESW | 1853-12-08 | FD | SESW | R:HAMILTON |
| 1770 | ANDERSON, Edmund | 21 | W½NW | 1848-12-02 | FD | W2NW | |
| 1767 | " " | 17 | SESE | 1848-12-02 | FD | SESE | |
| 1768 | " " | 20 | NENE | 1848-12-02 | FD | NENE | |
| 1769 | " " | 20 | SWNW | 1853-12-14 | FD | SWNW | R:HAMILTON |
| 1844 | ANDERSON, John | 21 | E½SE | 1833-12-18 | FD | E2SE | R:HAMILTON |
| 1954 | " " | 16 | | 1836-01-15 | SC | SECT14 | |
| 1980 | " " | 16 | | 1837-07-05 | SC | SECT11 | |
| 1992 | ANDERSON, Robert | 24 | NW | 1819-12-02 | FD | NW | R:TENNESSEE |
| 1991 | " " | 13 | SW | 1819-12-02 | FD | SW | R:TENNESSEE |
| 1699 | ASKEY, Andrew Jackson | 3 | W½NE | 1848-02-21 | FD | W2NE | |
| 1697 | " " | 3 | NWSE | 1848-02-21 | FD | NWSE | |
| 1698 | " " | 3 | SENE | 1848-02-21 | FD | SENE | |
| 1761 | BARNES, David | 21 | SESW | 1837-04-22 | FD | SESW | R:HAMILTON |
| 1810 | BARNES, James | 29 | NWNE | 1837-04-12 | FD | NWNE | R:HAMILTON |
| 2052 | BARNET, William | 2 | SESW | 1851-03-10 | FD | SESW | |
| 2050 | " " | 11 | N½NE | 1851-03-10 | FD | N2NE | |
| 2051 | " " | 11 | NENW | 1851-03-10 | FD | NENW | |
| 2020 | BARRON, Thomas B | 23 | N½SW | 1852-08-18 | FD | N2SW | |
| 2019 | BARROW, Sherod | 23 | SESW | 1853-11-24 | FD | SESW | R:HAMILTON |
| 2053 | BAUMGARDNER, William | 5 | SWNW | 1853-02-28 | FD | SWNW | R:HAMILTON |
| 1774 | BENTON, Elijah | 6 | SENE | 1852-01-07 | FD | SENE | |
| 1765 | " " | 6 | SENE | 1852-01-07 | FD | SENE | |
| 1772 | " " | 5 | S½NW | 1852-01-07 | FD | S2NW | |
| 1773 | " " | 6 | NESE | 1852-01-07 | FD | NESE | |
| 1764 | " " | 6 | NESE | 1852-01-07 | FD | NESE | |
| 1762 | BOURLAND, David | 27 | NWNE | 1851-04-05 | FD | NWNE | R:KENTUCKY |
| 1791 | BOYD, Henry H | 33 | NENW | 1845-02-19 | FD | NENW | R:HAMILTON |
| 2054 | BOYD, William | 8 | NWSE | 1851-02-01 | FD | NWSE | R:HAMILTON |
| 1710 | BRADFOR, George | 16 | | 1833-12-04 | SC | SECT6 | |

| ID | Individual in Patent | Sec. | Sec. Part | Purchase Date | Sale Type | IL Aliquot Part | For More Info . . . |
|---|---|---|---|---|---|---|---|
| 1954 | BRADFOR, George (Cont'd) | 16 | | 1833-12-04 | SC | SECT5 | |
| 1788 | BROWN, Hanis G | 9 | NWSW | 1853-08-12 | FD | NWSW | R:FRANKLIN |
| 1925 | BRUMLY, Larkin | 5 | SWSW | 1846-08-25 | FD | SWSW | R:HAMILTON |
| 1813 | BRYANT, James H | 12 | SWNW | 1851-04-16 | FD | SWNW | |
| 2055 | BUMGARDENER, William | 5 | NWNW | 1854-09-28 | FD | NWNW | R:HAMILTON |
| 1846 | BURTON, John C | 22 | W½SE | 1848-10-09 | FD | W2SE | |
| 1845 | " " | 22 | W½NE | 1848-10-09 | FD | W2NE | |
| 1847 | " | 27 | NENW | 1853-04-18 | FD | NENW | R:HAMILTON |
| 1848 | CALDWELL, John | 9 | NW | 1819-01-01 | FD | NW | R:SHAWNEETOWN |
| 1726 | CAMPBELL, Charles | 4 | SE | 1818-09-15 | FD | SE | R:SHAWNEETOWN |
| 1919 | CAMPBELL, Joseph | 21 | NENE | 1851-09-22 | FD | NENE | R:HAMILTON |
| 2057 | CAMPBELL, William | 24 | NWNE | 1837-04-20 | FD | NWNE | R:HAMILTON |
| 1708 | CARGIL, David | 32 | NWNE | 1850-01-28 | FD | NWNE | G:7 |
| 1707 | " " | 29 | SESW | 1850-01-28 | FD | SESW | G:7 |
| 1706 | " " | 29 | S½SE | 1850-01-28 | FD | S2SE | G:7 |
| 1929 | CARGIL, Lewis | 25 | NWNW | 1836-12-05 | FD | NWNW | R:HAMILTON |
| 1930 | CARGILL, Lewis | 25 | SWSE | 1853-10-27 | FD | SWSE | R:HAMILTON |
| 1955 | CARPENTER, Milton | 9 | S½NW | 1837-11-20 | FD | S2NW | R:HAMILTON |
| 1900 | " " | 16 | | 1838-08-04 | SC | SECT15 | |
| 1718 | CARROLL, | 25 | NENW | 1839-08-01 | FD | NENW | R:HAMILTON S:A |
| 1719 | " " | 25 | SWNW | 1839-08-01 | FD | SWNW | R:HAMILTON S:A |
| 1802 | CLARK, Isaac | 23 | NWNW | 1836-07-29 | FD | NWNW | R:HAMILTON |
| 1807 | CLARK, Isaac W | 25 | NWSW | 1854-03-14 | FD | NWSW | R:HAMILTON |
| 1994 | CLARK, Robin | 34 | SENE | 1839-10-31 | FD | SENE | R:HAMILTON |
| 1821 | CLUCK, James M | 31 | NWSW | 1853-01-11 | FD | NWSW | |
| 1822 | " " | 31 | SESW | 1853-05-05 | FD | SESW | R:HAMILTON |
| 1811 | COBB, James C | 33 | SESW | 1854-01-18 | FD | SESW | R:HAMILTON |
| 1704 | COKER, Anthony D | 34 | NWNW | 1851-04-20 | FD | NWNW | |
| 1703 | " " | 33 | NENE | 1851-04-20 | FD | NENE | |
| 1702 | " " | 27 | S½SW | 1851-04-20 | FD | S2SW | |
| 1705 | COKER, Anthony Doke | 8 | NWSW | 1850-03-29 | FD | NWSW | R:HAMILTON |
| 1720 | COKER, Catharine | 18 | NENW | 1850-08-13 | FD | NENW | R:HAMILTON S:F |
| 1721 | " " | 8 | SESW | 1850-08-13 | FD | SESW | R:HAMILTON S:F |
| 1882 | " " | 8 | SESW | 1850-08-13 | FD | SESW | R:HAMILTON S:F |
| 1743 | " " | 8 | SESW | 1850-08-13 | FD | SESW | R:HAMILTON S:F |
| 1728 | COKER, Charles | 24 | SWNW | 1839-08-29 | FD | SWNW | R:HAMILTON |
| 1727 | " " | 24 | E½NW | 1839-09-07 | FD | E2NW | R:HAMILTON |
| 1920 | COKER, Joseph | 7 | SWNE | 1851-03-14 | FD | SWNE | R:HAMILTON |
| 2023 | COTTINGHAM, Thomas | 11 | SENW | 1836-04-02 | FD | SENW | R:HAMILTON |
| 2021 | " " | 11 | NWNW | 1837-06-30 | FD | NWNW | R:HAMILTON |
| 2022 | " " | 11 | NWSE | 1839-01-28 | FD | NWSE | R:HAMILTON |
| 1790 | CRISEL, Henry | 22 | NWSW | 1834-05-29 | FD | NWSW | R:HAMILTON |
| 2044 | DAILEY, Vincent | 7 | NWSW | 1837-06-30 | FD | NWSW | R:HAMILTON |
| 1789 | DAILY, Harvy Jones | 8 | SWSW | 1850-07-09 | FD | SWSW | R:HAMILTON |
| 1867 | DAILY, John Jr | 5 | NESE | 1836-12-15 | FD | NESE | R:HAMILTON |
| 1951 | DAILY, Mastin W | 5 | NWSW | 1850-07-26 | FD | NWSW | R:HAMILTON |
| 2084 | DALE, Daniel | 19 | NWSW | 1851-03-25 | FD | NWSW | R:HAMILTON |
| 1756 | " " | 19 | NWSW | 1851-03-25 | FD | NWSW | R:HAMILTON |
| 1852 | DALE, John | 18 | SW | 1818-02-13 | FD | SW | R:WHITE |
| 1849 | " " | 18 | NESW | 1837-04-13 | FD | NESW | R:HAMILTON |
| 1853 | " " | 18 | SWNW | 1837-04-13 | SC | SWNW | R:HAMILTON |
| 1851 | " " | 18 | SESW | 1848-10-09 | FD | SESWVOID | |
| 1850 | " " | 18 | SESW | 1848-10-09 | FD | SESWVOID | |
| 1857 | " " | 19 | SWNW | 1848-10-09 | FD | SWNWVOID | |
| 2085 | " " | 19 | SWNW | 1848-10-09 | FD | SWNWVOID | |
| 1855 | " " | 19 | NENW | 1848-10-09 | FD | NENWVOID | |
| 1858 | " " | 19 | W½SW | 1848-10-09 | FD | W2SWVOID | |
| 1854 | " " | 19 | E½NW | 1850-09-06 | FD | E2NW | |
| 2083 | " " | 19 | E½NW | 1850-09-06 | FD | E2NW | |
| 1850 | " " | 18 | SESW | 1850-09-06 | FD | SESW | |
| 1851 | " " | 18 | SESW | 1850-09-06 | FD | SESW | |
| 1856 | " " | 19 | NWNW | 1850-09-06 | FD | NWNW | |
| 1860 | " " | 19 | NWNW | 1850-09-06 | FD | NWNW | |
| 1856 | DALE, John H | 19 | NWNW | 1853-11-16 | FD | NWNW | R:HAMILTON |
| 1860 | " " | 19 | NWNW | 1853-11-16 | FD | NWNW | R:HAMILTON |
| 1983 | DALE, Reuben | 18 | SENW | 1849-12-06 | FD | SENW | R:HAMILTON |
| 2030 | DAVIS, Alfred | 7 | NW | 1847-12-07 | FD | NW | |
| 1692 | " " | 7 | NW | 1847-12-07 | FD | NW | |
| 1691 | " " | 6 | SESW | 1850-03-29 | FD | SESW | R:HAMILTON |
| 1997 | DEETS, Samuel | 14 | NESW | 1851-04-02 | FD | NESW | R:HAMILTON |
| 1812 | DIAL, James | 30 | NENW | 1854-10-23 | FD | NENW | R:HAMILTON |
| 1922 | DONIPHAN, Joseph | 18 | NWNW | 1853-03-09 | FD | NWNW | |
| 2025 | DREW, Thomas | 1 | SWNW | 1851-09-22 | FD | SWNW | R:HAMILTON |

| ID | Individual in Patent | Sec. | Sec. Part | Purchase Date | Sale Type | IL Aliquot Part | For More Info . . . |
|---|---|---|---|---|---|---|---|
| 2024 | DREW, Thomas (Cont'd) | 1 | NWNW | 1851-12-12 | FD | NWNW | R:HAMILTON |
| 2058 | ECHOLDS, William | 6 | NW | 1850-07-18 | FD | NW | |
| 1933 | ECHOLS, Loftin | 5 | NENW | 1853-12-29 | FD | NENW | R:HAMILTON |
| 1936 | ECHOLS, Lofton | 8 | NENW | 1848-08-19 | FD | NENW | |
| 1935 | " " | 5 | SENW | 1848-08-19 | FD | SENW | |
| 1934 | " " | 5 | E½SW | 1848-08-19 | FD | E2SW | |
| 1685 | FLINT, Adrian | 31 | S½SE | 1853-12-16 | FD | S2SE | R:HAMILTON |
| 2059 | FLINT, William | 21 | SE | 1818-09-26 | FD | SE | R:WHITE |
| 1709 | FORD, Benjamin As | 9 | | 1831-07-04 | FD | ACFFR | |
| 1696 | FREIZE, Anderson C | 12 | NESE | 1854-11-27 | FD | NESE | R:POPE |
| 1832 | GARRISON, Jefferson | 3 | SWSE | 1852-11-29 | FD | SWSE | |
| 1831 | " " | 3 | NENE | 1852-12-18 | FD | NENE | R:HAMILTON |
| 1893 | GOFF, John R | 3 | W½SW | 1847-12-16 | FD | W2SW | |
| 1892 | " " | 3 | E½SE | 1847-12-16 | FD | E2SE | |
| 1990 | GOWDY, Robert A | 22 | SESW | 1837-03-18 | FD | SESW | R:HAMILTON |
| 1996 | GRANT, Roswell H | 18 | NW | 1818-08-06 | FD | NW | R:CINCINATTI |
| 1995 | " " | 18 | NE | 1818-08-06 | FD | NE | R:CINCINATTI |
| 1877 | " " | 21 | NE | 1820-02-09 | FD | NE | G:19 |
| 1785 | GROCE, George W | 2 | NENE | 1851-11-17 | FD | NENE | R:HAMILTON |
| 1805 | HARDGE, Isaac E | 33 | NWNW | 1848-06-26 | FD | NWNW | |
| 2075 | " " | 33 | SENW | 1848-06-26 | FD | SENW | |
| 2072 | " " | 33 | NWNW | 1848-06-26 | FD | NWNW | |
| 2069 | " " | 32 | NENE | 1848-06-26 | FD | NENE | |
| 1806 | " " | 33 | SENW | 1848-06-26 | FD | SENW | |
| 1803 | " " | 28 | SW | 1848-06-26 | FD | SW | |
| 1804 | " " | 32 | NENE | 1848-06-26 | FD | NENE | |
| 1859 | HARDY, John Garrett | 7 | NWNE | 1839-10-09 | FD | NWNE | R:HAMILTON |
| 1942 | HARPER, Mark | 30 | NWSW | 1852-08-18 | FD | NWSW | |
| 1943 | " " | 30 | SESW | 1855-09-24 | FD | SESW | R:HAMILTON |
| 1947 | HAWLEY, Paul G | 31 | SWSW | 1857-07-21 | FD | SWSW | G:22 |
| 1695 | " " | 31 | SWSW | 1857-07-21 | FD | SWSW | G:22 |
| 1814 | HAYNES, James | 14 | SE | 1818-12-14 | FD | SE | R:WHITE |
| 1861 | HAYS, John | 31 | N½SE | 1852-09-06 | FD | N2SE | |
| 1904 | " " | 31 | NESW | 1853-03-14 | FD | NESWVOID | |
| 1862 | " " | 31 | NESW | 1853-03-14 | FD | NESWVOID | |
| 1738 | HEARD, Charles H | 22 | SWNW | 1839-01-03 | FD | SWNW | R:HAMILTON |
| 1737 | " " | 22 | NESW | 1839-01-03 | FD | NESW | R:HAMILTON |
| 1742 | " " | 4 | SW | 1848-11-18 | FD | SW | |
| 1730 | " " | 12 | N½SE | 1848-11-18 | FD | N2SE | |
| 1731 | " " | 12 | SENW | 1848-11-18 | FD | SENW | |
| 1732 | " " | 12 | SWNE | 1848-11-18 | FD | SWNE | |
| 1733 | " " | 16 | NWNW | 1849-05-05 | FD | NWNW | |
| 1746 | " " | 9 | SEN½ | 1849-05-05 | FD | S2NE | |
| 1744 | " " | 9 | NENE | 1849-05-05 | FD | NENE | |
| 1735 | " " | 21 | SWSW | 1851-03-17 | FD | SWSW | R:HAMILTON |
| 1743 | " " | 8 | SESW | 1851-04-14 | FD | SESW | |
| 1721 | " " | 8 | SESW | 1851-04-14 | FD | SESW | |
| 1882 | " " | 8 | SESW | 1851-04-14 | FD | SESW | |
| 1729 | " " | 10 | NENW | 1853-02-24 | FD | NENW | R:HAMILTON |
| 1745 | " " | 9 | NWNW | 1853-02-24 | FD | NWNW | R:HAMILTON |
| 1740 | " " | 27 | | 1853-07-01 | FD | W2NWSZ | |
| 1740 | " " | 27 | | 1853-07-01 | FD | NWSESZ | |
| 1740 | " " | 27 | | 1853-07-01 | FD | SENWSZ | |
| 1736 | " " | 22 | | 1853-07-01 | FD | SWSWSZ | |
| 1740 | " " | 27 | | 1853-07-01 | FD | NESWSZ | |
| 1740 | " " | 27 | | 1853-07-01 | FD | SWNESZ | |
| 1734 | " " | 20 | NWSW | 1853-12-29 | FD | NWSW | R:HAMILTON |
| 1741 | " " | 36 | NENE | 1854-03-28 | FD | NENE | R:HAMILTON |
| 1739 | " " | 26 | S½ | 1854-09-20 | FD | S2 | R:HAMILTON |
| 1747 | HEARD, Charles Harvey | 10 | W½NE | 1836-12-15 | FD | W2NE | R:HAMILTON |
| 1748 | " " | 9 | E½SE | 1837-04-14 | FD | E2SE | R:HAMILTON |
| 1749 | HEARD, Charles Henry | 22 | E½NW | 1839-02-23 | FD | E2NW | R:HAMILTON |
| 1823 | HEARD, James M | 34 | SESW | 1854-04-25 | FD | SESW | R:HAMILTON |
| 1954 | HERD, John | 16 | | 1832-10-30 | SC | SECT12 | |
| 1834 | " " | 16 | | 1832-10-30 | SC | SECT12 | |
| 1750 | HILL, Charles | 25 | SENW | 1839-09-12 | FD | SENW | R:HAMILTON |
| 1793 | HITE, | 13 | NW | 1818-08-14 | FD | NW | S:A G:23 |
| 1792 | " " | 12 | S½ | 1818-08-14 | FD | S2 | S:A G:24 |
| 2004 | HOGG, Samuel | 31 | NE | 1818-02-19 | FD | NE | R:WHITE |
| 1715 | HOLLAND, Berryman | 5 | NWNE | 1853-02-26 | FD | NWNE | |
| 1982 | HOOD, Benjamin | 16 | | 1832-03-20 | SC | SECT4 | |
| 1711 | " " | 35 | NENW | 1839-09-16 | FD | NENW | R:HAMILTON |
| 2065 | HOOD, William | 35 | SWNW | 1853-01-15 | FD | SWNW | |

| ID | Individual in Patent | Sec. | Sec. Part | Purchase Date | Sale Type | IL Aliquot Part | For More Info . . . |
|----|---------------------|------|-----------|---------------|-----------|-----------------|---------------------|
| 2064 | HOOD, William (Cont'd) | 35 | SENW | 1855-07-09 | FD | SENW | R:HAMILTON |
| 2063 | " " | 35 | NWNW | 1855-07-09 | FD | NWNW | R:HAMILTON |
| 1712 | HOOVER, Nathan | 11 | SWNW | 1843-10-17 | FD | SWNW | G:25 |
| 1816 | HUNTER, James | 29 | NWNW | 1836-07-04 | FD | NWNW | R:HAMILTON |
| 1818 | " " | 30 | NENE | 1850-12-31 | FD | NENE | R:HAMILTON |
| 1918 | " " | 19 | SESE | 1850-12-31 | FD | SESE | R:HAMILTON |
| 1817 | " " | 29 | SWNW | 1850-12-31 | FD | SWNW | R:HAMILTON |
| 1815 | " " | 19 | SESE | 1850-12-31 | FD | SESE | R:HAMILTON |
| 1683 | HUTSON, Abraham | 23 | E½SE | 1829-04-28 | FD | E2SE | R:HAMILTON |
| 1956 | HUTSON, Moses | 25 | NE | 1847-11-30 | FD | NE | |
| 1957 | " " | 26 | NENE | 1853-12-05 | FD | NENE | R:HAMILTON |
| 2039 | HUTSON, Uel H | 25 | NESW | 1848-11-21 | FD | NESW | R:HAMILTON |
| 2038 | " " | 23 | W½SE | 1853-11-24 | FD | W2SE | R:HAMILTON |
| 2042 | HUTSON, Vel H | 26 | NWNW | 1853-12-02 | FD | NWNW | R:HAMILTON |
| 2041 | " " | 26 | NWNE | 1854-04-17 | FD | NWNE | R:HAMILTON |
| 2043 | " " | 26 | SWNE | 1854-05-02 | FD | SWNE | R:HAMILTON |
| 1712 | HYSSIS, Benjamin | 11 | SWNW | 1843-10-17 | FD | SWNW | G:25 |
| 2017 | INGRAM, Sewel | 6 | NWSE | 1841-09-23 | FD | NWSE | R:HAMILTON |
| 2016 | " " | 6 | NESW | 1850-05-04 | FD | NESW | R:HAMILTON |
| 2018 | " " | 6 | SWSE | 1851-04-23 | FD | SWSE | |
| 1684 | IRVIN, Abraham | 21 | SWNE | 1851-07-03 | FD | SWNE | |
| 1940 | IRVIN, Lucretia | 20 | NWNE | 1853-11-16 | FD | NWNE | R:HAMILTON S:F |
| 1953 | JONES, Michael | 23 | E½NW | 1818-05-06 | FD | E2NW | R:SHAWNEETOWN |
| 1700 | KIRKPATRICK, Andrew | 20 | SESW | 1895-10-11 | RR | SESW | |
| 1908 | " " | 20 | SESW | 1895-10-11 | RR | SESW | |
| 1819 | LANE, James Jr | 12 | SESE | 1839-01-23 | FD | SESE | R:HAMILTON |
| 1926 | LANE, Laven | 10 | SWNW | 1838-01-25 | FD | SWNW | R:HAMILTON |
| 1928 | LANE, Leven | 9 | W½SE | 1836-06-20 | FD | W2SE | R:HAMILTON |
| 1927 | LANE, Leven As | 10 | | 1831-07-04 | FD | SWACFFC | |
| 2078 | " " | 10 | | 1831-07-04 | FD | SWACFFC | |
| 1931 | LANE, Lewis | 21 | NWNE | 1851-09-12 | FD | NWNE | R:HAMILTON |
| 2090 | LANE, William West | 13 | NWNW | 1834-05-29 | FD | NWNW | R:HAMILTON |
| 1839 | LEAKY, Joel | 23 | NE | 1817-02-19 | FD | NE | R:GALLATIN |
| 2005 | LEECH, Samuel | 13 | NE | 1818-09-21 | FD | NE | R:SHAWNEETOWN |
| 1921 | LOCKHART, Joseph D | 17 | NWNE | 1851-03-17 | FD | NWNE | R:HAMILTON |
| 1778 | LOCKWOOD, Elsey R | 17 | NESE | 1838-02-14 | FD | NESE | R:HAMILTON |
| 1863 | LOCKWOOD, Jesse C | 16 | | 1832-03-10 | SC | SECT16 | |
| 1835 | LOCKWOOD, Jesse Close | 22 | NWNW | 1836-04-27 | FD | NWNW | R:HAMILTON |
| 1869 | LONG, John | 10 | E½NE | 1836-12-08 | FD | E2NE | R:HAMILTON |
| 1871 | " " | 12 | SWSW | 1836-12-13 | FD | SWSW | R:HAMILTON |
| 1870 | " " | 11 | NESE | 1839-01-23 | FD | NESE | R:HAMILTON |
| 2031 | LONG, Thomas M | 2 | NENW | 1852-08-19 | FD | NENW | |
| 1820 | LORIE, James Jr | 13 | NENW | 1837-08-01 | FD | NENW | R:HAMILTON |
| 1872 | MANGIS, John | 14 | SEN½ | 1849-12-11 | FD | S2NE | R:HAMILTON |
| 2006 | MANNING, Samuel | 32 | NESE | 1855-03-26 | FD | NESE | R:HAMILTON |
| 2013 | MANNING, Sarah | 32 | SWNE | 1851-11-19 | FD | SWNE | S:F |
| 2012 | " " | 32 | SENW | 1851-11-19 | FD | SENW | S:F |
| 2036 | MARSH, Thomas W | 19 | SWSE | 1853-11-02 | FD | SWSE | R:HAMILTON |
| 2035 | " " | 19 | SESW | 1853-11-02 | FD | SESW | R:HAMILTON |
| 2037 | " " | 30 | NWNE | 1854-10-23 | FD | NWNE | R:HAMILTON |
| 1981 | MARSHALL, Daniel | 16 | | 1834-01-06 | SC | SECT13 | |
| 1758 | " " | 15 | E½SE | 1836-05-16 | FD | E2SE | R:HAMILTON |
| 1759 | " " | 15 | W½SE | 1836-11-04 | FD | W2SE | R:HAMILTON |
| 1757 | " " | 14 | W½SE | 1839-03-12 | FD | W2SE | R:HAMILTON |
| 1875 | MARSHALL, John | 14 | N½ | 1818-09-21 | FD | N2 | R:SHAWNEETOWN |
| 1874 | " " | 11 | S½ | 1818-09-21 | FD | S2 | R:SHAWNEETOWN |
| 1873 | " " | 10 | SE | 1818-09-21 | FD | SE | R:SHAWNEETOWN |
| 1876 | " " | 15 | NE | 1818-09-21 | FD | NE | R:SHAWNEETOWN |
| 1760 | MARSHALL, John W | 16 | | 1836-03-08 | SC | SECT2 | |
| 1760 | " " | 16 | | 1836-03-08 | SC | SECT9 | |
| 1782 | " " | 16 | | 1836-03-08 | SC | SECT10 | |
| 1782 | " " | 16 | | 1836-03-08 | SC | SECT3 | |
| 1901 | MARSHALL, John Walker | 17 | E½NE | 1836-07-04 | FD | E2NE | R:HAMILTON |
| 2007 | MARSHALL, Samuel S | 2 | SENW | 1853-08-09 | FD | SENW | R:HAMILTON |
| 2056 | MATHENY, William C | 34 | S½NW | 1853-06-28 | FD | S2NW | R:HAMILTON |
| 1984 | MAULDING, Richard | 7 | SE | 1818-05-11 | FD | SE | R:WHITE |
| 1947 | MCDONALD, Mary A | 31 | SWSW | 1848-12-27 | FD | SWSW | S:F |
| 1695 | " " | 31 | SWSW | 1848-12-27 | FD | SWSW | S:F |
| 1787 | MCFARLAND, Gilbert | 7 | SWSW | 1839-03-28 | FD | SWSW | R:HAMILTON |
| 1824 | MCFARLAND, James | 7 | E½SW | 1839-03-28 | FD | E2SW | R:ST. CLAIR |
| 1948 | MCLEAN, Charles | 20 | E½SE | 1818-09-09 | FD | E2SE | R:KENTUCKY |
| 1752 | " " | 21 | SW | 1818-09-09 | FD | SW | R:KENTUCKY |
| 1753 | " " | 28 | NW | 1818-09-09 | FD | NW | R:KENTUCKY |

| ID | Individual in Patent | Sec. | Sec. Part | Purchase Date | Sale Type | IL Aliquot Part | For More Info . . . |
|---|---|---|---|---|---|---|---|
| 1751 | MCLEAN, Charles (Cont'd) | 20 | E½SE | 1818-09-09 | FD | E2SE | R:KENTUCKY |
| 1877 | MCLEAN, John | 21 | NE | 1820-02-09 | FD | NE | G:19 |
| 1927 | MCLEAN, William | 10 | | 1818-09-09 | FD | SWNTACVOFFR | |
| 2079 | "          " | 15 | NW | 1818-09-09 | FD | NW | R:KENTUCKY |
| 2078 | "          " | 10 | | 1818-09-09 | FD | SWNTACVOFFR | |
| 2001 | MCMAHAN, James | 13 | N½NE | 1851-04-05 | FD | N2NE | |
| 1825 | "          " | 13 | N½NE | 1851-04-05 | FD | N2NE | |
| 1833 | MCNAMER, Jeremiah | 12 | NE | 1819-02-10 | FD | NE | R:UNION |
| 1878 | MCNEMAR, John | 11 | SWSE | 1835-09-04 | FD | SWSE | R:HAMILTON |
| 1879 | "          " | 12 | SENE | 1836-03-17 | FD | SENE | R:HAMILTON |
| 1794 | MITCHEL, Ichabod | 24 | SWSE | 1853-08-16 | FD | SWSE | R:GALLATIN |
| 1797 | MITCHELL, Ichabod | 24 | E½NE | 1836-05-04 | FD | E2NE | R:HAMILTON |
| 1799 | "          " | 24 | SWNE | 1839-08-29 | FD | SWNE | R:HAMILTON |
| 1796 | "          " | 23 | SWSW | 1851-01-09 | FD | SWSW | R:HAMILTON |
| 1795 | "          " | 22 | SESE | 1851-03-05 | FD | SESE | R:HAMILTON |
| 1800 | "          " | 34 | W½SW | 1852-09-27 | FD | W2SW | |
| 1798 | "          " | 24 | SESE | 1853-03-22 | FD | SESE | |
| 1801 | MITCHELL, Ichaboo | 24 | NESE | 1850-02-25 | FD | NESE | R:HAMILTON |
| 1826 | MOORE, James | 5 | NENE | 1847-06-07 | FD | NENE | R:HAMILTON |
| 1837 | MOORE, Jesse | 1 | S½SE | 1837-03-15 | FD | S2SE | R:HAMILTON |
| 1836 | "          " | 1 | NESW | 1851-02-11 | FD | NESW | R:HAMILTON |
| 1838 | "          " | 1 | SENE | 1853-02-01 | FD | SENE | R:HAMILTON |
| 2014 | MOORE, Sarah | 1 | NWSE | 1838-12-05 | FD | NWSE | R:HAMILTON S:F |
| 2080 | MOORE, William | 1 | NENE | 1839-09-07 | FD | NENE | R:HAMILTON |
| 1978 | MORRIS, Allen | 32 | NWSW | 1849-08-30 | FD | NWSW | |
| 1693 | "          " | 32 | E½SW | 1849-08-30 | FD | E2SW | |
| 1694 | "          " | 32 | NWSW | 1849-08-30 | FD | NWSW | |
| 1777 | MORRIS, Elizabeth | 21 | NWSW | 1847-11-27 | FD | NWSW | R:HAMILTON S:F |
| 1751 | MORRIS, Mason | 20 | E½SE | 1837-04-12 | FD | E2SE | R:HAMILTON |
| 1948 | "          " | 20 | E½SE | 1837-04-12 | FD | E2SE | R:HAMILTON |
| 1950 | "          " | 20 | W½SE | 1849-03-20 | FD | W2SE | |
| 1949 | "          " | 20 | SEN½ | 1849-03-20 | FD | S2NE | |
| 2081 | MOULDING, William | 6 | N½NE | 1850-05-31 | FD | N2NE | |
| 2082 | "          " | 6 | SWNE | 1850-05-31 | FD | SWNE | |
| 1985 | MUNSELL, Richard | 13 | SENE | 1845-09-20 | FD | SENE | R:HAMILTON |
| 1986 | "          " | 24 | NWSW | 1854-10-03 | FD | NWSW | R:HAMILTON |
| 1881 | MURPHY, John | 8 | SENE | 1848-10-16 | FD | SENEVOID | |
| 1721 | "          " | 8 | SESW | 1848-10-16 | FD | SESWVOID | |
| 1882 | "          " | 8 | SESW | 1848-10-16 | FD | SESWVOID | |
| 1880 | "          " | 8 | NESE | 1848-10-16 | FD | NESEVOID | |
| 1916 | "          " | 8 | NESE | 1848-10-16 | FD | NESEVOID | |
| 1743 | "          " | 8 | SESW | 1848-10-16 | FD | SESWVOID | |
| 1883 | "          " | 8 | SWSE | 1848-10-16 | FD | SWSEVOID | |
| 2000 | MUSGRAVE, Samuel G | 12 | NWNE | 1834-02-19 | FD | NWNE | R:HAMILTON |
| 1962 | "          " | 12 | NWNE | 1834-02-19 | FD | NWNE | R:HAMILTON |
| 1999 | "          " | 12 | NENW | 1834-09-12 | FD | NENW | R:HAMILTON |
| 1998 | "          " | 1 | SESW | 1837-03-02 | FD | SESW | R:HAMILTON |
| 1962 | MUSKGRAVE, Nancy | 12 | NWNE | 1837-02-27 | FD | NWNE | R:HAMILTON S:F |
| 2000 | "          " | 12 | NWNE | 1837-02-27 | FD | NWNE | R:HAMILTON S:F |
| 1868 | NEWMAN, John L | 6 | NWSW | 1852-01-07 | FD | NWSW | |
| 1710 | OGLESBY, Reuban | 16 | | 1834-02-25 | SC | SECT1 | |
| 1980 | "          " | 16 | | 1834-10-13 | SC | SECT7 | |
| 1782 | "          " | 16 | | 1835-06-10 | SC | SECT8 | |
| 1905 | ONEAL, John William | 21 | NENW | 1842-01-22 | FD | NENW | R:HAMILTON |
| 1793 | ORMSBY, | 13 | NW | 1818-08-14 | FD | NW | S:A G:23 |
| 1792 | "          " | 12 | S½ | 1818-08-14 | FD | S2 | S:A G:24 |
| 2062 | PETMAN, William H | 34 | NESW | 1854-04-03 | FD | NESW | R:HAMILTON |
| 1754 | PHELPS, Charles | 27 | NENE | 1851-07-29 | FD | NENE | |
| 1884 | PHELPS, John | 36 | NWNE | 1851-02-26 | FD | NWNE | R:HAMILTON |
| 1755 | PITTMAN, Christopher | 34 | SESE | 1849-04-11 | FD | SESE | R:HAMILTON |
| 1945 | PLUNCKETT, Martha | 30 | NWNW | 1852-03-04 | FD | NWNW | S:F |
| 1885 | PRATT, John | 22 | NESE | 1852-09-24 | FD | NESE | |
| 1886 | "          " | 22 | SENE | 1852-09-24 | FD | SENE | |
| 1888 | PRESLEY, John | 33 | NWSE | 1851-09-22 | FD | NWSE | R:HAMILTON |
| 1887 | "          " | 33 | N½SW | 1852-10-06 | FD | N2SW | |
| 1889 | "          " | 33 | SWSW | 1854-03-25 | FD | SWSW | R:HAMILTON |
| 1890 | PROCTER, John | 14 | NWNE | 1836-03-12 | FD | NWNE | R:GALLATIN |
| 1713 | PROCTOR, Benjamin | 13 | SWNE | 1851-05-22 | FD | SWNE | R:HAMILTON |
| 1763 | PROCTOR, David | 1 | SE | 1819-01-14 | FD | SE | R:WHITE |
| 1891 | PROCTOR, John | 11 | SESE | 1836-03-12 | FD | SESE | R:GALLATIN |
| 1932 | PROCTOR, Little Page | 14 | SESW | 1836-06-29 | FD | SESW | R:HAMILTON |
| 2001 | PROCTOR, Samuel H | 13 | N½NE | 1848-11-27 | FD | N2NE | |
| 1825 | "          " | 13 | N½NE | 1848-11-27 | FD | N2NE | |

| ID | Individual in Patent | Sec. | Sec. Part | Purchase Date | Sale Type | IL Aliquot Part | For More Info . . . |
|----|---------------------|------|-----------|---------------|-----------|-----------------|---------------------|
| 2003 | PROCTOR, Samuel H T | 13 | S½NW | 1849-03-17 | FD | S2NW | |
| 2002 | " | " | 13 | E½SW | 1849-03-17 | FD | E2SW | |
| 1895 | RAFFERTY, John | 19 | NWNE | 1849-05-11 | FD | NWNE | R:HAMILTON |
| 1894 | " | " | 19 | NESE | 1854-10-23 | FD | NESE | R:HAMILTON |
| 1896 | " | " | 19 | SEN½ | 1854-10-23 | FD | S2NE | R:HAMILTON |
| 1987 | RAMBEAU, Richard | 36 | SWNE | 1851-10-07 | FD | SWNE | R:HAMILTON |
| 1988 | RAMBO, Richard | 25 | SESE | 1853-11-28 | FD | SESE | R:HAMILTON |
| 1771 | RATHBONE, Edward D | 21 | NESW | 1847-11-18 | FD | NESW | R:HAMILTON |
| 1938 | RATHBONE, Lorenzo | 21 | W½SE | 1836-05-11 | FD | W2SE | R:HAMILTON |
| 1937 | " | " | 21 | SENW | 1849-12-29 | FD | SENW | R:HAMILTON |
| 1939 | " | " | 28 | NENE | 1851-09-06 | FD | NENE | R:HAMILTON |
| 2040 | RATHBONE, Valentine | 28 | NWNE | 1847-11-29 | FD | NWNE | R:HAMILTON |
| 1774 | RICHARDSON, David | 6 | SENE | 1853-02-19 | FD | SENE | R:HAMILTON |
| 1765 | " | " | 6 | SENE | 1853-02-19 | FD | SENE | R:HAMILTON |
| 1773 | " | " | 6 | NESE | 1853-02-19 | FD | NESE | R:HAMILTON |
| 1764 | " | " | 6 | NESE | 1853-02-19 | FD | NESE | R:HAMILTON |
| 1864 | RITCHEY, John J | 24 | NESW | 1851-04-02 | FD | NESW | |
| 1865 | " | " | 24 | NWSE | 1851-04-02 | FD | NWSE | |
| 1866 | " | " | 24 | S½SW | 1851-04-02 | FD | S2SW | |
| 1944 | ROGERS, Mark W | 16 | L72 | 1851-03-15 | SC | LOT72 | |
| 1716 | ROMINE, Caroline | 28 | N½SE | 1853-06-16 | FD | N2SE | R:HAMILTON S:F G:34 |
| 1717 | " | " | 28 | SEN½ | 1853-06-16 | FD | S2NE | R:HAMILTON S:F G:34 |
| 1963 | ROMINE, Peter A | 28 | N½SW | 1853-06-16 | FD | N2SW | R:HAMILTON |
| 1716 | ROMINE, Sarah Ann | 28 | N½SE | 1853-06-16 | FD | N2SE | R:HAMILTON S:F G:34 |
| 1717 | " | " | 28 | SEN½ | 1853-06-16 | FD | S2NE | R:HAMILTON S:F G:34 |
| 1686 | SALLENGER, Alexander | 17 | S½SW | 1848-03-09 | FD | S2SW | |
| 1687 | " | " | 17 | W½SE | 1848-03-09 | FD | W2SE | |
| 1784 | SAUER, George | 31 | E½NE | 1859-10-29 | FD | E2NW | |
| 2033 | SCOTT, Thomas | 26 | SENW | 1837-03-16 | FD | SENW | R:HAMILTON |
| 2032 | " | " | 26 | NENW | 1844-04-24 | FD | NENWLS | |
| 2034 | " | " | 26 | SWNW | 1849-12-18 | FD | SWNW | R:HAMILTON |
| 2085 | SEPHENS, William S | 19 | SWNW | 1849-11-09 | FD | SWNW | |
| 2083 | " | " | 19 | E½NW | 1849-11-09 | FD | E2NW | |
| 1857 | " | " | 19 | SWNW | 1849-11-09 | FD | SWNW | |
| 1854 | " | " | 19 | E½NW | 1849-11-09 | FD | E2NW | |
| 2084 | " | " | 19 | NWSW | 1849-11-09 | FD | NWSW | |
| 1756 | " | " | 19 | NWSW | 1849-11-09 | FD | NWSW | |
| 1766 | SHARP, David | 3 | SW | 1852-07-13 | FD | SWLS | R:HAMILTON |
| 1958 | SHIRBEY, Moses Jr | 18 | E½NE | 1839-06-10 | FD | E2NE | R:HAMILTON |
| 1961 | SHIRLEY, Moses | 18 | SE | 1818-02-13 | FD | SE | R:KENTUCKY |
| 1960 | " | " | 18 | E½SE | 1836-06-17 | FD | E2SE | R:HAMILTON |
| 1959 | SHIRLEY, Moses Jr | 17 | NWNW | 1840-11-27 | FD | NWNW | R:HAMILTON |
| 2026 | SLOO, Thomas Jr | 3 | NW | 1818-05-30 | FD | NW | R:CINCINATTI |
| 2027 | " | " | 4 | NE | 1818-05-30 | FD | NE | R:CINCINATTI |
| 2028 | " | " | 4 | NW | 1818-05-30 | FD | NW | R:CINCINATTI |
| 2030 | " | " | 7 | NW | 1818-06-03 | FD | NW | R:CINCINATTI |
| 1692 | " | " | 7 | NW | 1818-06-03 | FD | NW | R:CINCINATTI |
| 2029 | " | " | 7 | NE | 1818-06-03 | FD | NE | R:CINCINATTI |
| 1947 | SMITH, Alonzo B | 31 | SWSW | 1857-07-21 | FD | SWSW | G:22 |
| 1695 | " | " | 31 | SWSW | 1857-07-21 | FD | SWSW | G:22 |
| 1815 | SMITH, Joseph B | 19 | SESE | 1857-06-17 | FD | SESE | |
| 1918 | " | " | 19 | SESE | 1857-06-17 | FD | SESE | |
| 1989 | SMITH, Richard W | 29 | NE | 1819-03-05 | FD | NE | R:WHITE |
| 1701 | SNIDER, Andrew | 1 | NENW | 1851-12-12 | FD | NENW | R:HAMILTON |
| 2087 | STADDEN, William | 31 | SWNW | 1873-05-16 | FD | SWNW | |
| 1722 | STANFIELD, Catherine | 5 | SESE | 1850-11-16 | FD | SESE | S:F |
| 1723 | " | " | 8 | E½NE | 1850-11-16 | FD | E2NE | S:F |
| 1724 | " | " | 8 | NWNE | 1850-11-16 | FD | NWNE | S:F |
| 2047 | " | " | 8 | NWNE | 1850-11-16 | FD | NWNE | S:F |
| 1725 | STANTON, Champ | 20 | N½NE | 1852-03-12 | FD | N2NW | |
| 2008 | STEELLE, Samuel | 6 | SWSW | 1850-07-29 | FD | SWSW | |
| 1804 | STEPHENS, William L | 32 | NENE | 1850-06-18 | FD | NENE | |
| 2072 | " | " | 33 | NWNW | 1850-06-18 | FD | NWNW | |
| 1805 | " | " | 33 | NWNW | 1850-06-18 | FD | NWNW | |
| 2066 | " | " | 28 | S½SW | 1850-06-18 | FD | S2SW | |
| 2069 | " | " | 32 | NENE | 1850-06-18 | FD | NENE | |
| 1806 | " | " | 33 | SENW | 1850-12-02 | FD | SENW | R:GALLATIN |
| 2075 | " | " | 33 | SENW | 1850-12-02 | FD | SENW | R:GALLATIN |
| 2076 | " | " | 33 | SWNE | 1851-04-25 | FD | SWNE | R:HAMILTON |
| 2070 | " | " | 32 | SENE | 1851-10-09 | FD | SENE | R:HAMILTON |
| 2068 | " | " | 28 | SWSE | 1853-11-18 | FD | SWSE | R:HAMILTON |
| 2071 | " | " | 33 | NESE | 1854-09-20 | FD | NESE | R:HAMILTON |
| 2067 | " | " | 28 | SESE | 1854-09-20 | FD | SESE | R:HAMILTON |

| ID | Individual in Patent | Sec. | Sec. Part | Purchase Date | Sale Type | IL Aliquot Part | For More Info . . . |
|----|---------------------|------|-----------|---------------|-----------|-----------------|---------------------|
| 2073 | STEPHENS, William L (Cont'd) | 33 | S½SE | 1854-09-20 | FD | S2SE | R:HAMILTON |
| 2074 | " " | 33 | SEN½ | 1854-09-20 | FD | S2NE | R:HAMILTON |
| 2086 | STEPHENS, William S | 33 | SWNW | 1854-03-13 | FD | SWNW | R:HAMILTON |
| 1827 | STEPHENSON, James W | 12 | NENE | 1850-11-22 | FD | NENE | R:HAMILTON |
| 1829 | " " | 2 | NWSE | 1852-03-20 | FD | NWSE | |
| 1828 | " " | 2 | NESW | 1852-03-20 | FD | NESW | |
| 1923 | STEPHENSON, Joseph M | 11 | SENE | 1850-11-22 | FD | SENE | R:HAMILTON |
| 2077 | STEVENS, William L | 33 | NWNE | 1850-07-23 | FD | NWNE | R:HAMILTON |
| 1688 | SULLINGER, Alexander | 17 | SWNE | 1851-10-02 | FD | SWNE | |
| 1793 | SULLIVAN, | 13 | NW | 1818-08-14 | FD | NW | S:A G:23 |
| 1792 | SULLIVAN, No Ft Nm | 12 | S½ | 1818-08-14 | FD | S2 | S:A G:24 |
| 1714 | TODD, Benjamin | 1 | NWSW | 1851-12-19 | FD | NWSW | R:HAMILTON |
| 1898 | TOWNSEND, John | 31 | NW | 1816-11-15 | FD | NW | R:WHITE |
| 1783 | TUBMAN, George M | 15 | SW | 1819-09-01 | FD | SW | R:CINCINATTI |
| 1899 | TUNSEND, John | 31 | E½NE | 1839-01-16 | FD | E2NE | R:HAMILTON |
| 2009 | VAUGH, Samuel | 2 | NWNE | 1852-12-07 | FD | NWNE | R:HAMILTON |
| 2010 | VAUGHAN, Samuel | 2 | SWNE | 1853-10-08 | FD | SWNE | R:HAMILTON |
| 2088 | WALLIS, William | 22 | NENE | 1839-08-19 | FD | NENE | R:HAMILTON |
| 2089 | " " | 23 | SWNW | 1839-08-29 | FD | SWNW | R:HAMILTON |
| 1706 | WARD, Argon | 29 | S½SE | 1850-01-28 | FD | S2SE | G:7 |
| 1708 | " " | 32 | NWNE | 1850-01-28 | FD | NWNE | G:7 |
| 1707 | " " | 29 | SESW | 1850-01-28 | FD | SESW | G:7 |
| 1902 | WEBB, John | 13 | SE | 1847-12-08 | FD | SE | |
| 1690 | WELDIN, Alfred B | 12 | NWNW | 1850-11-22 | FD | NWNW | R:HAMILTON |
| 1689 | " " | 1 | SWSW | 1850-11-22 | FD | SWSW | R:HAMILTON |
| 1830 | WELLS, James | 1 | W½NE | 1852-01-03 | FD | W2NE | |
| 1781 | WESTON, Fredrick B | 34 | N½SE | 1844-06-08 | FD | N2SE | R:HAMILTON |
| 2015 | WESTON, Sarah | 20 | SWSW | 1853-11-15 | FD | SWSW | R:FRANKLIN S:F |
| 2011 | WESTON, Sarah Ann | 34 | SWNE | 1844-06-18 | FD | SWNE | R:HAMILTON S:F |
| 1903 | WHEELER, John | 24 | NE | 1819-02-22 | FD | NE | R:WHITE |
| 2091 | WHEELER, Willis | 25 | NESE | 1838-02-27 | FD | NESE | R:HAMILTON |
| 1779 | WHITE, Evaline | 30 | SEN½ | 1847-11-27 | FD | S2NE | R:HAMILTON S:F |
| 1862 | WHITE, John | 31 | NESW | 1855-05-23 | FD | NESW | R:HAMILTON |
| 1904 | " " | 31 | NESW | 1855-05-23 | FD | NESW | R:HAMILTON |
| 1964 | WHITE, Precious | 19 | NENE | 1852-01-21 | FD | NENE | S:F |
| 1968 | WHITE, Preston | 30 | NESE | 1836-09-01 | FD | NESE | R:HAMILTON |
| 1975 | " " | 30 | W½SW | 1847-11-27 | FD | W2SW | |
| 1971 | " " | 30 | S½SE | 1847-11-27 | FD | S2SE | |
| 1970 | " " | 30 | NWSE | 1847-11-27 | FD | NWSE | R:HAMILTON |
| 1977 | " " | 32 | NWNW | 1848-12-29 | FD | NWNW | R:HAMILTON |
| 1706 | " " | 29 | S½SE | 1850-01-28 | FD | S2SE | G:7 |
| 1707 | " " | 29 | SESW | 1850-01-28 | FD | SESW | G:7 |
| 1708 | " " | 32 | NWNE | 1850-01-28 | FD | NWNE | G:7 |
| 1974 | " " | 30 | SWSW | 1850-02-25 | FD | SWSW | R:HAMILTON |
| 1967 | " " | 29 | NESW | 1852-03-04 | FD | NESW | R:HAMILTON |
| 1976 | " " | 32 | NENW | 1852-08-31 | FD | NENW | |
| 1973 | " " | 30 | SWNW | 1853-03-02 | FD | SWNW | R:HAMILTON |
| 1694 | " " | 32 | NWSW | 1853-03-02 | FD | NWSW | R:HAMILTON |
| 1978 | " " | 32 | NWSW | 1853-03-02 | FD | NWSW | R:HAMILTON |
| 1979 | " " | 32 | SWNW | 1853-03-02 | FD | SWNW | R:HAMILTON |
| 1972 | " " | 30 | SENW | 1853-11-16 | FD | SENW | R:HAMILTON |
| 1969 | " " | 30 | NESW | 1853-12-16 | FD | NESW | R:HAMILTON |
| 1965 | " " | 19 | NESW | 1853-12-16 | FD | NESW | R:HAMILTON |
| 1966 | " " | 19 | NWSE | 1853-12-16 | FD | NWSE | R:HAMILTON |
| 2049 | WILLIAMS, Wiley | 8 | S½NW | 1848-12-13 | FD | S2NW | |
| 2048 | " " | 8 | S½NW | 1848-12-13 | FD | S2NW | |
| 1724 | " " | 8 | NWNE | 1848-12-13 | FD | NWNE | |
| 2046 | " " | 7 | NENE | 1848-12-13 | FD | NENE | |
| 2047 | " " | 8 | NWNE | 1848-12-13 | FD | NWNE | |
| 2049 | " " | 8 | S½NW | 1849-03-01 | FD | S2NW | |
| 2048 | " " | 8 | S½NW | 1849-03-01 | FD | S2NW | |
| 2045 | " " | 7 | E½NE | 1849-03-01 | FD | E2NE | |
| 2060 | WILLIAMS, William G | 1 | NESE | 1836-11-28 | FD | NESE | R:HAMILTON |
| 2061 | " " | 1 | SENW | 1854-01-02 | FD | SENW | R:HAMILTON |
| 2093 | WILLIAMS, Wylie | 8 | NWNW | 1842-06-04 | FD | NWNW | R:HAMILTON |
| 2092 | " " | 6 | SESE | 1842-06-04 | FD | SESE | R:HAMILTON |
| 1897 | WILLIS, John S | 14 | W½SW | 1821-08-04 | FD | W2SW | R:FRANKLIN |
| 1952 | WILLIS, Merrel | 8 | SESE | 1839-11-19 | FD | SESE | R:HAMILTON |
| 1841 | WILSON, John A | 16 | L84 | 1851-03-15 | SC | LOT84 | |
| 1840 | " " | 16 | L73 | 1851-03-15 | SC | LOT73 | |
| 1993 | WITT, Robert | 14 | NENE | 1834-02-14 | FD | NENE | R:HAMILTON |
| 1906 | WOODRIDGE, John | 34 | NWNE | 1851-03-15 | FD | NWNE | |
| 1780 | WOODRUFF, Fielding | 2 | S½SE | 1851-04-15 | FD | S2SE | |

| ID | Individual in Patent | Sec. | Sec. Part | Purchase Date | Sale Type | IL Aliquot Part | For More Info . . . |
|----|----------------------|------|-----------|---------------|-----------|-----------------|---------------------|
| 1786 | WOODRUFF, George W | 11 | SWNE | 1850-12-23 | FD | SWNE | R:HAMILTON |
| 1907 | WOOLRIDGE, John | 27 | NWSW | 1851-11-24 | FD | NWSW | |
| 1776 | YOUNG, Elizabeth G | 2 | SENE | 1853-11-15 | FD | SENE | R:HAMILTON S:F |
| 1775 | "                " | 2 | NESE | 1853-11-15 | FD | NESE | R:HAMILTON S:F |

## Patent Map

**T5-S R6-E**
**3rd PM Meridian**

**Map Group 8**

## Township Statistics

| | | |
|---|---|---|
| Parcels Mapped | : | 411 |
| Number of Patents | : | 1 |
| Number of Individuals | : | 238 |
| Patentees Identified | : | 232 |
| Number of Surnames | : | 159 |
| Multi-Patentee Parcels | : | 10 |
| Oldest Patent Date | : | 11/15/1816 |
| Most Recent Patent | : | 10/11/1895 |
| Block/Lot Parcels | : | 16 |
| Cities and Towns | : | 3 |
| Cemeteries | : | 6 |

Patent map grid (Sections 4–33) showing landowner names and dates:

**Section 6:** ECHOLDS William 1850; MOULDING William 1850; MOULDING William 1850; RICHARDSON David 1853; BENTON Elijah 1852; NEWMAN John L 1852; INGRAM Sewel 1850; INGRAM Sewel 1841; RICHARDSON David 1853; BENTON Elijah 1852; STEELLE Samuel 1850; DAVIS Alfred 1850; INGRAM Sewel 1850; WILLIAMS Wylie 1842

**Section 5:** BUMGARDENER William 1854; ECHOLS Loftin 1853; HOLLAND Berryman 1853; MOORE James 1847; BAUMGARDNER William 1853; ECHOLS Lofton 1848; BENTON Elijah 1852; DAILY Mastin W 1850; ECHOLS Lofton 1848; BRUMLY Larkin 1846; DAILY John Jr 1836; STANFIELD Catherine 1850

**Section 4:** SLOO Thomas Jr 1818; SLOO Thomas Jr 1818; HEARD Charles H 1848; CAMPBELL Charles 1818

**Section 7:** DAVIS Alfred 1847; HARDY John Garrett 1839; WILLIAMS Wiley 1848; SLOO Thomas Jr 1818; SLOO Thomas Jr 1818; COKER Joseph 1851; WILLIAMS Wiley 1849; DAILEY Vincent 1837; MCFARLAND James 1839; MCFARLAND Gilbert 1839; MAULDING Richard 1818

**Section 8:** WILLIAMS Wylie 1842; ECHOLS Lofton 1848; WILLIAMS Wiley 1848; STANFIELD Catherine 1850; STANFIELD Catherine 1850; WILLIAMS Wiley 1849; WILLIAMS Wiley 1848; ALLEN Joseph 1853; MURPHY John 1848; COKER Anthony Doke 1850; BOYD William 1851; MURPHY John ALLEN 1848 Joseph 1850; DAILY Harvy Jones 1850; HEARD Charles H 1851; MURPHY John 1848; COKER Catharine 1850; MURPHY John 1848; WILLIS Merrel 1839

**Section 9:** HEARD Charles H 1853; ALLEN James 1837; ALLEN James 1837; HEARD Charles H 1849; CALDWELL John 1819; CARPENTER Milton 1837; HEARD Charles H 1849; BROWN Hanis G 1853; FORD Benjamin As 1831; HEARD Charles Harvey 1837; LANE Leven 1836

**Section 18:** DONIPHAN Joseph 1853; COKER Catharine 1850; SHIRBEY Moses Jr 1839; GRANT Roswell H 1818; DALE John 1837; GRANT Roswell H 1818; DALE Reuben 1849; DALE John 1818; DALE John DALE 1850 John 1837; SHIRLEY Moses 1836; SHIRLEY Moses 1818; DALE John 1848

**Section 17:** SHIRLEY Moses Jr 1840; LOCKHART Joseph D 1851; SULLINGER Alexander 1851; MARSHALL John Walker 1836; SALLENGER Alexander 1848; LOCKWOOD Elsey R 1838; SALLENGER Alexander 1848; ANDERSON Edmund 1848

**Section 16:** HEARD Charles H 1849

Lots-Sec. 16:
L72 ROGERS, Mark W 1851
L73 WILSON, John A 1851
L84 WILSON, John A 1851
S1 OGLESBY, Reuben 1834
S2 MARSHALL, John W 1836
S3 MARSHALL, John W 1836
S4 HOOD, Benjamin 1832
S5 BRADFOR, George 1833
S6 BRADFOR, George 1833
S7 OGLESBY, Reuben 1834
S8 OGLESBY, Reuben 1835
S9 MARSHALL, John W 1836
S10 MARSHALL, John W 1836
S11 ANDERSON, John 1836
S12 HERD, John 1832
S13 MARSHALL, Daniel 1834
S14 ANDERSON, John 1836
S15 CARPENTER, Milton 1838
S16 LOCKWOOD, Jesse C 1832

**Section 19:** DALE John 1850 DALE John H 1853; DALE John 1848; SEPHENS; RAFFERTY John 1849; WHITE Precious 1852; SEPHENS William S 1849 DALE John 1848; William S DALE 1849 John 1850; RAFFERTY John 1854; SEPHENS William S 1849 DALE Daniel 1851; WHITE Preston 1853; WHITE Preston 1853; RAFFERTY John 1854; DALE John 1848; MARSH Thomas W 1853; MARSH Thomas W 1853; HUNTER James 1850 SMITH Joseph B 1857

**Section 20:** STANTON Champ 1852; IRVIN Lucretia 1853; ANDERSON Edmund 1848; ANDERSON Edmund 1853; ALLEN Joseph 1855; MORRIS Mason 1849; HEARD Charles H 1853; ALLEN Joseph 1854; MORRIS Mason 1849; MCLEAN Charles 1818; MORRIS Mason 1837; WESTON Sarah 1853; KIRKPATRICK Andrew 1895 ALLAN Joseph 1852

**Section 21:** ONEAL John William 1842; LANE Lewis 1851; CAMPBELL Joseph 1851; ANDERSON Edmund 1848; RATHBONE Lorenzo 1849; IRVIN Abraham 1851; MCLEAN [19] John 1820; MORRIS Elizabeth 1847; RATHBONE Edward D 1847; MCLEAN Charles 1818; ANDERSON John 1833; FLINT William 1818; HEARD Charles H 1851; BARNES David 1837; RATHBONE Lorenzo 1836

**Section 30:** PLUNCKETT Martha 1852; DIAL James 1854; MARSH Thomas W 1854; HUNTER James 1850; WHITE Preston 1853; WHITE Preston 1853; WHITE Evaline 1847; HUNTER James 1850; HARPER Mark 1852; WHITE Preston 1853; WHITE Preston 1847; WHITE Preston 1836; WHITE Preston 1847; WHITE Preston 1847; HARPER Mark 1855; WHITE Preston 1847

**Section 29:** HUNTER James 1836; ALLAN Joseph 1852; BARNES James 1837; ALLEN Joseph 1854; SMITH Richard W 1819; WHITE Preston 1852; ALLEN Joseph 1852; WARD [7] Argon 1850

**Section 28:** ANDERSON Edmund 1848; RATHBONE Lorenzo 1849; RATHBONE Valentine 1847; RATHBONE Lorenzo 1851; MCLEAN Charles 1818; ROMINE [34] Caroline 1853; ROMINE Peter A 1853; HARDGE Isaac E 1848; ROMINE [34] Caroline 1853; STEPHENS William L 1850

**Section 31:** SAUER George 1859; TUNSEND John 1839; TOWNSEND John 1816; HOGG Samuel 1818; STADDEN William 1873; CLUCK James M 1853; WHITE HAYS John 1855 John 1853; HAYS John 1852; MCDONALD Mary A 1848 SMITH [22] Alonzo B 1857; CLUCK James M 1853; FLINT Adrian 1853

**Section 32:** WHITE Preston 1848; WHITE Preston 1852; WARD [7] Argon 1850; WHITE Preston 1853; MANNING Sarah 1851; MANNING Sarah 1851; MORRIS WHITE Allen Preston 1849 1853; MORRIS Allen 1849; ALLEN Joseph 1853

**Section 33:** HARDGE Isaac E 1848 STEPHENS William L 1850; HARDGE Isaac E 1848 STEPHENS William L 1850; BOYD Henry L 1845; STEVENS William L 1850; COKER Anthony D 1851; STEPHENS William L 1851; STEPHENS William S 1854; HARDGE Isaac E STEPHENS 1848 William L 1850; STEPHENS William L 1851; STEPHENS William L 1854; MANNING Samuel 1855; PRESLEY John 1852; PRESLEY John 1851; STEPHENS William L 1854; ALLEN Joseph 1853; PRESLEY John 1854; COBB James C 1854; STEPHENS William L 1854

## Section 3 / 2 / 1 (top row)

**Section 3**
- SLOO Thomas Jr 1818
- ASKEY Andrew Jackson 1848
- GARRISON Jefferson 1852
- ASKEY Andrew Jackson 1848
- ASKEY Andrew Jackson 1848
- GOFF John R 1847
- SHARP David 1852
- GARRISON Jefferson 1852
- GOFF John R 1847

**Section 2**
- LONG Thomas M 1852
- VAUGH Samuel 1852
- GROCE George W 1851
- MARSHALL Samuel S 1853
- VAUGHAN Samuel 1853
- YOUNG Elizabeth G 1853
- STEPHENSON James W 1852
- STEPHENSON James W 1852
- YOUNG Elizabeth G 1853
- BARNET William 1851
- WOODRUFF Fielding

**Section 1**
- DREW Thomas 1851
- SNIDER Andrew 1851
- WELLS James 1852
- MOORE William 1839
- DREW Thomas 1851
- WILLIAMS William G 1854
- MOORE Jesse 1853
- TODD Benjamin 1851
- MOORE Jesse 1851
- MOORE Sarah 1838
- WILLIAMS William G 1836
- WELDIN Alfred B 1850
- MUSGRAVE Samuel G 1837
- MOORE Jesse
- PROCTOR David 1819

## Section 10 / 11 / 12 (second row)

**Section 10**
- HEARD Charles H 1853
- LONG John 1836
- LANE Laven 1838
- HEARD Charles Harvey 1836
- LANE Leven As 1831
- MCLEAN William 1818
- MARSHALL John 1818

**Section 11**
- COTTINGHAM Thomas 1837
- BARNET William 1851
- BARNET William 1851
- HYSSIS [25] Benjamin 1843
- COTTINGHAM Thomas 1836
- WOODRUFF George W 1850
- STEPHENSON Joseph M 1850
- COTTINGHAM Thomas 1839
- LONG John 1839
- MARSHALL John 1818
- MCNEMAR John 1835
- PROCTOR John 1836

**Section 12**
- WELDIN Alfred B 1850
- MUSGRAVE Samuel G 1834
- MUSGRAVE Samuel G 1834 / MUSKGRAVE Nancy 1837
- STEPHENSON James W 1850
- MCNAMER 1850 Jeremiah 1819
- BRYANT James H 1851
- HEARD Charles H 1848
- HEARD Charles H 1848
- MCNEMAR John 1836
- HEARD Charles H 1848
- FREIZE Anderson C 1854
- HITE [24]
- LONG John 1836
- 1818
- LANE James Jr 1839

## Section 15 / 14 / 13 (third row)

**Section 15**
- MCLEAN William 1818
- MARSHALL John 1818
- TUBMAN George M 1819
- MARSHALL Daniel 1836
- MARSHALL Daniel 1836

**Section 14**
- PROCTER John 1836
- WITT Robert 1834
- MARSHALL John 1818
- MANGIS John 1849
- WILLIS John S 1821
- DEETS Samuel 1851
- MARSHALL Daniel 1839
- PROCTOR Little Page 1836
- HAYNES James 1818

**Section 13**
- LANE William West 1834
- LORIE James Jr 1837
- MCMAHAN James 1851
- PROCTOR Samuel H 1848
- HITE [23] 1818
- LEECH Samuel 1818
- PROCTOR Samuel H T 1849
- PROCTOR Benjamin 1851
- MUNSELL Richard 1845
- ANDERSON Robert 1819
- WEBB John 1847
- PROCTOR Samuel H T 1849
- 13

## Section 22 / 23 / 24 (fourth row)

**Section 22**
- LOCKWOOD Jesse Close 1836
- HEARD Charles Henry 1839
- WALLIS William 1839
- HEARD Charles H 1839
- BURTON John C 1848
- PRATT John 1852
- CRISEL Henry 1834
- HEARD Charles H 1839
- PRATT John 1852
- HEARD Charles H 1853
- GOWDY Robert A 1837
- BURTON John C 1848
- MITCHELL Ichabod 1851
- 22

**Section 23**
- CLARK Isaac 1836
- JONES Michael 1818
- WALLIS William 1839
- LEAKY Joel 1817
- 23
- BARRON Thomas B 1852
- HUTSON Uel H 1853
- HUTSON Abraham 1829
- MITCHELL Ichabod
- BARROW Sherod 1853

**Section 24**
- COKER Charles 1839
- CAMPBELL William 1837
- MITCHELL Ichabod 1836
- ANDERSON Robert 1819
- MITCHELL Ichabod 1839
- COKER Charles 1839
- WHEELER John 1819
- MUNSELL Richard 1854
- RITCHEY John J 1851
- RITCHEY John J 1851
- MITCHELL Ichaboo 1850
- RITCHEY John J 1851
- MITCHEL Ichabod 1853
- MITCHELL Ichabod 1853
- 24

## Section 27 / 26 / 25 (fifth row)

**Section 27**
- BURTON John C 1853
- BOURLAND David 1851
- PHELPS Charles 1851
- HEARD Charles H 1853
- HEARD Charles H 1853
- HEARD Charles H 1853
- WOOLRIDGE John 1851
- HEARD Charles H 1853
- HEARD Charles H 1853
- COKER Anthony D 1851
- 27

**Section 26**
- HUTSON Vel H 1853
- SCOTT Thomas 1844
- HUTSON Vel H 1854
- HUTSON Moses 1853
- SCOTT Thomas 1849
- SCOTT Thomas 1837
- HUTSON Vel H 1854
- 26
- HEARD Charles H 1854

**Section 25**
- CARGIL Lewis 1836
- CARROLL 1839
- HUTSON Moses 1847
- CARROLL 1839
- HILL Charles 1839
- 25
- CLARK Isaac W 1854
- HUTSON Uel H 1848
- ALLEN Larken B 1851
- WHEELER Willis 1838
- ALLEN Mark 1853
- CARGILL Lewis 1853
- RAMBO Richard 1853

## Section 34 / 35 / 36 (bottom row)

**Section 34**
- COKER Anthony D 1851
- WOODRIDGE John 1851
- MATHENY William C 1853
- WESTON Sarah Ann 1844
- CLARK Robin 1839
- 34
- PETMAN William H 1854
- WESTON Fredrick B 1844
- MITCHELL Ichabod 1852
- HEARD James M 1854
- PITTMAN Christopher 1849

**Section 35**
- HOOD William 1855
- HOOD Benjamin 1839
- HOOD William 1853
- HOOD William 1855
- 35

**Section 36**
- PHELPS John 1851
- HEARD Charles H 1854
- RAMBEAU Richard 1851
- ACORD Martin 1853
- 36

---

## Helpful Hints

1. This Map's INDEX can be found on the preceding pages.

2. Refer to Map "C" to see where this Township lies within Hamilton County, Illinois.

3. Numbers within square brackets [ ] denote a multi-patentee land parcel (multi-owner). Refer to Appendix "C" for a full list of members in this group.

4. Areas that look to be crowded with Patentees usually indicate multiple sales of the same parcel (re-issues), cancellations or voided transactions (that we map, anyway) or overlapping parcels. We opt to show even these ambiguous parcels, which oftentimes lead to research avenues not yet taken.

## Legend

- ———— Patent Boundary
- ▬▬▬▬ Section Boundary
- No Patents Found (or Outside County)
- 1., 2., 3., ... Lot Numbers (when beside a name)
- [ ] Group Number (see Appendix "C")

**Scale**: Section = 1 mile X 1 mile (generally, with some exceptions)

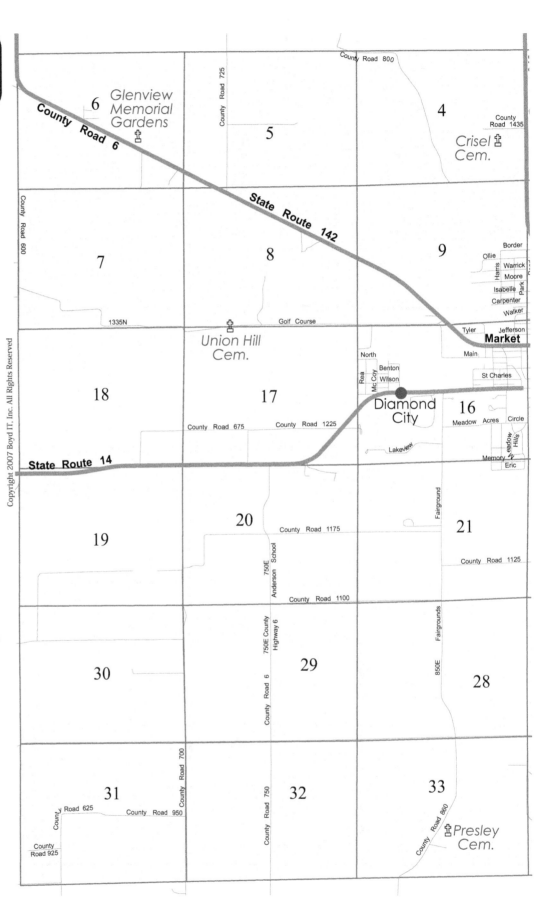

Road Map

T5-S  R6-E
3rd PM Meridian

Map  Group  8

Cities & Towns
Diamond City
Hoodville
McLeansboro

Cemeteries
Crisel Cemetery
Glenview Memorial Gardens
Hutson Cemetery
Presley Cemetery
Union Hill Cemetery
Independent Order of
  Oddfellows Cemetery

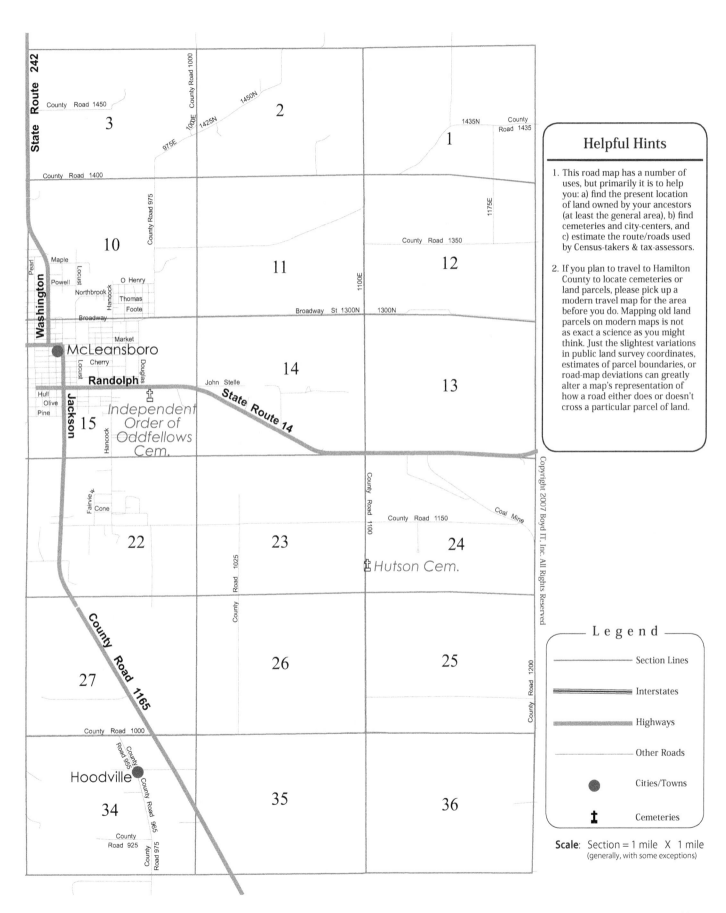

1. This road map has a number of uses, but primarily it is to help you: a) find the present location of land owned by your ancestors (at least the general area), b) find cemeteries and city-centers, and c) estimate the route/roads used by Census-takers & tax-assessors.

2. If you plan to travel to Hamilton County to locate cemeteries or land parcels, please pick up a modern travel map for the area before you do. Mapping old land parcels on modern maps is not as exact a science as you might think. Just the slightest variations in public land survey coordinates, estimates of parcel boundaries, or road-map deviations can greatly alter a map's representation of how a road either does or doesn't cross a particular parcel of land.

Copyright 2007 Boyd IT, Inc. All Rights Reserved

**L e g e n d**

——————— Section Lines

══════ Interstates

━━━━━ Highways

——————— Other Roads

● Cities/Towns

✝ Cemeteries

**Scale**: Section = 1 mile X 1 mile
(generally, with some exceptions)

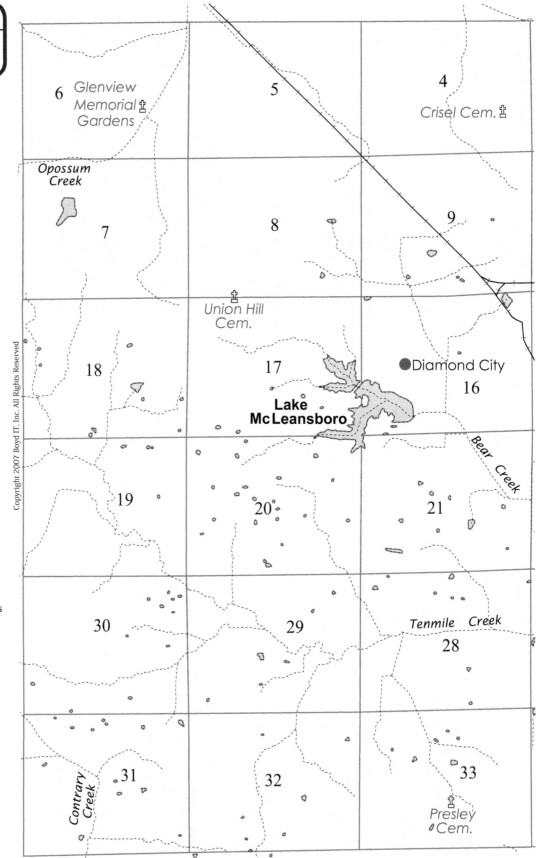

## Historical Map

T5-S R6-E
3rd PM Meridian

Map Group 8

### Cities & Towns
Diamond City
Hoodville
McLeansboro

### Cemeteries
Crisel Cemetery
Glenview Memorial Gardens
Hutson Cemetery
Presley Cemetery
Union Hill Cemetery
Independent Order of
  Oddfellows Cemetery

6

Glenview
Memorial
Gardens

Opossum
Creek

7

5

4

Crisel Cem.

8

9

Union Hill
Cem.

18

17

Lake
McLeansboro

●Diamond City

16

Bear Creek

19

20

21

30

29

Tenmile Creek

28

Contrary Creek

31

32

33

Presley
Cem.

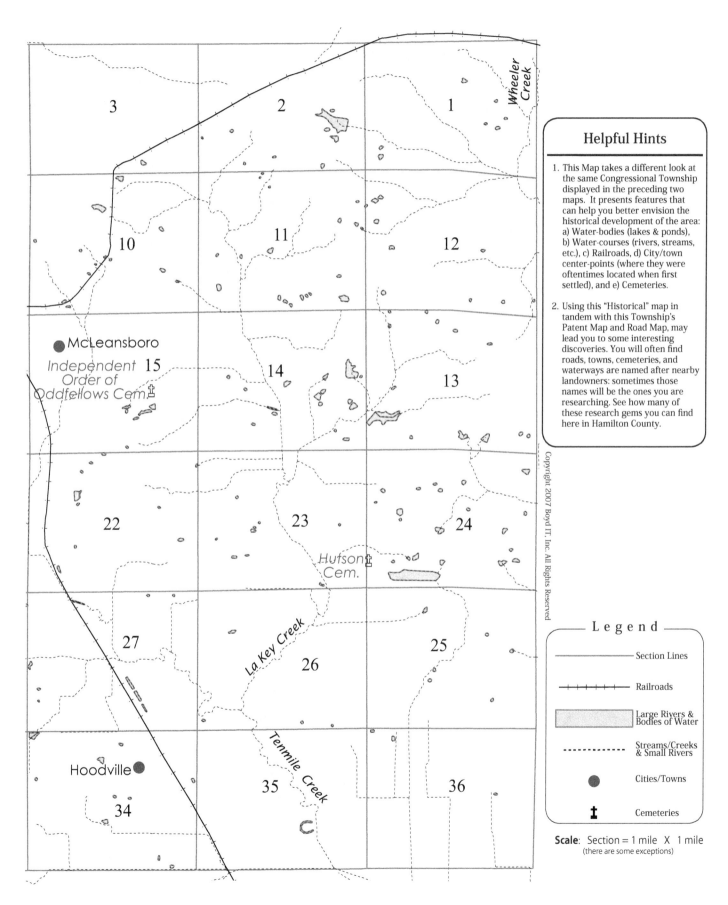

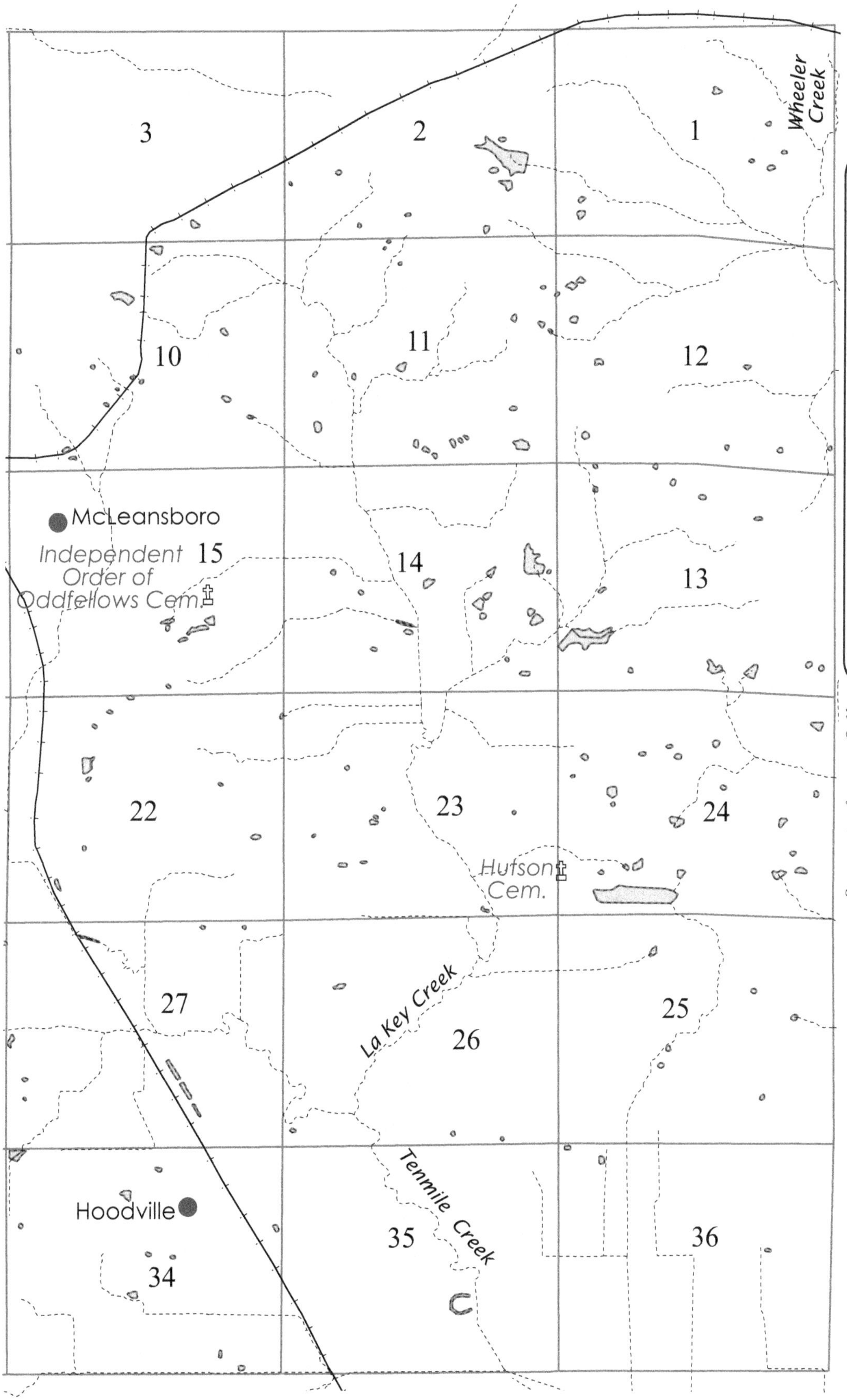
Wheeler Creek
3
2
1
10
11
12
McLeansboro
Independent Order of Oddfellows Cem.
15
14
13
22
23
24
Hufson Cem.
27
La Key Creek
26
25
Tenmile Creek
Hoodville
34
35
36



## Helpful Hints

1. This Map takes a different look at the same Congressional Township displayed in the preceding two maps. It presents features that can help you better envision the historical development of the area: a) Water-bodies (lakes & ponds), b) Water-courses (rivers, streams, etc.), c) Railroads, d) City/town center-points (where they were oftentimes located when first settled), and e) Cemeteries.

2. Using this "Historical" map in tandem with this Township's Patent Map and Road Map, may lead you to some interesting discoveries. You will often find roads, towns, cemeteries, and waterways are named after nearby landowners: sometimes those names will be the ones you are researching. See how many of these research gems you can find here in Hamilton County.

## Legend

- Section Lines
- Railroads
- Large Rivers & Bodies of Water
- Streams/Creeks & Small Rivers
- Cities/Towns
- Cemeteries

**Scale**: Section = 1 mile X 1 mile
(there are some exceptions)

## Map Group 9: Index to Land Patents

## Township 5-South Range 7-East (3rd PM)

After you locate an individual in this Index, take note of the Section and Section Part then proceed to the Land Patent map on the pages immediately following. You should have no difficulty locating the corresponding parcel of land.

The "For More Info" Column will lead you to more information about the underlying Patents. See the *Legend* at right, and the "How to Use this Book" chapter, for more information.

```
          LEGEND
      "For More Info . . ." column
G = Group  (Multi-Patentee Patent, see Appendix "C")
R = Residence
S = Social Status

See Appendix A for list of abbreviations used by the
Illinois State Archives in describing the place and
nature of these land patents.

Note: if the Abbreviations contain "L", "BL", "LOT",
or "BLOCK", the exact whereabouts of the parcel within
the section is not known.
```

| ID | Individual in Patent | Sec. | Sec. Part | Purchase Date | Sale Type | IL Aliquot Part | For More Info . . . |
|----|----------------------|------|-----------|---------------|-----------|-----------------|---------------------|
| 2110 | ALBIN, Allen H | 19 | E½NE | 1839-02-08 | FD | E2NE | R:GALLATIN |
| 2109 | " | 18 | E½SE | 1839-09-03 | FD | E2SE | R:HAMILTON |
| 2131 | ALLEN, Chaffin | 30 | SWSE | 1851-02-12 | FD | SWSE | R:HAMILTON |
| 2139 | ALLEN, David | 33 | NESW | 1846-08-25 | FD | NESW | R:HAMILTON |
| 2140 | " " | 33 | SENW | 1850-04-27 | FD | SENW | R:HAMILTON |
| 2177 | ALLEN, Ichabod | 30 | NWNW | 1837-12-22 | FD | NWNW | R:HAMILTON |
| 2199 | ALLEN, James | 16 | SWSW | 1838-08-04 | SC | SWSW | |
| 2200 | " " | 8 | SESE | 1847-08-14 | FD | SESE | R:HAMILTON |
| 2201 | " " | 9 | SWSW | 1851-04-15 | FD | SWSW | |
| 2221 | ALLEN, James J | 8 | SENE | 1852-04-23 | FD | SENE | |
| 2222 | " " | 9 | SWNW | 1852-04-23 | FD | SWNW | |
| 2248 | ALLEN, James R | 33 | NWSW | 1847-11-29 | FD | NWSW | R:HAMILTON |
| 2266 | ALLEN, John | 16 | NWSW | 1838-09-15 | SC | NWSW | |
| 2269 | " " | 21 | NESW | 1847-11-22 | FD | NESW | R:HAMILTON |
| 2267 | " " | 20 | E½NE | 1849-03-12 | FD | E2NE | |
| 2270 | " " | 21 | S½NW | 1849-03-12 | FD | S2NW | |
| 2268 | " " | 21 | NENW | 1851-04-15 | FD | NENW | |
| 2388 | ALLEN, Margaret | 33 | SWNW | 1840-06-24 | FD | SWNW | R:HAMILTON S:F |
| 2435 | ALLEN, Samuel | 11 | SWNE | 1840-06-05 | FD | SWNE | R:KENTUCKY |
| 2481 | ALLEN, William | 4 | W½SE | 1851-04-15 | FD | W2SE | |
| 2482 | " " | 9 | NENW | 1854-10-10 | FD | NENW | R:HAMILTON |
| 2208 | ANDERSON, James C | 28 | NENW | 1854-09-28 | FD | NENW | R:HAMILTON |
| 2207 | " " | 21 | SESW | 1854-09-28 | FD | SESW | R:HAMILTON |
| 2413 | ANDERSON, Orran Trigg | 27 | SWSW | 1836-09-02 | FD | SWSW | R:WHITE |
| 2412 | " " | 27 | NESW | 1837-01-21 | FD | NESW | R:WHITE |
| 2202 | ARTEBERRY, James | 9 | NWNE | 1854-10-10 | FD | NWNE | R:HAMILTON |
| 2276 | ARTESBERRY, John C | 11 | SENW | 1854-04-03 | FD | SENW | R:HAMILTON |
| 2277 | ATERBERRY, John C | 11 | SWNW | 1854-04-08 | FD | SWNW | R:HAMILTON |
| 2203 | ATTEBERRY, James | 9 | SENE | 1853-03-02 | FD | SENE | R:HAMILTON |
| 2204 | ATTERBURY, James | 9 | NENE | 1853-09-09 | FD | NENE | R:HAMILTON |
| 2271 | AVANT, John | 6 | NENE | 1851-07-21 | FD | NENE | |
| 2398 | BACK, Mitchell A | 11 | SWSW | 1855-05-05 | FD | SWSW | R:HAMILTON |
| 2147 | BADGER, Edmund W | 11 | NE | 1818-10-08 | FD | NE | R:WHITE |
| 2272 | BARKER, John | 11 | NWSW | 1851-08-06 | FD | NWSW | R:HAMILTON |
| 2156 | BARNES, Emberson | 22 | SWNW | 1847-11-16 | FD | SWNW | R:HAMILTON |
| 2155 | " " | 21 | NWSE | 1852-08-30 | FD | NWSE | R:HAMILTON |
| 2337 | " " | 21 | NWSE | 1852-08-30 | FD | NWSE | R:HAMILTON |
| 2256 | BARNETT, Jesse | 6 | SENW | 1854-10-12 | FD | SENW | R:HAMILTON |
| 2273 | BEARD, John | 5 | NWNW | 1852-12-04 | FD | NWNW | |
| 2274 | " | 5 | SWNW | 1854-01-16 | FD | SWNW | R:HAMILTON |
| 2483 | BECKERSTAFF, William | 15 | SWSE | 1854-03-17 | FD | SWSE | R:HAMILTON |
| 2206 | BENBROOK, James | 3 | NWNE | 1844-12-16 | FD | NWNE | R:HAMILTON |
| 2205 | " " | 1 | SESE | 1852-12-18 | FD | SESE | R:HAMILTON |
| 2233 | BENBROOK, James M | 1 | NESE | 1853-08-16 | FD | NESE | R:HAMILTON |
| 2456 | BENBROOK, Thomas C | 3 | SENE | 1851-04-28 | FD | SENE | R:HAMILTON |
| 2455 | " " | 3 | NESE | 1851-04-28 | FD | NESE | R:HAMILTON |

| ID | Individual in Patent | Sec. | Sec. Part | Purchase Date | Sale Type | IL Aliquot Part | For More Info . . . |
|---|---|---|---|---|---|---|---|
| 2454 | BENBROOK, Thomas C (Cont'd) | 2 | NWSW | 1852-12-15 | FD | NWSW | |
| 2172 | BICKERSTUFF, Hiram | 16 | E½NW | 1838-08-04 | SC | E2NW | |
| 2117 | BIGERSTAFF, Arden | 19 | N½NW | 1838-10-06 | FD | N2NW | R:HAMILTON |
| 2436 | BIGERSTAFF, Samuel | 13 | NW | 1820-04-07 | FD | NW | R:WHITE |
| 2475 | BIGERSTAFF, Westly | 23 | SWSE | 1833-03-15 | FD | SWSE | R:HAMILTON |
| 2108 | BIGGERSTAFF, Alfred | 13 | SESE | 1834-02-03 | FD | SESE | R:HAMILTON |
| 2173 | BIGGERSTAFF, Hiram | 15 | NESE | 1853-05-11 | FD | NESE | R:HAMILTON |
| 2347 | BIGGERSTAFF, Joshua | 15 | SESE | 1847-09-18 | FD | SESE | R:HAMILTON |
| 2349 | " | " | 22 | S½NE | 1849-08-21 | FD | S2NEVOID | |
| 2350 | " | " | 23 | S½SW | 1849-08-21 | FD | S2SWVOID | |
| 2348 | " | " | 22 | NENW | 1854-02-14 | FD | NENW | R:HAMILTON |
| 2351 | BIGGERSTAFF, Josuah | 22 | NWNE | 1849-09-08 | FD | NWNE | R:HAMILTON |
| 2387 | BIGGERSTAFF, Louisa | 5 | SWSE | 1853-09-02 | FD | SWSE | R:HAMILTON S:F G:4 |
| 2387 | BIGGERSTAFF, Malo M O | 5 | SWSE | 1853-09-02 | FD | SWSE | R:HAMILTON S:F G:4 |
| 2437 | BIGGERSTAFF, Samuel | 13 | NWNE | 1836-08-11 | FD | NWNE | R:HAMILTON |
| 2438 | " | " | 24 | SESE | 1850-03-28 | FD | SESE | R:HAMILTON |
| 2473 | BIGGERSTAFF, Wesley | 6 | SWNW | 1852-11-10 | FD | SWNW | R:HAMILTON |
| 2474 | BIGGERSTAFF, Westley | 6 | E½SW | 1838-10-12 | FD | E2SW | R:HAMILTON |
| 2404 | BLACK, Nancy | 3 | NWSW | 1852-02-18 | FD | NWSW | R:HAMILTON S:F |
| 2405 | " | " | 3 | SWSW | 1853-06-22 | FD | SWSW | R:HAMILTON S:F |
| 2275 | BOURLAND, John | 5 | | 1852-04-01 | FD | SWNET | |
| 2360 | BOWERS, Lemuel Gomers | 14 | NWSW | 1836-09-29 | FD | NWSW | R:WHITE |
| 2125 | BOYER, Calvin | 35 | NESW | 1855-03-26 | FD | NESW | R:HAMILTON |
| 2186 | BOYER, Isaac | 16 | L10 | 1854-02-25 | SC | LOT10NWSE | |
| 2439 | BOYER, Samuel | 35 | E½NW | 1838-11-07 | FD | E2NW | R:HAMILTON |
| 2442 | " | " | 35 | W½NE | 1838-11-07 | FD | W2NE | R:HAMILTON |
| 2441 | " | " | 35 | NWSE | 1838-11-28 | FD | NWSE | R:HAMILTON |
| 2440 | " | " | 35 | NWNW | 1838-11-28 | FD | NWNW | R:HAMILTON |
| 2484 | BRIANT, William | 17 | NWSW | 1837-03-13 | FD | NWSW | R:HAMILTON |
| 2486 | BRYANT, William | 21 | SWNE | 1851-04-26 | FD | SWNE | |
| 2525 | " | " | 17 | SWSE | 1854-02-27 | FD | SWSE | R:HAMILTON |
| 2485 | " | " | 17 | SWSE | 1854-02-27 | FD | SWSE | R:HAMILTON |
| 2449 | CAIN, William | 11 | SW | 1818-10-17 | FD | SW | G:6 |
| 2279 | CAMPBELL, John | 17 | NWNE | 1844-08-24 | FD | NWNE | R:HAMILTON |
| 2281 | " | " | 8 | SWSE | 1852-05-26 | FD | SWSE | |
| 2280 | " | " | 35 | NESE | 1853-12-03 | FD | NESE | R:HAMILTON |
| 2336 | CAMPBELL, Joseph | 21 | NENE | 1852-02-12 | FD | NENE | R:HAMILTON |
| 2155 | " | " | 21 | NWSE | 1854-01-02 | FD | NWSE | R:HAMILTON |
| 2337 | " | " | 21 | NWSE | 1854-01-02 | FD | NWSE | R:HAMILTON |
| 2491 | CAMPBELL, William | 17 | SWNW | 1837-04-20 | FD | SWNW | R:HAMILTON |
| 2492 | " | " | 19 | SWSW | 1851-06-05 | FD | SWSW | |
| 2502 | CAMPBELL, William H | 17 | E½NE | 1849-05-29 | FD | E2NE | |
| 2503 | " | " | 17 | E½SE | 1849-05-29 | FD | E2SE | |
| 2396 | CARPENTER, Milton | 29 | NENW | 1837-01-07 | FD | NENW | R:HAMILTON |
| 2401 | CHEEK, N C | 34 | | 1848-06-09 | FD | SEW | S:I |
| 2402 | " | " | 9 | N½ | 1848-06-09 | FD | N2 | S:I |
| 2403 | " | " | 9 | SW | 1848-06-09 | FD | SW | S:I G:9 |
| 2403 | CHEEK, Parmeleon | 9 | SW | 1848-06-09 | FD | SW | S:I G:9 |
| 2416 | CHEEK, Parmelon | 9 | N½SW | 1848-06-09 | FD | N2SW | G:10 |
| 2415 | " | " | 34 | SENW | 1848-06-09 | FD | SENW | G:10 |
| 2234 | " | " | 9 | N½SW | 1848-06-09 | FD | N2SW | G:10 |
| 2498 | CHEEK, William E | 34 | SENE | 1846-10-09 | FD | SENE | R:HAMILTON |
| 2416 | " | " | 9 | N½SW | 1848-06-09 | FD | N2SW | G:10 |
| 2415 | " | " | 34 | SENW | 1848-06-09 | FD | SENW | G:10 |
| 2234 | " | " | 9 | N½SW | 1848-06-09 | FD | N2SW | G:10 |
| 2403 | " | " | 9 | SW | 1848-06-09 | FD | SW | S:I G:9 |
| 2282 | CLEAVELIN, John | 19 | NWSE | 1838-04-23 | FD | NWSE | R:HAMILTON |
| 2452 | CLOUD, Silas | 5 | NENW | 1854-10-03 | FD | NENW | R:GALLATIN |
| 2451 | " | " | 5 | NE | 1854-10-03 | FD | NE | R:GALLATIN |
| 2132 | COKER, Charles | 27 | SWNW | 1836-04-22 | FD | SWNW | R:HAMILTON |
| 2416 | COKER, James M | 9 | N½SW | 1854-09-28 | FD | N2SW | R:HAMILTON |
| 2236 | " | " | 9 | SESE | 1854-09-28 | FD | SESE | R:HAMILTON |
| 2235 | " | " | 9 | SENW | 1854-09-28 | FD | SENW | R:HAMILTON |
| 2234 | " | " | 9 | N½SW | 1854-09-28 | FD | N2SW | R:HAMILTON |
| 2237 | " | " | 9 | SESW | 1854-09-28 | FD | SESW | R:HAMILTON |
| 2238 | " | " | 9 | W½SE | 1854-09-28 | FD | W2SE | R:HAMILTON |
| 2286 | COKER, John | 9 | NWNW | 1851-04-15 | FD | NWNW | |
| 2285 | " | " | 8 | NENE | 1851-04-15 | FD | NENE | |
| 2284 | " | " | 5 | SESE | 1851-04-15 | FD | SESE | |
| 2283 | " | " | 4 | SWSW | 1851-04-15 | FD | SWSW | |
| 2114 | CONNELLEY, Andrew | 25 | SEN½ | 1852-11-13 | FD | S2NE | |
| 2175 | CONNELLY, Hugh | 25 | NESE | 1844-04-24 | FD | NESELS | R:JEFFERSON |
| 2152 | COOK, Elizabeth Ann | 27 | NESE | 1838-11-07 | FD | NESE | R:HAMILTON S:F |

| ID | Individual in Patent | Sec. | Sec. Part | Purchase Date | Sale Type | IL Aliquot Part | For More Info . . . |
|---|---|---|---|---|---|---|---|
| 2288 | COOPER, John | 14 | W½NE | 1824-01-20 | FD | W2NE | R:OHIO |
| 2287 | " " | 11 | SE | 1824-01-20 | FD | SE | R:OHIO |
| 2289 | CRAIG, John | 35 | SESE | 1851-12-17 | FD | SESE | R:HAMILTON |
| 2493 | CRAIG, William | 35 | E½NE | 1842-07-20 | FD | E2NE | R:HAMILTON |
| 2494 | " " | 36 | NWSW | 1845-03-31 | FD | NWSW | R:HAMILTON |
| 2145 | CRAWFORD, Dawson T | 14 | NENE | 1853-03-23 | FD | NENE | |
| 2150 | CRISEL, Eliza | 30 | NWSW | 1854-10-27 | FD | NWSW | R:HAMILTON S:F |
| 2153 | CROOK, Elizabeth Ann | 26 | SWSW | 1837-01-14 | FD | SWSW | R:HAMILTON S:F |
| 2211 | CROOK, James | 27 | SESE | 1833-03-15 | FD | SESE | R:HAMILTON |
| 2210 | " " | 26 | NWSW | 1833-08-21 | FD | NWSW | R:HAMILTON |
| 2453 | CUSIC, Talitha T | 23 | NWNE | 1854-11-14 | FD | NWNE | R:HAMILTON S:F |
| 2133 | DAVIS, Charles | 10 | SENW | 1851-05-24 | FD | SENW | R:HAMILTON |
| 2160 | DAVIS, George | 3 | NWNW | 1853-01-28 | FD | NWNW | R:HAMILTON |
| 2291 | DAVIS, John | 3 | SWSE | 1852-02-24 | FD | SWSE | R:HAMILTON |
| 2290 | " " | 3 | SESW | 1853-01-11 | FD | SESW | |
| 2316 | DAVIS, John R | 10 | NWNW | 1852-11-15 | FD | NWNW | |
| 2459 | DAVIS, Thomas P | 20 | SE | 1847-11-22 | FD | SE | |
| 2462 | " " | 33 | N½NW | 1850-03-08 | FD | N2NW | |
| 2461 | " " | 33 | N½NE | 1850-03-08 | FD | N2NE | |
| 2460 | " " | 27 | NWNE | 1854-10-13 | FD | NWNE | R:HAMILTON |
| 2488 | DAVIS, William C | 11 | SESW | 1840-05-29 | FD | SESW | R:HAMILTON |
| 2487 | " " | 11 | NESW | 1852-02-05 | FD | NESW | R:HAMILTON |
| 2339 | DENNY, Joseph H | 20 | W½NE | 1847-12-07 | FD | W2NE | |
| 2338 | " " | 20 | E½NW | 1847-12-07 | FD | E2NW | |
| 2514 | DENNY, William L | 16 | L9 | 1838-08-04 | SC | LOT9S2SE | |
| 2458 | " " | 16 | L9 | 1838-08-04 | SC | LOT9S2SE | |
| 2515 | " " | 35 | SWNW | 1852-08-24 | FD | SWNW | |
| 2518 | DENNY, William Lewis | 21 | SENE | 1839-10-07 | FD | SENE | R:HAMILTON |
| 2519 | " " | 26 | SESE | 1850-03-06 | FD | SESE | R:HAMILTON |
| 2292 | DOBBS, John | 5 | NWSW | 1854-02-28 | FD | NWSW | R:HAMILTON |
| 2294 | " " | 6 | SENE | 1854-09-28 | FD | SENE | R:HAMILTON |
| 2293 | " " | 6 | NESE | 1854-09-28 | FD | NESE | R:HAMILTON |
| 2296 | DOCKER, John | 7 | W½NE | 1837-10-02 | FD | W2NE | R:GALLATIN |
| 2295 | " " | 7 | E½NE | 1838-02-19 | FD | E2NE | R:GALLATIN |
| 2297 | DREW, John | 1 | NE | 1818-04-20 | FD | NE | R:WHITE |
| 2298 | " " | 12 | NW | 1818-11-07 | FD | NW | R:WHITE |
| 2353 | DREW, Langston | 1 | SENW | 1832-09-24 | FD | SENW | R:HAMILTON |
| 2495 | DREW, William | 1 | NESW | 1834-05-30 | FD | NESW | R:HAMILTON |
| 2497 | " " | 1 | W½SE | 1837-02-02 | FD | W2SE | R:HAMILTON |
| 2496 | " " | 1 | NWSW | 1852-01-27 | FD | NWSW | |
| 2212 | ELLIS, James | 2 | NWNE | 1837-01-20 | FD | NWNE | R:GALLATIN |
| 2141 | ERWIN, David Lewis | 16 | L4 | 1854-03-02 | SC | L4NWNW | |
| 2472 | FARRIS, Thompson | 26 | SESW | 1837-03-31 | FD | SESW | R:HAMILTON |
| 2471 | " " | 25 | W½NW | 1842-03-14 | FD | W2NW | R:HAMILTON |
| 2470 | " " | 25 | SWSE | 1851-02-22 | FD | SWSE | R:HAMILTON |
| 2469 | " " | 25 | SENW | 1853-01-13 | FD | SENW | |
| 2468 | " " | 25 | NENW | 1853-02-10 | FD | NENW | |
| 2499 | FARRISS, William | 24 | W½NW | 1853-12-27 | FD | W2NW | R:HAMILTON |
| 2501 | FIELDS, William | 2 | SESE | 1854-01-02 | FD | SESE | R:HAMILTON |
| 2500 | " " | 12 | NWNE | 1854-02-22 | FD | NWNE | R:HAMILTON |
| 2142 | FITZGERRALD, Davis | 21 | NESE | 1848-04-10 | FD | NESE | |
| 2143 | " " | 22 | NESW | 1848-04-10 | FD | NESW | |
| 2144 | " " | 22 | W½SW | 1848-04-10 | FD | W2SW | |
| 2187 | FLOYD, Isaac | 25 | SWSW | 1853-01-15 | FD | SWSW | |
| 2188 | " " | 36 | SWNE | 1853-01-19 | FD | SWNE | |
| 2299 | FULLER, John | 8 | NESE | 1837-08-15 | FD | NESE | R:HAMILTON |
| 2420 | FULLER, Richard C | 22 | SESW | 1839-03-20 | FD | SESW | R:HAMILTON |
| 2115 | GARRISON, Andrew J | 24 | NWSE | 1839-10-21 | FD | NWSE | R:HAMILTON |
| 2163 | GARRISON, Gomer | 36 | NWNE | 1854-02-22 | FD | NWNE | R:WHITE |
| 2465 | GARRISON, Thomas W | 23 | SWNE | 1850-02-11 | FD | SWNE | R:HAMILTON |
| 2463 | " " | 23 | NESE | 1851-12-26 | FD | NESE | R:HAMILTON |
| 2464 | " " | 23 | SENE | 1852-11-29 | FD | SENE | |
| 2466 | GARRISON, Thomas Wain | 23 | NWSE | 1837-01-02 | FD | NWSE | R:HAMILTON |
| 2444 | GATES, Samuel E | 30 | SENW | 1853-12-08 | FD | SENW | R:HAMILTON |
| 2445 | " " | 31 | NENW | 1853-12-08 | FD | NENW | R:HAMILTON |
| 2414 | GETTINGS, Ozias D | 21 | SWSW | 1853-10-04 | FD | SWSW | R:HAMILTON |
| 2148 | GORDON, Elisha | 19 | NE | 1818-11-16 | FD | NE | R:WHITE |
| 2149 | " " | 6 | SE | 1819-09-11 | FD | SE | R:WHITE |
| 2278 | GOUDY, John C | 23 | SE | 1819-05-11 | FD | SE | R:TENNESSEE |
| 2354 | GOWDY, Leander F | 12 | SENE | 1849-09-29 | FD | SENE | R:HAMILTON |
| 2257 | GRAY, Jesse | 26 | W½NE | 1847-09-16 | FD | W2NE | R:HAMILTON |
| 2192 | GREEN, Isham | 5 | SWSW | 1851-08-25 | FD | SWSW | |
| 2193 | " " | 6 | SESE | 1851-08-25 | FD | SESE | |

| ID | Individual in Patent | Sec. | Sec. Part | Purchase Date | Sale Type | IL Aliquot Part | For More Info . . . |
|---|---|---|---|---|---|---|---|
| 2239 | GREENLER, James M | 23 | E½SW | 1849-09-05 | FD | E2SW | |
| 2240 | " | 26 | N½NW | 1849-09-05 | FD | N2NW | |
| 2215 | HALL, James | 30 | W½NW | 1818-09-21 | FD | W2NW | R:WHITE |
| 2417 | HAMPTON, Peter | 35 | NWSW | 1853-04-11 | FD | NWSW | R:HAMILTON |
| 2134 | HANAGAN, Daniel | 24 | NENE | 1850-11-07 | FD | NENE | R:HAMILTON |
| 2135 | HANNAGAN, Daniel | 13 | W½SE | 1853-01-28 | FD | W2SE | |
| 2146 | HAWTHORN, Edmond | 2 | SWNW | 1853-01-31 | FD | SWNW | R:HAMILTON |
| 2306 | HAYTER, John M | 7 | W½NW | 1850-03-05 | FD | W2NW | |
| 2305 | " | 7 | NENW | 1850-03-05 | FD | NENW | |
| 2304 | " | 6 | SWSW | 1850-03-05 | FD | SWSW | |
| 2300 | HEARIN, John | 25 | SESE | 1836-12-12 | FD | SESE | R:HAMILTON |
| 2258 | HIATT, Jesse | 17 | SW | 1818-11-02 | FD | SW | R:WHITE |
| 2259 | " | 28 | SW | 1819-02-04 | FD | SW | R:WHITE |
| 2447 | HILL, Samuel Jr | 36 | E½NW | 1839-03-19 | FD | E2NW | R:WHITE |
| 2220 | HOPSON, James | 1 | W½NE | 1830-09-10 | FD | W2NE | R:HAMILTON |
| 2508 | HOPSON, William | 13 | SWNE | 1838-11-23 | FD | SWNE | R:HAMILTON |
| 2506 | " | 13 | NENW | 1850-11-04 | FD | NENW | R:HAMILTON |
| 2507 | " | 13 | SENW | 1853-10-21 | FD | SENW | R:HAMILTON |
| 2352 | HUBBELL, Justus | 36 | E½NE | 1839-10-23 | FD | E2NE | R:HAMILTON |
| 2260 | HUNT, Jesse | 4 | NWNW | 1853-12-15 | FD | NWNW | R:HAMILTON |
| 2539 | JOHNSON, William Sen | 7 | SWNE | 1837-10-17 | FD | SWNE | R:WHITE |
| 2513 | JONES, William | 18 | NWSW | 1853-03-22 | FD | NWSW | R:HAMILTON |
| 2159 | KIRK, Fredrick | 12 | SWSE | 1852-02-07 | FD | SWSE | R:HAMILTON |
| 2369 | LAM, Lewis | 8 | W½SW | 1839-04-20 | FD | W2SW | R:FRANKLIN |
| 2224 | LAMBERT, James | 10 | SENE | 1849-11-13 | FD | SENE | |
| 2223 | " | 10 | N½NE | 1849-11-13 | FD | N2NE | |
| 2225 | " | 3 | SESE | 1849-11-13 | FD | SESE | |
| 2346 | LANE, James | 7 | SW | 1818-11-25 | FD | SW | R:WHITE |
| 2228 | " | 7 | SW | 1818-11-25 | FD | SW | R:WHITE |
| 2226 | " | 18 | NE | 1819-01-02 | FD | NE | R:WHITE |
| 2227 | " | 22 | SEN½ | 1867-02-02 | FD | S2NE | |
| 2265 | LANE, Joel Prince | 7 | SENW | 1837-05-15 | FD | SENW | R:HAMILTON |
| 2264 | " | 7 | NESE | 1839-08-08 | FD | NESE | R:HAMILTON |
| 2302 | LANE, John | 17 | NW | 1819-03-08 | FD | NW | R:GALLATIN |
| 2303 | " | 7 | SESE | 1837-10-17 | FD | SESE | R:HAMILTON |
| 2307 | LANE, John M | 18 | NENE | 1840-03-30 | FD | NENE | R:HAMILTON |
| 2328 | LANE, John W | 17 | NWSE | 1851-09-12 | FD | NWSE | R:HAMILTON |
| 2376 | LANE, Lewis | 18 | SWNE | 1833-05-18 | FD | SWNE | R:HAMILTON |
| 2372 | " | 18 | NENW | 1837-05-15 | FD | NENW | R:HAMILTON |
| 2377 | " | 18 | W½SE | 1838-01-25 | FD | W2SE | R:HAMILTON |
| 2379 | " | 8 | E½SW | 1839-09-13 | FD | E2SW | R:HAMILTON |
| 2371 | " | 17 | NENW | 1848-09-11 | FD | NENW | R:HAMILTON |
| 2380 | " | 8 | SESW | 1848-09-11 | FD | SESW | R:HAMILTON |
| 2446 | " | 18 | S½NW | 1850-11-04 | FD | S2NW | R:HAMILTON |
| 2374 | " | 18 | S½NW | 1850-11-04 | FD | S2NW | R:HAMILTON |
| 2375 | " | 18 | SENE | 1851-11-28 | FD | SENE | R:HAMILTON |
| 2378 | " | 7 | SWSE | 1853-09-28 | FD | SWSE | R:HAMILTON |
| 2373 | " | 18 | NWNE | 1853-09-28 | FD | NWNE | R:HAMILTON |
| 2370 | " | 14 | SENE | 1854-09-29 | FD | SENE | R:HAMILTON |
| 2457 | LANE, Thomas | 8 | SWNW | 1834-02-08 | FD | SWNW | R:HAMILTON |
| 2097 | LANSDEN, Abner | 36 | SE | 1818-09-08 | FD | SE | R:TENNESSEE |
| 2229 | LASATER, James | 36 | NESW | 1836-12-12 | FD | NESW | R:HAMILTON |
| 2230 | " | 36 | SESW | 1852-08-18 | FD | SESW | |
| 2448 | LEECH, Samuel | 18 | NW | 1818-09-21 | FD | NW | R:SHAWNEETOWN |
| 2094 | LLOYD, Abel | 9 | SWNE | 1855-04-04 | FD | SWNE | R:HAMILTON |
| 2096 | LOYD, Abel | 15 | W½NW | 1848-09-25 | FD | W2NW | |
| 2095 | " | 15 | S½SW | 1848-09-25 | FD | S2SW | |
| 2232 | LOYD, James | 23 | W½NW | 1849-01-18 | FD | W2NW | |
| 2231 | " | 14 | S½SW | 1849-01-18 | FD | S2SW | |
| 2530 | LOYD, William R | 9 | NESE | 1853-03-12 | FD | NESE | R:HAMILTON |
| 2195 | MABERRY, Jacob | 33 | NESE | 1836-03-31 | FD | NESE | R:HAMILTON |
| 2522 | MALON, William | 11 | NENE | 1833-06-05 | FD | NENE | R:HAMILTON |
| 2308 | MALONE, John | 11 | NENW | 1851-05-27 | FD | NENW | R:HAMILTON |
| 2418 | MALONE, Peter | 3 | SWNW | 1851-05-27 | FD | SWNW | R:HAMILTON |
| 2478 | MALONE, Whitson | 4 | SENW | 1850-12-18 | FD | SENW | R:HAMILTON |
| 2479 | " | 4 | SWNE | 1852-02-18 | FD | SWNE | R:HAMILTON |
| 2477 | " | 4 | NWNE | 1853-02-10 | FD | NWNE | R:HAMILTON |
| 2476 | " | 4 | NENE | 1854-10-13 | FD | NENE | R:HAMILTON |
| 2523 | MALONE, William | 11 | NWNE | 1836-04-04 | FD | NWNE | R:HAMILTON |
| 2524 | " | 11 | SEN½ | 1841-09-13 | FD | S2NE | R:HAMILTON |
| 2516 | MALONE, William L | 3 | NENE | 1854-10-13 | FD | NENE | R:HAMILTON |
| 2521 | MALONE, William Logan | 3 | SWNE | 1848-03-09 | FD | SWNE | R:HAMILTON |
| 2520 | " | 3 | SENW | 1848-03-09 | FD | SENW | R:HAMILTON |

| ID | Individual in Patent | Sec. | Sec. Part | Purchase Date | Sale Type | IL Aliquot Part | For More Info . . . |
|----|---------------------|------|-----------|---------------|-----------|-----------------|---------------------|
| 2168 | MANGIS, Henry | 18 | SWSW | 1851-05-28 | FD | SWSW | R:HAMILTON |
| 2112 | MANSELL, Allin | 24 | NENW | 1851-06-06 | FD | NENW | R:HAMILTON |
| 2485 | MANSELL, William | 17 | SWSE | 1853-02-05 | FD | SWSE | |
| 2525 | " " | 17 | SWSE | 1853-02-05 | FD | SWSE | |
| 2194 | MARKEL, Jacob J | 29 | W½SW | 1860-11-12 | FD | W2SW | |
| 2551 | MARTIN, Winningham | 22 | NWSE | 1851-10-13 | FD | NWSE | R:HAMILTON |
| 2191 | MATLOCK, Isaac N | 33 | SESE | 1854-01-28 | FD | SESE | R:HAMILTON |
| 2309 | MATLOCK, John | 33 | SWNE | 1847-11-23 | FD | SWNE | R:HAMILTON |
| 2162 | MAYBERRY, George T | 35 | SESW | 1853-02-15 | FD | SESW | |
| 2196 | MAYBERRY, Jacob | 33 | NWSE | 1837-01-09 | FD | NWSE | R:HAMILTON |
| 2526 | MAYBERRY, William | 25 | E½SW | 1848-03-02 | FD | E2SW | |
| 2527 | " " | 25 | NWSW | 1848-03-02 | FD | NWSW | |
| 2528 | " " | 26 | NESE | 1848-03-02 | FD | NESE | |
| 2126 | MCBROOM, Calvin M | 31 | NENE | 1852-06-24 | FD | NENE | R:HAMILTON |
| 2127 | MCBROWN, Calvin M | 31 | NWSE | 1853-09-13 | FD | NWSE | |
| 2128 | " " | 31 | SWNE | 1853-09-13 | FD | SWNE | |
| 2190 | MCBROWN, Isaac | 31 | SENE | 1840-05-25 | FD | SENE | R:HAMILTON |
| 2189 | " " | 31 | NESE | 1840-05-25 | FD | NESE | R:HAMILTON |
| 2406 | MCBROWN, Nancy | 31 | S½SE | 1853-02-04 | FD | S2SE | S:F |
| 2310 | MCCOBGAN, John | 6 | NWNW | 1839-11-28 | FD | NWNW | R:HAMILTON |
| 2106 | MCKNIGHT, Leander W | 24 | SENE | 1850-11-04 | FD | SENE | |
| 2107 | " " | 24 | W½NE | 1850-11-04 | FD | W2NE | |
| 2357 | " " | 24 | SENE | 1850-11-04 | FD | SENE | |
| 2355 | " " | 24 | NESE | 1850-11-04 | FD | NESE | |
| 2113 | " " | 24 | NESE | 1850-11-04 | FD | NESE | |
| 2359 | " " | 24 | W½NE | 1850-11-04 | FD | W2NE | |
| 2358 | " " | 24 | SESW | 1853-05-20 | FD | SESW | |
| 2356 | " " | 24 | NESW | 1854-06-01 | FD | NESW | R:HAMILTON |
| 2529 | MCKNIGHT, William P | 25 | N½NE | 1853-12-31 | FD | N2NE | R:HAMILTON |
| 2480 | MCLIN, William A | 12 | SE | 1819-05-01 | FD | SE | R:TENNESSEE |
| 2101 | METCALF, Abram | 1 | SWSW | 1851-02-01 | FD | SWSW | R:HAMILTON |
| 2103 | " " | 12 | SENW | 1853-01-28 | FD | SENW | R:HAMILTON |
| 2104 | " " | 12 | SWNE | 1854-02-15 | FD | SWNE | R:HAMILTON |
| 2102 | " " | 12 | NENE | 1854-02-15 | FD | NENE | R:HAMILTON |
| 2137 | METCALF, Daniel P | 12 | NWSW | 1852-02-13 | FD | NWSW | R:HAMILTON |
| 2136 | " " | 12 | NESW | 1853-03-18 | FD | NESW | R:HAMILTON |
| 2138 | " " | 12 | SWSW | 1854-01-24 | FD | SWSW | R:HAMILTON |
| 2510 | METCALF, William J | 1 | SWNW | 1851-02-01 | FD | SWNW | R:HAMILTON |
| 2509 | " " | 1 | NENW | 1851-04-03 | FD | NENW | R:HAMILTON |
| 2511 | " " | 2 | NESE | 1851-04-03 | FD | NESE | R:HAMILTON |
| 2512 | " " | 2 | SENE | 1851-04-03 | FD | SENE | R:HAMILTON |
| 2179 | MITCHELL, Ichabod | 7 | SE | 1818-11-17 | FD | SE | R:WHITE |
| 2178 | " " | 19 | SWNW | 1833-07-12 | FD | SWNW | R:HAMILTON |
| 2390 | MITCHELL, Mark M | 33 | SENE | 1853-03-10 | FD | SENE | |
| 2261 | MOORE, Jesse | 6 | NWSW | 1851-02-11 | FD | NWSW | R:HAMILTON |
| 2367 | MOORE, Lewis L | 15 | SENW | 1853-03-01 | FD | SENW | |
| 2366 | " " | 15 | NESW | 1853-03-01 | FD | NESW | |
| 2368 | " " | 15 | SESW | 1854-02-14 | FD | SESW | R:HAMILTON |
| 2111 | MUNSELL, Allen | 24 | SENW | 1854-04-10 | FD | SENW | R:HAMILTON |
| 2181 | MUNSELL, Ira | 13 | W½SW | 1830-09-15 | FD | W2SW | R:HAMILTON |
| 2182 | " " | 14 | E½SE | 1830-09-15 | FD | E2SE | R:HAMILTON |
| 2184 | " " | 14 | NW | 1838-03-23 | FD | NW | R:HAMILTON |
| 2185 | " " | 14 | W½SE | 1838-03-23 | FD | W2SE | R:HAMILTON |
| 2180 | " " | 13 | E½SW | 1838-03-23 | FD | E2SW | R:HAMILTON |
| 2183 | " " | 14 | NESW | 1844-12-06 | FD | NESW | R:HARDIN |
| 2399 | MUSGRAVE, Moses | 6 | NENW | 1853-02-11 | FD | NENW | |
| 2400 | MUSGROVE, Moses | 6 | NWNE | 1850-06-10 | FD | NWNE | |
| 2490 | MYERS, William C | 22 | SENW | 1851-02-12 | FD | SENW | R:HAMILTON |
| 2489 | " " | 22 | E½SE | 1853-03-23 | FD | E2SE | |
| 2301 | NATION, John L | 16 | L2 | 1853-09-21 | SC | LOT2NWNE | |
| 2458 | NATION, Thomas | 16 | L9 | 1853-09-21 | SC | LOT9NESE | |
| 2514 | " " | 16 | L9 | 1853-09-21 | SC | LOT9NESE | |
| 2355 | NATIONS, Anderson | 24 | NESE | 1853-08-18 | FD | NESE | R:HAMILTON |
| 2113 | " " | 24 | NESE | 1853-08-18 | FD | NESE | R:HAMILTON |
| 2549 | NELSON, Willis Hogan | 1 | SESW | 1836-09-09 | FD | SESW | R:HAMILTON |
| 2443 | ORR, Samuel Calhoun | 13 | NESE | 1837-02-16 | FD | NESE | R:HAMILTON |
| 2397 | PATTELLO, Milton G | 29 | W½SE | 1854-10-09 | FD | W2SE | R:GALLATIN |
| 2116 | PECK, Andrew | 8 | NESW | 1837-03-24 | FD | NESW | R:HAMILTON |
| 2157 | PEIRCE, Ezekiel | 2 | NESW | 1855-05-07 | FD | NESW | R:HAMILTON |
| 2151 | PERRYMAN, Elizabeth A | 27 | NWSE | 1848-06-17 | FD | NWSE | R:HAMILTON |
| 2209 | PERRYMAN, James C | 27 | SENW | 1853-12-03 | FD | SENW | R:HAMILTON |
| 2504 | PERRYMAN, William H | 26 | NESW | 1845-12-27 | FD | NESW | R:HAMILTON |
| 2505 | " " | 26 | SWNW | 1846-12-27 | FD | SWNW | R:HAMILTON |

| ID | Individual in Patent | Sec. | Sec. Part | Purchase Date | Sale Type | IL Aliquot Part | For More Info . . . |
|---|---|---|---|---|---|---|---|
| 2120 | PHIPPS, Benjamin | 24 | NWSW | 1852-04-20 | FD | NWSW | R:HAMILTON |
| 2341 | PHIPPS, Joseph | 27 | SWSE | 1842-06-06 | FD | SWSE | R:HAMILTON |
| 2340 | " " | 24 | SWSW | 1853-01-15 | FD | SWSW | |
| 2419 | PORCTOR, Reuben | 21 | NWNW | 1833-11-04 | FD | NWNW | R:HAMILTON |
| 2427 | PORTER, Robert M | 13 | NE | 1819-09-08 | FD | NE | R:WHITE |
| 2246 | POWELL, James | 10 | NESW | 1848-09-20 | FD | NESW | R:HAMILTON |
| 2247 | " | 10 | SE | 1848-09-20 | FD | SE | |
| 2359 | PRIMM, Alexander T | 24 | W½NE | 1858-08-23 | FD | W2NEVOID | |
| 2107 | " " | 24 | W½NE | 1858-08-23 | FD | W2NEVOID | |
| 2357 | " " | 24 | SENE | 1858-08-23 | FD | SENEVOID | |
| 2106 | " " | 24 | SENE | 1858-08-23 | FD | SENEVOID | |
| 2314 | PRINCE, John | 27 | SESW | 1836-04-22 | FD | SESW | R:HAMILTON |
| 2313 | " | 26 | SENW | 1836-10-18 | FD | SENW | R:HAMILTON |
| 2342 | PRINCE, Joseph Phipps | 26 | NWSE | 1846-01-24 | FD | NWSE | R:HAMILTON |
| 2383 | PRINCE, Lewis | 8 | NWSE | 1845-02-20 | FD | NWSE | R:GALLATIN |
| 2384 | " " | 8 | SWNE | 1848-09-11 | FD | SWNE | R:HAMILTON |
| 2382 | " " | 8 | NWNW | 1848-10-28 | FD | NWNW | R:HAMILTON |
| 2381 | " " | 8 | NWNE | 1854-10-04 | FD | NWNE | R:HAMILTON |
| 2408 | PRINCE, Nathaniel | 32 | SENE | 1845-01-08 | FD | SENE | R:HAMILTON |
| 2423 | PRINCE, Richard | 5 | SESW | 1852-05-20 | FD | SESW | |
| 2421 | PRINCE, Richard C | 5 | NESW | 1852-12-27 | FD | NESW | |
| 2422 | " " | 5 | SENW | 1854-10-04 | FD | SENW | R:HAMILTON |
| 2315 | PROCTOR, John | 5 | N½SE | 1854-10-01 | FD | N2SE | R:HAMILTON |
| 2344 | PROCTOR, Joseph | 8 | SE | 1819-04-28 | FD | SE | R:WHITE |
| 2343 | " " | 7 | NWSE | 1834-02-19 | FD | NWSE | R:HAMILTON |
| 2386 | PROCTOR, Littlepage | 21 | NW | 1818-11-18 | FD | NW | R:WHITE |
| 2446 | PROCTOR, Samuel H | 18 | S½NW | 1848-11-27 | FD | S2NW | |
| 2374 | " " | 18 | S½NW | 1848-11-27 | FD | S2NW | |
| 2123 | QUARLES, Brice C | 12 | | 1838-10-22 | FD | NWSWNT | R:HAMILTON |
| 2533 | RANKIN, William | 4 | SESW | 1852-01-21 | FD | SESW | R:HAMILTON |
| 2531 | " " | 4 | NESW | 1853-01-28 | FD | NESW | R:HAMILTON |
| 2532 | " " | 4 | NWSW | 1854-06-29 | FD | NWSW | R:HAMILTON |
| 2534 | " " | 4 | SWNW | 1854-07-17 | FD | SWNW | R:HAMILTON |
| 2118 | RAY, Arden W | 16 | L7 | 1853-01-10 | SC | LOT7SWNE | |
| 2119 | " " | 16 | L8 | 1854-03-02 | SC | LOT8SENE | |
| 2323 | RAY, John | 22 | NENE | 1837-06-06 | FD | NENE | R:WHITE |
| 2321 | " " | 15 | SWNE | 1844-12-10 | FD | SWNE | R:JOHNSON |
| 2322 | " " | 15 | SWNE | 1844-12-10 | FD | SWNE | R:JOHNSON |
| 2320 | " " | 15 | SENE | 1847-08-28 | FD | SENE | R:HAMILTON |
| 2322 | " " | 15 | SWNE | 1853-01-01 | FD | SWNE | R:HAMILTON |
| 2321 | " " | 15 | SWNE | 1853-01-01 | FD | SWNE | R:HAMILTON |
| 2318 | " " | 15 | NENW | 1853-02-07 | FD | NENW | R:HAMILTON |
| 2319 | " " | 15 | NWSE | 1853-08-16 | FD | NWSE | |
| 2317 | " " | 15 | NENE | 1854-03-03 | FD | NENE | R:HAMILTON |
| 2324 | RILEY, John | 29 | SENE | 1854-10-13 | FD | SENE | R:HAMILTON |
| 2537 | RILEY, William | 29 | NESE | 1836-04-04 | FD | NESE | R:HAMILTON |
| 2536 | " " | 29 | NENE | 1844-12-12 | FD | NENE | R:JOHNSON |
| 2538 | " " | 32 | NENE | 1847-09-28 | FD | NENE | R:HAMILTON |
| 2535 | " " | 22 | SWSE | 1851-05-14 | FD | SWSE | |
| 2105 | RITCHY, Adams | 29 | NW | 1818-09-22 | FD | NW | R:WHITE |
| 2250 | ROBERTS, Jane | 2 | S½SW | 1853-03-11 | FD | S2SW | S:F |
| 2251 | " " | 2 | SWSE | 1853-03-11 | FD | SWSE | S:F |
| 2249 | " " | 11 | NWNW | 1853-03-11 | FD | NWNW | S:F |
| 2407 | ROBINSON, Nathaniel B | 4 | W½NW | 1839-07-17 | FD | W2NW | R:FRANKLIN |
| 2252 | SHELTON, Jane | 27 | NWNW | 1842-06-06 | FD | NWNW | R:HAMILTON |
| 2253 | SHELTON, Jerimiah | 27 | E½NW | 1842-06-06 | FD | E2NW | R:HAMILTON |
| 2255 | " " | 28 | SESE | 1842-06-06 | FD | SESE | R:HAMILTON |
| 2254 | " " | 27 | NWSW | 1842-06-06 | FD | NWSW | R:HAMILTON |
| 2389 | SMALLWOOD, Margaret | 15 | W½SW | 1854-02-21 | FD | W2SW | R:HAMILTON S:F |
| 2130 | SNEAD, Carrol | 12 | SESE | 1849-12-29 | FD | SESE | R:HAMILTON |
| 2129 | " " | 12 | NESE | 1851-02-10 | FD | NESE | R:HAMILTON |
| 2333 | SNIDER, Joseph | 18 | NWNW | 1853-03-07 | FD | NWNWVOID | |
| 2228 | " " | 7 | SW | 1853-03-07 | FD | SWVOID | |
| 2345 | " " | 18 | NWNW | 1853-03-07 | FD | NWNWVOID | |
| 2346 | " " | 7 | SW | 1853-03-07 | FD | SWVOID | |
| 2158 | STEPHENS, Fanny | 16 | E½SW | 1838-08-04 | SC | E2SW | S:F |
| 2385 | STEPHENS, Little Page | 16 | L5 | 1851-03-10 | SC | LOT5SWNW | |
| 2517 | STEVENS, William L | 17 | SENW | 1837-09-30 | FD | SENW | R:HAMILTON |
| 2540 | STEWART, William | 10 | SWNE | 1847-07-06 | FD | SWNE | R:HAMILTON |
| 2326 | STOCKER, John | 27 | NENE | 1854-07-10 | FD | NENE | R:HAMILTON |
| 2325 | " " | 23 | W½SW | 1854-07-10 | FD | W2SW | R:HAMILTON |
| 2124 | STRAWMAT, Brooks | 12 | NENW | 1836-09-10 | FD | NENW | R:HAMILTON |
| 2176 | SWEARINGEN, Hugh | 36 | W½NW | 1851-11-24 | FD | W2NW | |

| ID | Individual in Patent | Sec. | Sec. Part | Purchase Date | Sale Type | IL Aliquot Part | For More Info . . . |
|---|---|---|---|---|---|---|---|
| 2361 | THOMAS, Lewis F | 2 | NENW | 1837-03-07 | FD | NENW | R:HAMILTON |
| 2363 | " " | 2 | SWNE | 1851-02-06 | FD | SWNE | R:HAMILTON |
| 2362 | " " | 2 | SENW | 1851-02-06 | FD | SENW | R:HAMILTON |
| 2364 | " " | 22 | NWNW | 1851-04-28 | FD | NWNW | R:HAMILTON |
| 2365 | " " | 4 | NENW | 1853-11-24 | FD | NENW | R:HAMILTON |
| 2434 | THOMAS, Samuel A | 4 | SESE | 1852-08-12 | FD | SESE | |
| 2433 | " " | 4 | SENE | 1854-01-21 | FD | SENE | R:HAMILTON |
| 2432 | " " | 4 | NESE | 1854-01-21 | FD | NESE | R:HAMILTON |
| 2161 | TODD, William Balch | 23 | E½NW | 1860-02-08 | FD | E2NW | G:39 |
| 2311 | TROUT, John N | 34 | SESE | 1852-04-23 | FD | SESE | R:HAMILTON |
| 2312 | " " | 35 | SWSW | 1853-01-25 | FD | SWSW | |
| 2197 | ULMER, Jacob | 10 | SWNW | 1853-03-31 | FD | SWNW | |
| 2327 | UPTON, John | 12 | W½NW | 1833-12-02 | FD | W2NW | R:WHITE |
| 2161 | VARNELL, George H | 23 | E½NW | 1860-02-08 | FD | E2NW | G:39 |
| 2449 | VIOLETT, Sanford | 11 | SW | 1818-10-17 | FD | SW | G:6 |
| 2154 | WEBB, Elizabeth | 34 | NWNW | 1839-01-26 | FD | NWNW | R:HAMILTON S:F |
| 2174 | WEBB, Holley R | 34 | SWNW | 1844-04-24 | FD | SWNW | S:F |
| 2391 | WEBB, Martin | 34 | NENW | 1839-01-26 | FD | NENW | R:HAMILTON |
| 2393 | " " | 34 | NWSE | 1846-02-04 | FD | NWSE | R:HAMILTON |
| 2392 | " " | 34 | NESE | 1853-01-25 | FD | NESE | |
| 2394 | " " | 34 | SWSE | 1854-02-22 | FD | SWSE | R:HAMILTON |
| 2410 | WEBB, Obid Hendrick | 34 | NWSW | 1837-01-02 | FD | NWSW | R:HAMILTON |
| 2409 | " " | 34 | NESW | 1840-05-18 | FD | NESW | R:HAMILTON |
| 2411 | " " | 34 | SWSW | 1853-01-17 | FD | SWSW | |
| 2198 | WESNER, Jacob | 10 | NWSW | 1855-03-26 | FD | NWSW | R:HAMILTON |
| 2098 | WHEELER, Abner P | 31 | SWNW | 1853-10-27 | FD | SWNW | R:HAMILTON |
| 2100 | WHEELER, Abner Pierce | 31 | NWNW | 1847-10-11 | FD | NWNW | R:HAMILTON |
| 2099 | " " | 30 | SWSW | 1847-10-11 | FD | SWSW | R:HAMILTON |
| 2164 | WHEELER, Hellen M | 30 | SWNW | 1851-02-13 | FD | SWNW | R:HAMILTON S:F |
| 2170 | WHEELER, Henry | 20 | NESW | 1836-04-02 | FD | NESW | R:HAMILTON |
| 2169 | " " | 19 | E½SE | 1851-01-20 | FD | E2SE | R:HAMILTON |
| 2171 | " " | 20 | SESW | 1851-01-20 | FD | SESW | R:HAMILTON |
| 2329 | WHEELER, John | 29 | SENW | 1832-09-12 | FD | SENW | R:HAMILTON |
| 2330 | " " | 29 | SESE | 1836-10-22 | FD | SESE | R:HAMILTON |
| 2426 | WHEELER, Robert L | 17 | SWSW | 1848-10-27 | FD | SWSW | |
| 2424 | " " | 17 | E½SW | 1848-10-27 | FD | E2SW | |
| 2425 | " " | 17 | SWNE | 1848-10-27 | FD | SWNE | |
| 2467 | WHEELER, Thomas | 19 | SE | 1819-02-22 | FD | SE | R:WHITE |
| 2545 | WHEELER, William | 20 | W½NW | 1818-07-17 | FD | W2NW | R:WHITE |
| 2543 | " " | 19 | SW | 1818-11-14 | FD | SW | R:WHITE |
| 2541 | " " | 17 | NWNW | 1837-07-06 | FD | NWNW | R:HAMILTON |
| 2542 | " " | 19 | NWSW | 1839-03-07 | FD | NWSW | R:HAMILTON |
| 2547 | " " | 33 | SESW | 1851-02-05 | FD | SESW | R:HAMILTON |
| 2548 | " " | 33 | SWSE | 1851-02-05 | FD | SWSE | R:HAMILTON |
| 2546 | " " | 30 | NENW | 1851-09-01 | FD | NENW | |
| 2544 | " " | 19 | SWSE | 1854-10-11 | FD | SWSE | R:HAMILTON |
| 2550 | WHEELER, Willis | 20 | SW | 1817-02-07 | FD | SW | R:WHITE |
| 2166 | WILLIAMS, Henry J | 29 | NWNE | 1845-02-28 | FD | NWNE | R:WHITE |
| 2167 | " " | 29 | SWNE | 1847-06-12 | FD | SWNE | R:HAMILTON |
| 2165 | " " | 28 | SESW | 1852-02-06 | FD | SESW | R:HAMILTON |
| 2395 | WILLIS, Merrel | 19 | SENW | 1832-09-12 | FD | SENW | R:HAMILTON |
| 2242 | WILSON, James M | 28 | NWSE | 1836-03-28 | FD | NWSE | R:HAMILTON |
| 2241 | " " | 28 | NESE | 1838-12-10 | FD | NESE | R:HAMILTON |
| 2244 | " " | 28 | SWSE | 1843-01-04 | FD | SWSE | R:HAMILTON |
| 2243 | " " | 28 | SWNE | 1850-02-06 | FD | SWNE | R:HAMILTON |
| 2345 | WILSON, Joseph C | 18 | NWNW | 1850-03-13 | FD | NWNW | |
| 2335 | " " | 7 | W½SW | 1850-03-13 | FD | W2SW | |
| 2334 | " " | 7 | NESW | 1850-03-13 | FD | NESW | |
| 2333 | " " | 18 | NWNW | 1850-03-13 | FD | NWNW | |
| 2428 | WILSON, Robert | 28 | NESW | 1838-12-21 | FD | NESW | R:WHITE |
| 2430 | " " | 28 | SENW | 1846-02-20 | FD | SENW | R:HAMILTON |
| 2431 | " " | 28 | SWNW | 1850-02-07 | FD | SWNW | R:HAMILTON |
| 2429 | " " | 28 | NWNW | 1852-03-10 | FD | NWNW | R:HAMILTON |
| 2450 | WILSON, Sarah | 28 | SENE | 1843-01-31 | FD | SENE | R:HAMILTON S:F |
| 2245 | WINCHESTER, James M | 18 | E½SW | 1851-05-30 | FD | E2SW | |
| 2331 | WRAY, John | 13 | SE | 1819-10-16 | FD | SE | R:GALLATIN |
| 2214 | WRIGHT, James H | 36 | SWSE | 1854-01-28 | FD | SWSE | R:HAMILTON |
| 2213 | " " | 35 | SWSE | 1854-01-28 | FD | SWSE | R:HAMILTON |
| 2219 | WRIGHT, James Henry | 26 | SWSE | 1849-03-26 | FD | SWSE | R:HAMILTON |
| 2217 | " " | 26 | NENE | 1851-12-18 | FD | NENE | R:HAMILTON |
| 2216 | " " | 23 | SESE | 1852-01-30 | FD | SESE | R:HAMILTON |
| 2218 | " " | 26 | SENE | 1852-07-23 | FD | SENE | R:HAMILTON |
| 2121 | YORK, Branson | 3 | NESW | 1852-02-26 | FD | NESW | R:HAMILTON |

| ID | Individual in Patent | Sec. | Sec. Part | Purchase Date | Sale Type | IL Aliquot Part | For More Info . . . |
|----|---------------------|------|-----------|---------------|-----------|-----------------|---------------------|
| 2122 | YORK, Branson (Cont'd) | 3 | NWSE | 1852-05-27 | FD | NWSE | |
| 2263 | YORK, Jesse | 2 | NENE | 1848-09-11 | FD | NENE | |
| 2262 | "        " | 1 | NWNW | 1851-02-08 | FD | NWNW | R:HAMILTON |
| 2332 | YORK, John | 3 | NENW | 1837-10-27 | FD | NENW | R:HAMILTON |

## Patent Map

**T5-S R7-E**
**3rd PM Meridian**

Map Group 9

## Township Statistics

| | | |
|---|---|---|
| Parcels Mapped | : | 458 |
| Number of Patents | : | 1 |
| Number of Individuals | : | 264 |
| Patentees Identified | : | 261 |
| Number of Surnames | : | 157 |
| Multi-Patentee Parcels | : | 6 |
| Oldest Patent Date | : | 2/7/1817 |
| Most Recent Patent | : | 2/2/1867 |
| Block/Lot Parcels | : | 8 |
| Cities and Towns | : | 5 |
| Cemeteries | : | 7 |

**Section 6:**
MCCOBGAN John 1839 · MUSGRAVE Moses 1853 · MUSGROVE Moses 1850 · AVANT John 1851 · BIGGERSTAFF Wesley 1852 · BARNETT Jesse 1854 · DOBBS John 1854 · MOORE Jesse 1851 · BIGGERSTAFF Westley 1838 · GORDON Elisha 1819 · DOBBS John 1854 · GREEN Isham 1851 · HAYTER John M 1850

**Section 5:**
BEARD John 1852 · CLOUD Silas 1854 · CLOUD Silas 1854 · BEARD John 1854 · PRINCE Richard C 1854 · BOURLAND John 1852 · DOBBS John 1854 · PRINCE Richard C 1852 · PROCTOR John 1854 · GREEN Isham 1851 · PRINCE Richard 1852 · BIGGERSTAFF [4] Louisa 1853 · COKER John 1851

**Section 4:**
HUNT Jesse 1853 · THOMAS Lewis F 1853 · MALONE Whitson 1853 · MALONE Whitson 1854 · ROBINSON Nathaniel B 1839 · RANKIN William 1854 · MALONE Whitson 1850 · MALONE Whitson 1852 · THOMAS Samuel A 1854 · RANKIN William 1854 · RANKIN William 1853 · ALLEN William 1851 · THOMAS Samuel A 1854 · COKER John 1851 · RANKIN William 1852 · THOMAS Samuel A 1852

**Section 7:**
HAYTER John M 1850 · HAYTER John M 1850 · DOCKER John 1837 · LANE Joel Prince 1837 · JOHNSON William Sen 1837 · DOCKER John 1838 · LANE James 1818 · WILSON Joseph C 1850 · PROCTOR Joseph 1834 · LANE Joel Prince 1839 · WILSON Joseph C 1850 · SNIDER Joseph 1853 · MITCHELL Ichabod 1818 · LANE Lewis 1853 · LANE John 1837

**Section 8:**
PRINCE Lewis 1848 · LANE Thomas 1834 · PECK Andrew 1837 · LAM Lewis 1839 · LANE Lewis 1848 · LANE Lewis 1839

**Section 9 area:**
PRINCE Lewis 1854 · COKER John 1851 · COKER John 1851 · ALLEN William 1854 · ARTEBERRY James 1854 · ATTERBURY James 1853 · PRINCE Lewis 1848 · ALLEN James J 1852 · ALLEN James J 1852 · COKER James M 1854 · CHEEK 1848 · LLOYD Abel 1855 · ATTEBERRY James 1853 · PRINCE Lewis 1845 · FULLER John 1837 · CHEEK [10] Parmelon 1848 · CHEEK [9] · COKER James M 1854 · LOYD William R 1853 · PROCTOR Joseph 1819 · CAMPBELL John 1852 · ALLEN James 1847 · ALLEN James 1851 · N C 1848 · COKER James M 1854 · COKER James M 1854

**Section 16:**
BICKERSTUFF Hiram 1838
Lots-Sec. 16
L2 NATION, John L 1853
L4 ERWIN, David Lewis 1854
L5 STEPHENS, Little Pag 1851
L7 RAY, Arden W 1853
L8 RAY, Arden W 1854
L9 DENNY, William L 1838
L9 NATION, Thomas 1853
L10 BOYER, Isaac 1854

**Section 17/18 area:**
SNIDER Joseph 1853 · WILSON Joseph C 1850 · LANE Lewis 1837 · LANE Lewis 1853 · LANE John M 1840 · WHEELER William 1837 · LANE John 1819 · LANE Lewis 1848 · CAMPBELL John 1844 · CAMPBELL William H 1849 · LEECH Samuel 1818 · PROCTOR Samuel H 1848 · LANE Lewis 1850 · LANE Lewis 1833 · LANE James 1819 · LANE Lewis 1851 · CAMPBELL William 1837 · STEVENS William L 1837 · WHEELER Robert L 1848 · JONES William 1853 · WINCHESTER James M 1851 · LANE Lewis 1838 · ALBIN Allen H 1839 · BRIANT William 1837 · WHEELER Robert L 1848 · LANE John W 1851 · CAMPBELL William H 1849 · MANGIS Henry 1851 · WHEELER Robert L 1848 · HIATT Jesse 1818 · BRYANT William 1854 · MANSELL William 1853 · ALLEN John 1838 · ALLEN James 1838 · STEPHENS Fanny 1838

**Section 21 area:**
PORCTOR Reuben 1833 · ALLEN John 1851 · CAMPBELL Joseph 1852 · PROCTOR Littlepage 1818 · ALLEN John 1849 · BRYANT William 1851 · DENNY William Lewis 1839 · ALLEN John 1847 · BARNES Emberson 1852 · CAMPBELL Joseph 1854 · FITZGERRALD Davis 1848 · GETTINGS Ozias D 1853 · ANDERSON James C 1854

**Section 19:**
BIGERSTAFF Arden 1838 · ALBIN Allen H 1839 · GORDON 1839 Elisha 1818 · MITCHELL Ichabod 1833 · WILLIS Merrel 1832 · WHEELER William 1818 · DENNY Joseph H 1847 · DENNY Joseph H 1847 · ALLEN John 1849 · WHEELER William 1839 · WHEELER William 1818 · CLEAVELIN John 1838 · WHEELER Thomas 1819 · WHEELER Henry 1851 · CAMPBELL William 1851 · WHEELER William 1854

**Section 20:**
WHEELER Willis 1817 · WHEELER Henry 1836 · DAVIS Thomas P 1847 · WHEELER Henry 1851

**Section 30:**
HALL James 1818 · ALLEN Ichabod 1837 · WHEELER William 1851 · WHEELER Hellen M 1851 · GATES Samuel E 1853 · CRISEL Eliza 1854 · WHEELER Abner Pierce 1847 · WHEELER Abner Pierce 1847 · GATES Samuel E 1853 · MCBROOM Calvin M 1852 · ALLEN Chaffin 1851

**Section 29:**
RITCHY Adams 1818 · CARPENTER Milton 1837 · WILLIAMS Henry J 1845 · RILEY William 1844 · WHEELER John 1832 · WILLIAMS Henry J 1847 · RILEY John 1854 · RILEY William 1836 · PATTELLO Milton G 1854 · WHEELER John 1836 · MARKEL Jacob J 1860

**Section 28:**
WILSON Robert 1852 · ANDERSON James C 1854 · WILSON Robert 1850 · WILSON Robert 1846 · WILSON James M 1850 · WILSON Sarah 1843 · HIATT Jesse 1819 · WILSON Robert 1838 · WILSON James M 1836 · WILSON James M 1838 · WILLIAMS Henry J 1852 · WILSON James M 1843 · SHELTON Jerimiah 1842

**Section 31:**
WHEELER Abner P 1853 · GATES Samuel E 1853 · MCBROWN Calvin M 1853 · MCBROWN Isaac 1840 · MCBROWN Calvin M 1853 · MCBROWN Isaac 1840 · MCBROWN Nancy 1853

**Section 32:**
RILEY William 1847 · PRINCE Nathaniel 1845

**Section 33:**
DAVIS Thomas P 1850 · DAVIS Thomas P 1850 · ALLEN Margaret 1840 · ALLEN David 1850 · MATLOCK John 1847 · MITCHELL Mark M 1853 · ALLEN James R 1847 · ALLEN David 1846 · MAYBERRY Jacob 1837 · MABERRY Jacob 1836 · WHEELER William 1851 · WHEELER William 1851 · MATLOCK Isaac N 1854

## Section 3
DAVIS George 1853 · YORK John 1837 · BENBROOK James 1844 · MALONE William L 1854
MALONE Peter 1851 · MALONE William Logan 1848 · MALONE William Logan · **3** · MALONE William Logan 1848 · BENBROOK Thomas C 1851
BLACK Nancy 1852 · YORK Branson 1852 · YORK Branson 1852 · BENBROOK Thomas C 1851
BLACK Nancy 1853 · DAVIS John 1853 · DAVIS John 1852 · LAMBERT James 1849

## Section 2
THOMAS Lewis F 1837 · ELLIS James 1837
HAWTHORN Edmond 1853 · THOMAS Lewis F 1851 · THOMAS Lewis F 1851
BENBROOK Thomas C 1852 · PEIRCE Ezekiel 1855 · **2**
ROBERTS Jane 1853 · ROBERTS Jane 1853

## Section 1
YORK Jesse 1848 · YORK Jesse 1851 · METCALF William J 1851 · HOPSON James 1830 · DREW John 1818
METCALF William J 1851 · METCALF William J 1851 · DREW Langston 1832
METCALF William J 1851 · DREW William 1852 · DREW William 1834 · **1** · BENBROOK James M 1853
FIELDS William 1854 · METCALF Abram 1851 · NELSON Willis Hogan 1836 · DREW William 1837 · BENBROOK James 1852

## Section 10
DAVIS John R 1852 · LAMBERT James 1849 · ROBERTS Jane 1853
ULMER Jacob 1853 · DAVIS Charles 1851 · STEWART William 1847 · LAMBERT James 1849
WESNER Jacob 1855 · POWELL James 1848 · **10** · POWELL James 1848

## Section 11
ROBERTS Jane 1853 · MALONE John 1851 · MALONE William 1836 · MALON William 1833
BADGER Edmund W 1818 · ATERBERRY John C 1854 · ARTESBERRY John C 1854 · ALLEN Samuel 1840 · MALONE William 1841
BARKER John 1851 · DAVIS William C 1852 · VIOLETT [6] Sanford 1818 · **11**
BACK Mitchell A 1855 · DAVIS William C 1840 · COOPER John 1824

## Section 12
STRAWMAT Brooks 1836 · FIELDS William 1854 · METCALF Abram 1854
UPTON John 1833 · DREW John 1818 · METCALF Abram 1853 · METCALF Abram 1854 · GOWDY Leander F 1849
QUARLES Brice C 1852 · METCALF Daniel P 1852 · METCALF Daniel P 1853 · MCLIN William A 1819 · SNEAD Carrol 1851 · **12**
METCALF Daniel P 1854 · KIRK Fredrick 1852 · SNEAD Carrol 1849

## Section 15
LOYD Abel 1848 · RAY John 1853 · RAY John 1854
MOORE Lewis L 1853 · RAY John 1844 · RAY John 1853 · RAY John 1847 · **15**
MOORE Lewis L 1853 · RAY John 1853 · BIGGERSTAFF Hiram 1853
SMALLWOOD Margaret 1854 · LOYD Abel 1848 · MOORE Lewis L 1854 · BECKERSTAFF William 1854 · BIGGERSTAFF Joshua 1847

## Section 14
MUNSELL Ira 1838 · COOPER John 1824 · CRAWFORD Dawson T 1853
LANE Lewis 1854 · **14**
BOWERS Lemuel Gomers 1836 · MUNSELL Ira 1844 · MUNSELL Ira 1838 · MUNSELL Ira 1830
LOYD James 1849

## Section 13
HOPSON William 1850 · BIGGERSTAFF Samuel 1836
BIGERSTAFF Samuel 1820 · HOPSON William 1853 · HOPSON William 1838 · PORTER Robert M 1819
**13** · HANNAGAN Daniel 1853 · ORR Samuel Calhoun 1837
MUNSELL Ira 1830 · MUNSELL Ira 1838 · WRAY John 1819 · BIGGERSTAFF Alfred 1834

## Section 22
THOMAS Lewis F 1851 · BIGGERSTAFF Joshua 1854 · BIGGERSTAFF Josuah 1849 · RAY John 1837
BARNES Emberson 1847 · MYERS William C 1851 · LANE James 1867 · BIGGERSTAFF Joshua 1849
FITZGERRALD Davis 1848 · MARTIN Winningham 1851 · MYERS William C 1853
FITZGERRALD Davis 1848 · FULLER Richard C 1839 · RILEY William 1851 · **22**

## Section 23
LOYD James 1849 · VARNELL [39] George H 1860 · CUSIC Talitha T 1854
**23** · GARRISON Thomas W 1850 · GARRISON Thomas W 1852
STOCKER John 1854 · GREENLER James M 1849 · GARRISON Thomas Wain 1837 · GOUDY 1851 · GARRISON Thomas W 1851 · John C 1819
BIGGERSTAFF Joshua 1849 · BIGERSTAFF Westly 1833 · WRIGHT James Henry 1852

## Section 24
FARRISS William 1853 · MANSELL Allin 1851 · MCKNIGHT Leander W 1850 · HANAGAN Daniel 1850
MUNSELL Allen 1854 · PRIMM Alexander T 1858 · MCKNIGHT Leander W 1850 · PRIMM Alexander T 1858
**24** · PHIPPS Benjamin 1852 · MCKNIGHT Leander W 1854 · GARRISON Andrew T 1839 · NATIONS Anderson 1853 · MCKNIGHT Leander W 1850
PHIPPS Joseph 1853 · MCKNIGHT Leander W 1853 · BIGGERSTAFF Samuel 1850

## Section 27
SHELTON Jane 1842 · SHELTON Jerimiah 1842 · DAVIS Thomas P 1854 · STOCKER John 1854
COKER Charles 1836 · PERRYMAN James C 1853 · **27**
SHELTON Jerimiah 1842 · ANDERSON Orran Trigg 1837 · PERRYMAN Elizabeth A 1848 · COOK Elizabeth Ann 1838
ANDERSON Orran Trigg 1836 · PRINCE John 1836 · PHIPPS Joseph 1842 · CROOK James 1833

## Section 26
GREENLER James M 1849 · GRAY Jesse 1847 · WRIGHT James Henry 1851
PERRYMAN William H 1846 · PRINCE John 1836 · **26** · WRIGHT James Henry 1852
CROOK James 1833 · PERRYMAN William H 1845 · PRINCE Joseph Phipps 1846 · MAYBERRY William 1848
CROOK Elizabeth Ann 1837 · FARRIS Thompson 1837 · WRIGHT James Henry 1849 · DENNY William Lewis 1850

## Section 25
MAYBERRY William 1848 · FARRIS Thompson 1853 · MCKNIGHT William P 1853
FARRIS Thompson 1842 · FARRIS Thompson 1853 · CONNELLEY Andrew 1852
**25** · CONNELLY Hugh 1844
FLOYD Isaac 1853 · MAYBERRY William 1848 · FARRIS Thompson 1851 · HEARIN John 1836

## Section 34
WEBB Elizabeth 1839 · WEBB Martin 1839
WEBB Holley R 1844 · CHEEK [10] Parmelon 1848 · CHEEK William E 1846 · **34**
WEBB Obid Hendrick 1837 · WEBB Obid Hendrick 1840 · WEBB Martin 1846 · WEBB Martin 1853
WEBB Obid Hendrick 1853 · CHEEK N C 1848 · WEBB Martin 1854 · TROUT John N 1852

## Section 35
BOYER Samuel 1838 · BOYER Samuel 1838
DENNY William L 1852 · BOYER Samuel 1838 · CRAIG William 1842 · **35**
HAMPTON Peter 1853 · BOYER Calvin 1855 · BOYER Samuel 1838 · CAMPBELL John 1853
TROUT John N 1853 · MAYBERRY George T 1853 · WRIGHT James H 1854 · CRAIG John 1851

## Section 36
SWEARINGEN Hugh 1851 · HILL Samuel Jr 1839 · GARRISON Gomer 1854 · HUBBELL Justus 1839
FLOYD Isaac 1853
CRAIG William 1845 · LASATER James 1836 · **36**
LASATER James 1852 · LANSDEN Abner 1818 · WRIGHT James H 1854

---

## Helpful Hints

1. This Map's INDEX can be found on the preceding pages.

2. Refer to Map "C" to see where this Township lies within Hamilton County, Illinois.

3. Numbers within square brackets [ ] denote a multi-patentee land parcel (multi-owner). Refer to Appendix "C" for a full list of members in this group.

4. Areas that look to be crowded with Patentees usually indicate multiple sales of the same parcel (re-issues), cancellations or voided transactions (that we map, anyway) or overlapping parcels. We opt to show even these ambiguous parcels, which oftentimes lead to research avenues not yet taken.

## Legend

— Patent Boundary
— Section Boundary
No Patents Found (or Outside County)
1., 2., 3., ... Lot Numbers (when beside a name)
[ ] Group Number (see Appendix "C")

**Scale**: Section = 1 mile X 1 mile (generally, with some exceptions)

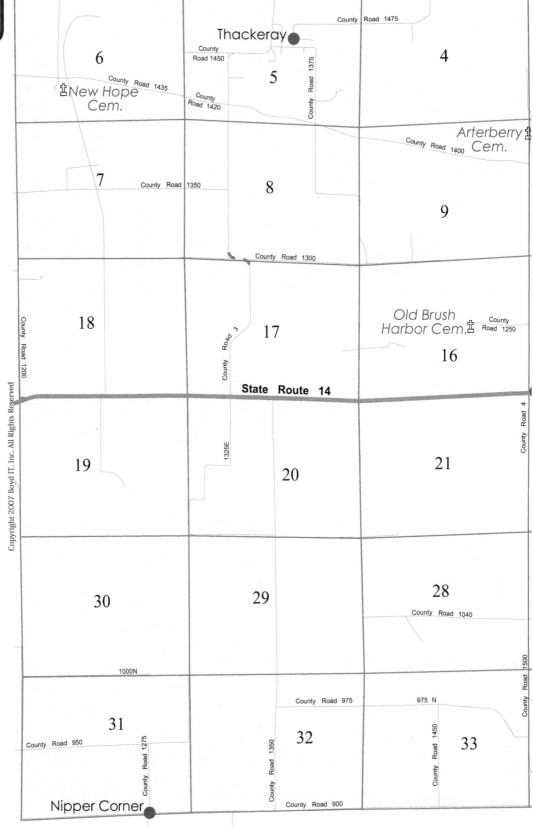

## Road Map

T5-S  R7-E
3rd PM Meridian

Map Group 9

### Cities & Towns
Jamestown (historical)
Logansport (historical)
Nipper Corner
Thackeray
Thurber

### Cemeteries
Arterberry Cemetery
Hopkins Cemetery
Munsell Cemetery
New Hope Cemetery
Old Brush Harbor Cemetery
Prince Cemetery
Webb Cemetery

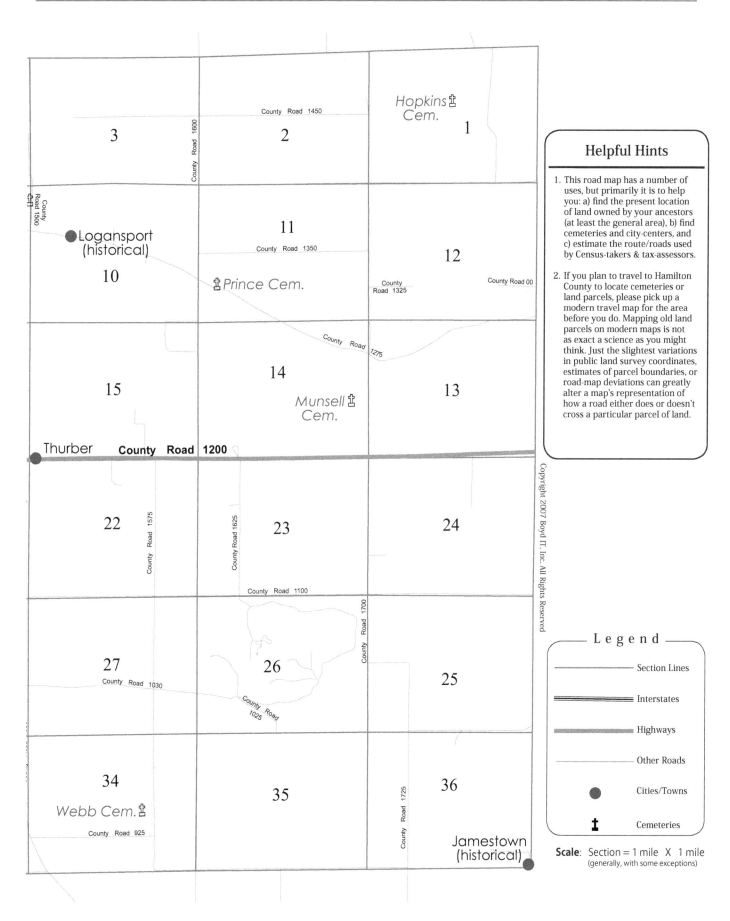

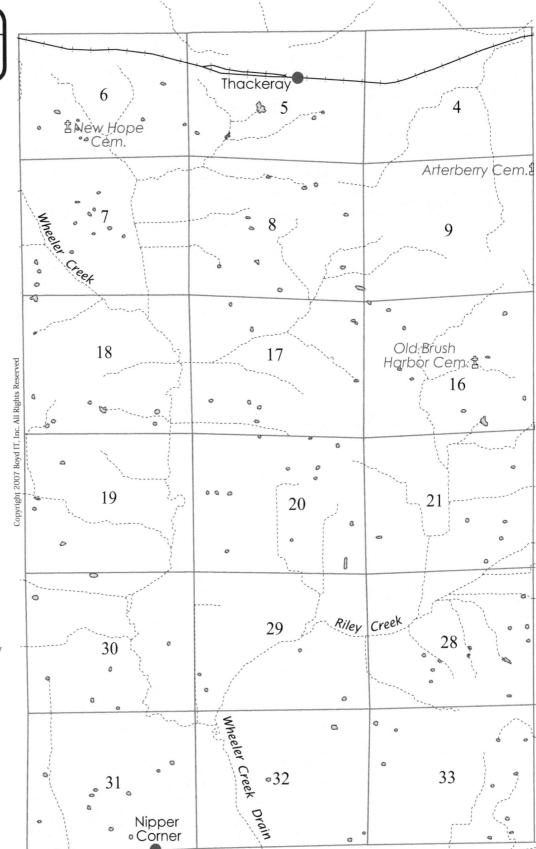

**Historical Map**

T5-S R7-E
3rd PM Meridian

Map Group 9

Thackeray

6

5

4

✝ New Hope Cem.

Arterberry Cem. ✝

**Cities & Towns**
Jamestown (historical)
Logansport (historical)
Nipper Corner
Thackeray
Thurber

7

8

9

Wheeler Creek

18

17

Old Brush Harbor Cem. ✝

16

Copyright 2007 Boyd IT, Inc. All Rights Reserved

19

20

21

**Cemeteries**
Arterberry Cemetery
Hopkins Cemetery
Munsell Cemetery
New Hope Cemetery
Old Brush Harbor Cemetery
Prince Cemetery
Webb Cemetery

30

29

Riley Creek

28

31

Wheeler Creek Drain

32

33

Nipper Corner

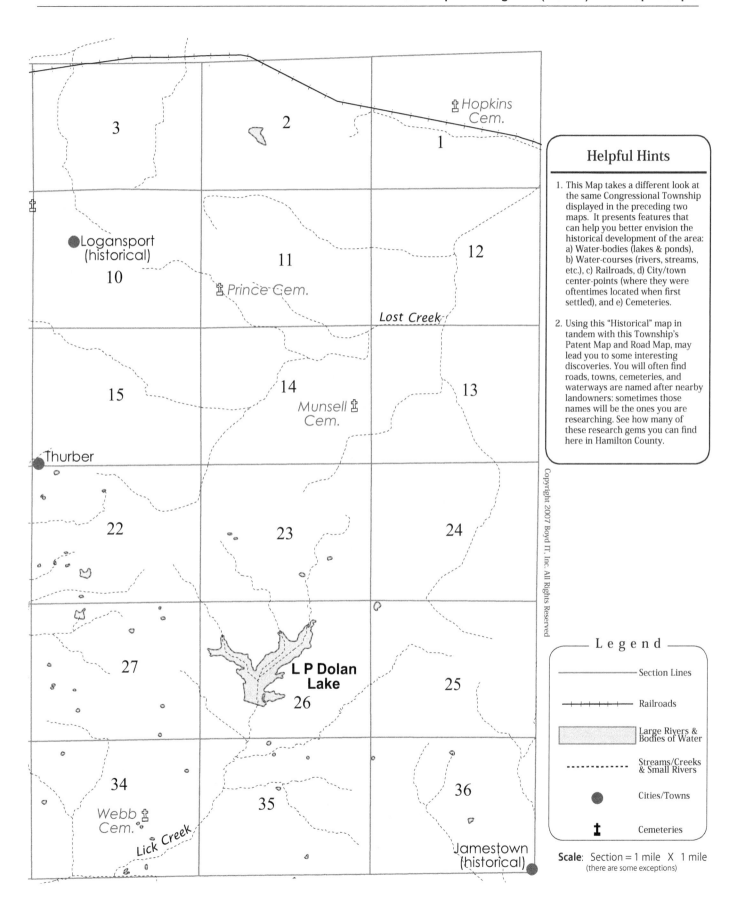

3

2

🜨 *Hopkins Cem.*

1

### Helpful Hints

1. This Map takes a different look at the same Congressional Township displayed in the preceding two maps. It presents features that can help you better envision the historical development of the area: a) Water-bodies (lakes & ponds), b) Water-courses (rivers, streams, etc.), c) Railroads, d) City/town center-points (where they were oftentimes located when first settled), and e) Cemeteries.

2. Using this "Historical" map in tandem with this Township's Patent Map and Road Map, may lead you to some interesting discoveries. You will often find roads, towns, cemeteries, and waterways are named after nearby landowners: sometimes those names will be the ones you are researching. See how many of these research gems you can find here in Hamilton County.

● Logansport (historical)

10

11

🜨 *Prince Cem.*

12

*Lost Creek*

15

14

Munsell 🜨 Cem.

13

● Thurber

22

23

24

27

**L P Dolan Lake**

26

25

34

35

36

Webb 🜨 Cem.

*Lick Creek*

Jamestown (historical) ●

### Legend

———— Section Lines

+++++ Railroads

▱ Large Rivers & Bodies of Water

----- Streams/Creeks & Small Rivers

● Cities/Towns

🜨 Cemeteries

**Scale**: Section = 1 mile X 1 mile
(there are some exceptions)

# Map Group 10: Index to Land Patents

## Township 6-South Range 5-East (3rd PM)

After you locate an individual in this Index, take note of the Section and Section Part then proceed to the Land Patent map on the pages immediately following. You should have no difficulty locating the corresponding parcel of land.

The "For More Info" Column will lead you to more information about the underlying Patents. See the *Legend* at right, and the "How to Use this Book" chapter, for more information.

```
                        LEGEND
            "For More Info . . . " column

G = Group  (Multi-Patentee Patent, see Appendix "C")
R = Residence
S = Social Status


See Appendix A for list of abbreviations used by the
Illinois State Archives in describing the place and
nature of these land patents.

Note: if the Abbreviations contain "L", "BL", "LOT",
or "BLOCK", the exact whereabouts of the parcel within
the section is not known.
```

| ID | Individual in Patent | Sec. | Sec. Part | Purchase Date | Sale Type | IL Aliquot Part | For More Info . . . |
|----|---------------------|------|-----------|---------------|-----------|-----------------|---------------------|
| 2877 | ALLEN, Robert Wilson | 26 | | 1848-12-11 | FD | SWNENT | R:HAMILTON |
| 2941 | ALLEN, William G | 26 | NWSE | 1853-10-12 | FD | NWSE | R:HAMILTON |
| 2676 | BAKER, Hiram | 36 | S½SW | 1849-01-01 | FD | S2SW | |
| 2675 | " " | 35 | E½SE | 1849-01-01 | FD | E2SE | |
| 2739 | BANES, James Milton | 18 | SWSW | 1850-01-03 | FD | SWSW | R:HAMILTON |
| 2959 | BANES, William T | 8 | SENE | 1854-10-27 | FD | SENE | R:HAMILTON |
| 2960 | BANES, William Thomas | 18 | SESW | 1850-01-03 | FD | SESW | R:HAMILTON |
| 2679 | BARKER, Hiram | 36 | NESW | 1836-05-07 | FD | NESW | R:HAMILTON |
| 2678 | " " | 35 | SENE | 1852-08-14 | FD | SENE | |
| 2681 | " " | 36 | SENW | 1853-03-17 | FD | SENW | R:HAMILTON |
| 2680 | " " | 36 | NWSW | 1853-08-22 | FD | NWSW | R:HAMILTON |
| 2682 | " " | 36 | SWNW | 1854-04-19 | FD | SWNW | R:HAMILTON |
| 2677 | " " | 35 | N½NE | 1854-10-09 | FD | N2NE | R:HAMILTON |
| 2755 | BARKER, John E | 35 | NWSE | 1853-10-13 | FD | NWSE | R:HAMILTON |
| 2754 | " " | 35 | NWNE | 1853-10-13 | FD | NWNE | R:HAMILTON |
| 2857 | BENTLEY, Osborn | 12 | NWSW | 1853-11-29 | FD | NWSW | |
| 2858 | BENTLY, Osborn | 12 | NESW | 1852-10-02 | FD | NESW | |
| 2848 | BILDERBACK, Nancy C | 15 | SENE | 1854-04-11 | FD | SENE | R:HAMILTON S:F |
| 2918 | BISHOP, William | 16 | L8 | 1850-02-20 | SC | LOT8SENE | |
| 2855 | BOYD, Noah | 6 | SENW | 1852-04-26 | FD | SENW | |
| 2856 | " " | 6 | W½NW | 1853-01-10 | FD | W2NW | |
| 2560 | BRADEN, Albert | 23 | NWNW | 1853-02-15 | FD | NWNW | |
| 2561 | " " | 23 | SENW | 1854-05-06 | FD | SENW | R:HAMILTON |
| 2555 | " " | 14 | SESW | 1854-09-23 | FD | SESW | R:HAMILTON |
| 2556 | " " | 15 | SESE | 1854-09-23 | FD | SESE | R:HAMILTON |
| 2557 | " " | 23 | N½SE | 1854-09-23 | FD | N2SE | R:HAMILTON |
| 2558 | " " | 23 | NENW | 1854-09-23 | FD | NENW | R:HAMILTON |
| 2559 | " " | 23 | NESW | 1854-09-23 | FD | NESW | R:HAMILTON |
| 2562 | " " | 23 | W½SW | 1854-09-23 | FD | W2SW | R:HAMILTON |
| 2574 | BRADEN, Alfred | 13 | SWSW | 1848-12-19 | FD | SWSW | |
| 2576 | " " | 14 | SESE | 1848-12-19 | FD | SESE | |
| 2577 | " " | 23 | NENE | 1848-12-19 | FD | NENE | |
| 2615 | " " | 13 | SWSW | 1848-12-19 | FD | SWSW | |
| 2578 | " " | 24 | NWNW | 1848-12-19 | FD | NWNW | |
| 2566 | " " | 1 | SENW | 1852-12-18 | FD | SENW | |
| 2575 | " " | 14 | NESE | 1853-11-15 | FD | NESE | R:HAMILTON |
| 2567 | " " | 11 | NESE | 1854-02-23 | FD | NESE | R:HAMILTON |
| 2568 | " " | 11 | NWSE | 1854-09-23 | FD | NWSE | R:HAMILTON |
| 2569 | " " | 11 | S½SE | 1854-09-23 | FD | S2SE | R:HAMILTON |
| 2570 | " " | 11 | SESW | 1854-09-23 | FD | SESW | R:HAMILTON |
| 2571 | " " | 11 | W½NW | 1854-09-23 | FD | W2NW | R:HAMILTON |
| 2572 | " " | 12 | SWSW | 1854-09-23 | FD | SWSW | R:HAMILTON |
| 2573 | " " | 13 | NWSW | 1854-09-23 | FD | NWSW | R:HAMILTON |
| 2697 | BRADEN, Jacob | 22 | SWSE | 1834-06-20 | FD | SWSE | R:HAMILTON |
| 2696 | " " | 22 | SESW | 1837-05-02 | FD | SESW | R:HAMILTON |
| 2700 | " " | 24 | N½NE | 1848-12-19 | FD | N2NE | |

| ID | Individual in Patent | Sec. | Sec. Part | Purchase Date | Sale Type | IL Aliquot Part | For More Info . . . |
|---|---|---|---|---|---|---|---|
| 2701 | BRADEN, Jacob (Cont'd) | 24 | NENW | 1848-12-19 | FD | NENW | |
| 2693 | "          " | 13 | SWSE | 1848-12-19 | FD | SWSE | |
| 2703 | "          " | 27 | NWNE | 1854-04-11 | FD | NWNE | R:HAMILTON |
| 2699 | "          " | 23 | SWNW | 1854-09-23 | FD | SWNW | R:HAMILTON |
| 2698 | "          " | 23 | E½SE | 1854-09-23 | FD | E2SE | R:HAMILTON |
| 2702 | "          " | 27 | NENE | 1854-09-23 | FD | NENE | R:HAMILTON |
| 2694 | "          " | 22 | E½SE | 1854-09-23 | FD | E2SE | R:HAMILTON |
| 2695 | "          " | 22 | NE | 1854-09-23 | FD | NE | R:HAMILTON |
| 2708 | BRADEN, Jacob Sen | 13 | E½SW | 1854-09-23 | FD | E2SW | R:HAMILTON |
| 2711 | "          " | 24 | SESE | 1854-09-23 | FD | SESE | R:HAMILTON |
| 2710 | "          " | 24 | SENE | 1854-09-23 | FD | SENE | R:HAMILTON |
| 2709 | "          " | 24 | N½SE | 1854-09-23 | FD | N2SE | R:HAMILTON |
| 2718 | BRADEN, James | 27 | SWNW | 1853-02-15 | FD | SWNW | |
| 2721 | "          " | 28 | SENE | 1853-09-02 | FD | SENE | R:HAMILTON |
| 2719 | "          " | 28 | NESE | 1853-11-01 | FD | NESE | R:HAMILTON |
| 2720 | "          " | 28 | NWSE | 1854-05-16 | FD | NWSE | R:HAMILTON |
| 2716 | "          " | 21 | S½NW | 1854-09-23 | FD | S2NW | R:HAMILTON |
| 2715 | "          " | 20 | SE | 1854-09-23 | FD | SE | R:HAMILTON |
| 2717 | "          " | 21 | W½SW | 1854-09-23 | FD | W2SW | R:HAMILTON |
| 2790 | BRADEN, John M | 14 | NWNE | 1853-02-15 | FD | NWNE | |
| 2789 | "          " | 14 | NENE | 1854-01-13 | FD | NENE | R:HAMILTON |
| 2846 | BRADEN, Nancy | 22 | SWSW | 1837-09-20 | FD | SWSW | R:HAMILTON S:F |
| 2845 | "          " | 22 | NWSE | 1837-09-20 | FD | NWSE | R:HAMILTON S:F |
| 2639 | BRANDON, George | 12 | N½NW | 1852-10-18 | FD | N2NW | |
| 2640 | "          " | 12 | SENE | 1852-10-18 | FD | SENE | |
| 2824 | BROYLES, Lewis S | 17 | SESE | 1850-12-29 | FD | SESE | R:HAMILTON |
| 2637 | BULLIN, Ezariah | 9 | NWNW | 1854-10-28 | FD | NWNW | R:HAMILTON |
| 2741 | BURLISON, James R | 31 | NW | 1854-10-27 | FD | NW | R:FRANKLIN |
| 2797 | BURLISON, John R | 31 | SENE | 1855-09-21 | FD | SENE | R:HAMILTON |
| 2749 | BURTON, John | 1 | NWNW | 1836-06-16 | FD | NWNW | R:HAMILTON |
| 2847 | BURTON, Nancy | 1 | NWNE | 1836-11-17 | FD | NWNE | R:HAMILTON S:F |
| 2735 | CAIN, James L | 17 | N½NE | 1854-10-25 | FD | N2NE | R:HAMILTON |
| 2722 | CALVIN, James | 4 | NWNW | 1851-09-08 | FD | NWNW | R:HAMILTON |
| 2746 | CALVIN, Job | 4 | NWSW | 1854-10-10 | FD | NWSW | R:HAMILTON |
| 2922 | CAMPBELL, William | 3 | NENW | 1851-04-18 | FD | NENW | |
| 2929 | CARLISLE, William | 29 | SENE | 1854-04-04 | FD | SENE | R:HAMILTON |
| 2927 | "          " | 29 | E½SE | 1854-04-04 | FD | E2SE | R:HAMILTON |
| 2924 | "          " | 28 | NESW | 1854-04-04 | FD | NESW | R:HAMILTON |
| 2926 | "          " | 28 | W½SW | 1854-04-04 | FD | W2SW | R:HAMILTON |
| 2925 | "          " | 28 | SWNW | 1855-03-26 | FD | SWNW | R:HAMILTON |
| 2928 | "          " | 29 | NWSE | 1855-03-26 | FD | NWSE | R:HAMILTON |
| 2923 | "          " | 28 | E½NW | 1855-03-26 | FD | E2NW | R:HAMILTON |
| 2816 | "          " | 29 | NWSE | 1855-03-26 | FD | NWSE | R:HAMILTON |
| 2601 | CARPENTER, Chester | 28 | NE | 1854-09-22 | FD | NE | R:HAMILTON |
| 2603 | "          " | 33 | N½SE | 1854-09-22 | FD | N2SE | R:HAMILTON |
| 2602 | "          " | 28 | S½SE | 1854-09-22 | FD | S2SE | R:HAMILTON |
| 2600 | "          " | 20 | NWNW | 1858-01-08 | FD | NWNW | |
| 2582 | CARTER, Anderson N | 30 | NENW | 1853-12-09 | FD | NENW | |
| 2819 | CARTER, Joseph | 33 | NW | 1854-09-26 | FD | NW | R:HAMILTON |
| 2726 | CLARK, James H | 22 | N½NW | 1855-08-18 | FD | N2NW | R:HAMILTON |
| 2643 | CLICK, George W | 30 | W½NW | 1855-09-14 | FD | W2NW | R:HAMILTON |
| 2752 | CLUCK, John | 2 | NWSE | 1851-11-14 | FD | NWSE | R:HAMILTON |
| 2751 | "          " | 2 | NWNE | 1851-12-12 | FD | NWNE | R:HAMILTON |
| 2742 | COFFEY, James W | 35 | SWSE | 1854-10-27 | FD | SWSE | R:HAMILTON |
| 2553 | COOK, Abraham | 7 | SESW | 1850-03-19 | FD | SESW | R:HAMILTON |
| 2554 | "          " | 7 | SWSW | 1855-09-12 | FD | SWSW | R:HAMILTON |
| 2683 | CORN, Hiram | 18 | W½NW | 1851-11-06 | FD | W2NW | |
| 2770 | CORN, John Harvey | 4 | NESE | 1851-02-21 | FD | NESE | R:HAMILTON |
| 2930 | CORN, William D | 18 | SWSE | 1849-03-17 | FD | SWSE | R:FRANKLIN |
| 2916 | CRABTREE, William A | 14 | SWNW | 1851-08-29 | FD | SWNW | |
| 2917 | "          " | 15 | SWNE | 1853-05-31 | FD | SWNE | R:HAMILTON |
| 2805 | CREEKMAN, John W | 15 | SWNW | 1855-09-06 | FD | SWNW | R:HAMILTON |
| 2804 | "          " | 15 | NWSW | 1855-09-06 | FD | NWSW | R:HAMILTON |
| 2860 | CULLY, Richard C | 31 | SW | 1854-10-27 | FD | SW | R:FRANKLIN |
| 2859 | "          " | 31 | NWSE | 1854-10-27 | FD | NWSE | R:FRANKLIN |
| 2823 | DAILEY, Lewis | 36 | NENE | 1853-09-13 | FD | NENE | |
| 2608 | DARNALL, David | 16 | L6 | 1850-02-20 | SC | L6SENW | |
| 2607 | "          " | 16 | L4 | 1850-02-20 | SC | LOT4NWNW | |
| 2609 | "          " | 6 | NESE | 1853-10-26 | FD | NESE | R:HAMILTON |
| 2610 | "          " | 8 | SESE | 1854-02-04 | FD | SESE | R:HAMILTON |
| 2723 | DARNALL, James | 16 | L3 | 1850-02-20 | SC | LOT3NENW | |
| 2730 | DARNALL, James H | 9 | SENW | 1850-12-02 | FD | SENW | R:HAMILTON |
| 2729 | "          " | 9 | NWSE | 1850-12-02 | FD | NWSE | R:HAMILTON |

| ID | Individual in Patent | Sec. | Sec. Part | Purchase Date | Sale Type | IL Aliquot Part | For More Info . . . |
|----|----------------------|------|-----------|---------------|-----------|-----------------|---------------------|
| 2728 | DARNALL, James H (Cont'd) | 9 | NENW | 1851-06-16 | FD | NENW | R:HAMILTON |
| 2727 | " | 8 | SWNE | 1853-01-14 | FD | SWNE | |
| 2897 | DARNALL, Thomas C | 9 | SWSE | 1853-12-15 | FD | SWSE | R:HAMILTON |
| 2896 | " " | 9 | SESW | 1854-02-22 | FD | SESW | R:HAMILTON |
| 2935 | DARNALL, William | 7 | NESW | 1853-10-26 | FD | NESW | R:HAMILTON |
| 2936 | " " | 7 | SENW | 1853-10-31 | FD | SENW | R:HAMILTON |
| 2934 | " " | 18 | W½NE | 1854-10-27 | FD | W2NE | R:HAMILTON |
| 2931 | " " | 17 | S½NW | 1854-10-27 | FD | S2NW | R:HAMILTON |
| 2774 | " " | 7 | SWSE | 1854-10-27 | FD | SWSE | R:HAMILTON G:13 |
| 2933 | " " | 18 | SENE | 1854-10-27 | FD | SENE | R:HAMILTON |
| 2932 | " " | 17 | SESW | 1854-10-27 | FD | SESW | R:HAMILTON |
| 2612 | DARNEL, David | 18 | NENE | 1851-10-28 | FD | NENE | R:HAMILTON |
| 2611 | " " | 17 | N½NW | 1851-10-28 | FD | N2NW | R:HAMILTON |
| 2614 | DARNELL, David | 8 | SWSE | 1853-11-24 | FD | SWSE | R:HAMILTON |
| 2613 | " " | 5 | SESW | 1853-11-24 | FD | SESW | R:HAMILTON |
| 2731 | DARNELL, James H | 7 | SWNW | 1853-12-20 | FD | SWNW | R:HAMILTON |
| 2732 | " " | 9 | SWNW | 1853-12-20 | FD | SWNW | R:HAMILTON |
| 2705 | DEAN, Jacob Clay | 36 | NESE | 1834-01-11 | FD | NESE | R:HAMILTON |
| 2706 | " " | 36 | NWSE | 1836-09-01 | FD | NWSE | R:HAMILTON |
| 2704 | DEEN, Jacob C | 36 | N½NE | 1850-06-29 | FD | N2NE | |
| 2753 | DRAKE, John | 5 | NENE | 1854-10-27 | FD | NENE | R:HAMILTON |
| 2638 | DUCKWORTH, Felix | 9 | W½NE | 1853-10-24 | FD | W2NE | R:HAMILTON |
| 2822 | DUCKWORTH, Julia Ann | 15 | SENW | 1851-11-12 | FD | SENW | R:HAMILTON S:F |
| 2901 | DUCKWORTH, Thomas | 16 | L15 | 1850-02-20 | SC | LOT15SWSE | |
| 2899 | " " | 16 | L11 | 1850-02-20 | SC | LOT11NESW | |
| 2900 | " " | 16 | L14 | 1850-02-20 | SC | L14SESW | |
| 2898 | " " | 10 | W½NW | 1850-03-07 | FD | W2NW | |
| 2903 | " " | 9 | E½NE | 1850-03-07 | FD | E2NE | |
| 2904 | " " | 9 | NESE | 1851-09-27 | FD | NESE | R:HAMILTON |
| 2902 | " " | 5 | SENW | 1852-01-15 | FD | SENW | |
| 2938 | DUCKWORTH, William | 16 | L2 | 1850-02-20 | SC | LOT2NWNE | |
| 2937 | " " | 16 | L1 | 1850-02-20 | SC | LOT1NENE | |
| 2840 | FANN, Moses | 4 | E½SW | 1853-07-26 | FD | E2SW | |
| 2583 | FAULKNER, Archibald | 23 | SW | 1853-12-22 | FD | SW | R:HAMILTON |
| 2605 | FAULKNER, Daniel | 23 | SE | 1853-12-22 | FD | SE | R:HAMILTON |
| 2895 | FAULKNER, Thomas B | 24 | SW | 1853-12-22 | FD | SW | R:HAMILTON |
| 2606 | FISHER, Daniel | 30 | NWSW | 1851-11-12 | FD | NWSW | R:HAMILTON |
| 2815 | FISHER, Jordan A | 29 | NWNW | 1852-10-30 | FD | NWNW | |
| 2813 | " " | 29 | S½NW | 1852-10-30 | FD | S2NW | |
| 2811 | " " | 29 | NWNW | 1852-10-30 | FD | NWNW | |
| 2812 | " " | 29 | NWSW | 1852-10-30 | FD | NWSW | |
| 2833 | FISHER, Jordon A | 30 | SENE | 1848-10-24 | FD | SENEVOID | |
| 2817 | " " | 29 | SWSE | 1848-10-24 | FD | SENWVOID | |
| 2890 | " " | 29 | SWSE | 1848-10-24 | FD | SENWVOID | |
| 2816 | " " | 29 | NWSE | 1848-10-24 | FD | NWSEVOID | |
| 2928 | " " | 29 | NWSE | 1848-10-24 | FD | NWSEVOID | |
| 2811 | " " | 29 | NWNW | 1848-10-24 | FD | NWNWVOID | |
| 2818 | " " | 30 | SENE | 1848-10-24 | FD | SENEVOID | |
| 2815 | " " | 29 | NWNW | 1848-10-24 | FD | NWNWVOID | |
| 2814 | " " | 29 | NENW | 1854-10-26 | FD | NENW | R:HAMILTON |
| 2940 | FISHER, William E | 20 | SWNW | 1854-10-26 | FD | SWNW | R:HAMILTON |
| 2939 | " " | 20 | NWSW | 1854-10-26 | FD | NWSW | R:HAMILTON |
| 2867 | FLANINKIN, Robert H | 36 | S½SE | 1850-01-25 | FD | S2SE | |
| 2885 | FLANNIKIN, Samuel W | 14 | NWSE | 1851-11-20 | FD | NWSE | |
| 2884 | " " | 14 | NESW | 1851-11-20 | FD | NESW | |
| 2656 | FLINT, Gilbert | 1 | SESE | 1852-07-29 | FD | SESE | |
| 2658 | " " | 12 | NENE | 1853-10-25 | FD | NENE | R:HAMILTON |
| 2657 | " " | 1 | SWSE | 1853-10-25 | FD | SWSE | R:HAMILTON |
| 2661 | " " | 28 | N½NE | 1854-09-22 | FD | N2NE | R:HAMILTON |
| 2660 | " " | 27 | NWNW | 1854-09-22 | FD | NWNW | R:HAMILTON |
| 2659 | " " | 27 | E½NW | 1854-09-22 | FD | E2NW | R:HAMILTON |
| 2662 | " " | 28 | SWNE | 1854-09-22 | FD | SWNE | R:HAMILTON |
| 2757 | FLINT, John | 1 | NESW | 1836-06-11 | FD | NESW | R:HAMILTON |
| 2756 | " " | 1 | N½SE | 1848-11-17 | FD | N2SE | |
| 2758 | " " | 1 | SEN½ | 1848-11-17 | FD | S2NE | |
| 2761 | " " | 34 | S½SW | 1854-09-23 | FD | S2SW | R:HAMILTON |
| 2760 | " " | 33 | SESW | 1854-09-23 | FD | SESW | R:HAMILTON |
| 2759 | " " | 33 | S½SE | 1854-09-23 | FD | S2SE | R:HAMILTON |
| 2849 | FLINT, Nancy | 1 | SESW | 1839-05-21 | FD | SESW | R:HAMILTON S:F |
| 2878 | FOSTER, Samuel | 20 | E½NE | 1853-01-26 | FD | E2NE | |
| 2879 | " " | 20 | NENW | 1855-04-02 | FD | NENW | R:HAMILTON |
| 2881 | " " | 21 | W½NE | 1855-04-02 | FD | W2NE | R:HAMILTON |
| 2880 | " " | 21 | NENW | 1855-04-02 | FD | NENW | R:HAMILTON |

| ID | Individual in Patent | Sec. | Sec. Part | Purchase Date | Sale Type | IL Aliquot Part | For More Info . . . |
|---|---|---|---|---|---|---|---|
| 2882 | FOSTER, Samuel R | 21 | NE | 1855-03-28 | FD | NE | R:HAMILTON |
| 2883 | FOSTER, Samuel Riley | 21 | E½SE | 1853-02-21 | FD | E2SE | |
| 2839 | GARNET, Moses B | 12 | NWSE | 1837-06-23 | FD | NWSE | R:HAMILTON |
| 2736 | GARVIN, James M | 10 | SENE | 1854-10-27 | FD | SENE | R:HAMILTON |
| 2915 | GARVIN, Wesley W | 11 | SWNW | 1853-10-31 | FD | SWNW | R:HAMILTON |
| 2961 | GARVIN, William W | 11 | SENW | 1853-10-17 | FD | SENW | R:HAMILTON |
| 2863 | GOWDY, Robert A | 34 | N½SW | 1854-09-20 | FD | N2SW | R:HAMILTON |
| 2864 | "          " | 34 | NWSE | 1854-09-20 | FD | NWSE | R:HAMILTON |
| 2865 | "          " | 34 | S½NW | 1854-09-20 | FD | S2NW | R:HAMILTON |
| 2866 | "          " | 34 | SEN½ | 1854-09-20 | FD | S2NE | R:HAMILTON |
| 2641 | GREEN, George G | 19 | N½NW | 1855-04-30 | FD | N2NW | R:HAMILTON |
| 2906 | GREEN, Thomas | 19 | SWNW | 1854-01-28 | FD | SWNW | R:FRANKLIN |
| 2748 | GRINESTAFF, John B | 31 | SWNE | 1852-05-24 | FD | SWNE | R:HAMILTON |
| 2685 | HALL, Hiram W | 2 | NW | 1847-11-27 | FD | NW | |
| 2687 | "          " | 3 | SWSE | 1853-03-12 | FD | SWSE | |
| 2684 | "          " | 10 | NENE | 1853-04-06 | FD | NENE | R:HAMILTON |
| 2686 | "          " | 3 | NENE | 1853-11-01 | FD | NENE | R:HAMILTON |
| 2763 | HALL, John | 5 | NENW | 1851-08-21 | FD | NENW | |
| 2764 | "          " | 5 | SENE | 1853-11-16 | FD | SENE | R:HAMILTON |
| 2801 | HALL, John T | 5 | NWSW | 1853-11-15 | FD | NWSW | R:HAMILTON |
| 2712 | HAMILTON, James B | 5 | W½NE | 1853-10-26 | FD | W2NE | R:HAMILTON |
| 2713 | "          " | 6 | SESE | 1853-10-26 | FD | SESE | R:HAMILTON |
| 2765 | HAMILTON, John | 11 | N½SW | 1854-09-27 | FD | N2SW | R:GALLATIN |
| 2766 | "          " | 11 | SWSW | 1854-09-27 | FD | SWSW | R:GALLATIN |
| 2767 | "          " | 14 | E½NW | 1854-09-27 | FD | E2NW | R:GALLATIN |
| 2768 | "          " | 14 | NWNW | 1854-09-27 | FD | NWNW | R:GALLATIN |
| 2769 | "          " | 14 | SEN½ | 1854-09-27 | FD | S2NE | R:GALLATIN |
| 2942 | "          " | 11 | N½SW | 1854-09-27 | FD | N2SW | R:GALLATIN |
| 2955 | "          " | 14 | SEN½ | 1854-09-27 | FD | S2NE | R:GALLATIN |
| 2584 | HANELSON, Benjamin W | 4 | NENE | 1854-02-13 | FD | NENE | R:HAMILTON |
| 2623 | HANNIKIN, Eevin G | 36 | SWNE | 1837-02-06 | FD | SWNE | R:HAMILTON |
| 2585 | HARRELSON, Benjamin W | 9 | SESE | 1855-08-20 | FD | SESE | R:HAMILTON |
| 2672 | HARRELSON, Herndon | 3 | NWNW | 1854-10-27 | FD | NWNW | R:HAMILTON |
| 2673 | "          " | 4 | SENE | 1854-10-27 | FD | SENE | R:HAMILTON |
| 2851 | HARRELSON, Nathaniel | 4 | NWNE | 1853-02-22 | FD | NWNE | R:HAMILTON |
| 2850 | "          " | 4 | NENW | 1854-02-15 | FD | NENW | R:HAMILTON |
| 2943 | HARRIS, William | 12 | SWSE | 1853-12-15 | FD | SWSE | R:HAMILTON |
| 2970 | HATCHET, Willis | 8 | NENW | 1852-08-07 | FD | NENW | R:HAMILTON |
| 2908 | HATCHETT, Thomas S | 7 | E½SE | 1854-10-27 | FD | E2SE | R:HAMILTON |
| 2909 | "          " | 7 | SENE | 1854-10-27 | FD | SENE | R:HAMILTON |
| 2972 | HATCHETT, Willis | 8 | NWNW | 1853-01-13 | FD | NWNW | |
| 2971 | "          " | 5 | SWSW | 1853-11-21 | FD | SWSW | R:HAMILTON |
| 2714 | HEARD, James B | 31 | NESE | 1854-04-19 | FD | NESE | R:HAMILTON |
| 2762 | HEARD, John H | 3 | NWNE | 1851-06-09 | FD | NWNE | |
| 2820 | HENSLEY, Joseph | 12 | E½NW | 1851-08-13 | FD | E2NW | |
| 2821 | "          " | 12 | W½NE | 1851-08-13 | FD | W2NE | |
| 2832 | HICKS, Martin S | 22 | S½NW | 1855-08-18 | FD | S2NW | R:HAMILTON |
| 2733 | HIDE, James H | 8 | SWNW | 1853-01-18 | FD | SWNW | |
| 2791 | HOLLEMAN, John M | 16 | L16 | 1850-02-20 | SC | LOT16SESE | |
| 2792 | "          " | 16 | L9 | 1850-02-20 | SC | LOT9NESE | |
| 2595 | HUNGATE, Charles | 19 | W½SE | 1848-07-17 | FD | W2SE | |
| 2591 | "          " | 19 | NESE | 1848-07-17 | FD | NESE | |
| 2592 | "          " | 19 | NESE | 1848-07-17 | FD | NESE | |
| 2598 | "          " | 30 | NENE | 1848-07-17 | FD | NENE | |
| 2958 | "          " | 30 | NENE | 1848-07-17 | FD | NENE | |
| 2596 | "          " | 19 | W½SE | 1848-07-17 | FD | W2SE | |
| 2591 | "          " | 19 | NESE | 1849-03-09 | FD | NESE | |
| 2592 | "          " | 19 | NESE | 1849-03-09 | FD | NESE | |
| 2950 | "          " | 19 | SWNE | 1849-03-09 | FD | SWNE | |
| 2596 | "          " | 19 | W½SE | 1849-03-09 | FD | W2SE | |
| 2594 | "          " | 19 | SWNE | 1849-03-09 | FD | SWNE | |
| 2595 | "          " | 19 | W½SE | 1849-03-09 | FD | W2SE | |
| 2597 | "          " | 2 | SESW | 1851-08-25 | FD | SESW | |
| 2593 | "          " | 19 | NESW | 1854-01-28 | FD | NESW | R:HAMILTON |
| 2947 | HUNGATE, William | 2 | SWSW | 1852-11-24 | FD | SWSW | |
| 2946 | "          " | 11 | NWNW | 1852-11-24 | FD | NWNW | |
| 2794 | "          " | 3 | SESE | 1853-03-16 | FD | SESE | |
| 2949 | "          " | 3 | SESE | 1853-03-16 | FD | SESE | |
| 2948 | "          " | 3 | SENE | 1854-10-04 | FD | SENE | R:HAMILTON |
| 2635 | HUNT, Henry | 12 | NWNW | 1853-04-11 | FD | NWNW | S:F G:26 |
| 2634 | "          " | 1 | SWSW | 1853-04-11 | FD | SWSW | S:F G:26 |
| 2634 | HUNT, Jane | 1 | SWSW | 1853-04-11 | FD | SWSW | S:F G:26 |
| 2635 | "          " | 12 | NWNW | 1853-04-11 | FD | NWNW | S:F G:26 |

| ID | Individual in Patent | Sec. | Sec. Part | Purchase Date | Sale Type | IL Aliquot Part | For More Info . . . |
|----|---------------------|------|-----------|---------------|-----------|-----------------|---------------------|
| 2634 | HUNT, Martha | 1 | SWSW | 1853-04-11 | FD | SWSW | S:F G:26 |
| 2635 | " " | 12 | NWNW | 1853-04-11 | FD | NWNW | S:F G:26 |
| 2634 | HUNT, Nancy A | 1 | SWSW | 1853-04-11 | FD | SWSW | S:F G:26 |
| 2635 | " " | 12 | NWNW | 1853-04-11 | FD | NWNW | S:F G:26 |
| 2636 | HUNTER, Ellen | 15 | N½NW | 1854-11-11 | FD | N2NW | R:HAMILTON S:F |
| 2734 | HYDE, James H | 8 | SENW | 1854-10-09 | FD | SENW | R:HAMILTON |
| 2778 | JOHNSEN, John L | 17 | SW | 1854-10-14 | FD | SW | R:HAMILTON |
| 2564 | JOHNSON, Alexander | 21 | NWSE | 1852-09-04 | FD | NWSE | |
| 2563 | " " | 21 | E½SW | 1852-09-04 | FD | E2SW | |
| 2565 | " " | 21 | SWSE | 1854-10-09 | FD | SWSE | R:HAMILTON |
| 2586 | JOHNSON, C A | 16 | L7 | 1850-02-20 | SC | LOT7SWNE | S:I |
| 2588 | JOHNSON, Charles A | 4 | W½SE | 1851-02-11 | FD | W2SE | R:HAMILTON |
| 2587 | " " | 4 | SESE | 1854-01-24 | FD | SESE | R:HAMILTON |
| 2590 | " " | 9 | W½SW | 1854-10-14 | FD | W2SW | R:HAMILTON |
| 2589 | " " | 8 | N½SE | 1854-10-14 | FD | N2SE | R:HAMILTON |
| 2624 | JOHNSON, Elhanan W | 19 | SESE | 1848-10-24 | FD | SESE | R:HAMILTON |
| 2626 | " " | 30 | W½NE | 1848-11-03 | FD | W2NE | |
| 2625 | " " | 30 | N½SE | 1848-11-03 | FD | N2SE | |
| 2633 | JOHNSON, Eliza | 26 | SWNW | 1837-07-26 | FD | SWNW | R:HAMILTON S:F |
| 2644 | JOHNSON, George W | 25 | NESE | 1836-04-30 | FD | NESE | R:HAMILTON |
| 2645 | " " | 25 | NWSE | 1837-01-04 | FD | NWSE | R:HAMILTON |
| 2651 | " " | 27 | SENE | 1848-02-04 | FD | SENE | R:HAMILTON |
| 2650 | " " | 27 | NWSW | 1848-02-04 | FD | NWSW | R:HAMILTON |
| 2649 | " " | 27 | NESE | 1849-06-15 | FD | NESE | R:HAMILTON |
| 2647 | " " | 26 | NWSW | 1851-02-06 | FD | NWSW | R:HAMILTON |
| 2652 | " " | 27 | SWSW | 1853-09-21 | FD | SWSW | R:HAMILTON |
| 2966 | " " | 26 | SENW | 1853-12-20 | FD | SENW | R:HAMILTON |
| 2648 | " " | 26 | SENW | 1853-12-20 | FD | SENW | R:HAMILTON |
| 2646 | " " | 26 | NWNW | 1854-05-11 | FD | NWNW | R:HAMILTON |
| 2912 | JOHNSON, John K | 31 | S½SE | 1854-09-26 | FD | S2SE | R:HAMILTON |
| 2777 | " " | 31 | S½SE | 1854-09-26 | FD | S2SE | R:HAMILTON |
| 2784 | JOHNSON, John Lewis | 36 | SENE | 1837-02-06 | FD | SENE | R:HAMILTON |
| 2780 | " " | 25 | SESE | 1851-01-24 | FD | SESE | R:HAMILTON |
| 2781 | " " | 27 | E½SW | 1853-08-22 | FD | E2SW | G:28 |
| 2782 | " " | 27 | NWSE | 1853-08-22 | FD | NWSE | G:28 |
| 2783 | " " | 27 | SWNE | 1853-08-22 | FD | SWNE | G:28 |
| 2786 | " " | 27 | E½SW | 1853-08-22 | FD | E2SW | G:28 |
| 2787 | " " | 27 | NWSE | 1853-08-22 | FD | NWSE | G:28 |
| 2788 | " " | 27 | SWNE | 1853-08-22 | FD | SWNE | G:28 |
| 2787 | " " | 27 | NWSE | 1857-08-25 | FD | NWSE | |
| 2781 | " " | 27 | E½SW | 1857-08-25 | FD | E2SW | |
| 2782 | " " | 27 | NWSE | 1857-08-25 | FD | NWSE | |
| 2786 | " " | 27 | E½SW | 1857-08-25 | FD | E2SW | |
| 2783 | " " | 27 | SWNE | 1857-08-28 | FD | SWNE | |
| 2788 | " " | 27 | SWNE | 1857-08-28 | FD | SWNE | |
| 2818 | JOHNSON, Mary | 30 | SENE | 1852-11-01 | FD | SENE | R:HAMILTON S:F |
| 2833 | " " | 30 | SENE | 1852-11-01 | FD | SENE | R:HAMILTON S:F |
| 2843 | JOHNSON, Moses | 31 | NWNE | 1852-09-23 | FD | NWNE | |
| 2841 | " " | 30 | SESW | 1854-09-25 | FD | SESW | R:HAMILTON |
| 2842 | " " | 30 | SWSE | 1854-09-25 | FD | SWSE | R:HAMILTON |
| 2874 | JOHNSON, Robert | 25 | NWSW | 1836-04-30 | FD | NWSW | R:HAMILTON |
| 2872 | " " | 16 | L10 | 1850-02-20 | SC | LOT10NWSE | |
| 2873 | " " | 25 | NESW | 1853-03-17 | FD | NESW | |
| 2875 | " " | 26 | NESE | 1853-03-17 | FD | NESE | |
| 2869 | JOHNSON, Robert H | 6 | NWSW | 1583-12-27 | FD | NWSW | R:HAMILTON |
| 2868 | " " | 6 | NESW | 1853-10-25 | FD | NESW | R:HAMILTON |
| 2871 | " " | 7 | NWSE | 1853-10-25 | FD | NWSE | R:HAMILTON |
| 2870 | " " | 6 | SWSW | 1854-09-26 | FD | SWSW | R:HAMILTON |
| 2771 | " " | 6 | SWSW | 1854-09-26 | FD | SWSW | R:HAMILTON |
| 2890 | JOHNSON, Solomon | 29 | SWSE | 1854-09-26 | FD | SWSE | R:WILLIAMSON |
| 2891 | " " | 32 | NE | 1854-09-26 | FD | NE | R:WILLIAMSON |
| 2892 | " " | 32 | NESW | 1854-09-26 | FD | NESW | R:WILLIAMSON |
| 2894 | " " | 32 | SENW | 1854-09-26 | FD | SENW | R:WILLIAMSON |
| 2817 | " " | 29 | SWSE | 1854-09-26 | FD | SWSE | R:WILLIAMSON |
| 2893 | " " | 32 | NWSE | 1854-09-26 | FD | NWSE | R:WILLIAMSON |
| 2907 | JOHNSON, Thomas M | 26 | SESE | 1854-02-21 | FD | SESE | R:HAMILTON |
| 2963 | JOHNSON, William W | 25 | SWNW | 1847-11-08 | FD | SWNW | R:HAMILTON |
| 2648 | " " | 26 | SENW | 1847-11-08 | FD | SENW | R:HAMILTON |
| 2966 | " " | 26 | SENW | 1847-11-08 | FD | SENW | R:HAMILTON |
| 2965 | " " | 26 | SENE | 1849-03-05 | FD | SENE | R:HAMILTON |
| 2967 | " " | 33 | NWSW | 1854-06-12 | FD | NWSW | R:HAMILTON |
| 2964 | " " | 26 | N½NE | 1854-10-07 | FD | N2NE | R:HAMILTON |
| 2962 | " " | 25 | N½NW | 1854-10-07 | FD | N2NW | R:HAMILTON |

| ID | Individual in Patent | Sec. | Sec. Part | Purchase Date | Sale Type | IL Aliquot Part | For More Info . . . |
|---|---|---|---|---|---|---|---|
| 2653 | JOHNSTON, George W | 26 | NENW | 1854-10-07 | FD | NENW | R:HAMILTON |
| 2654 | " " | 26 | NESW | 1854-10-07 | FD | NESW | R:HAMILTON |
| 2968 | JOHNSTON, William W | 32 | NESE | 1854-06-12 | FD | NESE | |
| 2690 | JONES, Hullem | 31 | NENE | 1854-02-15 | FD | NENE | R:INDIANA |
| 2691 | " " | 32 | SWNW | 1854-02-15 | FD | SWNW | R:INDIANA |
| 2689 | " " | 30 | SESE | 1854-02-15 | FD | SESE | R:INDIANA |
| 2622 | KINGTON, Edmund G | 29 | SWNE | 1851-08-26 | FD | SWNE | |
| 2620 | " " | 28 | NWNW | 1851-08-26 | FD | NWNW | |
| 2621 | " " | 29 | | 1851-08-29 | FD | NIM NE | |
| 2779 | LEE, John | 4 | SWNE | 1853-03-01 | FD | SWNE | |
| 2798 | LEE, John R | 4 | S½NW | 1854-10-10 | FD | S2NW | R:HAMILTON |
| 2782 | LEWIS, John | 27 | NWSE | 1853-08-22 | FD | NWSE | G:28 |
| 2783 | " " | 27 | SWNE | 1853-08-22 | FD | SWNE | G:28 |
| 2781 | " " | 27 | E½SW | 1853-08-22 | FD | E2SW | G:28 |
| 2788 | " " | 27 | SWNE | 1853-08-22 | FD | SWNE | G:28 |
| 2787 | " " | 27 | NWSE | 1853-08-22 | FD | NWSE | G:28 |
| 2786 | " " | 27 | E½SW | 1853-08-22 | FD | E2SW | G:28 |
| 2838 | MANNERS, Michael | 17 | N½SE | 1852-03-27 | FD | N2SE | |
| 2738 | MATHENY, James | 3 | SWNW | 1850-08-28 | FD | SWNW | R:HAMILTON |
| 2737 | " " | 3 | NESW | 1853-03-21 | FD | NESW | |
| 2635 | MAULDING, Elizabeth | 12 | NWNW | 1853-04-11 | FD | NWNW | S:F G:26 |
| 2634 | " " | 1 | SWSW | 1853-04-11 | FD | SWSW | S:F G:26 |
| 2617 | MCCLUSKY, David | 18 | NWSW | 1854-09-25 | FD | NWSW | R:FRANKLIN |
| 2616 | " " | 18 | N½SE | 1859-09-25 | FD | N2SE | R:FRANKLIN |
| 2615 | " " | 13 | SWSW | 1859-09-25 | FD | SWSW | R:FRANKLIN |
| 2574 | " " | 13 | SWSW | 1859-09-25 | FD | SWSW | R:FRANKLIN |
| 2618 | " " | 24 | NENE | 1859-09-25 | FD | NENE | R:FRANKLIN |
| 2635 | MCDANIEL, Susan | 12 | NWNW | 1853-04-11 | FD | NWNW | S:F G:26 |
| 2634 | " " | 1 | SWSW | 1853-04-11 | FD | SWSW | S:F G:26 |
| 2950 | MCKINZIE, William | 19 | SWNE | 1851-01-22 | FD | SWNE | R:WHITE |
| 2594 | " " | 19 | SWNE | 1851-01-22 | FD | SWNE | R:WHITE |
| 2724 | METHERY, James F | 20 | NESW | 1855-09-06 | FD | NESW | R:MORGAN |
| 2725 | " " | 20 | SENW | 1855-09-06 | FD | SENW | R:MORGAN |
| 2604 | MEZO, Constant | 17 | SENE | 1853-02-22 | FD | SENE | S:A |
| 2945 | MILLER, William Hiram | 30 | SWSW | 1851-01-24 | FD | SWSW | R:INDIANA |
| 2944 | " " | 30 | NESW | 1852-10-30 | FD | NESW | R:HAMILTON |
| 2951 | MILLS, William | 16 | L5 | 1850-02-20 | SC | LOT5SWNW | R:HAMILTON |
| 2599 | MOBLEY, Charles | 1 | NESE | 1851-04-22 | FD | NESE | R:WHITE |
| 2552 | MOORE, Aaron | 10 | NENW | 1851-12-10 | FD | NENW | |
| 2579 | MOORE, Alfred | 2 | NENE | 1850-04-05 | FD | NENE | |
| 2580 | " " | 35 | W½ | 1854-09-19 | FD | W2 | R:HAMILTON |
| 2919 | MOORE, William C | 11 | SWNE | 1853-04-06 | FD | SWNE | R:HAMILTON |
| 2920 | " " | 3 | SENW | 1853-10-28 | FD | SENW | R:HAMILTON |
| 2921 | " " | 3 | SWNE | 1853-10-28 | FD | SWNE | R:HAMILTON |
| 2740 | MOORMAN, James | 2 | SESE | 1852-12-16 | FD | SESE | |
| 2793 | NASH, John | 12 | SESW | 1853-06-25 | FD | SESW | |
| 2905 | NEILSON, Thomas F | 8 | SW | 1849-08-20 | FD | SW | |
| 2911 | ODELL, Uriah | 33 | | 1838-12-13 | FD | SWSWNT | R:HAMILTON |
| 2750 | OGLESBAY, John C | 17 | SWNE | 1851-09-05 | FD | SWNE | |
| 2913 | OGLESBY, Wade H | 15 | SWSE | 1854-08-02 | FD | SWSE | R:HAMILTON |
| 2688 | PAGE, Hosea B | 36 | NWNW | 1850-05-31 | FD | NWNW | R:HAMILTON |
| 2887 | PAGE, Sanford M | 19 | E½NE | 1854-10-27 | FD | E2NE | R:FRANKLIN |
| 2886 | " " | 18 | E½SE | 1854-10-27 | FD | E2SE | R:HAMILTON |
| 2889 | PAGE, Sanford R | 6 | NWSE | 1853-02-22 | FD | NWSE | R:HAMILTON |
| 2888 | " " | 5 | NWNW | 1853-11-24 | FD | NWNW | R:HAMILTON |
| 2914 | PGLESHY, Wade H | 15 | S½SW | 1854-10-09 | FD | S2SW | R:HAMILTON |
| 2707 | PHILIPS, Jacob Jr | 18 | SWNW | 1838-01-31 | FD | SWNW | R:JEFFERSON |
| 2794 | PHILIPS, John | 3 | SESE | 1853-11-01 | FD | SESE | R:HAMILTON |
| 2949 | " " | 3 | SESE | 1853-11-01 | FD | SESE | R:HAMILTON |
| 2795 | " " | 3 | SWSW | 1853-11-15 | FD | SWSW | R:HAMILTON |
| 2796 | PHILLIPS, John | 3 | NWSW | 1850-08-28 | FD | NWSW | R:HAMILTON |
| 2876 | PINER, Robert | 16 | L12 | 1850-02-20 | SC | LOT12NWSW | |
| 2581 | PYNOR, Amhos B | 17 | SWSE | 1853-11-07 | FD | SWSE | R:HAMILTON |
| 2771 | RICE, John J | 6 | SWSW | 1854-10-27 | FD | SWSW | R:HAMILTON |
| 2870 | " " | 6 | SWSW | 1854-10-27 | FD | SWSW | R:HAMILTON |
| 2772 | " " | 7 | NENE | 1854-10-27 | FD | NENE | R:HAMILTON |
| 2774 | " " | 7 | SWSE | 1854-10-27 | FD | SWSE | R:HAMILTON G:13 |
| 2773 | " " | 7 | NENW | 1854-10-27 | FD | NENW | R:HAMILTON |
| 2776 | RICE, John Jackson | 7 | NWNE | 1853-02-21 | FD | NWNE | |
| 2775 | " " | 6 | SESW | 1853-02-22 | FD | SESW | |
| 2802 | RICE, John T | 5 | SE | 1849-11-08 | FD | SE | |
| 2954 | ROHRER, William R | 6 | SWNE | 1854-09-26 | FD | SWNE | R:GALLATIN |
| 2952 | " " | 6 | E½NE | 1854-09-26 | FD | E2NE | R:GALLATIN |

| ID | Individual in Patent | Sec. | Sec. Part | Purchase Date | Sale Type | IL Aliquot Part | For More Info . . . |
|---|---|---|---|---|---|---|---|
| 2953 | ROHRER, William R (Cont'd) | 6 | SE | 1854-09-26 | FD | SE | R:GALLATIN |
| 2668 | ROSBOROUGH, Green | 32 | N½NW | 1854-02-15 | FD | N2NW | R:INDIANA |
| 2667 | " " | 29 | SWSW | 1854-02-15 | FD | SWSW | R:INDIANA |
| 2665 | " " | 19 | SENW | 1854-02-15 | FD | SENW | R:INDIANA |
| 2664 | " " | 19 | S½SW | 1854-02-15 | FD | S2SW | R:INDIANA |
| 2663 | " " | 19 | NWSW | 1854-02-15 | FD | NWSW | R:INDIANA |
| 2666 | " " | 29 | SESW | 1854-03-11 | FD | SESW | R:INDIANA |
| 2955 | ROSE, William | 14 | SEN½ | 1854-03-24 | FD | S2NE | R:OHIO |
| 2769 | " " | 14 | SEN½ | 1854-03-24 | FD | S2NE | R:OHIO |
| 2957 | " " | 23 | NWNE | 1854-03-24 | FD | NWNE | R:OHIO |
| 2956 | " " | 14 | SWSE | 1854-03-25 | FD | SWSE | R:OHIO |
| 2744 | RUDE, Jesse E | 23 | SENE | 1854-09-23 | FD | SENE | R:SALINE |
| 2747 | RUTTER, John A | 30 | SENW | 1850-03-29 | FD | SENW | R:HAMILTON |
| 2674 | SCOTT, Hezekiah | 10 | W½SW | 1854-09-26 | FD | W2SW | R:GALLATIN |
| 2844 | SHERLEY, Moses | 7 | NWNW | 1855-10-12 | FD | NWNW | R:HAMILTON |
| 2692 | SIMS, Isaac S | 8 | N½NE | 1854-09-20 | FD | N2NE | R:HAMILTON |
| 2800 | SIMS, John | 7 | SWNE | 1854-03-03 | FD | SWNE | R:HAMILTON |
| 2799 | SIMS, John S | 5 | SWNW | 1854-09-20 | FD | SWNW | R:HAMILTON |
| 2803 | SIMS, John T | 5 | NESW | 1853-10-26 | FD | NESW | R:HAMILTON |
| 2628 | SMITH, Eli | 18 | NWSE | 1849-02-22 | FD | NWSE | R:HAMILTON |
| 2632 | " " | 20 | SWSW | 1849-02-22 | FD | SWSW | R:HAMILTON |
| 2627 | " " | 16 | L13 | 1850-02-20 | SC | LOT13SWSW | |
| 2629 | " " | 18 | SENW | 1852-10-16 | FD | SENW | |
| 2630 | " " | 19 | NWNE | 1852-10-16 | FD | NWNEVOID | |
| 2631 | " " | 20 | SESW | 1853-04-23 | FD | SESW | R:HAMILTON |
| 2785 | SMITH, John Lewis | 1 | NENW | 1846-12-05 | FD | NENW | R:HAMILTON |
| 2831 | SPILLER, Martin B | 22 | N½SW | 1854-10-02 | FD | N2SW | R:HAMILTON |
| 2830 | " " | 13 | SWNE | 1855-08-13 | FD | SWNE | R:HAMILTON |
| 2829 | " " | 13 | SENW | 1855-08-13 | FD | SENW | R:HAMILTON |
| 2828 | " " | 13 | NENE | 1855-08-13 | FD | NENE | R:HAMILTON |
| 2826 | " " | 13 | NENE | 1855-08-13 | FD | NENE | R:HAMILTON |
| 2619 | STELLE, David | 18 | NESW | 1849-03-24 | FD | NESW | R:HAMILTON |
| 2826 | STEPHENSON, Madison | 13 | NENE | 1853-09-22 | FD | NENE | R:OHIO |
| 2825 | " " | 12 | SESE | 1853-09-22 | FD | SESE | R:OHIO |
| 2827 | " " | 13 | NENW | 1853-09-22 | FD | NENW | R:OHIO |
| 2828 | " " | 13 | NENE | 1853-09-22 | FD | NENE | R:OHIO |
| 2958 | STEWART, William | 30 | NENE | 1849-03-09 | FD | NENE | R:HAMILTON |
| 2598 | " " | 30 | NENE | 1849-03-09 | FD | NENE | R:HAMILTON |
| 2745 | TAYLOR, Jesse | 11 | NENE | 1852-10-30 | FD | NENE | |
| 2835 | TAYLOR, Mary | 11 | NWNE | 1853-01-12 | FD | NWNE | S:F |
| 2834 | " " | 11 | NENW | 1853-03-21 | FD | NENW | R:HAMILTON S:F |
| 2836 | " " | 11 | SENE | 1853-12-15 | FD | SENE | S:F |
| 2837 | " " | 12 | SWNW | 1853-12-15 | FD | SWNW | S:F |
| 2765 | TAYLOR, William H | 11 | N½SW | 1860-08-15 | FD | N2SW | |
| 2942 | " " | 11 | N½SW | 1860-08-15 | FD | N2SW | |
| 2743 | TURRENLIN, James W Et | 6 | NE | 1849-10-15 | FD | NE | |
| 2642 | VALENTINE, George | 10 | E½SE | 1852-12-17 | FD | E2SE | |
| 2655 | VALENTINE, George W | 10 | NESW | 1851-07-24 | FD | NESW | R:HAMILTON |
| 2853 | VALENTINE, Nicholas | 10 | W½NE | 1841-11-15 | FD | W2NE | R:GALLATIN |
| 2852 | " " | 10 | NWSE | 1851-03-17 | FD | NWSE | R:HAMILTON |
| 2669 | VALETINE, Nicholas | 10 | SENW | 1853-11-16 | FD | SENW | R:HAMILTON |
| 2854 | " " | 10 | SENW | 1853-11-16 | FD | SENW | R:HAMILTON |
| 2862 | WALLER, Richard | 33 | NESW | 1853-03-17 | FD | NESW | |
| 2861 | " " | 28 | SESW | 1855-05-14 | FD | SESW | R:HAMILTON |
| 2912 | WALLER, Uriah | 31 | S½SE | 1855-08-08 | FD | S2SE | R:HAMILTON |
| 2777 | " " | 31 | S½SE | 1855-08-08 | FD | S2SE | R:HAMILTON |
| 2969 | WALLER, William | 32 | S½SW | 1854-10-05 | FD | S2SW | R:HAMILTON |
| 2671 | WEEKS, Henry | 15 | N½NE | 1854-03-08 | FD | N2NE | R:HAMILTON |
| 2670 | " " | 10 | SWSE | 1854-03-17 | FD | SWSE | R:HAMILTON |
| 2669 | " " | 10 | SENW | 1854-08-08 | FD | SENW | R:HAMILTON |
| 2854 | " " | 10 | SENW | 1854-08-08 | FD | SENW | R:HAMILTON |
| 2910 | WILLIAMSON, Thomas | 7 | NWSW | 1852-11-01 | FD | NWSW | R:WAYNE |
| 2809 | WRIGHT, John | 29 | NESW | 1854-09-11 | FD | NESW | R:HAMILTON |
| 2810 | " " | 34 | N½NE | 1854-10-05 | FD | N2NE | R:HAMILTON |
| 2807 | " " | 26 | S½SW | 1854-10-05 | FD | S2SW | R:HAMILTON |
| 2806 | " " | 26 | N½NW | 1854-10-05 | FD | N2NW | R:HAMILTON |
| 2808 | " " | 27 | S½SE | 1854-10-05 | FD | S2SE | R:HAMILTON |

## Patent Map

**T6-S R5-E**
**3rd PM Meridian**

Map Group 10

## Township Statistics

| | | |
|---|---|---|
| Parcels Mapped | : | 421 |
| Number of Patents | : | 1 |
| Number of Individuals | : | 200 |
| Patentees Identified | : | 196 |
| Number of Surnames | : | 120 |
| Multi-Patentee Parcels | : | 6 |
| Oldest Patent Date | : | 12/27/1583 |
| Most Recent Patent | : | 8/15/1860 |
| Block/Lot Parcels | : | 16 |
| Cities and Towns | : | 4 |
| Cemeteries | : | 3 |

Copyright 2007 Boyd IT, Inc. All Rights Reserved

**Section 6**
BOYD Noah 1853
BOYD Noah
TURRENLIN James W Et 1849
ROHRER William R 1852
ROHRER William R 1854
JOHNSON Robert H 1583
JOHNSON Robert H 1853
PAGE Sanford R 1853
DARNALL David 1853
JOHNSON Robert H 1854
RICE John J 1854
ROHRER William R 1854
HAMILTON James B 1853

**Section 5**
PAGE Sanford R 1853
HALL John 1851
DRAKE John 1854
SIMS John S 1854
DUCKWORTH Thomas 1852
HAMILTON James B 1853 / HALL John 1853
HALL John T 1853
SIMS John T 1853
HATCHETT Willis 1853
DARNELL David 1853
RICE John T 1849

**Section 4**
CALVIN James 1851
HARRELSON Nathaniel 1854
HARRELSON Nathaniel 1853
HANELSON Benjamin W 1854
LEE John R 1854
LEE John 1853
HARRELSON Herndon 1854
CALVIN Job 1854
FANN Moses 1853
JOHNSON Charles A 1851
CORN John Harvey 1851
JOHNSON Charles A 1854

**Section 7**
SHERLEY Moses 1855
RICE John J 1854
RICE John Jackson 1853
RICE John J 1854
DARNELL James H 1853
DARNALL William 1853
SIMS John 1854
HATCHETT Thomas S 1854
WILLIAMSON Thomas 1852
DARNALL William 1853
JOHNSON Robert H 1853
HATCHETT Thomas S 1854
COOK Abraham 1855
COOK Abraham 1850
RICE [13] John J 1854

**Section 8**
HATCHETT Willis 1853
HATCHET Willis 1852
SIMS Isaac S 1854
HIDE James H 1853
HYDE James H 1854
DARNALL James H 1853
BANES William T 1854
NEILSON Thomas F 1849
DARNELL David 1853
DARNALL David 1854
JOHNSON Charles A 1854

**Section 9**
BULLIN Ezariah 1854
DARNALL James H 1851
DUCKWORTH Felix 1853
DUCKWORTH Thomas 1850
DARNELL James H 1853
DARNALL James H 1850
JOHNSON Charles A 1854
DARNALL James H 1850
DUCKWORTH Thomas 1851
DARNALL Thomas C 1854
DARNALL Thomas C 1853
HARRELSON Benjamin W 1855

**Section 18**
CORN Hiram 1851
DARNALL William 1854
DARNEL David 1851
PHILIPS Jacob Jr 1838
SMITH Eli 1852
DARNALL William 1854
MCCLUSKY David 1854
STELLE David 1849
SMITH Eli 1849 / MCCLUSKY David 1859
BANES James Milton 1850
BANES William Thomas 1850
CORN William D 1849
PAGE Sanford M 1854

**Section 17**
DARNEL David 1851
CAIN James L 1854
DARNALL William 1854
OGLESBAY John C 1851
MEZO Constant 1853
JOHNSEN John L 1854
MANNERS Michael 1852
DARNALL William 1854
PYNOR Amhos B 1853
BROYLES Lewis S 1850

**Section 16**
Lots-Sec. 16
L1 DUCKWORTH, William 1850
L2 DUCKWORTH, William 1850
L3 DARNALL, James 1850
L4 DARNALL, David 1850
L5 MILLS, William 1850
L6 DARNALL, David 1850
L7 JOHNSON, C A 1850
L8 BISHOP, William 1850
L9 HOLLEMAN, John M 1850
L10 JOHNSON, Robert 1850
L11 DUCKWORTH, Thomas 1850
L12 PINER, Robert 1850
L13 SMITH, Eli 1850
L14 DUCKWORTH, Thomas 1850
L15 DUCKWORTH, Thomas 1850
L16 HOLLEMAN, John M 1850

**Section 19**
GREEN George G 1855
SMITH Eli 1852
PAGE Sanford M 1854
GREEN Thomas 1854
ROSBOROUGH Green 1854 / HUNGATE Charles 1849 / MCKINZIE William 1851
ROSBOROUGH Green 1854
HUNGATE Charles 1848
HUNGATE Charles 1848 / HUNGATE Charles 1849
ROSBOROUGH Green 1854
HUNGATE Charles 1848 / HUNGATE Charles 1849
JOHNSON Elhanan W 1848

**Section 20**
CARPENTER Chester 1858
FOSTER Samuel 1855
FISHER William E 1854
METHERY James F 1855
FOSTER Samuel 1853
FISHER William E 1854
METHERY James F 1855
SMITH Eli 1849
SMITH Eli 1853

**Section 21**
FOSTER Samuel 1855
FOSTER Samuel 1855
BRADEN James 1854
BRADEN James 1854
JOHNSON Alexander 1852
FOSTER Samuel R 1855
JOHNSON Alexander 1852
JOHNSON Alexander 1854
FOSTER Samuel Riley 1853

**Section 30**
CLICK George W 1855
CARTER Anderson N 1853
JOHNSON Elhanan W 1848
HUNGATE Charles 1848 / STEWART William 1849 / JOHNSON Mary 1852 / FISHER Jordon A 1848
RUTTER John A 1850
FISHER Daniel 1851
MILLER William Hiram 1852
JOHNSON Elhanan W 1848
MILLER William Hiram 1851
JOHNSON Moses 1854 / JOHNSON Moses 1854
JONES Hullem 1854

**Section 29**
FISHER Jordon A 1854 / FISHER 1852 / Jordon A 1848
FISHER Jordon A 1854
KINGTON Edmund G 1851
FISHER Jordon A 1852
FISHER Jordon A 1848
KINGTON Edmund G 1851
CARLISLE William 1854
FISHER Jordon A 1852
WRIGHT John 1854
CARLISLE William 1855 / FISHER 1855 / Jordon A 1848
CARLISLE William 1854
ROSBOROUGH Green 1854
ROSBOROUGH Green 1854
JOHNSON Solomon 1854

**Section 28**
KINGTON Edmund G 1851
CARLISLE William 1855
FLINT Gilbert 1854
CARPENTER Chester 1854
CARLISLE William 1855
FLINT Gilbert 1854
BRADEN James 1853
CARLISLE William 1854
CARLISLE William 1854
BRADEN James 1854
BRADEN James 1853
WALLER Richard 1855
CARPENTER Chester 1854

**Section 31**
BURLISON James R 1854
JOHNSON Moses 1852
JONES Hullem 1854
GRINESTAFF John B 1852
BURLISON John R 1855
CULLY Richard C 1854
HEARD James B 1854
CULLY Richard C 1854
WALLER Uriah 1855

**Section 32**
ROSBOROUGH Green 1854
JOHNSON Solomon 1854
JONES Hullem 1854
JOHNSON Solomon 1854
JOHNSON Solomon 1854
JOHNSON Solomon 1854
JOHNSON Solomon 1854
JOHNSTON William W 1854
WALLER William 1854

**Section 33**
CARTER Joseph 1854
JOHNSON William W 1854
WALLER Richard 1853
CARPENTER Chester 1854
ODELL Uriah 1838
FLINT John 1854
FLINT John 1854

154

Copyright 2007 Boyd IT, Inc. All Rights Reserved

## Helpful Hints

1. This Map's INDEX can be found on the preceding pages.

2. Refer to Map "C" to see where this Township lies within Hamilton County, Illinois.

3. Numbers within square brackets [ ] denote a multi-patentee land parcel (multi-owner). Refer to Appendix "C" for a full list of members in this group.

4. Areas that look to be crowded with Patentees usually indicate multiple sales of the same parcel (re-issues), cancellations or voided transactions (that we map, anyway) or overlapping parcels. We opt to show even these ambiguous parcels, which oftentimes lead to research avenues not yet taken.

### Map Parcels

**Section 1 area:**
- HARRELSON Herndon 1854
- CAMPBELL William 1851
- HEARD John H 1851
- HALL Hiram W 1853
- CLUCK John 1851
- MOORE Alfred 1850
- BURTON John 1836
- SMITH John Lewis 1846
- BURTON Nancy 1836
- MATHENY James 1850
- MOORE William C 1853
- MOORE William C 1853
- HUNGATE William 1854
- HALL Hiram W 1847
- 2
- BRADEN Alfred 1852
- 1
- FLINT John 1848
- PHILLIPS John 1850
- MATHENY James 1853
- 3
- CLUCK John 1851
- FLINT John 1836
- FLINT John 1848
- MOBLEY Charles 1851
- PHILIPS John 1853
- PHILIPS John 1853
- HALL Hiram W 1853
- HUNGATE William 1853
- HUNGATE William 1852
- HUNGATE Charles 1851
- MOORMAN James 1852
- MAULDING [26] Elizabeth 1853
- FLINT Nancy 1839
- FLINT Gilbert 1853
- FLINT Gilbert 1852

**Section 10, 11, 12 area:**
- DUCKWORTH Thomas 1850
- MOORE Aaron 1851
- VALENTINE Nicholas 1841
- HALL Hiram W 1853
- HUNGATE William 1852
- TAYLOR Mary 1853
- TAYLOR Mary 1853
- TAYLOR Jesse 1852
- MAULDING [26] Elizabeth 1853
- BRANDON George 1852
- HENSLEY Joseph 1851
- FLINT Gilbert 1853
- VALETINE Nicholas 1853
- WEEKS Henry 1854
- GARVIN James M 1854
- BRADEN Alfred 1854
- GARVIN Wesley W 1853
- GARVIN William W 1853
- MOORE William C 1853
- TAYLOR Mary 1853
- TAYLOR Mary 1853
- HENSLEY Joseph 1851
- BRANDON George 1852
- 10
- 11
- 12
- SCOTT Hezekiah 1854
- VALENTINE George W 1851
- VALENTINE Nicholas 1851
- VALENTINE George 1852
- TAYLOR William H 1860
- HAMILTON John 1854
- BRADEN Alfred 1854
- BRADEN Alfred 1854
- BENTLEY Osborn 1853
- BENTLY Osborn 1852
- GARNET Moses B 1837
- WEEKS Henry 1854
- HAMILTON John 1854
- BRADEN Alfred 1854
- BRADEN Alfred 1854
- BRADEN Alfred 1854
- NASH John 1853
- HARRIS William 1853
- STEPHENSON Madison 1853

**Section 13, 14, 15 area:**
- HUNTER Ellen 1854
- WEEKS Henry 1854
- HAMILTON John 1854
- HAMILTON John 1854
- BRADEN John M 1853
- BRADEN John M 1854
- STEPHENSON Madison 1853
- SPILLER Martin B 1855
- STEPHENSON Madison 1853
- CREEKMAN John W 1855
- DUCKWORTH Julia Ann 1851
- CRABTREE William A 1853
- BILDERBACK Nancy C 1854
- CRABTREE William A 1851
- 14
- HAMILTON John 1854
- ROSE William 1854
- SPILLER Martin B 1855
- SPILLER Martin B 1855
- CREEKMAN John W 1855
- 15
- FLANNIKIN Samuel W 1851
- FLANNIKIN Samuel W 1851
- BRADEN Alfred 1853
- BRADEN Alfred 1854
- 13
- BRADEN Jacob Sen 1854
- BRADEN Jacob 1848
- PGLESHY Wade H 1854
- OGLESBY Wade H 1854
- BRADEN Albert 1854
- BRADEN Albert 1854
- ROSE William 1854
- BRADEN Alfred 1848
- MCCLUSKY David 1859
- BRADEN Alfred 1848
- BRADEN Jacob 1848

**Section 22, 23, 24 area:**
- CLARK James H 1855
- BRADEN Jacob 1854
- BRADEN Albert 1853
- BRADEN Albert 1854
- ROSE William 1854
- BRADEN Alfred 1848
- BRADEN Alfred 1848
- BRADEN Jacob 1848
- BRADEN Jacob 1848
- MCCLUSKY David 1859
- HICKS Martin S 1855
- 22
- BRADEN Jacob 1854
- BRADEN Albert 1854
- 23
- RUDE Jesse E 1854
- 24
- BRADEN Jacob Sen 1854
- SPILLER Martin B 1854
- BRADEN Nancy 1837
- BRADEN Jacob 1854
- BRADEN Albert 1854
- BRADEN Albert 1854
- BRADEN Albert 1854
- FAULKNER Thomas B 1853
- BRADEN Jacob Sen 1854
- BRADEN Nancy 1837
- BRADEN Jacob 1837
- BRADEN Jacob 1834
- FAULKNER Archibald 1853
- FAULKNER Daniel 1853
- BRADEN Jacob 1854
- BRADEN Jacob Sen 1854

**Section 25, 26, 27 area:**
- FLINT Gilbert 1854
- FLINT Gilbert 1854
- BRADEN Jacob 1854
- BRADEN Jacob 1854
- JOHNSTON George W 1854
- WRIGHT John 1854
- JOHNSTON George W 1854
- JOHNSON William W 1854
- JOHNSON William W 1854
- BRADEN James 1853
- 27
- JOHNSON John Lewis 1857
- LEWIS [28] 1857 John 1853
- JOHNSON George W 1848
- JOHNSON Eliza 1837
- JOHNSON 1853 William W 1847
- ALLEN Robert Wilson 1848
- JOHNSON William W 1849
- JOHNSON William W 1847
- 25
- JOHNSON George W 1848
- LEWIS [28] John 1853
- LEWIS [28] John 1857
- JOHNSON John Lewis 1853
- JOHNSON George W 1849
- JOHNSON George W 1851
- JOHNSON George W 1854
- ALLEN William G 1854
- JOHNSON Robert 1853
- JOHNSON Robert 1836
- JOHNSON Robert 1853
- JOHNSON George W 1837
- JOHNSON George W 1836
- JOHNSON George W 1853
- JOHNSON John Lewis 1857
- WRIGHT John 1854
- WRIGHT John 1854
- JOHNSON Thomas M 1854
- JOHNSON John Lewis 1851

**Section 34, 35, 36 area:**
- WRIGHT John 1854
- BARKER John E 1853
- BARKER Hiram 1854
- PAGE Hosea B 1850
- DEEN Jacob C 1850
- DAILEY Lewis 1853
- GOWDY Robert A 1854
- GOWDY Robert A 1854
- 34
- 35
- MOORE Alfred 1854
- BARKER Hiram 1852
- BARKER Hiram 1854
- BARKER Hiram 1853
- HANNIKIN Eevin G 1837
- JOHNSON John Lewis 1837
- GOWDY Robert A 1854
- GOWDY Robert A 1854
- BARKER John E 1853
- BAKER Hiram 1849
- BARKER Hiram 1853
- BARKER Hiram 1836
- DEAN Jacob Clay 1836
- DEAN Jacob Clay 1834
- FLINT John 1854
- COFFEY James W 1854
- 36
- BAKER Hiram 1849
- FLANINKIN Robert H 1850

## Legend

— Patent Boundary

— Section Boundary

No Patents Found (or Outside County)

1., 2., 3., ... Lot Numbers (when beside a name)

[ ] Group Number (see Appendix "C")

**Scale:** Section = 1 mile X 1 mile (generally, with some exceptions)

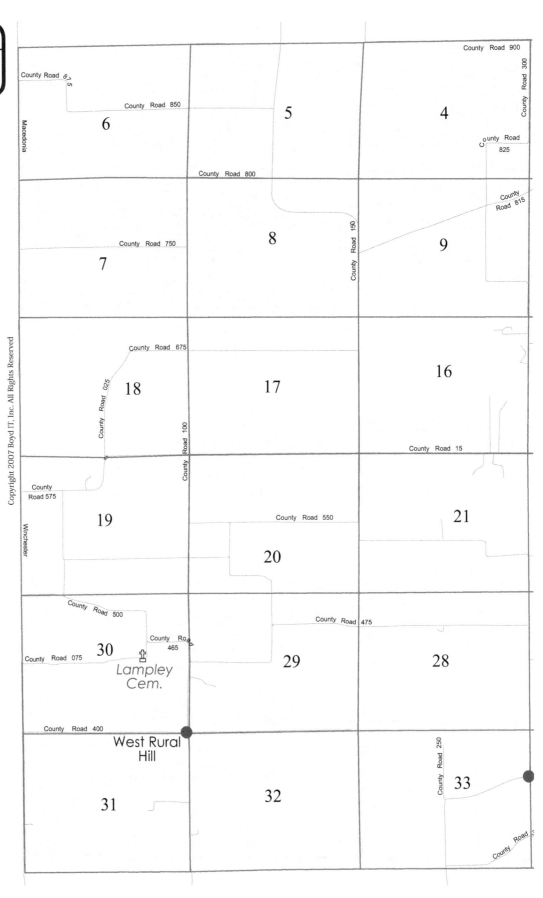

Road Map

T6-S  R5-E
3rd PM Meridian

Map Group 10

### Cities & Towns
Braden
Rural Hill
Tuckers Corners
West Rural Hill

### Cemeteries
Cartwright Cemetery
Knights Prairie Cemetery
Lampley Cemetery

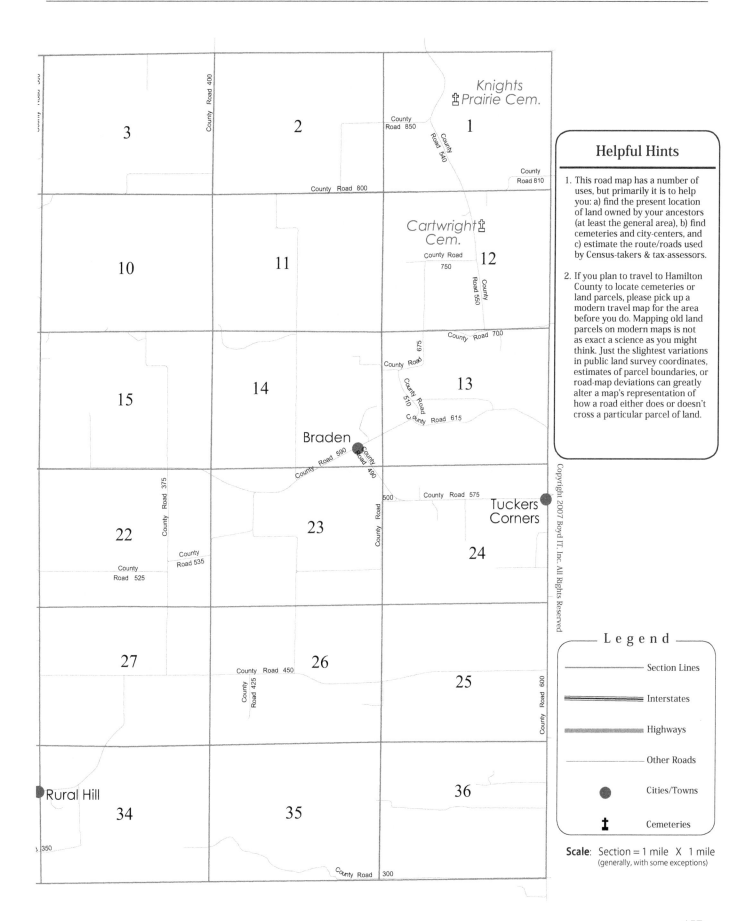

County Road 400

3

2

County Road 850

County Road 540

Knights ✝ Prairie Cem.

1

County Road 810

County Road 800

10

11

Cartwright ✝ Cem.

County Road 750

12

County Road 550

15

14

County Road 700

County Road 675

County Road

County Road 510

13

County Road 615

Braden

County Road 590

County Road 490

22

County Road 375

County Road 535

County Road 525

23

500

County Road

County Road 575

Tuckers Corners

24

27

County Road 450

County Road 425

26

25

County Road 600

Rural Hill

34

35

36

350

County Road 300

Copyright 2007 Boyd IT, Inc. All Rights Reserved

**Helpful Hints**

1. This road map has a number of uses, but primarily it is to help you: a) find the present location of land owned by your ancestors (at least the general area), b) find cemeteries and city-centers, and c) estimate the route/roads used by Census-takers & tax-assessors.

2. If you plan to travel to Hamilton County to locate cemeteries or land parcels, please pick up a modern travel map for the area before you do. Mapping old land parcels on modern maps is not as exact a science as you might think. Just the slightest variations in public land survey coordinates, estimates of parcel boundaries, or road-map deviations can greatly alter a map's representation of how a road either does or doesn't cross a particular parcel of land.

**L e g e n d**

Section Lines

Interstates

Highways

Other Roads

Cities/Towns

Cemeteries

**Scale:** Section = 1 mile X 1 mile
(generally, with some exceptions)

## Historical Map

T6-S  R5-E
3rd PM Meridian

Map Group 10

### Cities & Towns
Braden
Rural Hill
Tuckers Corners
West Rural Hill

### Cemeteries
Cartwright Cemetery
Knights Prairie Cemetery
Lampley Cemetery

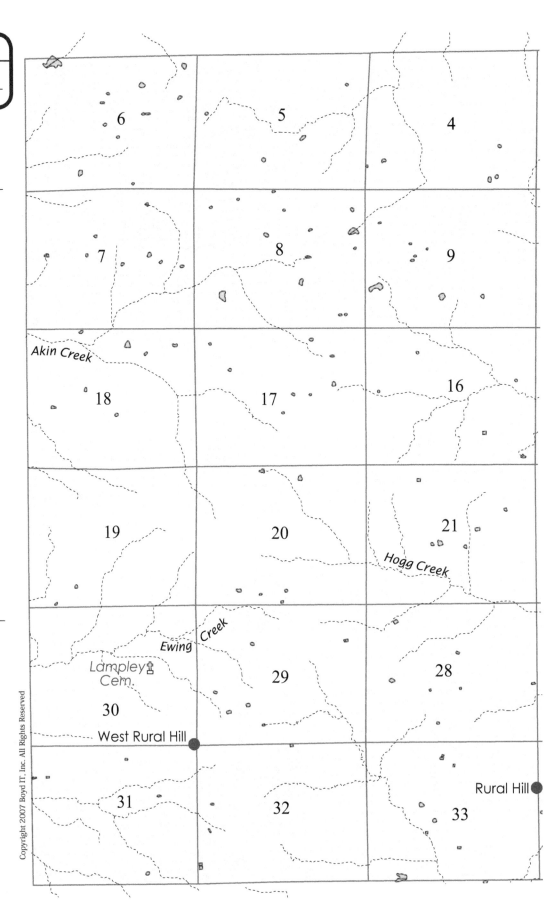

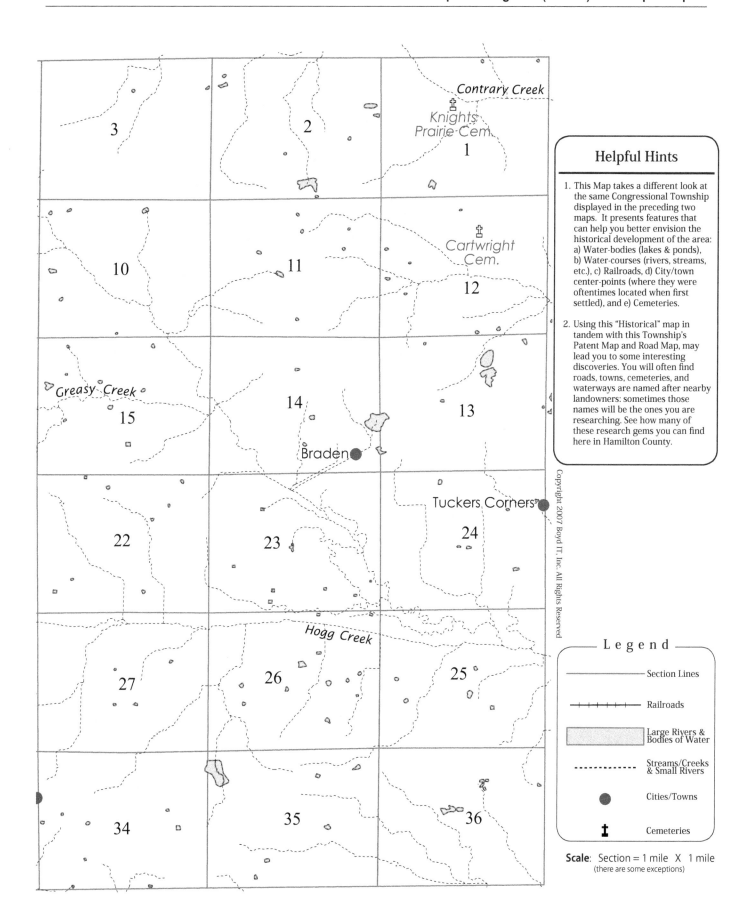

Contrary Creek

Knights
Prairie Cem.

3

2

1

10

11

Cartwright
Cem.

12

Greasy Creek

15

14

13

Braden

22

23

Tuckers Corners

24

Hogg Creek

27

26

25

34

35

36

### Helpful Hints

1. This Map takes a different look at the same Congressional Township displayed in the preceding two maps. It presents features that can help you better envision the historical development of the area: a) Water-bodies (lakes & ponds), b) Water-courses (rivers, streams, etc.), c) Railroads, d) City/town center-points (where they were oftentimes located when first settled), and e) Cemeteries.

2. Using this "Historical" map in tandem with this Township's Patent Map and Road Map, may lead you to some interesting discoveries. You will often find roads, towns, cemeteries, and waterways are named after nearby landowners: sometimes those names will be the ones you are researching. See how many of these research gems you can find here in Hamilton County.

### Legend

——————— Section Lines

+−+−+−+−+ Railroads

▨ Large Rivers & Bodies of Water

- - - - - - - Streams/Creeks & Small Rivers

● Cities/Towns

✝ Cemeteries

**Scale**: Section = 1 mile X 1 mile
(there are some exceptions)

# Map Group 11: Index to Land Patents

# Township 6-South Range 6-East (3rd PM)

After you locate an individual in this Index, take note of the Section and Section Part then proceed to the Land Patent map on the pages immediately following. You should have no difficulty locating the corresponding parcel of land.

The "For More Info" Column will lead you to more information about the underlying Patents. See the *Legend* at right, and the "How to Use this Book" chapter, for more information.

| ID | Individual in Patent | Sec. | Sec. Part | Purchase Date | Sale Type | IL Aliquot Part | For More Info . . . |
|---|---|---|---|---|---|---|---|
| 3143 | ALLEN, Joseph | 4 | N½SE | 1852-07-22 | FD | N2SE | |
| 3144 | " " | 4 | SESE | 1852-07-22 | FD | SESE | |
| 3145 | " " | 4 | SWNE | 1852-07-22 | FD | SWNE | |
| 3146 | " " | 5 | NWNE | 1853-01-11 | FD | NWNE | |
| 3007 | BARKER, Edmund | 34 | W½SE | 1832-08-21 | FD | W2SE | R:HAMILTON |
| 3188 | BARNES, Thomas | 14 | SWSE | 1853-11-03 | FD | SWSE | |
| 3013 | BARNETT, Elizabeth | 35 | SWNE | 1852-09-07 | FD | SWNE | S:F |
| 3098 | BETTS, John | 34 | SESE | 1853-11-24 | FD | SESE | R:HAMILTON |
| 3099 | " " | 34 | SWNE | 1855-09-17 | FD | SWNE | R:HAMILTON |
| 3061 | BLADES, James M | 31 | S½SE | 1854-09-25 | FD | S2SE | R:HAMILTON |
| 3045 | " " | 31 | SWNE | 1854-09-25 | FD | SWNE | R:HAMILTON |
| 3062 | " " | 31 | SWNE | 1854-09-25 | FD | SWNE | R:HAMILTON |
| 3024 | BRANDON, George | 7 | NWSW | 1852-10-18 | FD | NWSW | |
| 3025 | " " | 7 | SWNW | 1852-10-18 | FD | SWNW | |
| 3152 | BRUMLEY, Larkin | 5 | W½SE | 1847-12-08 | FD | W2SE | |
| 3151 | " " | 5 | SEN½ | 1847-12-08 | FD | S2NE | |
| 3174 | BUNNETT, Robert | 19 | SWNW | 1854-10-11 | FD | SWNW | R:HAMILTON |
| 3173 | " " | 19 | NENW | 1854-10-11 | FD | NENW | R:HAMILTON |
| 3172 | " " | 18 | W½SW | 1854-10-11 | FD | W2SW | R:HAMILTON |
| 3028 | BURNETT, George V | 35 | NWSW | 1849-06-01 | FD | NWSW | |
| 3027 | " " | 35 | NWSE | 1849-06-01 | FD | NWSE | |
| 3212 | " " | 35 | E½SW | 1849-06-01 | FD | E2SW | |
| 3213 | " " | 35 | NWSE | 1849-06-01 | FD | NWSE | |
| 3214 | " " | 35 | NWSW | 1849-06-01 | FD | NWSW | |
| 3026 | " " | 35 | E½SW | 1849-06-01 | FD | E2SW | |
| 3029 | " " | 35 | SENE | 1851-04-02 | FD | SENE | R:HAMILTON |
| 3050 | BURNETT, Jacob | 35 | SWSW | 1853-08-31 | FD | SWSW | R:HAMILTON |
| 3053 | BURNETT, James | 33 | NWSE | 1853-02-21 | FD | NWSE | R:HAMILTON |
| 3182 | BURNETT, Samuel H | 18 | SESW | 1853-10-06 | FD | SESW | R:HAMILTON |
| 3000 | CARGILL, David | 7 | SWSE | 1853-12-19 | FD | SWSE | R:HAMILTON |
| 3039 | " " | 7 | SWSE | 1853-12-19 | FD | SWSE | R:HAMILTON |
| 3018 | CARGILL, Elmira | 7 | S½SW | 1853-11-03 | FD | S2SW | R:HAMILTON S:F |
| 2998 | CARPENTER, Chester | 30 | NWNE | 1858-01-08 | FD | NWNE | |
| 2997 | " " | 19 | NWSW | 1858-01-08 | FD | NWSW | |
| 3161 | CHARLES, William | 5 | NESE | 1854-10-11 | FD | NESE | R:HAMILTON |
| 3226 | " " | 5 | SENE | 1854-10-11 | FD | SENE | R:HAMILTON |
| 3225 | " " | 5 | NESE | 1854-10-11 | FD | NESE | R:HAMILTON |
| 3121 | CHENNAULT, John N | 34 | SESW | 1836-04-13 | FD | SESW | R:HAMILTON |
| 3122 | " " | 34 | SWSW | 1836-05-25 | FD | SWSW | R:HAMILTON |
| 3096 | CLARK, John A | 6 | SENW | 1853-11-07 | FD | SENW | R:HAMILTON |
| 3097 | " " | 6 | SWNE | 1853-11-07 | FD | SWNE | R:HAMILTON |
| 3239 | CLARK, William Jr | 11 | SWNE | 1852-05-13 | FD | SWNE | |
| 3238 | " " | 11 | NWSE | 1852-05-13 | FD | NWSE | |
| 3100 | CLUCK, John | 7 | N½NE | 1853-12-31 | FD | N2NE | R:HAMILTON |
| 3058 | COBB, James G | 4 | NENW | 1853-12-12 | FD | NENW | R:HAMILTON |
| 3055 | COONS, James | 5 | NESW | 1855-03-29 | FD | NESW | R:HAMILTON |

| ID | Individual in Patent | Sec. | Sec. Part | Purchase Date | Sale Type | IL Aliquot Part | For More Info . . . |
|---|---|---|---|---|---|---|---|
| 3129 | COONS, John Sen | 5 | SWSW | 1854-02-10 | FD | SWSW | R:HAMILTON |
| 3128 | " | 5 | NWSW | 1855-03-27 | FD | NWSW | R:HAMILTON |
| 3221 | COONS, Warden | 16 | L14 | 1851-03-08 | SC | LOT14SESW | |
| 3222 | COONS, Warden Pope Jr | 6 | NESE | 1853-02-14 | FD | NESE | R:HAMILTON |
| 3002 | CORGILL, David | 18 | NWNE | 1853-12-13 | FD | NWNE | R:HAMILTON |
| 3001 | " | 18 | N½NW | 1853-12-13 | FD | N2NW | R:HAMILTON |
| 3189 | CUMMUNGS, Thomas | 4 | W½NW | 1851-08-25 | FD | W2NW | |
| 3153 | DANIEL, Levi | 4 | SENE | 1851-10-24 | FD | SENE | R:HAMILTON |
| 3052 | DEAN, Jacob Clay | 31 | W½SW | 1836-04-30 | FD | W2SW | R:HAMILTON |
| 3051 | DEEN, Jacob C | 31 | W½NW | 1850-06-29 | FD | W2NW | |
| 3102 | DEUVALL, John | 4 | SWSE | 1851-05-31 | FD | SWSE | R:HAMILTON |
| 3103 | " | 9 | W½NE | 1852-01-28 | FD | W2NE | R:HAMILTON |
| 3101 | " | 4 | SESW | 1854-10-09 | FD | SESW | R:HAMILTON |
| 3160 | DIGBY, Jane | 24 | SWSE | 1854-09-19 | FD | SWSE | R:HAMILTON S:F |
| 3093 | " | 24 | NWNE | 1854-09-19 | FD | NWNE | R:HAMILTON S:F |
| 3092 | " | 13 | SESW | 1854-09-19 | FD | SESW | R:HAMILTON S:F |
| 3094 | " | 24 | SWSE | 1854-09-19 | FD | SWSE | R:HAMILTON S:F |
| 3104 | DIGBY, John | 13 | NESW | 1854-08-01 | FD | NESW | R:HAMILTON |
| 3105 | " | 14 | NWNW | 1854-10-13 | FD | NWNW | R:HAMILTON |
| 3190 | DIGBY, Thomas | 11 | S½SE | 1841-10-07 | FD | S2SE | R:HAMILTON |
| 3191 | DUCKWORTH, Thomas | 16 | L15 | 1851-03-08 | SC | LOT15SWSE | |
| 3194 | " | 16 | L9 | 1851-03-08 | SC | LOT9NESE | |
| 3193 | " | 16 | L8 | 1851-03-08 | SC | LOT8SENE | |
| 3192 | " | 16 | L16 | 1851-03-08 | SC | LOT16SESE | |
| 3135 | DURAM, John W | 16 | L12 | 1851-03-08 | SC | LOT12NWSW | |
| 3134 | " | 16 | L11 | 1851-03-08 | SC | LOT11NESW | |
| 3136 | DURHAM, John W | 33 | SW | 1848-08-05 | FD | SW | |
| 3195 | EDWARDS, Thomas H | 11 | NWNE | 1851-10-11 | FD | NWNE | R:HAMILTON |
| 3196 | " | 2 | SESE | 1852-05-14 | FD | SESE | R:HAMILTON |
| 3197 | " | 9 | W½SE | 1853-01-11 | FD | W2SE | |
| 3227 | EMMERSON, William | 11 | NWSW | 1851-04-21 | FD | NWSW | R:HARDIN |
| 3094 | ESSARY, Nathan | 24 | SWSE | 1852-05-28 | FD | SWSE | R:HAMILTON |
| 3160 | " | 24 | SWSE | 1852-05-28 | FD | SWSE | R:HAMILTON |
| 3159 | " | 24 | SESE | 1853-02-13 | FD | SESE | |
| 3028 | EUILINSTINE, Tronquet | 35 | NWSW | 1859-10-01 | FD | NWSW | |
| 3027 | " | 35 | NWSE | 1859-10-01 | FD | NWSE | |
| 3212 | " | 35 | E½SW | 1859-10-01 | FD | E2SW | |
| 3026 | " | 35 | E½SW | 1859-10-01 | FD | E2SW | |
| 3214 | " | 35 | NWSW | 1859-10-01 | FD | NWSW | |
| 3213 | " | 35 | NWSE | 1859-10-01 | FD | NWSE | |
| 3010 | EWING, Elijah Dunn | 12 | E½SW | 1839-05-02 | FD | E2SW | R:FRANKLIN |
| 2993 | FAIRWEATHER, Charlott | 2 | SENW | 1853-01-27 | FD | SENW | S:F |
| 3057 | FAULKNER, James | 17 | NW | 1853-12-22 | FD | NW | R:HAMILTON |
| 3218 | FLINT, Albert | 18 | SENW | 1854-10-13 | FD | SENW | R:HAMILTON |
| 2975 | " | 18 | SWNE | 1854-10-13 | FD | SWNE | R:HAMILTON |
| 2974 | " | 18 | SENW | 1854-10-13 | FD | SENW | R:HAMILTON |
| 3106 | FLINT, John | 6 | NESW | 1853-10-25 | FD | NESW | R:HAMILTON |
| 3108 | " | 6 | SESW | 1853-11-01 | FD | SESW | R:HAMILTON |
| 3109 | " | 6 | SWSE | 1854-04-24 | FD | SWSE | R:HAMILTON |
| 3107 | " | 6 | NWSE | 1854-04-27 | FD | NWSE | R:HAMILTON |
| 3056 | GALLIHER, James F | 11 | NESW | 1837-06-02 | FD | NESW | R:HAMILTON |
| 3031 | GATES, Harvey L | 36 | SESE | 1854-09-20 | FD | SESE | R:HAMILTON |
| 3032 | GATES, Harvey S | 36 | SESW | 1852-11-11 | FD | SESW | |
| 3033 | " | 36 | SWSE | 1852-11-11 | FD | SWSE | |
| 3054 | HANCOCK, James C | 2 | NENE | 1854-10-13 | FD | NENE | R:SALINE |
| 3181 | HARRIS, Rollin | 24 | SENW | 1854-10-05 | FD | SENW | R:HAMILTON |
| 3180 | " | 24 | N½NW | 1854-10-05 | FD | N2NW | R:HAMILTON |
| 3179 | " | 14 | NWSE | 1854-10-05 | FD | NWSE | R:HAMILTON |
| 3178 | " | 14 | E½SE | 1854-10-05 | FD | E2SE | R:HAMILTON |
| 3177 | " | 13 | W½SW | 1854-10-05 | FD | W2SW | R:HAMILTON |
| 3048 | HEARD, Irend | 10 | NENE | 1841-10-07 | FD | NENE | R:HAMILTON |
| 3076 | HEARD, James M | 3 | SESE | 1837-03-31 | FD | SESE | R:HAMILTON |
| 3064 | " | 10 | NWNE | 1849-05-05 | FD | NWNE | |
| 3063 | " | 10 | NENW | 1849-05-05 | FD | NENW | |
| 3072 | " | 3 | E½SW | 1849-05-05 | FD | E2SW | |
| 3074 | " | 3 | SEN½ | 1849-09-29 | FD | S2NE | |
| 3075 | " | 3 | SENW | 1849-09-29 | FD | SENW | |
| 3071 | " | 2 | SWNW | 1849-09-29 | FD | SWNW | |
| 3068 | " | 16 | L13 | 1851-03-08 | SC | LOT13SWSW | |
| 3070 | " | 16 | L5 | 1851-03-08 | SC | LOT5SWNW | |
| 3067 | " | 16 | L1 | 1851-03-08 | SC | LOT1NENE | |
| 3069 | " | 16 | L4 | 1851-03-08 | SC | LOT4NWNWN | |
| 3066 | " | 11 | NWNW | 1851-04-21 | FD | NWNW | R:HARDIN |

| ID | Individual in Patent | Sec. | Sec. Part | Purchase Date | Sale Type | IL Aliquot Part | For More Info . . . |
|---|---|---|---|---|---|---|---|
| 3073 | HEARD, James M (Cont'd) | 3 | NENW | 1853-02-19 | FD | NENW | R:HAMILTON |
| 3079 | " " | 7 | SWNE | 1853-10-07 | FD | SWNE | R:HAMILTON |
| 3065 | " " | 10 | SENW | 1853-10-07 | FD | SENW | R:HAMILTON |
| 3078 | " " | 7 | SENE | 1854-03-25 | FD | SENE | R:HAMILTON |
| 3077 | " " | 36 | W½SW | 1854-09-20 | FD | W2SW | R:HAMILTON |
| 3081 | HEARD, James Mulheron | 3 | NESE | 1841-08-17 | FD | NESE | R:HAMILTON |
| 3082 | HEARD, James Mulhiron | 3 | W½SE | 1836-06-10 | FD | W2SE | R:HAMILTON |
| 3228 | HERRINGTON, William | 18 | NWSE | 1859-10-08 | FD | NWSE | |
| 3229 | HINSON, William | 35 | SESE | 1836-07-20 | FD | SESE | R:HAMILTON |
| 3185 | HOGG, Samuel | 21 | NW | 1816-12-09 | FD | NW | R:WHITE |
| 3184 | " " | 14 | NE | 1819-05-31 | FD | NE | R:WHITE |
| 3183 | " " | 11 | SW | 1819-11-08 | FD | SW | R:WHITE |
| 3020 | HUNT, Emily | 7 | NWNW | 1854-03-27 | FD | NWNW | R:HAMILTON S:F |
| 3019 | " " | 6 | W½SW | 1854-03-27 | FD | W2SW | R:HAMILTON S:F |
| 3059 | HUNTER, James | 14 | SWNE | 1850-12-31 | FD | SWNE | R:HAMILTON |
| 2999 | HUTCHINSON, Daniel | 14 | SENE | 1853-09-28 | FD | SENE | R:HAMILTON |
| 3163 | HUTSON, Pleasant | 5 | SWNE | 1853-08-21 | FD | SWNE | R:HAMILTON S:A |
| 3162 | " " | 5 | SENW | 1853-12-31 | FD | SENW | R:HAMILTON S:A |
| 3140 | JOHNSEN, John W | 24 | NESW | 1854-10-09 | FD | NESW | R:HAMILTON |
| 3138 | " " | 24 | N½SE | 1854-10-09 | FD | N2SE | R:HAMILTON |
| 3137 | " " | 13 | SESE | 1854-10-09 | FD | SESE | R:HAMILTON |
| 3139 | " " | 24 | NENE | 1854-10-09 | FD | NENE | R:HAMILTON |
| 3141 | " " | 24 | SEN½ | 1854-10-09 | FD | S2NE | R:HAMILTON |
| 3012 | JOHNSON, Eliza S | 17 | NESE | 1851-09-01 | FD | NESE | R:HAMILTON S:F |
| 3049 | JOHNSON, Isaac | 33 | E½SE | 1836-05-23 | FD | E2SE | R:HAMILTON |
| 3060 | JOHNSON, James | 28 | SWSE | 1853-07-30 | FD | SWSE | R:HAMILTON |
| 3112 | JOHNSON, John | 16 | L3 | 1851-03-10 | SC | LOT3NENW | |
| 3111 | " " | 16 | L2 | 1851-03-10 | SC | L2NWNE | |
| 3114 | " " | 20 | N½NE | 1851-09-01 | FD | N2NE | R:HAMILTON |
| 3113 | " " | 17 | S½SE | 1851-09-01 | FD | S2SE | R:HAMILTON |
| 3115 | " " | 20 | NENW | 1854-07-22 | FD | NENW | R:HAMILTON |
| 3116 | JOHNSON, John L | 19 | NENE | 1854-02-21 | FD | NENE | R:HAMILTON G:27 |
| 3117 | " " | 20 | NWNW | 1854-02-21 | FD | NWNW | R:HAMILTON G:27 |
| 3155 | JOHNSON, Margaret | 34 | SWNW | 1853-06-25 | FD | SWNW | R:HAMILTON S:F |
| 3236 | JOHNSON, William | 33 | W½NE | 1839-06-01 | FD | W2NE | R:HAMILTON |
| 3237 | " " | 34 | NWSW | 1850-08-19 | FD | NWSW | R:HAMILTON |
| 3235 | " " | 33 | SENE | 1850-08-19 | FD | SENE | R:HAMILTON |
| 3230 | " " | 16 | L10 | 1851-03-10 | SC | LOT10NWSE | |
| 3231 | " " | 16 | L6 | 1851-03-10 | SC | LOT6SENW | |
| 3232 | " " | 16 | L7 | 1851-03-10 | SC | L7SWNE | |
| 3233 | " " | 28 | SESE | 1853-02-28 | FD | SESE | |
| 3240 | " " | 28 | SESE | 1853-02-28 | FD | SESE | |
| 3234 | " " | 33 | NENE | 1853-02-28 | FD | NENE | |
| 3156 | JONES, Margaret S | 5 | NENE | 1854-01-04 | FD | NENE | R:HAMILTON S:F |
| 3198 | JONES, Thomas | 3 | W½NW | 1852-01-07 | FD | W2NW | |
| 3090 | KINNEAR, James Wood | 11 | E½NW | 1839-03-28 | FD | E2NW | R:OHIO |
| 3091 | " " | 11 | SWNW | 1839-03-28 | FD | SWNW | R:OHIO |
| 3080 | LASATER, James M | 30 | SESE | 1857-06-09 | FD | SESE | |
| 3036 | LASSWELL, Henry | 32 | NESW | 1836-10-07 | FD | NESW | R:HAMILTON |
| 3038 | " " | 32 | SWSE | 1838-05-23 | FD | SWSE | R:HAMILTON |
| 3037 | " " | 32 | S½SW | 1851-08-13 | FD | S2SW | |
| 3040 | LEONARD, Edward F | 29 | W½SE | 1860-06-15 | FD | W2SE | |
| 3008 | " " | 29 | W½SE | 1860-06-15 | FD | W2SE | |
| 3021 | LEWALLEN, Enoch | 33 | E½NW | 1850-08-13 | FD | E2NW | R:HAMILTON |
| 3117 | LEWIS, John | 20 | NWNW | 1854-02-21 | FD | NWNW | R:HAMILTON G:27 |
| 3116 | " " | 19 | NENE | 1854-02-21 | FD | NENE | R:HAMILTON G:27 |
| 3187 | LOCKHART, Theodore L | 32 | NWSE | 1853-12-21 | FD | NWSE | R:HAMILTON |
| 3120 | MAN, John | 35 | SWSE | 1849-05-24 | FD | SWSE | R:HAMILTON |
| 3119 | " " | 35 | NESE | 1852-03-24 | FD | NESE | R:HAMILTON |
| 3154 | " " | 35 | NESE | 1852-03-24 | FD | NESE | R:HAMILTON |
| 3244 | MANIER, William | 35 | SENW | 1853-11-11 | FD | SENW | R:HAMILTON |
| 2985 | MANN, Andrew | 36 | NWSW | 1853-01-27 | FD | NWSW | |
| 2978 | MAYBERRY, Anderson | 12 | SESW | 1851-05-31 | FD | SESW | R:HAMILTON |
| 3004 | MAYBERRY, David K | 13 | NWNE | 1836-06-01 | FD | NWNE | R:HAMILTON |
| 3003 | " " | 12 | SWSE | 1849-11-02 | FD | SWSE | R:HAMILTON |
| 3005 | MAYBERRY, David R | 12 | NWSE | 1852-03-25 | FD | NWSE | |
| 3034 | MAYBERRY, Henderson | 12 | SESE | 1836-06-01 | FD | SESE | R:HAMILTON |
| 3035 | " " | 13 | NENE | 1839-08-16 | FD | NENE | R:HAMILTON |
| 3158 | MAYBERRY, Michael | 1 | SWNW | 1839-08-21 | FD | SWNW | R:HAMILTON |
| 3022 | MCCOMBS, Gabriel | 29 | E½SW | 1853-09-29 | FD | E2SW | |
| 3023 | " " | 32 | N½NW | 1853-09-29 | FD | N2NW | |
| 2984 | MCDANIEL, Andrew J | 6 | SENE | 1854-10-13 | FD | SENE | R:HAMILTON |
| 2983 | " " | 5 | SWNW | 1854-10-13 | FD | SWNW | R:HAMILTON |

| ID | Individual in Patent | Sec. | Sec. Part | Purchase Date | Sale Type | IL Aliquot Part | For More Info . . . |
|---|---|---|---|---|---|---|---|
| 3157 | MCDONALD, Mary A | 6 | NWNW | 1848-12-27 | FD | NWNW | S:F |
| 3110 | MCGILL, John H | 32 | E½SE | 1851-11-19 | FD | E2SE | |
| 3215 | MCGUIER, Vincent | 30 | NWSW | 1835-12-22 | FD | NWSW | R:HAMILTON |
| 3220 | MCGUIRE, Vincent | 30 | SWSW | 1837-04-17 | FD | SWSW | R:HAMILTON |
| 2974 | " " | 18 | SENW | 1851-12-04 | FD | SENW | |
| 3218 | " " | 18 | SENW | 1851-12-04 | FD | SENW | |
| 3217 | " " | 18 | NESW | 1851-12-04 | FD | NESW | |
| 3216 | " " | 17 | SWSW | 1853-07-11 | FD | SWSW | |
| 3219 | " " | 18 | SESE | 1853-07-11 | FD | SESE | |
| 3147 | MEZO, Joseph | 18 | SWNW | 1854-01-13 | FD | SWNW | R:HAMILTON |
| 3223 | MEZO, William C | 17 | NWSW | 1854-10-23 | FD | NWSW | R:HAMILTON |
| 3224 | " " | 18 | NESE | 1854-10-23 | FD | NESE | R:HAMILTON |
| 3148 | MIZE, Joseph | 18 | SWSE | 1855-04-04 | FD | SWSE | R:HAMILTON |
| 2992 | MOBLEY, Charles | 4 | NWSW | 1836-01-14 | FD | NWSW | R:WHITE |
| 2977 | MORRIS, Allen | 5 | NENW | 1849-08-30 | FD | NENW | |
| 3011 | PARKER, Elijah | 11 | NW | 1819-01-08 | FD | NW | R:WHITE |
| 2973 | PIERCE, Abner | 13 | SENE | 1837-10-26 | FD | SENE | R:HAMILTON |
| 3118 | PITMAN, John M | 4 | NENE | 1854-04-28 | FD | NENE | R:HAMILTON |
| 2990 | PRESLEY, Burrell D | 5 | NWSE | 1855-08-13 | FD | NWSE | R:HAMILTON |
| 3124 | PRESLEY, John | 5 | SE | 1854-10-11 | FD | SE | R:HAMILTON |
| 3125 | " " | 5 | SESW | 1854-10-11 | FD | SESW | R:HAMILTON |
| 3126 | " " | 8 | NESW | 1854-10-11 | FD | NESW | R:HAMILTON |
| 3169 | " " | 8 | NESW | 1854-10-11 | FD | NESW | R:HAMILTON |
| 3123 | " " | 5 | E½NW | 1854-10-11 | FD | E2NW | R:HAMILTON |
| 3211 | RICE, Toliver G | 2 | SWSE | 1851-10-15 | FD | SWSE | R:MASSAC |
| 3006 | ROGERS, Edmond | 2 | NWSW | 1837-10-17 | FD | NWSW | R:IOWA |
| 3186 | ROGERS, Sirena | 2 | S½SW | 1839-10-24 | FD | S2SW | R:HAMILTON S:F |
| 3083 | RUSSELL, James | 32 | SENE | 1853-07-21 | FD | SENE | |
| 3084 | " " | 33 | SWNW | 1853-08-05 | FD | SWNW | R:HAMILTON |
| 3200 | RUSSELL, Thomas | 17 | NWSE | 1854-10-01 | FD | NWSE | R:HAMILTON |
| 3201 | " " | 17 | SEN½ | 1854-10-01 | FD | S2NE | R:HAMILTON |
| 3199 | " " | 17 | E½SW | 1854-10-01 | FD | E2SW | R:HAMILTON |
| 3119 | SCARLET, Lewis | 35 | NESE | 1851-08-30 | FD | NESE | |
| 3154 | " " | 35 | NESE | 1851-08-30 | FD | NESE | |
| 3085 | SCHOOLCRAFT, James | 11 | SESW | 1836-06-10 | FD | SESW | R:HAMILTON |
| 3086 | " " | 11 | SWSW | 1837-06-03 | FD | SWSW | R:HAMILTON |
| 3087 | " " | 14 | NENW | 1851-06-06 | FD | NENW | |
| 3245 | SCOTT, William | 15 | NENW | 1851-11-26 | FD | NENW | |
| 3225 | SHANNON, Oliver N | 5 | NESE | 1857-03-30 | FD | NESE | |
| 3161 | " " | 5 | NESE | 1857-03-30 | FD | NESE | |
| 2979 | SMITH, Andrew C | 31 | NENW | 1852-06-19 | FD | NENW | R:HAMILTON |
| 2981 | SMITH, Andrew E | 30 | SWSE | 1848-10-22 | FD | SWSE | G:35 |
| 2982 | " " | 31 | NWNE | 1848-10-22 | FD | NWNE | G:35 |
| 2980 | " " | 30 | E½SW | 1848-10-22 | FD | E2SW | G:35 |
| 2988 | SMITH, Augusta | 33 | SWSE | 1853-03-08 | FD | SWSE | |
| 2980 | SMITH, Charles A | 30 | E½SW | 1848-10-22 | FD | E2SW | G:35 |
| 2981 | " " | 30 | SWSE | 1848-10-22 | FD | SWSE | G:35 |
| 2982 | " " | 31 | NWNE | 1848-10-22 | FD | NWNE | G:35 |
| 3009 | SMITH, Eli | 30 | SENE | 1836-11-09 | FD | SENE | R:HAMILTON |
| 3008 | SMITH, Ira | 29 | W½SE | 1850-08-19 | FD | W2SE | |
| 3046 | " " | 32 | N½NE | 1850-08-19 | FD | N2NE | |
| 3040 | " " | 29 | W½SE | 1850-08-19 | FD | W2SE | |
| 3045 | " " | 31 | SWNE | 1852-06-19 | FD | SWNE | |
| 3042 | " " | 31 | NWSE | 1852-06-19 | FD | NWSE | |
| 3062 | " " | 31 | SWNE | 1852-06-19 | FD | SWNE | |
| 3044 | " " | 31 | SESW | 1853-01-19 | FD | SESW | |
| 3041 | " " | 31 | NESE | 1853-01-19 | FD | NESE | |
| 3043 | " " | 31 | SENE | 1854-03-27 | FD | SENE | R:HAMILTON |
| 3047 | " " | 32 | NWSW | 1854-03-27 | FD | NWSW | R:HAMILTON |
| 2995 | " " | 32 | NWSW | 1854-03-27 | FD | NWSW | R:HAMILTON |
| 3088 | SMITH, James | 29 | W½SW | 1854-10-24 | FD | W2SW | R:HAMILTON |
| 3130 | SMITH, John | 31 | NESW | 1833-12-23 | FD | NESW | R:HAMILTON |
| 3131 | " " | 31 | SENW | 1833-12-23 | FD | SENW | R:HAMILTON |
| 3127 | SMITH, John R | 32 | SENW | 1854-12-11 | FD | SENW | R:HAMILTON |
| 2996 | " " | 32 | SENW | 1854-12-11 | FD | SENW | R:HAMILTON |
| 3150 | SMITH, Katharine | 32 | SWNW | 1855-09-21 | FD | SWNW | R:HAMILTON S:F |
| 3149 | " " | 31 | NENE | 1855-09-21 | FD | NENE | R:HAMILTON S:F |
| 3203 | STANFIELD, Thomas | 4 | W½SW | 1850-12-17 | FD | W2SW | |
| 3204 | " " | 5 | SESE | 1850-12-17 | FD | SESE | |
| 3202 | " " | 4 | NESW | 1850-12-17 | FD | NESW | |
| 3205 | " " | 5 | SWSE | 1854-01-21 | FD | SWSE | R:HAMILTON |
| 3206 | " " | 8 | NE | 1854-10-09 | FD | NE | R:HAMILTON |
| 3243 | STEPHENS, William L | 4 | SEN½ | 1854-09-20 | FD | S2NE | R:HAMILTON |

| ID | Individual in Patent | Sec. | Sec. Part | Purchase Date | Sale Type | IL Aliquot Part | For More Info . . . |
|---|---|---|---|---|---|---|---|
| 3241 | STEPHENS, William L (Cont'd) | 4 | NESE | 1854-09-20 | FD | NESE | R:HAMILTON |
| 3242 | " " | 4 | NWNE | 1854-09-20 | FD | NWNE | R:HAMILTON |
| 3233 | " " | 28 | SESE | 1854-09-20 | FD | SESE | R:HAMILTON |
| 3240 | " " | 28 | SESE | 1854-09-20 | FD | SESE | R:HAMILTON |
| 3015 | TALLEE, Ellis | 5 | NWNW | 1848-10-14 | FD | NWNW | S:F |
| 3017 | " " | 6 | NENW | 1848-10-14 | FD | NENW | S:F |
| 3016 | " " | 6 | N½NE | 1848-10-14 | FD | N2NE | S:F |
| 2989 | TAYLOR, Benjamin J | 19 | NWNE | 1854-10-28 | FD | NWNE | R:HAMILTON |
| 3095 | TAYLOR, Jesse | 19 | NWNW | 1837-05-03 | FD | NWNW | R:HAMILTON |
| 2991 | THOMASON, Calvin P | 17 | SENE | 1853-12-19 | FD | SENE | R:WAYNE |
| 3014 | TINER, Elizabeth C | 15 | NE | 1852-06-14 | FD | NE | S:F |
| 3132 | TOWNSEND, John | 6 | SWNW | 1839-01-16 | FD | SWNW | R:HAMILTON |
| 3133 | TROUT, John | 4 | SENW | 1850-11-26 | FD | SENW | R:HAMILTON |
| 2996 | TURNER, Charlotte Et | 32 | SENW | 1854-01-11 | FD | SENW | S:F |
| 3127 | " " | 32 | SENW | 1854-01-11 | FD | SENW | S:F |
| 2995 | " " | 32 | NWSW | 1854-01-11 | FD | NWSW | S:F |
| 2994 | " " | 32 | E½SW | 1854-01-11 | FD | E2SW | S:F |
| 3047 | " " | 32 | NWSW | 1854-01-11 | FD | NWSW | S:F |
| 2976 | WHEELER, Alfred | 14 | NWNE | 1836-06-08 | FD | NWNE | R:HAMILTON |
| 3030 | WHEELER, George W | 13 | NESE | 1838-08-16 | FD | NESE | R:HAMILTON |
| 3089 | WHEELER, James | 14 | NENE | 1844-12-13 | FD | NENE | R:HAMILTON |
| 3175 | WHEELER, Robert L | 13 | NWSE | 1837-03-13 | FD | NWSE | R:HAMILTON |
| 3176 | " " | 13 | SWNE | 1837-03-13 | FD | SWNE | R:HAMILTON |
| 3208 | WHEELER, Thomas | 13 | N½NW | 1836-05-30 | FD | N2NW | R:HAMILTON |
| 3209 | " " | 13 | SENW | 1849-09-07 | FD | SENW | R:HAMILTON |
| 3210 | " " | 13 | SWNW | 1852-03-11 | FD | SWNW | R:HAMILTON |
| 3207 | " " | 12 | SWSW | 1853-06-09 | FD | SWSW | R:HAMILTON |
| 3164 | WHITE, Preston | 7 | E½NW | 1854-09-20 | FD | E2NW | R:HAMILTON |
| 3170 | " " | 8 | NWSW | 1854-09-20 | FD | NWSW | R:HAMILTON |
| 3166 | " " | 7 | NESW | 1854-09-20 | FD | NESW | R:HAMILTON |
| 3167 | " " | 8 | E½NW | 1854-09-20 | FD | E2NW | R:HAMILTON |
| 3165 | " " | 7 | N½SE | 1854-09-20 | FD | N2SE | R:HAMILTON |
| 3168 | " " | 8 | N½SE | 1854-09-20 | FD | N2SE | R:HAMILTON |
| 3126 | " " | 8 | NESW | 1854-09-20 | FD | NESW | R:HAMILTON |
| 3169 | " " | 8 | NESW | 1854-09-20 | FD | NESW | R:HAMILTON |
| 3171 | " " | 8 | W½NW | 1854-09-20 | FD | W2NW | R:HAMILTON |
| 2986 | WILLIAMS, Anna | 31 | NWSW | 1854-10-23 | FD | NWSW | R:POPE S:F |
| 2987 | " " | 31 | SWNW | 1854-10-23 | FD | SWNW | R:POPE S:F |
| 3000 | WILLIAMS, Horace | 7 | SWSW | 1857-05-30 | FD | SWSW | |
| 3039 | " " | 7 | SWSE | 1857-05-30 | FD | SWSE | |
| 3142 | WRIGHT, John | 36 | SWSW | 1852-04-03 | FD | SWSW | |

# Patent Map

**T6-S R6-E**
**3rd PM Meridian**

Map Group 11

## Township Statistics

| | | |
|---|---|---|
| Parcels Mapped | : | 273 |
| Number of Patents | : | 1 |
| Number of Individuals | : | 142 |
| Patentees Identified | : | 140 |
| Number of Surnames | : | 97 |
| Multi-Patentee Parcels | : | 5 |
| Oldest Patent Date | : | 12/9/1816 |
| Most Recent Patent | : | 6/15/1860 |
| Block/Lot Parcels | : | 16 |
| Cities and Towns | : | 2 |
| Cemeteries | : | 2 |

**Section 6**
MCDONALD Mary A 1848
TALLEE Ellis 1848
TALLEE Ellis 1848
TOWNSEND John 1839
CLARK John A 1853
CLARK John A 1853
MCDANIEL Andrew J 1854
HUNT Emily 1854
FLINT John 1853
FLINT John 1854
COONS Warden Pope Jr 1853
FLINT John 1853
FLINT John 1854

**Section 5**
TALLEE Ellis 1848
MORRIS Allen 1849
ALLEN Joseph 1853
JONES Margaret S 1854
MCDANIEL Andrew J 1854
HUTSON Pleasant PRESLEY 1853 John 1854
HUTSON Pleasant 1853
CHARLES William BRUMLEY 1854 Larkin 1847
COONS John Sen 1855
COONS James 1855
PRESLEY Burrell D BRUMLEY 1855 Larkin 1847
SHANNON Oliver N 1857 CHARLES William 1854
PRESLEY John 1854
COONS John Sen 1854
PRESLEY John 1854
STANFIELD Thomas 1854
STANFIELD Thomas 1850

**Section 4**
CUMMUNGS Thomas 1851
COBB James G 1853
STEPHENS William L 1854
PITMAN John M 1854
TROUT John 1850
ALLEN Joseph 1852
STEPHENS William L 1854 DANIEL Levi 1851
MOBLEY Charles 1836
STANFIELD Thomas 1850
ALLEN Joseph 1852
STEPHENS William L 1854
STANFIELD Thomas 1850
DEUVALL John 1854
DEUVALL John 1851
ALLEN Joseph 1852

**Section 7**
HUNT Emily 1854
WHITE Preston 1854
CLUCK John 1853
BRANDON George 1852
HEARD James M 1853
HEARD James M 1854
BRANDON George 1852
WHITE Preston 1854
WHITE Preston 1854
CARGILL Elmira 1853
CARGILL David 1853 WILLIAMS Horace 1857

**Section 8**
WHITE Preston 1854
WHITE Preston 1854
STANFIELD Thomas 1854
WHITE Preston 1854
PRESLEY John WHITE 1854 Preston 1854
WHITE Preston 1854

**Section 9**
DEUVALL John 1852
EDWARDS Thomas H 1853

**Section 18**
CORGILL David 1853
CORGILL David 1853
MEZO Joseph 1854
FLINT Vincent 1851 Albert 1854
FLINT Albert 1854
MCGUIRE Vincent 1851
HERRINGTON William 1859
MEZO William C 1854
BUNNETT Robert 1854
BURNETT Samuel H 1853
MIZE Joseph 1855
MCGUIRE Vincent 1853

**Section 17**
FAULKNER James 1853
RUSSELL Thomas 1854
THOMASON Calvin P 1853
MEZO William C 1854
RUSSELL Thomas 1854
RUSSELL Thomas 1854
JOHNSON Eliza S 1851
MCGUIRE Vincent 1853
JOHNSON John 1851

**Lots-Sec. 16**
| L1 | HEARD, James M | 1851 |
| L2 | JOHNSON, John | 1851 |
| L3 | JOHNSON, John | 1851 |
| L4 | HEARD, James M | 1851 |
| L5 | HEARD, James M | 1851 |
| L6 | JOHNSON, William | 1851 |
| L7 | JOHNSON, William | 1851 |
| L8 | DUCKWORTH, Thomas | 1851 |
| L9 | DUCKWORTH, Thomas | 1851 |
| L10 | JOHNSON, William | 1851 |
| L11 | DURAM, John W | 1851 |
| L12 | DURAM, John W | 1851 |
| L13 | HEARD, James M | 1851 |
| L14 | COONS, Warden | 1851 |
| L15 | DUCKWORTH, Thomas | 1851 |
| L16 | DUCKWORTH, Thomas | 1851 |

**Section 19**
TAYLOR Jesse 1837
BUNNETT Robert 1854
TAYLOR Benjamin J 1854
JOHNSON [27] John L 1854
BUNNETT Robert 1854
CARPENTER Chester 1858

**Section 20**
JOHNSON [27] John L 1854
JOHNSON John 1854
JOHNSON John 1854
JOHNSON John 1851

**Section 21**
HOGG Samuel 1816

**Section 30**
CARPENTER Chester 1858
SMITH Eli 1836
MCGUIER Vincent 1835
SMITH [35] Andrew E 1848
MCGUIRE Vincent 1837
SMITH [35] Andrew E 1848
LASATER James M 1857

**Section 29**
SMITH James 1854
MCCOMBS Gabriel 1853
SMITH Ira 1850
LEONARD Edward F 1860

**Section 28**
JOHNSON James 1853
JOHNSON William STEPHENS 1853 William L 1854

**Section 31**
DEEN Jacob C 1850
SMITH Andrew C 1852
SMITH [35] Andrew E 1848
SMITH Katharine 1855
WILLIAMS Anna 1854
SMITH John 1833
SMITH Ira 1852 BLADES James M 1854
SMITH Ira 1854
WILLIAMS Anna 1854
SMITH John 1833
SMITH Ira 1852
SMITH Ira 1853
DEAN Jacob Clay 1836
SMITH Ira 1853
BLADES James M 1854

**Section 32**
MCCOMBS Gabriel 1853
SMITH Ira 1850
SMITH Katharine 1855
TURNER Charlotte Et 1854 SMITH John R 1854
SMITH Ira TURNER 1854 Charlotte Et 1854
LASSWELL Henry 1836 TURNER Charlotte Et 1854
LASSWELL Henry 1851
32
LOCKHART Theodore L 1853
LASSWELL Henry 1838

**Section 33**
JOHNSON William 1853
JOHNSON William 1839
JOHNSON William 1850
RUSSELL James 1853
RUSSELL James 1853
LEWALLEN Enoch 1850
JOHNSON William 1853
MCGILL John H 1851
DURHAM John W 1848
BURNETT James 1853
SMITH Augusta 1853
JOHNSON Isaac 1836

| | | | | |
|---|---|---|---|---|
| JONES Thomas 1852 | HEARD James M 1853 | | HANCOCK James C 1854 | MAYBERRY Michael 1839 |

**Section 3**

HEARD James M 1849 | 3 | HEARD James M 1849

HEARD James M 1849 | HEARD James Mulheron 1841 / HEARD James Mulhiron 1836 | HEARD James Mulheron 1841

HEARD James M 1837

**Section 2**

HEARD James M 1849 | FAIRWEATHER Charlott 1853

ROGERS Edmond 1837 | 2

ROGERS Sirena 1839 | RICE Toliver G 1851 | EDWARDS Thomas H 1852

**Section 1**

MAYBERRY Michael 1839 | 1

**Section 10**

HEARD James M 1849 | HEARD James M 1849 | HEARD Irend 1841

HEARD James M 1853

10

**Section 11**

HEARD James M 1851 | KINNEAR James Wood 1839 | EDWARDS Thomas H 1851

PARKER Elijah 1819

KINNEAR James Wood 1839

CLARK William Jr 1852

11

EMMERSON William 1851 | GALLIHER James F 1837 | CLARK William Jr 1852

HOGG Samuel 1819

SCHOOLCRAFT James 1837 | SCHOOLCRAFT James 1836 | DIGBY Thomas 1841

**Section 12**

12

EWING Elijah Dunn 1839 | MAYBERRY David R 1852

WHEELER Thomas 1853 | MAYBERRY Anderson 1851 | MAYBERRY David K 1849 | MAYBERRY Henderson 1836

**Section 15**

SCOTT William 1851

TINER Elizabeth C 1852

15

**Section 14**

DIGBY John 1854 | SCHOOLCRAFT James 1851 | WHEELER Alfred 1836 | WHEELER James 1844

14

HUNTER James 1850 | HUTCHINSON HOGG Daniel 1853 Samuel 1819

HARRIS Rollin 1854 | HARRIS Rollin 1854

BARNES Thomas 1853

**Section 13**

WHEELER Thomas 1836

MAYBERRY David K 1836 | MAYBERRY Henderson 1839

WHEELER Thomas 1852 | WHEELER Thomas 1849 | WHEELER Robert L 1837 | PIERCE Abner 1837

13

HARRIS Rollin 1854 | DIGBY John 1854 | WHEELER Robert L 1837 | WHEELER George W 1838

DIGBY Jane 1854 | JOHNSEN John W 1854

**Section 22**

22

**Section 23**

23

**Section 24**

HARRIS Rollin 1854 | DIGBY Jane 1854 | JOHNSEN John W 1854

HARRIS Rollin 1854 | 24 | JOHNSEN John W 1854

JOHNSEN John W 1854 | JOHNSEN John W 1854

ESSARY Nathan 1852

DIGBY Jane 1854 | ESSARY Nathan 1853

**Section 27**

27

**Section 26**

26

**Section 25**

25

**Section 34**

34

JOHNSON Margaret 1853 | BETTS John 1855

JOHNSON William 1850

CHENNAULT John N 1836 | CHENNAULT John N 1836 | BARKER Edmund 1832 | BETTS John 1853

**Section 35**

MANIER William 1853 | 35 | BARNETT Elizabeth 1852 | BURNETT George V 1851

BURNETT George V 1849 EUILINSTINE Tronquet 1859 | EUILINSTINE Tronquet 1859 | BURNETT George V 1849 EUILINSTINE Tronquet 1859 | SCARLET Lewis 1851 MAN John 1852

BURNETT Jacob 1853 | BURNETT George V 1849 | MAN John 1849 | HINSON William 1836

**Section 36**

36

MANN Andrew 1853

WRIGHT John 1852 HEARD James M 1854 | GATES Harvey S 1852 | GATES Harvey S 1852 | GATES Harvey L 1854

## Helpful Hints

1. This Map's INDEX can be found on the preceding pages.

2. Refer to Map "C" to see where this Township lies within Hamilton County, Illinois.

3. Numbers within square brackets [ ] denote a multi-patentee land parcel (multi-owner). Refer to Appendix "C" for a full list of members in this group.

4. Areas that look to be crowded with Patentees usually indicate multiple sales of the same parcel (re-issues), cancellations or voided transactions (that we map, anyway) or overlapping parcels. We opt to show even these ambiguous parcels, which oftentimes lead to research avenues not yet taken.

## Legend

———————— Patent Boundary

━━━━━━━━ Section Boundary

No Patents Found (or Outside County)

1., 2., 3., ...  Lot Numbers (when beside a name)

[ ]  Group Number (see Appendix "C")

**Scale**: Section = 1 mile X 1 mile (generally, with some exceptions)

### Road Map

T6-S   R6-E
3rd PM Meridian

Map Group 11

**Cities & Towns**

Dale
Olga

**Cemeteries**

Digby Cemetery
Marys Chapel Cemetery

Copyright 2007 Boyd IT, Inc. All Rights Reserved

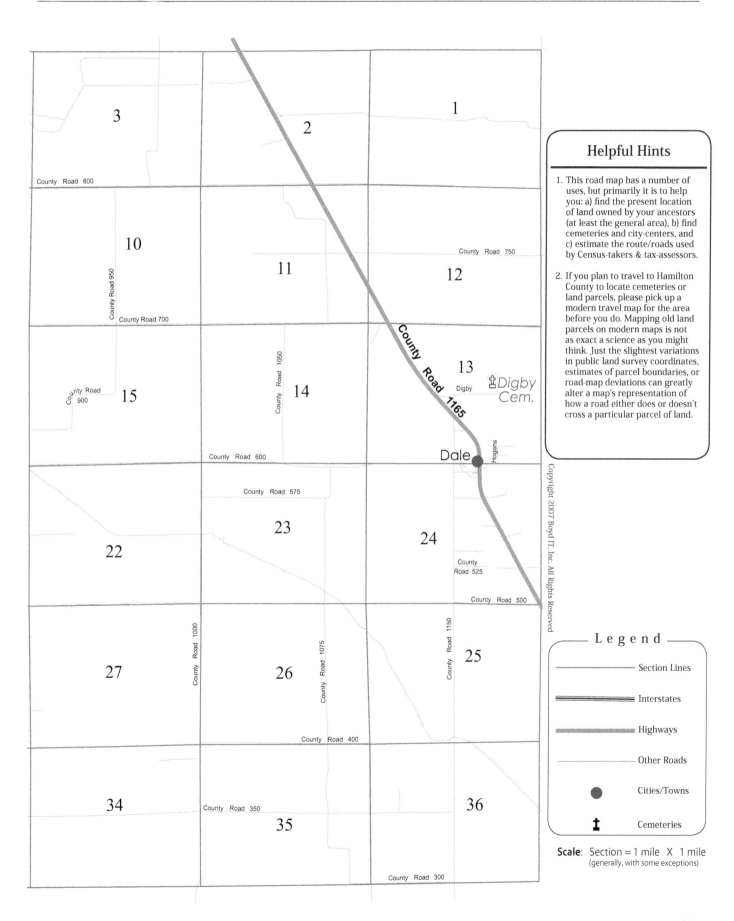

County Road 800

3

2

1

10

County Road 950

County Road 700

County Road 750

11

12

County Road 1050

13

County Road 900

15

14

Digby

🖽 Digby Cem.

County Road 600

Dale ●

Hogans

County Road 575

22

23

24

County Road 525

County Road 500

County Road 1000

County Road 1075

County Road 1150

27

26

25

County Road 400

County Road 350

34

35

36

County Road 300

Copyright 2007 Boyd IT, Inc. All Rights Reserved

### Helpful Hints

1. This road map has a number of uses, but primarily it is to help you: a) find the present location of land owned by your ancestors (at least the general area), b) find cemeteries and city-centers, and c) estimate the route/roads used by Census-takers & tax-assessors.

2. If you plan to travel to Hamilton County to locate cemeteries or land parcels, please pick up a modern travel map for the area before you do. Mapping old land parcels on modern maps is not as exact a science as you might think. Just the slightest variations in public land survey coordinates, estimates of parcel boundaries, or road-map deviations can greatly alter a map's representation of how a road either does or doesn't cross a particular parcel of land.

### L e g e n d

| | |
|---|---|
| ——— | Section Lines |
| ═══ | Interstates |
| ━━━ | Highways |
| —— | Other Roads |
| ● | Cities/Towns |
| ✝ | Cemeteries |

**Scale**: Section = 1 mile X 1 mile
(generally, with some exceptions)

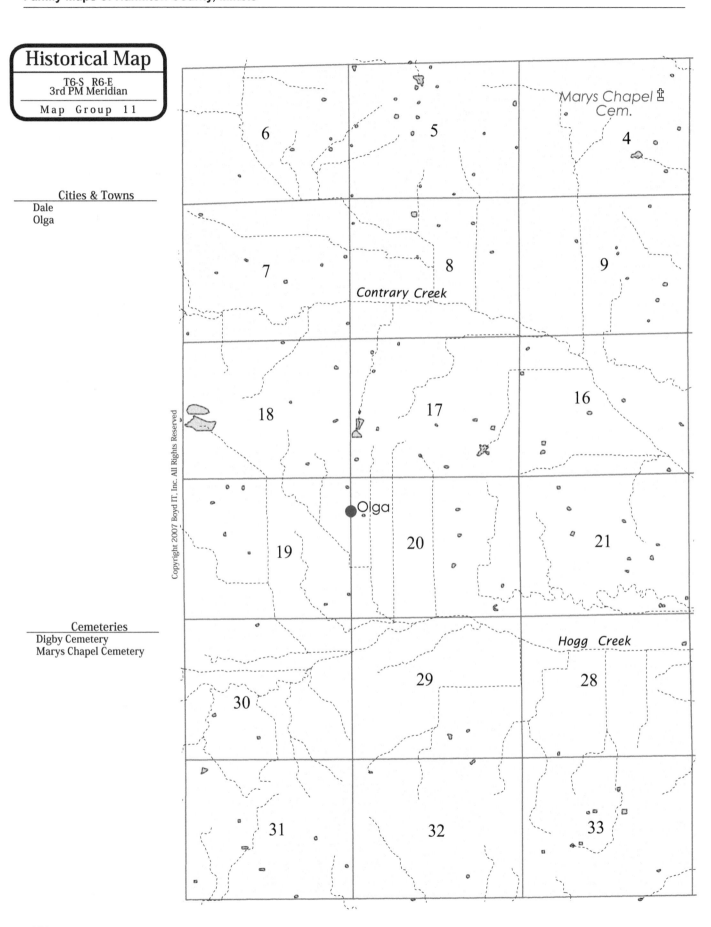

**Historical Map**

T6-S R6-E
3rd PM Meridian

Map Group 11

Cities & Towns
Dale
Olga

Cemeteries
Digby Cemetery
Marys Chapel Cemetery

Marys Chapel ⚏ Cem.

6    5    4

7    8    9

Contrary Creek

18    17    16

● Olga

19    20    21

Hogg Creek

30    29    28

31    32    33

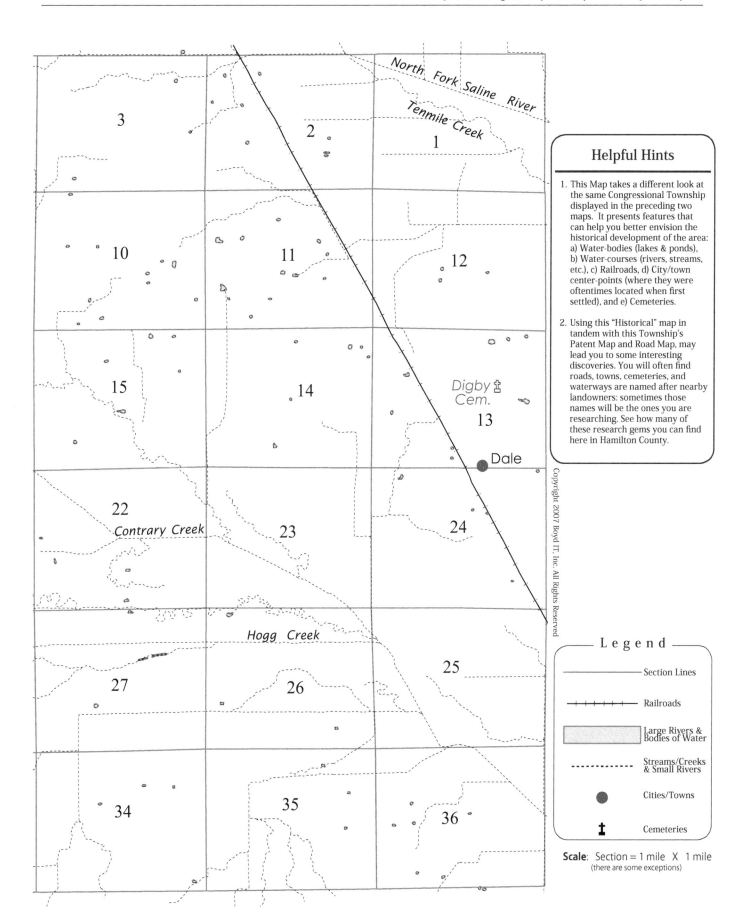

3

2

1

North Fork Saline River

Tenmile Creek

10

11

12

15

14

Digby ✝
Cem.

13

Dale

22

Contrary Creek

23

24

Hogg Creek

27

26

25

34

35

36

## Helpful Hints

1. This Map takes a different look at the same Congressional Township displayed in the preceding two maps. It presents features that can help you better envision the historical development of the area: a) Water-bodies (lakes & ponds), b) Water-courses (rivers, streams, etc.), c) Railroads, d) City/town center-points (where they were oftentimes located when first settled), and e) Cemeteries.

2. Using this "Historical" map in tandem with this Township's Patent Map and Road Map, may lead you to some interesting discoveries. You will often find roads, towns, cemeteries, and waterways are named after nearby landowners: sometimes those names will be the ones you are researching. See how many of these research gems you can find here in Hamilton County.

## Legend

———————— Section Lines

+–+–+–+–+ Railroads

▭ Large Rivers & Bodies of Water

- - - - - - Streams/Creeks & Small Rivers

● Cities/Towns

✝ Cemeteries

**Scale**: Section = 1 mile X 1 mile
(there are some exceptions)

## Map Group 12:  Index to Land Patents

## Township 6-South Range 7-East (3rd PM)

After you locate an individual in this Index, take note of the Section and Section Part then proceed to the Land Patent map on the pages immediately following. You should have no difficulty locating the corresponding parcel of land.

The "For More Info" Column will lead you to more information about the underlying Patents. See the *Legend* at right, and the "How to Use this Book" chapter, for more information.

```
┌─────────────────────────────────────────────────────┐
│                      LEGEND                          │
│           "For More Info . . . " column              │
│  ─────────────────────────────────────────────────   │
│  G = Group (Multi-Patentee Patent, see Appendix "C") │
│  R = Residence                                       │
│  S = Social Status                                   │
│                                                      │
│                                                      │
│  See Appendix A for list of abbreviations used by the│
│  Illinois State Archives in describing the place and │
│  nature of these land patents.                       │
│                                                      │
│  Note: if the Abbreviations contain "L", "BL", "LOT",│
│  or "BLOCK", the exact whereabouts of the parcel with-│
│  in the section is not known.                        │
└─────────────────────────────────────────────────────┘
```

| ID | Individual in Patent | Sec. | Sec. Part | Purchase Date | Sale Type | IL Aliquot Part | For More Info . . . |
|----|---------------------|------|-----------|---------------|-----------|-----------------|---------------------|
| 3434 | ALEXANDER, Mastin | 6 | SENE | 1851-07-11 | FD | SENE | |
| 3378 | ALLEN, John | 3 | SENE | 1836-12-14 | FD | SENE | R:HAMILTON |
| 3377 | "          " | 3 | NENE | 1850-04-27 | FD | NENE | R:HAMILTON |
| 3376 | "          " | 2 | SWNW | 1854-01-14 | FD | SWNW | R:HAMILTON |
| 3478 | ANDERSON, William B | 1 | SW | 1819-05-11 | FD | SW | R:TENNESSEE |
| 3379 | AVERETT, John | 10 | E½NW | 1829-03-23 | FD | E2NW | R:HAMILTON |
| 3475 | BAGLY, William A | 36 | NENE | 1848-02-14 | FD | NENE | R:WHITE |
| 3374 | BALLARD, Joel | 3 | SENW | 1847-11-29 | FD | SENW | R:HAMILTON |
| 3373 | "          " | 3 | NWNW | 1853-11-11 | FD | NWNW | R:HAMILTON |
| 3479 | BEATY, William | 25 | W½NE | 1837-01-23 | FD | W2NE | R:WHITE |
| 3354 | BLAKE, James M | 24 | N½NE | 1848-11-24 | FD | N2NE | |
| 3355 | "          " | 24 | NENW | 1848-11-24 | FD | NENW | |
| 3353 | "          " | 13 | SESW | 1848-11-24 | FD | SESW | |
| 3352 | "          " | 13 | NESW | 1851-07-16 | FD | NESW | |
| 3351 | "          " | 11 | NWSW | 1853-01-13 | FD | NWSW | |
| 3357 | BLAKE, James Madison | 13 | SWSE | 1836-04-16 | FD | SWSE | R:HAMILTON |
| 3358 | "          " | 24 | NESE | 1848-06-27 | FD | NESE | R:HAMILTON |
| 3309 | BOLARJACK, Harvey F | 10 | SEN½ | 1854-10-13 | FD | S2NE | R:WHITE |
| 3310 | "          " | 11 | W½NW | 1854-10-13 | FD | W2NW | R:WHITE |
| 3458 | BRILL, S S Gn | 13 | NESE | 1853-10-06 | FD | NESE | S:I |
| 3460 | BRILL, Soloman Scott | 24 | SENE | 1848-06-19 | FD | SENE | R:WHITE |
| 3463 | BRILL, Solomon S | 13 | SENE | 1854-01-09 | FD | SENE | R:HAMILTON |
| 3266 | CARPENTER, Chester | 8 | SESE | 1858-01-08 | FD | SESE | |
| 3265 | "          " | 32 | SESE | 1858-01-08 | FD | SESE | |
| 3324 | CLARK, Isaac H | 23 | SENW | 1853-02-07 | FD | SENW | |
| 3325 | CLARK, Isaac Hynes | 23 | NENW | 1850-04-08 | FD | NENW | R:HAMILTON |
| 3326 | "          " | 23 | NWNE | 1853-03-07 | FD | NWNE | |
| 3375 | "          " | 23 | NWNE | 1853-03-07 | FD | NWNE | |
| 3384 | CROUSE, John | 35 | NWNW | 1839-12-17 | FD | NWNW | R:HAMILTON |
| 3383 | "          " | 26 | SWSW | 1840-02-01 | FD | SWSW | R:HAMILTON |
| 3382 | DEBOARD, John C | 12 | NESW | 1854-10-13 | FD | NESW | R:HAMILTON |
| 3385 | DELAP, John | 1 | NENE | 1852-07-21 | FD | NENE | |
| 3486 | DENNY, William L | 3 | NESE | 1854-10-03 | FD | NESE | R:HAMILTON |
| 3485 | "          " | 2 | NWSW | 1854-10-03 | FD | NWSW | R:HAMILTON |
| 3476 | DOCHOR, William A | 35 | NWNE | 1840-04-03 | FD | NWNE | R:WAYNE |
| 3477 | DOCKER, William A | 26 | W½SE | 1840-03-11 | FD | W2SE | R:GALLATIN |
| 3386 | FAIRWEATHER, John | 22 | NENW | 1853-03-16 | FD | NENW | |
| 3388 | FAIRWEATHERS, John | 22 | NWNE | 1851-02-22 | FD | NWNE | R:HAMILTON |
| 3387 | "          " | 15 | SWSE | 1854-01-02 | FD | SWSE | R:HAMILTON |
| 3251 | FORD, Abram | 34 | SESE | 1837-01-16 | FD | SESE | R:HAMILTON |
| 3502 | FORD, Wodly | 34 | NESE | 1853-01-17 | FD | NESE | |
| 3442 | GHOLSON, Newton | 16 | L2 | 1851-03-02 | SC | LOT2NWNE | |
| 3443 | "          " | 16 | L3 | 1851-03-02 | SC | LOT3NENW | |
| 3451 | GHOLSON, Reuben E | 16 | L1 | 1850-09-22 | SC | LOT1NENE | |
| 3484 | GOSSETT, William J | 14 | SWNW | 1853-05-19 | FD | SWNW | |
| 3488 | GOTT, Anthony | 15 | SENE | 1852-02-17 | FD | SENE | |

| ID | Individual in Patent | Sec. | Sec. Part | Purchase Date | Sale Type | IL Aliquot Part | For More Info . . . |
|----|---------------------|------|-----------|---------------|-----------|-----------------|---------------------|
| 3257 | GOTT, Anthony (Cont'd) | 15 | SENE | 1852-02-17 | FD | SENE | |
| 3258 | GOTT, Anthony Wayne | 25 | SENE | 1836-11-29 | FD | SENE | R:HAMILTON |
| 3259 | " " | 25 | SESW | 1839-01-08 | FD | SESW | R:HAMILTON |
| 3261 | " " | 26 | E½SE | 1849-03-21 | FD | E2SE | |
| 3260 | " " | 25 | W½SW | 1849-03-21 | FD | W2SW | |
| 3322 | GREATHOUSE, Hiram | 35 | NWSE | 1832-09-12 | FD | NWSE | R:HAMILTON |
| 3275 | GRIFFITH, David C | 9 | NWNE | 1851-03-20 | FD | NWNE | R:HAMILTON |
| 3277 | " " | 9 | SESW | 1851-03-20 | FD | SESW | R:HAMILTON |
| 3274 | " " | 9 | NENW | 1853-03-04 | FD | NENW | |
| 3276 | " " | 9 | NWNW | 1853-04-11 | FD | NWNW | |
| 3253 | GRIMES, Adonijah | 26 | SESW | 1836-06-01 | FD | SESW | R:HAMILTON |
| 3254 | " | 35 | NENW | 1837-08-16 | FD | NENW | R:GALLATIN |
| 3450 | GRIMES, Rachael | 25 | SWSW | 1840-03-11 | FD | SWSW | R:HAMILTON S:F |
| 3459 | GRIMES, Sarah Jane | 26 | NESW | 1838-11-01 | FD | NESW | R:HAMILTON S:F |
| 3480 | GROSS, William | 27 | NE | 1848-02-29 | FD | NE | |
| 3481 | GROVES, William | 14 | SWSW | 1851-10-25 | FD | SWSW | R:HAMILTON |
| 3280 | HAMILTON, Edmund | 35 | SWNW | 1836-01-11 | FD | SWNW | R:HAMILTON |
| 3279 | " | 35 | SENW | 1836-02-01 | FD | SENW | R:HAMILTON |
| 3430 | HAMILTON, Maria | 34 | SENE | 1840-02-01 | FD | SENE | R:HAMILTON S:F |
| 3366 | HANDEESTER, Jesse | 13 | NWSE | 1849-04-03 | FD | NWSE | R:HAMILTON |
| 3367 | HARDESTER, Jesse | 24 | NWNW | 1849-11-23 | FD | NWNW | R:HAMILTON |
| 3267 | HARDESTY, Christopher | 36 | E½NW | 1821-03-24 | FD | E2NW | R:WHITE |
| 3268 | " " | 36 | W½NW | 1837-04-22 | FD | W2NW | R:HAMILTON |
| 3482 | HARDESTY, William | 35 | SWSE | 1836-01-27 | FD | SWSE | R:HAMILTON |
| 3270 | HARDISTY, Christopher | 13 | SWNE | 1853-02-02 | FD | SWNE | |
| 3269 | " " | 13 | SENW | 1853-02-02 | FD | SENW | |
| 3308 | HARDISTY, George W | 35 | SESE | 1854-01-04 | FD | SESE | R:HAMILTON |
| 3368 | HARDISTY, Jesse | 24 | S½NW | 1836-12-07 | FD | S2NW | R:HAMILTON |
| 3483 | HARDISTY, William | 35 | SW | 1819-01-27 | FD | SW | R:WHITE |
| 3401 | HARRISON, Thomas P | 25 | SWNW | 1839-07-24 | FD | SWNW | R:FRANKLIN |
| 3472 | " " | 25 | SWNW | 1839-07-24 | FD | SWNW | R:FRANKLIN |
| 3312 | HARROWOOD, Henry | 18 | SESW | 1853-06-09 | FD | SESW | R:HAMILTON |
| 3313 | " " | 19 | | 1853-06-09 | FD | NWNESZ | |
| 3391 | HEARD, John H | 16 | L11 | 1851-09-16 | SC | LOT11NESW | |
| 3393 | " " | 16 | L13 | 1851-09-16 | SC | LOT13SWSW | |
| 3390 | " " | 16 | L10 | 1851-09-16 | SC | LOT10NWSE | |
| 3394 | " " | 16 | L14 | 1851-09-16 | SC | LOT14SESW | |
| 3395 | " " | 16 | L15 | 1851-09-16 | SC | LOT15SWSE | |
| 3399 | " " | 16 | L6 | 1851-09-16 | SC | LOT6SENW | |
| 3392 | " " | 16 | L12 | 1851-09-16 | SC | LOT12NWSW | |
| 3398 | " " | 16 | L5 | 1851-09-16 | SC | LOT5SWNW | |
| 3397 | " " | 16 | L4 | 1851-09-16 | SC | LOT4NWNW | |
| 3396 | " " | 16 | L16 | 1851-09-16 | SC | LOT16SESE | |
| 3347 | HOWARD, James | 35 | SWSW | 1836-02-05 | FD | SWSW | R:HAMILTON |
| 3418 | HOWARD, Joseph | 35 | NWSW | 1836-07-22 | FD | NWSW | R:HAMILTON |
| 3501 | HOWARD, Wilson L | 36 | NESW | 1848-11-30 | FD | NESW | R:HAMILTON |
| 3348 | HUGHES, James | 22 | NWSE | 1853-03-12 | FD | NWSE | |
| 3350 | HUGHS, James | 22 | SWSE | 1848-03-01 | FD | SWSE | R:HAMILTON |
| 3349 | " " | 22 | NESW | 1851-03-14 | FD | NESW | R:HAMILTON |
| 3433 | JESTEES, Martin | 3 | NWSE | 1855-07-19 | FD | NWSE | R:HAMILTON |
| 3402 | JOHNSON, John J | 1 | NWSE | 1852-08-05 | FD | NWSE | |
| 3474 | KITEHEY, Wiley S | 36 | NWNE | 1848-10-30 | FD | NWNE | R:HAMILTON |
| 3252 | LASATER, Absolom | 2 | NWNW | 1837-07-28 | FD | NWNW | R:HAMILTON |
| 3278 | LASATER, David H | 1 | NWNE | 1854-02-22 | FD | NWNE | R:HAMILTON |
| 3294 | LASATER, Enos Allen | 5 | NENW | 1841-09-30 | FD | NENW | R:WHITE |
| 3329 | LASATER, Jacob B | 1 | SENE | 1853-02-07 | FD | SENE | |
| 3337 | LASATER, James C | 1 | SWNW | 1854-03-25 | FD | SWNW | G:30 |
| 3416 | LASATER, Jonathan A | 15 | W½NW | 1851-03-25 | FD | W2NW | |
| 3417 | " " | 15 | W½SW | 1851-03-25 | FD | W2SW | |
| 3337 | LASATER, Rebecca Jane | 1 | SWNW | 1854-03-25 | FD | SWNW | G:30 |
| 3337 | LASATER, Robert W | 1 | SWNW | 1854-03-25 | FD | SWNW | G:30 |
| 3337 | LASATER, Sarah Ann | 1 | SWNW | 1854-03-25 | FD | SWNW | G:30 |
| 3464 | LASATER, Stanford A | 9 | SWNW | 1857-07-31 | FD | SWNW | |
| 3337 | LASATER, Thomas J | 1 | SWNW | 1854-03-25 | FD | SWNW | G:30 |
| 3471 | MARGRAVE, Thomas | 1 | NENW | 1854-02-18 | FD | NENW | R:HAMILTON |
| 3403 | MATLOCK, John | 3 | NESW | 1852-04-23 | FD | NESW | R:HAMILTON |
| 3405 | " " | 3 | SWNW | 1852-06-29 | FD | SWNW | R:HAMILTON |
| 3404 | " " | 3 | SWNE | 1853-01-11 | FD | SWNE | |
| 3299 | MAYBERRY, Frederick | 14 | SW | 1819-01-27 | FD | SW | R:WHITE |
| 3295 | " " | 14 | NENW | 1832-10-10 | FD | NENW | R:HAMILTON |
| 3298 | " " | 14 | NWSW | 1833-09-25 | FD | NWSW | R:HAMILTON |
| 3296 | " " | 14 | NWNE | 1836-12-10 | FD | NWNE | R:HAMILTON |
| 3297 | " " | 14 | NWNW | 1848-03-02 | FD | NWNW | R:HAMILTON |

| ID | Individual in Patent | Sec. | Sec. Part | Purchase Date | Sale Type | IL Aliquot Part | For More Info . . . |
|---|---|---|---|---|---|---|---|
| 3302 | MAYBERRY, George T | 2 | NENW | 1853-02-15 | FD | NENW | |
| 3303 | " " | 2 | SENW | 1854-04-05 | FD | SENW | R:HAMILTON |
| 3311 | MAYBERRY, Henderson | 18 | NWNW | 1852-07-06 | FD | NWNW | |
| 3315 | MAYBERRY, Henry J | 26 | NENW | 1849-03-31 | FD | NENW | R:HAMILTON |
| 3316 | " " | 26 | SENW | 1851-01-14 | FD | SENW | R:HAMILTON |
| 3314 | " " | 22 | SENW | 1853-03-12 | FD | SENW | |
| 3332 | MAYBERRY, Jacob | 23 | NWNW | 1848-03-27 | FD | NWNW | |
| 3331 | " " | 22 | E½NE | 1848-03-27 | FD | E2NE | |
| 3330 | " " | 15 | SESE | 1848-03-27 | FD | SESE | |
| 3335 | MAYBERRY, James A | 23 | SESW | 1851-01-06 | FD | SESW | R:HAMILTON |
| 3334 | " " | 22 | SWNE | 1853-02-11 | FD | SWNE | |
| 3369 | MAYBERRY, James H | 10 | NWSE | 1854-01-27 | FD | NWSE | R:HAMILTON |
| 3339 | " " | 10 | NWSE | 1854-01-27 | FD | NWSE | R:HAMILTON |
| 3340 | " " | 3 | SESW | 1854-01-27 | FD | SESW | R:HAMILTON |
| 3338 | " " | 10 | NESW | 1854-01-27 | FD | NESW | R:HAMILTON |
| 3421 | MAYBERRY, Lemual G | 9 | SENE | 1849-08-20 | FD | SENE | R:HAMILTON |
| 3425 | MAYBERRY, Lemuel G | 9 | NENE | 1851-02-17 | FD | NENE | R:HAMILTON |
| 3422 | " " | 10 | NWSW | 1853-03-01 | FD | NWSW | |
| 3426 | " " | 9 | NESE | 1853-03-01 | FD | NESE | |
| 3424 | " " | 10 | SESE | 1854-10-04 | FD | SESE | R:HAMILTON |
| 3423 | " " | 10 | S½SW | 1854-10-04 | FD | S2SW | R:HAMILTON |
| 3435 | MAYBERRY, Michael | 15 | E½NW | 1848-03-17 | FD | E2NW | |
| 3436 | " " | 15 | E½SW | 1848-03-17 | FD | E2SW | |
| 3438 | " " | 16 | L9 | 1851-04-05 | SC | LOT9NESE | |
| 3437 | " " | 15 | SWNE | 1853-03-31 | FD | SWNE | |
| 3440 | MAYBERRY, Militia | 14 | SWNE | 1839-08-08 | FD | SWNE | R:HAMILTON S:F |
| 3439 | " " | 14 | SENW | 1839-08-08 | FD | SENW | R:HAMILTON S:F |
| 3462 | MAYBERRY, Solomon | 26 | NWNE | 1836-12-10 | FD | NWNE | R:HAMILTON |
| 3461 | " " | 23 | SWNW | 1853-02-11 | FD | SWNW | |
| 3488 | MAYBERRY, William | 15 | SENE | 1837-02-13 | FD | SENE | R:HAMILTON |
| 3257 | " " | 15 | SENE | 1837-02-13 | FD | SENE | R:HAMILTON |
| 3487 | " " | 14 | NWSE | 1839-12-02 | FD | NWSE | R:HAMILTON |
| 3489 | " " | 26 | N½SE | 1854-10-07 | FD | N2SE | R:HAMILTON |
| 3457 | MCBROOM, Robert M | 6 | NENE | 1851-01-21 | FD | NENE | R:HAMILTON |
| 3256 | MCCAWLLEY, Andrew J | 11 | SWSE | 1847-07-07 | FD | SWSE | R:POPE |
| 3336 | " " | 11 | SWSE | 1847-07-07 | FD | SWSE | R:POPE |
| 3361 | MCDOWELL, Eliza W | 13 | W½SW | 1858-04-10 | FD | W2SW | S:F |
| 3283 | " " | 13 | W½SW | 1858-04-10 | FD | W2SW | S:F |
| 3282 | " " | 13 | SWNW | 1858-04-10 | FD | SWNW | S:F |
| 3360 | " " | 13 | SWNW | 1858-04-10 | FD | SWNW | S:F |
| 3490 | MCILVANE, William | 9 | SWSE | 1854-02-24 | FD | SWSE | R:HAMILTON |
| 3247 | MCKENZIE, Aaron S | 36 | SWNE | 1846-12-29 | FD | SWNE | R:HAMILTON |
| 3246 | " " | 13 | NWNW | 1854-04-13 | FD | NWNW | R:HAMILTON |
| 3362 | MCKENZIE, James V | 25 | NENE | 1836-11-28 | FD | NENE | R:HAMILTON |
| 3365 | MCKENZIE, Jesse B T | 13 | NENE | 1840-11-12 | FD | NENE | R:HAMILTON |
| 3491 | MCKENZIE, William | 12 | SESE | 1836-12-12 | FD | SESE | R:HAMILTON |
| 3492 | " " | 13 | SESE | 1846-11-10 | FD | SESE | R:WHITE |
| 3427 | " " | 13 | SESE | 1846-11-10 | FD | SESE | R:WHITE |
| 3248 | MCKINGY, Aaron Shelby | 36 | NWSE | 1848-10-04 | FD | NWSE | R:HAMILTON |
| 3493 | MCKINSIE, William | 14 | SWSE | 1851-12-20 | FD | SWSE | R:HAMILTON |
| 3363 | MCKINZIE, James V | 24 | SESE | 1834-07-26 | FD | SESE | R:HAMILTON |
| 3494 | MCKINZIE, William | 12 | W½SW | 1853-03-24 | FD | W2SW | |
| 3281 | MCMAHAN, Edward | 10 | NWNE | 1848-06-15 | FD | NWNE | R:HAMILTON |
| 3454 | MCMAHAN, Reuben | 9 | E½SW | 1848-09-26 | FD | E2SW | |
| 3456 | " " | 9 | SWNE | 1848-09-26 | FD | SWNE | |
| 3455 | " " | 9 | NWSE | 1848-09-26 | FD | NWSE | |
| 3452 | " " | 10 | NENE | 1850-03-11 | FD | NENE | R:HAMILTON |
| 3453 | " " | 3 | SWSE | 1854-04-28 | FD | SWSE | R:HAMILTON |
| 3466 | MCMAHAN, Stephen | 3 | SESE | 1853-11-26 | FD | SESE | |
| 3465 | " " | 2 | SWSW | 1855-05-29 | FD | SWSW | R:HAMILTON |
| 3359 | MCMAHON, James | 10 | NESE | 1855-06-11 | FD | NESE | R:HAMILTON |
| 3323 | MCMURTRY, Horace | 25 | | 1838-10-05 | FD | NWNWPA | R:HAMILTON |
| 3472 | MCMURTRY, John Henry | 25 | SWNW | 1847-12-23 | FD | SWNW | R:HAMILTON |
| 3401 | " " | 25 | SWNW | 1847-12-23 | FD | SWNW | R:HAMILTON |
| 3400 | " " | 25 | SENW | 1849-02-21 | FD | SENW | R:HAMILTON |
| 3411 | MILLER, John W | 12 | SESW | 1848-06-20 | FD | SESW | |
| 3412 | " " | 12 | SWSE | 1848-06-20 | FD | SWSE | |
| 3413 | " " | 13 | NENW | 1848-06-20 | FD | NENW | |
| 3414 | " " | 13 | NWNE | 1848-06-20 | FD | NWNE | |
| 3449 | MILLER, Peter | 1 | NE | 1818-11-13 | FD | NE | R:WHITE |
| 3271 | MILLSBAUGH, Daniel G | 24 | W½SE | 1837-01-23 | FD | W2SE | R:WHITE |
| 3360 | MILLSPAUGH, James | 13 | SWNW | 1854-09-29 | FD | SWNW | R:WHITE |
| 3361 | " " | 13 | W½SW | 1854-09-29 | FD | W2SW | R:WHITE |

| ID | Individual in Patent | Sec. | Sec. Part | Purchase Date | Sale Type | IL Aliquot Part | For More Info . . . |
|---|---|---|---|---|---|---|---|
| 3283 | MILLSPAUGH, James (Cont'd) | 13 | W½SW | 1854-09-29 | FD | W2SW | R:WHITE |
| 3282 | " " | 13 | SWNW | 1854-09-29 | FD | SWNW | R:WHITE |
| 3370 | MILLSPAUGH, Joan | 10 | S½SE | 1854-09-29 | FD | S2SE | R:WHITE |
| 3372 | " " | 11 | SWSW | 1854-09-29 | FD | SWSW | R:WHITE |
| 3371 | " " | 11 | E½SW | 1854-09-29 | FD | E2SW | R:WHITE |
| 3369 | " " | 10 | NWSE | 1854-09-29 | FD | NWSE | R:WHITE |
| 3339 | " " | 10 | NWSE | 1854-09-29 | FD | NWSE | R:WHITE |
| 3406 | MILLSPAUGH, John | 14 | E½NE | 1853-01-01 | FD | E2NE | |
| 3407 | " " | 15 | N½NE | 1854-09-29 | FD | N2NE | R:WHITE |
| 3389 | MILLSPAUGH, John G | 25 | NENW | 1836-12-05 | FD | NENW | R:HAMILTON |
| 3428 | MOORES, Loammi | 24 | SWNE | 1847-02-23 | FD | SWNE | R:HAMILTON |
| 3264 | MORRIS, Benjamin F | 23 | SWNE | 1849-08-20 | FD | SWNE | |
| 3263 | " " | 23 | E½NE | 1849-08-20 | FD | E2NE | |
| 3262 | " " | 14 | SESE | 1849-08-20 | FD | SESE | |
| 3336 | MORRIS, James A | 11 | SWSE | 1853-02-09 | FD | SWSE | |
| 3256 | " " | 11 | SWSE | 1853-02-09 | FD | SWSE | |
| 3255 | NATIONS, Anderson | 1 | SWNE | 1852-01-28 | FD | SWNE | |
| 3272 | POWELL, Daniel | 25 | SE | 1819-02-17 | FD | SE | R:KENTUCKY |
| 3273 | " " | 36 | E½SE | 1836-04-09 | FD | E2SE | R:WHITE |
| 3469 | POWELL, Thomas J | 36 | SENE | 1848-10-30 | FD | SENE | R:WHITE |
| 3470 | " " | 36 | SWSE | 1849-03-13 | FD | SWSE | R:WHITE |
| 3467 | " " | 16 | L7 | 1851-01-21 | SC | LOT7SWNE | |
| 3468 | " " | 16 | L8 | 1851-01-21 | SC | LOT8SENE | |
| 3318 | PRINCE, Henry W | 2 | NWSE | 1854-07-22 | FD | NWSE | R:HAMILTON |
| 3319 | " " | 2 | SWNE | 1854-07-28 | FD | SWNE | R:HAMILTON |
| 3419 | PRINCE, Joseph P | 2 | NESW | 1854-07-17 | FD | NESW | R:HAMILTON |
| 3420 | " " | 2 | SWSE | 1854-10-03 | FD | SWSE | R:HAMILTON |
| 3441 | RAPARD, Nelson F | 27 | NESE | 1852-12-29 | FD | NESE | |
| 3492 | REINER, Lewis | 13 | SESE | 1854-08-03 | FD | SESE | R:HARDIN |
| 3427 | " " | 13 | SESE | 1854-08-03 | FD | SESE | R:HARDIN |
| 3289 | SIGLER, Emanuel | 12 | NENW | 1837-01-09 | FD | NENW | R:HAMILTON |
| 3286 | " " | 11 | NENE | 1848-03-23 | FD | NENE | |
| 3293 | " " | 2 | SESE | 1848-03-23 | FD | SESE | |
| 3292 | " " | 12 | W½NW | 1848-03-23 | FD | W2NW | |
| 3291 | " " | 12 | SWNE | 1851-12-13 | FD | SWNE | R:HAMILTON |
| 3287 | " " | 11 | NESE | 1854-10-04 | FD | NESE | R:HAMILTON |
| 3290 | " " | 12 | SENW | 1854-10-04 | FD | SENW | R:HAMILTON |
| 3288 | " " | 11 | SENE | 1854-10-04 | FD | SENE | R:HAMILTON |
| 3328 | SIGLER, Isaac | 12 | SENE | 1836-04-07 | FD | SENE | R:HAMILTON |
| 3327 | " " | 12 | NWNE | 1836-04-07 | FD | NWNE | R:HAMILTON |
| 3409 | SIGLER, John | 12 | NESE | 1836-04-04 | FD | NESE | R:HAMILTON |
| 3410 | " " | 12 | NWSE | 1849-10-10 | FD | NWSE | R:HAMILTON |
| 3429 | SIGLER, Manuel | 12 | NENE | 1853-12-13 | FD | NENE | R:HAMILTON |
| 3284 | SLOAN, Elizabeth | 3 | SWSW | 1846-08-25 | FD | SWSW | R:HAMILTON S:F |
| 3250 | STONE, John | 24 | SW | 1817-02-01 | FD | SW | R:WHITE G:37 |
| 3408 | STORY, John N | 26 | NWSW | 1854-11-27 | FD | NWSW | R:HAMILTON |
| 3432 | STORY, Marsah | 11 | W½NE | 1853-01-22 | FD | W2NE | |
| 3431 | " " | 11 | E½NW | 1853-01-22 | FD | E2NW | |
| 3250 | STOVALL, Abraham | 24 | SW | 1817-02-01 | FD | SW | R:WHITE G:37 |
| 3380 | STOVALL, John B | 23 | SE | 1816-12-19 | FD | SE | R:WHITE |
| 3381 | " " | 26 | NE | 1816-12-28 | FD | NE | R:WHITE |
| 3249 | TROUSDALE, Abner L | 1 | SWSE | 1852-02-09 | FD | SWSE | |
| 3333 | TROUT, Jacob | 26 | NENE | 1840-03-23 | FD | NENE | R:HAMILTON |
| 3300 | VARNELL, George H | 36 | SESW | 1860-11-03 | FD | SESWVOID | |
| 3301 | " " | 36 | W½SW | 1860-11-03 | FD | W2SWVOID | |
| 3306 | VICKERS, George | 23 | NWSW | 1853-06-16 | FD | NWSW | |
| 3305 | " " | 23 | NESW | 1854-03-04 | FD | NESW | R:HAMILTON |
| 3307 | " " | 23 | SWSW | 1854-04-27 | FD | SWSW | |
| 3304 | " " | 22 | E½SE | 1854-10-24 | FD | E2SE | R:HAMILTON |
| 3473 | VICKERS, Thomas | 26 | SEN½ | 1852-01-19 | FD | S2NE | |
| 3499 | VICKERS, William | 35 | SWNE | 1836-11-14 | FD | SWNE | R:TENNESSEE |
| 3498 | " " | 35 | SENE | 1843-12-21 | FD | SENE | R:HAMILTON |
| 3496 | " " | 31 | NENE | 1851-12-29 | FD | NENE | |
| 3497 | " " | 35 | NESE | 1853-06-16 | FD | NESE | |
| 3317 | WAYBERRY, Henry J | 26 | W½NW | 1854-10-07 | FD | W2NW | R:HAMILTON |
| 3445 | WEBB, Obed H | 3 | NENW | 1853-12-27 | FD | NENW | R:HAMILTON |
| 3444 | " " | 1 | SENW | 1854-02-22 | FD | SENW | R:HAMILTON |
| 3448 | WEBB, Obed Hendrick | 4 | E½SE | 1847-11-29 | FD | E2SE | R:HAMILTON |
| 3447 | " " | 3 | NWSW | 1849-03-07 | FD | NWSW | R:HAMILTON |
| 3446 | " " | 3 | NWNE | 1852-04-12 | FD | NWNE | R:HAMILTON |
| 3285 | WHEELER, Elizabeth W | 19 | NWNW | 1853-01-11 | FD | NWNW | S:F |
| 3320 | WHEELER, Henry | 5 | NWSW | 1851-11-26 | FD | NWSW | |
| 3321 | " " | 5 | SESW | 1853-03-31 | FD | SESW | |

| ID | Individual in Patent | Sec. | Sec. Part | Purchase Date | Sale Type | IL Aliquot Part | For More Info . . . |
|---|---|---|---|---|---|---|---|
| 3364 | WHEELER, James | 18 | SENW | 1836-06-07 | FD | SENW | R:HAMILTON |
| 3495 | WHEELER, William T | 18 | SWNW | 1851-01-22 | FD | SWNW | R:HAMILTON G:41 |
| 3500 | WHEELER, Willis | 10 | NW | 1818-11-20 | FD | NW | R:WHITE |
| 3495 | WHEELER, Willis Abner | 18 | SWNW | 1851-01-22 | FD | SWNW | R:HAMILTON G:41 |
| 3326 | WILKINS, John A | 23 | NWNE | 1852-09-04 | FD | NWNE | |
| 3375 | " " | 23 | NWNE | 1852-09-04 | FD | NWNE | |
| 3415 | WINKLER, John | 1 | NESE | 1850-01-16 | FD | NESEVOID | R:HAMILTON |
| 3356 | WOOSLEY, James M | 2 | SESW | 1854-02-06 | FD | SESW | R:HAMILTON |
| 3345 | WRIGHT, James H | 2 | SENE | 1854-01-28 | FD | SENE | R:HAMILTON |
| 3343 | " " | 2 | NESE | 1854-01-28 | FD | NESE | R:HAMILTON |
| 3342 | " " | 2 | NENE | 1854-01-28 | FD | NENE | R:HAMILTON |
| 3344 | " " | 2 | NWNE | 1854-02-02 | FD | NWNE | R:HAMILTON |
| 3341 | " " | 1 | NWNW | 1854-02-02 | FD | NWNW | R:HAMILTON |
| 3346 | WRIGHT, James Henry | 10 | W½NW | 1844-04-24 | FD | W2NW | |

Patent Map

T6-S R7-E
3rd PM Meridian

Map Group 12

## Township Statistics

| | | |
|---|---|---|
| Parcels Mapped | : | 257 |
| Number of Patents | : | 1 |
| Number of Individuals | : | 150 |
| Patentees Identified | : | 144 |
| Number of Surnames | : | 84 |
| Multi-Patentee Parcels | : | 3 |
| Oldest Patent Date | : | 12/19/1816 |
| Most Recent Patent | : | 11/3/1860 |
| Block/Lot Parcels | : | 16 |
| Cities and Towns | : | 0 |
| Cemeteries | : | 2 |

Map grid:

**6** — MCBROOM Robert M 1851; ALEXANDER Mastin 1851

**5** — LASATER Enos Allen 1841; WHEELER Henry 1851; WHEELER Henry 1853

**4** — WEBB Obed Hendrick 1847

**7**

**8** — CARPENTER Chester 1858

**9** — GRIFFITH David C 1853; GRIFFITH David C 1853; GRIFFITH David C 1851; MAYBERRY Lemuel G 1851; LASATER Stanford A 1857; MCMAHAN Reuben 1848; MAYBERRY Lemuel G 1849; MCMAHAN Reuben 1848; MCMAHAN Reuben 1848; MAYBERRY Lemuel G 1853; GRIFFITH David C 1851; MCILVANE William 1854

**18** — MAYBERRY Henderson 1852; WHEELER [41] William T 1851; WHEELER James 1836; HARROWOOD Henry 1853

**17**

**16**

Lots-Sec. 16
| | | | |
|---|---|---|---|
| L1 | GHOLSON, Reuben E | 1850 |
| L2 | GHOLSON, Newton | 1851 |
| L3 | GHOLSON, Newton | 1851 |
| L4 | HEARD, John H | 1851 |
| L5 | HEARD, John H | 1851 |
| L6 | HEARD, John H | 1851 |
| L7 | POWELL, Thomas J | 1851 |
| L8 | POWELL, Thomas J | 1851 |
| L9 | MAYBERRY, Michael | 1851 |
| L10 | HEARD, John H | 1851 |
| L11 | HEARD, John H | 1851 |
| L12 | HEARD, John H | 1851 |
| L13 | HEARD, John H | 1851 |
| L14 | HEARD, John H | 1851 |
| L15 | HEARD, John H | 1851 |
| L16 | HEARD, John H | 1851 |

**19** — WHEELER Elizabeth W 1853; HARROWOOD Henry 1853

**20**

**21**

**30**

**29**

**28**

**31**

**32** — VICKERS William 1851; CARPENTER Chester 1858

**33**

## Map Grid

**Section 3**

| BALLARD Joel 1853 | WEBB Obed H 1853 | WEBB Obed Hendrick 1852 | ALLEN John 1850 |
| MATLOCK John 1852 | BALLARD Joel 1847 | MATLOCK John 1853 | ALLEN John 1836 |
| WEBB Obed Hendrick 1849 | MATLOCK John 1852 | JESTEES Martin 1855 | DENNY William L 1854 |
| SLOAN Elizabeth 1846 | MAYBERRY James H 1854 | MCMAHAN Reuben 1854 | MCMAHAN Stephen 1853 |

**Section 2**

| LASATER Absolom 1837 | MAYBERRY George T 1853 | WRIGHT James H 1854 | WRIGHT James H 1854 |
| ALLEN John 1854 | MAYBERRY George T 1854 | PRINCE Henry W 1854 | WRIGHT James H 1854 |
| DENNY William L 1854 | PRINCE Joseph P 1854 | PRINCE Henry W 1854 | WRIGHT James H 1854 |
| MCMAHAN Stephen 1855 | WOOSLEY James M 1854 | PRINCE Joseph P 1854 | SIGLER Emanuel 1848 |

**Section 1**

| WRIGHT James H 1854 | MARGRAVE Thomas 1854 | LASATER David H 1854 | DELAP MILLER Peter 1852 / 1818 |
| LASATER [30] James C 1854 | WEBB Obed H 1854 | NATIONS Anderson 1852 | LASATER Jacob B 1853 |
| ANDERSON William B 1819 | | JOHNSON John J 1852 | WINKLER John 1850 |
| | | TROUSDALE Abner L 1852 | |

**Section 10**

| WHEELER Willis 1818 / AVERETT John 1829 | MCMAHAN Edward 1848 | MCMAHAN Reuben 1850 |
| WRIGHT James Henry 1844 | BOLARJACK Harvey F 1854 | |
| MAYBERRY Lemuel G 1853 | MILLSPAUGH Joan 1854 / MAYBERRY James H 1854 | MCMAHON James 1855 |
| MAYBERRY Lemuel G 1854 | MILLSPAUGH Joan 1854 | MAYBERRY Lemuel G 1854 |

**Section 11**

| BOLARJACK Harvey F 1854 | STORY Marsah 1853 | SIGLER Emanuel 1848 |
| STORY Marsah 1853 | | SIGLER Emanuel 1854 |
| BLAKE James M 1853 | MILLSPAUGH Joan 1854 / MORRIS James A 1853 / MCCAWLLEY Andrew J 1847 | SIGLER Emanuel 1854 |

**Section 12**

| SIGLER Emanuel 1837 | SIGLER Isaac 1836 | SIGLER Manuel 1853 |
| SIGLER Emanuel 1848 | SIGLER Emanuel 1854 | SIGLER Emanuel 1851 | SIGLER Isaac 1836 |
| MCKINZIE William 1853 | DEBOARD John C 1854 | SIGLER John 1849 | SIGLER John 1836 |
| | MILLER John W 1848 | MILLER John W 1848 | MCKENZIE William 1836 |

**Section 15**

| MAYBERRY Michael 1848 | MILLSPAUGH John 1854 | |
| LASATER Jonathan A 1851 | MAYBERRY Michael 1853 | MAYBERRY William 1837 / GOTT Anthony 1852 |
| | FAIRWEATHERS John 1854 | MAYBERRY Jacob 1848 |
| LASATER Jonathan A 1851 | MAYBERRY Michael 1848 | |

**Section 14**

| MAYBERRY Frederick 1848 | MAYBERRY Frederick 1832 | MAYBERRY Frederick 1836 |
| GOSSETT William J 1853 | MAYBERRY Militia 1839 | MAYBERRY Militia 1839 | MILLSPAUGH John 1853 |
| MAYBERRY Frederick 1833 | MAYBERRY Frederick 1819 | MAYBERRY William 1839 |
| GROVES William 1851 | MCKINSIE William 1851 | MORRIS Benjamin F 1849 |

**Section 13**

| MCKENZIE Aaron S 1854 | MILLER John W 1848 | MILLER John W 1848 | MCKENZIE Jesse B T 1840 |
| MCDOWELL Eliza W 1858 / MILLSPAUGH James 1854 | HARDISTY Christopher 1853 | HARDISTY Christopher 1853 | BRILL Solomon S 1854 |
| MILLSPAUGH James 1854 | BLAKE James M 1851 | HANDEESTER Jesse 1849 | BRILL S S Gn 1853 |
| MCDOWELL Eliza W 1858 | BLAKE James M 1848 | BLAKE James Madison 1836 / MCKENZIE William 1846 | REINER Lewis 1854 |

**Section 22**

| FAIRWEATHER John 1854 | FAIRWEATHERS John 1851 | MAYBERRY Jacob 1848 |
| MAYBERRY Henry J 1853 | MAYBERRY James A 1853 | |
| HUGHS James 1851 | HUGHES James 1853 | VICKERS George 1854 |
| | HUGHS James 1848 | |

**Section 23**

| MAYBERRY Jacob 1848 | CLARK Isaac Hynes 1850 | WILKINS John A 1852 / CLARK Isaac Hynes | MORRIS Benjamin F 1849 |
| MAYBERRY Solomon 1853 | CLARK Isaac H 1853 | MORRIS Benjamin F 1849 | |
| VICKERS George 1853 | VICKERS George 1854 | | |
| VICKERS George 1854 | MAYBERRY James A 1851 | STOVALL John B 1816 | |

**Section 24**

| HARDESTER Jesse 1849 | BLAKE James M 1848 | BLAKE James M 1848 |
| HARDISTY Jesse 1836 | MOORES Loammi 1847 | BRILL Soloman Scott 1848 |
| STOVALL [37] Abraham 1817 | MILLSBAUGH Daniel G 1837 | BLAKE James Madison 1848 |
| | | MCKINZIE James V 1834 |

**Section 27**

| GROSS William 1848 | WAYBERRY Henry J 1854 |
| RAPARD Nelson F 1852 | |

**Section 26**

| MAYBERRY Henry J 1849 | MAYBERRY Solomon 1836 | TROUT Jacob 1840 |
| MAYBERRY Henry J 1851 | STOVALL John B 1816 | VICKERS Thomas 1852 |
| STORY John N 1854 | GRIMES Sarah Jane 1838 | MAYBERRY William 1854 |
| CROUSE John 1840 | GRIMES Adonijah 1836 | DOCKER William A 1840 |

**Section 25**

| MCMURTRY Horace 1838 | MILLSPAUGH John G 1836 | BEATY William 1837 | MCKENZIE James V 1836 |
| HARRISON Thomas P 1839 / MCMURTRY John Henry 1847 | MCMURTRY John Henry 1849 | | GOTT Anthony Wayne 1836 |
| GOTT Anthony Wayne 1849 | | POWELL Daniel 1819 | |
| GRIMES Rachael 1840 | GOTT Anthony Wayne 1849 | | |

**Section 34**

| | |

**Section 35**

| CROUSE John 1839 | GRIMES Adonijah 1837 | DOCHOR William A 1840 |
| HAMILTON Maria 1840 | HAMILTON Edmund 1836 | HAMILTON Edmund 1836 | VICKERS William 1836 / VICKERS William 1843 |
| FORD Wodly 1853 | HOWARD Joseph 1836 | GREATHOUSE Hiram 1832 | VICKERS William 1853 |
| FORD Abram 1837 | HOWARD James 1836 | HARDISTY William 1819 | HARDISTY William 1836 / HARDISTY George W 1854 |

**Section 36**

| HARDESTY Christopher 1837 | HARDESTY Christopher 1821 | KITEHEY Wiley S 1848 | BAGLY William A 1848 |
| | | MCKENZIE Aaron S 1846 | POWELL Thomas J 1848 |
| VARNELL George H 1860 | HOWARD Wilson L 1848 | MCKINGY Aaron Shelby 1848 | POWELL Daniel 1836 |
| VARNELL George H 1860 | VARNELL George H 1860 | POWELL Thomas J 1849 | |

---

## Helpful Hints

1. This Map's INDEX can be found on the preceding pages.

2. Refer to Map "C" to see where this Township lies within Hamilton County, Illinois.

3. Numbers within square brackets [ ] denote a multi-patentee land parcel (multi-owner). Refer to Appendix "C" for a full list of members in this group.

4. Areas that look to be crowded with Patentees usually indicate multiple sales of the same parcel (re-issues), cancellations or voided transactions (that we map, anyway) or overlapping parcels. We opt to show even these ambiguous parcels, which oftentimes lead to research avenues not yet taken.

## Legend

- Patent Boundary
- Section Boundary
- No Patents Found (or Outside County)
- 1., 2., 3., ... Lot Numbers (when beside a name)
- [ ] Group Number (see Appendix "C")

**Scale**: Section = 1 mile X 1 mile (generally, with some exceptions)

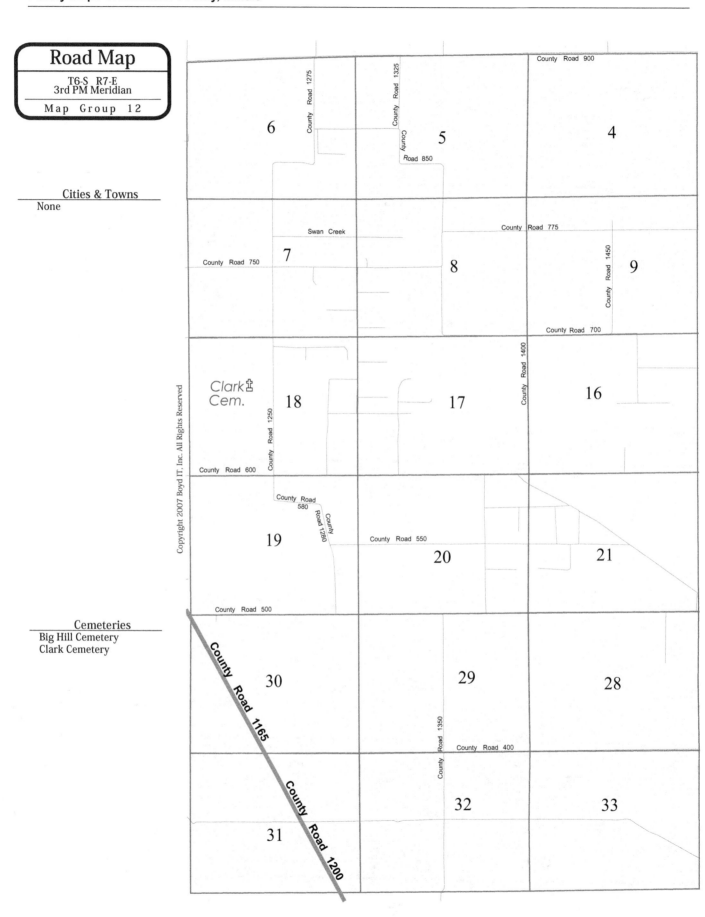

Road Map

T6-S  R7-E
3rd PM Meridian

Map Group 12

Cities & Towns
None

Cemeteries
Big Hill Cemetery
Clark Cemetery

County Road 1275

County Road 1325

County Road 900

6

County Road

Road 850

5

4

Swan Creek

County Road 775

County Road 750

7

8

County Road 1450

9

County Road 700

County Road 1400

Clark Cem.

18

17

16

County Road 1250

County Road 600

County Road 580

County Road 1280

County Road 550

19

20

21

County Road 500

Copyright 2007 Boyd IT, Inc. All Rights Reserved

County Road 1165

30

29

28

County Road 1350

County Road 400

County Road 1200

31

32

33

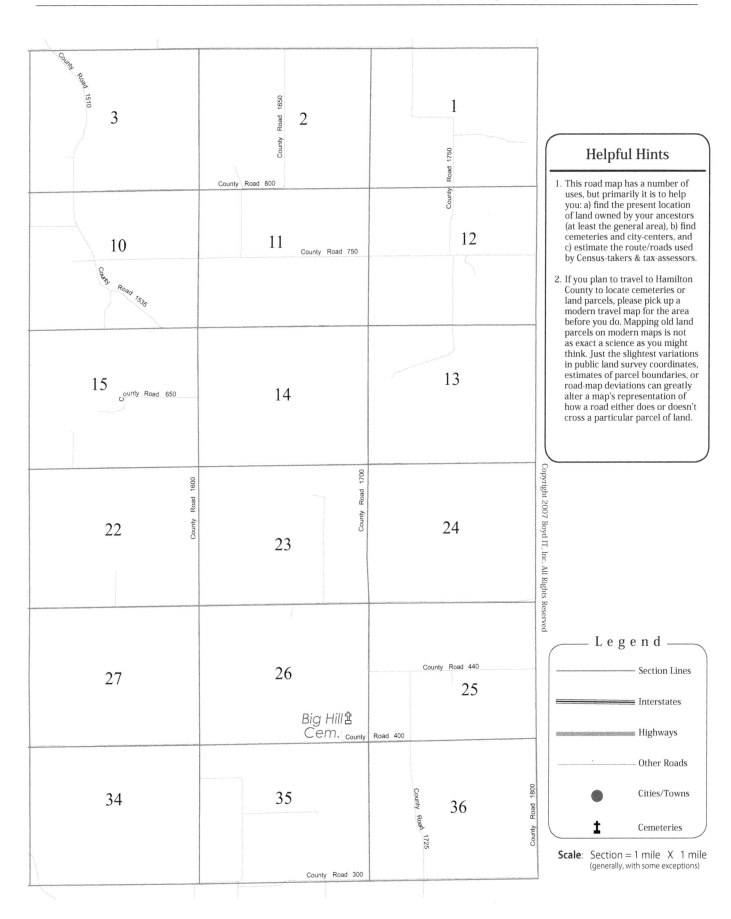

County Road 1510

3

County Road 1650

2

1

County Road 1750

County Road 800

10

11

County Road 750

12

County Road 1535

15

County Road 650

14

13

22

County Road 1600

23

County Road 1700

24

27

26

County Road 440

25

Big Hill
Cem.

County Road 400

34

35

County Road 1725

36

County Road 1800

County Road 300

## Helpful Hints

1. This road map has a number of uses, but primarily it is to help you: a) find the present location of land owned by your ancestors (at least the general area), b) find cemeteries and city-centers, and c) estimate the route/roads used by Census-takers & tax-assessors.

2. If you plan to travel to Hamilton County to locate cemeteries or land parcels, please pick up a modern travel map for the area before you do. Mapping old land parcels on modern maps is not as exact a science as you might think. Just the slightest variations in public land survey coordinates, estimates of parcel boundaries, or road-map deviations can greatly alter a map's representation of how a road either does or doesn't cross a particular parcel of land.

### Legend

| | |
|---|---|
| ———————— | Section Lines |
| ════════════ | Interstates |
| ▬▬▬▬▬▬▬▬ | Highways |
| ———————— | Other Roads |
| ● | Cities/Towns |
| ✝ | Cemeteries |

**Scale**: Section = 1 mile X 1 mile
(generally, with some exceptions)

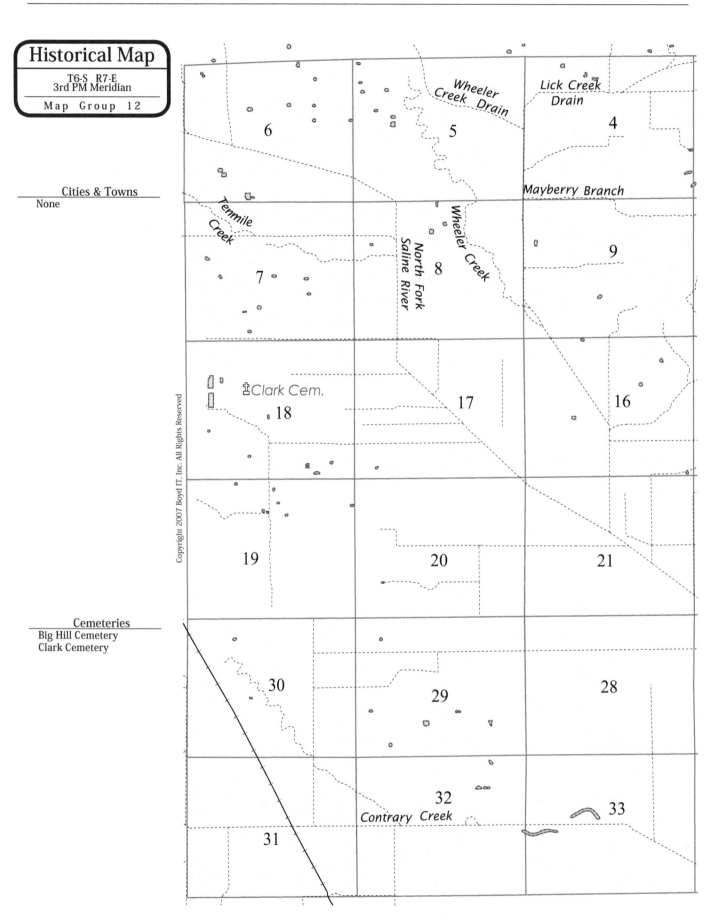

## Historical Map

T6-S  R7-E
3rd PM Meridian

Map Group 12

### Cities & Towns
None

### Cemeteries
Big Hill Cemetery
Clark Cemetery

Wheeler Creek Drain

Lick Creek Drain

6

5

4

Mayberry Branch

Tenmile Creek

Wheeler Creek

North Fork Saline River

7

8

9

⚱ Clark Cem.

18

17

16

19

20

21

30

29

28

32

33

Contrary Creek

31

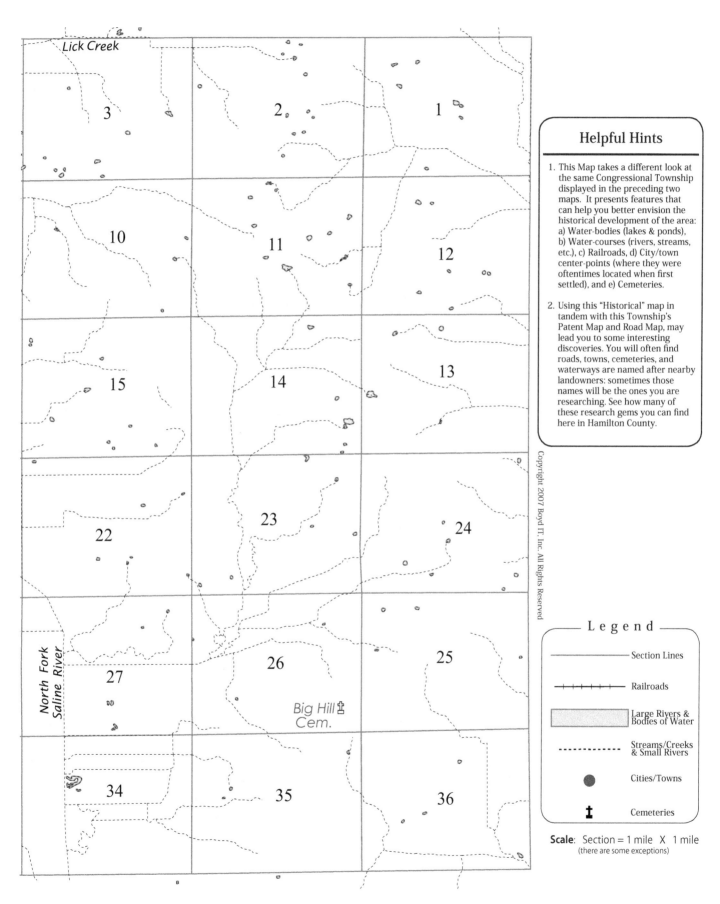

### Helpful Hints

1. This Map takes a different look at the same Congressional Township displayed in the preceding two maps. It presents features that can help you better envision the historical development of the area: a) Water-bodies (lakes & ponds), b) Water-courses (rivers, streams, etc.), c) Railroads, d) City/town center-points (where they were oftentimes located when first settled), and e) Cemeteries.

2. Using this "Historical" map in tandem with this Township's Patent Map and Road Map, may lead you to some interesting discoveries. You will often find roads, towns, cemeteries, and waterways are named after nearby landowners: sometimes those names will be the ones you are researching. See how many of these research gems you can find here in Hamilton County.

**L e g e n d**

| | |
|---|---|
| | Section Lines |
| +++++ | Railroads |
| | Large Rivers & Bodies of Water |
| - - - - - | Streams/Creeks & Small Rivers |
| ● | Cities/Towns |
| ‡ | Cemeteries |

**Scale**: Section = 1 mile X 1 mile
(there are some exceptions)

Lick Creek

North Fork Saline River

Big Hill ‡ Cem.

## Map Group 13: Index to Land Patents

## Township 7-South Range 5-East (3rd PM)

After you locate an individual in this Index, take note of the Section and Section Part then proceed to the Land Patent map on the pages immediately following. You should have no difficulty locating the corresponding parcel of land.

The "For More Info" Column will lead you to more information about the underlying Patents. See the *Legend* at right, and the "How to Use this Book" chapter, for more information.

```
┌─────────────────────────────────────────────────────┐
│                     LEGEND                           │
│           "For More Info . . . " column              │
│  ─────────────────────────────────────────────────   │
│  G = Group  (Multi-Patentee Patent, see Appendix "C")│
│  R = Residence                                       │
│  S = Social Status                                   │
│                                                      │
│  See Appendix A for list of abbreviations used by the│
│  Illinois State Archives in describing the place and │
│  nature of these land patents.                       │
│                                                      │
│  Note: if the Abbreviations contain "L", "BL", "LOT",│
│  or "BLOCK", the exact whereabouts of the parcel     │
│  within the section is not known.                    │
└─────────────────────────────────────────────────────┘
```

| ID | Individual in Patent | Sec. | Sec. Part | Purchase Date | Sale Type | IL Aliquot Part | For More Info . . . |
|---|---|---|---|---|---|---|---|
| 3513 | AARON, Benjamin | 12 | SESW | 1849-10-25 | FD | SESW | R:HAMILTON |
| 3514 | " " | 12 | SWSW | 1854-05-27 | FD | SWSW | R:HAMILTON |
| 3515 | " " | 13 | NWNW | 1854-05-27 | FD | NWNW | R:HAMILTON |
| 3712 | " " | 12 | SWSW | 1854-05-27 | FD | SWSW | R:HAMILTON |
| 3713 | " " | 13 | NWNW | 1854-05-27 | FD | NWNW | R:HAMILTON |
| 3512 | " " | 11 | SESE | 1854-06-10 | FD | SESE | R:HAMILTON |
| 3630 | ALLEN, John L | 6 | W½SE | 1853-12-12 | FD | W2SE | G:1 |
| 3630 | ALLEN, Lucy | 6 | W½SE | 1853-12-12 | FD | W2SE | G:1 |
| 3630 | ALLEN, Moses P | 6 | W½SE | 1853-12-12 | FD | W2SE | G:1 |
| 3630 | ALLEN, Ruth L | 6 | W½SE | 1853-12-12 | FD | W2SE | G:1 |
| 3717 | ANDERSON, William G | 11 | SENW | 1854-06-12 | SW | SENW | |
| 3718 | " " | 11 | SWNW | 1854-06-12 | SW | SWNW | |
| 3516 | ARON, Benjamin | 13 | SWNW | 1855-10-20 | FD | SWNW | R:HAMILTON |
| 3561 | BENNETT, Jacob | 18 | E½NE | 1852-05-11 | FD | E2NE | |
| 3562 | " " | 18 | W½NE | 1855-03-26 | FD | W2NE | R:HAMILTON |
| 3565 | BRADSHAN, James C | 14 | S½SW | 1852-03-02 | FD | S2SW | |
| 3709 | BROWN, William C | 12 | SWSE | 1853-05-30 | FD | SWSE | R:HAMILTON |
| 3710 | " " | 13 | E½NW | 1854-10-27 | FD | E2NW | R:HAMILTON |
| 3711 | " " | 13 | W½NE | 1854-10-27 | FD | W2NE | R:HAMILTON |
| 3708 | " " | 12 | NWSE | 1854-10-27 | FD | NWSE | R:HAMILTON |
| 3719 | BURNETT, William G | 1 | SWNE | 1853-12-20 | FD | SWNE | R:HAMILTON |
| 3645 | CANTRELL, Jonathan L | 8 | E½SW | 1853-02-03 | FD | E2SW | |
| 3646 | " " | 8 | SWSE | 1853-02-03 | FD | SWSE | |
| 3549 | CARNER, George | 17 | SWSE | 1854-11-28 | FD | SWSE | R:SALINE |
| 3527 | CARPENTER, Chester | 16 | L11 | 1857-04-09 | SC | LOT11NESW | G:8 |
| 3539 | " " | 16 | L9 | 1857-04-09 | SC | LOT9NESE | G:8 |
| 3538 | " " | 16 | L8 | 1857-04-09 | SC | LOT8SENE | G:8 |
| 3524 | " " | 16 | L5 | 1857-04-09 | SC | L5SWNW | |
| 3583 | " " | 16 | L5 | 1857-04-09 | SC | L5SWNW | |
| 3525 | " " | 16 | L1 | 1857-04-09 | SC | LOT1NENE | G:8 |
| 3537 | " " | 16 | L7 | 1857-04-09 | SC | LOT7SWNE | G:8 |
| 3532 | " " | 16 | L16 | 1857-04-09 | SC | LOT16SESE | G:8 |
| 3529 | " " | 16 | L13 | 1857-04-09 | SC | LOT13SWSW | G:8 |
| 3530 | " " | 16 | L14 | 1857-04-09 | SC | LOT14SESW | G:8 |
| 3531 | " " | 16 | L15 | 1857-04-09 | SC | LOT15SWSE | G:8 |
| 3536 | " " | 16 | L6 | 1857-04-09 | SC | LOT6SENW | G:8 |
| 3533 | " " | 16 | L2 | 1857-04-09 | SC | LOT2NWNE | G:8 |
| 3534 | " " | 16 | L3 | 1857-04-09 | SC | LOT3NENW | G:8 |
| 3528 | " " | 16 | L12 | 1857-04-09 | SC | LOT12NWSW | G:8 |
| 3535 | " " | 16 | L4 | 1857-04-09 | SC | LOT4NWNW | G:8 |
| 3526 | " " | 16 | L10 | 1857-04-09 | SC | LOT10NWSE | G:8 |
| 3685 | CATTSEL, Price | 4 | NWNW | 1838-11-24 | FD | NWNW | R:HAMILTON |
| 3523 | CAVANAUGH, Charles | 7 | SE | 1855-10-02 | FD | SE | R:JEFFERSON |
| 3660 | CLARK, Josiah | 5 | S½SE | 1854-10-06 | FD | S2SE | R:WHITE |
| 3727 | " " | 5 | S½SE | 1854-10-06 | FD | S2SE | R:WHITE |
| 3661 | " " | 8 | NE | 1854-10-06 | FD | NE | R:WHITE |

| ID | Individual in Patent | Sec. | Sec. Part | Purchase Date | Sale Type | IL Aliquot Part | For More Info . . . |
|---|---|---|---|---|---|---|---|
| 3547 | COFFER, Eli | 12 | NENW | 1850-11-04 | FD | NENW | |
| 3546 | " " | 12 | N½NE | 1850-11-04 | FD | N2NE | |
| 3595 | COFFEY, James W | 1 | NWNW | 1853-10-12 | FD | NWNW | |
| 3596 | " " | 2 | NENE | 1853-10-12 | FD | NENE | |
| 3720 | COLLINS, William H | 18 | NENW | 1859-08-25 | FD | NENW | |
| 3692 | COMPTON, Samuel | 1 | SENE | 1851-12-16 | FD | SENE | |
| 3592 | CORDER, James S | 18 | SWSW | 1853-05-25 | FD | SWSW | |
| 3618 | DAVIS, John | 3 | NENW | 1853-01-26 | FD | NENW | R:HAMILTON |
| 3648 | DAWES, Joseph | 12 | E½SE | 1852-05-31 | FD | E2SE | |
| 3647 | " " | 12 | E½SE | 1852-05-31 | FD | E2SE | |
| 3520 | FANNING, Buttsford | 9 | S½ | 1854-10-23 | FD | S2 | R:HAMILTON |
| 3689 | FLANIKIN, Robert H | 1 | S½NW | 1854-10-27 | FD | S2NW | R:HAMILTON |
| 3690 | FLANINKIN, Robert H | 1 | NENW | 1850-01-25 | FD | NENW | |
| 3691 | " " | 1 | NWNE | 1850-01-25 | FD | NWNE | |
| 3597 | FLANNIKEN, James W | 1 | NENE | 1837-05-02 | FD | NENE | R:HAMILTON |
| 3600 | FLANNIKIN, James W | 5 | NESW | 1851-11-08 | FD | NESW | |
| 3669 | " " | 5 | NESW | 1851-11-08 | FD | NESW | |
| 3598 | " " | 3 | NWSE | 1852-10-02 | FD | NWSE | |
| 3599 | " " | 3 | SWNE | 1852-10-02 | FD | SWNE | |
| 3602 | FLANNIKIN, Jarrus W | 3 | SWSE | 1855-03-26 | FD | SWSE | R:HAMILTON |
| 3550 | FLOYD, George W | 8 | N½SE | 1855-07-17 | FD | N2SE | R:WHITE |
| 3716 | FORESTER, William F | 2 | NWNW | 1852-12-10 | FD | NWNW | R:WHITE |
| 3559 | GALBRAITH, Henry | 7 | NWNW | 1852-07-31 | FD | NWNW | |
| 3558 | " " | 6 | SWSW | 1852-07-31 | FD | SWSW | |
| 3619 | GALBRAITH, John | 17 | E½SW | 1853-02-11 | FD | E2SW | |
| 3579 | GALBREATH, James | 18 | SESW | 1854-01-27 | FD | SESW | R:FRANKLIN |
| 3578 | " " | 18 | NWSE | 1854-01-27 | FD | NWSE | R:FRANKLIN |
| 3673 | GHOLSTEN, Lucinda | 14 | NE | 1854-10-23 | FD | NE | R:WHITE S:F |
| 3663 | GRAVES, Lewis | 17 | NWSW | 1853-01-28 | FD | NWSW | |
| 3664 | " " | 18 | NESE | 1853-01-28 | FD | NESE | |
| 3506 | GRAY, Alexander | 1 | N½SE | 1853-10-28 | FD | N2SE | |
| 3511 | GRAY, Basil S | 1 | SWSE | 1853-10-28 | FD | SWSE | R:JOHNSON |
| 3522 | HALL, Calvin | 7 | SWSE | 1854-10-26 | FD | SWSE | R:HAMILTON |
| 3521 | " " | 7 | E½SE | 1854-10-26 | FD | E2SE | R:HAMILTON |
| 3620 | HALL, John | 8 | W½SW | 1854-10-27 | FD | W2SW | R:SALINE |
| 3728 | HALL, Wilson H | 10 | NWSW | 1854-11-25 | FD | NWSW | R:SALINE |
| 3518 | HANCOCK, Bennet | 17 | SESW | 1832-10-12 | FD | SESW | R:GALLATIN |
| 3519 | HANCOK, Bennet | 17 | SWSW | 1833-02-06 | FD | SWSW | R:GALLATIN |
| 3517 | HARRIS, Benjamin | 6 | W½SE | 1855-06-12 | FD | W2SE | R:HAMILTON |
| 3662 | HARRISON, Lemuel | 13 | NENE | 1853-03-07 | FD | NENE | R:FRANKLIN |
| 3650 | " " | 13 | NENE | 1853-03-07 | FD | NENE | R:FRANKLIN |
| 3687 | HEARD, Richard | 6 | E½NE | 1855-03-30 | FD | E2NE | R:HAMILTON |
| 3686 | " " | 5 | W½NW | 1855-03-30 | FD | W2NW | R:HAMILTON |
| 3697 | HIGGINS, Thomas H | 14 | SEN½ | 1857-04-15 | FD | S2NE | |
| 3721 | HOLDERLY, William | 5 | S½SW | 1854-10-06 | FD | S2SW | R:WHITE |
| 3722 | " " | 8 | NW | 1854-10-06 | FD | NW | R:WHITE |
| 3509 | HOLLADAY, Alfred V | 13 | SESW | 1854-11-10 | FD | SESW | R:HAMILTON |
| 3508 | " " | 13 | NWSE | 1854-11-10 | FD | NWSE | R:HAMILTON |
| 3581 | HOLLAND, James | 13 | NESE | 1854-03-15 | FD | NESE | R:HARDIN |
| 3674 | HUFF, Lydia | 5 | SENE | 1851-08-20 | FD | SENE | S:F |
| 3693 | HUFFSTATLER, Solomon | 10 | N½NE | 1854-10-13 | FD | N2NE | R:HAMILTON |
| 3694 | " " | 10 | SENE | 1854-10-13 | FD | SENE | R:HAMILTON |
| 3621 | IRBY, John | 4 | N½SW | 1848-10-06 | FD | N2SW | |
| 3622 | " " | 4 | NWSE | 1848-10-06 | FD | NWSE | |
| 3623 | " " | 4 | SWNE | 1848-10-06 | FD | SWNE | |
| 3624 | " " | 5 | SWNE | 1854-01-04 | FD | SWNE | R:HAMILTON |
| 3625 | " " | 9 | NWNW | 1855-08-04 | FD | NWNW | R:HAMILTON |
| 3627 | " " | 9 | SWNW | 1855-08-06 | FD | SWNW | R:HAMILTON |
| 3626 | " " | 9 | SWNE | 1855-08-06 | FD | SWNE | R:HAMILTON |
| 3683 | " " | 9 | SWNW | 1855-08-06 | FD | SWNW | R:HAMILTON |
| 3566 | IRLY, James D | 4 | S½SW | 1849-10-01 | FD | S2SW | |
| 3567 | " " | 4 | SWSE | 1849-10-01 | FD | SWSE | |
| 3568 | " " | 9 | NWNE | 1849-10-01 | FD | NWNE | |
| 3540 | JOHNS, Dabney W | 2 | NESW | 1853-08-22 | FD | NESW | R:HAMILTON |
| 3541 | " " | 2 | NWSE | 1854-03-16 | FD | NWSE | R:HAMILTON |
| 3555 | JOHNS, Granville | 1 | NESW | 1854-06-16 | FD | NESW | R:HAMILTON |
| 3570 | JOHNS, James D | 2 | NESE | 1853-02-03 | FD | NESE | |
| 3571 | " " | 2 | SENE | 1853-02-03 | FD | SENE | |
| 3569 | " " | 1 | NWSW | 1853-11-18 | FD | NWSW | R:HAMILTON |
| 3572 | " " | 2 | SESE | 1854-10-26 | FD | SESE | R:HAMILTON |
| 3667 | JOHNS, Lewis H | 12 | SWNW | 1852-05-31 | FD | SWNW | |
| 3666 | " " | 12 | NWNW | 1852-07-03 | FD | NWNW | |
| 3665 | " " | 1 | S½SW | 1853-10-14 | FD | S2SW | R:HAMILTON |

| ID | Individual in Patent | Sec. | Sec. Part | Purchase Date | Sale Type | IL Aliquot Part | For More Info . . . |
|---|---|---|---|---|---|---|---|
| 3503 | JOHNSON, Aaron | 2 | E½NW | 1853-08-26 | FD | E2NW | R:HAMILTON |
| 3504 | " " | 2 | W½NW | 1854-10-07 | FD | W2NW | R:HAMILTON |
| 3702 | JONES, John | 11 | NWSE | 1854-04-08 | SW | NWSE | |
| 3682 | " " | 11 | SWSE | 1854-04-08 | SW | SWSE | |
| 3628 | " " | 11 | NWSE | 1854-04-08 | SW | NWSE | |
| 3629 | " " | 11 | SWSE | 1854-04-08 | SW | SWSE | |
| 3675 | KELLEY, Mary Jane | 6 | SESE | 1853-09-29 | FD | SESE | R:HAMILTON S:F |
| 3698 | KELLEY, Thomas | 7 | NENW | 1853-08-04 | FD | NENW | R:HAMILTON |
| 3723 | KELLEY, William | 6 | NESW | 1853-09-02 | FD | NESW | R:HAMILTON |
| 3543 | KNIGHT, David D | 7 | SWSW | 1853-08-01 | FD | SWSW | R:HAMILTON |
| 3542 | " " | 18 | NWNW | 1854-11-25 | FD | NWNW | R:HAMILTON |
| 3582 | KNIGHT, James | 18 | SESE | 1854-11-27 | FD | SESE | R:HAMILTON |
| 3609 | KNIGHT, Jessaman J | 8 | N½SW | 1854-10-07 | FD | N2SW | R:HAMILTON |
| 3611 | " " | 8 | NWSE | 1854-10-07 | FD | NWSE | R:HAMILTON |
| 3610 | " " | 8 | NENW | 1854-10-07 | FD | NENW | R:HAMILTON |
| 3612 | " " | 8 | SENW | 1854-10-07 | FD | SENW | R:HAMILTON |
| 3613 | " " | 8 | SESW | 1854-10-07 | FD | SESW | R:HAMILTON |
| 3724 | KNIGHT, William S | 7 | SWNW | 1853-08-25 | FD | SWNW | R:HAMILTON |
| 3580 | LAMKIN, James H | 3 | SESE | 1853-12-05 | FD | SESE | R:HAMILTON |
| 3670 | LANE, Lewis | 9 | NENW | 1851-10-10 | FD | NENW | |
| 3600 | " " | 5 | NESW | 1854-10-27 | FD | NESW | R:HAMILTON |
| 3668 | " " | 5 | E½NW | 1854-10-27 | FD | E2NW | R:HAMILTON |
| 3669 | " " | 5 | NESW | 1854-10-27 | FD | NESW | R:HAMILTON |
| 3514 | LANE, William Carroll | 12 | SWSW | 1853-02-22 | FD | SWSWVOID | |
| 3712 | " " | 12 | SWSW | 1853-02-22 | FD | SWSWVOID | |
| 3713 | " " | 13 | NWNW | 1853-02-22 | FD | NWNWVOID | |
| 3515 | " " | 13 | NWNW | 1853-02-22 | FD | NWNWVOID | |
| 3563 | LANES, Jacob | 3 | NENE | 1855-11-06 | FD | NENE | R:HAMILTON |
| 3628 | LASATER, Thomas S | 11 | NWSE | 1854-10-13 | FD | NWSE | R:HAMILTON |
| 3701 | " " | 11 | E½SW | 1854-10-13 | FD | E2SW | R:HAMILTON |
| 3702 | " " | 11 | NWSE | 1854-10-13 | FD | NWSE | R:HAMILTON |
| 3533 | LASSATER, James M | 16 | L2 | 1857-04-09 | SC | LOT2NWNE | G:8 |
| 3532 | " " | 16 | L16 | 1857-04-09 | SC | LOT16SESE | G:8 |
| 3531 | " " | 16 | L15 | 1857-04-09 | SC | LOT15SWSE | G:8 |
| 3529 | " " | 16 | L13 | 1857-04-09 | SC | LOT13SWSW | G:8 |
| 3525 | " " | 16 | L1 | 1857-04-09 | SC | LOT1NENE | G:8 |
| 3528 | " " | 16 | L12 | 1857-04-09 | SC | LOT12NWSW | G:8 |
| 3527 | " " | 16 | L11 | 1857-04-09 | SC | LOT11NESW | G:8 |
| 3526 | " " | 16 | L10 | 1857-04-09 | SC | LOT10NWSE | G:8 |
| 3524 | " " | 16 | L5 | 1857-04-09 | SC | LOT5SWNW | |
| 3530 | " " | 16 | L14 | 1857-04-09 | SC | LOT14SESW | G:8 |
| 3535 | " " | 16 | L4 | 1857-04-09 | SC | LOT4NWNW | G:8 |
| 3534 | " " | 16 | L3 | 1857-04-09 | SC | LOT3NENW | G:8 |
| 3583 | " " | 16 | L5 | 1857-04-09 | SC | LOT5SWNW | |
| 3536 | " " | 16 | L6 | 1857-04-09 | SC | LOT6SENW | G:8 |
| 3537 | " " | 16 | L7 | 1857-04-09 | SC | LOT7SWNE | G:8 |
| 3539 | " " | 16 | L9 | 1857-04-09 | SC | LOT9NESE | G:8 |
| 3538 | " " | 16 | L8 | 1857-04-09 | SC | LOT8SENE | G:8 |
| 3650 | LAWS, Joseph | 13 | NENE | 1854-04-15 | FD | NENE | R:HAMILTON |
| 3662 | " " | 13 | NENE | 1854-04-15 | FD | NENE | R:HAMILTON |
| 3651 | " " | 13 | SENE | 1854-10-25 | FD | SENE | R:HAMILTON |
| 3649 | " " | 12 | SENE | 1854-10-25 | FD | SENE | R:HAMILTON |
| 3647 | " " | 12 | E½SE | 1858-02-03 | FD | E2SE | |
| 3648 | " " | 12 | E½SE | 1858-02-03 | FD | E2SE | |
| 3573 | LEWIS, James D | 3 | NESE | 1853-09-21 | FD | NESE | R:HAMILTON |
| 3605 | LEWIS, Jeremiah | 3 | SENE | 1852-04-26 | FD | SENE | |
| 3606 | LEWIS, Jeremiah T F | 11 | NE | 1849-11-19 | FD | NE | |
| 3608 | " " | 2 | SWSE | 1853-10-19 | FD | SWSE | R:HAMILTON |
| 3607 | " " | 12 | SENW | 1854-02-15 | FD | SENW | R:HAMILTON |
| 3680 | LYNCH, Matthew | 15 | S½NW | 1854-11-10 | FD | S2NW | R:HAMILTON |
| 3681 | " " | 15 | W½NE | 1854-11-10 | FD | W2NE | R:HAMILTON |
| 3556 | MARICLE, Harvey J | 13 | N½SW | 1854-11-10 | FD | N2SW | R:HAMILTON |
| 3557 | " " | 13 | SWSW | 1854-11-10 | FD | SWSW | R:HAMILTON |
| 3604 | MARTIN, Jason | 10 | SESE | 1851-02-28 | FD | SESE | R:HAMILTON |
| 3603 | " " | 10 | NESE | 1852-02-16 | FD | NESE | |
| 3507 | MCCREERY, Alexander | 17 | NWNW | 1853-11-17 | FD | NWNW | R:FRANKLIN |
| 3707 | MCDONALD, William B | 5 | N½SE | 1851-10-10 | FD | N2SE | |
| 3631 | MCFARLAND, John | 17 | E½NW | 1849-03-27 | FD | E2NW | R:HAMILTON |
| 3633 | " " | 17 | SWNW | 1853-11-28 | FD | SWNW | R:HAMILTON |
| 3632 | " " | 17 | SWNE | 1854-04-17 | FD | SWNE | R:HAMILTON |
| 3684 | MCFARLAND, Polly | 17 | SESE | 1854-11-25 | FD | SESE | R:HAMILTON S:F |
| 3653 | MELTON, Joseph | 7 | SWNE | 1854-02-17 | FD | SWNE | R:HAMILTON |
| 3652 | " " | 7 | SENE | 1854-11-25 | FD | SENE | R:HAMILTON |

| ID | Individual in Patent | Sec. | Sec. Part | Purchase Date | Sale Type | IL Aliquot Part | For More Info . . . |
|---|---|---|---|---|---|---|---|
| 3688 | MELTON, Richard | 2 | W½NE | 1851-06-21 | FD | W2NE | |
| 3510 | ODEL, Anny | 9 | NENE | 1851-07-01 | FD | NENE | R:WILLIAMSON S:F |
| 3584 | ODELL, James | 4 | SWNW | 1838-12-13 | FD | SWNW | R:HAMILTON |
| 3704 | ODELL, Uriah | 4 | | 1838-12-13 | FD | SESENT | R:HAMILTON |
| 3586 | ODLE, James | 3 | NWSW | 1849-04-12 | FD | NWSW | |
| 3590 | " " | 4 | NESE | 1849-04-12 | FD | NESE | |
| 3588 | " " | 3 | SWNW | 1849-04-12 | FD | SWNW | |
| 3591 | " " | 4 | SENE | 1849-04-12 | FD | SENE | |
| 3589 | " " | 4 | NENE | 1852-03-29 | FD | NENE | R:HAMILTON |
| 3587 | " " | 3 | SENW | 1852-05-14 | FD | SENW | R:HAMILTON |
| 3585 | " " | 3 | NWNE | 1854-04-15 | FD | NWNE | R:HAMILTON |
| 3601 | ODLE, Jarrus | 3 | NWNW | 1854-03-26 | FD | NWNW | R:HAMILTON |
| 3634 | ODLE, John | 10 | N½NW | 1852-10-02 | FD | N2NW | |
| 3636 | " " | 3 | S½SW | 1853-01-28 | FD | S2SW | |
| 3637 | " " | 9 | SENE | 1853-02-03 | FD | SENE | |
| 3635 | " " | 10 | SWNW | 1853-02-03 | FD | SWNW | |
| 3575 | ORGAN, James F | 14 | W½SE | 1852-07-14 | FD | W2SE | |
| 3574 | " " | 14 | NWSW | 1853-04-04 | FD | NWSW | |
| 3577 | PEMBERTON, James F | 2 | SWSW | 1854-02-15 | FD | SWSW | R:HAMILTON |
| 3576 | " " | 2 | NWSW | 1854-02-25 | FD | NWSW | R:HAMILTON |
| 3616 | PEMBERTON, Jesse | 12 | NWSW | 1854-02-06 | FD | NWSW | R:HAMILTON |
| 3615 | " " | 12 | NESW | 1854-02-06 | FD | NESW | R:HAMILTON |
| 3614 | " " | 11 | NESE | 1854-02-21 | FD | NESE | R:HAMILTON |
| 3657 | PEMBERTON, Joshua | 10 | SWSW | 1854-04-11 | FD | SWSW | R:SALINE |
| 3658 | " " | 14 | NENW | 1854-06-14 | FD | NENW | |
| 3659 | " " | 14 | SENW | 1854-11-14 | FD | SENW | R:HAMILTON |
| 3679 | PEMBERTON, Mathew W | 14 | N½NE | 1857-03-13 | FD | N2NE | |
| 3682 | PEMBERTON, Matthew W | 11 | SWSE | 1854-05-19 | FD | SWSE | R:HAMILTON |
| 3629 | " " | 11 | SWSE | 1854-05-19 | FD | SWSE | R:HAMILTON |
| 3700 | PEMBERTON, Thomas | 10 | SWNE | 1853-08-26 | FD | SWNE | R:HAMILTON |
| 3656 | " " | 10 | SWNE | 1853-08-26 | FD | SWNE | R:HAMILTON |
| 3564 | RECTOR, Jacob | 4 | SENW | 1852-01-06 | FD | SENW | |
| 3560 | RUMSEY, Henry | 18 | SWSE | 1837-03-25 | FD | SWSE | R:GALLATIN |
| 3638 | SACKBERGER, John | 6 | N½SW | 1854-10-14 | FD | N2SW | R:GALLATIN |
| 3639 | " " | 6 | NW | 1854-10-14 | FD | NW | R:GALLATIN |
| 3706 | SARRELLS, Walter | 18 | SWNW | 1853-03-01 | FD | SWNW | |
| 3705 | " " | 18 | NWSW | 1853-03-01 | FD | NWSW | |
| 3548 | SMITH, Elijah | 11 | NW | 1851-11-11 | FD | NW | |
| 3700 | SMITH, Joseph | 10 | SWNE | 1851-11-14 | FD | SWNE | |
| 3656 | " " | 10 | SWNE | 1851-11-14 | FD | SWNE | |
| 3654 | " " | 10 | NESW | 1851-11-14 | FD | NESW | |
| 3655 | " " | 10 | SENW | 1851-11-14 | FD | SENW | |
| 3726 | SPAIN, John A | 5 | NWSW | 1855-11-05 | FD | NWSW | R:HAMILTON |
| 3617 | " " | 5 | NWSW | 1855-11-05 | FD | NWSW | R:HAMILTON |
| 3695 | SPAIN, Stephen F | 18 | NESW | 1853-11-04 | FD | NESW | R:SALINE |
| 3703 | SPAIN, Thomas | 7 | N½NE | 1854-11-25 | FD | N2NE | R:HAMILTON |
| 3699 | SPAIN, Thomas N | 18 | SENW | 1855-03-29 | FD | SENW | R:HAMILTON |
| 3683 | SWAIN, Michael | 9 | SWNW | 1855-07-20 | FD | SWNW | R:KENTUCKY |
| 3627 | " " | 9 | SWNW | 1855-07-20 | FD | SWNW | R:KENTUCKY |
| 3544 | TATE, David | 15 | NESE | 1853-09-16 | FD | NESE | R:SALINE |
| 3545 | " " | 5 | SESE | 1854-11-14 | FD | SESE | R:HAMILTON |
| 3552 | TATE, George W | 15 | E½NE | 1849-05-02 | FD | E2NE | |
| 3551 | " " | 14 | W½NW | 1849-05-02 | FD | W2NW | |
| 3640 | TATE, John | 15 | SENW | 1854-11-10 | FD | SENW | R:SALINE |
| 3641 | " " | 15 | SWSE | 1854-11-10 | FD | SWSE | R:SALINE |
| 3642 | " " | 15 | N½NW | 1854-11-10 | FD | N2NW | R:SALINE G:38 |
| 3643 | TATE, John V | 14 | NESW | 1853-09-16 | FD | NESW | R:SALINE |
| 3644 | " " | 14 | SESE | 1853-09-16 | FD | SESE | R:SALINE |
| 3714 | TATE, William D | 10 | SESW | 1854-04-17 | FD | SESW | R:HAMILTON |
| 3715 | " " | 10 | SWSE | 1854-04-17 | FD | SWSE | R:HAMILTON |
| 3642 | " " | 15 | N½NW | 1854-11-10 | FD | N2NW | R:SALINE G:38 |
| 3672 | WALLER, Lewis | 4 | NWNE | 1853-12-13 | FD | NWNE | R:HAMILTON |
| 3671 | " " | 4 | NENW | 1853-12-13 | FD | NENW | R:HAMILTON |
| 3727 | WALLER, William | 5 | S½SE | 1854-10-05 | FD | S2SE | R:HAMILTON |
| 3726 | " " | 5 | NWSW | 1854-10-05 | FD | NWSW | R:HAMILTON |
| 3660 | " " | 5 | S½SE | 1854-10-05 | FD | S2SE | R:HAMILTON |
| 3617 | " " | 5 | NWSW | 1854-10-05 | FD | NWSW | R:HAMILTON |
| 3725 | " " | 5 | N½NE | 1854-10-05 | FD | N2NE | R:HAMILTON |
| 3676 | WHORLOW, Mary | 17 | E½NE | 1854-11-10 | FD | E2NE | R:HAMILTON S:F |
| 3677 | " " | 17 | N½SE | 1854-11-10 | FD | N2SE | R:HAMILTON S:F |
| 3678 | " " | 8 | SESE | 1854-11-10 | FD | SESE | R:HAMILTON S:F |
| 3696 | WIGGINS, Thomas A | 14 | NESE | 1854-11-14 | FD | NESE | R:HAMILTON |
| 3553 | WILLIAMS, George W | 11 | NESW | 1854-04-12 | SW | NESW | |

| ID | Individual in Patent | Sec. | Sec. Part | Purchase Date | Sale Type | IL Aliquot Part | For More Info . . . |
|------|-----------------------------|------|-------|------------|------|------|-------------|
| 3554 | WILLIAMS, George W (Cont'd) | 11 | SESW | 1854-04-12 | SW | SESW | |
| 3594 | WINN, James T | 15 | SW | 1854-11-10 | FD | SW | R:HAMILTON |
| 3593 | " " | 15 | NWSE | 1854-11-10 | FD | NWSE | R:HAMILTON |
| 3505 | WOLF, Adam A | 11 | W½SW | 1854-03-01 | FD | W2SW | R:HAMILTON |
| 3729 | WOOLSEY, Zepaniah | 1 | SESE | 1851-09-27 | FD | SESE | |

# Patent Map

### T7-S  R5-E
### 3rd PM Meridian

Map  Group  13

## Township Statistics

| | | |
|---|---|---|
| Parcels Mapped | : | 227 |
| Number of Patents | : | 1 |
| Number of Individuals | : | 124 |
| Patentees Identified | : | 123 |
| Number of Surnames | : | 86 |
| Multi-Patentee Parcels | : | 17 |
| Oldest Patent Date | : | 10/12/1832 |
| Most Recent Patent | : | 8/25/1859 |
| Block/Lot Parcels | : | 17 |
| Cities and Towns | : | 2 |
| Cemeteries | : | 2 |

Note: the area contained in this map amounts to far less than a full Township. Therefore, its contents are completely on this single page (instead of a "normal" 2-page spread).

## Legend

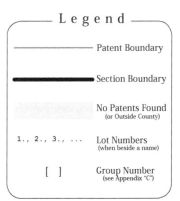

——————— Patent Boundary

——————— Section Boundary

No Patents Found
(or Outside County)

1., 2., 3., ...   Lot Numbers
(when beside a name)

[ ]   Group Number
(see Appendix "C")

**Scale**: Section = 1 mile X 1 mile
(generally, with some exceptions)

N

## Road Map

**T7-S R5-E**
**3rd PM Meridian**

Map Group 13

Note: the area contained in this map amounts to far less than a full Township. Therefore, its contents are completely on this single page (instead of a "normal" 2-page spread).

### Cities & Towns
Cornerville
University

### Cemeteries
Good Hope Cemetery
Winn Cemetery

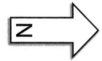

### Legend

| | |
|---|---|
| ——————— | Section Lines |
| ═══════ | Interstates |
| ━━━━━━━ | Highways |
| ————— | Other Roads |
| ● | Cities/Towns |
| ✝ | Cemeteries |

**Scale**: Section = 1 mile X 1 mile
(generally, with some exceptions)

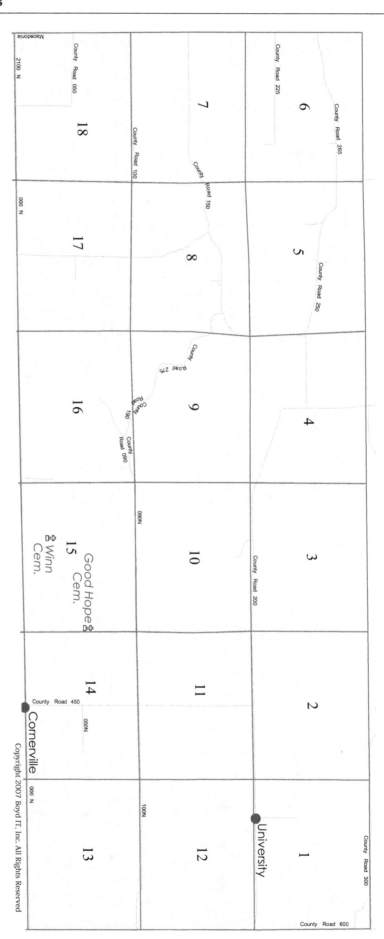

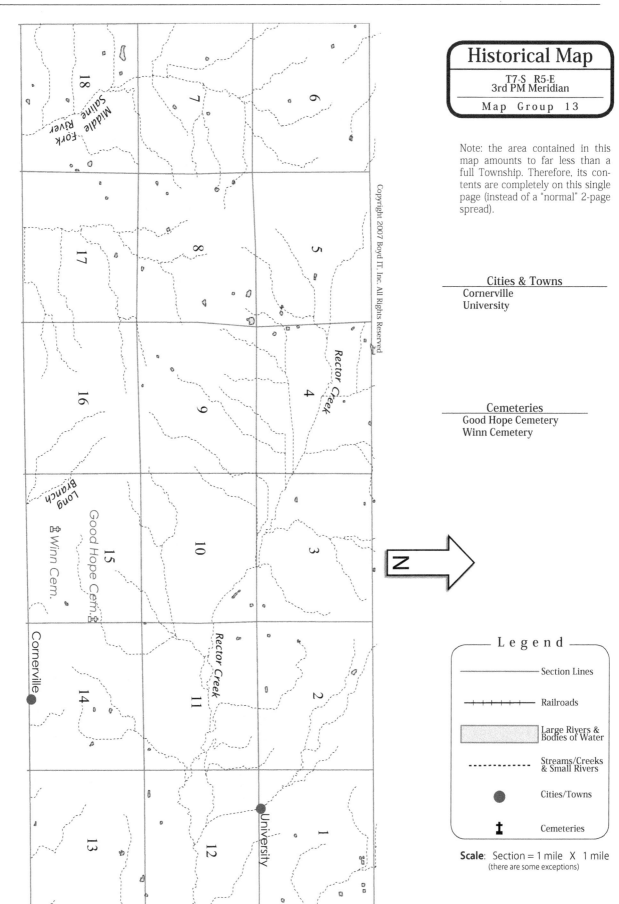

## Historical Map

T7-S R5-E
3rd PM Meridian

Map Group 13

Note: the area contained in this map amounts to far less than a full Township. Therefore, its contents are completely on this single page (instead of a "normal" 2-page spread).

### Cities & Towns
Cornerville
University

### Cemeteries
Good Hope Cemetery
Winn Cemetery

N

### Legend

Section Lines

Railroads

Large Rivers & Bodies of Water

Streams/Creeks & Small Rivers

Cities/Towns

Cemeteries

**Scale**: Section = 1 mile X 1 mile
(there are some exceptions)

## Map Group 14: Index to Land Patents

## Township 7-South Range 6-East (3rd PM)

After you locate an individual in this Index, take note of the Section and Section Part then proceed to the Land Patent map on the pages immediately following. You should have no difficulty locating the corresponding parcel of land.

The "For More Info" Column will lead you to more information about the underlying Patents. See the *Legend* at right, and the "How to Use this Book" chapter, for more information.

```
                    LEGEND
          "For More Info . . . " column
G = Group  (Multi-Patentee Patent, see Appendix "C")
R = Residence
S = Social Status

See Appendix A for list of abbreviations used by the
Illinois State Archives in describing the place and
nature of these land patents.

Note: if the Abbreviations contain "L", "BL", "LOT",
or "BLOCK", the exact whereabouts of the parcel within
the section is not known.
```

| ID | Individual in Patent | Sec. | Sec. Part | Purchase Date | Sale Type | IL Aliquot Part | For More Info . . . |
|---|---|---|---|---|---|---|---|
| 3747 | AARON, Benjamin | 18 | NWNE | 1836-07-04 | FD | NWNE | R:HAMILTON |
| 3766 | ADAMS, Elisha | 17 | NW | 1819-10-01 | FD | NW | R:KENTUCKY |
| 3767 | " " | 7 | SE | 1819-10-01 | FD | SE | R:KENTUCKY |
| 3897 | ADAMS, Nelson R | 15 | SESW | 1858-04-09 | FD | SESW | |
| 3898 | " " | 15 | W½SE | 1858-04-09 | FD | W2SE | |
| 3771 | ALLEN, Francis | 13 | SWNW | 1852-02-26 | FD | SWNW | |
| 3772 | " | 14 | SENE | 1852-02-26 | FD | SENE | |
| 3812 | ALLEN, James | 10 | E½SE | 1852-03-02 | FD | E2SE | |
| 3937 | ALLEN, William B W | 11 | SESE | 1852-03-02 | FD | SESE | R:HAMILTON |
| 3939 | " " | 11 | SWSE | 1854-06-02 | FD | SWSE | R:HAMILTON |
| 3940 | " " | 14 | NWNE | 1854-06-02 | FD | NWNE | R:HAMILTON |
| 3938 | " " | 11 | SESW | 1854-10-04 | FD | SESW | R:HAMILTON |
| 3965 | ALLEN, Wwilliam B W | 14 | NENW | 1854-10-04 | FD | NENW | R:HAMILTON |
| 3761 | BARKER, Edmund | 3 | NWNE | 1837-12-09 | FD | NWNE | R:GALLATIN |
| 3806 | BARKER, Jacob | 1 | NESW | 1833-09-30 | FD | NESW | R:HAMILTON |
| 3807 | " " | 1 | SESW | 1837-01-19 | FD | SESW | R:HAMILTON |
| 3840 | BARKER, John | 3 | E½NW | 1836-04-15 | FD | E2NW | R:HAMILTON |
| 3841 | " " | 3 | NESW | 1836-04-15 | FD | NESW | R:HAMILTON |
| 3843 | " " | 3 | W½NW | 1836-04-23 | FD | W2NW | R:HAMILTON |
| 3842 | " " | 3 | NWSW | 1836-05-07 | FD | NWSW | R:HAMILTON |
| 3837 | " " | 1 | E½NW | 1838-12-31 | FD | E2NW | R:HAMILTON |
| 3838 | " " | 1 | NWSW | 1851-04-28 | FD | NWSW | R:HAMILTON |
| 3839 | " " | 1 | SWSW | 1852-03-27 | FD | SWSW | R:HAMILTON |
| 3927 | BARKER, Thomas | 1 | W½SE | 1832-02-06 | FD | W2SE | R:HAMILTON |
| 3926 | " " | 1 | SEN½ | 1836-05-16 | FD | S2NE | R:HAMILTON |
| 3924 | " " | 1 | NESE | 1837-01-19 | FD | NESE | R:HAMILTON |
| 3925 | " " | 1 | NWNE | 1849-05-21 | FD | NWNE | R:HAMILTON |
| 3923 | " " | 1 | NENE | 1853-12-02 | FD | NENE | R:HAMILTON |
| 3825 | BLADES, James M | 6 | N½NE | 1854-09-25 | FD | N2NE | R:HAMILTON |
| 3844 | BRADEN, John | 1 | SESE | 1836-06-15 | FD | SESE | R:HAMILTON |
| 3928 | BRADEN, Thomas | 2 | NWNW | 1836-04-23 | FD | NWNW | R:HAMILTON |
| 3929 | " " | 2 | W½SW | 1838-12-27 | FD | W2SW | R:HAMILTON |
| 3882 | BRIAN, Joseph H | 9 | SENW | 1852-08-21 | FD | SENW | |
| 3881 | " " | 9 | NESW | 1852-08-21 | FD | NESW | |
| 3808 | BURNETT, Jacob | 4 | SWNW | 1837-11-21 | FD | SWNW | R:HAMILTON |
| 3911 | CANTRELL, Sampson B | 11 | NESW | 1852-10-18 | FD | NESWVOID | |
| 3912 | " " | 11 | SWNW | 1853-03-10 | FD | SWNW | R:HAMILTON |
| 3762 | COFFEE, Eli | 6 | SESW | 1853-03-04 | FD | SESW | R:HAMILTON |
| 3763 | COFFER, Eli | 7 | NWNW | 1850-11-04 | FD | NWNW | |
| 3814 | DAEN, James | 18 | SENE | 1851-06-07 | FD | SENE | R:HAMILTON |
| 3759 | DAVIS, Dicy | 10 | SENE | 1837-06-05 | FD | SENE | R:GALLATIN S:F |
| 3760 | " " | 3 | SWSE | 1837-06-05 | FD | SWSE | R:GALLATIN S:F |
| 3764 | DAVIS, Elijah | 8 | E½SE | 1854-10-04 | FD | E2SE | R:HAMILTON |
| 3817 | " " | 8 | SWSW | 1854-10-04 | FD | SWSW | R:HAMILTON |
| 3765 | " " | 8 | SWSW | 1854-10-04 | FD | SWSW | R:HAMILTON |
| 3794 | DAVIS, Henry | 11 | NWSW | 1852-10-07 | FD | NWSW | |

| ID | Individual in Patent | Sec. | Sec. Part | Purchase Date | Sale Type | IL Aliquot Part | For More Info . . . |
|---|---|---|---|---|---|---|---|
| 3795 | DAVIS, Henry (Cont'd) | 11 | SWSW | 1854-05-03 | FD | SWSW | R:HAMILTON |
| 3798 | " " | 15 | E½NE | 1854-10-04 | FD | E2NE | R:HAMILTON |
| 3796 | " " | 14 | SENW | 1854-10-04 | FD | SENW | R:HAMILTON |
| 3797 | " " | 14 | W½NW | 1854-10-04 | FD | W2NW | R:HAMILTON |
| 3815 | DAVIS, James | 9 | SWSE | 1854-02-06 | FD | SWSE | R:WILLIAMSON |
| 3850 | DAVIS, John | 10 | W½NE | 1836-05-25 | FD | W2NE | R:HAMILTON |
| 3853 | " " | 9 | SWNW | 1836-06-15 | FD | SWNW | R:HAMILTON |
| 3852 | " " | 9 | NWSW | 1836-06-15 | FD | NWSW | R:HAMILTON |
| 3851 | " " | 11 | NWNW | 1852-02-11 | FD | NWNW | R:HAMILTON |
| 3848 | " " | 10 | NENE | 1852-02-11 | FD | NENE | R:HAMILTON |
| 3849 | " " | 10 | NENW | 1853-01-26 | FD | NENW | |
| 3862 | DAVIS, John J | 11 | SENW | 1838-03-30 | FD | SENW | R:HAMILTON |
| 3865 | DAVIS, John Jr | 15 | NWNW | 1854-04-03 | FD | NWNW | R:HAMILTON |
| 3863 | " " | 15 | E½NW | 1854-10-04 | FD | E2NW | R:HAMILTON |
| 3864 | " " | 15 | N½SW | 1854-10-04 | FD | N2SW | R:HAMILTON |
| 3866 | " " | 15 | SWNW | 1854-10-04 | FD | SWNW | R:HAMILTON |
| 3885 | DAVIS, Josephus | 15 | W½NE | 1854-10-04 | FD | W2NE | R:HAMILTON |
| 3884 | " " | 10 | E½SW | 1854-10-04 | FD | E2SW | R:HAMILTON |
| 3816 | DEAN, James | 5 | SESW | 1852-09-29 | FD | SESW | |
| 3809 | DEEN, Jacob | 5 | NWSE | 1852-03-12 | FD | NWSE | R:JOHNSON |
| 3810 | " " | 8 | NWNE | 1854-01-13 | FD | NWNE | R:HAMILTON |
| 3817 | DEEN, James | 8 | SWSW | 1838-03-21 | FD | SWSW | R:HAMILTON |
| 3765 | " " | 8 | SWSW | 1838-03-21 | FD | SWSW | R:HAMILTON |
| 3942 | DEEN, William | 18 | NENE | 1835-07-27 | FD | NENE | R:GALLATIN |
| 3944 | " " | 8 | SESW | 1847-10-07 | FD | SESW | R:HAMILTON |
| 3943 | " " | 8 | NENW | 1852-10-02 | FD | NENW | |
| 3945 | " " | 8 | SWNE | 1853-02-10 | FD | SWNE | |
| 3811 | DEER, Jacob | 5 | SWSE | 1849-03-29 | FD | SWSE | R:HAMILTON |
| 3892 | DOUGLAS, Margaret | 1 | W½NW | 1852-03-24 | FD | W2NW | S:F |
| 3946 | DUN, William | 8 | SENW | 1853-11-21 | FD | SENW | R:HAMILTON |
| 3741 | DURHAM, Asahel | 15 | SWSW | 1839-09-19 | FD | SWSW | R:GALLATIN |
| 3742 | " " | 16 | L15 | 1840-12-29 | SC | LOT15 | |
| 3743 | " " | 16 | L16 | 1840-12-29 | SC | LOT16 | |
| 3854 | FENTCH, John H | 9 | NESE | 1855-04-23 | FD | NESE | R:HAMILTON |
| 3855 | FOUTCH, John H | 10 | SWSW | 1852-02-11 | FD | SWSW | |
| 3790 | GAINES, Gilson W | 12 | SENW | 1852-08-28 | FD | SENW | |
| 3745 | GHOLSON, Asberry | 4 | SWNE | 1853-01-22 | FD | SWNE | G:18 |
| 3744 | " " | 4 | SENW | 1853-01-22 | FD | SENW | G:18 |
| 3745 | GHOLSON, Ely | 4 | SWNE | 1853-01-22 | FD | SWNE | G:18 |
| 3744 | " " | 4 | SENW | 1853-01-22 | FD | SENW | G:18 |
| 3745 | GHOLSON, James T | 4 | SWNE | 1853-01-22 | FD | SWNE | G:18 |
| 3744 | " " | 4 | SENW | 1853-01-22 | FD | SENW | G:18 |
| 3744 | GHOLSON, John | 4 | SENW | 1853-01-22 | FD | SENW | G:18 |
| 3745 | " " | 4 | SWNE | 1853-01-22 | FD | SWNE | G:18 |
| 3730 | GRAVES, A D | 12 | SWSW | 1849-10-29 | FD | SWSW | S:I G:20 |
| 3732 | " " | 13 | NWNE | 1849-10-29 | FD | NWNE | S:I G:20 |
| 3731 | " " | 13 | N½NW | 1849-10-29 | FD | N2NW | S:I G:20 |
| 3776 | " " | 13 | N½NW | 1849-10-29 | FD | N2NW | S:I G:20 |
| 3777 | " " | 13 | NWNE | 1849-10-29 | FD | NWNE | S:I G:20 |
| 3737 | GRAY, Alexander | 6 | NWSW | 1854-03-04 | FD | NWSW | R:HAMILTON |
| 3735 | GRIMES, Adonijah | 13 | NENE | 1854-02-13 | FD | NENE | R:HAMILTON |
| 3736 | " " | 13 | SENE | 1854-09-19 | FD | SENE | R:HAMILTON |
| 3733 | GRIMES, Adonijah C | 13 | SWNE | 1852-03-02 | FD | SWNE | |
| 3734 | GRIMES, Adonijah D | 13 | SE | 1854-09-19 | FD | SE | R:HAMILTON |
| 3813 | GRIMES, James C | 13 | SENW | 1854-02-08 | FD | SENW | R:HAMILTON |
| 3781 | GRISWOLD, Gilbert | 4 | SW | 1818-11-09 | FD | SW | R:NEW HAMPSHIRE |
| 3784 | " " | 2 | W½NE | 1819-07-01 | FD | W2NE | G:21 |
| 3833 | " " | 2 | W½NE | 1819-07-01 | FD | W2NE | G:21 |
| 3783 | " " | 2 | E½NE | 1819-07-22 | FD | E2NE | G:21 |
| 3778 | " " | 3 | NWSE | 1836-06-01 | FD | NWSE | R:HAMILTON |
| 3779 | " " | 3 | SWNE | 1836-06-01 | FD | SWNE | R:HAMILTON |
| 3780 | " " | 4 | E½SW | 1837-12-16 | FD | E2SW | R:HAMILTON |
| 3785 | " " | 6 | SWSE | 1840-04-08 | FD | SWSE | R:HAMILTON |
| 3782 | " " | 6 | SWSE | 1840-04-08 | FD | SWSE | R:HAMILTON |
| 3782 | GRISWOLD, Gilbert Jr | 6 | SWSE | 1853-01-28 | FD | SWSE | |
| 3786 | " " | 7 | NWNE | 1853-01-28 | FD | NWNE | |
| 3785 | " " | 6 | SWSE | 1853-01-28 | FD | SWSE | |
| 3788 | " " | 7 | SEN½ | 1854-10-03 | FD | S2NE | R:JOHNSON |
| 3787 | " " | 7 | S½NW | 1854-10-03 | FD | S2NW | R:JOHNSON |
| 3789 | GRISWOLD, Gilbert Sen | 4 | SWSE | 1851-05-17 | FD | SWSE | R:HAMILTON |
| 3919 | GRISWOLD, Sarah | 4 | NWNE | 1855-11-03 | FD | NWNE | R:GALLATIN S:F |
| 3933 | GRISWOLD, Thomas S | 5 | SESE | 1839-11-18 | FD | SESE | R:HAMILTON |
| 3935 | GRISWOLD, Thomas Sloo | 4 | SENE | 1853-05-17 | FD | SENE | R:HAMILTON |

| ID | Individual in Patent | Sec. | Sec. Part | Purchase Date | Sale Type | IL Aliquot Part | For More Info . . . |
|---|---|---|---|---|---|---|---|
| 3936 | GRISWOLD, Tilitha | 4 | NWSE | 1854-02-02 | FD | NWSE | R:HAMILTON |
| 3900 | HALL, Polly | 10 | NWSW | 1853-01-22 | FD | NWSW | S:F |
| 3901 | "         " | 10 | W½NW | 1853-01-22 | FD | W2NW | S:F |
| 3902 | "         " | 3 | SWSW | 1853-01-22 | FD | SWSW | S:F |
| 3913 | HALL, Samuel L | 9 | NE | 1852-08-14 | FD | NE | |
| 3915 | "         " | 9 | NWSE | 1853-10-18 | FD | NWSE | R:HAMILTON |
| 3914 | "         " | 9 | NENW | 1854-01-17 | FD | NENW | R:HAMILTON |
| 3922 | HALL, Terry | 11 | SEN½ | 1849-10-11 | FD | S2NE | |
| 3921 | "         " | 11 | N½SE | 1849-10-11 | FD | N2SE | |
| 3799 | HARDESTER, Henry | 12 | NESW | 1836-11-02 | FD | NESW | R:HAMILTON |
| 3896 | HARDISBY, Nancy | 12 | NESE | 1845-07-19 | FD | NESE | R:HAMILTON S:F |
| 3753 | HARDISTY, Christopher | 10 | W½SE | 1852-02-14 | FD | W2SE | |
| 3754 | "         " | 12 | SESE | 1853-01-28 | FD | SESE | |
| 3800 | HARDISTY, Henry | 14 | NENE | 1853-03-07 | FD | NENE | |
| 3755 | HARISTY, Christopher | 12 | NWSE | 1846-01-09 | FD | NWSE | R:HAMILTON |
| 3751 | HARTESTER, Christophe | 12 | SESW | 1832-10-20 | FD | SESW | R:HAMILTON |
| 3752 | "         " | 12 | SWSE | 1832-10-20 | FD | SWSE | R:HAMILTON |
| 3732 | HARVESTER, Henry | 13 | NWNE | 1849-10-29 | FD | NWNE | S:I G:20 |
| 3776 | "         " | 13 | N½NW | 1849-10-29 | FD | N2NW | S:I G:20 |
| 3730 | "         " | 12 | SWSW | 1849-10-29 | FD | SWSW | S:I G:20 |
| 3777 | "         " | 13 | NWNE | 1849-10-29 | FD | NWNE | S:I G:20 |
| 3731 | "         " | 13 | N½NW | 1849-10-29 | FD | N2NW | S:I G:20 |
| 3920 | HENSON, Susannah | 4 | NESE | 1839-10-16 | FD | NESE | R:HAMILTON S:F |
| 3773 | HICKS, George | 4 | NENW | 1854-10-25 | FD | NENW | R:HAMILTON |
| 3952 | HINSON, William | 2 | NENE | 1836-07-25 | FD | NENE | R:HAMILTON |
| 3784 | HOGG, Samuel | 2 | W½NE | 1819-07-01 | FD | W2NE | G:21 |
| 3833 | "         " | 2 | W½NE | 1819-07-01 | FD | W2NE | G:21 |
| 3783 | "         " | 2 | E½NE | 1819-07-22 | FD | E2NE | G:21 |
| 3818 | HOLLAND, James | 18 | NWSW | 1852-04-02 | FD | NWSW | |
| 3803 | JONES, Hezekiah R | 8 | NWNW | 1851-02-05 | FD | NWNW | R:HAMILTON |
| 3804 | "         " | 8 | SWNW | 1853-02-07 | FD | SWNWVOID | |
| 3802 | "         " | 7 | NENE | 1853-02-07 | FD | NENE | |
| 3805 | KANE, Hugh | 16 | L13 | 1851-10-21 | SC | LOT13SWSW | |
| 3750 | LANE, Charles | 17 | NESE | 1854-01-17 | FD | NESE | R:HAMILTON |
| 3757 | LANE, Dabney | 17 | E½NW | 1836-06-15 | FD | E2NW | R:HAMILTON |
| 3739 | LANE, James | 18 | SWSE | 1848-12-29 | FD | SWSE | R:SALINE |
| 3822 | "         " | 18 | SWSE | 1848-12-29 | FD | SWSE | R:SALINE |
| 3823 | "         " | 7 | SWSW | 1851-07-26 | FD | SWSW | |
| 3821 | "         " | 17 | SENE | 1854-02-23 | FD | SENE | R:HAMILTON |
| 3869 | LANE, John | 8 | SWSE | 1850-04-15 | FD | SWSE | R:HAMILTON |
| 3868 | "         " | 17 | NWSE | 1851-01-24 | FD | NWSE | R:HAMILTON |
| 3867 | "         " | 17 | NENE | 1853-02-10 | FD | NENE | |
| 3857 | LANE, John H | 8 | N½SW | 1853-02-01 | FD | N2SW | |
| 3856 | "         " | 17 | SESE | 1855-11-06 | FD | SESE | R:HAMILTON |
| 3860 | LANE, John Henry | 17 | NWSW | 1851-01-07 | FD | NWSW | R:HAMILTON |
| 3861 | "         " | 18 | SESE | 1852-03-05 | FD | SESE | R:SALINE |
| 3890 | LANE, Lewis | 7 | SESE | 1833-05-21 | FD | SESE | R:HAMILTON |
| 3888 | "         " | 17 | W½NE | 1835-12-12 | FD | W2NE | R:HAMILTON |
| 3891 | "         " | 7 | SWSE | 1835-12-22 | FD | SWSE | R:HAMILTON |
| 3889 | "         " | 17 | W½NW | 1836-02-04 | FD | W2NW | R:HAMILTON |
| 3886 | "         " | 16 | L2 | 1839-07-20 | SC | L2 | |
| 3887 | "         " | 16 | L7 | 1839-07-20 | SC | L7 | |
| 3931 | LANE, Thomas | 18 | E½SW | 1840-06-15 | FD | E2SW | R:GALLATIN |
| 3932 | "         " | 18 | SWSW | 1854-09-26 | FD | SWSW | R:HAMILTON |
| 3930 | "         " | 13 | SESE | 1854-09-26 | FD | SESE | R:HAMILTON |
| 3801 | LASSWELL, Henry | 5 | W½NW | 1851-08-13 | FD | W2NW | |
| 3748 | LASWELL, Benjamin F | 6 | SENE | 1853-10-08 | FD | SENE | R:HAMILTON |
| 3836 | LAWS, Joel | 5 | NWSW | 1853-12-23 | FD | NWSW | R:HAMILTON |
| 3819 | LEWIS, James J | 18 | NENW | 1853-10-11 | FD | NENW | R:HAMILTON |
| 3820 | LEWIS, James Jackson | 18 | SENW | 1849-11-19 | FD | SENW | R:HAMILTON |
| 3893 | LEWIS, Momy V | 6 | NESW | 1853-10-11 | FD | NESW | R:HAMILTON |
| 3895 | LEWIS, Moury Vickers | 6 | W½NW | 1851-02-17 | FD | W2NW | R:HAMILTON |
| 3894 | "         " | 6 | SENW | 1853-03-26 | FD | SENW | R:HAMILTON |
| 3941 | LITTLE, William Clay | 18 | NESE | 1851-01-09 | FD | NESE | R:SALINE |
| 3962 | LITTLE, Willis | 16 | L9 | 1839-07-20 | SC | L9 | |
| 3961 | "         " | 16 | L4 | 1839-07-20 | SC | L4 | |
| 3960 | "         " | 16 | L3 | 1839-07-20 | SC | L3 | |
| 3959 | "         " | 16 | L10 | 1839-07-20 | SC | LOT10 | |
| 3963 | "         " | 16 | L5 | 1841-07-21 | SC | L5 | |
| 3964 | "         " | 16 | L14 | 1843-07-21 | SC | LOT14 | |
| 3872 | LOCKHART, John | 5 | W½NE | 1830-12-18 | FD | W2NE | R:HAMILTON |
| 3870 | "         " | 5 | NENE | 1836-06-17 | FD | NENE | R:HAMILTON |
| 3871 | "         " | 5 | SENE | 1839-06-08 | FD | SENE | R:HAMILTON |

| ID | Individual in Patent | Sec. | Sec. Part | Purchase Date | Sale Type | IL Aliquot Part | For More Info . . . |
|---|---|---|---|---|---|---|---|
| 3824 | LONE, James | 7 | SESW | 1849-09-19 | FD | SESW | R:HAMILTON |
| 3770 | MARTIN, Enoch Jr | 9 | SESW | 1839-07-26 | FD | SESW | R:HAMILTON |
| 3758 | MAUG, Dennis | 14 | E½SW | 1858-03-29 | FD | E2SW | |
| 3883 | MCCOMB, Joseph | 6 | NENW | 1853-02-22 | FD | NENW | R:GEORGIA |
| 3858 | MCGILL, John H | 3 | SESE | 1851-01-15 | FD | SESE | R:HAMILTON |
| 3910 | MCGILL, Robert | 3 | SESW | 1852-10-01 | FD | SESW | |
| 3774 | MOTT, George W | 18 | NWNW | 1850-04-15 | FD | NWNW | R:HAMILTON |
| 3775 | "         " | 18 | SWNW | 1851-09-03 | FD | SWNW | R:HAMILTON |
| 3908 | OGDEN, Rensler B | 7 | NWSW | 1853-04-01 | FD | NWSW | R:HAMILTON |
| 3907 | "         " | 7 | NESW | 1853-04-22 | FD | NESW | R:HAMILTON |
| 3909 | OGDON, Rensler B | 7 | N½SE | 1841-11-03 | FD | N2SE | R:PHILADELPHIA |
| 3749 | OHUMACHT, Bernhard | 14 | SEN½ | 1858-03-29 | FD | S2NE | |
| 3740 | PATRIDGE, Ariel | 4 | SESE | 1839-10-10 | FD | SESE | R:HAMILTON |
| 3949 | PATTON, Zadoc C | 16 | L1 | 1852-03-08 | SC | LOT1NENE | |
| 3966 | "         " | 16 | L1 | 1852-03-08 | SC | LOT1NENE | |
| 3791 | PENNINGTON, Harvey D | 13 | NESW | 1854-02-17 | FD | NESW | R:HAMILTON |
| 3792 | "         " | 13 | W½SW | 1854-10-04 | FD | W2SW | R:HAMILTON |
| 3793 | PENNINGTON, Henry D | 13 | SESW | 1853-12-13 | FD | SESW | |
| 3756 | PORTER, Clemence H | 2 | SESE | 1850-07-20 | FD | SESE | R:HAMILTON |
| 3739 | PRYOR, Anderson | 18 | SWSE | 1833-07-06 | FD | SWSE | R:HAMILTON |
| 3822 | "         " | 18 | SWSE | 1833-07-06 | FD | SWSE | R:HAMILTON |
| 3738 | "         " | 18 | NWSE | 1837-12-27 | FD | NWSE | R:HAMILTON |
| 3953 | PULLIAM, William P | 17 | NESW | 1851-01-07 | FD | NESW | R:SALINE |
| 3954 | "         " | 17 | S½SW | 1851-07-26 | FD | S2SW | |
| 3955 | PULLIAN, William P | 16 | L12 | 1851-10-15 | SC | LOT12NWSW | |
| 3847 | RICHESON, John D | 7 | NENW | 1853-02-07 | FD | NENW | |
| 3916 | RITCHEY, Samuel M | 6 | SESE | 1853-12-21 | FD | SESE | R:HAMILTON |
| 3918 | RITCHY, Samuel M | 5 | SWSW | 1854-10-03 | FD | SWSW | R:HAMILTON |
| 3917 | "         " | 5 | NESE | 1854-10-03 | FD | NESE | R:HAMILTON |
| 3958 | "         " | 5 | NESE | 1854-10-03 | FD | NESE | R:HAMILTON |
| 3732 | RIVES, George W | 13 | NWNE | 1858-07-06 | FD | NWNE | G:33 |
| 3777 | "         " | 13 | NWNE | 1858-07-06 | FD | NWNE | G:33 |
| 3731 | "         " | 13 | N½NW | 1858-07-06 | FD | N2NW | G:33 |
| 3776 | "         " | 13 | N½NW | 1858-07-06 | FD | N2NW | G:33 |
| 3906 | ROBERTS, Reason D | 12 | SWNW | 1851-01-25 | FD | SWNW | R:HAMILTON |
| 3904 | "         " | 12 | NWNW | 1852-05-22 | FD | NWNW | R:HAMILTON |
| 3905 | "         " | 12 | NWSW | 1852-09-11 | FD | NWSW | |
| 3949 | ROBERTS, William H | 16 | L1 | 1851-10-15 | SC | LOT1NENE | |
| 3950 | "         " | 16 | L8 | 1851-10-15 | SC | LOT8SENE | |
| 3966 | "         " | 16 | L1 | 1851-10-15 | SC | LOT1NENE | |
| 3951 | "         " | 9 | SESE | 1853-03-07 | FD | SESE | |
| 3947 | "         " | 14 | N½SE | 1854-10-04 | FD | N2SE | R:HAMILTON |
| 3948 | "         " | 14 | SWNE | 1854-10-04 | FD | SWNE | R:HAMILTON |
| 3768 | SANDERS, Elisha | 3 | NESE | 1836-07-09 | FD | NESE | R:HAMILTON |
| 3769 | "         " | 3 | SENE | 1837-05-22 | FD | SENE | R:HAMILTON |
| 3876 | SCHOOLCRAFT, John | 12 | E½NE | 1836-04-15 | FD | E2NE | R:HAMILTON |
| 3877 | "         " | 12 | NENW | 1837-07-01 | FD | NENW | R:HAMILTON |
| 3934 | SCOTT, Thomas | 5 | E½NW | 1855-08-13 | FD | E2NW | R:HAMILTON |
| 3874 | SHASTEEN, John Rennet | 2 | SWNW | 1848-12-15 | FD | SWNW | R:HAMILTON |
| 3875 | "         " | 3 | NENE | 1848-12-15 | FD | NENE | R:HAMILTON |
| 3746 | SMITH, Augusta | 4 | NENE | 1855-03-27 | FD | NENE | R:HAMILTON |
| 3879 | SMITH, John | 16 | L6 | 1851-10-15 | SC | LOT6SENW | |
| 3878 | "         " | 16 | L11 | 1851-10-15 | SC | LOT11NESW | |
| 3776 | SMITH, John A | 13 | N½NW | 1858-07-06 | FD | N2NW | G:33 |
| 3732 | "         " | 13 | NWNE | 1858-07-06 | FD | NWNE | G:33 |
| 3731 | "         " | 13 | N½NW | 1858-07-06 | FD | N2NW | G:33 |
| 3777 | "         " | 13 | NWNE | 1858-07-06 | FD | NWNE | G:33 |
| 3846 | SMITH, John C | 15 | E½SE | 1858-04-09 | FD | E2SEVOID | |
| 3845 | "         " | 14 | W½SW | 1858-04-09 | FD | W2SWVOID | |
| 3859 | SMITH, John H | 10 | SENW | 1851-09-02 | FD | SENW | |
| 3873 | SMITH, John R | 4 | NWNW | 1853-08-03 | FD | NWNW | R:HAMILTON |
| 3903 | SMITH, Randolph | 9 | SW | 1818-11-23 | FD | SW | R:WHITE |
| 3956 | SULLIVAN, William P | 17 | SWSE | 1855-03-29 | FD | SWSE | R:SALINE |
| 3899 | SWEET, Peleg | 8 | NE | 1820-01-05 | FD | NE | R:WHITE |
| 3957 | SWEETEN, William | 17 | SW | 1819-11-03 | FD | SW | R:WHITE |
| 3826 | TICKNER, James P | 9 | NWNW | 1839-08-27 | FD | NWNW | R:HAMILTON |
| 3833 | TWIGG, James | 2 | W½NE | 1836-05-28 | FD | W2NE | R:HAMILTON |
| 3784 | "         " | 2 | W½NE | 1836-05-28 | FD | W2NE | R:HAMILTON |
| 3830 | "         " | 2 | NESE | 1837-01-21 | FD | NESE | R:HAMILTON |
| 3829 | "         " | 2 | NENW | 1837-01-21 | FD | NENW | R:HAMILTON |
| 3831 | "         " | 2 | SENE | 1839-06-20 | FD | SENE | R:HAMILTON |
| 3834 | "         " | 2 | W½SE | 1839-06-20 | FD | W2SE | R:HAMILTON |
| 3827 | "         " | 11 | NENW | 1850-06-18 | FD | NENW | |

| ID | Individual in Patent | Sec. | Sec. Part | Purchase Date | Sale Type | IL Aliquot Part | For More Info . . . |
|---|---|---|---|---|---|---|---|
| 3828 | TWIGG, James (Cont'd) | 2 | E½SW | 1850-06-18 | FD | E2SW | |
| 3832 | "            " | 2 | SENW | 1850-06-18 | FD | SENW | |
| 3835 | TWIGGS, James | 11 | N½NE | 1852-09-07 | FD | N2NE | |
| 3917 | WILLIAMS, William | 5 | NESE | 1847-04-05 | FD | NESE | R:HAMILTON |
| 3958 | "            " | 5 | NESE | 1847-04-05 | FD | NESE | R:HAMILTON |
| 3880 | WILSON, John | 12 | NE | 1819-03-01 | FD | NE | R:WHITE |
| 3967 | WOOLSEY, Zepaniah | 6 | SWSW | 1851-09-27 | FD | SWSW | |

## Patent Map

**T7-S R6-E**
**3rd PM Meridian**

Map Group 14

## Township Statistics

| | | |
|---|---|---|
| Parcels Mapped | : | 238 |
| Number of Patents | : | 1 |
| Number of Individuals | : | 135 |
| Patentees Identified | : | 130 |
| Number of Surnames | : | 83 |
| Multi-Patentee Parcels | : | 9 |
| Oldest Patent Date | : | 11/9/1818 |
| Most Recent Patent | : | 7/6/1858 |
| Block/Lot Parcels | : | 17 |
| Cities and Towns | : | 1 |
| Cemeteries | : | 2 |

Note: the area contained in this map amounts to far less than a full Township. Therefore, its contents are completely on this single page (instead of a "normal" 2-page spread).

Copyright 2007 Boyd IT, Inc. All Rights Reserved

## Legend

——— Patent Boundary

▬▬▬ Section Boundary

No Patents Found (or Outside County)

1., 2., 3., ... Lot Numbers (when beside a name)

[ ] Group Number (see Appendix "C")

**Scale**: Section = 1 mile X 1 mile (generally, with some exceptions)

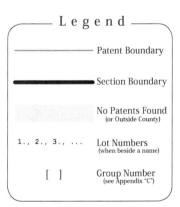

N

197

## Road Map

### T7-S  R6-E
### 3rd PM Meridian

Map Group 14

Note: the area contained in this map amounts to far less than a full Township. Therefore, its contents are completely on this single page (instead of a "normal" 2-page spread).

### Cities & Towns
Walpole

### Cemeteries
Barker Cemetery
Roberts Cemetery

### Legend

| | |
|---|---|
| ——————— | Section Lines |
| ══════════ | Interstates |
| ━━━━━━━━ | Highways |
| ——————— | Other Roads |
| ● | Cities/Towns |
| ⚱ | Cemeteries |

**Scale**: Section = 1 mile X 1 mile
(generally, with some exceptions)

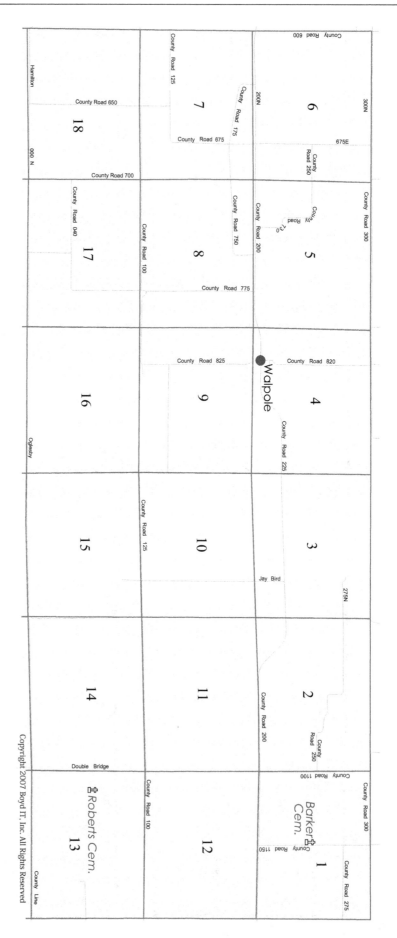

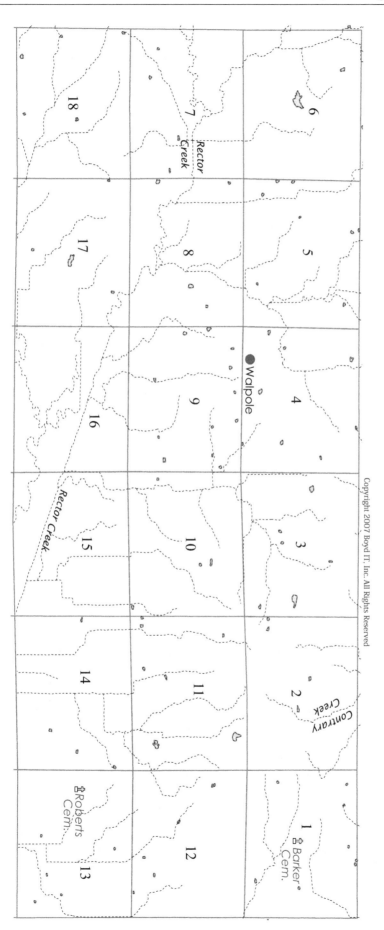

## Historical Map

**T7-S  R6-E**
**3rd PM Meridian**

Map Group 14

Note: the area contained in this map amounts to far less than a full Township. Therefore, its contents are completely on this single page (instead of a "normal" 2-page spread).

### Cities & Towns
Walpole

### Cemeteries
Barker Cemetery
Roberts Cemetery

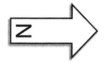

### Legend

— Section Lines

+++++ Railroads

▭ Large Rivers & Bodies of Water

- - - - Streams/Creeks & Small Rivers

● Cities/Towns

✝ Cemeteries

**Scale**: Section = 1 mile  X  1 mile
(there are some exceptions)

## Map Group 15: Index to Land Patents

## Township 7-South Range 7-East (3rd PM)

After you locate an individual in this Index, take note of the Section and Section Part then proceed to the Land Patent map on the pages immediately following. You should have no difficulty locating the corresponding parcel of land.

The "For More Info" Column will lead you to more information about the underlying Patents. See the *Legend* at right, and the "How to Use this Book" chapter, for more information.

```
                    LEGEND
            "For More Info . . . " column
G = Group (Multi-Patentee Patent, see Appendix "C")
R = Residence
S = Social Status


See Appendix A for list of abbreviations used by the
Illinois State Archives in describing the place and
nature of these land patents.

Note: if the Abbreviations contain "L", "BL", "LOT",
or "BLOCK", the exact whereabouts of the parcel within
the section is not known.
```

| ID | Individual in Patent | Sec. | Sec. Part | Purchase Date | Sale Type | IL Aliquot Part | For More Info . . . |
|----|---------------------|------|-----------|---------------|-----------|-----------------|---------------------|
| 4107 | ALDEN, Royal | 16 | L12 | 1849-07-09 | SC | L12NWSW | |
| 4108 | " " | 16 | L13 | 1849-07-09 | SC | LOT13SWSW | |
| 4034 | ALLEN, James | 7 | NWNE | 1852-02-18 | FD | NWNE | |
| 4090 | ALLEN, Malina | 7 | SWNE | 1836-04-18 | FD | SWNE | R:HAMILTON S:F |
| 4113 | ALLEN, Thomas Hart B | 7 | SENW | 1837-04-10 | FD | SENW | R:HAMILTON |
| 4131 | ALLEN, Zachariah | 17 | E½SE | 1837-04-21 | FD | E2SE | R:GALLATIN |
| 4003 | BARKER, David | 7 | NENW | 1852-10-26 | FD | NENW | |
| 4033 | BARKER, Jacob | 6 | SESW | 1851-12-22 | FD | SESW | R:HAMILTON |
| 4111 | BARKER, Thomas | 6 | NWSW | 1849-11-05 | FD | NWSW | R:HAMILTON |
| 4112 | " " | 6 | SWNW | 1855-04-02 | FD | SWNW | R:HAMILTON |
| 4021 | BELL, Franklin | 1 | NENW | 1845-09-25 | FD | NENW | R:HAMILTON |
| 4056 | BRADEN, John | 6 | SWSW | 1837-05-02 | FD | SWSW | R:HAMILTON |
| 3984 | CARPENTER, Chester | 18 | SWSW | 1858-01-08 | FD | SWSW | |
| 4089 | CLEAVELAND, Macajah | 15 | NWNW | 1854-04-03 | FD | NWNW | R:HAMILTON |
| 4060 | COOK, John | 1 | W½NE | 1829-05-05 | FD | W2NE | R:HAMILTON |
| 4057 | " " | 1 | SENE | 1836-12-12 | FD | SENE | R:HAMILTON |
| 4058 | " " | 1 | SENW | 1848-01-05 | FD | SENW | R:HAMILTON |
| 4059 | " " | 1 | SWNW | 1853-12-07 | FD | SWNW | R:HAMILTON |
| 4071 | COOK, John Jr | 1 | NENE | 1850-01-21 | FD | NENE | R:HAMILTON |
| 3983 | DAVIS, Catharine | 1 | NWSE | 1842-01-06 | FD | NWSE | R:HAMILTON S:F |
| 4047 | DAVIS, James Stedman | 12 | NENE | 1849-02-24 | FD | NENE | R:HAMILTON |
| 4074 | DAVIS, John Sledmun | 1 | E½SE | 1842-01-06 | FD | E2SE | R:HAMILTON |
| 4075 | DAVIS, John Stidman | 12 | SENE | 1837-01-07 | FD | SENE | R:HAMILTON |
| 4076 | DAVIS, John Stidmun | 12 | E½SW | 1836-01-14 | FD | E2SW | R:HAMILTON |
| 4061 | DOUGLAS, John | 17 | E½NW | 1826-06-09 | FD | E2NW | R:GALLATIN |
| 3989 | DOUGLASS, Daniel D | 7 | W½SE | 1836-04-08 | FD | W2SE | R:PUTNAM |
| 3988 | " " | 17 | W½NE | 1836-04-08 | FD | W2NE | R:PUTNAM |
| 4035 | DOUGLASS, James | 17 | NWSW | 1836-04-05 | FD | NWSW | R:HAMILTON |
| 4036 | " " | 17 | W½NW | 1836-04-05 | FD | W2NW | R:HAMILTON |
| 4038 | " " | 8 | SWNW | 1836-04-14 | FD | SWNW | R:GALLATIN |
| 4037 | " " | 7 | E½NE | 1837-03-27 | FD | E2NE | R:HAMILTON |
| 4063 | DOUGLASS, John | 8 | W½SW | 1827-05-15 | FD | W2SW | R:GALLATIN |
| 4062 | " " | 7 | E½SE | 1828-08-01 | FD | E2SE | R:GALLATIN |
| 4079 | EDWARDS, John Y C | 4 | NWNW | 1853-01-25 | FD | NWNW | |
| 4130 | FORD, Woodley | 3 | NESE | 1851-12-04 | FD | NESE | R:HAMILTON |
| 4064 | GEORGE, John | 13 | E½SE | 1827-08-28 | FD | E2SE | R:HAMILTON |
| 4091 | GHOLSEN, Marine F | 18 | NESW | 1854-09-21 | FD | NESW | R:HAMILTON |
| 4092 | " " | 18 | SWNE | 1854-09-21 | FD | SWNE | R:HAMILTON |
| 4018 | GHOLSON, Eli | 16 | W½NW | 1838-08-04 | SC | W2NW | |
| 4019 | GHOLSON, Ely | 17 | NE | 1836-04-18 | FD | NE | R:HAMILTON |
| 4039 | GHOLSON, James | 16 | E½NW | 1838-08-04 | SC | E2NW | |
| 4093 | GHOLSON, Marine F | 18 | NENW | 1854-02-08 | FD | NENW | R:HAMILTON |
| 4095 | GHOLSON, Marnie F | 18 | SENW | 1854-02-13 | FD | SENW | R:HAMILTON |
| 4099 | GHOLSON, Milton | 8 | SENW | 1837-03-21 | FD | SENW | R:HAMILTON |
| 4098 | " " | 10 | SWSW | 1838-02-14 | FD | SWSW | R:HAMILTON |
| 4102 | GHOLSON, Nathaniel | 16 | W½SE | 1838-08-04 | SC | W2SE | |

| ID | Individual in Patent | Sec. | Sec. Part | Purchase Date | Sale Type | IL Aliquot Part | For More Info . . . |
|----|----------------------|------|-----------|---------------|-----------|-----------------|---------------------|
| 4101 | GHOLSON, Nathaniel (Cont'd) | 16 | NENE | 1838-08-04 | SC | NENE | |
| 4122 | GHOLSON, Wesley W | 16 | E½SW | 1838-08-04 | SC | E2SW | |
| 4123 | GHOLSON, William | 7 | NESW | 1836-04-11 | FD | NESW | R:HAMILTON |
| 3974 | GIBSON, Amos | 15 | NWNE | 1854-04-03 | FD | NWNE | R:HAMILTON |
| 3993 | GIBSON, Daniel | 2 | SENW | 1848-07-07 | FD | SENW | |
| 3996 | " " | 2 | W½SW | 1848-07-07 | FD | W2SW | |
| 3991 | " " | 2 | NESW | 1848-07-07 | FD | NESW | |
| 3995 | " " | 2 | W½SW | 1848-07-07 | FD | W2SW | |
| 3994 | " " | 2 | SENW | 1848-07-07 | FD | SENW | |
| 3992 | " " | 2 | NESW | 1848-07-07 | FD | NESW | |
| 3991 | " " | 2 | NESW | 1849-03-30 | FD | NESW | |
| 3992 | " " | 2 | NESW | 1849-03-30 | FD | NESW | |
| 3994 | " " | 2 | SENW | 1849-03-30 | FD | SENW | |
| 3995 | " " | 2 | W½SW | 1849-03-30 | FD | W2SW | |
| 3996 | " " | 2 | W½SW | 1849-03-30 | FD | W2SW | |
| 3993 | " " | 2 | SENW | 1849-03-30 | FD | SENW | |
| 4048 | GIBSON, James W | 15 | NENW | 1854-04-03 | FD | NENW | R:HAMILTON |
| 4049 | " " | 15 | SWNE | 1855-04-13 | FD | SWNE | R:HAMILTON |
| 4106 | GIBSON, Robert | 2 | SESW | 1836-04-18 | FD | SESW | R:HAMILTON |
| 4020 | GREGG, Francis | 14 | E½SE | 1836-04-18 | FD | E2SE | R:GALLATIN |
| 4030 | GREGG, Hugh | 17 | NESW | 1836-04-18 | FD | NESW | R:HAMILTON |
| 4031 | " " | 17 | W½SE | 1837-03-27 | FD | W2SE | R:HAMILTON |
| 3972 | GRIMES, Adonijah | 18 | SWNW | 1854-09-19 | FD | SWNW | R:HAMILTON |
| 4066 | HADLEY, John | 1 | NESW | 1853-10-15 | FD | NESW | R:HAMILTON |
| 4097 | HALEY, Meeks | 6 | W½SE | 1851-06-27 | FD | W2SE | R:GALLATIN |
| 4042 | HARDESTY, James | 2 | NENW | 1836-07-08 | FD | NENW | R:HAMILTON |
| 4126 | HARDESTY, William | 2 | NWNE | 1836-01-27 | FD | NWNE | R:HAMILTON |
| 3986 | HARDISTY, Christopher | 7 | NWSW | 1853-01-28 | FD | NWSW | |
| 3985 | " " | 11 | SWSW | 1853-11-11 | FD | SWSW | R:HAMILTON |
| 4029 | HARDISTY, Henry | 7 | SWSW | 1854-02-13 | FD | SWSW | R:HAMILTON |
| 4051 | HARDISTY, Jesse B | 11 | SENE | 1848-10-21 | FD | SENE | R:HAMILTON |
| 4124 | HARDISTY, William H | 2 | NENE | 1854-01-04 | FD | NENE | R:HAMILTON |
| 4114 | HOLLOWAY, Thomas | 2 | SE | 1829-04-30 | FD | SE | R:HAMILTON |
| 3976 | HOOD, Anderson | 16 | L9 | 1849-07-09 | SC | LOT9NESE | |
| 3975 | " " | 15 | N½SW | 1855-05-17 | FD | N2SW | R:HAMILTON |
| 3981 | HOOD, Benjamin | 16 | L1 | 1849-07-09 | SC | LOT1NENE | |
| 3982 | " " | 16 | L8 | 1849-07-09 | SC | LOT8SENE | |
| 3980 | " " | 15 | SENW | 1855-06-12 | FD | SENW | R:HAMILTON |
| 4127 | HOOD, William | 16 | L10 | 1849-07-09 | SC | LOT10NWSE | |
| 4080 | HOWARD, Joseph | 2 | SWNE | 1852-03-23 | FD | SWNE | |
| 4070 | JOHNSON, John J | 3 | SESE | 1853-02-21 | FD | SESE | R:HAMILTON |
| 4069 | " " | 11 | NWSW | 1853-03-02 | FD | NWSW | |
| 4067 | " " | 10 | NESE | 1853-03-02 | FD | NESE | |
| 4068 | " " | 10 | SESE | 1854-03-31 | FD | SESE | R:HAMILTON |
| 4105 | JOHNSON, Robert A | 18 | NWNE | 1854-02-13 | FD | NWNE | R:HAMILTON |
| 3987 | KEASLER, Clauinda | 13 | SESW | 1853-07-13 | FD | SESW | R:HAMILTON S:F |
| 4005 | KEASLER, David | 14 | W½NE | 1837-11-28 | FD | W2NE | R:HAMILTON |
| 4004 | " " | 14 | SENE | 1854-01-03 | FD | SENE | R:HAMILTON |
| 3971 | KEENEY, Abel | 15 | SENE | 1856-06-27 | FD | SENE | |
| 3970 | " " | 15 | N½SE | 1856-06-27 | FD | N2SE | |
| 4012 | KESLER, David | 13 | W½NE | 1833-12-11 | FD | W2NE | R:HAMILTON |
| 4013 | " " | 13 | W½SE | 1836-04-08 | FD | W2SE | R:HAMILTON |
| 4009 | " " | 12 | W½NE | 1836-04-22 | FD | W2NE | R:HAMILTON |
| 4010 | " " | 12 | W½SW | 1836-08-04 | FD | W2SW | R:HAMILTON |
| 4008 | " " | 12 | E½SE | 1837-03-20 | FD | E2SE | R:HAMILTON |
| 4007 | " " | 10 | W½NE | 1837-03-20 | FD | W2NE | R:HAMILTON |
| 4006 | " " | 10 | E½SW | 1837-03-20 | FD | E2SW | R:HAMILTON |
| 4011 | " " | 13 | NESW | 1837-05-29 | FD | NESW | R:HAMILTON |
| 4014 | " " | 14 | NENE | 1837-12-30 | FD | NENE | R:HAMILTON |
| 4043 | LANHAM, James I | 9 | NWSE | 1852-10-15 | FD | NWSE | |
| 4072 | LANHAM, John | 9 | NESW | 1837-04-28 | FD | NESW | R:HAMILTON |
| 4077 | LANHAM, John T | 10 | NWSW | 1855-04-13 | FD | NWSW | R:HAMILTON |
| 4081 | LANHAM, Joseph S | 9 | SESW | 1852-09-23 | FD | SESW | |
| 4045 | LASATER, James M | 3 | NWSE | 1857-06-09 | FD | NWSE | |
| 4044 | " " | 18 | NWSW | 1857-06-09 | FD | NWSW | |
| 3968 | MCKENZIE, Aaron | 2 | SENE | 1853-04-26 | FD | SENE | |
| 3969 | MCKINZIE, Aaron S | 10 | NENE | 1851-11-29 | FD | NENE | R:HAMILTON |
| 4065 | MCMURTRY, John H | 15 | NENE | 1583-12-28 | FD | NENE | R:HAMILTON |
| 4087 | MCMURTRY, Logan | 11 | NENE | 1852-09-01 | FD | NENE | |
| 4088 | " " | 11 | NESW | 1853-03-12 | FD | NESW | |
| 4022 | MEYER, Frederick | 3 | NWNE | 1855-10-26 | FD | NWNE | R:INDIANA |
| 4100 | MORRIS, Nancy | 1 | W½SW | 1848-12-01 | FD | W2SW | R:HAMILTON S:F |
| 4050 | OGLESBY, James W | 15 | SWSW | 1854-04-24 | FD | SWSW | R:SALINE |

| ID | Individual in Patent | Sec. | Sec. Part | Purchase Date | Sale Type | IL Aliquot Part | For More Info . . . |
|---|---|---|---|---|---|---|---|
| 4024 | PORTER, Grayson | 6 | SESE | 1854-03-30 | FD | SESE | R:SALINE |
| 4028 | PORTER, Hardin | 8 | NENE | 1837-03-06 | FD | NENE | R:HAMILTON |
| 4025 | " " | 15 | SWNW | 1838-07-20 | FD | SWNW | R:HAMILTON |
| 4026 | " " | 4 | SWSW | 1851-08-15 | FD | SWSW | R:HAMILTON |
| 4027 | " " | 5 | SESE | 1852-10-15 | FD | SESE | |
| 4086 | PORTER, Lewis | 9 | W½NW | 1837-03-18 | FD | W2NW | R:HAMILTON |
| 4094 | PORTER, Mark M | 8 | SENE | 1852-10-15 | FD | SENE | |
| 4096 | PORTER, Mason | 6 | NESE | 1837-09-12 | FD | NESE | R:HAMILTON |
| 4116 | PORTER, Thomas J | 9 | SENW | 1852-09-22 | FD | SENW | R:HAMILTON |
| 4115 | " " | 9 | NE | 1855-05-23 | FD | NE | R:HAMILTON |
| 4118 | PORTER, Thompson | 16 | W½NE | 1839-08-17 | SC | W2NE | |
| 4120 | PORTER, Tomzen | 8 | SESE | 1832-11-08 | FD | SESE | R:HAMILTON |
| 4119 | " " | 8 | NESE | 1836-04-18 | FD | NESE | R:HAMILTON |
| 4128 | PORTER, William | 10 | W½SE | 1837-10-19 | FD | W2SE | R:HAMILTON |
| 4001 | POWELL, Daniel | 8 | W½SE | 1836-04-09 | FD | W2SE | R:WHITE |
| 4000 | " " | 8 | E½SW | 1836-04-09 | FD | E2SW | R:WHITE |
| 3997 | " " | 17 | E½NE | 1836-04-09 | FD | E2NE | R:WHITE |
| 4002 | " " | 9 | W½SW | 1836-04-09 | FD | W2SW | R:WHITE |
| 3999 | " " | 3 | E½NE | 1839-02-25 | FD | E2NE | R:WHITE |
| 3998 | " " | 18 | E½NE | 1853-12-06 | FD | E2NE | R:WHITE |
| 4046 | RIDGWAY, James Olden | 3 | SWSE | 1837-10-28 | FD | SWSE | R:HAMILTON |
| 3990 | RILEY, Daniel Earp | 14 | SWSE | 1837-01-13 | FD | SWSE | R:HAMILTON |
| 4032 | RILEY, Ira Ellis | 14 | NWSE | 1836-06-17 | FD | NWSE | R:HAMILTON |
| 4110 | RILEY, Sarah | 13 | E½NE | 1836-03-29 | FD | E2NE | R:HAMILTON S:F |
| 4103 | RUPARD, Nelson | 2 | SWNW | 1836-07-22 | FD | SWNW | R:HAMILTON |
| 4104 | RUSSARD, Peter | 2 | NWNW | 1836-02-05 | FD | NWNW | R:HAMILTON |
| 4073 | SCHOOLCRAFT, John | 7 | W½NW | 1837-04-22 | FD | W2NW | R:HAMILTON |
| 4082 | SMITH, Joseph | 10 | NWSE | 1851-11-14 | FD | NWSE | |
| 4117 | SMITH, Thomas | 6 | NESW | 1854-10-04 | FD | NESW | R:HAMILTON |
| 4121 | STEVENS, Vachel | 11 | NWSE | 1852-11-17 | FD | NWSE | |
| 4125 | STOREY, William H | 10 | SENE | 1836-12-09 | FD | SENE | R:HAMILTON |
| 4053 | STOVALL, John B | 11 | NW | 1815-02-13 | FD | NW | R:GALLATIN |
| 4055 | " " | 12 | NW | 1816-12-28 | FD | NW | R:GALLATIN |
| 4054 | " " | 11 | SE | 1818-07-03 | FD | SE | R:WHITE |
| 4052 | " " | 11 | NE | 1818-11-26 | FD | NE | R:WHITE |
| 4023 | VARNELL, George H | 1 | NWNW | 1860-11-03 | FD | NWNWVOID | |
| 4078 | WATSON, John | 13 | SE | 1820-03-17 | FD | SE | G:40 |
| 4078 | WATSON, Robert | 13 | SE | 1820-03-17 | FD | SE | G:40 |
| 4129 | WATSON, William | 13 | NW | 1815-11-07 | FD | NW | R:GALLATIN |
| 3973 | WILLIAMS, Alexander | 13 | W½SW | 1831-04-06 | FD | W2SW | R:GALLATIN |
| 4016 | WILSON, David | 18 | NWSE | 1836-04-14 | FD | NWSE | R:HAMILTON |
| 4015 | " " | 18 | E½SE | 1836-04-14 | FD | E2SE | R:HAMILTON |
| 4109 | WILSON, Samuel | 7 | SESW | 1837-03-27 | FD | SESW | R:HAMILTON |
| 4017 | WOOD, Edward | 12 | W½SE | 1837-01-04 | FD | W2SE | R:HAMILTON |
| 3978 | YOUNG, Andrew I | 14 | NWSW | 1855-03-31 | FD | NWSW | R:HAMILTON |
| 3977 | " " | 14 | E½NW | 1855-03-31 | FD | E2NW | R:HAMILTON |
| 3979 | YOUNG, Andrew J | 14 | W½NW | 1853-10-20 | FD | W2NW | R:HAMILTON |
| 4040 | YOUNG, James H | 1 | SESW | 1853-03-08 | FD | SESW | R:HAMILTON |
| 4041 | " " | 11 | SESW | 1853-03-16 | FD | SESW | |
| 4083 | YOUNG, Joseph | 11 | SWSE | 1847-07-19 | FD | SWSE | R:HAMILTON |
| 4085 | " " | 16 | L16 | 1849-07-09 | SC | LOT16SESE | |
| 4084 | " " | 16 | L15 | 1849-07-09 | SC | LOT15SWSE | |

# Patent Map

### T7-S  R7-E
### 3rd PM Meridian

## Map Group 15

## Township Statistics

| | | |
|---|---|---|
| Parcels Mapped | : | 164 |
| Number of Patents | : | 1 |
| Number of Individuals | : | 108 |
| Patentees Identified | : | 107 |
| Number of Surnames | : | 55 |
| Multi-Patentee Parcels | : | 1 |
| Oldest Patent Date | : | 12/28/1583 |
| Most Recent Patent | : | 11/3/1860 |
| Block/Lot Parcels | : | 8 |
| Cities and Towns | : | 2 |
| Cemeteries | : | 6 |

Note: the area contained in this map amounts to far less than a full Township. Therefore, its contents are completely on this single page (instead of a "normal" 2-page spread).

## Legend

| | |
|---|---|
| ———————— | Patent Boundary |
| ▬▬▬▬▬▬ | Section Boundary |
| (shaded) | No Patents Found (or Outside County) |
| 1., 2., 3., ... | Lot Numbers (when beside a name) |
| [ ] | Group Number (see Appendix "C") |

**Scale**: Section = 1 mile X 1 mile
(generally, with some exceptions)

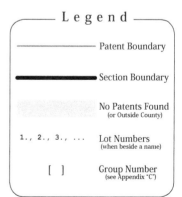

203

## Road Map

### T7-S  R7-E
### 3rd PM Meridian

Map Group 15

Note: the area contained in this map amounts to far less than a full Township. Therefore, its contents are completely on this single page (instead of a "normal" 2-page spread).

### Cities & Towns
Broughton
Rectorville (historical)

### Cemeteries
Cook Cemetery
Gholson Cemetery
Keasler Cemetery
Lantham Cemetery
Morris Cemetery
Wolfe Cemetery

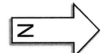

### Legend

—————— Section Lines

━━━━━━ Interstates

━━━━━━ Highways

—————— Other Roads

● Cities/Towns

✝ Cemeteries

**Scale**: Section = 1 mile X 1 mile
(generally, with some exceptions)

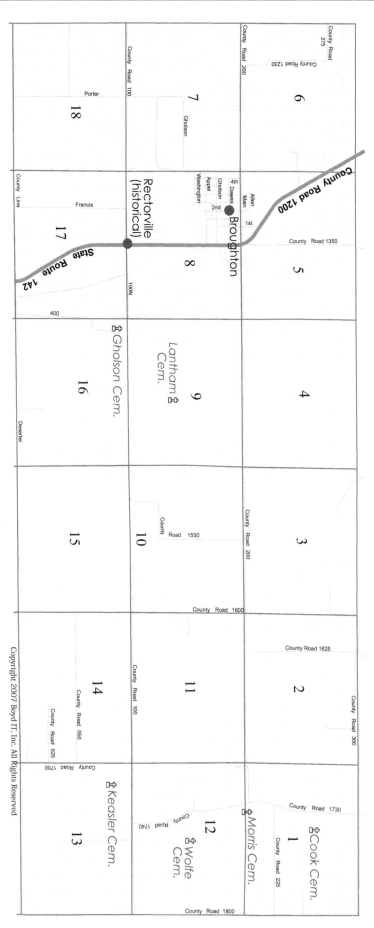

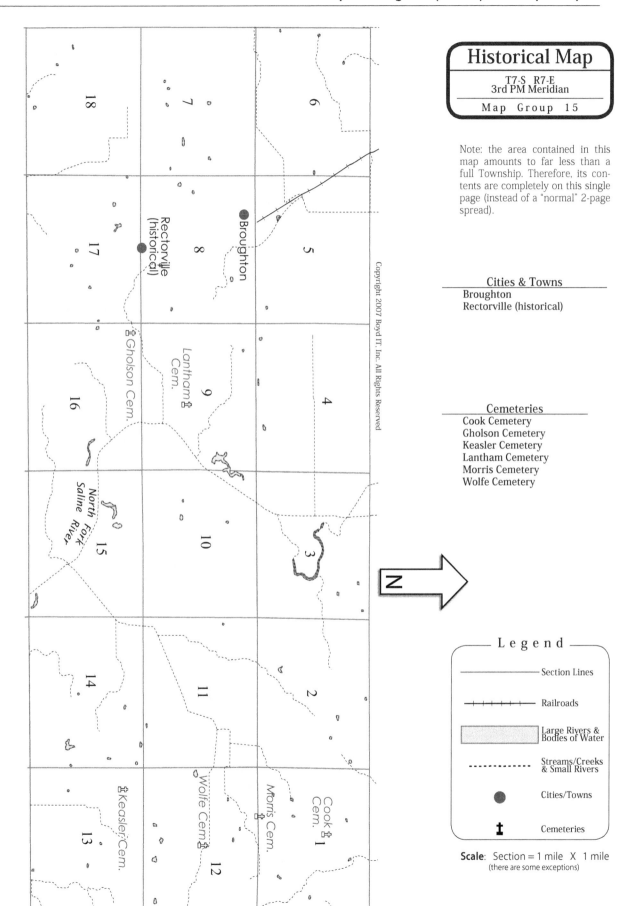

## Historical Map

T7-S R7-E
3rd PM Meridian

Map Group 15

Note: the area contained in this map amounts to far less than a full Township. Therefore, its contents are completely on this single page (instead of a "normal" 2-page spread).

### Cities & Towns
Broughton
Rectorville (historical)

### Cemeteries
Cook Cemetery
Gholson Cemetery
Keasler Cemetery
Lantham Cemetery
Morris Cemetery
Wolfe Cemetery

N

### Legend
——————— Section Lines

+++++++ Railroads

▭ Large Rivers & Bodies of Water

- - - - - - Streams/Creeks & Small Rivers

● Cities/Towns

✝ Cemeteries

**Scale**: Section = 1 mile X 1 mile
(there are some exceptions)

# Appendices

# Appendix A - Illinois Archives Abbreviations

The following abbreviations are used by the Illinois State Archives in describing the nature and locations of the land-patents in their "Tract Indexes" at www.cyberdriveillinois.com. Most line-items in the Patent Indexes in this volume will contain one or more of these abbreviations. When multiple abbreviations are used, no space will be found between each (and that can sometimes be confusing). Many of these are fairly easy to decipher, but many ambiguities exist. Only after reviewing a copy of the original land-patent can one be certain of the meaning of any given abbreviations.

| Abbrev. | Description |
|---|---|
| A | assumed |
| AA | acres assumed |
| AB | Alton & Shelbyville Railroad |
| AC | act |
| AD | addition |
| AG | Agricultural College |
| AI | alias |
| AL | others |
| AM | Alton & Mt. Carmel Railroad |
| AN | Administrator |
| APR | Apple River |
| AR | Army |
| ART | artillery |
| AS | assignee |
| ASC | associate |
| ASM | assemble |
| ASS | association |
| AT | attorney (lawyer) |
| AW | Alton & Shawneetown Railroad |
| B | block, outblock, inblock, bank |
| BAP | Baptist |
| BET | between |
| BL | block, outblock, inblock, boundary line |
| BMR | Big Muddy River |
| BNK | bank |
| BO | board |
| BR | British |
| BRO | brothers |
| BT | Baptist |
| BUXTON ISL | Buxton Island |
| C | claim |
| CA | Catholic |
| CALR | Calumet River |
| CARB | carbon |
| CE | center |
| CEM | cemetery |
| CEN | central |
| CENT | Centralia |
| CFT | counterfeit |
| CG | Congregation(al) |
| CH | Church |
| CHI | Chicago |
| CHR | Christian |
| CI | Centralia |
| CK | creek |
| CL | college |
| CM | Commerce Street, County Microfilm |
| CN | canal |
| CNTY | county |
| CO | company |

| Abbrev. | Description |
|---|---|
| COM | Commission(er)(s) |
| COR | corner |
| CP | captive |
| CPE | cape |
| CR | corner |
| CT | cattle |
| CY | city |
| D | deceased veteran of War of 1812 |
| DANE CNTY | Dane County |
| DD | date-of-deed |
| DE | date |
| DESR | Des Plaines River |
| DG | DuPage |
| DH | detached |
| DI | description |
| DIIO | description incomplete |
| DINT | description notation |
| DIV | division |
| DO | donation |
| DP | date-of-purchase |
| DPT | detached part |
| DQ | DuQuoin |
| DR | doctor |
| DS | discount |
| DT | district |
| DU | Dutch |
| E | East |
| E2 | East half |
| EC | excess |
| EDGE | Edgewood |
| EL | Eldena |
| EMP | emporium |
| END | end |
| EP | Episcopal |
| ES | estate |
| ET | and |
| ET AL | and others |
| ETG | unknown symbol meaning |
| EV | Evangelical |
| EX | executor |
| EXCPT | except |
| F | feet |
| FD | federal |
| FEED | feeder |
| FEL | Fellons |
| FFR | forfeited land redeemed |
| FK | Franklin Street |
| FL | float |
| FNB | First National Bank |
| FO | forgery |

| Abbrev. | Description | Abbrev. | Description |
|---------|-------------|---------|-------------|
| FOR | Forrestor | MA | money assumed |
| FR | fractional | MAIN | main |
| FS | forfeited land stock | MANT | Manteno |
| FT | first | MANUF | manufacture(r)(s)(ing) |
| FUL | Fulton | MARS | Marshal(l) |
| FV | Fox River | MATT | Matthiessen |
| FX | Fox River | ME | Methodist |
| GAL | Galena | MID | middle |
| GD | guard | MIN | mining |
| GEN | General | MISSR | Mississippi River |
| GER | German | MLK | Milwaukee |
| GIR | Girardeau | MNLD | mainland |
| GLD | gold | MO | Missouri |
| GN | guardian | MT | military tract |
| GR | grand | MU | Minuscule |
| GT | Gratiot Street | N | North |
| H | heir of deceased veteran of War of 1812 | N2 | North half |
| HEG | Hegeler | NAT | national |
| HO | house | NE | Northeast |
| HR | heir or heirs | NEG | Negro |
| HS | Homestead | NM | name |
| I | initials | NMA | name assumed |
| IBL | Indian boundary line | NO | number |
| IC | included | NR | Nora |
| IL | inlot | NT | note |
| ILL | Illinois | NW | Northwest |
| ILLR | Illinois River | OA | Ottawa |
| IM | improvement | OD | Odin |
| IN | Indian | OF | office |
| INST | institute | OL | outlot |
| IO | incomplete | OT | original town |
| IR | Iroquois River | P | [unknown currency] |
| ISL | island | PA | paper |
| JL | Joliet | PE | Presbyterian |
| JOHNS ISL | Johns Island | PECK | Pecatonica River |
| JR | Junior | PEN | Pennsylvannia |
| KA | Kankakee | PET | petroleum |
| KANKR | Kankakee River | PLK | plank |
| KNOX CNTY | Knox County | PM | [unknown currency] |
| KP | Kappa | PNT | patent |
| KSRR | Kaskaskia River | PR | Plum River |
| L | lot, outlot, inlot, line | PRA | prairie |
| LA | Loda | PRE | pre-emption |
| LD | land | PRES | president |
| LG | lodge | PT | part |
| LI | listed | PY | payment |
| LIB | liberal | R | river |
| LK | Lake | RAILRD | railroad |
| LL | little | RC | recorded |
| LNT | Lieutenant | RD | railroad |
| LO | lot, outlot, inlot | RE | reservation |
| LOC | locust | REL | real |
| LOCK | lock | REV | ecclesiastical title, Reverend, Bishop, etc. |
| LP | Lockport | | |
| LS | (military) land scrip or LaSalle | RI | reinstated |
| LT | left | RIC | Richview |
| LU | Lutheran | RIP | ripple |
| LUT | Lutheran | RL | release |
| M | money | RM | redeemed |

| Abbrev. | Description |
|---------|-------------|
| RO | Roman |
| RP | receipt |
| RQ | relinquished |
| RR | Rock River or railroad |
| RS | residence |
| RT | right |
| RTW | right of way |
| RV | reserved |
| S | South |
| S2 | South half |
| SA | saline |
| SAND | Sandoval |
| SANGR | Sangamon River |
| SC | section or school |
| SD | side |
| SE | Southeast |
| SECT | section (640 acres) |
| SEN | senior |
| SH | Shawneetown |
| SIDE | side |
| SIL | silver |
| SK | stock |
| SL | saline, slough or sublot |
| SM | seminary |
| SN | senior |
| SOC | society |
| SPR | Spoon River |
| SR | Sugar River |
| ST | state |
| STC | St. Charles |
| STCK | Stillman Creek |
| STIS | St. Isadore (Church) |
| STP | St. Paul |
| STPET | St. Peter |
| SUBD | subdivision |
| SUP | Superintendent |
| SURV | survey |
| SW | Southwest or swamp |
| SX | settlement |
| SY | sale |
| TAB | tabernacle |
| TB | timber |
| TE | treaty |
| TF | transferred |
| TIMLT | timberlot |
| TN | town |
| TOL | Tolono |
| TOW | tower |
| TR | trustees |
| TRA | transportation |
| TS | township |
| TT | tract |
| TX | tax |
| TY | treasury |
| UN | Unitarian |
| UNKWN | Unknown |
| V | void, canceled, etc. |
| VC | Vincennes |
| VI | village |

| Abbrev. | Description |
|---------|-------------|
| VO | void, canceled, etc. |
| VOID | void, canceled, etc. |
| W | West |
| W2 | West half |
| WA | warrant |
| WAR | CNTY Warren County |
| WB | Wabash |
| WP | Wapella |
| WT | Water Street |
| X | exclusive |

# Appendix B - Section Parts (Aliquot Parts)

The following represent the various abbreviations we have found thus far in describing the parts of a Public Land Section. Some of these are very obscure and rarely used, but we wanted to list them for just that reason. A full section is 1 square mile or 640 acres.

| Section Part | Description | Acres |
|---|---|---|
| \<none\> | Full Acre (if no Section Part is listed, presumed a full Section) | 640 |
| \<1-??\> | A number represents a Lot Number and can be of various sizes | ? |
| E½ | East Half-Section | 320 |
| E½E½ | East Half of East Half-Section | 160 |
| E½E½SE | East Half of East Half of Southeast Quarter-Section | 40 |
| E½N½ | East Half of North Half-Section | 160 |
| E½NE | East Half of Northeast Quarter-Section | 80 |
| E½NENE | East Half of Northeast Quarter of Northeast Quarter-Section | 20 |
| E½NENW | East Half of Northeast Quarter of Northwest Quarter-Section | 20 |
| E½NESE | East Half of Northeast Quarter of Southeast Quarter-Section | 20 |
| E½NESW | East Half of Northeast Quarter of Southwest Quarter-Section | 20 |
| E½NW | East Half of Northwest Quarter-Section | 80 |
| E½NWNE | East Half of Northwest Quarter of Northeast Quarter-Section | 20 |
| E½NWNW | East Half of Northwest Quarter of Northwest Quarter-Section | 20 |
| E½NWSE | East Half of Northwest Quarter of Southeast Quarter-Section | 20 |
| E½NWSW | East Half of Northwest Quarter of Southwest Quarter-Section | 20 |
| E½S½ | East Half of South Half-Section | 160 |
| E½SE | East Half of Southeast Quarter-Section | 80 |
| E½SENE | East Half of Southeast Quarter of Northeast Quarter-Section | 20 |
| E½SENW | East Half of Southeast Quarter of Northwest Quarter-Section | 20 |
| E½SESE | East Half of Southeast Quarter of Southeast Quarter-Section | 20 |
| E½SESW | East Half of Southeast Quarter of Southwest Quarter-Section | 20 |
| E½SW | East Half of Southwest Quarter-Section | 80 |
| E½SWNE | East Half of Southwest Quarter of Northeast Quarter-Section | 20 |
| E½SWNW | East Half of Southwest Quarter of Northwest Quarter-Section | 20 |
| E½SWSE | East Half of Southwest Quarter of Southeast Quarter-Section | 20 |
| E½SWSW | East Half of Southwest Quarter of Southwest Quarter-Section | 20 |
| E½W½ | East Half of West Half-Section | 160 |
| N½ | North Half-Section | 320 |
| N½E½NE | North Half of East Half of Northeast Quarter-Section | 40 |
| N½E½NW | North Half of East Half of Northwest Quarter-Section | 40 |
| N½E½SE | North Half of East Half of Southeast Quarter-Section | 40 |
| N½E½SW | North Half of East Half of Southwest Quarter-Section | 40 |
| N½N½ | North Half of North Half-Section | 160 |
| N½NE | North Half of Northeast Quarter-Section | 80 |
| N½NENE | North Half of Northeast Quarter of Northeast Quarter-Section | 20 |
| N½NENW | North Half of Northeast Quarter of Northwest Quarter-Section | 20 |
| N½NESE | North Half of Northeast Quarter of Southeast Quarter-Section | 20 |
| N½NESW | North Half of Northeast Quarter of Southwest Quarter-Section | 20 |
| N½NW | North Half of Northwest Quarter-Section | 80 |
| N½NWNE | North Half of Northwest Quarter of Northeast Quarter-Section | 20 |
| N½NWNW | North Half of Northwest Quarter of Northwest Quarter-Section | 20 |
| N½NWSE | North Half of Northwest Quarter of Southeast Quarter-Section | 20 |
| N½NWSW | North Half of Northwest Quarter of Southwest Quarter-Section | 20 |
| N½S½ | North Half of South Half-Section | 160 |
| N½SE | North Half of Southeast Quarter-Section | 80 |
| N½SENE | North Half of Southeast Quarter of Northeast Quarter-Section | 20 |
| N½SENW | North Half of Southeast Quarter of Northwest Quarter-Section | 20 |
| N½SESE | North Half of Southeast Quarter of Southeast Quarter-Section | 20 |

| Section Part | Description | Acres |
|---|---|---|
| N½SESW | North Half of Southeast Quarter of Southwest Quarter-Section | 20 |
| N½SESW | North Half of Southeast Quarter of Southwest Quarter-Section | 20 |
| N½SW | North Half of Southwest Quarter-Section | 80 |
| N½SWNE | North Half of Southwest Quarter of Northeast Quarter-Section | 20 |
| N½SWNW | North Half of Southwest Quarter of Northwest Quarter-Section | 20 |
| N½SWSE | North Half of Southwest Quarter of Southeast Quarter-Section | 20 |
| N½SWSE | North Half of Southwest Quarter of Southeast Quarter-Section | 20 |
| N½SWSW | North Half of Southwest Quarter of Southwest Quarter-Section | 20 |
| N½W½NW | North Half of West Half of Northwest Quarter-Section | 40 |
| N½W½SE | North Half of West Half of Southeast Quarter-Section | 40 |
| N½W½SW | North Half of West Half of Southwest Quarter-Section | 40 |
| NE | Northeast Quarter-Section | 160 |
| NEN½ | Northeast Quarter of North Half-Section | 80 |
| NENE | Northeast Quarter of Northeast Quarter-Section | 40 |
| NENENE | Northeast Quarter of Northeast Quarter of Northeast Quarter | 10 |
| NENENW | Northeast Quarter of Northeast Quarter of Northwest Quarter | 10 |
| NENESE | Northeast Quarter of Northeast Quarter of Southeast Quarter | 10 |
| NENESW | Northeast Quarter of Northeast Quarter of Southwest Quarter | 10 |
| NENW | Northeast Quarter of Northwest Quarter-Section | 40 |
| NENWNE | Northeast Quarter of Northwest Quarter of Northeast Quarter | 10 |
| NENWNW | Northeast Quarter of Northwest Quarter of Northwest Quarter | 10 |
| NENWSE | Northeast Quarter of Northwest Quarter of Southeast Quarter | 10 |
| NENWSW | Northeast Quarter of Northwest Quarter of Southwest Quarter | 10 |
| NESE | Northeast Quarter of Southeast Quarter-Section | 40 |
| NESENE | Northeast Quarter of Southeast Quarter of Northeast Quarter | 10 |
| NESENW | Northeast Quarter of Southeast Quarter of Northwest Quarter | 10 |
| NESESE | Northeast Quarter of Southeast Quarter of Southeast Quarter | 10 |
| NESESW | Northeast Quarter of Southeast Quarter of Southwest Quarter | 10 |
| NESW | Northeast Quarter of Southwest Quarter-Section | 40 |
| NESWNE | Northeast Quarter of Southwest Quarter of Northeast Quarter | 10 |
| NESWNW | Northeast Quarter of Southwest Quarter of Northwest Quarter | 10 |
| NESWSE | Northeast Quarter of Southwest Quarter of Southeast Quarter | 10 |
| NESWSW | Northeast Quarter of Southwest Quarter of Southwest Quarter | 10 |
| NW | Northwest Quarter-Section | 160 |
| NWE½ | Northwest Quarter of Eastern Half-Section | 80 |
| NWN½ | Northwest Quarter of North Half-Section | 80 |
| NWNE | Northwest Quarter of Northeast Quarter-Section | 40 |
| NWNENE | Northwest Quarter of Northeast Quarter of Northeast Quarter | 10 |
| NWNENW | Northwest Quarter of Northeast Quarter of Northwest Quarter | 10 |
| NWNESE | Northwest Quarter of Northeast Quarter of Southeast Quarter | 10 |
| NWNESW | Northwest Quarter of Northeast Quarter of Southwest Quarter | 10 |
| NWNW | Northwest Quarter of Northwest Quarter-Section | 40 |
| NWNWNE | Northwest Quarter of Northwest Quarter of Northeast Quarter | 10 |
| NWNWNW | Northwest Quarter of Northwest Quarter of Northwest Quarter | 10 |
| NWNWSE | Northwest Quarter of Northwest Quarter of Southeast Quarter | 10 |
| NWNWSW | Northwest Quarter of Northwest Quarter of Southwest Quarter | 10 |
| NWSE | Northwest Quarter of Southeast Quarter-Section | 40 |
| NWSENE | Northwest Quarter of Southeast Quarter of Northeast Quarter | 10 |
| NWSENW | Northwest Quarter of Southeast Quarter of Northwest Quarter | 10 |
| NWSESE | Northwest Quarter of Southeast Quarter of Southeast Quarter | 10 |
| NWSESW | Northwest Quarter of Southeast Quarter of Southwest Quarter | 10 |
| NWSW | Northwest Quarter of Southwest Quarter-Section | 40 |
| NWSWNE | Northwest Quarter of Southwest Quarter of Northeast Quarter | 10 |
| NWSWNW | Northwest Quarter of Southwest Quarter of Northwest Quarter | 10 |
| NWSWSE | Northwest Quarter of Southwest Quarter of Southeast Quarter | 10 |
| NWSWSW | Northwest Quarter of Southwest Quarter of Southwest Quarter | 10 |
| S½ | South Half-Section | 320 |
| S½E½NE | South Half of East Half of Northeast Quarter-Section | 40 |
| S½E½NW | South Half of East Half of Northwest Quarter-Section | 40 |
| S½E½SE | South Half of East Half of Southeast Quarter-Section | 40 |

| Section Part | Description | Acres |
|---|---|---|
| S½E½SW | South Half of East Half of Southwest Quarter-Section | 40 |
| S½N½ | South Half of North Half-Section | 160 |
| S½NE | South Half of Northeast Quarter-Section | 80 |
| S½NENE | South Half of Northeast Quarter of Northeast Quarter-Section | 20 |
| S½NENW | South Half of Northeast Quarter of Northwest Quarter-Section | 20 |
| S½NESE | South Half of Northeast Quarter of Southeast Quarter-Section | 20 |
| S½NESW | South Half of Northeast Quarter of Southwest Quarter-Section | 20 |
| S½NW | South Half of Northwest Quarter-Section | 80 |
| S½NWNE | South Half of Northwest Quarter of Northeast Quarter-Section | 20 |
| S½NWNW | South Half of Northwest Quarter of Northwest Quarter-Section | 20 |
| S½NWSE | South Half of Northwest Quarter of Southeast Quarter-Section | 20 |
| S½NWSW | South Half of Northwest Quarter of Southwest Quarter-Section | 20 |
| S½S½ | South Half of South Half-Section | 160 |
| S½SE | South Half of Southeast Quarter-Section | 80 |
| S½SENE | South Half of Southeast Quarter of Northeast Quarter-Section | 20 |
| S½SENW | South Half of Southeast Quarter of Northwest Quarter-Section | 20 |
| S½SESE | South Half of Southeast Quarter of Southeast Quarter-Section | 20 |
| S½SESW | South Half of Southeast Quarter of Southwest Quarter-Section | 20 |
| S½SESW | South Half of Southeast Quarter of Southwest Quarter-Section | 20 |
| S½SW | South Half of Southwest Quarter-Section | 80 |
| S½SWNE | South Half of Southwest Quarter of Northeast Quarter-Section | 20 |
| S½SWNW | South Half of Southwest Quarter of Northwest Quarter-Section | 20 |
| S½SWSE | South Half of Southwest Quarter of Southeast Quarter-Section | 20 |
| S½SWSE | South Half of Southwest Quarter of Southeast Quarter-Section | 20 |
| S½SWSW | South Half of Southwest Quarter of Southwest Quarter-Section | 20 |
| S½W½NE | South Half of West Half of Northeast Quarter-Section | 40 |
| S½W½NW | South Half of West Half of Northwest Quarter-Section | 40 |
| S½W½SE | South Half of West Half of Southeast Quarter-Section | 40 |
| S½W½SW | South Half of West Half of Southwest Quarter-Section | 40 |
| SE | Southeast Quarter Section | 160 |
| SEN½ | Southeast Quarter of North Half-Section | 80 |
| SENE | Southeast Quarter of Northeast Quarter-Section | 40 |
| SENENE | Southeast Quarter of Northeast Quarter of Northeast Quarter | 10 |
| SENENW | Southeast Quarter of Northeast Quarter of Northwest Quarter | 10 |
| SENESE | Southeast Quarter of Northeast Quarter of Southeast Quarter | 10 |
| SENESW | Southeast Quarter of Northeast Quarter of Southwest Quarter | 10 |
| SENW | Southeast Quarter of Northwest Quarter-Section | 40 |
| SENWNE | Southeast Quarter of Northwest Quarter of Northeast Quarter | 10 |
| SENWNW | Southeast Quarter of Northwest Quarter of Northwest Quarter | 10 |
| SENWSE | Souteast Quarter of Northwest Quarter of Southeast Quarter | 10 |
| SENWSW | Southeast Quarter of Northwest Quarter of Southwest Quarter | 10 |
| SESE | Southeast Quarter of Southeast Quarter-Section | 40 |
| SESENE | SoutheastQuarter of Southeast Quarter of Northeast Quarter | 10 |
| SESENW | Southeast Quarter of Southeast Quarter of Northwest Quarter | 10 |
| SESESE | Southeast Quarter of Southeast Quarter of Southeast Quarter | 10 |
| SESESW | Southeast Quarter of Southeast Quarter of Southwest Quarter | 10 |
| SESW | Southeast Quarter of Southwest Quarter-Section | 40 |
| SESWNE | Southeast Quarter of Southwest Quarter of Northeast Quarter | 10 |
| SESWNW | Southeast Quarter of Southwest Quarter of Northwest Quarter | 10 |
| SESWSE | Southeast Quarter of Southwest Quarter of Southeast Quarter | 10 |
| SESWSW | Southeast Quarter of Southwest Quarter of Southwest Quarter | 10 |
| SW | Southwest Quarter-Section | 160 |
| SWNE | Southwest Quarter of Northeast Quarter-Section | 40 |
| SWNENE | Southwest Quarter of Northeast Quarter of Northeast Quarter | 10 |
| SWNENW | Southwest Quarter of Northeast Quarter of Northwest Quarter | 10 |
| SWNESE | Southwest Quarter of Northeast Quarter of Southeast Quarter | 10 |
| SWNESW | Southwest Quarter of Northeast Quarter of Southwest Quarter | 10 |
| SWNW | Southwest Quarter of Northwest Quarter-Section | 40 |
| SWNWNE | Southwest Quarter of Northwest Quarter of Northeast Quarter | 10 |
| SWNWNW | Southwest Quarter of Northwest Quarter of Northwest Quarter | 10 |

| Section Part | Description | Acres |
|---|---|---|
| SWNWSE | Southwest Quarter of Northwest Quarter of Southeast Quarter | 10 |
| SWNWSW | Southwest Quarter of Northwest Quarter of Southwest Quarter | 10 |
| SWSE | Southwest Quarter of Southeast Quarter-Section | 40 |
| SWSENE | Southwest Quarter of Southeast Quarter of Northeast Quarter | 10 |
| SWSENW | Southwest Quarter of Southeast Quarter of Northwest Quarter | 10 |
| SWSESE | Southwest Quarter of Southeast Quarter of Southeast Quarter | 10 |
| SWSESW | Southwest Quarter of Southeast Quarter of Southwest Quarter | 10 |
| SWSW | Southwest Quarter of Southwest Quarter-Section | 40 |
| SWSWNE | Southwest Quarter of Southwest Quarter of Northeast Quarter | 10 |
| SWSWNW | Southwest Quarter of Southwest Quarter of Northwest Quarter | 10 |
| SWSWSE | Southwest Quarter of Southwest Quarter of Southeast Quarter | 10 |
| SWSWSW | Southwest Quarter of Southwest Quarter of Southwest Quarter | 10 |
| W½ | West Half-Section | 320 |
| W½E½ | West Half of East Half-Section | 160 |
| W½N½ | West Half of North Half-Section (same as NW) | 160 |
| W½NE | West Half of Northeast Quarter | 80 |
| W½NENE | West Half of Northeast Quarter of Northeast Quarter-Section | 20 |
| W½NENW | West Half of Northeast Quarter of Northwest Quarter-Section | 20 |
| W½NESE | West Half of Northeast Quarter of Southeast Quarter-Section | 20 |
| W½NESW | West Half of Northeast Quarter of Southwest Quarter-Section | 20 |
| W½NW | West Half of Northwest Quarter-Section | 80 |
| W½NWNE | West Half of Northwest Quarter of Northeast Quarter-Section | 20 |
| W½NWNW | West Half of Northwest Quarter of Northwest Quarter-Section | 20 |
| W½NWSE | West Half of Northwest Quarter of Southeast Quarter-Section | 20 |
| W½NWSW | West Half of Northwest Quarter of Southwest Quarter-Section | 20 |
| W½S½ | West Half of South Half-Section | 160 |
| W½SE | West Half of Southeast Quarter-Section | 80 |
| W½SENE | West Half of Southeast Quarter of Northeast Quarter-Section | 20 |
| W½SENW | West Half of Southeast Quarter of Northwest Quarter-Section | 20 |
| W½SESE | West Half of Southeast Quarter of Southeast Quarter-Section | 20 |
| W½SESW | West Half of Southeast Quarter of Southwest Quarter-Section | 20 |
| W½SW | West Half of Southwest Quarter-Section | 80 |
| W½SWNE | West Half of Southwest Quarter of Northeast Quarter-Section | 20 |
| W½SWNW | West Half of Southwest Quarter of Northwest Quarter-Section | 20 |
| W½SWSE | West Half of Southwest Quarter of Southeast Quarter-Section | 20 |
| W½SWSW | West Half of Southwest Quarter of Southwest Quarter-Section | 20 |
| W½W½ | West Half of West Half-Section | 160 |

# Appendix C - Multi-Patentee Groups

The following index presents groups of people who jointly received patents in Hamilton County, Illinois. The Group Numbers are used in the Patent Maps and their Indexes so that you may then turn to this Appendix in order to identify all the members of the each buying group.

**Group Number 1**
ALLEN, John L; ALLEN, Lucy; ALLEN, Moses P;
ALLEN, Ruth L

**Group Number 2**
ALLEN, William B; TALLER, James

**Group Number 3**
BIGGERSTAFF, Lewis L; BIGGERSTAFF, Lucy;
BIGGERSTAFF, Mary E; BIGGERSTAFF, Milo M

**Group Number 4**
BIGGERSTAFF, Louisa; BIGGERSTAFF, Malo M O

**Group Number 5**
BUCK, Warner; CROUCH, Adam

**Group Number 6**
CAIN, William; VIOLETT, Sanford

**Group Number 7**
CARGIL, David; WARD, Argon; WHITE, Preston

**Group Number 8**
CARPENTER, Chester; LASSATER, James M

**Group Number 9**
CHEEK, N C; CHEEK, Parmeleon; CHEEK, William E

**Group Number 10**
CHEEK, Parmelon; CHEEK, William E

**Group Number 11**
CROSS, John; CROSS, John C

**Group Number 12**
CROUCH, Cloyd; LEWIS, Wilson

**Group Number 13**
DARNALL, William; RICE, John J

**Group Number 14**
DAVIS, Elizabeth; DAVIS, Joseph

**Group Number 15**
FOSTER, Isaac; WILBANKS, Robert A D

**Group Number 16**
GARRISON, Henry G; GARRISON, John A

**Group Number 17**
GARRISON, Jefferson; GARRISON, William

**Group Number 18**
GHOLSON, Asberry; GHOLSON, Ely; GHOLSON, James
T; GHOLSON, John

**Group Number 19**
GRANT, Roswell H; MCLEAN, John

**Group Number 20**
GRAVES, A D; HARVESTER, Henry

**Group Number 21**
GRISWOLD, Gilbert; HOGG, Samuel

**Group Number 22**
HAWLEY, Paul G; SMITH, Alonzo B

**Group Number 23**
HITE, ; ORMSBY, ; SULLIVAN,

**Group Number 24**
HITE, ; ORMSBY,; SULLIVAN, No Ft Nm

**Group Number 25**
HOOVER, Nathan; HYSSIS, Benjamin

**Group Number 26**
HUNT, Henry; HUNT, Jane; HUNT, Martha; HUNT,
Nancy A; MAULDING, Elizabeth; MCDANIEL, Susan

**Group Number 27**
JOHNSON, John L; LEWIS, John

**Group Number 28**
JOHNSON, John Lewis; LEWIS, John

**Group Number 29**
LANE, James; MUSGRAVE, Robert J

**Group Number 30**
LASATER, James C; LASATER, Rebecca Jane;
LASATER, Robert W; LASATER, Sarah Ann; LASATER,
Thomas J

**Group Number 31**
PINKSTON, William; ROO, Shelton

**Group Number 32**
PROCOT, Samuel M; PROCTOR, Samuel L M

**Group Number 33**
RIVES, George W; SMITH, John A

**Group Number 34**
ROMINE, Caroline; ROMINE, Sarah Ann

**Group Number 35**
SMITH, Andrew E; SMITH, Charles A

**Group Number 36**
STALL, James; STALL, Lawrence

**Group Number 37**
STONE, John; STOVALL, Abraham

**Group Number 38**
TATE, John; TATE, William D

**Group Number 39**
TODD, William Balch; VARNELL, George H

**Group Number 40**
WATSON, John; WATSON, Robert

**Group Number 41**
WHEELER, William T; WHEELER, Willis Abner

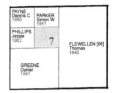

# Extra! Extra! (about our Indexes)

We purposefully do not have an all-name index in the back of this volume so that our readers do not miss one of the best uses of this book: finding misspelled names among more specialized indexes.

Without repeating the text of our "How-to" chapter, we have nonetheless tried to assist our more anxious researchers by delivering a short-cut to the two county-wide Surname Indexes, the second of which will lead you to all-name indexes for each Congressional Township mapped in this volume :

*For your convenience, the "How To Use this Book" Chart on page 2 is repeated on the reverse of this page.*

We should be releasing new titles every week for the foreseeable future. We urge you to write, fax, call, or email us any time for a current list of titles. Of course, our web-page will always have the most current information about current and upcoming books.

Arphax Publishing Co.
2210 Research Park Blvd.
Norman, Oklahoma 73069
(800) 681-5298 toll-free
(405) 366-6181 local
(405) 366-8184 fax
info@arphax.com

**www.arphax.com**

## How to Use This Book - A Graphical Summary

### Part I
# "The Big Picture"

Map A ▸ *Counties in the State*

Map B ▸ *Surrounding Counties*

Map C ▸ *Congressional Townships (Map Groups) in the County*

Map D ▸ *Cities & Towns in the County*

Map E ▸ *Cemeteries in the County*

Surnames in the County ▸ *Number of Land-Parcels for Each Surname*

Surname/Township Index ▸ *Directs you to Township Map Groups in Part II*

*The <u>Surname/Township Index</u> can direct you to any number of* **Township Map Groups**

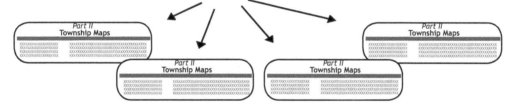

### Part II
# Township Map Groups
### *(1 for each Township in the County)*

Each Township Map Group contains all four of of the following tools . . .

Land Patent Index ▸ *Every-name Index of Patents Mapped in this Township*

Land Patent Map ▸ *Map of Patents as listed in above Index*

Road Map ▸ *Map of Roads, City-centers, and Cemeteries in the Township*

Historical Map ▸ *Map of Railroads, Lakes, Rivers, Creeks, City-Centers, and Cemeteries*

# Appendices

Appendix A ▸ *Illinois State Archives Abbreviations*

Appendix B ▸ *Section-Parts / Aliquot Parts (a comprehensive list)*

Appendix C ▸ *Multi-patentee Groups (Individuals within Buying Groups)*

Printed in the USA
CPSIA information can be obtained
at www.ICGtesting.com
LVHW081948180724
785661LV00024B/286